The SAGE Handbook of

International Social Work

The SAGE Handbook of

International Social Work

Edited by

Karen Lyons, Terry Hokenstad,
Manohar Pawar, Nathalie Huegler
and Nigel Hall

Los Angeles | London | New Delhi
Singapore | Washington DC

First published 2012

SAGE Publications Ltd
1 Oliver's Yard
55 City Road
London EC1Y 1SP

SAGE Publications Inc.
2455 Teller Road
Thousand Oaks, California 91320

SAGE Publications India Pvt Ltd
B 1/I 1 Mohan Cooperative Industrial Area
Mathura Road, Post Bag 7
New Delhi 110 044

SAGE Publications Asia-Pacific Pte Ltd
3 Church Street
10–04 Samsung Hub
Singapore 049483

Library of Congress Control Number: 2011941086

British Library Cataloguing in Publication data

A catalogue record for this book is available from the British Library

ISBN 978-0-85702-333-9

Typeset by Cenveo Publisher Services
Printed by MPG Books Group, Bodmin, Cornwall
Printed on paper from sustainable resources

Contents

Notes on the Editors

Karen Lyons began her career as a school social worker before entering academic work. From 1978 to 2000 she was responsible for professional social work education at the University of East London (UK) including undertaking research, writing and developing post-qualifying programmes. Involvement from the 1980s in European exchange programmes and anti-racist teaching led to a particular interest in international social work. She has contributed to social work developments and educational programmes in a wide range of countries since the 1990s and was a member of the Board of the International Association of Schools of Social Work (2000–2004). Karen Lyons has had varied editorial board experience and in 2004 was appointed Editor-in-Chief of the journal *International Social Work* (until 2009). As an Emeritus Professor at London Metropolitan University, she continues to undertake doctoral supervision and examination, editing and writing.

Terry Hokenstad is a Distinguished University Professor at Case Western Reserve University (USA) and holds the title of Ralph S. and Dorothy P. Schmitt Professor in the Mandel School of Applied Social Sciences. He has given special attention to the internationalisation of social work and the challenge of an ageing world in a career spanning more than four decades. He has uniquely combined these two areas of expertise in his teaching and writing, as well as in his leadership roles at the United Nations and in national and international organisations, e.g. the (US) Council on Social Work Education and the International Association of Schools of Social Work. Terry Hokenstad has authored and edited numerous books, articles, chapters, and monographs in the fields of comparative social welfare, care of older people, and social work practice and education. In addition, he has served as a former Editor-in-Chief of *International Social Work* and as a member of the editorial board for a number of other scholarly journals.

Manohar Pawar is Professor of Social Work at the School of Humanities and Social Sciences, Charles Sturt University (NSW, Australia) and is president of the Asia-Pacific branch of the International Consortium for Social Development. He has nearly 30 years of experience in social work education, research and practice in Australia and India. Professor Pawar has received various awards, including the citation award for outstanding contribution to student learning (2008, from the Australian Learning and Teaching Council); and Quality of Life Award (2001, from the Association of Commonwealth Universities). Current areas of interest include international social work, development and policy; social consequences of climate change; informal care and ageing; NGOs and community development. Publications include: International Social Work (Sage, 2006), *Community Development in Asia and the Pacific* (Routledge, 2010), *Social Development* (Routledge, 2010) and International Social Work (2nd edition, Sage, 2012).

Nathalie Huegler trained as a social worker and social pedagogue in Germany and has since worked with young refugees in different settings, including in London local authorities, and currently as a senior social worker in a charity which provides rehabilitation and campaigns for the rights of survivors of torture. Following a Master's in international social work and refugee studies, she is undertaking doctoral research at London Metropolitan University about social work with separated children in Germany and the UK and the role of human rights. Other current and past activities include teaching and supervision on social work courses, co-authoring a number of publications and editorial assistance for the journal, *International Social Work*.

Nigel Hall is a Senior Lecturer at the School of Social Work, Kingston University, London (UK), and has both academic and practical experience of social work in the UK, Zimbabwe and other African countries. Nigel has represented the International Federation of Social Workers (IFSW) over many years in several capacities, most recently with responsibility for publications. He is also a Board member of the Commonwealth Organisation for Social Work (COSW). Nigel has authored and edited a variety of publications on HIV/AIDS, development, poverty alleviation and social work. He is presently the IFSW representative to the Editorial Policy Committee of *International Social Work*.

Notes on the Contributors

Tatsuru Akimoto is Director & Professor of the Social Work Research Institute, Asian Centre for Welfare in Society, Japan College of Social Work (since 2010) and is also Professor Emeritus, Japan Women's University. He is currently President of the Asia Pacific Association of Social Work Education (APASWE); and is a regional Vice-President of the International Association of Schools of Social Work (IASSW). For two decades he was Professor at, Japan Women's University. In addition to social work and international social work, his special interests include 'work and employment' and he was an Employment Promotion Expert for the International Labour Organisation (1992–1994). He has published a number of books and articles including 'The unipolar world and inequality: implications for social work', in *International Social Work* (2007).

Sahar Sulieman Al-Makhamreh was awarded her PhD in social work by Warwick University (UK) and has been a lecturer on the BA social work programme at Al-Balqa Applied University in Jordan since 2005. She is also Head of the Social Work Department and Assistant Dean (Development and Planning) at Princess Rahma University College and Al-Balqa Applied University. She is a co-founder of the Jordanian Association of Social Workers. Her main areas of research are: developing and professionalising social work; inter-professional relationships; health inequality; localising practice; cultural and gender sensitivity in Middle Eastern social work practice.

Margaret Alston commenced as Head of Department of Social Work at Monash University (Australia) in 2008, and has since established the Gender, Leadership and Social Sustainability (GLASS) Research Unit. She has served on various national Boards (e.g. the Family Services Council and the National Women's Advisory Group overseeing the Rural Women's Policy Unit in the Department of Primary Industries and Energy). In the past decade her expert status has involved her in work with the Gender Division of the UN FAO in Rome, the Commission for the Status of Women in New York and UN-Habitat meeting in Kenya. Her writing, speeches and media commentary focus on rural social conditions, climate change and gender issues.

Harjeet Badwall from Toronto (Canada) has been a practising social worker for 18 years in the areas of community health, social justice, and working with survivors of violence. She is a doctoral candidate, specialising in the area of critical race studies at the Ontario Institute for Studies in Education/University of Toronto, and is a faculty member at York University's School of Social Work. Harjeet Badwall's research explores the racial and colonial dimensions of social work theories and practices. Her doctoral thesis explores the narratives of racialised social workers and their encounters with race and racism in the field.

Liz Beddoe is Associate Professor in the School of Counselling, Human Services and Social Work at the University of Auckland (New Zealand). Her interests include critical perspectives on social work education, professional supervision, the sociology of occupations, the social work professionalisation project, learning discourses, interprofessional learning and practitioner research. She has published articles on supervision and professional issues in New Zealand and international journals. Recent publications include *Best Practice in Professional Supervision: a Guide for the Helping Professions* (2010) with Allyson Davys, and *Mapping Knowledge for Social Work Practice: Critical Intersections*, with Jane Maidment (2009).

Fred H. Besthorn is Associate Professor of Social Work at Wichita State University School of Social Work (USA). He has presented numerous papers at national and international conferences in addition to publications. His interests include developing a theoretical framework for the integration of a deep ecological awareness with social work policy and practice, including conducting research on the relationship between environmental degradation and the social, physical, economic and spiritual impact on at-risk populations. He is the founder of The Global Alliance for a Deep-Ecological Social Work – a forum for concerned social workers sharing a commitment to incorporating deeper environmental awareness into traditional social work practice.

Jennifer Bourassa obtained a Master's degree in Social Work at the University of Calgary (Canada). She is currently practising as a social worker with the Canadian forces. She previously worked for Alberta Health Services in a variety of roles including: Crisis Intervention Therapist, Brief Therapist, Community Developer and Emergency and Disaster Preparedness Consultant. Jennifer Bourassa has 17 years disaster experience working in countries such as Canada, the United States, Puerto Rico, Indonesia and Haiti. In 2009 her article 'Psychosocial interventions with mass populations: a social work perspective', was published in *International Social Work*, discussing the importance of utilising participatory methodology with disaster-impacted populations.

Wendy Bowles is Associate Professor of Social Work at Charles Sturt University and is a social worker with experience in the disability field. Her teaching and research interests cover the broad terrain of social work theory, practice and ethics with a focus on rural and regional practice. Two books written with colleagues include *Ethical Practice in Social Work* and *Research for Social Workers – An Introduction to Methods*. Wendy has served a full term as member of the National Ethics Committee of the Australian Association of Social Workers and is involved in professional practice issues in social work.

Paul Bywaters is Emeritus Professor of Social Work at Coventry University and Honorary Professor at the University of Warwick (both in the UK). He was co-founder and the first convenor of the international Social Work and Health Inequalities Network (www.warwick.ac.uk/go/swhin). Apart from his teaching, research and administrative roles in social work education, he has written extensively about social work and health over the past 25 years. His recent publications include *Social Work and Global Health Inequalities* (Policy Press, 2009); and he was the co-author of the revised International Federation of Social Workers' policy statement on Health, ratified in 2008.

Ruby Chau is an independent researcher. She is formerly Assistant Professor at the University of Hong Kong and Lecturer at the University of Sheffield (UK). She is a registered social worker in Hong Kong and has worked in NGOs in Hong Kong and the UK. Her main research interests include social exclusion, social diversity and welfare mix. She has conducted research in Hong Kong, China and the UK; and published in internationally renowned academic journals and refereed books.

David Cox is a retired Professor of Social Work, La Trobe University (Australia). He worked as a social worker with refugees and migrants for nearly 20 years before moving into academic social work. He worked in a variety of Australian universities over approximately a 30-year period, teaching and writing about social work with immigrants, international social work and social development.

Cindy Davis is an Associate Professor in Social Work at the University of Tennessee (USA). Her primary area of research is health and international social work. After receiving her PhD from the University of California at Los Angeles, she spent two years backpacking across Africa and Asia. She then completed a post-doctoral fellowship in clinical psychology at the Chinese University of Hong Kong. Cindy Davis has since served as a behavioural scientist at the National Health and Medical Research Centre's National Breast Cancer Centre in Australia. She has published extensively in the area of health and international issues.

Murli Desai obtained her doctorate in Social Work from Washington University in St Louis (USA). From 1984 she was on the faculty of the Tata Institute of Social Sciences, Mumbai (India), taking voluntary retirement in 2006 as Professor and Head of its Social Work Education and Practice Cell. In 2007–2008, she worked as a Senior Visiting Fellow in the Department of Social Work, National University of Singapore and the following year, she worked as a Professor in the Department of Social Welfare, Seoul National University of South Korea. She has authored three books, edited six books and guest-edited ten special issues of journals on different themes in social work and social development.

Lena Dominelli as Professor in Applied Social Sciences and Associate Director at the Institute of Hazards, Risk and Resilience Research, Durham University (UK), heads the Vulnerability and Resilience Programme. She has a wealth of experience as an educator, researcher and practitioner and has published widely in social work, social policy and sociology. Her latest book is *Green Social Work*. She is recognised as a leading figure in social work education globally and was elected President of the International Association of Schools of Social Work (IASSW) from 1996 to 2004. She is currently chair of IASSW's Committees on Disaster Interventions and Climate Change. She has received various honours including a medal in 2002 from the French Senate and an honorary doctorate in 2008 from the University of KwaZulu-Natal (South Africa).

Heather Fraser works as a Senior Lecturer in the Discipline of Social Work and Social Planning at Flinders University, South Australia, after years spent teaching social work in Melbourne, Cairns and Winnipeg (Canada). She teaches topics such as Reasons for Social Work, Integrity in Social Work, Social Work with Diverse Populations and Social Work with Addictions. Her practice experience relates predominantly to women and children, particularly in areas related to violence and abuse. Author of the book, *In the Name of Love, Women's Narratives of Love and Abuse* (2008), Heather Fraser identifies as a narrative feminist who works from a critical perspective.

John R. Graham is Murray Fraser Professor of Community Economic Development, Faculty of Social Work, University of Calgary (Canada). He has published extensively on spirituality and social work, international social work, and social policy analysis.

Gerda Heck is currently a post-doctoral research fellow in an international, transdisciplinary research project, 'Global Prayers' at the University of Frankfurt/Oder (Germany), investigating the role of (neo-)Pentecostal church communities on the migration routes of Congolese migrants. In her doctoral thesis (2006) she discussed the phenomenon of undocumented immigration in Germany and the USA, mainly focusing on the development of the respective migration regimes, the public discussion on the subject and the influencing thereof by relevant initiatives. Since 2007 she has been conducting research on the shifts in EU migration policy towards North African countries and the strategies of sub-Saharan migrants on the migration routes towards Europe.

Staffan Höjer is a Social Work Professor in the Department of Social Work at the University of Gothenburg (Sweden). His main research areas concern the development of social work knowledge, organisational development and professionalisation in social work. His publications reflect these interests and include a cross-national analysis of models of supervision. He also has a special interest in international social work: he has undertaken research in Cuba and is currently involved in PhD supervision in Sweden, Rwanda and Uganda. He has been involved in the CERTS project (about doctoral studies in Europe) and is currently Deputy Editor of the *European Journal of Social Work.*

Jennifer Holder Dolly was for many years a Lecturer in Social Work and the Coordinator of Graduate Studies at the University of the West Indies, St Augustine. She is currently the Clinical Director and joint owner of a behaviour change consulting firm. She has also worked intensively in disaster recovery and management roles, heading the social sector recovery effort in Grenada after Hurricane Ivan. She has consulted with private, public and non-governmental organisations and conducted a range of psycho-educational and personal development workshops. Dr Holder Dolly has researched and presented many papers at regional and international conferences and workshops.

Richard Hugman is Professor of Social Work at the University of New South Wales (Australia). He has been a social work practitioner, researcher and teacher in Australia and the UK and has published widely in the field, both as an author and as an editor. Since 2004 he has been a consultant to UNICEF Vietnam on the development of professional social work in Vietnam. Richard is currently the chair of the Permanent Committee on Ethics of the International Federation of Social Workers. Recent publications include *Understanding International Social Work* (2010).

Marion Huxtable spent 29 years as a school social worker advocating for school children. She contributed to her profession by serving on Boards of state and regional professional associations, publishing in professional journals and books and serving as a consulting editor for *Social Work in Education* (now *Children and Schools*). Twenty years ago, she developed the International Network for School Social Work to give school social workers and their professional associations a way of communicating with peers around the world. It has grown to include 46 countries. She continues to operate the Network to foster international interaction among school social workers.

Jeff Karabanow is a Professor of Social Work at Dalhousie University (Canada) in the Faculty of Health Professions. He has worked with homeless young people in Toronto, Montreal, Halifax and Guatemala. He has undertaken research in various locations and published numerous academic articles about housing stability, service delivery systems, street health and homeless youth culture. He has completed a film documentary looking at the plight of street youth in

Guatemala City and several animated shorts on Canadian street youth culture. His most recent work is *Leaving the Streets:Stories of Canadian Youth* published in 2010 (Fernwood Press).

Synnove Karvinen-Niinikoski is a Professor of Social Work at the University of Helsinki (Finland), engaged in promoting the integration of teaching, research and professional development. Special interests include development of critical practice and reflexive expertise, and she is engaged in practice research and learning and researcher education. In 1998 Synnove Karvinen-Niinikoski was elected the first President of the Finnish Society for Social Work Research and she received the Biannual Nordic Prize for Social Work Educators in 2009. Since 2010 she has been a member of the Board of the International Association of Schools of Social Work; and up to 2012 Vice President of the European Resource Centre for Research in Social Work (CERTS).

Linda Kreitzer began her Social Work career in 1978 in the United States and migrated to Britain in 1981 where she worked in social service departments for over a decade. Between 1994 and 1996 she taught social work at the University of Ghana, leaving to undertake a Master's degree in international social work at the University of Calgary (Canada), specifically looking at refugee issues. After a year's work in Armenia she returned to Calgary to undertake PhD research. The focus of her doctorate (awarded in 2004) was the development of a culturally appropriate social work curriculum at the University of Ghana, Legon. She is currently an Associate Professor at the University of Calgary, Edmonton, Canada.

Susan Lawrence qualified as a social worker in 1976 and has been a social work educator since 1991, she is currently Principal Lecturer in International Social Work at London Metropolitan University (UK). She has been actively involved in European social work research, networks and exchanges throughout her career and is Course Director of the MA in Comparative European Social Studies (MACESS) and Course Leader of the Professional Doctorate in International Social Work. Susan Lawrence is currently President of the European Association of Schools of Social Work and Regional Vice-President of International Association of Schools of Social Work (IASSW). She has published in the area of international social work and is on the editorial Board of the *European Journal of Social Work.*

Kathryn Libal is Assistant Professor in Community Organisation at the University of Connecticut School of Social Work (USA). An anthropologist by training, she has conducted historical and ethnographic research on women's and children's rights in Turkey. Recently she has collaborated with Dr Scott Harding on research regarding non-governmental organisation advocacy for Iraqi refugees. She also writes on the US human rights movement, with a focus on children's economic rights, and has co-edited the book, *Human Rights in the United States: Beyond Exceptionalism* (2011). She teaches courses on social policy, human oppression and human rights.

Reima Ana Maglajlic was a Senior Lecturer in Social Work at Swansea University (Wales) (2007–2011). Prior to this she worked as a consultant and activist across south-east Europe, but primarily in Bosnia and Herzegovina. Her doctoral research used participatory action research with service users, students and practitioners in England and Bosnia to explore social work education. Her main interests and experiences focus on working on the reform of social care services, in societies 'in transition' and/or affected by political conflict. In 2011 she became the Research and Monitoring Director at the Mental Disability Advocacy Centre, an international non-governmental organisation based in Budapest, Hungary.

Kathleen Manion has lived and worked in various countries and studied psychology and community development in Canada and international social work in England. She undertook cross-national research into commercial sexual exploitation of girls in London, Sydney and Vancouver for her doctoral degree and was awarded her PhD by the University of East London in 2006. She has since relocated to New Zealand where she works for the Ministry of Social Development.

Golam M. Mathbor is the Associate Dean of the School of Humanities and Social Sciences, and Professor in the School of Social Work at Monmouth University (USA). Currently, he is Vice President of the American Institute of Bangladesh Studies (AIBS), and of the International Consortium for Social Development (ICSD). He has taught in Austria, Bangladesh, Canada, Latvia, Kosovo and the USA and his teaching areas include research methods, programme evaluation, social welfare policy and planning, management of non-governmental organisations, migration and intercultural cooperation, and international social work. Areas of research include disaster relief and management, international social development and international social work. Golam Mathbor has published extensively on disaster relief and other topics including most recently, *Effective Community Participation in Coastal Development.*

Jennifer McKinnon is an Associate Professor at Charles Sturt University (Australia). She has a social work practice background in hospitals and mental health, as well as in youth work and private practice, and has been an academic since 1992. Her doctoral studies were on the topic of the social/environmental nexus in social work practice, which is also now her major research focus. Jennifer has published widely on the topic of social justice and environmental justice, and has presented at many international conferences. She has also published on the topic of social work practice in schools, and is the co-editor of two editions of *Social Work: Fields of Practice* (Oxford University Press).

Lengwe-Katembula J. Mwansa is a Professor at the University of Botswana in the Department of Social Work. He began his teaching career in social work in 1996 after completing his PhD (awarded by Brandeis University, USA). He has taught in several universities and held various portfolios including headship of the Department of Social Work at the Universities of Zambia and Botswana 1998–1991 and 1999–2005, respectively; Presidency of Southern African Social Sciences Conference (1994–1999); and recently, the Presidency of the Association of Schools of Social Work in Africa (2005–2010), His areas of interest and publications include social policy (health policy), youth, social work education in Africa, and non-governmental organisations.

James Midgley is Harry and Riva Specht Professor of Public Social Services at the School of Social Welfare, University of California, Berkeley (USA). He has published widely on issues of social development, international social welfare and social policy. Recent books include *The Handbook of Social Policy*, Sage, 2009 (co-editor, Michelle Livermore); *Social Work and Social Development*, Oxford University Press, 2010 (co-editor, Amy Conley); *Grassroots Social Security in Asia*, Routledge, 2011 (co-editor, Mitsuhiko Hosaka) and *Colonialism and Welfare: Social Policy and the British Imperial Legacy,* Edward Elgar, 2011 (co-editor, David Piachaud). He is a Fellow of the *American Academy of Social Work and Social Welfare* and an Honorary Professor at the Hong Kong Polytechnic University; Nihon Fukishi University in Japan; the University of Johannesburg, South Africa; and Sun Yat-sen University in China.

Joan Orme is Emeritus Professor of Social Work at Glasgow University and Visiting Professor at the University of Southampton (UK). She has been a member of the Board of the International Association of Schools of Social Work and has worked with colleagues in Australia, Finland, New Zealand, Poland and the USA. Her research includes workloads, care management and aspects of social work practice and education and she has published on social work practice and research and feminism. She co-edited the *Sage Handbook of Social Work Research* (2010) and co-authored (with David Shemmings) *Developing Research Based Social Work Practice* (Palgrave Macmillan, 2010).

Henry Parada is an Associate Professor at Ryerson University (Canada) where he teaches Theories of Social Work Practices, Transformative Social Work, International Social Work, Graduate Research Seminar and Child Welfare. Henry's research interests include: analysis of institutional practices; social work epistemology; and institutional ethnography methodology. He has published in the area of child protection and governance of workers and clients, institutional ethnography, the construction of subject locations, and community social work and education in Latin American. He has undertaken a variety of research projects with funding from various sources including the Canadian International Development Agency (CIDA), Latin American and Caribbean Exchange Grant (LACREG), UNICEF-Santo Domingo and SSHRC International Opportunity Fund.

Malcolm Payne is Policy and Development Adviser, St Christopher's Hospice (London, UK) where he was previously Director of Psycho-social and Spiritual Care. He has broad experience of social work, having worked in probation, social work, community work and management, consulting on teamwork in health and social care organisations. He was Professor and Head of Applied Community Studies, Manchester Metropolitan University, for many years, during which he was involved in child and mental health service advocacy projects, research and international social work. Among his recent books are: *Modern Social Work Theory*; *Humanistic Social Work*; *Citizenship Social Work with Older People* and *Social Work in End-of-Life and Palliative Care* (with Margaret Reith). He has visiting/honorary academic appointments at a number of UK and European Universities, including Opole University, Poland, and Kingston University, UK.

Michael Preston-Shoot is Professor of Social Work and Dean of the Faculty of Health and Social Sciences at the University of Bedfordshire (UK). He has worked in social work education since 1988 following a career as a social worker. He has been Editor of *Social Work Education;* Managing Editor of the *European Journal of Social Work;* and is a Founding Editor of *Ethics and Social Welfare*. He has written and researched widely on law and social work, and on social work education and practice. Currently, he is an independent chair of two local Safeguarding Boards (Children, Vulnerable Adults) and sits on the governing body of an NHS Trust and of the National Skills Academy for Social Care.

Shulamit Ramon is mental health research lead at the University of Hertfordshire and Emeritus Professor at Anglia Ruskin University (UK). A social worker and clinical psychologist by training, Shulamit Ramon has researched mental health and social work issues, introducing user involvement in research and education internationally. She has focused on introducing social work education to post-communist countries in the 1990s (Ukraine, Russia, Azerbaijan), and on the impact of political conflict on social work since 2000. She has recently edited the book *Social Work in the Context of Political Conflict* (2008); has led two related

International Association of Schools of Social Work (IASSW) projects on this issue, and has researched the impact of the end of intifada on Israeli Arab and Jewish social workers.

Narda Razack is an Associate Dean (Faculty of Liberal Arts and Professional Studies) and Associate Professor in the School of Social Work, York University (Canada). She has extensive experience in research, teaching and administration. She has published in the areas of critical race and oppression, international social work and field education; and co-edited *Social Justice: A Journal of Crime, Conflict and World Order*. Narda Razack currently co-directs a CURA-funded project, 'Assets Coming Together for Youth: Linking Research, Policy and Action for Positive Youth Development'; and is a team member on a Canadian International Development Agency (CIDA)-funded project, 'Social Work in Nigeria'. Research areas include: North–South relations, globalisation and international social work, critical race theory, post-colonialism and equity in administration.

Taly Reininger is a Professor of Social Work at the Universidad Andres Bello in Santiago (Chile). She received her MSW from the University of Wisconsin (USA). Currently she teaches Field Placement Seminars and Foundations of Social Work and is embarking on her research and writing career.

Amy Restorick Roberts is a doctoral candidate at the Mandel School of Applied Social Sciences at Case Western Reserve University in Cleveland, Ohio. She is currently in preparation for an academic career in gerontological social work research and education to improve the quality of life of older adults.

Letnie Rock completed her doctoral studies at Fordham University, New York (USA) and after a period in practice is a Lecturer in Social Work and Head of the Department of Government, Sociology and Social Work at the University of the West Indies (Cave Hill Campus, Barbados). She is currently the President of the Caribbean Association of Social Work Educators, a member of the Editorial Board of the *Caribbean Journal of Social Work* and of the Boards of the North American and Caribbean Association of Schools of Social Work and of the International Association of Schools of Social Work. Research and publications to date have primarily been in the fields of child abuse and neglect, domestic violence, disaster management and social work practice.

Mahia Saracostti Schwartzman qualified as a social worker and with a Master's in Business Administration of Pontificia Universidad Católica de Chile, before being awarded her PhD in Social Welfare at City University of New York. She is currently Director of Social Work at the Universidad Autónoma de Chile in Santiago, and has held posts at various Chilean Universities previously. She has been member of the Editorial Board of *International Social Work*, and is a faculty advisor at Hunter College School of Social Work, New York, as well as a consultant for the Inter-American Development Bank and for the European Union. She has published in specialised journals, newspapers and books.

Uma A. Segal is Professor in the School of Social Work at the University of Missouri, St Louis (USA). Her Areas of research are immigrant and refugee concerns, Asian American acculturation, and cross-national issues in family violence. In 2004, Uma Segal was appointed Editor of the *Journal of Immigrant & Refugee Studies* and redirected it toward an international, interdisciplinary focus in exploring human migration. She serves as resident scholar on immigration for the Advisory Board of the Katherine A. Kendall Institute (KAKI) of the (US) Council on Social Work Education; and co-edited *Immigration Worldwide* with Elliott and Mayadas in 2010.

Micheal L. Shier qualified as a social worker (BSW) before completing his MSW and is now a PhD student at the University of Pennsylvania (USA) researching human service organisations and service delivery outcomes. He is currently working as a research associate at the University of Calgary and Doctoral Research Fellow at University of Pennsylvania. He has co-authored articles on the subjects of spirituality and religion in social work, the lived experiences of vulnerable populations, and practice-based experiences of social workers in diverse contexts.

John Solas is currently Senior Lecturer in Human Services and Counselling at the University of Southern Queensland (Australia). John previously lectured on social policy at Monash University and human rights at Queensland University of Technology. He was a member of the Centre for Rural, Social and Economic Research Centre at Central Queensland University and of the Health and Well-Being Research Group at Ballarat University. While Head of Social Work and Welfare Studies at Charles Darwin University, he was a representative on the Northern Land Council where his research and advocacy were instrumental in improving the delivery of primary health care services to Indigenous communities in Central and Northern regions of Australia. John has published widely on social work theory and practice. Among his major works is *The Deconstruction of Educational Practice in Social Work*.

Cynthia Akorfa Sottie gained her MSW at West Virginia University in the United States in 1996 and completed her PhD in Social work at Queens University in Belfast in 2010. She has been teaching at the Department of Social Work, University of Ghana since 2000. Her main area of research interest is child and family welfare with specific interest in ways of helping young people from disadvantaged backgrounds break out of the cycle of poverty and overcome vulnerability when social and economic conditions place severe limits on opportunities.

Silvia Staub-Bernasconi is a member of the Academic Board and Lecturer of the European network programme, INDOSOW (International Doctoral Studies in Social Work), following eight years as Director of the Master's programme `Social Work as Human Rights Profession' in Berlin. She has been a Professor at the Technical University in Berlin teaching Social Work Theory and Human Rights Practice since 1997. Initially she qualified as a social worker in Zurich, gaining a UN-Fellowship to study social work in the USA. She subsequently practised in New York and Zurich, including study visits (e.g. to Birmingham (UK), Rio de Janeiro (Brazil, U of California/Santa Cruz). From 1967 to 1997 she was Professor of social work at the Zurich School, while studying sociology, psychological pedagogy and social ethics, finishing her studies with a Ph.D. in sociology at the University of Zurich. She published widely on social problems, social work as discipline and profession, social work and human rights/social justice, theories of power and empowerment. At the Joint World Conference on Social Work in Hong Kong she received the "Kathleen Kendall Award 2010".

Decha Sungkawan is Associate Professor of Social Welfare and Criminal Justice at the Faculty of Social Administration, Thammasat University, Thailand where he teaches social work, social welfare, social policy, criminology and criminal justice. His research interests and publications have addressed the interrelated issues of social work and social welfare and criminal justice. He has been involved in several studies and development projects in Thailand including the projects on human rights plan education, community justice, restorative and transitional justice, conflict resolution and reconciliation, drug control policy, offenders and drug addicts rehabilitation programmes, victim compensation and reparation, human trafficking, refugees and migrant workers, disabilities and older persons, family violence, volunteer network and social work education. He holds Ph from the School of Social Service Administration, the

University of Chicago. Presently, he is the Dean of the Faculty of Social Administration, Thammasat University.

Ming-sum Tsui is a Professor of Social Work and Leader of the Doctor of Social Work (DSW) Programme in the Department of Applied Social Sciences, Hong Kong Polytechnic University. His research interests include social work supervision, social work theory and practice, human service management, substance abuse, and international social work practice. Ming-sum Tsui has published more than 100 pieces of research works, including 11 books and 50 journal articles. He is involved in editorial or reviewing work for 20 professional/academic journals. Recently, his article 'From resilience to resistance: A reconstruction of the strengths perspective in social work practice', published in *International Social Work* was awarded the Frank Turner Prize - Best Paper in 2010.

Khuajin Ulziitungalag is Professor in the Social Work Department at the State University of Education in Ulaanbaatar, Mongolia (where she has worked since 1997). Her teaching includes courses on Macro Social Work Practice, Child Protection, and Human Rights and Social Work. Khuajin Ulziitungalag's research is informed by her previous social work experience with maltreated children in public and private settings and focuses on child protection in the social welfare system. She is currently working to adapt a community-based child protection service aimed at increasing community participation in protecting children.

Julia M. Watkins is the Executive Director of the Council on Social Work Education (USA). She serves as treasurer of the International Association of Schools of Social Work. Previous positions have included President of the American University in Bulgaria (1993–2003), Professor of Social Work, and interim Vice President for Academic Affairs and Dean of the College of Social And Behavioural Sciences at the University of Maine. Other leadership positions have included President of the Alliance of Universities for Democracy and President of the Association of American International Colleges and Universities. She received the MSW and a PhD in Educational Psychology from the University of Utah.

Joseph Wronka is Professor of Social Work at Springfield College in Massachusetts (USA). He is also Permanent Representative to the United Nations in Geneva for the International Association of Schools of Social Work (IASSW). He has also taught extensively on the college level; practiced in inner cities and Indigenous communities; and presented his work in roughly 13 countries. He is a Fulbright Senior Specialist in social work with specialties in poverty, social justice, human rights, psychology, and phenomenology. His doctorate in social policy is from Brandeis; his Master's is in existential-phenomenology from Duquesne. He also studied the phenomenology of the performing musician at the University of Nice.

Darja Zaviršek is Chair of the Department for Research on Social Justice and Inclusion at the University of Ljubljana, Faculty of Social Work (Slovenia) and Chair of the *Indosow* programme (International Doctoral Studies in Social Work). In 2002 she was appointed Honorary Professor of the University of Applied Sciences Alice Salomon, in Berlin. She initiated the Eastern European Sub-Regional Association of the European Association of Schools of Social Work (EASSW) serving as its President since 2008. She has been on the Board of the International Association of Schools of Social Work (IASSW) since 2003. Areas of research and publications include: disability and mental health; gender and violence; history of social work; diversity studies, ethnographic research and international social work.

Editorial Advisory Board

List of Tables and Figures

TABLES

Preface and Acknowledgements

An invitation from Sage in late 2009 to put in a proposal to produce a Handbook of this kind was both exciting and challenging. As (initially four) prospective co-editors (KL, TH, MP and Nathalie H), we had all been engrossed in the subject of 'International Social Work' for various lengths of time: we all knew of each others' work, though had not worked together on a task such as this, with the exception of Karen and Nathalie who had gained recent experience editing the journal *International Social Work*. We received comprehensive – if sometimes conflicting – feedback from a number of reviewers on the initial proposal, for which we thank them, and proceeded to draft the final outline for the Handbook, according to the publisher's guidelines, with indicative content shaped by our own ideas and the feedback.

The first challenge was to identify social workers around the world who would be knowledgeable about the subject area and would be active editorial advisors. We asked the people we approached whether they might be willing to write specific chapters – or could assist us in identifying other authors – and also to contribute to the reviewing of drafts. A major vote of thanks, therefore, is to the members of the Editorial Advisory Board (see page xxi) who, almost without exception undertook the tasks they had volunteered for, or agreed to, promptly and helpfully. Special thanks go to those who undertook more than their fair share of reviewing or who subsequently agreed to contribute to the appendices or to the final stages of the editing process itself (of which more later).

Recruiting authors was an interesting process which took longer than we had anticipated. Apart from immediately raising queries about our ambitious time-scale(!), this also provided some insights into which were 'popular topics' and which seemed 'unknown' or not conceptualised in the way we were proposing. However, together with offers from individual editors as well as members of the advisory board, we eventually 'signed up' authors for Chapters 2 to 30, the first one being the editors' responsibility. We decided early on that we would encourage co-authorship of these long chapters on a variety of criteria. We particularly favoured cross-national collaborations, but it was not always possible for lead authors to arrange this and did not always work so smoothly where we prompted authors not known to each other to work together – although some such arrangements worked very well (in terms of both the process and outcome). Another criterion was the more familiar one of an experienced author working with a junior colleague, which has also produced some good chapters. Finally, some authors either chose to work alone or were left to do so if others were unable to deliver on previous agreements. While we very much appreciate the contributions of all the authors, we are particularly grateful to people who were solo authors (not by choice) and to others who came on board later in the writing stage due to intended authors finding themselves unavailable for some reason.

The phrase 'stuff happens' was very apt at various stages of this Handbook's production and helped give perspective when events threatened to raise blood pressure or produce grey hairs. Apart from 'losing' occasional authors, the editors themselves were not immune from work pressures and personal events – sometimes anticipated and sometimes not – which impinge on the smooth flow of work. And of course, particularly given the nature of the Handbook, people were occasionally away at conferences or undertaking work abroad, sometimes affording time to meet but at other times making e-mail contact difficult in the short-term. In addition, at various stages, individual editors moved house; had new responsibilities in 'the day job'; had to attend funerals or mind sick children; and even had a first baby. It was this last event, coupled with the fact that our initial planned submission date had had to be renegotiated, which prompted recruitment of a fifth editor (Nigel H.) who, drawing on his own experience (in international work and editing, as well as his role on the editorial advisory board), was able to make a significant contribution to the final stages of editorial work.

So we have reached the point when the Handbook goes into production, if not in record time, at least in a timeframe which, we hope, means that material (often drafted in 2010 but revised in 2011) will still be topical and up-to-date when published. We are, of course, grateful to staff at Sage – for giving us the chance to work on this very stimulating project, for agreeing to revised schedules and the addition of a fifth editor – as well as for the more formal tasks which publishers undertake, including marketing and production. We also express thanks to long-suffering partners and families who are familiar with the demands that work regularly places on us and who, nevertheless, support our endeavours.

As is customary, we accept responsibility for any errors which we might not have spotted. However, we are also pleased that we have been able to encourage diverse voices and views in this Handbook. Our approach to analysing and developing different aspects of 'international social work' has been largely thematic (with the exception of the chapters in the Regional Perspectives section), and including authors from a range of countries and beyond the English-speaking world has resulted in examples from many countries and use of literature which might not otherwise be widely accessible. Nevertheless, we regret that 'coverage' could not be comprehensive and hope that some notable omissions will be addressed in alternative or subsequent texts. As co-editors, sharing a common language (English in its various forms), we have varied personal heritages and bring professional experience from different national contexts contributing to sometimes differing interpretations or emphases in relation to our common theme. We agreed early on that it is not possible to give one definitive answer to the question, 'what is international social work' but (apart from our own attempts to address this question in Chapter 1) authors have explicitly or implicitly also considered this question from their own perspectives. While we expect that individual readers will 'dip' into the Handbook to read the chapter(s) of most interest to them, we think that the whole also adds up to a wide-ranging consideration of a topic which increasing numbers of social workers will need to be informed about. We therefore believe that this is an important contribution to considering the value base and developing theory and practice in the broadly defined field of international social work.

Karen Lyons—UK (Ireland), Terry Hokenstad—USA, Manohar Pawar—Australia (India), Nathalie Huegler—UK (Germany), Nigel Hall—UK (Zimbabwe)

November 2011

1

Setting the Scene

Nathalie Huegler, Karen Lyons
and Manohar Pawar

INTRODUCTION

In an increasingly interdependent world, the domains of social work, social development and the social professions, more generally, are not immune from the global processes affecting whole societies and, more specifically, national welfare systems – or the lack of them – and the living standards and life chances of individuals, families, groups and communities. It is increasingly acknowledged that 'social work' is influenced by global trends and that many social problems are either common to different societies, or have an international dimension or even involve social professionals in transnational activities and international mobility. It is therefore timely to produce a Handbook which addresses the social issues which have an international aetiology or dimension; which analyses the international organisations, conventions and policies which impact on regional, transnational and national/local (social) developments; and which interrogates and illustrates a term which has a long genesis but unclear definition, 'international social work'.

The purpose of this chapter is to orientate readers to the broad field of 'international social work', partly through offering a brief introduction to its origins and exponents, and centrally through exploring the various meanings that can be ascribed to the term, and some of the related concepts, e.g. 'international perspectives'; 'comparative social welfare'; and 'social professionals'. We also present a preliminary analysis of some of the concerns and constructs which have particular significance in this context (e.g. globalisation and 'glocalisation'; indigenisation; the global North and global South) and suggest that ideas of 'space' and 'time' are salient concepts in social work (i.e. geographical and historical factors in macro terms but also the micro space and time elements of individual and community lives). The role of constructs such as race, ethnicity, culture and religion in the context of globalisation and their relevance for international social work are discussed as are the relationship between values, diversity and power relations. Also, as a precursor to more detailed discussions later, we sketch out some of the important trends and comparative data about global issues which provide a backdrop to social interventions at global, regional and local levels. Finally, we describe the organisation of the book and give a brief preview of its contents.

Overall, this Handbook provides a 'state of the art' analysis of 'international social work' as a specialist form of professional practice. However, in a global context, the practices of all social professionals are increasingly influenced by macro-economic and political forces and informed by international conventions and the inter-relationships between nations and transnational communities. The Handbook also uses an international lens to view social work as a local activity and sometimes takes a comparative perspective to illustrate the diversity of social work theories and practices across the world. We should clarify now that 'social work' is used in this Handbook as a generic term for a diverse occupational group which takes many forms across the globe. The emphasis of work varies between countries and regions as do the challenges; social professionals have different training opportunities and traditions and are known by different titles; and they are employed in a varied range of settings and agencies with different conditions regarding public expectations, esteem and regulation. Even apparently shared values may be contested in the context of particular (national) cultures and agreement about a shared/international value base which does not simply perpetuate 'Western' ideologies and power (relative to the interests and claims of indigenous and/or minority populations) is an on-going challenge.[1]

The Handbook is 'international' both in terms of the wide range of countries from which the authors are drawn and also through the use of examples in the chapters which help elaborate both national differences and also shared concerns and practices. The latter identify social work as a recognisable activity in many countries of the world. For example, 92 national associations of social workers have chosen to join the International Federation of Social Workers

(IFSW) while schools of social work from up to 100 countries are members of the International Association of Schools of Social Work (IASSW). A third international body, the International Council of Social Welfare (ICSW), comprising, predominantly, national umbrella or lead organisations representing third sector or non-governmental organisations (NGOs) and international organisations in more than 70 countries, reflects a similarly wide geographical spread of social work and development initiatives. These three bodies are important in giving a voice, internationally, to social workers and those involved in social development and are (at the time of writing) engaged in developing a 'global agenda' for social work (see websites of the three organisations and later).

The aims of the Handbook can therefore be summarised as follows:

- to critically review and advance our understanding of the term 'international social work' as both a specialist form of practice and as a way of better appreciating local conditions and developing local practice
- to analyse and draw on related concepts, such as international perspectives; comparative social welfare; and transnational social work to illustrate both commonalities and diversity globally
- to present key social issues relevant to social work in international, historical and contemporary perspectives and identify particular practices in social work and social development which have international dimensions
- to indicate potential directions for research, education and practice in the fields of international, comparative and transnational social work.

KEY TERMS AND CONCEPTS USED IN THIS HANDBOOK

We start by analysing and defining some terms and concepts which will be used in this chapter and in the handbook overall. The key concept at the heart of this handbook, naturally, is 'international social work' itself but, before considering this term, it is useful to look at some of the related concepts which form the basis for considering international social work.

What do we understand by 'international'?

A central term which needs to be defined in the context of this Handbook is *'international'* – and particularly the question of how this relates to similar terms (sometimes used interchangeably) such as *'transnational'*, *'cross-national'* or *'global'*. An obvious commonality among the first three terms is that they all make reference to the concept of the nation-state, a link which is significant for social work both historically and currently, as we will discuss later. Healy (2001: 5) has provided a helpful distinction between the terms 'global' and 'international', stating that the former indicates a concern for the world as a whole, while 'international' involves issues and relationships between two or more nations (or their citizens), or which transcend national boundaries and viewpoints. The transcendence of national boundaries is emphasised even more strongly by the term 'transnational', which departs from the view of the nation-state as a 'container' for political, economic, social and cultural activities and relationships and instead focuses on practices, organisations, networks and flows, which create on-going interconnections across borders, particularly on the micro-level of human relationships (e.g. through transnational migration networks) (Glick Schiller and Levitt, 2006). Cross-national, on the other hand, often refers to comparisons or transactions between a (limited) number of nation-states (Healy, 2001).

Along with various terms that indicate some form of border crossing (whether actual or more 'virtual'), this introduction also needs to consider the various 'spatial' units 'below' and 'beyond' the nation-state which are of relevance to (international) social work. The growth of literature in the international social work field in recent years has sparked (or perhaps rekindled) debates about what might be appropriate 'locations' of social work, and whether suggesting a 'global' frame of reference for the profession is – in polarised forms – a necessity of our time (Ife, 2001) or a project of (at best) unrealistic vanity or (at worst) imperialism by a selected elite of academics from economically privileged countries (Webb, 2003; Haug, 2005; Gray and Webb, 2007) The tensions brought out by these debates reflect both the many contentions inherent in the practice and theory of social work as such (from the micro- through to the macro-level), as well as the contradictions and complexities, which characterise various spatial units. Few people would probably dispute the statement that social work has been and is a 'locality-bound' (as well as time-specific) activity (Lyons, 1999), but quite what constitutes a *'locality'* is a less well-defined and even contested notion. We can imagine various meanings ranging from fairly small human settlements (e.g. a village or, an urban neighbourhood); the 'local' level of a whole city or urban or rural conglomerations of several hundred thousand or even a few million inhabitants which have been grouped together as administrative units; through to the level of a society delimited by national borders. More often than not 'local' seems to be defined mainly in relation to other spatial contexts, for example, as an opposite to 'global' (Dominelli, 2010).[2]

Distinguishing 'regions'

Another example of a term which can be ambiguous is *'region'* – which in some contexts denotes different areas within a country, but which we mainly use in this Handbook to refer to different continental regions of the world. Grouping countries into regions or even finding appropriate names to describe regions is far from straight-forward, and the difficulties brought about by such attempts (which we have nevertheless made) are highlighted in most of the 'regional perspectives' chapters in Section 5 of this Handbook.

On the point of language, we also need to acknowledge that any discussion which seeks to compare or contrast different parts of the world in terms of economic and political power relations involves word choices which are contentious. In this chapter, and elsewhere, we tend to use the terms 'global North' and 'global South' to distinguish between countries which (usually based on historically developed power dynamics, e.g. through colonialism) are relatively rich and powerful in the international arena, and those that have tended to be economically and politically marginalised – often because their resources were (or continue to be) exploited by other nations. While this distinction reflects, to some extent, actual geographical locations of the countries and regions in either the northern or southern hemisphere of the world, like any dichotomy, this categorisation has exceptions (e.g. Australia or New Zealand as relatively wealthy nations in the geographical South) and blurred boundaries (e.g. the status of poor nations in rich regions, such as some states in Eastern Europe). The notion of 'rich' and 'poor' nations itself is relativised through the fact that there are privileged 'elites' in the South (for instance, the relatively small number of billionaires in India continues to grow, while the vast majority still live on less than $US2 per day (e.g. Agrawal, 2011) and excluded populations in the North. Other 'typologies' used in this Handbook include that of 'Western' nations (or concepts and ideas which originated there) which usually denotes a similar 'area' to that described by the term global North. 'Western' is sometimes contrasted with 'Eastern', but more often with 'non-Western', which already alludes to some of the difficulties associated with this particular term. A further common distinction used by the UN is that of 'developed' relative to 'developing' regions or countries. This suggests a certain progressional path in which countries with access to more resources are considered to have moved 'further along' than those with less resources. While many may view this as unproblematic when

comparing the economic 'output' and technological 'advances' of certain countries, the difficulty with this terminology is that it can suggest inferiority or 'backwardness' in the context of social or cultural issues, with negative implications for attitudes and behaviours towards populations in countries so described. Perhaps the terms, 'industrialised' (or post-industrial) and 'industrialising' convey a more neutral description. Distinctions can also be made more overtly on the basis of economic wealth as in the terms 'minority world' and 'majority world', sometimes referred to as the 'one-thirds' and 'two-thirds' world (Sewpaul and Jones, 2004). These terms reflect the considerable inequality of resource distribution across the globe as well as the fact that a minority of the world's population sustains luxurious life styles on the very basis that these are unattainable for the remaining majority. Each of these dichotomies seems to have its particular problems and the various notions can be contested. Therefore, in editing this Handbook, we have refrained from seeking to establish a standardised vocabulary but suggest that linguistic diversity within even the Anglophone literature (not to mention the literature in other languages) is a reality and a testimony to the richness of ideas and concepts in social work, as well as providing its own challenges.

Globalisation – what does it mean and is it relevant?

Turning to another key concept for this Handbook, the term 'globalisation' (see Chapter 2), continues to generate debate about its meaning, range and even its existence or novelty status, as well as its relation to social reform and social work (Teeple, 2000; Payne and Askeland, 2008). Among the many different views and perspectives are those which view globalisation predominantly as an economic process spreading capitalist ideas and modes of production as well as integrating local markets into a wider global market, and those which consider it to be a more multidimensional process which has social, political, cultural and environmental (or spatial) aspects and consequences that are as important as the economic ones. There are also different views on the role of nation-states within globalisation – ranging from the notion that states are losing power and influence to transnational corporations, which are free to set their own conditions, through to the argument that globalisation has done relatively little to influence the existing international power dynamics among nation-states, with Western states remaining privileged in profiting from capitalist structures and retaining their hegemony in organisations such as the International Monetary Fund (IMF), the World Bank and even the United Nations (UN). However, in relation to this last point, the increasing economic power of the BRIC countries (Brazil, Russia, India and China) is set to challenge established power positions in the world order. Midgley (2008) argues that some of the literature on globalisation (including that from within the social work field) has tended to provide an oversimplified presentation of the processes involved, ignoring the complexities and often paradoxical nature of the phenomenon. He contrasts different positions, particularly in the context of globalisation's impact on culture: the first perspective highlights the destructive nature of globalisation (particularly through the worldwide and unbridled spread of capitalism) leading to global disorder, cultural fragmentation, the erosion of social ties and the end of certainty and continuity. The second perspective argues that globalisation leads to increasing convergence and homogenisation of values and practices, perpetuating cultural imperialism and a dominance of Western values such as individualism, rationalisation and standardisation in many domains of human life, while at the same time producing international like-minded 'elites'. A third perspective focuses on the 'backlash' against the dominance of Western values leading to polarisation and conflict, fuelled by growing economic disparities and uncertainties. Finally, the fourth perspective emphasises the emergence of new, hybridised cultural patterns resulting from the fusion of indigenous and exogenous values and practices – particularly through migration and the media.

Midgley (2008) considers the inconclusiveness of these various positions and the lack of a single perspective as problematic, including social work. On the other hand, one could argue that such differences reflect the dialectical nature of globalisation. For example, seemingly opposite trends of 'localisation' (such as the growing identification with and return to traditional values and practices in some communities, and the search for locally based solutions by social and environmental movements) can be considered, in a 'both/and'-perspective, as an inherent part of the same set of processes (or the other side of the coin). An expression of this is the term 'glocalisation' (Robertson, 1995) – representing the impact of the global on the local and vice versa (e.g. Lawrence et al., 2009; Hugman et al., 2010).

As much as mirroring the tensions between modern and postmodern world-views, the different positions described above also reflect some of the continuing debates and issues relevant to international social work, including on-going concerns about professional imperialism; the advantages or disadvantages of seeking 'global' frameworks; the role of international perspectives in local social work; as well as indigenisation and authentisation of social work practice (referring, respectively, to the adaptation of concepts to make them more relevant to local circumstances, and to the creation of local professional models (Hugman, 2010). These are themes which run through this Handbook, and we return to them in later sections of this chapter.

Social work and social professions

We have already indicated that there are varied understandings of social work, which are, to some extent, reflected in how the term is used in different chapters of this Handbook. In the UK and some other Anglophone countries, a fairly narrow understanding of social work, usually related to work with a techno-bureaucratic and individualistic focus, has evolved which can be contrasted with other countries where social development or community work are given more prominence. These different understandings have given rise to debates about whether there is an international common 'core' of social work, including its value base, or whether it is too contextually different to be considered 'an international profession' (Webb, 2003) and also to attempts to provide alternative terms which are inclusive of a wider range of titles and do not privilege one over another, including the notion of 'social professions'.

Considering the root or core notion,

the word 'social' is generic, broad and all encompassing. The root of the word is found in Latin, where socius (noun) means 'ally, confederate', but also, by extension, 'sharer, partner and companion'. Its adjective socialis means 'of or belonging to, companionship, sociable, social'. The Shorter Oxford English Dictionary lists four meanings for the word 'social' that emphasize, respectively: 'belonging; mutuality; group living; and activities to improve conditions of a society by addressing problems and issues (Pawar and Cox, 2010: 14).

All of these meanings, not least the last, are relevant to the practices of social professionals across the world and are important in distinguishing our activities from those of professionals whose primary concern is with the health or education of individuals and populations.

Considering the term 'social professions', more specifically, this originated from European exchange and network programmes (Seibel and Lorenz, 1998) and has been helpful in facilitating more inclusive discussions in Europe about the various professional titles and qualifications of those working in the social welfare field. These include, for example, social pedagogues (e.g. Germany and Denmark), community development workers (e.g. UK) and animators (e.g. Netherlands and France). On the other hand, some authors (e.g. Lorenz, 2006) have also noted and critiqued a trend in some countries towards an ever increasing diversity of titles, which specify the exact group of people with whom social professionals will be working (e.g. degrees specifically in work with children and families, or older people), leading to concerns about the fragmentation and even deprofessionalisation of the generic field of social work (Staub-Bernasconi, 2006; see also Chapter 27), related to the marketisation and managerialism evident in social work organisation and practices in many countries since the late twentieth century (Dominelli, 1996).

These latter trends are also reflected in the growth of relatively new occupational titles and groupings which in some countries both subsume and extend beyond the 'boundaries' of 'professional' social work, such as care management (with its origins in the US) and the social care sector, the latter term now used in the UK to include but extend beyond social work (Higham, 2005). To some extent these terms also reflect the views of society and even social workers themselves as to the nature of social work and whether (and in what form) professional education is a prerequisite in the 'organisation and delivery of services' or whether more inclusive and 'less elitist' forms are preferred. For instance, professionally qualified social workers may find themselves employed in international non-governmental organisations (INGOs) delivering welfare and humanitarian assistance to specific populations and working alongside others who make no claim to this title; and similar issues arise in relation to the notion of social development. Lavelette and Ioakimidis (2011: 139–42) have suggested use of the terms, 'official social work' (carried out by qualified and possibly licenced staff) and 'popular social work', the latter term being used to describe the campaigning and human rights work recognisable in both the origins of social work and currently in the international arena, for instance, in Palestine.

Social development – is it social work?

Since the 1960s, the UN has played a major role in popularising the social development approach through its various bodies (e.g. the Commission for Social Development; International Labour Organisation (ILO); United Nations Development Programme (UNDP); Research Institute for Social Development; the World Bank; the World Summit on Social Development). In 2010, at the joint world conference of IFSW, IASSW and ICSW, social development sat alongside social work in the title and content as well as in the emerging agenda. However, social development has remained a contested concept and it has had a mixed reception, for instance, among social work educators, and thus it is important to establish a common understanding of the term, notwithstanding the challenges to developing its practice. As with some other concepts, it is sometimes easier to say (and important to clarify) what it is not, so social development does not mean development of just one individual, one family, one neighbourhood, one community, one corporation, one nation, one nation-state or one region; nor does it mean development of just one aspect of any entity, such as the economic or political, to the neglect of other aspects. It is rather the collective and inclusive (Miah, 2008) development of the whole entity, whatever that entity might be: the use of the term 'development' raises questions as to whether biological notions of growth, advancement and maturity can be 'transferred' to the social context – to communities, societies and institutions. It may be that there are value connotations and power relationships implied in the term and we shall be returning to these when considering some overarching constructs.

Meanwhile, there are varied definitions of social development in existence which Pawar and Cox (2010) have flexibly grouped under three categories. The first of these emphasises, among other things, systematic planning and the link between social and economic development (e.g. Midgley, 1995; Patel, 2005). A second group of definitions emphasises that bringing about structural change is the core element of social development (e.g. Todaro, 1997). A third focus is on realizing human potential, meeting needs and achieving a satisfactory quality of life (e.g. Mohan and Sharma, 1985; Davis 2004). One of the critical issues in defining social development is its relationship with economic development. Is economic development embedded in social development, or is social development complementary to economic development? The 1995 World Summit on Social Development distinguishes the two and sees social development (without defining it) as necessary to complement economic development: the UNDP *Human Development Reports* reflect a similar view. Some definitions seem to capture this issue by suggesting that social and economic development are different but at the same time juxtaposed, but, as some authors have noted, the social has become subordinated to the economic in some countries (e.g. the UK; see Walker, 1996).

An analysis of different definitions suggests that some authors focus on processes, some on outcomes, and some on both. Some definitions include the meaning and purpose of social development, and what needs to be done to achieve it, whereas others cover only one aspect of it. Overall, we suggest that social development is about systematically introducing a planned (sometimes radical) change process, releasing human potential, transforming people's determination, reorganizing and reorienting structures and strengthening the capacity of people and their institutions to meet human needs. Additional goals include reducing inequalities and problems, creating opportunities and empowering people, achieving human welfare and well-being, improving relationships between people and their institutions, and, finally, ensuring economic development. Midgley's (1995) categorisation of social development into eight key characteristics is useful here. Four of these characteristics address the issue of process – positive change, progressive development, intervention through organized efforts and economic development. The other four characteristics refer to interdisciplinary theoretical bases, ideologically oriented strategies, an inclusive or universal scope, and the welfare goals of social development.

There seems to be little disagreement with the goals of social development but there is less clarity about how these goals, values, strategies and processes can be implemented and achieved in the field. Also, the demonstration that social development can be practised and achieved in the 'one-thirds' world and is not only relevant to 'developing countries' is a significant challenge. Pawar and Cox (2010: 27–34) suggest that social development practice involves understanding and changing current conditions by setting and following clear goals (well-being or quality of life and freedom to realise the potential); values (human dignity, human rights and obligations, diversity and human link with nature); and processes (participatory and empowering); and by developing and implementing plans and strategies that are multilevel (international to local) and multidimensional (including cultural, political, economic, ecological, education, health, housing, equity groups and citizens and their institutions). We suggest that these goals, values, processes and practices surely resonate with 'social work'.

PERSPECTIVES ON INTERNATIONAL SOCIAL WORK

In this section, we consider understandings and manifestations of the central concept of this Handbook, international social work; and also look at a related concept, comparative social welfare. However, we start with a brief overview of international social work from a historical perspective, as a precursor to the historical dimensions alluded to more specifically by authors in some of the following chapters.

International social work in historical perspective

It can be argued that social work has a long history as 'an international profession' and the recounting of this history, including of the first individual exchanges and then of congresses leading to the formation of international associations, reflects a strong European and American bias in its origins (Kendall, 2000; Healy, 2001) with implications for subsequent developments in other parts of the world. However, the beginnings of international social work as a form of practice were also evident in the establishment of the International Social Services organisation in 1924 (Lyons, 1999).

Many authors in this text and elsewhere refer to the origins of welfare provisions and 'social work interventions' in religious institutions and philanthropic activities, and the roots of social work in charitable organisations were indeed strongly represented in many countries (Lorenz, 1994). But in some countries, there were also early indications of the 'care/control' dichotomy, that is, the direct intervention of the state through national legislation and/or delegation of responsibilities to 'local authorities' (whether as big as states or provinces or as small as counties and parishes) for provision of 'relief' (of those most afflicted by poverty) and restraint (e.g. of 'wayward' or 'immoral' youth). One such example was the 1834 (New) Poor Law and provision of workhouses in the UK, providing both care and control in relation to the very poor, and which subsequently gave rise to separate forms of (state) care, e.g. for elders, or people with mental illness or physical disabilities (Young and Ashton, 1963).

Additionally, also important were the campaigning activists (individuals and groups) who sought to change not individuals but the conditions in which whole minorities existed, whose heirs can be seen in the community activists who challenge or even enter politics today (Lavalette and Ioakimidis, 2011). An expanded view of social work's European origins around the turn of the twentieth century is provided by Lorenz (1994), who identified four strands in these initiatives – the Judeo–Christian heritage; early protagonists of opportunities for women; the trade union movement; and philanthropy. Of course, the particular histories of social work in individual countries vary, both in length and in the degree to which each of these three or four strands was evident or dominant, but internationally, the role of European countries in colonisation – and later of the US through its economic and political power – have been important in influencing the shape of welfare systems and the development of social work, including through professional education and preferred research paradigms. (See later chapters including those in Section 5.)

Given the origins of social work in the context of industrialisation, urbanisation and then mass migration, it is not surprising that the earliest examples of 'international activities' were the visits of individuals to other countries within Europe or across the Atlantic to learn about social work elsewhere and share experiences. The establishment of professional relationships between leading figures of the time sometimes resulted from meetings at international conferences; for instance, Jane Addams (US) and Alice Solomon (Germany) apparently met at an International Congress of Women held in Germany in 1904 (Healy, 2001). International conferences also became the basis in the 1920s for the establishment of the three professional bodies referred to in the introduction. Their more precise origins can be located in the 'Paris Conference', or more accurately, an International Social Welfare Fortnight, which included an International Conference of Social Work and a section on social work education. As a result of this, the International Conference of Social Work developed into ICSW, while the International Committee of Schools of Social Work developed into IASSW (Healy, 2001). The IFSW was to have a more chequered path and later establishment, the work of the International

Permanent Secretariat of Social Workers having been disrupted by the Second World War (1939–45) and IFSW not taking its current form and title until 1956 (Lawrence et al., 2009). The relative strengths of each and the relationships between the three associations have varied over time but, at the time of writing, the organisations which had a common origin nearly a century ago are again working collaboratively on establishing a common agenda and providing all aspects of social work with a stronger voice.

For the best part of the twentieth century, then, the history and development of 'international social work' was associated with individual and group exchange programmes; establishment of cross-national professional networks; and specialist or regional organisations also concerned with 'exchange' (e.g. through conferences or research programmes). Some of this development took place within the context of, or associated, with social work education and research. For instance, a project was carried out in the mid-twentieth century by eminent figures such as Katherine Kendall (US) and Eileen Younghusband (UK), on behalf of the IASSW and under the auspices of the UN: this resulted in four major reports about developments in social work education worldwide (Kendall, 1998; Lyons, 2008). However, the establishment of social work (education) in many countries of the global South resulted from the efforts of missionaries and other 'western' influences rather than developing from indigenous roots (see Chapter 8), leaving a legacy of concerns about the relevance of curricula and practices and the need to develop more authentic ones. International social work was also frequently perceived as something that individuals who 'worked abroad' did – often for INGOs – which again, until recently, tended to be seen as an opportunity open mainly to relatively affluent social workers from the Global North going to less-developed countries. However, more recent studies suggest some changes in the patterns of labour migration in social work in the twenty-first century resulting in concerns about the 'brain drain' (from sending countries) and exploitation of 'overseas workers' rather than the potential for 'professional imperialism' in North–South movements (Lyons and Littlechild, 2006; Welbourne et al., 2007).

It is perhaps only in the last 20–30 years that social work has paid more attention to power imbalances inherent in international relations between states and the implications for the personal/professional relationships between those 'on the ground', as we discuss later. Meanwhile, it is useful to identify some resources available to investigate historical aspects of international social work. These are relatively few and tend to be found in the documents and texts relating to the history of social work in particular countries (that is providing a comparative rather than an international perspective). However, there are also the (largely unexplored) records of the international associations themselves (but see, for instance, Kniephoff-Knebel and Seibel, 2008). In addition, an increasing number of journals, articles and books have accumulated over (mainly) the past 30 years.

The earliest journal devoted to international social work (though not specifically its history) was *International Social Work,* established in 1957 by the three international associations, initially mainly as a service to members (Lyons, 2007). However, as Healy and Thomas (2007) noted in their retrospective analysis of contributions, only a relatively small proportion of articles have been directly concerned with developing our understanding of the notion of international social work and, latterly, with the implications of globalisation. (More generally, the journal has provided a significant number of national case examples from which to learn about comparative aspects of social work, welfare and development trends and initiatives). There has also been some growth in regional journals (for instance, in Africa, the Caribbean and the Asia Pacific), although the first such English language, one relating to Europe, was not established until 1992 (*Social Work in Europe*) and subsequently

merged with a slightly later publication (*European Journal of Social Work*) in 2002. The latter journal provided an important source of information about key figures in the history of social work in several European countries through its 'Historical Portraits' series. These served a useful purpose in enabling readers in many Central and East European (CEE) countries to 'reclaim' their social work history and revealed to West Europeans the important roles played by, for instance, Polish and Czech national figures in developing social work in Europe, as did some of the material in the book about IASSW presidents (Seibel, 2008).

The concept of international social work

The concept of international social work is contested and still evolving but requires analysis and development for educational and research purposes as well as practice. The ambiguous or different meanings of international social work are partly due to the way 'social work' itself is variously defined and understood in different countries and regions, notwithstanding the 'international definition of social work' agreed by the IFSW and IASSW (see Appendix 1). Here, it is important to distinguish between this definition and the definition of 'international social work', which is the focus of this discussion.

Although the term 'international social work' was first used in 1943 by George Warren (Xu, 2006), the preceding section illustrates the ways in which an international dimension, in the form of exchange or transfer of knowledge and practices, was present in social work from its earliest days. Until the 1920s or so, emerging social work knowledge was mainly shared within the North but subsequently (1920s to 1940s), social work knowledge and models were also being transferred from the North to the South and the internationalisation of social work was also strengthened by representatives from Latin America and Asia at the 1928 Paris meeting.

During the 1940s to 1960s, and particularly following the Second World War, a particular kind of international social work peaked, in terms of transfer of education, practice and welfare administration models and skills, mostly from the North to the South. This occurred with support from UN organisations and INGOs, and receptive governments of new nation-states: it was not until over a decade later that the direction of this linear flow was criticised as professional imperialism (Midgley, 1981). Additionally, a recent analysis of documents relating to the post-war establishment of social work in Greece also highlights the strong connection between the political interests of wealthy and powerful nations and developments in welfare elsewhere (Lavalette and Ioakimidis, 2011).

Since the 1990s and with the advent of globalisation, the term 'international social work' has been applied to different forms of practice, with more attention paid to power differentials and ethical dimensions, and some efforts to correct the unidirectional flow, at least theoretically (Cox and Pawar, 2006; Xu, 2006; Healy, 2008; Hugman, 2010). Core issues (e.g. poverty, unemployment, health concerns, ecological issues, migration and globalisation) are recognised as impacting both in the North and the South (though in different degrees and forms), and there has been an increasing realisation that interdependence, mutual learning and sharing are essential. A review of relevant literature shows various understandings and definitions of international social work (Hokenstad et al., 1992; Johnson, 1996; Pawar, 1998; Lyons, 1999; Healy, 2001; Ahmadi, 2003; Cox and Pawar, 2006; Lyons et al., 2006; Xu, 2006; Payne and Askeland, 2008; Hugman, 2010) largely reflecting developments in different periods as summarised above. In the mid-1990s, a survey across 400 schools of social work in 20 countries by Nagy and Falk gave rise to a wide range of ideas about the 'meaning' of international social work (summarised in 12 categories in Lyons, 1999). Rather than repeating the whole range of definitions, we have chosen to focus on two

relatively recent ones provided in international social work texts (Cox and Pawar, 2006; Healy, 2008) as most relevant to both the North and the South contexts and also to contemporary developments. In addition, we consider the related notion of 'international perspectives' and look at the five elements of international social work identified by Hugman (2010). The latter appear to synthesise various concepts and certain basic principles that are crucial for international social work.

Healy (2001: 7) defined international social work as 'international professional pratice and the capacity for international action by the social work profession and its members. International action has four dimensions: internationally related domestic practice and advocacy, professional exchange, international practice, and international policy development and advocacy'. Cox and Pawar (2006: 20) defined it as

> ...the promotion of social work education and practice globally and locally, with the purpose of building a truly integrated international profession that reflects social work's capacity to respond appropriately and effectively, in education and practice terms, to the various global challenges that are having a significant impact on the well-being of large sections of the world's population.

Although the two definitions are complementary, Healy's definition emphasises professional practice in the international context and the social work profession's and social workers' capacity for international action in four specific areas, although these might be seen as somewhat restrictive. However, one of the interesting aspects of Healy's definition is the idea that practising international social work does not necessarily involve working abroad or in an INGO as some aspects of international social work practice, e.g. refugee resettlement, international adoption and responses to human trafficking, are likely to be undertaken as 'domestic activities'.

Cox and Pawar's international social work concept focuses on social work education and practice both at global and local levels so as to build the social work profession and its capacity internationally in such a way that it is able to address both global and local challenges concerning the well-being of the whole population. Although these definitions seem to cover both the North and the South, a critical examination of them may raise the question of their applicability in the South as they appear to have been defined in Northern contexts reflecting Northern concerns (Pawar, 2010). There are also those within the North who question the appropriateness of the term 'international social work' and argue for more work to develop a theory and practice that examine processes and the diverse ways in which the global and the local interact (e.g. Dominelli, 2010) or who advocate the notion of social work internationalism, rather than international social work (Lavalette and Ioakimidis, 2011).

Perhaps it is also appropriate to mention here the related notion of 'international perspectives' on social work as discussed by Lyons et al. (2006) and Lawrence et al. (2009). These authors suggest that local practices can – and should – be viewed through an international lens or that knowledge about international events and different cultures should inform local practices, e.g. with newly arrived and even established minority ethnic populations. Thus, while not all social workers will choose to engage in 'international social work' as a specialist activity – or be drawn into transnational social work by chance – the internationalisation of social problems will require increasing numbers of social professionals to have knowledge about international conditions and current affairs in order to understand the concerns of the service users and respond appropriately. In addition, increasing numbers will find it necessary to develop their comparative knowledge of welfare systems and social work services if they are to engage in transnational activities in specialist areas of work which might previously have been seen as restricted to the national scene e.g. transnational fostering (Lyons, 2006).

By analysing a range of definitions, Hugman (2010: 18–20) has delineated five core elements in international social work. These are: (1) the practice of social work in a country other than the home country of the social worker; (2) working with individuals, families and communities whose origins are in a country other than that where the social worker is practising; (3) working in international organisations; (4) collaborations between countries in which social workers exchange ideas or work together on projects that cross national borders; and (5) practices that address locally issues that originate in globalised social systems. Although the five elements may be implicit in the above definitions, the delineation in this way helps facilitate the understanding of international social work, not least as being addressed in this Handbook.

Comparative perspectives

Finally, in this section, we should consider a closely related notion that has already been mentioned or implied and has particular significance to international social work when applied to welfare systems, social policies and research, as well as the national organisation and practice of social work, that is, the term 'comparative'. Comparative social welfare is a concept closely connected to, but distinct from, international social work which can be an important source of knowledge (Hokenstad et al., 1992; Hoefer, 1996).

Social welfare is a broad and comprehensive concept that connotes how (ways and means) individuals, families, communities, organisations and the nation-state meet needs and address social issues, particularly of marginalised and disadvantaged groups in a society. In the global North, relatively more literature and research are available on the state's contribution to social welfare through a range of (social) policies and provisions relating to education, health, housing, poverty and income support, and to vulnerable groups such as children, older people or people with disabilities (Esping-Anderson,

1990; Hill, 1996; Castles, 1998; Goodin et al., 2000; Cochrane et al., 2001). Such (social) policies and provisions vary from one nation-state to another depending upon their socioeconomic and political contexts, and, although the wealth of the country is a major determinant of the role of the state in providing a range of welfare services, political ideology has also assumed greater significance in patterns of welfare provision in the North, with greater emphasis being placed on individual responsibility, private markets and the role of the voluntary/not for profit sector, including a growing number of social enterprises (see Chapter 7).

Comparative social welfare is the term generally applied to comparative analysis of the welfare policies and provisions of two or more nation-states to identify common trends and differences; and to develop insights to further improve policy or to replicate it elsewhere. It often has an interdisciplinary research orientation, and insights gained from such comparative analysis can be used in international social work in terms of developing social work education; designing welfare policies and programmes; and preparing personnel for delivering services, particularly in countries where welfare systems are less established.

The appropriate focus of comparative social welfare research (sometimes also referred to as cross-national research) is a matter of debate since comparing welfare systems can be the basis for generalisations and development of theories; for understanding the causes of global miseries; and for devising intervention strategies and programmes (Rodgers, 1977; Mohan, 1986). However, most of the comparative social welfare analysis is undertaken where national comparative data sets are (easily) available, ignoring welfare trends and issues in countries without such readily available data sets. This kind of comparative social welfare has resulted in partial understanding of welfare systems around the world. Beyond comparing national aggregate data sets, micro or local level analysis is also needed to understand the contribution of welfare programmes to reducing inequality and alleviating poverty, and to demonstrate how people and communities live without well-developed welfare systems and provisions. Social welfare outcomes are as important as welfare expenditure. Hill (1996: 56) also concludes that micro-policy analysis is needed to explore how different nation-states and their welfare systems deal with the same issues, e.g. the needs of single-parent families, the encouragement of labour market participation or the control of professional power.

The subject matter of international social work as related to the comparative concept generally focuses on building capacity in the social work profession and extending an understanding of the roles and activities of social workers in national contexts (e.g. Weiss-Gal and Welbourne, 2008), sometimes with a view to developing policies and practices in different parts of the world. However, there have also been longer standing examples of comparative research into social work education and also practices, for instance, in Europe (Brauns and Kramer, 1991; Cooper et al., 1995).

Given the comparative social welfare approach or methodology and the substance of comparison, we suggest that international social work and comparative social welfare can be distinguished, but are linked and often mutually useful. However, it may be noted that international social work can be done without being comparative in a methodological sense (although comparisons do occur at a cognitive level among international social workers), and comparative analysis can be undertaken without including international aspects.

SOME OVERARCHING THEMES FOR INTERNATIONAL SOCIAL WORK

Previous sections have highlighted that international social work is not a clearly defined or unambiguous concept. The literature shows multiple definitions, identifying different 'strands' and issues. For an action-orientated profession, it is not surprising that the focus has often been on what international social workers 'do'. Another way of approaching the subject is to identify some of the underlying themes which frame professional action in an interconnected world. This is particularly important given concerns about discourses which have neglected to analyse the power relations inherent in ideas of international social work (e.g. Haug, 2005). In this section, we discuss three overarching themes (theoretical frameworks) that we think are important.

There have been previous attempts to identify theoretical frameworks which underpin the (still contested) concept of international social work. For example, Cox and Pawar (2006) suggest a conceptual framework based on four different inter-related perspectives. Globalisation provides the overall context within which international social work is set, with both unifying and divisive elements and globalising and localising tendencies; the authors suggest that the concept of '*world citizenship*' can reconcile these different aspects. *Human rights* provide the second perspective, setting out a fundamental value base for social work; while an *ecological perspective* (and within it the principle of sustainability) represents the link between humanity and nature. Finally, the authors argue that a *social development* perspective (meaning the enhancement of the well-being of people in a society), utilising various levels of intervention, should be the 'sense of direction' for international social work.

We acknowledge the existing diversity of theoretical frameworks and definitions of international social work and do not seek to provide a unitary 'frame' for the concept. Rather, based on existing debates and our own understandings, we identify three dimensions or overarching themes which seem relevant.

• First, we consider *'space'* as a key theme for social work, particularly for any discussion about international dimensions of the discipline and profession. This is reflected in the IFSW/IASSW 'international definition' of social work, which refers to the interaction of people and their environments as a key 'location' of social work. Important conceptual issues in this context include, for example, the changing characters of some spatial units in the context of globalisation and localisation, as well as issues of mobility or 'migrations' and their relevance for social work.

• A second key theme is *'time'* – which we consider both on the macro-level of historical global developments relevant to contemporary international social work (and possibly for future directions), as well as on the micro-level of human experience – in particular, the impact of transnational practices on life courses.

• As a third overarching theme, it is vital for any analysis of international social work to engage with issues of *'human diversity'* and the *'power relations'* which manifest themselves through inequality and the exclusion and oppression of some groups by others. In this context, key issues include debates about the privileging of ideas and knowledge from the global North over that of the global South, coined in the term 'professional imperialism' (Midgley, 1981), as well as questions about the 'universality' of social work and the concept of the indigenisation of approaches.

Finally, rather than being an additional theme, we suggest that spatial, time-related and diversity-related constructs interact and interconnect, and that the notion of 'intersectionality' is a useful lens for analysing issues related to international social work. References to intersectionality in the social work field are increasing – particularly in relation to gender issues (see, for example, the IIFSW's (2010) policy paper on women) – and a new international journal (*Intersectionalities*, http://journals.library. mun.ca/ojs/index.php/IJ) is calling for papers for its first edition, at the time of writing. Given the complexity of international social work, intersectionality provides a useful framework for considering how the three selected themes interact and interlink. This means applying spatial, historical, life course, diversity and power relations lenses to practice, education, research, and policy regarding international social work, and based on these, considering dilemmas on macro- and micro-levels in ways which are contextually relevant.

'Space' as a relevant concept for social work

'Space' (or locality) has played a part in social work since its very beginnings. In its origins, the living conditions of those in poverty in the urban slums of European cities (formed in the wake of the 'industrial revolution') provided a key focus for the interventions of 'social work pioneers'. The issue of professional 'location' was evident from early on, reflected in different paradigms of 'professional distance' (the Charity Organisation Society's approach of avoiding 'too much' empathy with welfare recipients) and relative physical 'closeness' (the Settlement movement's emphasis on living among 'the poor').

It is relevant here to distinguish between different dimensions of space. For example, Bourdieu (1999) described 'physical space' (the site where people are physically present) and 'social space' (people's relationships or symbolic 'locations' in relation to other actors and objects). The two notions are connected in that a person's social position is often reflected in the type of physical space (e.g. living space) they occupy. The question of the contexts in which people are 'located' (or not), in physical, social or symbolic terms, has been recognised as a significant issue for social work – not least through ecological approaches which consider the interaction of people and their environments. Spatscheck and Wolf-Ostermann (2009) argue that in Germany, for example, a social space orientation in social work has become common in recent decades. An example is the concept of 'life world' (*Lebenswelt*)-oriented social work (e.g. Grunwald and Thiersch, 2009), which is located in those 'places' where individuals (or communities) experience and try to make sense of the impact of 'the wider world' on their day-to-day lives.

A relevant issue for (international) social work is the on-going danger of the life world becoming 'colonised' by the state and its systems – including by social work professionals (Hayes and Houston, 2007).

Globalisation leads both to compressions and extensions of social spaces. For example, membership in 'virtual communities', using media such as the internet, may lead to people thousands of miles apart feeling more connected to each other than to next-door neighbours. On the other hand, changed livelihood strategies, not least migration, have influenced social relationships and the make-up of social spaces in many different ways. For example, migration has made family-based care more complicated, in relation to care of young children or relatives who are elderly or otherwise vulnerable. Such situations can lead to the creation of transnational social spaces characterised by on-going interactions (whether virtually or physically) across borders (Köngeter, 2010); these movements and networks are relevant for social workers both from local and international perspectives.

A spatial perspective involves considering different units of reference, ranging from the 'macro' to the 'micro' level. At the macro level, the spatial unit of the nation state is particularly significant as, from this, we define 'international' (see above). Additionally, states were the bases for the establishment of different welfare regimes when social work itself was emerging as a 'modern profession' in Europe and North America (Hugman, 2010). Anderson (1991) has described nation states as 'imagined communities' and they have had a relatively short existence (in the overall course of history) but this does not diminish the contemporary powerfulness of this concept. Despite the influences of globalisation, a world not 'ordered' by nation-states is hard to imagine (see Chapter 6).

Citizenship (i.e. 'belonging' to the defined territory of a nation) remains an important factor for access to welfare. 'Deviation' from defined norms (e.g. being economically active and productive in capitalist nations) is likely to lead to exclusion as an 'undeserving' member of society, while others, such as migrants (who challenge the notion of national citizenship), may be denied access to citizenship – or even to the very territory of the state (Hugman et al., 2010). While capital flows and activities of transnational corporations are relatively unrestricted by national borders, the movement of people is subject to policing and restrictive controls (Glick Schiller and Levitt, 2006). Bauman (1998) has suggested that globalisation increases the differences between the 'globalised rich' who are able to buy into the technological advances of travel and communication to overcome restrictions of time and space and the 'localised poor' who lack such resources and are thus condemned to remain in undesirable spaces such as urban ghettos (slums or favelas). Such limitations on physical and social mobility are not new, and are indeed connected with the history of social work in some countries, where the movement of the poor between localities was restricted by welfare systems designed to keep them in their 'place' (e.g. Garrett, 2006).

Today's limitations on human mobility disproportionately affect movements from the global South to the North. Another concept by Bauman (1998) – that of 'tourists' and 'vagabonds' – is applied by Hugman et al. (2010) to international professional mobility within social work. The movement of social workers from the global North to the South is most likely to take place in a context where professionals are seen as experts, or at least as contributors to local social development, who share their knowledge before returning to their own countries; as such, these international social workers travel largely as 'tourists'. This contrasts with the treatment of migrants from the South in the global North who are most often placed in the roles of 'vagabonds' (witness the detention of asylum seekers in many Western countries). However, even for

professional social workers from the global South, their role may be undervalued and the sharing of knowledge they bring may not be expected (Lyons and Littlechild, 2006) so that, when conditions (in the local labour market) change, recruitment schemes decline and the movements of those seeking to migrate are restricted. Such differential values placed on the contributions of social workers from different regions of the world risks perpetuating notions of professional imperialism. Hugman et al. (2010: 634) argue that international social work can involve various forms of border crossings: those which are *transcending* (they emphasise ideas about the commonalities of the human condition – but in doing so risk succumbing to idealistic notions); those which focus on *transmitting* ideas and concepts from one locality to another (a process which currently tends to privilege positions originating from the global North); border crossings which aim at *transforming* power relationships; and those which are considered as *transgressions* – as out of place and therefore inferior or undesirable.

Finally, the increase in international initiatives by nation-states operating under the umbrella of the UN and the growth of international networks and movements (including, for instance, people concerned with disability rights or protection of the environment) have led some to identify a global civil society. Additionally, they argue that citizenship should not be tied to individual states, but that citizenship obligations (of the state) should be shared internationally (e.g. Lister, 1998). Such thinking led Oxfam to devise a curriculum for 'global citizenship' (including an understanding of how the world works) on the basis of which global citizens would act on a range of levels (local to global) to promote, for example, human rights and eco-justice (Oxfam, 1997). Notions of social space are thus extended to the global level with obvious relevance for international social work, notwithstanding the cautions identified by Hugman et al. (2010).

'Time'– human development in macro- and micro-dimensions

Social work has been acknowledged as an activity set in a specific time context (Lyons, 1999) and, as suggested, time-related perspectives, on the macro-level of historical developments and on the micro-level of the human life course, are useful concepts for international social work. Historically, forces of colonialism, which privileged 'whiteness' (see Chapter 8) while oppressing indigenous populations, were instrumental in spreading administrative systems and structures linked to the establishment of social work to many countries in the global South (e.g. see Chapter 24). Even in postcolonial times, the origins and continuing dominance of Western ideas influence the status and development of the profession, particularly in the context of debates about internationalisation and indigenisation (e.g. Gray and Coates, 2010).

One critique of some of the discourses concerning international social work has been the lack of a critical analysis of this historical legacy (e.g. Haug, 2005), represented in the gap which exists between the profession's stated value commitments (e.g. to social justice and human rights) and examples of practices which have been (and in some cases still are) oppressive. Tensions between professional values and actual practice are, of course, not just an issue for *international* social work, nor are the tensions which exist between micro- and macroperspectives (evident in social work's origins and with the former having achieved dominance in the global North), but both are significant in debates concerning the 'export' of social work ideas and practices (Hugman, 2010).

Lorenz (2007) argues that an uncritical relationship with history within social work can lead to an over-emphasis on rationalised order and bureaucratic systematisation at the cost of a concern for understanding the uniqueness of people and communities. Apart from colonial legacies, there are other examples of the relevance of historical consciousness for reflections on social work's potential roles: in relation to conflict and displacement professionals have not only been guilty of coercion and collaboration during the dark times of National Socialism and the Holocaust, but have also been active in resistance taking personal risks to save others (Lorenz, 2007). In contemporary conflict situations, as well as in work with displaced populations, social workers continue to face challenges which may (or may not) result in practice conforming to the values of social justice and human rights (Briskman and Cemlyn, 2005; see also Chapter 19).

Turning from the 'macro-level' of historical awareness to the micro-level of human experience, the impact of transnationalisation and globalisation on communities and individuals becomes clear when considered from a life course perspective (see Section 4). Beck (2000: 74) refers to 'biographical glocalisation' when describing processes where 'global' developments enter the 'local' level of people's everyday lives. Heinz and Krüger (2001) define the life course as stages and transitions from birth to death, which are influenced by culture, structural and institutional factors, as well as subjective meaning making. Some early studies in the life course field have been criticised as Eurocentric (Robinson, 2002) and gender-biased (Heinz and Krüger, 2001), but more recent research has aimed to make this concept more contextually relevant, including by focusing on transnational practices. These may occur when families live apart (in different countries) not just on a short-term basis, but maintain roles and relationships across distances, including as parents or as carers for sick or elderly relatives (Köngeter, 2010). On the other hand, globalisation processes have also been blamed for the progressive commodification of care relationships in the global North, with evidence of an increase in extra-familial care for the very young, sick or elderly. Such developments are connected with a transnationalisation of life courses. For example, family members in some Western countries and the Middle East are looked after by carers from the global South who often leave behind their own family members, including dependent children (Midgley, 2008; and e.g. Chapters 6 and 27).

Diversity and power relationships in an international context

The diversity of human experience is a major concern for international social work, especially since, throughout history, difference has been used to create divisions and oppression based on the unequal distribution of power. Social work has relied on different constructs, mainly from the social sciences, to analyse how difference affects people's access to resources and overall wellbeing. A (non-exhaustive) acronym currently used in some contexts refers to a variety of constructs as the 'Social GRRAACCEESS' (gender, race, religion, age, ability, class, culture, ethnicity, education, sexuality and spirituality) (Burnham, 1993). We can only consider the implications for international social work of some of these constructs in this chapter, although all receive attention at other points in the Handbook.

The focus has tended to shift between constructs in different countries and at different times, with criticism that certain forms of oppression have received attention to the exclusion of others. For example, in British and North American social work, a focus on anti-racist social work in the 1980s was later subsumed under broader 'anti-discriminatory practice' and 'equality-of-oppressions' frameworks. Some argue that this has weakened the acknowledgement of racial oppression and of the related collective histories of the struggle for racial equality (Graham and Schiele, 2010). 'Class', an issue which was clearly very relevant to the earliest (nineteenth century) contexts of social work, has been noted as a now (unjustifiably) more marginalised concept, with the focus instead turning to issues of poverty and social exclusion (Strier, 2009; Ferguson, 2011).

In respect of gender-specific social work, some of the early 'pioneers' of social work in Europe (e.g. Alice Salomon in Germany) were influential in highlighting the role of women in the profession (Kuhlmann, 2001), and this was advanced through the feminist movements of the 1960s and 1970s. In more recent years, explorations of masculinity and the role of men in societies and in social work have also become more widespread (e.g. Pease and Pringle, 2001). However, gender is a good example of how constructs can have different meanings in different cultural contexts. There is a risk that contested practices rooted in some communities of the global South are oversimplified by those in the global North. The Beijing Platform for Action after the 1995 World Conference for Women was a milestone in devising common agendas supported by women from both the South and the North (e.g. in relation to domestic violence). However, problems persist. For instance, the practice of female genital cutting (FGC) takes place in the context of local complex realities: it can be endorsed by powerful members of a community but equally is being opposed by black women's movements in both the South and the North (Khaja et al., 2009). It has been made illegal by many western countries but its continuing practice among some immigrant communities presents dilemmas for social workers who have responsibility for safeguarding children's welfare but also need to consider the consequences for girls 'rescued' from situations where FGC could happen (Dustin and Davies, 2007).

The concern that some bases for discrimination were being privileged over others has led to increasing acknowledgement that different forms of inequality and oppression (based on the range of human diversity) are interconnected, as expressed in the concept of 'intersectionality'. This emerged from black women's rights movements and critiqued the lack of acknowledgement of other forms of oppression (e.g. based on race or class) in mainstream feminism (Verloo, 2006). The concept fits well with postmodern perspectives on inequality, since it is concerned with how various aspects of a person's identity inter-relate to lead to particular experiences of oppression. Intersectionality can prevent homogenising interpretations; hierarchies among forms of oppression; and approaches that address specific inequalities in isolation – or make mistaken assumptions of similarity about the ways they are experienced. Intersectionality also involves considering spatial and historical contexts of oppression, including the location of inequalities in public and private spheres and the various levels at which they are reproduced (e.g. interpersonal, identity, symbolic, organisational and structural levels) (Verloo, 2006).

Concerns about issues raised by respectful acknowledgement of diversity have also led (particularly in the global North) to an increased emphasis being placed on the need for social workers to be 'culturally competent' or 'culturally sensitive' (e.g. when working with minority ethnic groups) although the concept of anti-oppressive practice (Dominelli, 2002) better acknowledges both the varied bases for discrimination and the power differentials inherent in professional relationships with minority groups. However, considerations of culture, in particular, are important in various forms of international social work, where concerns about overriding or ignoring local cultures can occur, for example, in the transfer of knowledge for social work education or when practising in an INGO outside one's home country.

Additionally, in debates about indigenisation and authentisation (particularly in countries of the global South), 'culture' tends to take centre stage (Gray and Coates, 2010). It is important to remember the definitional diversity of 'culture' and to be mindful of the risk of treating it as an essentialised and fixed aspect of identity. In this context, approaches to indigenisation can become exclusionary themselves depending on who holds the power to define what is 'culturally relevant'. If developed within national contexts, ethnocentric perspectives, which ignore the

increasingly multicultural reality of societies today, can be reinforced (see Chapter 2). Connected are debates about the tension between universalist and relativist approaches to value frameworks: the adoption of a pluralist approach recognises the existence of sometimes competing (and possibly even contradictory) positions, but places emphasis on contextually relevant (or authentic) attempts to resolve dilemma situations that may arise from this diversity (Healy, 2007; and Chapter 9).

One concept which is missing from the above acronym as a separate entity is language. Issues associated with language were identified in social work by feminist authors drawing on the work of Dale Spender in the 1980s. However, Harrison (2006) argues that language has since been neglected in social work generally, despite its significance as a marker of identity and its centrality for practice (both in seemingly 'monolingual' contexts and in the multilingual reality of societies). Similarly, there has been relatively less attention to language in the debate about international social work compared with other constructs, but it raises clear issues of power differentials and the privileging of some languages. This is most evident in the continuing predominance of Anglophone traditions and the dominance of the English language at international conferences or in publications, and in the assumptions made by some (monolingually) Anglophone practitioners and academics about the translatability and transferability of concepts (Harrison, 2006; see also Chapter 2). The journal, *International Social Work*, now has abstracts translated into French, Spanish, Chinese, Arabic and Russian, but English remains the language for manuscript submissions. However, (and in addition to debates about the risks of linguistic professional imperialism) the apparently homogenising character of a 'lingua franca' masks the increasing processes of differentiation (both locally and globally) affecting languages in general, and English in particular, which has given rise to the term 'Globish'.

These issues indicate that international social work must continually consider its potential for the transformation of power relationships (Hugman et al., 2010). How this might be achieved remains an open but increasingly active debate: at its core are questions about the universality (or common core) of social work given its many different manifestations globally. In this context, internationalising social work risks overemphasising notions of universality (e.g. in terms of 'common' standards or ethical frameworks) (Gray and Fook, 2004), particularly when the transfer of ideas and concepts is unidirectional (i.e. from the global North to the South). On the other hand (just as 'globalisation' suggests an oversimplified picture of homogenisation of the whole world in accordance with 'Western' values), the notion of 'Western social work' as a monolithic entity can be critiqued as negating the many different strands that exist. For instance, within a region such as Europe there is no single common theoretical or methodological base; and even where social work is strictly regulated and standardised (such as in England), there is more diversity than might be expected.

As editors of a handbook of international social work, we consider that there are, at least, some commonalities to be found among the issues and themes, which social professionals in different localities around the world address, but that this does not prevent acknowledgment of the vast diversity that exists among the many different contexts of social work. If social work (in whatever form or location) is to be effective at the points where people interact with their environments (or have a 'life-world' orientation), a principle aim has to be for it to be 'culturally' (or contextually) relevant – and thus flexible in trying to understand the particular circumstances and subjective patterns of meaning of each individual, family or community. This sometimes requires engaging in dialogical practice or 'cultural translation work' (Staub-Bernasconi, 1995: 303) across diverse perspectives. It seems that the earlier mentioned

micro-level metaphor of working against a 'colonisation' of the life world holds equally true when applied to the macro-context of international social work.

SOME CURRENT CONTEXTUAL TRENDS AND ISSUES

Many of the most significant conditions affecting human existence and social life around the world – and their relevance to social work – are addressed in the chapters that follow. However, in this section, we identify some of the main trends and issues that provide the backdrop to welfare provisions and the activities of social professionals globally. Perhaps most obvious to social professionals internationally are the glaring inequalities in power and the distribution of wealth, as well as access to and use of resources, both between but also within countries (see e.g. Chapters 5 and 12). In addition, the media disseminate news globally about conflicts (notably in the 'Middle East'); disasters (often related to environmental concerns); and the activities of 'terrorists' or freedom fighters (often based on opposing religious ideologies or ethnic identities).

Many social professionals have direct or indirect experience of migration and acknowledge the rise of the internet (a source of the rapid growth and exchange of knowledge) and information and communications technologies (ICT) generally. ICT can be a valuable aid, including for maintaining family and community links across national borders; and for the creation of virtual worlds/communities (including of professionals). However, there are also negative uses, including increased access to (child) pornography and international communications about other criminal activities. For example, some social professionals are specifically involved in addressing the after-effects of the international trades in arms, drugs and people. Many of these factors are inter-related and the ways in which they are separated and presented aim primarily to provide clarity across complex fields. The contextual factors we shall consider briefly here are the natural environment and disasters; the global economy and international relations; and demographic factors and migration.

The natural environment and disasters

In recent history (late nineteenth and twentieth century), explorers, anthropologists and other 'Westerners' have tended to think of indigenous peoples and traditional communities as having a close connection with their natural habitats to which they have adapted over centuries (e.g. the Inuit in the North of Canada and the Aborigines in Australia). The relationship between communities and their environments in countries which have industrialised (a process which began in the seventeenth century, reaching its peak in the nineteenth century in many European countries and still continuing today, not least in Brazil, India and China) has been far less in tune with – and respectful of – the natural environment. It has been characterised by the sense that 'man' can control the environment and is at liberty to exploit the natural resources of the world for personal, national or corporate gain. Natural resources range from the most fundamental of life-sustaining elements – air and water – to other 'products' – e.g. coal, oil, gas and 'precious metals'. While the last have been mined for centuries and were previously the cause of colonial expansion and conflict, coal, oil and gas have fuelled first the industrial and then the technological revolutions and the accumulation of gross wealth of the few as well as 'living standards', which are expected to show generational 'improvements' for many, while, at the same time, further disadvantaging many more. Sometimes the relationship between extraction of resources and increased wealth is a direct one and sometimes not. For instance, Norway as a country/society

has benefitted from the extraction of North Sea oil and gas; but few Nigerians have benefitted from the considerable oil fields and petroleum refineries of the Niger Delta, which, on the contrary, have been a source of local distress and conflict (Omeje, 2008).

While social work pioneers in the nineteenth and early twentieth centuries linked *local* environmental conditions (e.g. foul air and water) to the disease and squalor which characterised the living conditions of 'the urban poor', it is only in the last few decades that there has been increasing awareness of widespread damage to the environment globally; the interconnected nature of responsibilities for exploitation of resources; and the (often differential) impact which misuse of natural resources is having on people across the globe (see also Chapters 3 and 16). The most obvious and concerning, though disputed, factor is climate change in so far as this is related to human activity. 'Global warming' is now a widely accepted phenomenon and its impact has been discussed by economists and political scientists (Stern, 2009; Giddens, 2009). Environmental sustainability is one of the Millennium Development Goals (MDGs, see Appendix 6) but relatively little attention has been paid at inter-governmental level to one of its significant causes – widespread deforestation. A recent UN report claimed that, although there has been some recent decrease in deforestation, 'the rate remains alarming' (UN News, 2010).

Large forested areas have traditionally acted like sponges, soaking up and recirculating water and moist air, as well as preventing soil erosion caused by rapid run-off. Not only do large-scale logging enterprises affect the local eco-system and livelihoods of indigenous people but floods and droughts can also occur great distances from the original sites of deforestation (e.g. increased flooding in the monsoon season in Bangladesh and the silting up of the Bay of Bengal has been attributed to tree felling in the foothills of the Himalayas) (Lyons, 1999). Deforestation, as well as the release of increased levels of carbon dioxide and other pollutants into the atmosphere, are also responsible for damage to the ozone layer (protecting us from the sun's rays) posing serious threat to people everywhere. Thus, the natural environment is being denuded and damaged by forces as diverse as (often multinational) corporations; the policies of national governments (through fiscal and regulatory powers nationally as well as their role in supporting or blocking international policy responses); and the demands of the better-off citizens of the world for consumer goods and luxuries of all kinds, as well as 'endless supplies' of water, oil and other power sources needed for heating/cooling and lighting workplaces and institutions and running communications and transport systems.

Similarly, the damage to a nuclear power station in 2011 in Japan, caused by an earthquake in the Pacific and resultant tsunami, reminded us that contamination of air and water supplies (in this case by radioactive substances) spreads the risk of death and disease to a much wider population over a longer period of time than might initially be apparent. Witness the after effects of the high cancer rates following the nuclear plant disaster in Chernobyl (Ukraine) in 1986. Even higher rates of death and disease were attributed to the release of pesticides from the Union Carbide factory in Bhopal (India) in 1985 but in that case the disaster was attributed to multinational corporate policy and human error rather than 'natural causes' (Lyons, 1999). However, as the Japanese example demonstrates, there is often a link between naturally caused disasters and ones which might be categorised as 'man-made'.

Returning to the issue of climate change, specifically, there is evidence more generally of increased instances of extreme weather conditions (wider temperature ranges and drought or excessive rainfall) in many locations, which cause 'local' disasters sometimes of considerable magnitude. When disasters can be predicted the effects may be different according to people's capacity to buy their way out of trouble – so, for instance,

drought leading to crop failure and the need for overseas aid to avert mass starvation typically affects poor people in poor countries but food insecurity is an issue affecting increasing numbers of people in many more locations. In other cases, natural disasters are not predictable and no respecters of national power or individual wealth.

The global economy and international relations

As previously mentioned, a key feature of the notion of globalisation is the extent to which national economies and the fiscal fortunes of people around the world are dominated by capitalism. The widespread neo-liberal belief in the rights and power of 'the market' have created or sustained a situation in which global corporations have come to dominate not just the extraction of natural resources and production of commodities but also international banking systems and increasingly also provision of services in the welfare sector (particularly health care, partly through the link with pharmaceutical industries, and also making inroads into education and social services).

Through the twentieth century, national governments have sought to establish international (rather than bilateral) forums for achieving agreements and maintaining 'peaceful co-existence', but the powers of 'big business' have continued to grow and the extent to which national governments or international agencies can influence corporate decisions and actions is minimal. This seems to have been demonstrated in the global North when the recent (2008) banking crisis resulted in a massive downturn in the economies (and thus employment opportunities for individuals) of many large and wealthy nations (not least the US) and the virtual bankruptcy and serious recession of several smaller countries (e.g. Iceland and Greece).

The job opportunities and thus financial fortunes of whole communities, if not whole nations, have been influenced by the whims of multinational corporations which have been free to relocate from wealthy countries to poorer ones where they can take advantage of low wages and minimal state interference (e.g. with regard to health and safety regulations). Individual countries have sometimes offered state inducements (e.g. through the tax system) to firms to relocate, particularly if they wish to attract particular kinds of 'industry'. For example, this was the basis of Ireland's change in fortunes from a country of low employment and high emigration up to the 1980s to one of nearly full employment and immigration into the early twenty-first century. At this stage some of the multinational companies previously attracted were already transferring operations to countries where labour costs were considerably lower (e.g. India) leaving the Irish economy heavily dependent on service industries and an overheated construction industry and vulnerable to the impending banking crisis.[3]

An overriding feature of the current world order is the extent to which economies, political systems, multinational corporations and major international bodies are (still) dominated by the thinking and interests of the global North. The conference held at Bretton Woods (in the US) in 1944, attended by 44 nations, laid the basis not only for the UN but also for the IMF; the World Bank; and the General Agreement on Trade and Tariffs (GATT) (Hewitt, 1992) and this situation was compounded in 1961 with the establishment of the Organisation for Economic Co-operation and Development (OECD) with membership then drawn from 25 'advanced industrial economies'. Subsequently, a number of smaller/less powerful nations formed the Group of 77 (within the UN) aiming to reach a common position on a range of issues, including the environment (Vogler, 1997: 230).

For a period of a few decades the influence of 'the West' was counter-balanced to some extent by the competing ideology of communism as espoused by the USSR, China and other states (e.g. Cuba and Vietnam). However, the break-up of the Soviet bloc

since 1989 and the gradual adoption by many countries of a more mixed economy (even if still sometimes espousing a communist political system) has seen various shifts in trading relationships and markets. This has been particularly marked in Europe where many CEE countries were 'in transition', both politically and economically, in the 1990s, and had achieved national goals of integration into the European Union by 2007 (allowing for a greater degree of labour mobility than would previously have been the case). While people living in North and West European countries still generally have better employment prospects and more disposable income than those in the CEE states, the difference has decreased and is relatively less marked at the time of writing (2011) for the people of Greece, Ireland and Portugal. These three countries have had to seek loans from the European Central Bank to shore up their banking systems since 2008: they had previously been identified as being 'at risk' in terms of the redistribution of the benefits of EU membership with its expansion eastwards (Lyons et al., 2006: 29).

However, overall, the dominance of countries of the global North (and often of countries where English is the official language) is being challenged by the fast growing power of Brazil, India and China (and to a lesser extent Russia) – all countries with a range of natural resources; considerable manufacturing capacity (partly based on a labour force drawn from rural migration and others who are increasingly well-educated, as well as by the policies of global corporations) and, of course, huge and expanding internal as well as external markets.

One of the significant debates related to the state of national economies, relative stages of 'development' and bilateral or international interventions has been that expressed as 'aid or trade'. While various forms of aid were promoted as a 'responsibility' of wealthier nations to poorer ones, it was also increasingly recognised as a mechanism for ensuring 'loyalty' of recipient countries to donor countries and in many cases also had direct 'pay-offs' for donor countries in terms of purchase of goods and services by the countries to which aid was being provided. In addition, there have been allegations of corruption among either government officials or personnel in INGOs responsible for the administration of aid schemes. The reputation of 'aid' is indeed tarnished although there are still considerable efforts to encourage donor giving (whether by governments, private enterprise, charities or the general public) and to provide seed corn money for sustainable projects, not least for people in many African countries which tend to have the lowest rates of urbanisation and industrialisation and the highest rates of poverty and disease.

Trade might therefore be a better avenue for the sustainable development of poor nations – but, even if the countries most in need have commodities or manufactured goods to sell, trading conditions do not operate in their favour. The exploitation of natural resources which marked the colonial era has tended to continue and in some cases been increased by the international agreement on Trade Related aspects of Intellectual Property Rights (TRIPs) and the attempt by global companies (e.g. in the pharmaceutical field) to patent the raw materials used for generations in traditional medicine (Manion, 2005). In addition, trading agreements and processes are also liable to corruption. There has therefore been a shift in the attention of the UNDP and other agencies to the need for governments and INGOs to declare and demonstrate their commitment to 'good governance'.

A major goal of the UN and a major aspect of the field of international relations is the preservation – or restoration – of peace. Peace is a pre-requisite for economic stability within and between countries but has also been associated with the promotion of democratic societies and the reduction of human rights abuses. However, the latter decades of the twentieth century and the first decade of the twenty-first have been far from peaceful in many parts of the world, and 'humanitarian aid' has come to be associated as much with the relief of people caught up in conflict

as those struggling with the after effects of disasters.

Some global population trends, poverty, conflict and migration

With medical advances and improved living standards for many, the world population continues to grow and now stands at just under 6.9 billion (UN Population Database), notwithstanding scientific and natural forces enabling or causing reductions. Factors affecting population change range from improved birth control techniques and the strategies of individual governments to limit population growth on the one hand to the effects of diseases such as malaria or AIDS on the other, as well as the previously mentioned consequences of disasters – or poverty and conflicts (see later). In addition, the age distribution across the world is changing. While a general tendency towards 'the greying of the planet' may be shifting in particular countries, birth rates, longevity and the size of the adult population available to contribute to the economy, civil society and the care needs of societies vary enormously. In general terms, a decrease in the birth rate and increased longevity in post-industrial societies has led to a need for immigrant labour (although this may be met in the short or longer term by migration within regions) while other factors, not least poverty and conflict, continue to encourage migration, particularly between countries in the global South as well as to the global North.

Although relative poverty is experienced by sometimes rural but more often urban populations in the global North, the majority of the poorest people in the world live in the global South but are impacted by the events and policies of the global North. The UN Millennium Development Goals Report states that

an estimated 1.4 billion people were still living in extreme poverty in 2005. Moreover, the effects of the global financial crisis are likely to persist: poverty rates will be slightly higher in 2015 and even beyond, to 2020, than they would have been had the world economy grown steadily at its pre-crisis pace (UNDESA, 2010: 4).

The number of people who were undernourished in 2008 may be as high as 915 million and exceed 1 billion in 2009: about 25 per cent of infants and children are under weight due to lack food and quality food (UNDESA, 2010). Over half of the people in Sub-Saharan Africa and about two-fifths of people in Southern Asia live on less than $1.25 per day. An analysis according to the Multidimensional Poverty Index (MPI) shows that about 1.7 billion people from 104 countries – a third of their entire population – live in multidimensional poverty. The analysis further shows that half of the world's poor live in South Asia (51 per cent or 844 million people) and one-quarter in Africa (28 per cent or 458 million). Despite economic growth of the country as a whole, there are more poor people in eight Indian states alone (421 million) than in the 26 poorest African countries combined (410 million). Niger has the greatest intensity and incidence of poverty in any one country, with 93 per cent of the population classified as poor. Nairobi has the same level of poverty as the Dominican Republic, whereas Kenya's rural northeast is poorer than Niger (UNDP, 2010). This suggests that rural poverty remains stubbornly high (sometimes leading to internal migration) but requiring interventions at international, national and local levels. Various strategies already referred to, e.g. aid and trade, improvement of governance, and social development, are required in a concerted form to meet the basic human needs of individuals (sustenance and shelter) and develop the services and infrastructures which can build capacity in societies (e.g. health, education and employment opportunities).

However, natural conditions, colonial history, current neglect or exploitation and corrupt governments are only some of the causes of poverty. Conflict and violence can be seen as both the causes and consequences of poverty; and, as Mahatma Gandhi once said, poverty itself is a form of violence. Conflicts are broadly classified into inter- and intra-state, which may include civil war, communal clashes, inter-group fighting, political violence (organised armed violence by the state against civilians) and terrorism (Hazen, 2008). Over the decade 2000–2009, only three of the total of 30 major armed conflicts have been interstate, though many armed conflicts to some extent are international due to their engagement in international trade, e.g. in arms, drugs, diamonds (Bray, 2005).

A BBC website reports that every minute two people are killed around the world (BBC, 2011), and in 2010, major armed conflicts were active in 15 locations globally. These included four countries in Africa (Rwanda, Somalia, Sudan and Uganda), three in America (Colombia, Peru and the USA), five in Asia (Afghanistan, India, Myanmar, Pakistan and the Philippines) and three in Middle East (Iraq, Israel and Turkey) (Stockholm International Peace Research Institute, 2011), and further unrest in the Middle East at the time of writing (2011) has added to this list (e.g. Egypt and Libya). In addition, the BBC list includes Chechnya, DR Congo, Georgia, Laos, Nagorno-Karabakh and Nepal. The historical context and causes of conflict and violence differ from one country to another. However, some of the common grounds for the majority of conflicts are claims and counter-claims over disputed territories (and their resources), political and government control, political rights, extreme suppression by ruling elites, discriminatory policies and practices against minority racial, ethnic and religious groups, corrupt governments (see Hazen, 2008) and unwillingness to share power and see the growth and development of traditionally disadvantaged groups (Pawar, 2010). Whatever the causes of conflict, one consequence is inevitably migration, usually across neighbouring borders, but sometimes through more organised or clandestine routes as 'official' or unofficial refugees to more distant countries in the global North.

According to a Global Trends report (UNHCR, 2010), 43.3 million people were forcibly displaced in 2009, the highest number of people uprooted by conflict and persecution since the mid-1990s. Of these, 15.2 million were refugees while internally displaced persons grew by 4 per cent to 27.1 million. On-going and unresolved conflicts in Afghanistan, Somalia and DR Congo and stagnated situations in Sudan and Iraq significantly reduced the chances of repatriation (Guterres, 2010). In addition, about 5.5 million refugees were in protracted situations, under the UNHCR care; and approximately 6.6 to 12 million people had become stateless. The report also indicated that the number of individual asylum claims worldwide grew to nearly 1 million, with South Africa receiving more than 222,000 new claims last year, making it the single largest asylum destination in the world. It is also important to note a new trend: increasing numbers of refugees are living in cities of the global South, challenging the notion that refugees are 'inundating' the industrialized developed nations.

The issues of poverty, conflict and migration (in its various forms) are of increasing relevance for social professionals, whether working in international or local contexts, and will all be the subject of more detailed attention in later chapters. Increased levels of people smuggling and trafficking; the growth of transnational (cross-cultural) marriages (arranged through agencies); theft for sale of organs; exploitative practices in inter-country adoptions are all examples of social issues related to these three factors and facilitated by use of information and communication technologies and global networks, posing actual or potential challenges for practitioners, as well as policy makers, legislators and justice systems nationally and internationally.

STRUCTURE AND CONTENTS

As mentioned in the introduction, the Handbook aims to present a comprehensive

account of different aspects of the globalised context within which all social workers now operate and to advance ideas about the purposes and forms of international social work. We have therefore taken a thematic approach to the overall structure (five sections) and the 30 chapters, rather than adopting a more comparative approach (presentation and analyses of national situations) – although authors have drawn on examples from a wide variety of countries as relevant. In identifying the focus of chapters, we recognised the inter-related nature of many of the themes discussed but also sought to provide clarity and different perspectives through grouping the chapters into five sections. The sections themselves provide overarching frameworks for chapters addressing, in turn, (1) the more theoretical aspects of concepts and processes; (2) professional contexts and approaches; (3) key issues and settings; (4) the life course; and (5) regional perspectives, respectively, as further elaborated in the preface to each section.

We also recruited authors from a wide range of countries to ensure a range of expertise (based on different national traditions and experiences); and to enhance international dialogue (where two or more colleagues worked together cross-nationally) and access to a greater range of literature. It is likely that readers will find some 'overlaps' between material in the different sections and chapters which, however, can also be read as 'free-standing' units. Finally, we selected themes for six general appendices according to the topics which have most often been referred to in different chapters.

In relation to individual chapters, authors have interpreted the general guidelines provided in various ways and we have employed a relatively light editorial touch so that chapters reflect their distinct contributions. We took an initial decision not to have chapters dedicated to diversity and anti-oppressive practices in relation to particular minorities (e.g. based on gender, sexuality or disability) but asked all authors to address issues of diversity and anti-oppressive practice in ways most relevant to their topics: we have also introduced material on the cross-cutting themes of diversity and power-relationships in this introductory chapter. Notwithstanding some reference to the historical aspects of their topic, the focus of the chapters is primarily on contemporary aspects of international social work – or international and comparative perspectives on social work; on the social issues which engage social workers at national, regional and international levels; and on the challenges and future directions possible for 'international social work'.

In Section 1 (*Key concepts and processes*), Chapter 2, Dominelli writes on globalisation and the related but often contradictory processes of indigenisation and their relevance for international social work. Alston and Besthorn, in Chapter 3, discuss issues concerning environment and sustainability: given the link between a healthy environment and human well-being (and even survival) they urge greater engagement of social workers with this topic. In Chapter 4, Wronka and Staub-Bernasconi consider human rights in international context. From an initial description of the major international instruments defining human rights, they propose (more overt) integration of this topic into social work education curricula and practices. Chapter 5, authored by Desai and Solas, focuses on poverty, development and social justice: they argue for development policies and practices that are gender aware, sustainable and rights based. In Chapter 6, Segal and Heck discuss issues of migration, minorities and citizenship. As well as historical perspectives on migration, the authors consider notions of citizenship and the nation-state; and conclude with the implications for social work in this inherently international field.

Section 2 (*Professional contexts*) opens with Chapter 7 by Payne who considers the political and organisational contexts of social work internationally. He suggests that different political values give rise to different welfare regimes, which in turn result in different 'social works', which are themselves variously organised in terms of the settings in which they operate. In Chapter 8, Badwall and Razack look at social work theories, particularly critical perspectives and new challenges. They suggest that the development of social work (theories and practices) illustrates the white bias and American/European influence which still dominates thinking and practices in the profession. Hugman and Bowles, in Chapter 9, debate issues of social work values, ethics and professional regulation and describe how these are closely related but distinct. They ask whether a single (global) statement of ethics is plausible, and conclude that shared conversations about values and ethics in social work internationally are important. Chapter 10 by Hokenstad is concerned with social work education in a global context. The chapter includes historical and comparative perspectives as well as discussing the notion of 'international social work' in relation to curriculum changes and opportunities for student exchange and other learning opportunities. Orme and Karvinen-Niinikoski, in Chapter 11, look at the issue of social work research from an international perspective. They include discussion of different traditions and methodological approaches and ethical considerations needed as well as the resources for comparative and international research.

In Section 3 (*Key issues for social work internationally*), Akimoto and Sungkawan (Chapter 12) consider the connections between social work, economic conditions and livelihoods. They describe the significant variations in work opportunities and forms of employment and comment on the scope for greater involvement of social and development workers in this field. In Chapter 13, Bywaters and Davis discuss health issues pertinent to social work internationally. They define health as a human right and therefore a matter of concern for all social workers, with scope for international action. Huxtable, Sottie and Ulziitungalag, in Chapter 14, present material about social work and education, primarily as a specialism supporting the school system of different countries. The authors give various examples of school social work, particularly in Ghana and Mongolia, and identify some challenges and changes in this field. In Chapter 15, Preston-Shoot and Höjer focus on social work, justice and protection systems and the extent to which issues of discrimination and equality are addressed in national legislation. They describe social work as a moral activity with a widespread role in protecting adults and children at risk of abuse or neglect. In Chapter 16, McKinnon explores social work and changing environments, commenting on the ways in which environmental, social and economic environments are inter-related. Shier and Graham, in Chapter 17, examine religion, culture and spirituality, defining each as distinct though related. They identify religion and/or spirituality as important in the well-being of some individuals and communities and central in some cultures: they are thus significant in anti-oppressive social work. In Chapter 18, Mathbor and Bourassa discuss disaster management and humanitarian action and suggest that social workers have a role in both pre-and post-disaster phases of interventions. The authors stress the importance of participatory techniques and the inclusion of survivors in all phases of the recovery processes. Ramon and Maglajlic, in Chapter 19, focus on social work, conflict and displacement – a neglected but important field for social work engagement. They identify examples of resilience alongside the more damaging effects on individuals and communities and advocate greater attention to this topic in social work education.

Opening Section 4 (*Life-course perspectives*), Desai, in Chapter 20, considers the changing contexts and forms of families. The author identifies key issues and challenges for families in contemporary societies, including the increase in the number of transnational families. Rock, Karabanow and Manion, in Chapter 21, explore childhood and youth in an international context, stressing that childhood is a social construct which varies over time and place. The authors identify three 'groups' of children and young

people who are vulnerable (but also often resilient) – children who are orphaned or affected by HIV/AIDS; those who are affected by disasters; and street children. In Chapter 22, Chau applies a life-course perspective to the stage of adulthood. She looks at the two major institutions that contribute to adult identity and roles, namely, family and work; and identifies significant changes in adults' likely experiences in the labour market. Hokenstad and Roberts, in Chapter 23, consider old age in a global context, noting increases in longevity and in the numbers of people over 60, with particular challenges arising from the increased numbers of 'frail elderly' people. Alongside their special responsibilities in relation to elder abuse and neglect, the authors identify three internationally identified priority directions for social workers.

In Section 5 (*Regional perspectives*) in Chapter 24 on Africa, Mwansa and Kreitzer present a brief summary of the colonial histories prevalent in this continent, which have had enduring consequences for social policy and social work (education). They refer to the considerable levels of poverty and range of social problems in the continent and the challenges to developing appropriate services and indigenous practices. Pawar with Tsui, in Chapter 25 on Southern and Eastern Asia, include a focus on the extent to which social work has developed national associations and whether these are linked to regional and international bodies. They provide examples from many countries of developments and issues in social work and education, with particular reference to India and China. In Chapter 26 on Australasia, Beddoe and Fraser describe the uneven and different developments in social work related to the very different socioeconomic conditions in Australia and New Zealand relative to the island nations of the South West Pacific. They include some reference to professional associations and to social worker mobility within and outside the region. Zaviršek and Lawrence discuss, in Chapter 27, the national, ethnic and linguistic diversity of Europe and the origins of social work as well as current challenges. Despite EU policies and engagement of social work in exchange programmes there is no common recognition of social work qualifications, but there are shared concerns, including developments in anti-oppressive values and practices. In Chapter 28, on the Middle East, Al-Makhamreh and Libal give examples of social work developments in a number of countries including particularly Egypt, Israel, Jordan and Turkey. They convey the complexities and inequalities of the region and illustrate efforts to develop forms of social work which are more in tune with its needs and cultural traditions. In the chapter on Latin America, Chapter 29, Saracostti, Reininger and Parada describe the effects of political and economic events in different countries on social work. A core issue is the poverty and marginalisation of the majority of the region's population and the need to develop indigenous services and practices free of international neo-liberal interventions. Finally, Watkins and Holder Dolly, in Chapter 30 on North America and the Caribbean, describe well-developed and regulated (but different) forms of social work in the US and Canada. The socioeconomic situation of the Caribbean islands is markedly different (and their histories are varied) resulting in differences in the concerns and developments of social work in this sub-region.

CONCLUDING SUMMARY

We have aimed in this chapter to introduce some material which has general relevance across the Handbook and to orientate the reader to the more detailed discussions that follow. Essential to this task has been a consideration of some terms which are basic to furthering our understanding of the notion of international social work. In relation to the core theme, we suggest that 'international social work' does not have a single meaning, but is rather a concept which has been used over time to describe different forms of practice and which currently has important meanings, in the context of globalisation, for social workers operating at local levels as well as those involved in work which transcends or crosses national boundaries. We have identified the themes of space, time and diversity as having salience to international social work and also identified (and linked) some current trends and issues, which we consider to be particularly relevant to this field of activity, research and education. Finally, we said something about the structure and contents of the Handbook and noted the inclusion of examples of national and regional issues and practices relevant to the main theme. Significant among these is the examination of international bodies, policies and practices, in the political and socioeconomic fields which impact on international social work, and with which social workers can usefully engage, whether working locally or internationally. We conclude that international social work is a value-based activity, which requires social professionals to be knowledgeable about the global context, critically aware of issues of diversity and power and internationalist in their pursuance of human rights and social justice.

NOTES

1　Many examples are given later in the Handbook but these include: social work education models in southern countries that are critiqued as professional imperialism; human rights that are questioned from a cultural relativism point of view; structural adjustment packages of the World Bank that are perceived as the imposition of western fiscal measures on poor countries.

2　We can note here the associated term, 'community', also a highly contested notion. While 'communities' are sometimes assumed to be homogeneous populations (with similar interests and values) sharing a defined space, they are more often collections of individuals and smaller 'groups' holding more or less power in a given context. They are therefore sometimes the site of rivalries and resentments if not outright conflict. In addition, they may be 'communities of interest', not bounded by physical location, and/or be virtual communities.

3   The epithet 'emerald tiger' was both a play on Ireland's traditional title as 'the Emerald Isle', but also an acknowledgement of the considerable speed with which it moved from a low economic base to an expanding one, reminiscent of the 'Asian Tigers' before it.

REFERENCES

Agrawal, P. (2011) 'India needs an equality tax', *Financial Times Online*, 1 April 2011, http://www.ft.com/cms/s/2/f44a9528-5c3d-11e0-8f48-00144feab49a.html#axzz1YKIX2OL1.

Ahmadi, N. (2003) 'Globalisation of consciousness and new challenges for international social work', *International Journal of Social Welfare*, 12(1): 14–23.

Anderson, B. (1991) *Imagined Communities, Reflections on the Origin and Spread of Nationalism*. London: Verso.

Bauman, Z. (1998) *Globalization: The Human Consequences*. Cambridge: Polity Press.

BBC (2011) *One Day of War*, retrieved on 12 March 2011, from http://news.bbc.co.uk/2/shared/spl/hi/programmes/this_world/one_day_of_war/clickable_map/html/introduction.stm.

Beck, U. (2000) *What is Globalization?* Cambridge: Polity Press.

Bourdieu, P. (1999) 'Site effects', in P. Bourdieu (1999) *The Weight of the World: Social Suffering in Contemporary Society*. Cambridge: Polity Press.

Brauns, H.-J. and Kramer, D. (1991) 'Social work education and professional development', in M. Hill, (ed.), *Social Work in the European Community: The Social Policy and Practice Contexts*. London: Jessica Kingsley.

Bray, J. (2005) 'International companies and post-conflict reconstruction: cross-sectoral comparisons', Social Development papers: Conflict Prevention and Reconstruction, paper no. 22. World Bank: Washington. Retrieved on 11 March 2011, from http://siteresources.worldbank.org/INTCPR/214578-111996036679/20482471/WP22_RevisedWeb.pdf

Briskman, L. and Cemlyn, S. (2005) 'Reclaiming humanity for asylum-seekers: a social work response', *International Social Work*, 48(6): 714–24.

Burnham, J. (1993), 'Systemic supervision: the evolution of reflexivity in the context of the supervisory relationship', *Human Systems*, 4: 349–81.

Castles, F.G. (1998) *Comparative Public Policy: Patterns of Post-war Transformation*. Cheltenham: Edward Elgar.

Cochrane, A., Clarke, J. and Gewirtz, S. (eds) (2001) *Comparing Welfare States*. 2nd edn. London: Sage.

Cooper, A., Hetherington, R., Baistow, K., Pitts, J. and Spriggs, A. (1995) *Positive Child Protection: A View from Abroad*. Lyme Regis: Russell House Publishing.

Cox, D. and Pawar, M. (2006) *International Social Work: Issues, Strategies and Programs*. London: Sage.

Davis, G. (2004) 'A history of the social development network in the World Bank, 1973–2002', http://siteresources.worldbank.org/EXTSOCIALDEVELOPMENT/Resources/244362-1164107274725/3182370-1164201144397/SocialDevelopment-History.pdf?resourceurlname=SocialDevelopment-History.pdf (accessed 6 June 2008).

Dominelli, L. (1996) 'Deprofessionalising social work: anti-oppressive practice, competencies and post-modernism', *British Journal of Social Work*, 26(2): 153–75.

Dominelli, L. (2002) *Anti-oppressive Social Work Theory and Practices*. Basingstoke: Palgrave Macmillan.

Dominelli, L. (2010) *Social Work in a Globalising World*. Cambridge: Polity Press.

Dustin, D. and Davies, L. (2007) 'Female genital cutting and children's rights: implications for social work practice', *Child Care in Practice*, 13(1): 3–16.

Esping-Andersen, G. (1990) *The Three Worlds of Welfare Capitalism*. Cambridge: Polity Press.

Ferguson, I. (2011) 'Why class (still) matters', in M. Lavalette (ed.), *Radical Social Work Today: Social Work at the Crossroads*. Bristol/Portland, OR: The Policy Press.

Garrett, P. (2006) 'Protecting children in a globalized world: 'race' and 'place' in the Laming Report on the Death of Victoria Climbié', *Journal of Social Work*, 6(3): 315–36.

Giddens, A. (2009) *The Politics of Climate Change*. Cambridge: Polity Press.

Glick Schiller, N. and Levitt, P. (2006) *Haven't We Heard This Somewhere Before? A Substantive View of Transnational Migration Studies by Way of a Reply to Waldinger and Fitzgerald*. Princeton University: Center for Migration and Development Working Paper Series.

Goodin, R., Headey, B., Muffels, R. and Dirven, H.J. (2000) *The Real Worlds of Welfare Capitalism*. Cambridge: Cambridge University Press.

Graham, M. and Schiele, J.H. (2010) 'Equality-of-oppressions and anti-discriminatory models in social work: reflections from the USA and UK', *European Journal of Social Work*, 13(2): 231–44.

Gray, M. and Coates, J. (2010) "Indigenization" and knowledge development: extending the debate', *International Social Work,* 53(5): 613–27.

Gray, M. and Fook, J. (2004) 'The quest for a universal social work: some issues and implications', *Social Work Education,* 23(5): 625–44.

Gray, M. and Webb, S.A. (2007) 'Global double standards in social work: a critical review', *Social Work and Society,* 8 March, http://www.socmag.net/?p=56.

Grunwald, K. and Thiersch, H. (2009) 'The concept of the "lifeworld orientation" for social work and social care', *Journal of Social Work Practice*, 23(2): 131–46.

Guterres, A. (2010) 'Number of forcibly displaced rises to 43.3 million last year, the highest level since mid-1990s', retrieved on 13 March 2011, from http://www.unhcr.org/4c176c969.html.

Harrison, G. (2006) 'Broadening the conceptual lens on language in social work: difference, diversity and English as a global language', *British Journal of Social Work*, 6(3): 401–18.

Haug, E. (2005) 'Critical reflections on the emerging discourse of international social work', *International Social Work,* 48(2): 126–35.

Hayes, D. and Houston, S. (2007) '''Lifeworld", "system" and family group conferences: Habermas's contribution to discourse in child protection', *British Journal of Social Work*, 37(6): 987–1006.

Hazen, J.M. (2008) *Armed Violence in Asia and the Pacific: An Overview of Costs, Causes and Consequences.* Briefing paper. UNDP, http://www.undp.org/cpr/documents/armed_violence/AV_AsiaPacific_2008.pdf (accessed 9 November 2008).

Healy, L. (2001) *International Social Work: Professional Action in an Interdependent World.* Oxford: Oxford University Press.

Healy, L. (2007) 'Universalism and cultural relativism in social work ethics', *International Social Work,* 50(1): 11–26.

Healy, L. (2008) *International Social Work: Professional Action in an Interdependent World.* 2nd edn. New York: Oxford University Press.

Healy, L.M. and Thomas, R. (2007) 'International social work: a retrospective in the 50th year', *International Social Work,* 50(5): 581–96.

Heinz, W. and Krüger, H. (2001) 'Life course: innovations and challenges for social research', *Current Sociology,* 49(2): 29–45.

Hewitt, V. (1992) *The international politics of South Asia.* Manchester: Manchester University Press.

Higham, P. (2005) *What is Important about Social Work and Social Care?* Paper for the Assembly for Social Care and Social Work Education, Training and Research, http://www.ssrg.org.uk/assembly/files/patriciahigham.pdf.

Hill, M. (1996) *Social Policy: A Comparative Analysis.* London: Prentice Hall.

Hoefer, R. (1996) 'A conceptual model for studying social welfare policy comparatively', *Journal of Social Work Education*, 32(1): 101–13.

Hokenstad, M.C., Khinduka, S.K. and Midgley, J. (eds) (1992). *Profiles in International Social Work.* Washington: National Association of Social Workers Press.

Hugman, R. (2010) *Understanding International Social Work: A Critical Analysis.* Basingstoke, Palgrave-Macmillan.

Hugman, R., Moosa-Mitha, M. and Moyo, O. (2010) 'Towards a borderless social work: reconsidering notions of international social work', *International Social Work,* 53(5): 629–43.

Ife, J. (2001) 'Local and global practice: relocating social work as a human rights profession in the new global order', *European Journal of Social Work*, 4(1): 5–15.

IFSW (International Federation of Social Workers). (2010) *International Policy on Women.* http://www.ifsw.org/p38000218.html.

Johnson, H.W. (1996) 'International activity in undergraduate social work education in the United States', *International Social Work,* 39(2): 189–99.

Kendall, K. (1998) *IASSW: The First Fifty Years 1928–78. A Tribute to the Founders.* Alexandria, VA: IASSW/CSWE.

Kendall, K. (2000) *Social Work Education: Its Origins in Europe.* Alexandria, VA: CSWE

Khaja, K., Barkdull, C., Augustine, M. and Cunningham, D. (2009). 'Female genital cutting: African women speak out', *International Social Work,* 52(6): 727–41.

Kniephoff-Knebel, A. and Seibel, F. (2008) 'Establishing international cooperation in social work education: the first decade of the International Committee of Schools for Social Work (CSSW)', *International Social Work*, 51(6): 790–812.

Köngeter, S. (2010) 'Transnationalism', *Social Work & Society*, 8(1): 177–81.

Kuhlmann, C. (2001) 'Historical portraits of important European leaders in social work: Alice Salomon 1872–1948 – Germany', *European Journal of Social Work*, 4(1): 65–75.

Lavalette, M. (ed.) (2011) *Radical Social Work Today: Social Work at the Crossroads.* Bristol/Portland, OR: The Policy Press.

Lavalette, M. and Ioakimidis, V. (2011) 'International social work or social work internationalism? Radical social work in global perspective', in M. Lavalette (ed.), *Radical Social Work Today: Social Work at the Crossroads*. Bristol/Portland, OR: The Policy Press. pp. 135–52.

Lawrence, S., Lyons, K., Simpson, G. and Huegler, N. (2009) *Introducing International Social Work*. Exeter: Learning Matters.

Lister, R. (1998) 'Citizenship, social work and social action', *European Journal of Social Work*, 1(1): 5–18.

Lorenz, W. (1994) *Social Work in a Changing Europe*. London: Routledge.

Lorenz, W. (2006) 'Education for the social professions', in K. Lyons and S. Lawrence (eds), *Social Work in Europe: Educating for Change*. Birmingham: Venture Press/BASW.

Lorenz, W. (2007) 'Practising history: memory and contemporary professional practice', *International Social Work*, 50(5): 597–612.

Lyons, K. (1999) *International Social Work: Themes and Perspectives*. Aldershot: Ashgate.

Lyons, K. (2006) 'Globalization and social work: international and local implications', *British Journal of Social Work*, 36(3): 365–80.

Lyons, K. (2007) 'Editorial', *International Social Work* 50(1): 5–9.

Lyons, K. (2008) 'Eileen Younghusband, 1961–1968', in F. Seibel (ed.), *Global Leaders for Social Work Education: the IASSW Presidents 1928–2008*. Brno: Albert.

Lyons, K. and Littlechild, B. (eds) (2006) *International Labour Mobility in Social Work*. BASW Monograph. Birmingham: Venture Press.

Lyons, K., Manion, K. and Carlsen, M. (2006) *International Perspectives on Social Work*. Basingstoke: Palgrave Macmillan.

Manion, H.K. (2005) 'A global perspective on intellectual property rights: a social work view', *International Social Work*, 48(1): 77–88.

Miah, M.R. (2008) 'Social development', in T. Mizrahi and L.E. Davis (eds), *Encyclopedia of Social Work*. New York: NASW and Oxford University Press.

Midgley, J. (1981) *Professional Imperialism: Social Work in the Third World*. London: Heinemann.

Midgley, J. (1995) *Social Development: The Development Perspective in Social Work*. London: Sage.

Midgley, J. (2008) 'Perspectives on globalization and culture: implications for international social work practice', *Journal of Global Social Work Practice* 1 (1), http://www.globalsocialwork.org/vol1no1_Midgley.html.

Mohan, B. (1986) 'Unraveling comparative social welfare', in B. Mohan (ed.), *Toward Comparative Social Welfare*. Cambridge: MA: Schenkman. pp. 1–110.

Mohan, B. and Sharma, P. (1985) 'On human oppression and social development', *Social Development Issues*, Spring, IX, 1: 12–23.

Omeje, K. (ed.) (2008) *Extractive Economies and Conflicts in the Global South*. Aldershot: Ashgate.

Oxfam (1997) *A Curriculum for Global Citizenship*. Oxford: Oxfam UK and Ireland.

Patel, L. (2005) *Social Welfare and Social Development in South Africa*. Cape Town: OUP.

Pawar, M. (1998) 'International Social Work', *AASW NSW Branch Newsletter*, December 1998.

Pawar, M. (2010) 'Looking outwards: teaching international social work in Asia', *International Journal of Social Work Education*, 29(8): 896–909.

Pawar, M. and Cox (eds), (2010) 'Social development', in M. Pawar and D. Cox. *Social Development: Critical Themes and Perspectives*. New York: Routledge. pp.13–36.

Payne, M. and Askeland, G.A. (2008) *Globalization and International Social Work: Postmodern Change and Challenge*. Aldershot: Ashgate.

Pease, B. and Pringle, K. (eds) (2001) *A Man's World? Changing Men's Practices in a Globalized World*. London, New York: Zed Books.

Robertson, R. (1995) 'Glocalization: time–space and homogeneity–heterogeneity', in M. Featherstone, S. Lash and R. Robertson (eds), *Global Modernities*. London: Sage.

Robinson, L. (2002) 'Social work through the life course', in R. Adams, L. Dominelli and M. Payne (eds), *Social Work: Themes, Issues and Critical Debates*. 2nd edn. Basingstoke: Palgrave. pp. 84–94.

Rodgers, B. (1977) 'Comparative studies in social policy and administration', in H. Heisler, (ed.), *Foundations of Social Administration*. London: Macmillan. pp. 196–220.

Seibel, F. (ed.) (2008) *Global Leaders for Social Work Education: The IASSW Presidents 1928–2008*. Brno: Albert.

Seibel, F. and Lorenz, W. (1998) *Social Professions for a Social Europe: ERASMUS Evaluation Conference 1996*. Frankfurt: IKO.

Sewpaul, V. and Jones, D. (2004) 'Global standards for social work education and training', *Social Work Education*, 23(5): 493–513.

Spatscheck, C. and Wolf-Ostermann, K. (2009) *Social Space Analyses and the Socio-Spatial Paradigm in Social Work*. Lunds: Lunds University Working Paper Series.

Staub-Bernasconi, S. (1995) *Systemtheorie, Soziale Probleme und Soziale Arbeit: Lokal, National, International. Oder: vom Ende der Bescheidenheit.* Bern: Paul Haupt.

Staub-Bernasconi, S. (2006) 'Social work as a profession: cross-national similarities and differences', in: I. Weiss and P. Welbourne (eds), *Social Work as a Profession: A Comparative Cross-national Perspective.* Birmingham: Venture Press.

Stern, N. (2009) *The Global Deal: Climate Change and the Creation of a New Era of Progress and Prosperity.* New York/Philadelphia: Public Affairs/Perseus Books.

Strier, R. (2009) 'Class-competent social work: a preliminary definition', *International Journal of Social Welfare,* 18(3): 237–42.

Stockholm International Peace Research Institute (2011) *Yearbook 2011,* available online: http://www.sipri.org/yearbook/2011/02/02A.

Teeple, G. (2000) *Globalization and the Decline of Social Reform: Into the 21st Century* 2nd edn. Aurora, ON: Garamond Press.

Todaro, M.P. (1997) *Economic Development.* Reading, Mass.: Addison-Wesley.

United Nations Department of Economic and Social Affairs (UNDESA) (2010) 'The Millennium Development Goals Report 2010', Retrieved 11 March 2011, http://www.un.org/millenniumgoals/pdf/MDG%20Report%202010%20En%20r15%20-low%20res%2020100615%20-.pdf

United Nations Development Programme (UNDP) (2010) *Human Development Report 2010.* New York: Oxford University Press.

United Nations High Commissioner for Refugees (UNHCR) (2010) *2009 Global Trends: Refugees, Asylum-seekers, Returnees, Internally Displaced and Stateless Persons.* www.unhcr.org/statistics.

UN News (2010) *Deforestation now in Decline but Rate Remains Alarming, UN Agency Says.* www.un.org/apps/news/story.asp?NEWSID=34195.

Verloo, M. (2006) 'Multiple inequalities, intersectionality and the European Union', *European Journal of Women's Studies,* 13(3): 211–28.

Vogler, J. (1997) 'Environment and natural resources', in B. White, R. Little and M. Smith (eds), *Issues in World Politics.* Basingstoke: Macmillan Press.

Walker, A. (ed.) (1996) *The New Generational Contract, Intergenerational Relations, Old Age and Welfare.* London: University College London Press.

Webb, S. (2003) 'Local orders and global chaos in social work', *European Journal of Social Work,* 6(2): 191–204.

Weiss-Gal, I. and Welbourne, P. (2008) 'The profession of social work: cross national approach', *International Journal of Social Welfare,* 17(4): 281–99.

Welbourne, P., Harrison, G. and Forde, D. (2007) 'Social work in the UK and the global labour market: recruitment, practice and ethical considerations', *International Social Work,* 50(1): 27–40.

Xu, Q. (2006). 'Defining international social work: a social service agency perspective', *International Social Work,* 49(6): 679–92.

Young, A. and Ashton, E. (1963) *British Social Work in the 19th Century.* 2nd edn. London: Routledge and Kegan Paul Ltd.

Concepts, Processes and Values

Karen Lyons

INTRODUCTION TO SECTION 1: CONCEPTS, PROCESSES AND VALUES

The practice of social work – in all its forms – is framed by a variety of external contextual factors and processes, as well as being underpinned by theoretical concepts and value positions. For many social professionals these relate primarily to the national or 'domestic' situations in which they operate. However, in considering international social work (in the various forms suggested in Chapter 1), we must explore issues and processes evident in the wider geographical context of the world and consider the concepts and values which have international recognition and salience. In relation to values, two in particular have overarching significance for the roles and activities of social professionals (whether operating locally or at international level) namely, human rights and social justice. These are often linked together, including in the international definition of social work (see Appendix 1), but can be treated separately (as we have chosen

to do in this Handbook), given their scope, importance and relationship to other themes.

Chapters in this section aim to identify the main 'external' and 'macro' concepts and processes which determine or influence the various forms of social work observable around the world. More specifically, we have selected global themes which require or enable social professionals to operate in international environments; to practice transnationally; or to recognise the international dimensions of their local concerns. Given the way in which international social work could be seen primarily as transferring ideas and practices from 'developed' to 'developing' countries (Lavalette and Ioakimidis, 2011) and considering the ongoing concerns about professional imperialism, it is important to develop an increased understanding of global processes and international interactions and to apply professional values to the practices of those engaged in social work and development. Together the chapters therefore provide a theoretical basis for concepts which are frequently referred to in the subsequent chapters of this Handbook and also provide a value base from which to interrogate ideas and practices in the field of international social work.

A major aspect of the international context is globalisation which can be linked to the opposing processes of indigenisation, as addressed by Dominelli in Chapter 2. Globalisation is now recognised as having a major impact on welfare systems and thus on the role of social workers, both through the economic conditions created in different continental regions and individual countries, and through the trends promoted towards political and cultural hegemony (Payne and Askeland, 2008). But the local impact of globalisation is variable within and between countries, favouring the interests of some, while hugely disadvantaging other populations. The efforts of people at local and international levels to resist the homogenising and damaging effects of globalisation have led, among other things, to increased recognition of the rights of indigenous populations who have been oppressed either as indigenous minorities in their own homelands or as majority populations, previously colonised and subject to ongoing economic exploitation and professional imperialism. Dominelli urges social workers to understand the implications of such processes and ally themselves with groups resisting the damaging effects of globalisation and advocating for respect for indigenous values and development of appropriate practices in the context of internationalism.

A second contextual theme relates to concerns (not universally shared) about the environment and sustainability and these are the focus of Alston and Besthorn's chapter (Chapter 3). Environmental issues are related to economic globalisation (through exploitation of the earth's natural resources for individual and, often multinational, corporate profit); as well as damage to local and global environments and weather systems (caused in part by the processes of production of goods for ever increasing markets). The finite nature of natural resources and fragility of eco-systems have led to increased attention to the concept of sustainability. While international bodies and national governments have a major responsibility for redressing and regulating excesses and promoting sustainable measures, Alston and Besthorn suggest that social workers can operate in tandem with local communities and international movements to highlight damaging social consequences of environmental and climate change and lobby for sustainable practices.

In relation to human rights, it is only relatively recently (since the mid-20th century) that there has been international recognition of the universal nature of the most basic of human needs and of the particular needs of populations subject to discrimination (on whatever grounds). Wronka and Staub-Bernasconi (Chapter 4) describe a wide range of international declarations and conventions, primarily (but not exclusively) articulated by the United Nations (see also Appendix 5). They also identify the establishment of mechanisms to monitor their implementation. Such declarations and monitoring devices have sometimes been sufficient to encourage development of national policies which support human rights but there are still many opportunities for social professionals to ally themselves with other groups to identify and challenge violations. Additionally, while human rights may be understood as an individual matter (and tend to be so interpreted by many social workers in the global North), the rights of oppressed minority groups (and even of the majority population in some societies) suggest that there is both scope and need for interventions of a more strategic and possibly transnational kind, requiring more attention to this field in the education of social professionals, as advocated by the authors.

This last point is also highly relevant in relation to social justice which, in Chapter 5 by Desai and Solas, is linked to a discussion about social development. The concept of social justice has had less prominence than human rights on the global stage, but was recognised in the Millennium Development

Goals (see Appendix 6), just over a decade ago. Substantial economic inequalities are evident within societies as well as between them but in the international context the differences are stark between countries of the global North and global South. Desai and Solas therefore analyse the meaning of terms used in development discourses and the different paradigms influencing the transfer of resources to less developed countries via international and bilateral arrangements. Social inequalities reflect economic ones and, again, while social professionals alone are unlikely to be able adequately to address social exclusion or effect social justice nationally or internationally, nevertheless, the authors suggest that adherence to the value of social justice between different groups in any society and worldwide must underpin social work policies and practices locally and internationally.

The last major concept selected for inclusion in this section is migration, as discussed by Segal and Heck (Chapter 6). As well as having demonstrable relationships with the effects of globalisation, environmental damage and poverty – and constituting a focus for the application of values and policies related to human rights and social justice – the plight of international migrants was an early focus for the development of international and local social work and services. After an analysis of the role of the nation state and notions of citizenship, the authors describe the varied causes, effects, forms and patterns of migration and note that the experience of refugees and other migrants constitutes an important, though sometimes neglected, focus for social work. This is particularly so in a world where there has been a hardening of public attitudes in many societies towards people who cross

borders, particularly from the global South to more affluent nations. Segal and Heck suggest that social professionals need to respond more appropriately to national and international policies and systems affecting migrants. In addition, the multi-ethnic composition of many societies requires development of value-based and culturally competent practices in working with minority and transnational communities.

Chapters in this section therefore introduce a range of topics which are important in laying the theoretical and contextual bases for the following sections and chapters. In some cases other authors (in the following sections) return to a particular theme addressed in Section 1 and develop the material further, for example, as it relates to social work practice, or explore it from a different perspective: in other cases the chapters in this section provide a more detailed analysis of values (such as human rights and social justice) that are referred to in less detail but frequently elsewhere in the Handbook. Either way the chapters can be read as 'stand-alone' contributions but they each have significant relationships with ensuing chapters and provide an essential basis for enhancing our understanding of – and rationale for – international social work.

REFERENCES

Lavalette, M. and Ioakimidis, V. (2011) 'International social work or social work internationalism? Radical social work in global perspective', in M. Lavelette (ed.), *Radical Social Work Today: Social Work at the Crossroads.* Bristol: The Policy Press.

Payne, M. and Askeland, G. (2008) *Gobalization and International Social Work: Post-modern Change and Challenge.* Aldershot: Ashgate.

2

Globalisation and Indigenisation: Reconciling the Irreconcilable in Social Work?

Lena Dominelli

INTRODUCTION

Social work enhances human and environmental well-being by delivering appropriate services and advocating for change in the interests of people and planet earth. Expressed locally, nationally and internationally, this remit links practitioners to humanity's highest ideals and is reshaped constantly under pressure from: professionalisation; public expectations; service users' demands; political and socioeconomic forces; and interactions across local–global borders. Social workers utilise the theories and practice of a heterogeneous profession to provide services in specific geographic localities; advocate for the well-being of peoples excluded by social divisions, such as age, gender, class, 'race' or ethnicity; critique policies that limit access to social power and resources; and control deviant populations. These roles are contradictory and trap practitioners in 'care-control' dilemmas highlighted in the radical social work movement of the 1970s (Bailey and

Brake, 1975) and currently resurfacing in the UK (Lavalette, 2011) and elsewhere. Opposing injustice configures social work as a politicised profession and creates tensions over reconciling the irreconcilable in both local and international practice. The latter occurs when social workers cross borders to assist, for example, in humanitarian disasters (Desai, 2007); support endeavours overseas (Humphreys, 1996); become migrant workers (Devo, 2006); or engage in transnational activities (Dominelli, 2012).

In this chapter, I explore the complex realities of practice and tensions faced by social workers upholding human rights and advocating for social justice as they negotiate local/national and international domains. I unpack the concepts of globalisation, internationalising practices and indigenisation to reveal social workers' complicated positioning arising from: calls for liberation and self-definition; heterogeneous, interdependent relations; and global homogenisation. Globalisation and indigenisation present opportunities and challenges for practitioners attempting empowering, locality specific and culturally relevant approaches. These carry implications for international social work when exchanging practitioners, faculty, student and curricula.

HISTORICAL AND CONTEXTUAL BACKGROUND

The social work profession had its origins in Europe in the late 19th century (Kendall, 2000) as a handmaiden of the state (Lorenz, 1994) and spread globally through colonising state agendas and altruistic impulses. Colonisation had taken root from the 17th century, altering local socioeconomic formations and Europeanising indigenous lifestyles, in every other continent. From the 19th century social workers became involved through institutions including nation-states and military, religious, voluntary and educational organisations, where controlling mechanisms replaced caring ones. Such oppressive practices ranged from turning indigenous peoples in Australia, Canada, Aotearoa/New Zealand, and United States into white Europeans, including by removing children from families and denying their cultures, languages, and religions (Haig-Brown, 1988; Humphreys, 1996; Grande, 2004) to oppressing minorities in Nazi Germany (Lorenz, 1994). In addition, migration from Europe was fostered by war or persecution as well as directly, by charity organisations. For example, Barnardo's, created in Victorian times, sent poor children (allegedly orphans) to Commonwealth countries, where, in foster homes or orphanages, many were abused (Bagnell, 2001).

Colonists also imposed educational materials which were considered to be superior to any existing and suggesting that their contents were universally applicable, regardless of local contexts or cultures. This tradition that was later evident in the establishment of social work education outside Europe and

North America and has persisted (Yip, 2005, see also Section 5). French, Spanish, Portuguese, Dutch and English were colonising languages in earlier exchanges and English has since become the dominant 'global' language, not least in social work. This reality excludes those not speaking it.

The beginnings of social work as an international profession arose when social workers crossed borders. For example, Jane Addams (US) and, a generation later, Eileen Younghusband (UK), used transatlantic exchanges to draw inspiration from visits to projects and colleagues abroad. The founding meeting of what would become the International Association of Schools of Social Work (IASSW), International Federation of Social Workers (IFSW), and International Council of Social Welfare (ICSW) in Paris in 1928 included social work amongst several 'social' professions (such as psychiatry). In addition to European and North American participants, representation from the world's other major regions – Latin America, Asia and Africa, raised the profession's profile internationally, although (Western) Europeans dominated numerically. Participants spoke in the three official Western European languages of the UN's predecessor, the League of Nations – English, French and Spanish. (The UN has since expanded this repertoire to include Arabic, Chinese and Russian.) Parity of usage for each heritage language is impossible without substantial resources for mother tongue translations that acknowledge their worth. Language is an issue about equality because it encapsulates power relations, cultural assumptions and worldviews that can become expressions of unfair internationalising practices (Dominelli, 2004a). Nonetheless, the question persists, how do people communicate with each other across borders while recognising each other's heritage language? As mentioned, language deprivation became an instrument of oppression in colonising indigenous peoples and English has risen to dominance spatially and in particular spheres. But this dominance is not necessarily enduring: other languages, for example, Greek and Latin, lost continental dominance when their empires declined. Today, Chinese is spoken by larger numbers of people than English (Ethnologue Survey, 1999) and, as the power balances reflected in geo political and economic relations shift, so could language dominance.

Today IASSW, ICSW and IFSW express commitment to international social work through raising its professional status; sharing models of practice, curricula, and personnel within a framework of human rights and social justice; and observing UN charters and conventions. Social work's global reach is affirmed by the Directory of the International Association of Schools of Social Work that locates tertiary level social work in 74 countries, and International Federation of Social Workers' claim of 1.5 million members worldwide.[1]

However, practitioners' activities, loosely referred to as 'international social work' are contested and reflect ambiguities about how it is constituted or carried out. Internationally, social work's noble ideals have sometimes provided needed services and been welcomed. But they have also been misused to perpetuate oppressive practices under the colonising ambitions of imperial powers (Ioakimidis, 2010); foster capitalist social relations in non-capitalist societies (Midgley, 1995); and suppress indigenous cultures (Haig-Brown, 1988). These outcomes require critical scrutiny (Grande, 2004) because ongoing concerns about the exploitative capacities of market forces to subordinate human needs cause recipients in the global South to suspect Western 'goodwill gestures' (Shiva, 2003).

The Victorian philanthropic organisations espousing Western superiority and models that imposed 'civilising' influences on those different from them have since elicited demands for indigenisation to check Western dominance and celebrate local achievements (Yip, 2005). Practitioners, squeezed by local pressures emanating from the nation-state alongside global ones, confront complex historical legacies that complicate relationships

between local and global (Payne and Askeland, 2008). Indigenous people's negative evaluations of practice are endorsed by other service users. During the 1960s, activists in 'new' social movements declared social workers oppressive for not challenging negative labelling and social stigmatisation; others have since felt thwarted by the privileging of expert power and inadequate resourcing (Dominelli, 2002).

Globalisation, indigenisation and internationalisation are separate but linked grand narratives of modernity. Post-modernity eschews grand narratives without acknowledging its own – having none. Its tenets usefully highlight the unique and specific in social work. The emphasis in post-modernity on individualisation limits the potential for social change where collective action is necessary. Activists in 'new' social movements utilise collective action for transformative change locally and internationally (Noble, 2007). Social workers undertake collective action internationally to create social capital, tackle structural inequalities and promote social inclusion. These activities enable practitioners to transcend individual victimhood by promoting agency through mutually beneficial internationalising practices within contingent and contextualised choices. Social workers eschewing hegemonic social relations innovate to develop practice which supersedes colonising concepts, policies and practices.

EXPLORING CONTESTED CONCEPTS, MEANINGS AND INTERPRETATIONS

How international social work, internationalisation, globalisation, internationalising practices and indigenisation are defined matters because the terrain they cover shapes policy and practice. Globalisation, used broadly, describes socioeconomic processes that transcend national boundaries. For many, globalisation is fundamentally an economic process of market integration (Sklair, 1998) that ultimately affects all social institutions including universities and social work practice. Internationalisation refers to processes, objectives, practices, behaviours, challenges and strategies that expose interdependencies in the local–global nexus (Dominelli, 2000a). Whether beneficial or exploitative, their meanings vary across different institutions (Knight, 1997; Callan, 1998; Lyons et al., 2006). Indigenisation celebrates local traditions, relationships and practices and allows peoples to self-define (Grande, 2004). Some see indigenisation as rejecting cultural homogeneity perpetrated through globalisation (Gray et al., 2009). Others argue that indigenisation predates globalisation, currently expressed as neo-liberalism. They deem indigenisation as a resistance movement protecting pre-capitalist social relations from being undermined by modernity while transforming these and situating indigenous people as active agents in contemporary capitalist societies (Grande, 2004).

International social work

'International social work' is a slippery phrase with various meanings. IASSW and IFSW jointly agreed an 'international' definition of social work in 2001 which is not, however, the same as 'international social work'. Some authors (e.g. Healy, 1988; Healy and Link, 2005) have highlighted curricula exchanges as central to international social work. Lyons (1999) suggested that the local and global become linked through international seminars and conferences, comparative studies spanning policies, values and practice; knowledge about international organisations; and struggles for social justice and human rights while Healy (2001, 2008) describes social work as an international profession that is active internationally through practice and advocacy work; relates domestic practice to international issues; and engages in professional exchanges. Lyons et al. (2006), like Cox and Pawar (2006), examine processes whereby international social work

provides perspectives for exploring specific issues that cross borders although practitioners intervene locally, e.g. people-trafficking. Others have suggested that studying social work practice or working in a country other than one's own constitutes 'international social work'. However, as Razack (2002) points out, the term can mean crossing national frontiers and doing over 'there' what was done at home under *assumptions* that the domestic practices are better and transferrable.

Borrmann et al. (2007) focus on international contexts in social work, e.g. social workers crossing borders to administer aid during natural disasters like earthquakes. But poorly delivered humanitarian aid (Hancock, 1996) and inappropriate support for local community and social development problematise social work interventions in the global South (Mohanty, 2003). Interactions between the local and global also become evident when similar issues are faced by social workers across several locations (Lawrence et al., 2009), e.g. caring for older people who migrate to join their families. A recent comparative study examined similarities and differences in social work values and methods to see which traverse different contexts and settings. The researchers identified commonalities around values, methods and issues whether practitioners practised in the global North or global South but found significant differences in historical trajectories; public support for social work; professional development; and accountability (Weiss and Welbourne, 2007). Similarities enable people from different countries to talk 'social work' together; understand what is being discussed; and consider the significance of differentiated contexts as expressed locally. Contexts are fluid and change as new events (re)shape practice locally and internationally, e.g. mass migrations, terrorist acts, failures in safeguarding children. Those social workers exposed for failing to protect children under their care tarnish practitioners' image at home and abroad (Gove, 1995; Laming, 2009).

Lack of clarity and consensus around the term international social work, has prompted calls for a re-theorisation of the 'international' to promote mutuality in exchange processes (Dominelli, 2000a). However, a reframing of 'international social work' as interactions between the global and local to produce new theories and practice has proven elusive to conceptualise adequately because it encompasses many different strands, levels and activities. Multinational corporations and nation-states co-opt social workers to impose exploitative practices upon local communities. Grass-roots resistance to exploitation complicates how social workers are perceived and what they can do overseas. For instance, attacks on humanitarian aid workers illustrate how altruistic intentions become entangled in local political power struggles: 278 humanitarian aid workers were killed or violently assaulted in 2009.[2] National policy rulings may complicate the global situation by requiring social workers to take sides when they would rather not. In *Holder vs Humanitarian Law* the US Supreme Court ruled that providing material support (including training and expert advice) to designated foreign terrorist organisations was a federal crime. Giving medical supplies to injured child soldiers could contravene this injunction although it is likely that the children have been abducted, placed in terrorising militias and forced to commit atrocities against others (including their families and tribes). In other situations withholding aid could undermine resistance to exploitative practices, e.g. domestic violence situations involving women seeking asylum (Kassindja and Miller-Bashir, 1998). Resistance becomes emancipatory social work (Dominelli, 1997) when local players become aware of the forces depriving them of resources, power and self-determination and develop the capacity to take action (Freire, 1972). Indigenisation is one form of emancipatory practice.

Globalisation

Globalisation is fuelled by modern technology, profit motives, and belief in a single world market. The General Agreement on Trades and Services (GATS) authorised by the World Trade Organisation (WTO) demands the privatisation of health, education and social services globally, with implications for international social work. Cox (1981) defined globalisation as an economic system that straddles the globe, integrates different socio-economic formations into one homogeneous whole, operates internationally and impacts upon localities. Held et al. (1999) suggest there is no homogeneous global system because significant variations exist in the economies of different societies. Others include public life when defining globalisation, but exclude private domains, e.g. Giddens and Hutton (2000) and Hirst et al. (2009). Some conceptualise globalisation as the spread of capitalist social relations to all spheres of public and private life (Dominelli, 2004a). Including both private and public elements is crucial for social workers whose activities in 'the social' straddle both, as evidenced by their work with survivors of violence in their homes; armed conflicts; or journeying across borders. Critiques of neo-liberalism, e.g. Netto (2006) in Latin America and Sewpaul and Holscher (2004) in South Africa, argue that globalisation causes havoc throughout the world.

International institutions like the World Bank (WB) and International Monetary Fund (IMF) promote internationalising practices that increase economic and social integration into one global system through neo-liberal, market-driven globalisation. These institutions stress poverty alleviation but serve the global South poorly despite initiatives such as the Structural Adjustment Programmes (SAPs) of the 1980s, Poverty Reduction Strategies (PRSs) of the 1990s, and Millennium Development Goals (MDGs) of 2000. In Africa, SAPs exacerbated poverty by demanding balanced state budgets and individual self-sufficiency enforced by removing welfare subsidies. SAPs led to disinvestment, high inflation rates, distorted structural reforms including land redistribution, poverty and social unrest (Bieberich, 2008). Narrowly focused poverty alleviation strategies lack capacity to promote human and social development unlike the wider ambitions declared at Copenhagen's Social Development Conference in 1995 that IASSW, ICSW and IFSW endorsed. Except for increases in school enrolment or lifting people in China and India out of poverty, MDGs are not being met (Correll, 2008).

While policies under PSRs and MDGs have aimed to promote poverty reduction and improvements in primary education and health, sub-Saharan Africa remains the world's least developed region, arguably due to the legacy of colonialism, compounded more recently by the impact of globalising forces and the policies of institutions dominated by the global North. Most countries have low and/or stagnant human development index scores; significant proportions of people living below the now official poverty line of $US1–25 a day (it was US$1–00 until very recently); chronic illnesses like malaria, TB, HIV/AIDS undermining family relationships; low life expectancy; and high rates of maternal and infant deaths (UNDP, 2009). These statistics are complicated by unreliable governance structures, political unrest and armed conflicts that produce large numbers of refugees (ICAR, 2005). Half the world's internally displaced population is in Africa (Handley et al., 2009).

The interplay between internationalisation and globalisation in social work takes various forms (Dominelli, 2010). Cultural diffusion and rapprochement are contradicted by increasingly nationalist tendencies; market mechanisms are prioritised over social relations affecting all aspects of life; migration increases as a response to economic hardship and armed conflict; environmental degradation results from favouring economic development over social progress; violence is used to resolve domestic and external conflicts; general economic integration spreads market forces across borders; growing protectionism and exclusion occurs between and within countries; rapid technological change introduces new forms of social exclusion (e.g. digital divides); urban–rural disparities increase; and urbanisation and economic centralisation undermine local environmental capacities to support growing populations (Dominelli, 2012).

In many countries global forces have shaped local social work practice by bringing 'new' managerialist business practices and market discipline into settings that previously ignored profit motives; disempowering social workers through a mismatch between resources available and needs assessments; increasing techno-bureaucratic practices through performance indicators and efficiency measures; eroding relational social work by shifting practitioner-service user relationships to those of commissioning services from private sector and voluntary agencies; commodifying relationships between service users and state through a quasi-market that treats them as consumers with choices and control; modernisation, private provisions and choice, e.g. personalisation agendas with individual budgets that turn service users into employers and unpaid tax collectors responsible for collecting taxes, national insurance and superannuation contributions from those they 'employ' to provide personal care; reducing solidarity in service provisions through residual public services that target the neediest of the needy; encouraging individual responsibility and self-sufficiency in meeting one's welfare needs whilst the state, preoccupied with competitiveness, opens welfare provisions to international corporations for making profit; increasing the impact of the 'international' on local practice through the internationalisation of social problems like poverty, organised crime, drug trade, arms trade, trafficking in women and children, and spread of diseases; decreasing service provisions for asylum seekers; and increasing numbers of social workers training in one country but working in another (Dominelli, 2004b,c).

Internationalising practices

Globalisation as economic integration across geographical terrains differs from internationalisation. 'Internationalisation' and 'globalisation' are sometimes used interchangeably and are readily confused. Although interrelated, they are different phenomena. Sklair (1998) suggests it is unsound to confuse globalisation with internationalisation which involves more holistic and interactive cross-national processes in networks that encompass all aspects of social life including culture and histories (Yang, 2002).

Disciplines like education, social policy and sociology have defined internationalising practices, whereas, to date, social work has not. In its positive forms, I define internationalisation as those processes whereby people interact across national borders, cultures, traditions and everyday life routines through organisations that link the local with the global and vice-versa to promote human well-being through egalitarian practices. In negative developments, internationalisation creates processes of cross-border exchanges that undermine human well-being through the imposition of inappropriate theories, curricula, methods, paradigms of professional practice, socio-economic and political formations and cultural expression including language and religion. Both versions coexist; highlight contexts within which internationalisation occurs; and invite questions about who is involved, why they are involved and how; and who benefits.

As suggested earlier, internationalising practices in social work include a history of oppression rooted in colonising practices (that integrated non-capitalist economies into a capitalist economic regime for imperialist countries to access land, resources and cheap labour [Kwo, 1984]) as well as supportive engagement during crises. Thus, internationalisation is a controversial, complicated, multi-layered process traversing various settings, countries and contexts. Institutions of higher education and professions like social work are increasingly involved in processes of internationalisation. A trawl of websites exposes 'internationalisation' as a buzzword in mission statements of universities and civil

society organisations throughout the world, appearing in their values, policies, institutional strategies, and satellite campuses, e.g. Harvard University's Villa i Tatti in Italy and the Shanghai Centre in China. In some places local residents have responded to such initiatives by demanding locally controlled processes of interaction; and such actions have created empowering paradigms for practice. Feminist (Mohanty, 2003) and indigenous practices are amongst these (Grande, 2004).

Globalisation and internationalisation are distinct processes with overlapping elements like prioritising market-discipline in areas of life hitherto excluded from it. Privatised social services, private criminal justice provisions, and competition between nation-states (re)shape individual and organisational behaviours in market-oriented directions. These marketise 'the social' and subordinate it to economic rationalities that reflect international and global processes favoured by GATS. The internationalisation of the nation-state, civil society organisations, universities and professions like social work indicate the dominance of economic imperatives internationally, often detrimentally for localities (Calhoun et al., 2011).

The complexities, ambiguities and rigidities of interactions across borders need exploration through empirical research that assesses the effectiveness of different approaches to internationalisation. It must unpack internationalising practices in social work conceptually and practically to identify locally empowering forms of internationalised institutional and professional practices.[2] The emphasis on the local is important because this is the space where everyday life practices occur. Globalisation and internationalisation are eliciting counter-movements of resistance to homogenising tendencies and reduced local uniqueness, e.g. indigenous movements, anti-globalisation movements and resistance to the Multilateral Agreement on Investment (MAI) (Khor, 1998). Some social workers are engaging with such resistances.

Internationally, IASSW and IFSW aim to promote egalitarian internationalising practices, for example, by advocating equality, mutuality and interdependency in curricula exchanges and culturally relevant social work in the Global Standards document (Sewpaul and Jones, 2004; see Appendix 3). IFSW has policy statements on globalisation and the environment, and indigenous people. These affirm peace and human rights-based sustainable development; and oppose policies that destroy people's welfare, e.g. SAPs. An edited collection published by IFSW, *Social Work Around the World III*, highlights the negative consequences of globalisation (Tan and Rowlands, 2004).

Interventions across borders may jeopardise mutuality through unintended consequences. This occurred in the 1990s when Western academics advised on curricula in Eastern Europe, while charging sizeable fees drawn from foreign reserves badly needed locally to purchase technological equipment from abroad and sometimes ignoring previous traditions (which existed before USSR domination). In 2010, non-governmental organisations (NGOs) attending the UN's Climate Change Conference in Cancun listened to President Calderon praise the event as carbon neutral while delegates froze in air-conditioned rooms when it was 35°C outdoors.

Egalitarian values, difficult to uphold in international social work, are significant in forming reciprocal partnerships between the global South and global North. Indigenous people warn that equality and mutuality are not always evident, for example, when multinational companies override indigenous concerns about developing the Amazon Basin (Griffith, 2010). This is a stark illustration of the lack of reciprocity or equality in North–South relations that social workers cannot alter alone.

Indigenisation

Indigenisation is an empowering practice in social work that has spread globally (Dominelli, 2004a; Gray et al., 2009).

Its local expressions vary from place to place, as in the following examples. In Malaysia, indigenous practice focuses on Asian values rooted in the extended family and united national entity (Ahmad, 2009). First Nations peoples in Canada base their indigenous practices on the band and relationships between people and their physical and spiritual environments, often expressed through the Medicine Wheel (Green and Thomas, 2007; Cyr, 2007). The Maoris emphasise kinship-based caring traditions (Tait-Rolleston and Pehi-Barlow, 2001). Bolivia's indigenous peoples protect their environment from predatory industrialisation (Griffith, 2010). Indigenisation strongly resists injustice, denial of human rights, and disparagement of local cultures, customs, languages and communities by reclaiming past traditions and affirming the dynamic creation of new forms under the control of indigenous peoples. Celebrating traditional cultures has been central to this resistance which has included highlighting appalling treatment experienced in residential schools (Haig-Brown, 1988), developed new theories for practice (Cyr, 2007) and created indigenous social work (Green and Thomas, 2007).

Social workers can learn from different traditions. For instance, indigenous practices, such as the Medicine Wheel and Family Group Conferences, have significantly affected practice by being mainstreamed, including internationally. Other locality specific practices have potential for transnational learning. For example, Britain's *Every Child Matters* agenda, highlighting principles for working with children – be healthy, stay safe, enjoy and achieve; make a positive contribution, achieve economic well-being – echoes a rights-based agenda for children and exemplifies this. It also prioritises integrated services; early years preventative services (through Sure Start centres) and flexible service provision; and promotes evidence-based practice and continued professional development (Coughlan, 2009: 20). Social pedagogy, as practised in several

European countries (e.g. France, Denmark, Finland and Germany) offers other paradigms for preventative work and relationship building in everyday routines (Oxtoby, 2009).

Information technologies associated with globalisation assist communication processes that facilitate learning across borders. Human agency shapes technologies for specific situations as empowering or disempowering. 'Risk' mitigation procedures (Swift and Callahan, 2009) become technologies of globalisation that promise certainty in an uncertain world. Their positive dimension remains unfulfilled because risk assessments ignore change that secures social justice, e.g. altering adult power relations to empower children. Swift and Callahan (2009) conclude that economic growth and development is crucial to securing social justice, a lesson that resonates in Western countries as well as the global South. Media frenzies around failed child protection undermine social work's status globally when demonising individual social workers, for example, in the case of Peter Connelly's untimely death in the UK when his mother, her boyfriend and his brother killed him in 2007 (Laming, 2009). Public castigation of individuals is unlikely if social workers are respected and failure is attributed to systems rather than individuals (Taylor, 2009: 18).

Indigenisation in social work resists the imposition of European social work models upon non-capitalist cultural modes of helping and preserves other locality specific cultural caring traditions (Yip, 2005). Indigenisation is conceptually problematic because it depends on what population is being described, who is using it and a people's purpose in utilising it. The term applied negative labelling to indigenous identities under colonisation; underplays complicated relationships of interdependence between peoples; focuses on binaries based on superiority and inferiority; and has been appropriated by hegemonic groups like the British National Party (BNP) and similar political entities endorsing white dominance elsewhere (Dominelli, 2000a, 2004a). The terms 'locality specific, culturally relevant social work', and using indigenous peoples' own words for their discourses, are preferred (Dominelli, 1997) to affirm indigenous peoples' strengths and resistance to colonisation, and avoid white supremacist associations with indigeneity.

European supremacist groups argue that white 'indigenous' people have lost cultures and status in their 'own' society (Dominelli, 2004a). Britain's BNP reasserts the privileging of white English, Scottish and Welsh populations currently feeling undermined by sharing resources and power in a multicultural UK (Griffin, 2009). Such supremacists refer to the 'original' inhabitants of a land and essentialise identity as a pure, singular and unchanging entity. White supremacist arguments are nonsensical. The origins of humankind can be traced to Africa from where different groups migrated to inhabit different landscapes (Rincorn, 2011): this evolution makes all people descendants of migrants who have settled in particular territories at different points in time. Migratory processes continue, albeit they are now controlled at the boundaries of nation-states through immigration controls or internally within them. Rural–urban migration in China illustrates the latter process. Human cultures, formed through interactions with others, are dynamic and changing. Empowering social workers engage with these realities while rejecting colonising practices that impose inappropriate theories and practices against the wishes of local people. Migration enables people to learn from others, rework gained knowledge and make it their own (Dominelli, 2004a).

PROMOTING INTERNATIONAL SOCIAL WORK PRACTICE

Social workers' involvement in internationalising practices is complicated when emphasis is placed on personal change and does not tackle structural inequalities (Hoogvelt, 2007) but it is sometimes easier for practitioners to implement individually based therapeutic interventions than collective action for structural change (Bishop, 2001).

Today's financial crisis, the epitome of internationalised institutional practices, undermines human well-being globally. For example, in 2008, Britons paid £1.5 trillion in public funds to bail-out the financial sector (Waugh, 2009). Government expenditures on banks have risen through interest payments accrued on monies borrowed, with funds for education, health and other public services being severely reduced. Such policies undermine public order and people's well-being. In 2010, public expenditure cuts caused protests in Ireland, Iceland, Greece, France and elsewhere. Banks make limited contributions to tax revenues that pay for social services, e.g. Barclays Bank paid £113 million in UK corporation tax after profits of £11.6bn. Had it paid the Organisation for Economic Co-operation and Development's (OECD) corporate tax rate, it would have contributed £3bn (Treanor, 2011: 12), making more funds available for social and health services needed by people and determined by them. Global collective action involving social workers could demand transparency and accountability from banks.

Practitioners can promote positive internationalising practices rooted in egalitarianism and empowering participation. Empowerment becomes political when supporting collective social action that advances egalitarian practices. Adams (2008) defines empowerment as a change process that tackles inegalitarian power relations and develops people's individual and community capacities to control their lives. Empowering processes support marginalised people to achieve self-determination in decision-making; valorising and normalising their views and social roles; assessing contexts and risks; and tackling power differentials, oppression, discrimination and low incomes locally and internationally (Rocha, 1997; Dominelli, 2002; Vene Klasen et al., 2004).

However, empowerment is not a panacea for social ills. Empowerment processes disempower people if they are individualistic, tokenistic, bureaucratic or consumerist (Dominelli, 2000b). Oliver (1992) highlights its limitations by arguing that professionals can only avoid disempowering others. Several strategies need to be employed. Professionals themselves need to be empowered. Binaries classifying claimants for publicly funded services as 'deserving' or 'undeserving' should be eschewed. The actions of claimants and service users need to be embedded in principles of agency, empowerment, social justice, human rights, reciprocity, solidarity, interdependence and equality. And, critical reflexion whereby people maximize their strengths and create opportunities for self-expression and change, locally and internationally, needs to be endorsed. For indigenous people, this includes their cultures and traditions (Dominelli, 2004a).

To advocate effectively for structural change, social workers must engage policymakers and local people in activities that redistribute power and resources to marginalised groups, within a country and outside it. Radical social workers and anti-oppressive practitioners have encouraged such initiatives since the 1970s (Dominelli, 2010). The politics of recognition and redistribution of wealth and resources are internationalising practices that celebrate diverse identities and citizenship-based empowerment locally and internationally (Ife, 2001). Achieving these goals links the local and global, challenging practitioners and educators to take a broad view of them. In promoting these, professionals have to engage with media hostility that disparages social work and reflects (and shapes) public opinion that deleteriously undermines claims for assistance. In relation to the latter, asylum seekers have been physically attacked in Europe; Tamils have been refused refuge in Canada (Coyne, 2010); refugees from Albania and Tunisia have drowned while trying to get to Italy (VOA News, 2009); and there has been resistance to people seeking refuge in Australia

(O'Connor, 2010). Border controls at points of entry endanger life by turning away people taking enormous risks to reach safe destinations. In some countries, e.g. the UK, internal controls limiting welfare support for asylum seekers also promote surveillance by social workers while substantially increasing destitution and homelessness post-arrival (Vickers, 2011).

These internationalising practices expose limits to solidarity globally. National governments' failure to reduce greenhouse gas emissions (Dessler and Parson, 2010), in order to safeguard planet earth for future generations, reveal problems in securing collaborative solutions within and between countries because national self-interest trumps interdependencies amongst nations. Government responses to asylum seekers and climate change illustrate the difficulties of redistributing resources within a framework of human rights and social justice (Fowler, 2009) when national self-interest blocks empowering practice (Houston, 2008) and present international social work with dilemmas.

Women link the local and global

Women are affected worse than men by the negative impacts of globalisation and internationalising practices: they are disproportionately poor, have the highest illiteracy rates and poorest health outcomes globally (UNDP, 2009). However, women actively resist the negative consequences of globalisation, nationally and internationally. They have demanded changes in patriarchal social relations to tackle domestic issues, including poverty and violence. Their struggles became transnational when women sought strong international alliances and commonalities while retaining roots in local concerns and traditions. They fostered regional organisations that turned national concerns over poverty, violence and polluting environments into international ones, e.g. FEMNET (African Women's Development and Communication Network), WiLDAF (Women in Law and Development in Africa), FAWE (Forum for African Women Educationalists), AAWORD (Association of African Women for Research and Development) in Africa; and *Encuentros* (regional meetings) in Latin America. Women's activities have problematised relationships between the local and global; created egalitarian relationships amongst different women; eliminated hierarchical relationships between women; and promoted empowering processes in women's interactions (Shiva, 2003). Women's activism has led to changes at the UN level. For instance, the UN has targeted women in social development and poverty alleviation drives to guarantee that benefits reach families, especially children; declared the Decade for Women; and held conferences to address inequalities between men and women. These initiatives culminated in the Beijing Agenda for Action in 1995 with follow-up sessions every five years since. IASSW, IFSW and ICSW have participated in these deliberations; and women's actions and movements in many parts of the world have been actively supported by social workers, the majority of whom are themselves women.

However, women's multiple and fluid identities are absent in many programmes devised by international institutions. The IMF, WB and international non-governmental organisations (INGOs) ignore how place and social divisions shape women's experiences of oppression differently. The MDGs treat women across the world as having the same health and educational needs. Unitary views of women are powerful when translated into social policies locally, nationally and internationally and incorporated into professional practice. Women have critiqued international institutions for ignoring their diversity, differentiated needs, local strengths, knowledge and capacities in solving problems (Mohanty, 1991). For example, Frohmader (2002) and Parker (2006) exposed marginalisation of disabled women in the International

Covenant on Economic, Social and Cultural Rights (ICESCR) and Standard Rules on the Equalization of Opportunities for Persons with a Disability. Recently, women have critiqued the lack of attention given to gender in the United Nation's climate change talks. For example, in Durban, South Africa, the Asia Pacific Forum on Women, Law and Development held a press conference on this issue. The Chair of the IASSW Climate Change Committee helped draft the statement used at it.

Nation-states, internationalised and integrated into the world economy, prioritise market discipline and competition (Cox, 1981); commission services from global voluntary, not-for-profit and commercial providers; become major employers of low-paid women; and commodify their relationships with citizens, and between social workers and service users. In the global South, neo-liberalism undermines social development (Sewpaul and Holscher, 2004; Netto, 2006). Commodifying trends have replaced relational social work with techno-bureaucratic social work in European countries as diverse as Sweden and Italy (Folgheraiter, 2004). In the UK, bureaucratic social work undermines statutory services especially in child protection (Laming, 2009) and encourages professionals to migrate to the voluntary sector, with consequences for staff turnover and vacancies (Dominelli, 2004a; Unison, 2009). Current cuts in social welfare in many countries have profound effects on women workers, carers, and service users, who form the majority in all these categories.

Both female and male social workers have participated in and opposed service marketisation. Their opposition to hegemonic models creates new theories and practices for domestic and overseas consumption. These include innovative indigenous practices, e.g., Family Group Conferences, developed through Maori critiques of dominant practice in Aotearoa/New Zealand, have spread to countries ranging from the USA to Hong Kong; spirituality has been highlighted

and mainstreamed in education and practice in secular countries (Holloway and Moss, 2010); indigenous methodologies are spreading globally (Green and Thomas, 2007); and Eastern philosophies have been reinvigorating societies (Mehta and Yasas, 1990). Practitioners and academics argue for gender equality by innovating; joining anti-globalisation movements; arguing for social justice and human rights-based practice locally, nationally and internationally; forming alliances and partnerships with service users and community groups; and strengthening relationships with key international institutions through organisations such as IASSW, ICSW and IFSW.

Internationalising the Professional Work Force

Increased international labour mobility is one side-effect of globalisation (as well as the relocation of industries and services) and this has promoted harmonisation in professional qualifications to encourage such labour mobility. For instance, in Europe, the Bologna Process (the Italian city where the Treaty was signed in 1999) sought parity in tertiary level qualifications; introduced degree progression (bachelor to masters and subsequently PhD level); and modularised credit structures to increase professional mobility across Europe (http://www.ehea.info). The European Union has agreements to integrate higher education institutions in Europe with those in North America (Transatlantic Exchange Partnership (TEP) and Atlantis), Asia, Australia and Aotearoa/New Zealand (Industrialised Countries Instrument Education Cooperation Programme [ICI-ECP]) and Latin America. These internationalising practices include social work projects that exchange staff, students and curricula and teach joint degrees (Dominelli and Bernard, 2003; Dominelli, 2007).

Social workers constitute migrant workers, sometimes called international social workers, employed in countries other than that in which they trained (White, 2007). In the UK, 10 percent (6884) of practitioners are overseas workers recruited to reduce vacancy rates and maintain sectors like child protection (Mickel, 2009: 16). This trend may not continue. The numbers of those from overseas registered with the regulatory authority in England, the General Social Care Council, dropped from 1425 in 2006 to 518 in 2009. Applicants must have qualifications equivalent to Britain's social work degree and 13 days of post-qualifying training. Tighter immigration controls, criticism of predatory employer practices, and publication of stressful experiences by existing workers have influenced this reduction. Of those qualifying overseas, 60 percent are from Australia, South Africa, the USA and India (Mickel, 2009: 16). Social workers also exit the UK for higher paid work in the USA and Canada (White, 2007).

Social worker mobility has implications for both sending and receiving countries. Active recruitment by local authorities and recruiting agencies attracted 50 percent of trained Zimbabwean practitioners to Birmingham in the UK earlier this century (Devo, 2006), with significant implications for services in Zimbabwe. In addition, many of those recruited found inadequate arrangements for their arrival in terms of housing, induction, job preparation, and career progression (Sithole, 2011). In another example, care services for older Western Europeans would collapse without Eastern European migrant labour. As immigration constraints on workers from outside Europe have intensified, Eastern European recruitment has become more attractive. Filipino workers fulfil similar roles in social care in North America. Potentially, such worker mobility is not a one-way process in terms of skills and knowledge exchange. Migrant workers' transferable skills can help internationalise the workforce and promote two-way exchanges in social work theory and practice, if the prior experience and cultural competence of such 'international social workers' are recognised.

CONCLUSIONS

International social work, a contested concept, faces challenges and opportunities in enhancing human well-being and environmental security in a globalising world. Affirming citizenship-based welfare entitlements and tackling structural inequalities require global united action by social work educators and practitioners to change public discourses and influence international institutions as suggested in IASSW, ICSW and IFSW's global agenda. Such action can reverse social work's historical legacy of oppressing indigenous and other marginalised groups and develop a professional voice independent of state or corporate interference.

Internationalisation and economic globalisation challenge social workers to reconcile the irreconcilable and to promote egalitarianism when negotiating processes of indigenisation in the context of international social problems and privatised social services. Educating and training practitioners (including migrant workers) and facilitating their acquisition of the skills to act as empowered and empowering professionals can enable them to meet service users' expectations about social justice, human rights and citizenship-based entitlements and promote egalitarian interactions in social work locally and internationally.

USEFUL WEBSITES

AAWORD: http://www.afdevinfo.com/htmlreports/org/org_61353.html, accessed 3 March 2011.
FAWE: www.fawe.org, accessed 3 March 2011.
FEMNET: http://www.femnet.or.ke, accessed on 3 March 2011.
Encuentros: http://www.wri-irg.org/node/3693, accessed 3 March 2011.
IASSW: www.iassw-aiets.org, accessed 21 Dec 2010.
IFSW: www.ifsw.org, accessed 21 Dec 2010.
IASSW-IFSW: Global Standards, Ethics Document and Definition of Social Work (2004) all available on

www.iassw-aiets.org or www.ifsw.org, accessed
21 Dec 2010.
United Nations: www.un.org, accessed 21 Dec 2010.
WiLDAF: http://www.wildaf.org, accessed 2 March
2011.

NOTES

1. See websites: www.iassw-aiets.org and http://
ifsw.org
2 See websites: http://www.patronusanalytical.
com/aid%20worker%20fatalities/Fatal%20
Incidents%20Aid%20Workers%20DB/Fatal%20
Incidents%20data.html, accessed 3 March 2011.
3 For example, Durham University's project,
Internationalising Institutional and Professional
Practices, funded by the UK's Economic and Social
Research Council from January 2009 to August 2012.

REFERENCES

Adams, R. (2008) *Empowerment, Participation and
Social Work*, (4th edn). Basingstoke: Palgrave
Macmillan.
Ahmad, S. (2009) *Culture, Power and Resistance:
Post-Colonialism, Autobiography and Malaysian
Independence*. PhD thesis, Durham University,
Department of Applied Social Sciences.
Bagnell, K. (2001) *The Little Immigrants: the
Orphans Who Came to Canada*. Toronto: Dundurn
Press.
Bailey, R. and Brake, M. (1975) *Radical Social Work*.
London: Edward Arnold.
Bieberich, V. (2008) 'Structural adjustment policies and
stability in sub-Saharan Africa: moving forward',
Think International, 1(1): 60–70.
Bishop, A. (2001) *Becoming an Ally*. Halifax: Fernwood
Press. First published in 1996.
Borrmann, S., Klassen, M. and Spatscheck, C. (eds)
(2007) *International Social Work: Social Problems,
Cultural Issues and Social Work Education*. Opladen,
Germany: Barbara Budrich Publishers.
Calhoun, A., Whitmore, E. and Wilson, M. (2011)
Activism that Works. Halifax: Fernwood Publishing.
Callan, H. (1998) 'Internationalisation in Europe', in
P. Scott (ed.), *The Globalisation of Higher Education*.
Buckingham: Open University Press.
Correll, D. (2008) 'The politics of poverty and social
development', *International Social Work*, 51(4):
453–66.

Coughlan, J. (2009) 'English lessons', *Community Care*,
19 March: 20.
Cox, R. (1981) 'Social forces, states, and world orders:
beyond international relations theory', *Millenium*, 12
(2): 146–57.
Cox, D. and Pawar, M. (2006) *International Social
Work: Issues, Strategies and Programs*. London:
Sage.
Coyne, A. (2010) 'Call it the "bottom of the boat" test',
MacLean's Magazine, 30 August: 33–4.
Cyr, G. (2007) 'An indigenist and anti-colonialist frame-
work for practice', in L. Dominelli (ed.), *Revitalising
Communities in a Globalising World*. Aldershot:
Ashgate.
Desai, A. (2007) 'Disaster and social work responses',
in L. Dominelli (ed.) *Revitalising Communities in a
Globalising World*. Aldershot: Ashgate.
Dessler, A. and Parson, E. (2010) *The Science and
Politics of Global Climate Change: a Guide to the
Debate*. Cambridge: Cambridge University Press.
(1st edn, 2006.)
Devo, J. (2006) 'Out of Africa into Birmingham:
Zimbabwean social workers talk to *Professional
Social Work*', *Professional Social Work*, August 1:
12–3.
Dominelli, L. (1997) *Sociology for Social Work*. London:
Macmillan.
Dominelli, L. (2000a) 'International comparisons in
social work', in R. Pearce and J. Weinstein (eds),
*Innovative Education and Training for Care
Professionals: a Providers' Guide*. London: Jessica
Kingsley. pp. 25–42.
Dominelli, L. (2000b) 'Empowerment: help or hindrance
in professional relationships?', in D. Ford and
P. Stepney (eds), *Social Work Models, Methods
and Theories: a Framework for Practice*. Lyme
Regis: Russell House Publishing. pp. 125–38.
Dominelli, L. (2002) *Anti-Oppressive Social Work
Theory and Practice*. London: Palgrave Macmillan.
Dominelli, L. (2004a) *Social Work: Theory and
Practice in a Changing Profession*. Cambridge: Polity
Press.
Dominelli, L. (2004b) 'Crossing international divides:
language and communication within international
settings', *Social Work Education*, 23(5): 515–25.
Dominelli, L. (2004c) 'Practising social work in a
globalising world', in N.T. Tan and A. Rowlands
(eds), *Social Work around the World III*. Berne:
International Federation of Social Workers.
Dominelli, L. (2007) 'Challenges in internationalising
social work curricula', in L. Dominelli (ed.) *Revitalising
Communities in a Globalising World*. Aldershot:
Ashgate.

Dominelli, L. (2010) *Social Work in a Globalising World*. Cambridge: Polity Press.

Dominelli, L. (2012) *Green Social Work*. Cambridge: Polity Press.

Dominelli, L. and Thomas B.W. (eds) (2003) *Broadening Horizons: International Exchanges in Social Work*. Aldershot: Ashgate.

Ethnologue Survey. (1999) *The World's Most Widely Spoken Languages*, http://www2.ignatius.edu/faculty/turner/worldlang.htm, accessed 2 March 2011.

Folgheraiter, F. (2004) *Relational Social Work: Toward Network and Societal Practices*. London: Jessica Kingsley Publishers.

Fowler, B. (2009) 'The recognition/redistribution debate and Bourdieu's theory of practice', *Theory, Culture and Society*, 26(1): 144–56.

Freire, P. (1972) *Pedagogy of the Oppressed*. Harmondsworth: Penguin.

Frohmader, C. (2002) *There is No Justice – Just Us! The Status of Women with Disabilities in Australia*. Tasmania: Women with Disabilities Australia.

Giddens, A. and Hutton, W. (eds) (2000) *On the Edge: Living with Global Capitalism*. London: Vintage.

Grande, S. (2004) *Red Pedagogy: Native American and Political Thought*. Lanham, MD: Rowman & Littlefield.

Gray, M., Coates, J. and Yellow Bird, M. (2009) *Indigenous Social Work around the World: Towards Culturally Relevant Education and Practice*. Aldershot: Ashgate.

Griffin, N. (2009) 'BNP scures two European seats', *BBC News* 8 June. Also on http://news.bbc.co.uk/2/hi/uk_news/politics/8088381.stm, accessed 3 March 2011.

Griffith, A. (2010) 'Latin American struggles between Aboriginal rights and national priorities', *Cutting Edge News*, 21 June. Also on http://www.thecuttingedgenews.com/index.php?article=12292, accessed 3 Mar 2011.

Green, J. and Thomas, R. (2007) 'Learning through our children, healing for our children: best practice in First Nations communities', in L. Dominelli (ed.), *Revitalising Communities in a Globalising World*. Aldershot: Ashgate.

Gove, T. (1995) *The Gove Inquiry into Child Protection in British Columbia*. Victoria: Queen's Printer.

Haig-Brown, C. (1988) *Resistance and Renewal: Surviving the Indian Residential School*. Vancouver: Arsenal Pulp Press.

Hancock, G. (1996) *Lords of Poverty: the Power, Prestige, and Corruption of the International Aid Business*. New York: Atlantic Monthly Press.

Handley, G., Higgins, K., Sharma, B., Bird, K. and Cammack, D. (2009) *Poverty and Poverty Reduction in Sub-Saharan Africa: an Overview of the Issue*. Working Paper 299. London: Overseas Development Institute.

Healy, L. (1988) 'Curriculum building in international social work: towards preparing professionals for a global age', *Journal of Social Work Education*, 24(3): 221–8.

Healy, L. (2001) *International Social Work: Professional Action in an Interdependent World*. Oxford: Oxford University Press.

Healy, L. (2008) *International Social Work: Professional Action in an Interdependent World*. Oxford: Oxford University Press. (1st edn, 2001.)

Healy, L. M. and Link, R. (2005) *Teaching International Content: Curriculum Resources for Social Work Education*. Alexandria, VA: Council on Social Work Education.

Held, D., McGrew, T., Goldblatt, D. and Perraton, J. (1999) *Global Transformations: Politics, Economics and Culture*. Cambridge: Polity Press.

Hirst, P., Thompson, G. and Bromley, S. (2009) *Globalization in Question*, 3rd edn. Cambridge: Polity Press.

Holloway, M. and Moss, B. (2010) *Spirituality and Social Work*. London: Palgrave.

Hoogvelt, A. (2007) 'Globalisation and imperialism: wars and humanitarian intervention', in L. Dominelli (ed.), *Revitalising Communities in a Globalising World*. Aldershot: Ashgate.

Houston, S. (2008) 'Beyond *Homo economicus*: recognition, self-realization and social work', *British Journal of Social Work*, 40: 841–57.

Humphreys, M. (1996) *Empty Cradles*. London: Corgi.

ICAR. (2005) *Destitution*. http://www.icar.org.uk/?lid=6575, accessed 3 March 2011.

Ife, J. (2001) 'Local and global practice: relocating social work as a human rights profession in a new global order', *European Journal of Social Work*, 4(1): 515–21.

Ioakimidis, V. (2010) 'Expanding imperialism, exporting expertise: international social work and the Greek project', *International Social Work*, 54(4): 505–19.

Kassindja, F. and Miller-Basher, L. (1998) *Do They Hear You When You Cry?* New York: Delacourt Press.

Kendall, K. (2000) *Social Work Education: Its Origins in Europe*. Alexandria, VA: Council on Social Work Education.

Khor, M. (1998) 'MAI', in *Third World Network*. Also on http://ictsd.org/i/news/bridgesweekly/93603, accessed 1 June 2005.

Knight, J. (1997) 'Internationalisation of higher educa-
tion: a conceptual framework', in J. Knight and H. De
Wit (eds), *Internationalisation of Higher Education in
Asia Pacific Countries*. Amsterdam: EAIE.

Kwo, E.M. (1984) 'Community education and community development in Cameroon: the British colonial
experience, 1922–1961', *Community Development
Journal*, 19(4): 204–13.

Laming, H. (2009) *The Protection of Children in
England: a Progress Report*. London: DCSF.

Lavalette, M. (ed.) (2011) *Radical Social Work Today*.
Bristol, Policy Press.

Lawrence, S., Lyons, K., Simpson, G. and Huegler, N.
(2009) *Introducing International Social Work:
Transforming Social Work Practice*. Exeter: Learning
Matters.

Lorenz, W. (1994) *Social Work in a Changing Europe*.
London: Routledge.

Lyons, K. (1999) *International Social Work: Themes and
Perspectives*. Aldershot: Ashgate.

Lyons, K., Manion, K. and Carlsen, M. (2006)
*International Perspectives on Social Work: Global
Conditions and Local Practice*. Basingstoke: Palgrave
Macmillan.

Mehta, V. and Yasas, F. (eds) (1990) *Feminist Visions
in Social Work*. Pune, India: Streevani/The
International Association of Schools of Social Work.

Mickel, A. (2009) 'Global marketplace puts up the
barriers', *Community Care*, 19 March: 16–7.

Midgley, J. (1995) *Social Development: the Development
Perspective in Social Welfare*. Thousand Oaks, CA:
Sage. (First published in 1981.)

Mohanty, C.T. (1991) 'Cartographies of struggle: third
world women and the politics of feminism', in C.T.
Mohanty, A. Russo and L. Torres (eds), *Third World
Women and the Politics of Feminism*. Bloomington:
Indiana University Press.

Mohanty, C.T. (2003) *Feminism Without Borders:
Decolonizing Theory, Practicing Solidarity*. London:
Duke University Press.

Netto, P. (2006) *The Challenges and Opportunities of
Neoliberalism: a Marxist Perspective*. Paper given at
IASSW Congress, Santiago, Chile, 15–18 July.

Noble, C. (2007) 'Social work, collective action and
social movements: re-thematising the local–global
nexus', in L. Dominelli (ed.), *Revitalising Communities
in a Globalising World*. Aldershot: Ashgate.

O'Connor, P. (2010) *Up to 50 Refugees Drown off
Australian Coast*, on http://www.wsws.org/articles/
2010/dec2010/refu-d16.shtml, accessed 2 March
2011.

Oliver, M. (1992) *The Politics of Disablement*. London:
Macmillan.

Oxtoby, K. (2009) 'Continental Divide', *Community
Care*, 19 March: 22–4.

Parker, S. (2006) 'International justice: the United
Nations, human rights and disability', *Journal of
Comparative Social Welfare*, 22(1): 63–78.

Payne, M. and Askeland, G. (2008) *Globalization and
International Social Work*. Aldershot: Ashgate.

Razack, N. (2002) *Transforming the Field: Critical
Antiracist and Anti-Oppressive Perspectives for the
Human Services Practicum*. Halifax: Fernwood
Publishing.

Rincorn, P. (2011) 'Humans "left Africa much earlier"',
BBC News, 27 January. Also on http://www.
bbc.co.uk/news/science-environment-12300228,
accessed 2 March 2011.

Rocha, E. (1997) 'A ladder of empowerment', *Journal
of Planning Education and Research*, 17(1):
31–44.

Sewpaul, V. and Holscher, D. (2004) *Social Work in
Times of Neoliberalism*. Pretoria: Van Schaik.

Sewpaul, V. and Jones, D. (2004) 'Global standards for
social work education and training', *Social Work
Education*, 23(5): 493–513.

Sithole, M. (2011) *Zimbabwean Social Workers in
Large City Council*. Durham: Durham University,
PhD thesis.

Shiva, V. (2003) 'Food rights, free trade and fascism',
in M. Gibney (ed.), *Globalising Rights*. Oxford:
Oxford University Press.

Sklair, L. (1998) *Competing Conceptions of Globalisation*. Montreal: World Congress of Sociology.

Swift, K. and Callahan, M. (2009) *At Risk: Social Justice
in Child Welfare and Other Human Services*. Toronto:
University of Toronto Press.

Tait-Rolleston, W. and Pehi-Barlow, S. (2001) 'A Maori
Social Work Construct' in L. Dominelli, W. Lorenz
and H. Soydan (eds), *Beyond Racial Divides*.
Aldershot: Ashgate.

Tan, T.N. and Rowlands, A. (eds) (2004) *Social Work
Around the World, III*. Berne: IFSW.

Taylor, A. (2009) 'It wouldn't happen there', *Community
Care*, 19 March: 18–9.

Treanor, J. (2011) 'Lib-Dem peer to demand more
transparency over bank taxes', *The Guardian*, 19
February: 12.

UNDP (United Nations Development Programme).
(2009) *Overcoming Barriers: Human Mobility and
Development*. New York: UNDP.

Unison. (2009) *Survey of Social Workers*.

Vene Klasen, L., Miller, V., Clark, C. and Reilly, R.
(2004) 'Rights-based approaches and beyond: the
challenge of linking rights and participation', *IDS
Working Paper*, 235: 1–52.

Vickers, T. (2011) *Asylum Seekers and the British State*. Durham: Durham University, PhD Thesis.

VOA News. (2009) *Eritreans Rescued at Sea off Italian Island,* on http://www.voanews.com/english/news/a-13-2009-08-20-voa33-68659057.html

Waugh, P. (2009) 'Bailout of banks to cost taxpayer £1,500,000,000,000', *London Evening Standard*, 19 February.

Weiss, I. and Welbourne, P. (eds) (2007) *Social Work as a Profession: a Comparative Cross-Cultural Perspective*. Birmingham: Venture Press, BASW, IASSW.

White, R. (2007) 'Challenges and opportunities for social workers in the transnational labour force', in L. Dominelli (ed.), *Revitalising Communities in a Globalising World*. Aldershot: Ashgate.

Yang, R. (2002) 'University internationalisation: its meanings, rationales and implications', *Intercultural Education*, 13(1): 81–95.

Yip, K.S. (2005) 'A dynamic Asian response to globalization in cross-cultural social work', *International Social Work*, 48(5): 593–607.

3

Environment and Sustainability

Margaret Alston and Fred H. Besthorn

INTRODUCTION

Overworked and highly stressed social workers might reasonably wonder whether pressing environmental issues are really their concern. Of course, we are all interested at some level but isn't environmental work the work of environmentalists? And, does our professional focus on environmental issues serve any useful purpose except to alarm already taxed social workers laboring with a plethora of 'real life' problems of the world's most vulnerable peoples? We think yes. Indeed, we are convinced, along with a growing number of social workers from around the world (Alston and McKinnon, 2005; Besthorn, 2001, 2008; Coates, 2003; Hoff and McNutt, 1994; Lysack, 2007; McKinnon, 2005, 2008; Ungar, 2002; van-Wormer and Besthorn, 2010; Zapf, 2009), that it is of utmost importance that a deeper environmental awareness become a major part of how international social work understands itself and its practice domains. This chapter focuses on the environment as an emerging domain of social work practice, gives an historical overview, analyses social sustainability and notes the significance of a human rights focus to address the significant social outcomes and the rights of vulnerable groups.

Recent cataclysmic environmental events like the Haitian Earthquake of 2009, the Deep Water Horizon oil spill of 2010, hurricane Katrina of 2005, and the horrific tsunami event off the Indian Ocean of 2004 and another affecting Japan in 2011 have claimed an estimated 400,000 lives, caused billions in economic and infrastructure damage, displaced millions of people from their homes and caused nearly unfathomable damage to delicate ecological systems. These are just five of the most recent but growing number of stark reminders that the world community is reaching a critical threshold in its relationship to the natural environment.

The wholesale destruction of world's ecosystems has grown to such an extent that human-induced destructive activity now threatens the very survival of the human species. The list of deeply troubling ecological disturbances encompasses such vital concerns as overpopulation, global warming, depletion of the ozone layer, wetland and coastal estuarial erosion, water pollution, air pollution, species extinction, loss of genetic diversity, overfishing, toxic waste, poisonous effects of chemical-based fertilizers and pesticides, desertification, environmentally displaced persons due to the collapse of strategic ecological systems, famine, global pandemics, and dozens of less well-publicized but nonetheless troubling environmental issues (van Wormer and Besthorn, 2010). According to the World Watch Institute (Flavin et al., 2002), the human species may no longer be able to control permanent ecological decline. Thus the environment and the consequences of its destruction are of critical importance to international social work.

Recent history would suggest that the world community, and in particular the modern industrialized and industrializing nations of the global North, are not yet willing to respond in meaningful ways to the global environmental crisis. The failure to reach substantive or binding agreement on core climatic concerns at the Copenhagen Climate Accords of 2009 and subsequent global meetings is just one example. This inability to respond even in the face of mounting evidence that a global crisis of epic proportions is upon us suggests some collective conceptual myopia that the world community and social work must seriously consider. First, environmental crises are not just, at their most elemental level, crises of biology. Rather, they are crises of community, of society, of spirit, and of an unrestrained ideological commitment to a set of values that have become inherently destructive to earth systems. Second, solutions to planetary decline must consist of more than new international policy agreements, calls for more corporate responsibility, more personal restraint, or the development of a handful of ecologically friendly technologies. Indeed, because the environmental crisis evolved in the context of community, society, and historical patterns of production and consumption, the solution to environmental problems involves a transformation of both individual consciousness and the major social bases of environmental degradation (van Wormer and Besthorn, 2010). As long as dominant social and economic relationships remain unquestioned, little progress will be made toward meaningful environmental action.

RECENT HISTORICAL LEGACY: PERSON AND ENVIRONMENT

Social work's person/environment models have been guiding frameworks of professional practice for at least the last 30–40 years. In the early 1970s, social work began to separate itself from other helping professionals by claiming as their particular jurisdiction a unique and dual concern for both person and environment. Unfortunately, in practice the person/environment orientation has become challenging partly because of the difficulty associated with attending equally to personal and environmental issues (Besthorn, 2001; Saleebey, 1992; Weick, 1981).

Social work's persistent historical tendency has been to focus on knowledge and skills directed to the personal domain while the encompassing scope of environment has become constricted. Much of what social work finds tiresome in fulfilling its primary goal of optimising realisation of person-in-environment has to do with its struggle to thoroughly conceptualise and act upon both its personal and especially its environmental commitments (Graham et al., 2009).

This conceptual difficulty has been most striking in social work's difficulty in integrating a comprehensive understanding of the natural environment and its influence on individual and collective development as well as issues of social and economic justice. Social work's person/environment emphases have been routinely affirmed in the professional literature and in leading social work textbooks for several generations (Germain and Gitterman, 1980; Germain, 1991). With few exceptions these earlier social work source materials had little explicit or comprehensive discussion of the natural environment (Robbins et al., 2006). The major difficulty with many of social work's primary conceptual sources was their tendency to restrict the definition of environment to limited interpersonal or social realms (Coates, 2003; McKinnon, 2001). In reality the natural environment was generally under-valued or simply became the benign backdrop for more fundamentally important social processes.

This conceptual short-sightedness began to change in the mid- to late 1990s. Social work theorists Maria Hoff and John McNutt (1994), John Coates and Mary McKay (1995), Fred Besthorn (1997) and Mary Rogge (1994) were among the first social workers in North America to begin exploring the theoretical and practice linkages between environmentalism and social work. These theorists began to systematically and comprehensively extend social work's definition of environment to include a deeper connection with the natural world. This link was not really made in Australia until the first decade of the 2000s despite major environmental trauma resulting from drought. It was the impact of significant environmental crises that led to a search for social work's place in this field (Alston, 2009; Alston and McKinnon, 2005; McKinnon, 2005, 2008). Thus, for a growing number of social workers in developed countries, the recognition began to emerge that the natural environment shares a complex and evolutionary link to personal and social development. Social workers were beginning to address the implications of nature's degradation, especially on poor and vulnerable populations, and to explore its aesthetic and mythic value for informing social work theory and practice.

Building on the work of social theorists and ecologists like Thomas Berry (1988), Frija Capra (1996), Edward O. Wilson (1984), Leonardo Boff (1997), and Herman Daly (1990), social workers were slowly beginning to see the importance of an expanded definition of our historic environmental construct. Many were beginning to view the natural environment not as backdrop to other matters but as centrepiece – interlocking spheres of activity made up of interconnected elements. Human life itself and human social development were increasingly seen as integrally related to, dependent upon, and emergent from the natural environment. Natural ecosystems consist of several interconnected layers including the geosphere, hydrosphere, atmosphere, biosphere, and noosphere (Hoff and McNutt, 1994). The first of these refer to facets of the soil, water, air, and biological species which impinge on human survivability. The noosphere, on the other hand, represents a deeper, atavistic and perhaps even a genetically predisposed connectedness with nature which lies beyond physical dependence but which is nonetheless absolutely indispensable for human development and survival (Besthorn and Saleebey, 2003; Wilson, 1984).

SOCIAL WORK, NATURE AND THE MODERNIST PROJECT

Social work's emerging understanding of the natural environment as both physically and metaphorically crucial to survival was beginning to strongly suggest to the profession that nature affects not only our biological existence but the character of all our relationships. Social work was slowly coming to the realization that both practically and philosophically, our understanding of environment has consequences for the way we perceive ourselves and how we conduct ourselves in interaction with others.

As suggested, social work has had difficulty articulating the implications of an expanded perspective of environment even though the profession conceives of itself as uniquely situated at the interface of both person and environment. The failure of social work to attend to the relevance of the natural environment has all too often continued to command our professional allegiance even as disparate peoples and cultures all around the world are sensing a growing awareness of a deep alienation between humans and natural systems and that the disastrous consequences of this estrangement are becoming ever more profound. For at least the last decade the perception has been widening that humanity must transform its way of relating to the environment, must change its exploitative and extractive *economic* enterprises, and must again begin defining itself in terms which include a resonate relationship with the natural world. This interdependency of humans and the natural world represents a kind of primordial connectedness which endures beyond cultures, religion and time itself.

Social work scholar, John Coates, has suggested that social work has been slow to respond to environmental concerns largely because it has been so deeply entrenched in the philosophical assumptions and economic values of modernity. Coates suggests that modern social work has become a 'domesticated profession' (2003: 38). That is, it has been so thoroughly indoctrinated in modernist ideas of control over nature, unending progress and unrestrained development that the profession has been reduced to being the hand-maiden of the dominant socio-economic order.

The modern period in history flowed from the humanistic resurgence of the Renaissance and emancipatory aims of the Enlightenment. Modernism, as a cultural system of beliefs, is associated with the philosophy of Rene Descartes and Francis Bacon as well as the scientific discoveries of Galileo and Isaac Newton. Modernism is often equated with the scientific worldview and the technological advances of industrial capitalism (Besthorn, 1997). For a western world emerging from millennia of religious violence, superstition and suppression of creative thought, science and technology represented a powerful and successful new approach to controlling nature and expanding culture. The focus on mathematical description, analytical thought, deductive reasoning, the neutrality of the observer, the precision of empirical observation and quantification of objective data had come to dominate every aspect of western culture.

Closely associated with these core values of modernity is the belief that nature and society could be conceptualized as machines with interchangeable parts. This approach cast social workers and many other professionals in the role of expert mechanics that, with technical skill backed by science, could control the vicissitudes of environment and the thorny problem of human relationships and thus repair the malfunctioning machine (Mosher, 2009). This mechanistic, reductionist view of reality created a dualistic perception of phenomenon. Dualism is a deeply engrained pattern of thought that tends to see all things as categorical opposites such as good/bad, us/them, nature/human. Unfortunately, this way of thinking has tended to separate humans from nature and led to a gross misperception that humans are not members of the natural world. Indeed, it has also resulted in a widely held view in modern culture that humans are the pinnacle of creation – set apart, separate from the rest of the natural order. This human-centered or anthropocentric view of humankind in relationship to the natural world tends to lead to a prioritization of individual need over community need and a valuing of that which is near and dear to the exclusion of all others – human or otherwise. As Coates (2003) points out, it is easier to justify exploiting nature when human beings see themselves as separate and above nature.

While our embeddedness in the values and assumptions of modernism has obscured our memory of our tie to the natural world, a need is being expressed globally, in nearly every profession and in all cultures, to find a way to regain entry into nature. Social work is no different and must necessarily engage with the environment and its fragile balance. Before leaving this discussion we make the critical reflection that social work as a profession developed with little understanding of indigenous knowledge of the delicate balance of ecosystems and our need to work in harmony with the earth. It is beyond the scope of this chapter to address this issue more fully and we refer readers to Chapter 2 and 16 of this text. However, we make the observation that social work must engage with indigenous knowledge and culture and a critical first step is to indigenise our curricula and ensure more engagement of indigenous workers in education and practice programmes. We turn now to one of the many promising avenues of social work involvement in issues of the environment – the emerging focus on sustainability (Mary, 2008).

SUSTAINABILITY

In 1987 the World Commission on Environment and Development (WCED) released *Our Common Future,* a report that has since become more commonly known as the Brundtland Report. This report alerted the world to the dangers inherent in the wholesale pursuit of economic growth without adequate attention to the limitations of natural and non-renewable resources and with limited attention to the outcomes for people. The oft-quoted definition of sustainable development draws from this report which describes it as: '... a development that meets the needs of the present without compromising the ability of future generations to meet their own needs' (WCED, 1987: 46). Thus the report draws attention to the need to preserve for future generations the ability to sustain quality of life by protecting and sustaining our resources and yet not necessarily defraying economic development. Two of the defining principles of the Brundtland Report are the need to redistribute resources toward poorer nations to create global equity and intergenerational equity between current and future generations. Essentially these two issues have become the moral imperatives that have underpinned ongoing discussions of sustainability. For social workers, what is of critical interest is that the report draws attention to three components of sustainable development – environmental protection, economic security and social equity, thereby giving equal and critical attention to social sustainability.

There has been a great deal of debate on the notion of sustainability since this report, a debate made more urgent in recent times by the threat of irreversible climate change and resource depletion. Much of this debate has focused on environmental and economic growth and those shaping the construction of sustainable development tend to be politicians, scientists, environmentalists and economists. Social sustainability has been very much sidelined in the years since the Brundtland Report was released. Thus the lack of attention to social equity has limited discussion of the likely impacts on the people and communities most affected by ongoing and rapid escalation of resource depletion and climate change – most likely to be indigenous peoples, the rural poor and impoverished women. Significantly, polluting factories and industries are located in impoverished areas where those most affected are silenced by their need for employment. Perhaps this is the reason that there is belated attention to the role of social workers in addressing issues of sustainability and a lack of acknowledgement that sustainable development might well be a key area for social workers.

In an earlier work on the issue of the intertwining of the environmental, economic and social aspects of sustainability a number of definitional factors are noted:

- sustainability involves a balance between environmental, economic and social priorities;
- sustainability is a relative concept that denotes progression towards a preferred future rather than a defined end point;
- sustainability is a contested term and commentators give greater or lesser focus to the three elements – environmental, economic and social; and
- indicators of sustainable communities are not consistently reliable (Cocklin and Alston, 2003: 3).

Nonetheless we can say with some certainty that the notion of *social sustainability* has been largely missing from the language of sustainable development and risks disappearing without attention from social scientists and social workers. Black, writing in an Australian context notes that social sustainability relates to 'the extent to which social values, social identities, social relationships and social institutions are capable of being maintained into the future' (2005: 25). This definition presupposes an ordered development into the future but also alerts us to the social upheavals that might arise from a lack of global equity in relation to major changes including climate change, and diminishing access to clean water and food. Perhaps a better definition might be *the extent to which people across the globe can be free from poverty and live in security with adequate access to clean water and food whilst maintaining social identities, social relationships and social institutions*. Such a definition shifts the focus of sustainability from environmental and economic resources to people and communities across the globe and alerts us to the need for attention to global poverty and food and water security.

The idea of social sustainability also opens up for scrutiny those who are *socially excluded*. Social exclusion is a much broader concept than poverty and refers to those people who cannot participate in society for reasons beyond their control despite their desire to participate (Burchardt, 2000). Thus, in a world characterised by rising global inequities in relation to resource access, there are increasing numbers of people who are excluded from participation in even a basic ordered existence. A UK report noted in 2005 that there are over a billion people living on less than a dollar a day, over 800 million who are malnourished and over two and a half billion who lack access to basic sanitation (HM Government, 2005). Such a world is unsustainable and implies a significant threat to world order. History provides ample evidence of more powerful groups overturning others. Therefore it is not unreasonable to suggest, as Murray et al. (2006) do, that social sustainability is not an innocent concept and rests on the tensions between

capitalism and social justice. History has shown us time and time again that economic gain overrides altruistic notions of social justice. Thus social sustainability implies that people will live locally and globally in a constant struggle for harmony in a world currently operating at unsustainable levels (Murray et al., 2006).

Two complex environmental issues which impact many millions around the world are the loss of bio-diversity and the high ecological costs of war.

LOSS OF BIO-DIVERSITY AND ECOLOGICAL AFTERMATH OF WAR

The term *biodiversity* refers to the variability among living organisms that maintains the health of each. Excellent illustrations of biodiversity can be found among the still remaining tall grass prairie lands of the US central plains region and the vast remote areas of Australia. These verdant ecosystems which feature a wide variety of native species have maintained a yearly bio-equilibrium for literally thousands of years. They have become a living example of how healthy ecosystems function and increasingly provide a template for emerging forms of sustainable agriculture, organic farming and rural revitalization.

With publication of *Silent Spring,* Rachel Carson (1962) presented compelling data on the ecological impact of chemical pollution. Carson's work was so influential for its time because it was one of the first to convincingly link exploitation of the environmental to human health (Dorsey and Thormodsgard, 2003). The title of her book refers to the silencing of springtime songbirds due to the spraying of insecticides and herbicides.

The impetus for seeking to learn from biologically diverse nature-scapes and development of sustainable land practice is to support the creation of healthy environments free from synthetic fertilizers, pesticides, and herbicides and the avoidance of mono-cropping (van Wormer and Besthorn, 2010). Non-profit research and development organisations working for years to put the ecological lessons of bio-diverse prairie/range land into practice are The Land Institute of Salina, Kansas (Land Institute, 2002) and Desert Knowledge in Australia. The Land Institute's sustainable agri-practices feature perennial crops whose year-round, deeply embedded root systems hold the life-giving topsoil. They grow and are sustained in an environment reminiscent of native grasslands. Desert Knowledge seeks to create sustainable environments and lifestyles for desert people in remote parts of Australia.

Conventional farming practices have traditionally been wasteful in terms of land usage. Additionally, only a tiny fraction of chemical pesticides reach their targets, and insects, having developed resistance, are destroying crops at an increasing rate. To force some of the last remaining nutritive life out of the depleted soil, farmers use an incredible amount of chemical fertilizers – many of them highly toxic – that seep into rural waterways, drinking water, soil, and air (Despommier, 2009). Soil that is depleted of its recuperative power and of the organic matter that anchors it, washes or is blown away precipitously through water and wind erosion. Without healthy soil, we are without food – literally. Ninety percent of US cropland is losing soil as a result of unsustainable conventional farming practices that have become the norm in American agribusiness over the last 70 years (Land Institute, 2002). A similar process is underway in Australia where droughts have led to major dust storms as top soils blow away and tons of productive soil finds its way to cities and coastlands.

In response to an international call for a scientific assessment of the health of the world's soil and ecosystems, the Millennium Ecosystem Assessment (Mooney et al., 2005) was conducted. Over 1000 researchers from 95 nations contributed to this effort. Unique to this report was the emphasis on protecting bio-diversity while at the same time enhancing human well-being by eradicating poverty and hunger (van Wormer and Besthorn, 2010). The report's findings chronicling the loss of biodiversity remind us that biodiversity is a requirement for all life on the planet. Major findings from the assessment are that:

- humans have radically altered ecosystems over the past 70 years;
- about 75% of the world's commercial fisheries have been fully overexploited;
- more land has been converted to cropland since 1950 than during the agricultural revolution of the 19th century;
- species extinction is unparalleled;
- sixty percent of world ecosystem bio-benefits have been degraded;
- about 20% of world coral reefs were lost in just 20 years;
- nutrient pollution, from chemical fertilizers, has led to the contamination of water and depletion of topsoil;
- water availability is projected to decrease in many regions leading to social conflicts; and
- poverty and hunger will result for the world's poorest people without the development of sustainable practices.

According to the ecosystems assessment report, human societies can ease the strain on nature through changes in consumption patterns, better education, new technologies, reduction in the use of fertilisers and pesticides, and higher prices placed on industry and agriculture for exploiting practices.

Perhaps the most harmful form of abuse of the earth comes from the ravages of war.

Unlike modern industrialism's prodding assault on nature, the goal of which is to control nature for human consumption, wars against people often involve a deliberate attack on the natural environment as a part of a military *bring-the-enemy-to-its-knees* campaign (van Wormer and Besthorn, 2010). Throughout history, the natural environment has been one of war's worst and most frequent casualties. Romans spread salt on the fields of Carthage in order to defeat the Carthaginians; Sherman's troops marched to the sea in the waning days of the US Civil

War, pillaging and burning a large swath of Georgia as they moved ahead; Allied and Axis powers did untold damage to natural systems, literally across the face of the earth, during World War II; the United States defoliated Vietnamese jungles; and Saddam Hussein set fire to the oilfields in Kuwait. Long after wars are over, major unanticipated effects may occur. Fischer (1993) reminds us of the 'Just Cause' invasion of Panama in 1989, which, along with imposed US sanctions, broke the economy, causing the people to deplete remaining land resources and cut protected forests in order to survive. Just as war leads to environmental decimation, so depleting the environment produces ethnic and territorial conflict as people are pitted against each other to secure the last remaining resources. Waves of refugees fleeing war zones further ravage environmental reserves (Besthorn and Meyer, 2010).

Today, according to Australian physician, Helen Caldicott (2000), the United States and its other Western Allies, with their massive arsenal of nuclear and biological weapons, are the most ominous threat to world peace and the environment. The use of depleted uranium in recent wars is a case in point. This product is used by the military because of its high density, which enables it to penetrate hardened targets. Such toxic weaponry constitutes a weapon of *ongoing* mass destruction in terms of destruction of human life and long-term radioactive contamination. Literally, they are the weapons which keep on killing. For years after a war has ended they kill the victors as well as the vanquished. The use of depleted-uranium ordinance in the Iraqi War has affected not only the combatants and civilians but also their children – causing infertility, skeletal deformities, leukemia, and testicular and brain cancers (Nixon, 2005). Depleted uranium vaporises when it hits a target. Once released, the microscopic particles are easily spread by the wind and literally can be transported across the globe by the upper-level jet stream. Depleted uranium is strongly suspected as a cause of Gulf War syndrome, the

assortment of health problems that has affected many members of the military (National Gulf War Resource Center at www. ngwrc.org).

In light of the catastrophic global consequences of war for the physical and social environment, the Sierra Club of North America (historically focused on protection of natural environments) has issued statements not only on behalf of the environment, but also for disarmament and the end of war (May, 2002). All responsible persons are beginning to recognize the interconnected association between wars (whether local, regional or global) and decimated natural environments.

CLIMATE CHANGE, POPULATION GROWTH AND FOOD INSECURITY

We reiterate that it is not only wars where mankind has been instrumental in the destruction of the environment. The assault on the environment through major industrial development has caused unprecedented harm and potentially irreversible climate change. Climate change refers to the observed changes in weather patterns resulting from the build up of greenhouse gases in the atmosphere which results from the burning of fossil fuels, deforestation and the production of mining waste and results in melting of the icecaps, rising seas levels and extreme weather events (IPCC, 2007). The build up of greenhouse gases was first recognized during the 1970s and has increased by 70% since that time with predictions that it will rise significantly in the coming decades unless radical action is adopted. In 1988 the United Nations established the Intergovernmental Panel on Climate Change (IPCC), a body that has produced several scientific reports on the extent of climate change and its likely impacts since that time. The IPCC was awarded the Nobel Peace Prize in 2007 for alerting the world to the very real possibility of irreversible climate change.

As a result of the work of the IPCC, the United Nations Framework Convention on Climate Change (UNFCC) was adopted in 1997 and nations were urged to sign up to reducing greenhouse gas emissions in what has become known as the Kyoto Protocol. Kyoto has been signed by several nations across the world and there is genuine agreement that a reduction in greenhouse gases is essential to future sustainable development. However, tensions have arisen between developed and developing nations around the issue of which countries should be responsible for reducing emissions and which should be given some leeway to develop industrially. Many developing nations argue that the developed countries such as the United States and Australia are the largest emitters and should therefore be the countries with higher reduction targets. They also argue that economic development depends very much on their own ability to continue to produce greenhouse gas emissions as their industries develop. Some developing countries also argue that those responsible for the emissions should be the ones to solve the problem. As a result of these political tensions, the Climate Change Forum held in Copenhagen in 2009 failed to achieve world agreement on significant and enforceable greenhouse gas reduction targets. There is much dismay across the world that this failure may result in dire forecasts of things to come.

While the scientific community is largely of the view that climate change is man-made, there are sceptics who dispute whether climate change is anything more than a normal, although extreme, cyclical pattern of weather events (see, for example, Plimer, 2009). What is clear is that evidence of climate change, or climate variability for those who prefer the sceptics view, is emerging across the world. Climate variability has resulted in both *incremental* climate change including drought and desertification processes, and in *cataclysmic* climate events including flooding and bush-fires. Weather patterns are more unpredictable, extreme weather events are occurring with greater regularity and at more extreme levels, temperatures are rising, as are sea levels, and food productive capacity is destabilized by uncertain weather. Water access is reduced in many parts of the world including the Murray–Darling Basin area of Australia and many Pacific Island countries.

While climate change is a major global problem, its links to other significant world trends is compounding the outcomes for people and communities. For example, the United Nations Population Fund (UNFPA) noted in 2007 that the world's population had tipped for the first time into being predominantly urban (UNFPA, 2007) and that a majority of urban poor live in slum dwellings on the edges of cities with insufficient access to clean water and nutritious food. Predictions are that the population will rise further from 6 billion to 9 billion by 2050, and at the same time life expectancy is rising in many countries (UNDP, 2008). The highest population rises are in poorer countries such as those in the African continent. Our planet is facing unprecedented pressure from population growth alone. Coupled with climate variability and significant world poverty, there is significant pressure on resources to sustain world population growth. Water and food insecurity are growing and the ability to access food and clean water is reducing for many people. In 2008, Britain's Chief Scientific Adviser, Professor John Beddington, described food and water insecurity as 'the elephant in the room' (Smith and Elliot, 2008) and, in the same year, the UN's Under-Secretary-General for Humanitarian Affairs, Sir John Holmes, warned that increasing food prices, food scarcity and rising fuel prices are creating civil unrest in vulnerable countries. In the early months of 2008, for instance, there were food riots in Egypt, Haiti, the Ivory Coast, Cameroon, Mauritania, Mozambique, Senegal, Uzbekistan, Yemen, Bolivia and Indonesia (Adams, 2008).

Water insecurity is also a problem recognised by the International Fund for Agricultural Development (IFAD, 2007) which notes that most of the world's 1.2 billion poor (two-thirds of whom are women) live in areas where water is scarce and they do not have access to safe, reliable water. They further argue that one-third of the world's population is experiencing some form of water shortage.

The impacts of these factors on health and well-being are evident. In developing countries, this includes higher mortality rates, malnutrition and disease (FAO, 2007) and in developed countries higher morbidity rates, health and mental health consequences (Alston, 2010; Alston and Kent, 2006). There are also health impacts from airborne disease, exposure to higher temperatures and unclean water.

Another consequence of these factors working together is a rise in the numbers of 'climate refugees' – those people fleeing areas where food and water insecurity are evident, fleeing to neighbouring countries to live in refugee camps (Besthorn and Meyer, 2010) In both developing and developed countries, we are also seeing migrations of people from rural to urban areas in search of work to support families unable to make a living in agricultural production.

There is no doubt that climate change, its environmental consequences and its intersection with population growth and rising world poverty is having significant social consequences and affecting social sustainability across the world. How social work might respond effectively is the subject of the next section.

SOCIAL WORK – HUMAN RIGHTS AND ANTI-OPPRESSIVE PRACTICE

We have produced a strong case for critical global issues that are shaping unsustainable global responses and threatening world order. We have also argued for the need for social sustainability to be a central part of global sustainable development into the future – for a much stronger focus on people. In this section we urge social workers to view the environment and its attendant issues as a significant part of their future work and for social workers to take a lead in building social sustainability. Social workers are committed to social justice as a key element of their work and are dedicated to ensuring human rights are protected – they can become key change agents in attending to environmental degradation and refocusing attention to the person in the *environment*. There is no doubt that the pressure on the environment from unsustainable economic development and the depletion of natural resources is resulting in significant social disruption and human rights abuses. We argue that attention to human-rights-based practice and anti-oppressive practice is the basis for social work in the area of environment and sustainability.

The work of Paulo Friere (1972) is instructive in drawing attention to the structural constraints that shape and structure people's life chances. Food and water insecurity are evident constraints and Freire's notion of conscientisation – or the need to raise critical awareness amongst people about the social, political and economic realities that constrain and shape oppression – is highly relevant. Leonard's (1997) notion of emancipatory practice is also relevant, a practice he defines as empowering people to make positive changes in their lives and to advocate on their behalf for adequate resources. Drawing on these concepts, Ife (2001) defines a human rights based practice as one that focuses on the fundamental rights of people as opposed to their perceived deficits, a perspective that allows us to see the citizenship rights of people who are abused by a lack of access to clean food and water, to adequate services and infrastructure, to health outcomes and education, to employment and other taken for granted quality of life indicators.

Drawing on the three generations of human rights articulated through the United Nations Declaration of Human Rights, Ife draws our attention to the third generation of rights that articulates collective actions such as the right to a healthy environment, intergenerational equity and sustainability. Thus the environment is very much recognised as an area of human rights practice and environmental degradation and resource depletion are sites of social work activity.

Anti-oppressive practice builds on similar ideas, noting that the individual is central to practice. It articulates the types of structural issues associated with individual disadvantage and works for radical social change based on equality (Healy, 2005). Oppression is viewed as a reflection of wider structural disadvantage and is based on power imbalances between people – men and women, for example. Anti-oppressive practice can therefore be used to determine structural disadvantage within and between countries based on inequitable access to resources and on inequitable accounting of responsibility for resource depletion.

The term glocal practice has been used to describe the link between local contextual issues and global factors (Harris and Chou, 2001; McDonald, 2006). Social workers can become the voice of resistance, working with people at local levels to expose the impacts of global realities. Thus there is room for 'glocal' practice that draws on a human rights framework and champions the voice of the marginalised in relation to ongoing sustainable development and, in particular, social sustainability.

To avoid the exploitation of the impoverished and malnourished, social workers should focus attention on social sustainability at all levels to ensure that people at an individual, community and national level have adequate and fair access to resources that will improve their participation and quality of life. Thus the focus is on building individual and community *resilience* and addressing *community capacity building*.

Resilience describes the way people and communities respond to vulnerability and their capacity to react to adversity (Eckersley, 2009). If circumstances are such that people are diminished in their daily lives and their health is affected then their capacity to embrace change is deeply affected. Thus resilience can be *reactive* where people and communities resist change, continuing unsustainable practices. Examples of reactive resilience abound and include practices such as the many people who draw on unclean water sources in the slum areas of large cities. Resilience can also be *proactive* when people and communities acknowledge change is inevitable and they work toward more positive futures (Handmer and Dovers, 2009). Proactive resilience addresses processes that limit sustainability, challenges social structures that disadvantage, treats the causes of potential dysfunction and moves communities toward greater social sustainability. Examples of proactive resilience also abound and include the building of more secure clean water catchments in areas such as the Pacific Island countries (Barnett and Campbell, 2009). The role of social workers in building proactive resilience is obvious and includes assisting people at individual, community and national levels to ensure social sustainability. Another area where social workers are particularly skilled is in the area of *community capacity building*.

Community capacity building builds on the notion of social sustainability, moving communities toward a preferred and sustainable future. It focuses on an assets-based approach working with communities to develop their strengths. It has been defined as 'the interaction of human capital, organisational resources and social capital existing within a given community that can be leveraged to solve collective problems and improve or maintain the wellbeing of that community' (Chaskin et al., 2001: 7).

Black and Hughes (2001: 7) prefer the term *community strengthening* and define it as 'the extent to which resources and processes within a community maintain and enhance both individual and collective wellbeing in ways consistent with the principles of equity, comprehensiveness, participation, self-reliance and social responsibility'.

Various strategies can be used to empower local people to develop their own solutions to complex environmental problems emerging from resource depletion and changing environmental contexts (see, for example, Taylor et al., 2008).

CONCLUSION

There is irrefutable evidence that the environment is under threat and that sustainability may be an ever-receding dream. We have argued for social workers to view the environment as a critical focus for practice, as part of their world view when addressing their professional persona and as the missing piece in the person and environment nexus, without which the survival of our species is under threat. However, we finish this chapter with a degree of optimism because we see from our differing perspectives in two continents on different sides of the world and in different hemispheres, that all is not yet lost. We stand on the cusp of a global catastrophe, still able to pull back from the precipice and still with the capacity to reverse our mistakes.

We are both passionate in our belief that social workers can play a critical role in bringing forward a different way of viewing the world, of linking people, place and policy, and of using their practice skills to reshape society. We argue that this will take place in many spheres through grassroots activism and advocacy, through community capacity building, building individual and community resilience, through conscientisation and human rights practice, through advocating for changed national and international policies and through building a world where the link between people and the physical environment is re-established and revalued.

There will necessarily be a new world order in the 21st century. Social workers can act to ensure it is a healing and compassionate one, and one which values our environment, our natural resources, our diverse cultures and our people and that the significance of

social sustainability is an overarching piece in the landscape of the future.

REFERENCES

Adams, D. (2008) 'UN warns of a hungry and less stable world: food riots likely to be more frequent', *The Age*, 10 April: 12.

Alston, M. (2009) *Innovative Human Services: Changing Landscapes*. Melbourne: Pan Macmillan.

Alston, M. (2010) 'Rural male suicide in Australia', *Social Science and Medicine*, published online; doi:10.1016/j.socscimed.2010.04.036.

Alston, M. and Kent, J. (2006) *Impact of Drought on Rural and Remote Education Access: a Report to DEST and Rural Education Fund of FRRR*. Wagga Wagga: Centre for Rural Social Research, Charles Sturt University.

Alston, M. and McKinnon, J (eds) (2005) *Social Work: Fields of Practice*. 2nd edn. Melbourne: Oxford University Press.

Barnett, J. and Campbell, A. (2009) *Climate Change and Small Island States*. Australia: Earthscan.

Berry, T. (1988) *The Dream of the Earth*. San Francisco: Sierra Books.

Besthorn, F.H. (1997) *Reconceptualizing Social Work's Person-in-Environment Perspective: Explorations in Radical Environmental Thought*. University of Kansas, Lawrence. Unpublished doctoral dissertation.

Besthorn, F.H. (2001) 'Transpersonal psychology and deep ecological philosophy: exploring linkages and applications for social work', in E.R. Canda and E.D. Smith (eds), *Transpersonal Perspectives on Spirituality in Social Work*. Binghamton, NY: Haworth Press. pp. 23–44.

Besthorn, F.H. (2008) 'Environment and social work practice', in *Encyclopedia of Social Work-20th Edition* (vol. 2). New York: Oxford University Press. pp. 132–6.

Besthorn, F.H. and Meyer, E. (2010) 'Environmentally displaced persons: broadening social work's helping imperative', *Journal of Critical Social Work*, 11(3): 123–38. Retrieved from http://www.uwindsor.ca/criticalsocialwork/2010-volume-11-no-3.

Besthorn, F.H. and Saleebey, D. (2003) 'Nature, genetics and the biophilia connection: exploring linkages with social work values and practice', *Advances in Social Work*, 4(1): 1–18.

Black, A. (2005) 'Rural communities and sustainability', in C. Cocklin and J. Dibden (eds), *Sustainability and*

Change in Rural Australia. Sydney: UNSW Press. pp. 20–37.

Black, A. and Hughes, P. (2001) *The Identification and Analysis of Indicators of Community Strengthening and Analysis.* Occasional Paper No 3, Department of Family and Community Services, Canberra.

Boff, L. (1997) *Cry of the Earth, Cry of the Poor.* Marynoll, NY: Orbis Books.

Burchardt, T. (2000) 'Social exclusion: concepts and evidence', in D. Gordon and P. Townsend (eds), *Breadline Europe: the Measurement of Poverty.* Bristol: Policy Press. pp. 385–406.

Caldicott, H. (2000) *The New Nuclear Danger: George W. Bush's Military-Industrial Complex.* Queensland, Australia: University of Queensland Press.

Capra, F. (1996) *The Web of Life: A New Scientific Understanding of Living Systems.* New York: Anchor Books.

Carson, R. (1962) *Silent Spring.* Boston, MA: Mariner Books. [1st. Pub. Houghton Mifflin, 1962].

Chaskin, R.J., Brown, P., Venkatesh, S. and Vidal, A. (2001) *Building Community Capacity.* Edison NJ: Aldine Transaction.

Coates, J. (2003) *Ecology and Social Work: Toward a New Paradigm.* Halifax, Nova Scotia: Fernwood.

Coates, J and McKay, M. (1995) 'Toward a new pedagogy for social transformation', *Journal of Progressive Human Services,* 6(1): 27–44.

Cocklin, C. and Alston, M. (2003) 'Introduction', in C. Cocklin and M. Alston (eds), *Community Sustainability: a Question of Capital.* Wagga Wagga: Centre for Rural Social Research.

Daly, H. (1990) 'Toward some operational principles of sustainable development', *Ecological Economics,* 2: 1–6.

Despommier, D. (2009) 'The rise of vertical farms', *Scientific American Magazine,* November: 80–7.

Dorsey, E. and Thormodsgard, M. (2003) Rachel Carson Wanred Us, Ms, v 12, Winter 2002: 42–5.

Eckersley, R. (2009) 'Population health: the forgotten dimension of social resilience', in S. Cork (ed.), *Brighter Prospects: Enhancing the Resilience of Australia.* Australia 21 Shaping the Future. Weston: ACT. pp. 36–40. http://www.australia21.org.au/pdf/A21%20Brighter%20Prospects%20Report.pdf.

Fischer, E. (1993) 'War and the environment', in J. Allen (ed.), *Environment 93/94* (12th edn). Guilford, CT: Dushkin. pp. 73–88.

Flavin, C., French, H. and Gardner, G. (eds) (2002) *The Worldwatch Institute State of the World: 2002.* New York: Norton.

FAO (Food and Agricultural Organisation.) (2007) *Gender and Climate Change: Existing Research and Knowledge Gaps.* Rome: Gender and Population Division, FAO.

Freire, P. (1972) *Pedagogy of the Oppressed.* Harmondsworth: Penguin.

Germain, C.B. (1991) *Human Behavior in the Social Environment: an Ecological View.* New York: Columbia University Press.

Germain, C.B. and Gitterman, A. (1980) *The Life Model of Social Work Practice.* New York: Columbia University Press.

Graham, J., Swift, K. and Delaney, R. (2009) *Canadian Social Policy: an Introduction.* 3rd edn. Toronto: Pearson Education.

Handmer, J. and Dovers, S. (2009) 'A typology of resilience: rethinking institutions for sustainable development', in E.L.F. Schipper and I. Burton (eds), *Adaptation to Climate Change.* London: Earthscan Publishing for a Sustainable Future.

Harris, J. and Chou, Y-C. (2001) 'Globalization or glocalization? Community care in Taiwan and Britain', *European Journal of Social Work,* 4(2): 161–72.

Healy, K. (2005) 'Social work theories in context: A critical introduction'. Hampshire, UK: Palgrave MacMillan.

HM Government. (2005) *Securing the Future: Delivering UK Sustainable Development,* Strategy presented to parliament by the Secretary of State for Environment, Food and Rural Affairs by command of Her Majesty, March 2005. Norwich: HMSO.

Hoff, M. and McNutt, J. (eds) (1994) *The Global Environmental Crisis: Implications for Social Welfare and Social Work.* Brookfield, VT: Avebury. pp. 36–52.

IFAD (International Fund for Agricultural Development). (2007) *Gender and Water.* Rome, Italy: IFAD.

Ife, J. (2001) *Human Rights and Social Work: Towards Rights-Based Practice.* Cambridge: Cambridge University Press.

IPCC (Intergovernmental Panel on Climate Change). (2007) *Climate Change 2007: Mitigation of Climate Change.* Geneva: IPCC Secretariat. www.ipcc.ch.

Land Institute. (2002) 'Natural systems agriculture', *Land Institute Newsletter,* 1–2.

Leonard, P. (1997) *Postmodern Welfare: Reconstructing an Emancipatory Project.* London: Sage.

Lysack, M. (2007) 'Family therapy, the ecological self and global warming'. *Context,* 91: 9–11.

Mary, N. (2008) *Social Work in a Sustainable World.* Chicago: Lyceum Books Inc.

May, E. (2002) *Sierra Club in the US.* Press release, 11 December. Retrieved from http://www.sierraclub.ca/national/programs/atmosphere-energy/climate.

McDonald, C. (2006) *Challenging Social Work: the Context of Practice.* Hampshire: Palgrave Macmillan.

McKinnon, J. (2001) 'Social work and the environment', in M. Alston and J. McKinnon (eds), *Social Work: Fields of Practice.* Melbourne: Oxford University Press. pp. 193–205.

McKinnon, J. (2005) 'Social work, sustainability, and the environment', in M. Alston and J. McKinnon (eds), *Social Work: Fields of Practice.* 2nd edn. Melbourne: Oxford University Press. pp. 225–36.

McKinnon, J. (2008) 'Exploring the nexus between social work and the environment', *Australian Social Work,* 61(3): 256–68.

Mooney, H., Cropper, A. and Reid, W. (2005) 'Confronting the human dilemma', *Nature,* 434(3): 561–2.

Mosher, C. (2009) *A New Paradigm for Sustainability and Social Justice.* Paper presented at the meeting of the International Eco-Conference: Building Bridges Crossing Boundaries, May 2009, Calgary, AB, Canada.

Murray, J., Dey, C. and Lenzen, M. (2006) *Systems for Social Sustainability Global Connectedness and the Tuvalu Test,* University of Sydney, Integrated Sustainability Analysis, ISA Research Paper 02–06, School of Physics, University of Sydney, Sydney. http://www.isa.org.usyd.edu.au/publications/documents/Murray_et_al_2006_Tuvalu_Test.pdf, accessed 24 July 2010.

Nixon, R. (2005) 'Our tools of war, turned blindly against ourselves', *Chronicle of Higher Education,* 51(24): B7–11.

Plimer, I. (2009) *Heaven and Earth.* Australia: Connor Court.

Robbins, S.P., Chatterjee, P. and Canda, E.R. (2006) *Contemporary Human Behavior Theory: a Critical Perspective For Social Work.* 2nd edn. Boston: Allyn & Bacon.

Rogge, M. (1994) 'Environmental injustice: social welfare and toxic waste', in M. Hoff and J. McNutt (eds), *The Global Environmental Crisis: Implications for Social Welfare and Social Work.* Aldershot, UK: Ashgate. pp. 53–74.

Saleebey, D. (1992) Biology's challenge to social work: embodying the person-in-environment perspective', *Social Work,* 37(2): 112–8.

Smith, L. and Elliott, F. (2008) *Rush for Biofuels Threatens Starvation on a Global Scale.* Times On-Line, 7 March. http://forests.org/shared/reader/welcome.aspx?linkid=94234&keybold=biofuel%20rainforests, accessed 2 April 2008.

Taylor, J., Wilkinson, D. and Cheers, B. (2008) *Working with Communities in Health and Human Services.* Melbourne: Oxford University Press.

UNDP (United Nations Development Programme). (2008) *The World at Six Billion.* Department of Economic and Social Affairs Population Division. http://www.un.org/esa/population/publications/sixbillion/sixbillion.htm.

UNFPA (United Nations Population Fund). (2007) *State of the World Population 2007: Unleashing the Potential of Urban Growth.* United Nations: UNFPA.

Ungar, M. (2002) 'A deeper, more social ecological social work practice', *Social Service Review,* 76(3): 480–97.

Van Wormer, K. and Besthorn, F.H. (2010) *Human Behavior and the Social Environment: Macro Level: Groups, Communities, and Organizations.* New York: Oxford University Press.

WCED (World Commission on Environment and Development). (1987) *The Bruntland Report: Our Common Future.* Oxford: Oxford University Press.

Weick, A. (1981) 'Reframing the person-in-environment perspective', *Social Work,* 26(2): 140–5.

Wilson, E.O. (1984) *Biophilia: The Human Bond with Other Species.* Cambridge, MA: MIT Press.

Zapf, M. (2009) *Social Work and the Environment: Understanding People and Place.* Toronto: Canadian Scholars Press.

4

Human Rights

Joseph Wronka and Silvia Staub Bernasconi

INTRODUCTION

This chapter approaches the issue of human rights by first emphasising that social work from its inception has been called a 'human rights profession'. It then examines major United Nations (UN) human rights documents and institutional mechanisms that could assist in creating a socially just world, ultimately a global human rights culture, defined as a lived awareness of human rights principles in one's mind and heart, and dragged into the everyday life (Wronka, 2008, see Appendix 5). It then elaborates upon the importance of integrating human rights into social work theory and praxis, enlarging among other things social work's double mandate of the client and society, to include the profession itself.

SOCIAL WORK'S COMMITMENT TO HUMAN RIGHTS

Social work has traditionally had a commitment to social justice, an important, but rather amorphous concept. Indeed, human rights ought to provide the necessary contours of social justice, serving ultimately as its pillars (Reichert, 2007; Wronka, 2008). Indeed, the International Federation of Social Workers (IFSW) has called social work 'a human rights profession, having as its basic tenet the intrinsic value of every human being' (UN, 1994: 3). Recognising that both IFSW and the International Association of Schools of Social Work (IASSW) 'have an enduring commitment to the principles of social justice . . . in particular work in the area of human rights' (IFSW, 2002), they formed a Joint Commission on Human Rights in Geneva in 2002. Most recently, IFSW, IASSW and the International Council on Social Welfare (ICSW) drew up a *Global Agenda for Social Work and Social Development: Towards an Engagement Agenda – Mobilization of Social Workers, Social Work Educators, and Policy Practitioners and Developers for Global Social Change* (2010), which stressed looking at the 'Dignity and worth of the person' [and] 'human rights issues in relation to social, economic, cultural, and political situations' (2010: 4). Clearly, human rights, which ultimately are the legal mandate to fulfil human need, thereby promoting human development (Gil, 1998; Wronka, 1998) are a priority for the profession.

HUMAN RIGHTS DOCUMENTS

From the latin *docere* (meaning 'to teach'), documents provide an excellent means to create awareness about human rights. Viewed in their historical contexts, in 1938, US President Roosevelt called the Conference of Evian to stop the abuses of the Third Reich. The conference failed because other countries did not want to bring attention to their own atrocities like public lynching in the US, the Soviet Union's *Gulag*, and France's policies of torture in Africa. What ensued was the killing of ten million innocent people, primarily Jews, but also Gypsies and one quarter of Poland's population, among others. Increasingly 'sophisticated' weaponry culminated in the atomic bombings of Hiroshima and Nagasaki. An overall estimated 72 million people died (World War II Casualties, 2011). To prevent such atrocities from recurring the UN was formed on 24 October 1945.

Initially reluctant, the General Assembly endorsed the *Universal Declaration of Human Rights* (UDHR) with no dissent on 10 December 1948. A compromise among various historical epochs and philosophical and spiritual systems, the Universal Declaration consists of five crucial notions. The first is human dignity (Article 1); the second is non-discrimination (Article 2); both notions reflect essential strands of some of the world's major religions, like the Judaic–Christian–Islamic tradition, Hinduism, and Buddhism, mirroring also social work's emphasis upon spirituality and respect for cultural diversity. Thus, the only criterion to have one's dignity and rights is one's humanity, not one's gender, national or social origin, language, circumstances of birth, or other status. The third notion is civil and political rights (Articles 3–21), like freedoms of speech, the press, peaceful assembly and expression, largely mirroring the Age of Enlightenment and the US Bill of Rights. The fourth notion is that of economic, social, and cultural rights (Articles 22–27), such as rights to meaningful and gainful employment, rest and leisure, adequate shelter, medical care, security in old age and education, mirroring for the most part the Age of Industrialisation and the Soviet constitution of 1923. Finally, there is the notion of solidarity rights (Articles 28–30). Still in the process of conceptual elaboration, these rights are the product of post-modernism, reflecting the failure of domestic sovereignty. Emphasising duties to the community and intergovernmental cooperation, they have come to mean rights to humanitarian disaster relief, international distributive justice, self-determination, development, protection of the cultural and common heritages of humanity (like places of worship, the oceans, mountains and space) and the right to environmental sustainability. Those rights are interdependent and strikingly similar to priorities of the *Global Agenda* mentioned earlier, which includes not only human dignity, but also eradicating social and economic inequalities, and promoting environmental sustainability and the importance of human relationships.

The human rights triptych

Rene Cassin, often referred to as the father of human rights, felt that human rights could be best understood as a triptych. The centre panel is the *Universal Declaration*, the authoritative definition of human rights standards; the right panel is the documents following it, such as guiding principles, declarations, and conventions; and the left panel consists of implementation measures, generally institutional mechanisms, such as monitoring mechanisms, world conferences, and the Universal Periodic Review of the Human Rights Council.

The right panel then consists of documents like the *Guiding Principles to Eradicate Extreme Poverty*, the *Declarations on the Protection of Persons with Mental Illness* (1991) and the *Rights of Indigenous Peoples* (2007). Documents with stronger judicial force are generally called conventions or covenants, which have the status of 'treaty'. Some countries, like the US in its Supremacy Clause, have statements in their constitutions that assert that treaties when ratified shall 'become the Supreme Law of the Land.... And the judges bound thereby' (Article VI).

Presently, there are eight major conventions: the *International Convention on Civil and Political Rights* (ICCPR, adopted in 1966); the *International Convention on Economic, Social, and Cultural Rights* (ICESCR; 1966); the *Covenant Against Torture* (CAT; 1984); the *Convention on the Elimination of Discrimination Against Women* (CEDAW; 1979) *Convention on the Eradication of Racial Discrimination* (CERD; 1965); the *Rights of the Child* (CRC; 1989); the *Convention on Migrant Workers* (CMW; 1990); and the *Convention on People with Disabilities* (CPD; 2006).

Those conventions also have themes which in general illuminate the *Universal Declaration*. For instance, the ICCPR asserts, *inter alia*, themes of rights to self-determination; the enjoyment of one's culture; use of one's language; and the prohibition of slavery. CESCR asserts rights to full and productive employment at fair wages; to adequate food, clothing, housing; to take part in cultural life and the advancement of science; and the right to education to the full development of the human personality. CAT asserts principles of due process for the accused and the non-invocation of pretext for torture. CEDAW asserts the need for the modification of social and cultural patterns to eliminate the idea of superiority or inferiority of either sex and to promote equality of men and women in employment. CERD condemns racial discrimination or apartheid and any propaganda asserting the superiority of one race. CRC gives priority to the best interests of the child, asserting respect for the views of the child, and that all treatment for children shall be done in a positive, humane and expeditious manner. *Declaration on the Rights of Indigenous Peoples* asserts redress for deprivations of cultural values and ethnic identities; full guarantees against genocide; and the right to

strengthen distinctive spiritual and material relations with lands, waters and seas. The *Protection for Persons with Mental Illness* asserts the need for appropriate disclosure of treatment in form and language understood by the patient and medication meeting the best health needs of the patient, not to be given for the convenience of others (Wronka, 2008).

Institutional mechanisms in the promotion of human rights

From the Latin *institutio* (meaning 'arrangement'), institutions are arrangements society has developed to promote goals it values. The most important institutional arrangement is the UN, a voluntary organisation of governments in tandem with non-governmental organisations (NGOs). It also spawned regional organisations, most notably the Council of Europe (CE), the Organisation of American States (OAS), the African Union (AU) and, in its infancy, the Association of Southeast Asian Nations (ASEAN), whose aims are also to promote human rights, as defined above, but with varying degrees of regional differences.

UN HUMAN RIGHTS MACHINERY

Overseeing the entire human rights machinery at the UN is the Office of the High Commissioner of Human Rights, established on 20 December 1993. Presently, the High Commissioner is Ms Navanethem Pillay, a lawyer and social activist from South Africa. Its purpose is to facilitate all UN human rights initiatives among governments and NGOs in a spirit of cooperation (UN High Commissioner for Human Rights, 2010).

The Human Rights Council (HRC), which meets over 10 weeks periodically throughout the year in Geneva, is a major institutional arrangement. Formed on 15 March 2006 it replaced the Human Rights Commission, which appeared too politicised. In June 2007 it adopted an Institutional Building Package (UN Human Rights Council, 2010) consisting of open debates before the HRC; the Universal Periodic Review (UPR, 2010), whose purpose is to examine the human rights situation in states comprising the UN on a rotating basis every four years; an Advisory Committee which provides expertise on thematic human rights issues affecting the global community; a complaints procedure, allowing individuals and organisations to bring complaints to the attention of the HRC; and treaty-based mechanisms to promote human rights.

Open debates

In full session, the HRC asks governments and NGOs to bring matters to the Council's attention. Thus, they may bring up the importance of the role of civil society in policy formation; the necessity to release political prisoners; the eradication of violence against women and of extreme poverty; the promotion of gay and lesbian marriage; and concerns about the effects of savage capitalism or continuing exploitation of the Third World by the US and the EU. In 2010, IASSW praised US President Obama for his words 'the UN is indispensable' and asked him to apologise for slavery and genocide against Indigenous Peoples, much like Australian President Hugh McCracken apologised to the Aborigines and the Holy See apologised for the role of Christianity in the Holocaust. The IASSW also called for governments to adopt the *Guiding Principles for the Eradication of Extreme Poverty*, urging that governments eventually consider a convention to abolish extreme poverty (CAEP), given that roughly one billion people go to bed hungry each night (Wronka, 2010, 2012).

The Universal Periodic Review

Based upon the idea of equal treatment for all countries, the UPR provides governments with the opportunity to declare actions they have taken to improve human rights; share their best practices; and respond to the concerns of governments and NGOs. 'Troikas' (three states, chosen by lots) assist the government under review, by grouping together related questions to ensure an orderly and smooth review generally lasting an entire morning or afternoon session. Basically, states address human rights obligations as asserted by the UN charter, the UDHR, and other voluntary commitments it has made, such as ratification of human rights conventions. After the report is accepted, each state has four years to implement the recommendations of the HRC (Universal Periodic Review, 2010).

Whereas traditionally educators and activists stressed documents (certainly an important endeavour), the webcasting of the open debates and the UPR – and, at the time of writing, talk of broadcasting other aspects of this institutional package – make this machinery an excellent means to promote discussion and spark debate, so fundamental to values formation. Presently, UPR, and other UN webcasts can be found on the internet at: http://www.humanrightsculture.org/Links.html. It is important for social workers to be aware of ongoing technological developments here.

The Advisory Committee

Composed of 18 experts whose mandate is to interact with states and civil society, this committee serves largely as a think-tank and focuses mainly on research-based evidence concerning human rights violations globally. The HRC charges this committee with the responsibility of prioritising human rights issues that need addressing, without relinquishing the interdependency and indivisibility of human rights. Recently, its main thematic issues were human rights training and education, the right to food, missing persons, and leprosy related discrimination.

A preliminary study, for example, on the right to food on 22 February 2010 acknowledged the 2004 study of the Special

Rapporteur on the Right to Food which warned about a high concentration of control by a few multinational firms in all sectors of the food chain; production, trade, processing, marketing, and retail. Asserting that the right to food is ultimately the right to be able to feed oneself with dignity, this latest report acknowledges that prior to the recent economic and food crisis, those living in extreme poverty decreased from 1.8 billion in 1990 to 1.4 billion in 2005. Yet, this decline was largely attributable to progress in China. In fact, more than half of the sub-Saharan Africa remains below the poverty line and Southern Asia still has 39 percent of its population living in extreme poverty. Acknowledging the interrelatedness of hunger with the environment, it lamented global change and biofuels development, which will affect the four dimensions of food security: availability, accessibility, stability and utilisation (Advisory Committee, 2010). Although not noted in the report, India is the country of the world's first trillionaire.

The 1503 complaints procedure

The aim of this procedure is to address consistent patterns of gross and reliably attested human rights violations in any part of the world, where domestic remedies have been exhausted, and under any circumstance. This procedure is unique and widely accepted as effective due in large measure to its confidential nature. Communications, the preferred parlance of the working groups of this committee, must *inter alia* not be politically motivated; must have factual description of the violations, not based exclusively on the mass media; and must not contain abusive language.

Since its inception in 1972 it has examined situations in at least 86 countries, roughly 27 in Africa; 27 in Asia; 16 in Latin America; 10 in Eastern Europe; and 6 in Western Europe (Steiner et al., 2007). Basically, this procedure is shrouded in secrecy. One knows only of countries that are before these working groups, but not the issues. However, it is possible to guess; for example, in the instance of Latin America, this procedure may have played a dominant role in resolving some of its 'dirty wars' of the late 1970s.

Treaty-based mechanisms

Technically, these mechanisms are not part of the deliberations of the HRC. Yet, they are extremely important because they can show a country's commitment to human rights principles, as defined by various conventions that have the status of a treaty as mentioned briefly earlier in this chapter. As in research, where one triangulates the data to get at it from various ways, these treaty-based mechanisms are another way to creatively engage in dialogue with governments to express positive aspects of a country's functioning, yet express some concerns in open forum.

Treaties are the outcome of the collective wisdom of governments and civil society, posing strong obligations upon governments. Signing a treaty signifies a government's willingness to consider it for ratification. Once ratified, it ought to become law for that country. One can easily see here how the 'mobilisation of shame' may urge a country to ratify a document. The US, for example, apart from Somalia (which currently doesn't have the governmental capacity for ratification) is the only country in the world not to ratify the Convention on the Rights of the Child (CRC), in part because it feels that the family, not government, has the duty to take up the obligations in relation to economic well-being, health, education and special needs involved in raising children (Fellmeth, 2002). In the US, roughly 20% of children live in poverty.

On occasion, NGOs submit shadow reports in parallel with or in response to government reports. One example is the report *Racial Injustice and Crimes Against Humanity in Alaska* (Barnes, 2008) by the Indigenous Peoples and Nations Coalition. It cited the 1955 Tee-Hit-Ton decision of the US Supreme

Court (348 US 272), which asserted that Alaska was for the settlement of the white race. It also cited a 'hole in impunity' (Barnes, 2008: 20) for all American Indians, Alaska Native, and Kanaka Maoli Hawaiians. In 2006 the treaty-based human rights committee for CERD called upon the US to reconcile the Tee-Hit-Ton decision and asked for a formal apology to the Indigenous Peoples of Hawaii. Another shadow report was by Mind Freedom and Law Project International (Minkowitz et al., 2006) on *Forced Drugging, Electroshock, and Mental Health Screening of Children*. It questioned why recently trained child psychiatrists prescribe psychotropic drugs to 9 out of 10 children without active and appropriate informed consent; identified mass screening for emotional and behavioural issues as questionable; and found that the administration of electroshock occurred twice as often for women as for men. In part, these concerns were in response to the *Guiding Principles for the Protection of Persons with Mental Illness* and the *Convention on People with Disabilities* (CPD).

REGIONAL INSTITUTIONAL ARRANGEMENTS

Often referred to as human rights 'regimes', the most notable are the Council of Europe; the Organisation of American States (OAS); the African Union (AU); and (currently in formation) the Association of South Eastern Asian Nations (ASEAN). Europe, perhaps because of centuries of conflict and wars waged on its landscape, has ostensibly the most developed system of human rights laws and enforcement mechanisms, through its CE, which monitors the implementation of the *European Convention of Human Rights* (1950). Most noteworthy is the *European Social Charter* (adopted in 1961 and revised in 1996) which strongly supports an extensive array of economic, social, and cultural rights pertaining to, for example, safe and healthy working conditions; dignity at work; vocational guidance; equal opportunities and equal treatment for all; and protections against poverty, viewed largely in Europe as social exclusion from participation in policy formation and implementation. It also has its own monitoring procedures (Winkler, 2006), but like the UN, such procedures are ultimately only valuable if supported by public sentiment. Given a long history in Europe of commitments to health care, cultural development, and education, there appears a strong consensus to promote and defend human rights as defined by the Charter.

The most noteworthy document of the OAS is the *American Convention on Human Rights* (1969) with its *Protocol on Human Rights in the Area of Economic, Social, and Cultural Rights* (Protocol of San Salvador, 1988). It strongly emphasises family protection measures, such as special care and assistance for parents before and after childbirth; adequate nutrition for children; and special programmes of family training to help create a stable and positive environment for children to develop with values of understanding, solidarity, respect, and responsibility. The Inter-American Commission on Human Rights is responsible for enforcing that document. For the most part, however, the general populace in the Americas is unaware of the initiatives of the OAS (Wronka, 2008).

The AU has at its heart the *African Charter on Human and Peoples' Rights* (the Banjul Charter, 1986). As a legacy of the horrors of the transatlantic slave trade, this document appears to emphasise solidarity rights, with the unquestionable right to self-determination. Thus, it focuses on the rights of colonised and oppressed people to free themselves from the bonds of domination, which include foreign exploitation by international monopolies, by resorting to any means recognised by the international community. AU is responsible for enforcing the African Charter in the general style of negotiation inherent in African culture. Rampant extreme poverty appears to have prevented the general populace from learning about those documents (Wronka, 2008).

FROM THE GLOBAL TO THE EVERYDAY LIFE

Human rights, which represent a crystallisation of values, and the documents and machinery to assist in their implementation, are only as good as the public will to actualise them. As with the events of 9/11 in New York and natural disasters of increasing frequency (such as tsunamis in the South Pacific and the earthquakes in Japan, India, Kashmir, Chile, and Haiti), the world can definitively decide to step up to help those in need. The human condition moves toward altruism in times of emergency; we need to become aware that overcoming class, caste, religion, national origin or other status has similar urgency. The time is now for what social activist Dorothy Day called a 'revolution of the heart' (Day, 2010).

In eradicating social and individual malaises, social work, particularly Advanced Generalist Practice (in the US), often adheres to multipronged levels of intervention (Gil, 1998). Further described as the 'meta-macro' (global); macro (whole population); mezzo (at risk); micro (clinical); and 'meta-micro' (everyday life), these interventions (Wronka, 2008) can get much sustenance from human rights principles. For example, social workers can engage in activities that might consist of urging governments to ratify and implement conventions and the writing of shadow reports; ensuring that administrative and clinical policies and practices adhere to internationally accepted criteria; and, above all, incorporating these values into our everyday lives.

The implications of human rights documents and machinery may seem daunting, especially given the intricacies such as narrow definitions of the problem, hypocrisy of governments, the sanitisation of oppression, and cultural relativism (see Wronka, 2008). Governments, for instance, may lambaste others for violations, while ignoring their own: simply put, cultures do things differently. However, creating a human rights culture requires vision, courage, peace, humility and everlasting love, as eloquently enunciated by the great spiritual leader of the Lakota Sioux, Crazy Horse. Finally, as the late Mother Theresa often reminded us, we must 'Do good anyway'. If social work is true to its mission for social justice and social change, human rights can expand our symbolic consciousness (Gil, 1998), from a more parochial zeitgeist into a truly global consciousness, improving the quality of life for every person, everywhere.

The next section elaborates upon human rights as historically fundamental to social work calling for substantive inclusion of this powerful idea into the curriculum.

HUMAN RIGHTS AS A REGULATORY CONCEPT FOR CURRICULA BUILDING FOR SOCIAL WORK THEORY AND PRACTICE

Historical documents legitimising the human rights approach in social work

Human rights are not a completely new topic for social work. For example, Jane Addams, in *A New Consciousness and an Ancient Evil* (1912), writes about prostitution not as a moral issue, but as a global socio-economic enterprise for organised slavery, referring also to the origin of human rights and other struggles to eradicate slavery in the US and advocating for individual freedom in general. Many social workers also struggled for women's and social rights at a national level in the early 20th century. Defining war as the violation of every human right, the organised protest against World War I at the Women's Congress of The Hague (1915), presided by Jane Addams, was another international milestone (Addams et al., 1916). In England, Eglantine Jebb drafted a *Convention of Children's Rights* which the League of Nations endorsed in 1924, a forerunner to the UN's *Convention on Children's Rights* (CRC) ratified in 1989. Also, the theme of the International Conference on Social Welfare (1968) in Helsinki was 'Social Welfare and Human Rights'. In the Proceedings its president Eugen Pusic stated:

> If there is one basic value premise for all the professions in the field of welfare it is the affirmation of human rights. And if there is one major complex of technical problems common to all the sectors of the field – from casework to social security and from delinquency to rehabilitation – it is the question of how to implement, protect, and make real their human rights in the everyday life of people under stress. (Pusic, 1969: v–vi)

In 1992 (in preparation for the UN World Conference on Human Rights in Vienna and the Decade of Human Rights Education which began in 1995), a manual appeared, entitled *Human Rights and Social Work*. This was a cooperative effort between the UN Centre in Geneva, IFSW and IASSW. Roughly Ten years later IFSW published *Social Work and the Rights of the Child – a Professional Training Manual on the UN Convention* (2002). At the turn of the 21st century, IFSW and IASSW presented the consensual "International Definition of the Social Work Profession"; and subsequently agreed upon a statement about "Ethics in Social Work" and "Global Standards for the Education and Training of the Social Work Profession". These three documents, referring all to human rights, were collected – in a supplement to the journal *International Social Work* (2007). The actual definition of social work is:

> The social work profession promotes social change, problem solving in human relationships and the empowerment and liberation of people to enhance well-being. Utilising theories of human behaviour and social systems, social work intervenes at the points where people interact with their environments. Principles of human rights and social justice are fundamental to social work.

Furthermore, but not exhaustively, the Committee of Ministers of the European Council made recommendations to the member states 'to promote the inclusion of obligatory human rights courses in social work curricula and ensure in particular their implementation in social work practice' (CE, 2001 and 2003). The newest document, conceived by IFSW's European region, is about Standards in *Social Work Practice Meeting Human Rights* (IFSW, 2010 – www.ifsw.org/europe).

Taking seriously this obvious importance of human rights to the profession, it does not seem enough to only add some lectures, seminars or practice competences about UN issues or regional organisations to the bachelor's, master's or doctoral curricula in social work. It appears necessary to integrate this powerful idea of human rights into the construction of curricula which would include the necessary knowledge, values and skills; and to create a human rights culture in education and practice, a viable challenge for the 21st century and beyond.

Human rights as knowledge, values and skills for professional action

An action-oriented scientific human discipline must answer the following epistemological questions that lead to professional competencies: (1) What human rights violations can be identified? (2) how can one explain them? (3) what is the meaning of human dignity as it pertains to human rights, arguably its ethical basis? (4) is it possible to avoid Western colonialism in the name of the universality of human rights? (5) what role do human rights play for the professional mandate and the tasks of social work? and (6) what skills, procedures, and methods are needed to implement human rights effectively?

Human rights violations as an additional dimension of the object base and diagnostic categories of social work

Historically and culturally, human rights, the development of their philosophical, religious and ethical base as well as their political-revolutionary social movements are answers to grave experiences of injustice, extreme physical harm, and the powerlessness of individuals, groups and social minorities to act against such injustices. Human rights make us conscious of what human beings are capable of doing to each other, not only within social interactions pertaining to fear, pain, humiliation, social exclusion, torture, psychological destruction till to physical extermination; but also as structural violence through norms and social rules which allow discrimination and privileges, the tyranny of exploitation, cultural colonisation, classism, sexism and racism; and as unfair procedures where responsibility is diffused, if not entirely denied (Galtung, 1975), as asserted in the Nuremburg trials.

Three aspects of diagnoses here are of special relevance and will be examined further: first, the fact that vulnerability is a main characteristic of social work clients; second, the complex relationship between victims and victimisers; and third, economic, social and cultural rights as a special focus of social work.

Vulnerability as a main characteristic social work clients

The UN defines 'vulnerability' in part as follows: 'People … are vulnerable if there is loss or limitation of opportunities to take part in the normal life of the community on an equal level owing to physical or social barriers' (UN, 2003).

It is an interesting coincidence that the situations of individuals covered by the UN documents discussed earlier are almost identical with the situations and problems of those who are clients of social work, namely people who are unemployed or in poverty; women; migrants and their families; political refugees; and exploited children. They and other groups, are victims of racism, religious or ideological/political intolerance, persecution, homo/xenophobia, sometimes resulting in such atrocities as organised trafficking and degrading, arbitrary and despotic procedures (including, but not limited to, coerced prostitution, slavery, and torture).

Vulnerable groups are especially likely to be cast as scapegoats for experienced or feared structural threats (downward social mobility) and to be the subjects of disrespect and intolerance. Yet, prejudice must already exist against particular individuals or groups before scapegoating commences. Individuals in question must appear too weak to fight back successfully when attacked and society must sanction (positively) the scapegoating through its own institutional structures (Saenger, 1953, in Blumenfeld and Raymond, 2003: 24). Thus, the discipline of social work must consider systematic research concerning these vulnerable groups, their objective situation, as well as their subjective interpretation of it, and their attempts to deal with such injustices in everyday life.

The complex relationship between victims and victimisers

The difference between victims and offenders is not always clear-cut. Victims of violence in childhood may become offenders as adults and parents. It is also not always clear whether welfare agencies and social workers are actually implementing their official humanistic philosophy and ethical codes for the well-being of their clients. Agencies can get instrumentalised by political/state or economic powers, by, for example, implementing fascist, apartheid, authoritarian, or today's neoliberal ideology. This holds also for so-called faith-based agencies, which may demonstrate repressive family moral ethics, homophobic attitudes or abuse of power (e.g. as in cases of sexual abuse of children by priests). A human rights orientation would require an impartial assessment, that does not adhere to any loyalties towards, for example, a 'holy order' or particular political regimes: and human needs must not be commodified and subordinated to structural violence (see 'the triple mandate' below).

Economic, social and cultural rights as a special focus of social work assessment

Many (if not most) social work clients are economically disadvantaged and deprived of social rights (Staub-Bernasconi, 2007). With its focus on social rights, social work has to struggle with the difficulty that the violation of liberty and democratic rights, often referred to as civil and political rights (as discussed above), most often mobilise international public coalitions of NGOs (e.g. Amnesty International), journalists and individual activists. However, there is almost no lobby for the world-wide violation of social rights (Pogge, 2008; Kahn, 2009; Staub-Bernasconi, 2007; Steiner and Alston, 2007:237–322). It is unfortunate also that, lacking worker protection (as enunciated in human rights documents), social workers themselves may play a part in violations, for example, when they must cut the necessary grants to zero because of mostly minor failures of cooperation, or, after a specified duration for welfare funding. Yet, according to their triple mandate, they should be able to refuse these political claims (see later).

Finally, it is important to be aware that a human rights orientation doesn't replace, but is complementary to, the assessment process. To avoid inflating the idea of human rights to a moral guillotine, it is necessary to develop scales for their assessment, defining minor, middle, and grave violations.

Human rights and the basic scientific discipline of social work

There are several aspects to consider here. First, there is a lot of social research about victims of human rights violations. They give answers to the question: What are the psychological, social/socioeconomic and cultural explanations for becoming a victim (Adams et al. 2000)? But it is necessary, also, to have knowledge about the individual actor who can become an exploiter; rapist; oppressor; dictator; torturer; a trafficker of refugees, women, and children; or a devotedly obeying functionary, employee, or soldier. What is their biography? What were the decisive moments for such a 'career' and what kind of experiences might change their thinking and behaviour for the better? Second, what are the processes of building a power structure with social rules which produce structural violence, e.g. 'legalised' discrimination, exploitation etc. (Galtung, 1975; Staub-Bernasconi, 2010a)? Third, what determines the development and institutionalisation of cultural/religious beliefs, constitutional laws/rules such as apartheid or the Nurnberg Laws of Nazi Germany which legitimate discrimination, oppression, persecution and even extermination? Fourth, what are the theories and images of human beings and society which can be inhuman, when implemented? Such theories can include not only the extreme, fatal case of eugenics and racism in ethnology, psychiatry and social work (Kappeler, 2000), but also some psychological theories that define individuals as purely incentive driven, egocentric utilitarian human beings, pursuing uniquely economic interests. An alternative to this would be individuals with biological, psychological, social, cultural, including spiritual needs. This means with a broad potential of feelings and awareness, learning, judging and – last but not least – having moral capabilities and social competencies that can be cooperative as well as conflictive in social relationships. Fifth, what are the images and theories of society which reduce society to a totalising 'social body', with 'clashes' between civilisations and 'holistic cultures' where the individual is only a puppet of society or culture. All these theoretical approaches are, in a mild version, incomplete and reductionist, but in a strong version disastrous, when applied for diagnostic, explanatory, social policy and intervention purposes.

Human dignity as 'meta-value' for human rights and practice

The value base of human rights (since World War II) refers to human dignity as meta-value (Pollmann, 2010). This holds also for social work ethical codes. One can distinguish two different traditions here: one relies on a heteronomous concept of a transcendental dowry and law as an objective value which is due to a pre-factual existence given by God or nature. The 'utopian' Marxism has replaced the revelation of the divine laws with the deterministic (economic) laws of history (Tiedemann, 2006: 58). In contrast to this thinking there is the autonomous concept of human dignity. Kant, as its most prominent representative, postulated the moral autonomy of human beings which leads to the claim to institutionalise this autonomy as a general freedom pertaining to rights and equality-based participation in defining legislation ('gleichberechtigte republikanische Mitgesetzgebung') (Bielefeldt, 1998: 15).

According to Tiedemann (2006) the autonomous foundations cannot be reconciled with the heteronomous ones. Yet, it is possible to consider the unconditional respect for human dignity as a secularisation of the idea of the unconditional acceptance of women and men by God. And this unconditionality holds also for the respect, protection and fulfillment of human rights. It is important to remember, however, that human rights had to be fought for against the church, leaving a historical trail of injustice and blood. Still today, some churches stand for human rights in public, but violate them internally according to their own moral traditions and laws. But, referring to the Kantian conception of human dignity: what about human beings who do not (yet) have (or may have lost) the capacity for critical reflection and reasoning, such as little children, individuals with mental illnesses or comatose patients? Margalit (1996: 23) defines human dignity therefore as unconditional respect in interactions as well as being institutionalised in fair social rules

of societal power-structures which guarantee this respect.

In sum, none of the definitions of human dignity can be called truly universal. This has led different authors to refer to human needs shared by all human beings as the only universal base for the justification of the universality of human rights which can escape the reproach of Western colonialism (Nussbaum, 2002; Galtung, 1974; Pogge, 2008; Obrecht, 2007; Staub-Bernasconi, 2010). This joins a broad consensual theoretical tradition of social work which claims the crucial importance of human needs (Ife, 2001; Healy, 2001; Reichert, 2003, 2007; Wronka, 2008; Staub-Bernasconi, 1995, 2008, 2010a,b).

Yet, it is important to differentiate between needs which are universal and the forms and means of their satisfaction, their transformation into wishes, goals and interests are influenced by the context: cultural values, socialisation norms, accessible socio-economic resources etc (Staub-Bernasconi 2010b, 2011). Thus human rights cannot be the property of western/occidental or oriental/asiatic societies, philosophies or religions, because they really mean all human beings as human beings (Bielefeldt, 1998, 2007) without discrimination. And tolerance according to this theoretical argumentation ends where cultural/religious values, norms and laws violate the satisfaction of universal human needs, requiring protection through human rights policies and practices.

Dilemmas for social work implementing human rights

It is a fallacy that implementation of human rights can be uncontested. For instance, the right to social justice requires sacrifices from those who have more than others and thus restricts their right for land-property, capital or other scarce resources. In the case of divorce or children placed in a foster family because of mentally ill or abusing parents, one has to respect the rights of both parties which are not always compatible (Prior, 2003). Another dilemma may be the right to socio-economic development versus environmental protection.

Other dilemmas stem from the different continental declarations of human rights, such as the African Banjul, Islamic or Asian Charters. They all agree first on the universal and indivisible character of human rights, but then claim the primacy of their own cultural values which means that the values of the state philosophy (e.g. stability and harmony or divine laws) and/or the family (its cultural or religious morality) take precedence in the case of conflicts over the universal claims of the UN Charter and human rights documents in general. The 'West' or 'North' has to understand that these contextual interpretations of human rights are more than a plausible reaction to the colonial history of all of these countries by the North, its economic, military and cultural hegemony, its double-morality and now its neoliberal colonialism. A prominent, actual example is the coercion of countries of the global South to open their borders to 'free' trade by the World Trade Organisation while the Northern ones close them by demanding unacceptable import taxation. Or witness the establishment of exploitative and repressive management systems in some world factories in Asia (e.g. by corporations such as Dell, Apple, Hewlett Packard) while the headquarters sit mainly in the 'North', taking their freedom and civil rights for granted (Ngai and Hulin, 2010).

From the 'double-mandate' to the 'professional triple mandate' of social work

An important consequence of these considerations is the reformulation of the mandate of social work. Social work, as a profession ethically bound by human rights, no longer simply has the commonly recognised double mandate of care and control, given by the agency and the client(s). It must add a third mandate given by the profession itself with the following components: first, a scientific description and explanation base for interventions, methods and policies, which can solve or prevent social problems, and second, an ethical base, i.e. a professional code of ethics, which, as was shown above, contains human rights and social justice as main guidelines (Staub-Bernasconi, 2010a: 198ff.) This scientifically and ethically based third mandate constitutes the relative autonomy of each helping profession and, if necessary, allows for the modification or refusal of illegitimate claims and mandates from society, social agencies and clients. In states without functioning social legislation, in failed or corrupt states, it can become the base for the formulation of a mandate of its own. Cases in point are the women of Hull House; the feminist movement for shelters for victims of violence; the transformation of the suffering of Indigenous Peoples, blacks, asylum seekers, landless people into issues; social legislation and freedom rights; but also the activities of social workers in the African National Congress (ANC) during apartheid. Last but not least, the third mandate is also a base for the critical questioning of local, national/constitutional and international laws. Are they (only) legal or/and also legitimate? (Habermas 1996, Wronka, 1998).

Ultimately, the triple mandate could move critical or radical social work from its marginal position into the centre of social work. It may hopefully end the ceaseless debate, about whether the profession has to be political *or* professional; whether it must solve problems of individuals *or* should work for social/structural change, so that there is no longer an 'either/or' divide, but rather a skilful combination of both (Lavalette and Ferguson, 2007). Yet, the implementation of the third mandate is not without risks for individuals. It can mean the end of a career; the loss of one's job with no possibility of getting a new post; living with cyber and other threats in this technological age; even physical attacks against one's person and/or loved ones and collaborators; imprisonment or death.

Actors, procedures and methods

Historically the state is the target for claims about human rights: it has the duty to respect, to protect and to fulfil them by providing the necessary resources. And it has to implement them unconditionally – a norm which isn't fulfilled especially in relation to social rights. Other, more recent targets are economic organisations with enormous power, religious organisations, etc. Yet, a human rights orientation can't develop if there are no well-informed, human rights-educated citizens and professionals who are competent to build up multiple networks and political pressure groups promoting concerted action between actors on the macro, mezzo, and micro levels using the different UN instruments (Wronka, 2008: 114–20).

The particular professional roles, activities and methods for social workers are: (1) *empowerment* of individuals and groups, such as persons with disabilities, internally or externally displaced persons or communities, inhabitants of favelas and ghettos, to combat discriminatory practice and fight for education, meaningful and gainful employment and a basic worldwide income (Freire 1974; Cox and Pawar, 2006; Pogge, 2008); (2) *advocacy* for clients who aren't able to speak for themselves, such as children who have been trafficked or abused; child soldiers; patients; undocumented or irregular immigrants; and prisoners. This would necessitate the initiation of *organisational advocacy* by social movements, social agencies, NGOs and academia (Taylor, 1987; Briskman, 2010); (3) *capability-training* by means of education, mediation and the use of resources, particularly information dissemination (Montada and Kals, 2001), (4) public consciousness-raising, campaigning, lobbying – based on effective knowledge about human rights documents and international implementation procedures, like the Universal

Periodic Review or individual complaints etc. (Prasad, 2011). All this should be accompanied by social work research and action for social justice (Humphries, 2008), constructed from the pillars of human rights.

CONCLUSION

Social work in the 21st century and beyond can and should be a part of a worldwide community, consisting of billions of individuals, groups, networks, organisations on the local, national, and inter-/transnational level committed to a Global Agenda of Engagement as called for in part by Article 28 of the *Universal Declaration of Human Rights*: 'Everyone is entitled to a social and international order in which the rights and freedoms set forth in this Declaration can be fully realized'.

REFERENCES

Adams, M., Blumenfeld, W.J., Castaneda, R., Hackman, H.W., Peters, M.L. and Zúñiga, X. (eds) (2000) *Readings for Diversity and Social Justice. An Anthology on Racism, Anti-Semitism, Sexism, Heterosexism, Ableism, and Classism.* London: Routledge.

Addams, J. (1912) *A New Consciousness and an Ancient Evil.* New York: Macmillan.

Addams, J., Balch, E.G. and Hamilton, A. (1916) *Women at The Hague. The International Congress of Women and its Results.* New York: Macmillan.

Advisory Committee, (2010) *Preliminary Study on Discrimination in the Context of the Right to Food.* Available at: www2.ohchr.org/english/bodies/hrcouncil/advisorycommittee/right_to_food.htm accessed 21 July 2010.

Alinsky, S. (1969) *Reveille for Radicals.* New York: Vintage.

Alinsky, Saul D. (1971) *Rules for Radicals. A Pragmatic Primer for Realistic Radicals.* New York: Random House.

Barnes, R. (2008) *Report of the Indigenous Peoples and Nations Coalition: Racial Injustice and Crimes Against Humanity in Alaska: Article 15 of CERD Urgent Action.* Available from: angull2002@yahoo.com

Bielefeldt, H. (1998) *Philosophie der Menschenrechte.* Darmstadt: Primus.

Bielefeldt, H. (2007) *Menschenrechte in der Einwanderungsgesellschaft – Plädoyer für einen aufgeklärten Multikulturalismus*, Transcript, Bielefeld.

Briskman, L. (2010) *Recasting Social Work: Human Rights and Political Activism*, Eileen Younghusband Lecture, World Conference of IASSW, Durban. Unpublished Manuscript, Curtin University. Perth, Australia.

Council of Europe (CE). (2001) *Recommendation Rec(2001)1 of the Committee of Ministers to Member States on Social Workers. Adopted by the Committee of Ministers on 17 January 2001 at the 737th meeting of the Ministers' Deputies.* https://wcd.coe.int/wcd/ViewDoc.jsp?id=180283&Lang=en.

Cox, D. and Pawar, M. (2006) *International Social Work. Issues, Strategies and Programs*. London/UK: Sage.

Day, D. (2010) *Select Writings of Dorothy Day*. Retrieved from: http://www.catholicworker.org/dorothyday/, accessed 23 July 2010.

Fellmeth, R. (2002) *Civil Rights and Remedies: How the US Legal System Affects Children*. Atlanta, GA: Clarity.

Freire, P. (1974) *Education: The Practice of Freedom*. London: Writers and Readers.

Galtung, J. (1975) *Strukturelle Gewalt. Beiträge zur Friedens- und Konfliktforschung*. Hamburg: Reinbeck.

Galtung, J. (1994) *Menschenrechte – anders gesehen*. Frankfurt: Suhrkamp.

Gil, D. (1998) *Confronting Social Injustice: Concepts and Strategies for Social Workers*. New York: Columbia University Press.

Global Agenda for Social Work and Social Development (2010) Retrieved from: http://www.globalsocialagenda.org/, accessed 29 March 2011.

Habermas, J. (1996) *Between Facts and Norms*. Cambridge/Mass: MIT Press.

Healy, L.M. (2001) *International Social Work*. New York: Oxford University Press.

Humphries, B. (2008) *Social Work Research for Social Justice*. Hampshire, Palgrave.

Ife, J. (2001) *Human Rights and Social Work. Towards Rights-Based Practice*. Cambridge: Cambridge University Press.

IFSW (International Federation of Social Workers) (2002) *Joint IFSW/IASSW Human Rights Commission: IFSW General Meeting*. Geneva, Switzerland, 10–12 July 2002. http://www.ifsw.org/p38000256.html.

IFSW (International Federation of Social Workers) (2010) *Standards in Social Work Practice Meeting Human Rights*. Berlin: International Federation of Social Workers European Region.

Kahn, I. (2009) *The Unheard Truth. Poverty and Human Rights*. London/New York: Norton.

Kappeler, M. (2000) *Der schreckliche Traum vom vollkommenen Menschen. Rassenhygiene und Eugenik in der Sozialen Arbeit*. Marburg: Schüren, Presseverlag.

Lavalette, M. and Ferguson, I. (eds) (2007) *International Social Work and the Radical Tradition*. Birmingham: Venture Press.

Margalit, A. (1996) *The Decent Society*. Cambridge, MA: Harvard University Press.

Minkowitz, T., Galves, A., Kovary, M. and Remba, E. (2006) *Alternative Report on Forced Drugging, Forced Electroshock, and Mental Health Screening of Children*, cited in Wronka J. (2008).

Montada, L. and Kals, E. (2001) *Mediation*. Weinheim/Basel: Beltz.

Ngai, P. and Hulin, L. (2010) 'Unfinished proletarization: self, anger, and class – Action among the second generation of peasant-workers in present-day China, In *Modern China*, XX(X) 1–17, London: Sage. pp. 1–24.

Nussbaum, M. (2011) *Creating Capabilities. The Human Development Approach*. Cambridge: Harvard University Press.

Obrecht, W. (2007) *Umrisse einer biopsychosozialen Theorie menschlicher Bedürfnisse*. Wien: Typoscript MBA der Wirtschaftsuniversität Wien.

Pogge, T. (2008) 'Das Recht auf ein Existenzminimum', in I. Richter (ed.), *Transnationale Menschenrechte. Schritte zu einer weltweiten Verwirklichung der Menschenrechte*. Opladen: Barbara Budrich. pp. 121–38. *World Poverty and Human Rights: Cosmopolitan Responsibilities and Reform*, Cambridge, Policy Press.

Pollmann, A. (2010) 'Menschenwürde und Barbarei. Zu den Folgen eines gewaltsamen Umbruchs in der Geschichte der Menschenrechte', *Journal for Human Rights*, 1: 26–45.

Prasad, N. (2011) *Mit Recht gegen Gewalt. Die UN-Menschenrechte und ihre Bedeutung für die Soziale Arbeit*. Ein Handbuch für die Praxis, Opladen & Farmington Hills/MI: Barbara Budrich.

Prior, P.M. (2003) 'Removing children from the care of adults with diagnosed mental illnesses – a clash of human rights?', *European Journal of Social Work*, 2: 179–90.

Pusic, E. (1969) 'Foreword', in Council of Social Welfare, *Social Welfare and Human Rights, Proceedings of the XIVth International Conference on Social Welfare*, Helsinki, Finland, August 1968. pp: v–vii.

Reichert, E. (2003) *Social Work and Human Rights*, New York: Columbia University Press.

Reichert, E. (ed.) (2012) *Challenges in Human Rights. A Social Work Perspective.* 2nd edn. New York: Columbia University Press.

Roosevelt, E. (1958) *Remarks by Eleanor Roosevelt on presentation of booklet In Your Hands to the UN Commission on Human Rights.* Retrieved from: http://quotationsbook.com/quote/45532/, accessed 21 July 2010.

Saenger, Gerhart (2000) The Social Psychology of Prejudice, In: Blumenfeld, W.J. and Raymond, D. (2000) 'Prejudice and discrimination', in M. Adams, W.J. Blumenfeld, R. Castaneda, H.W. (eds), *Readings for Diversity and Social Justice. An Anthology on Racism, Anti-Semitism, Sexism, Heterosexism, Ableism, and Classism.* London: Routledge. pp. 21–30.

Staub-Bernasconi, S. (1995) 'Das fachliche Selbstverständnis Sozialer Arbeit – Wege aus der Bescheidenheit. Soziale Arbeit als "Human Rights Profession"', in W.R. Wendt (ed.) *Soziale Arbeit im Wandel ihres Selbstverständnisses: Profession und Identität.* Freiburg: Lambertus, i.Br. pp. 57–80.

Staub-Bernasconi, S. (2007) 'Economic and social rights: the neglected human rights', in E. Reichert (ed.), *Challenges in Human Rights. A Social Work Perspective.* New York: Columbia University Press. pp. 128–61.

Staub-Bernasconi, S. (2008) 'Soziale Arbeit und Menschenrechte – Oder: Was haben Menschenrechte in der Sozialen Arbeit zu suchen?', *Widersprüche*, 107: 9–32.

Staub-Bernasconi, S. (2010a) *Soziale Arbeit als Handlungswissenschaft.* 2nd edn. Bern/Stuttgart/Wien: UTB/Haupt.

Staub-Bernasconi, S. (2010b) 'Human rights and social work – philosophical and ethical reflections about a possible dialogue between East Asia and the West', *Journal of Ethics and Social Welfare*, 5(4): 331–47.

Staub-Bernasconi, S. (2011) *Human Rights and Social Work – Philosophical and Ethical Reflections About a Possible Dialogue Between East Asia And The West*, Journal of Ethics and Social Welfare, Vol. 5, No. 4, pp. 331–347.

Steiner, H., Alston, P. and Goodman, R. (2007). *International Human Rights in Context: Law, Politics, Morals.* 3rd edn. New York: Oxford University Press.

Taylor, E.D. (1987) *From Issue to Action. An Advocacy Program Model.* Lancaster/USA: Family and Children's Service.

Tiedemann, P. (2006) *Was ist Menschenwürde?* Darmstadt: Wissenschaftliche Buchgesellschaft.

UN (United Nations) (2003) *Ad Hoc Committee on a Comprehensive and Integral International Convention on Protection and Promotion of the Rights and Dignity of Persons with Disabilities: Issues and Emerging Trends Related to the Advancement of Persons with Disabilitie*s. Report of the Secretary-General. New York, 16–27 June 2003. A/AC.265/2003/1, C.10.

UN High Commissioner for Human Rights. (2010) Retrieved from www.ohchr.org, accessed 21 July 2010.

UN Human Rights Council. (2010) Retrieved from: http://en.wikipedia.org/wiki/United_Nations_Human_Rights_Council, accessed 19 July 2010.

US Department of State Report on Human Rights Practices (1993) Washington, DC.

Universal Periodic Review Highlights. (2010) *Review of Sweden, May 7 afternoon session.* Retrieved from: http://www.ohchr.org/EN/HRBodies/UPR/Pages/Highlights7May2010pm.aspx, accessed 2 July 2010.

Universal Periodic Review. (2010) Retrieved from: www.upr-info.org, accessed 20 July 2010.

Weissbrodt, D., Fitzpatrick, J., Newman, F., Hoffman, M. and Rumsey, M. (2001). *International Human Rights: Law, Policy, and Process.* Cincinnati, OH: Anderson.

Winkler, G. (2006) *The Council of Europe.* New York: Springer.

World War II Casualties, Wikipedia. (2011). Retrieved from: http://en.wikipedia.org/wiki/World_War_II_casualties, accessed 29 March 2011.

Wronka, J. (1998). *Human Rights and Social Policy in the 21st Century: a History of the Idea of Human Rights and Comparison of the United Nations Universal Declaration of Human Rights with United States Federal and State Constitutions*, rev. edn. Lanham, MD: University Press of America.

Wronka, J. (2008). *Human Rights and Social Justice: Social Action and Service for the Helping and Health Professions.* Available at: www.humanrightsculture.org. Thousand Oaks, CA: Sage.

Wronka, J. (2010, 2012). *Statement by the International Association of Schools of Social Work before the 13th Session of the Human Rights Council.* Available at: www.humanrightsculture.org.

5

Poverty, Development and Social Justice

Murli Desai and John Solas

INTRODUCTION

The commentary on the international definition of social work states that 'In solidarity with those who are disadvantaged, the profession strives to alleviate poverty and to liberate vulnerable and oppressed people in order to promote social inclusion.' (International Federation of Social Workers (IFSW) and International Association of Schools of Social Work (IASSW), 2000; see Appendix 1). The *Global Standards for the Education and Training of the Social Work Profession* adopted in 2004 by the IFSW and IASSW state that a core purpose of social work is to 'Engage in social and political action to impact social policy and economic development, and to effect change by critiquing and eliminating inequalities'. The domain of social work in this document includes 'A critical understanding of how socio-structural inadequacies, discrimination, oppression, and social, political and economic injustices impact human functioning and development at all levels, including the global' (IFSW and IASSW, 2004; see Appendix 3).

Commensurate with these commitments is the profession's pursuit of social justice. IFSW's *Code of Ethics* (1999) (also adopted by the IASSW in 2004) states that 'social workers have a responsibility to promote social justice, in relation to society generally, and in relation to the people with whom they work' (IFSW, 2005: 2; see Appendix 2). This means challenging negative discrimination[1] on the basis of characteristics such as ability, age, culture, sex, socioeconomic status, political opinions, racial or other physical characteristics, sexual orientation, or spiritual beliefs. It also means recognizing and respecting ethnic and cultural diversity; distributing resources equitably and according to need; challenging policies and practices which are oppressive, unfair or harmful; and working in solidarity towards an inclusive society (see Appendices 1, 2 and 3).

This chapter focuses on social work's engagement in social and political action to advance development, alleviate poverty and secure justice for all, especially vulnerable and oppressed people. The achievement of these aims requires a critical understanding of how socio-structural disadvantages that restrain human flourishing at local, regional and global levels are caused and counteracted. After a critical analysis of how poverty and social exclusion take place at the societal as well as global levels, and review of the international paradigm of economic development, the chapter examines the paradigm shift from economic to social development reflected in the United Nations (UN) decades of development and poverty eradication, through people-centred ideologies and social development policy directions. Progress made in human development and poverty eradication around the world is indicated through measures of social development. The chapter ends with the discussion of the integration of social justice ideals in the development discourse as an imperative for eradication of poverty and social exclusion in the world.

PERSPECTIVES ON POVERTY

Poverty is a social construct: its definition varies according to whoever formulates the definition (Rist, 2008: 230) and also according to time and place. The historical origins of state concern about poverty can be traced back to the Elizabethan Poor Law (England, 1601). According to this law, 'the poor' were helpless people with prolonged needs – 'orphans', 'the handicapped', the chronically ill and the 'feeble aged' (Leiby, 1987). Some were perceived as 'worthy' (of charitable relief) but others (able-bodied adults) were deemed 'unworthy', but both were considered responsible for their poverty. While the notions of 'worthy' or 'unworthy' have lingered on and resurfaced in different times and places in a variety of policy measures, this historical concept of poverty has been challenged and alternative explanations have been provided by critical thinkers.

A major challenge to the Elizabethan concept was provided by Karl Marx in his (19th century) theory of historical materialism.

This propounded that, depending on the mode of production, the social system contains a ruling class whose position is derived primarily from controlling the economic surplus (Newman, 2005). In the agricultural phase of society, the need for labour led to the practise of marriage, slavery and serfdom, institutionalising inequality and poverty. With the change from predominantly agricultural to industrial production, the capitalist class owns the means of production, distribution and exchange while working class people live by exchanging their socialised labour with the capital class for wages (Grusky and Takata, 1992).

More recent descriptions and explanations of poverty have been advanced in Brazil by Paulo Friere (1972) and by Amartya Sen from India (1999). Friere's early sharing of the life of poor people led him to identify the 'culture of silence' of the dispossessed: he saw ignorance and lethargy as the direct products of the system of economic, social and political domination, and the paternalism of which poor people are victims. Rather than being encouraged and equipped to know and respond to the realities of their world, people are kept 'submerged' in a situation in which critical awareness and response are practically impossible (Schaull, 1972). According to Freire (1972), self-deprecation is another characteristic of oppressed people, derived from their internalisation of the opinion of their oppressors. Sen (1999: 20–1) views poverty as a deprivation of basic capabilities, rather than just related to income, as reflected in premature mortality, significant undernourishment, persistent morbidity, widespread illiteracy and other disadvantages. Similarly, unemployment is not merely a deficiency of income that can be made up through state transfers: it is also a source of far-reaching effects on individual freedom, initiative and skills. Unemployment contributes to social exclusion of some groups and leads to losses of self-confidence and reliance, and diminishes psychological and physical health. This perspective concentrates on deprivations that are intrinsically important unlike low income which is only instrumentally important.

Post-modernist thinking has led to more complex understandings of the roots of poverty based on a multi-dimensional understanding of social stratification, related to other factors, e.g. race and gender, and not only class. In the Marxist analysis, property relations obscured ethnic ones, but now it is property that begins to seem derivative while ethnicity and gender seem to be more fundamental sources of stratification (Grusky and Takata, 1992). Prejudicing ideologies (e.g. ageism and ethnocentrism) justify role stereotypes, hierarchy, intolerance, and discrimination and, thereby, justify violence. These prejudicing ideologies have led to marginalisation of women, children, elderly, disabled, indigenous people, the non-white races, and other groups in poverty. The vulnerable groups are powerless with reference to control over resources due to the roles that they have historically performed, which are justified by the prejudicing ideologies of the dominant groups (Desai, 2002).

Most recently, the term 'social exclusion' has tended to displace 'poverty'. The term originated in Europe in about the last decade of the 20th century, and has been associated with a greater emphasis on spatial exclusion. It has been defined by the Department of International Development as:

> a process by which certain groups are systematically disadvantaged because they are discriminated against on the basis of their ethnicity, race, religion, sexual orientation, caste, descent, gender, age, disability, HIV status, migrant status or where they live. Discrimination occurs in public institutions, such as the legal system or education and health services, as well as social institutions like the household (DFID, 2005: 3).

Socially excluded people are often denied opportunities to increase their income and escape from poverty by their own efforts. So, even though the economy may grow and general income levels may rise, excluded people are likely to be left behind, and make up an increasing proportion of those who remain in poverty. Poverty reduction policies often fail to reach them unless they are specifically designed to do so. According to the *UN Report on the World's Social Situation* (2010), the concept of social exclusion contributes to an understanding of the nature of poverty and helps identify the causes of poverty that otherwise may have been neglected.

THE SOCIAL CONSTRUCTION OF UNDERDEVELOPMENT AND DEVELOPMENT

The focus on poverty at the global level has often been expressed as 'underdevelopment' and this is another social construction that has started a long journey in the field of international development.

'Development' meant different things to different people until after World War II in 1949, when the United States President, Harry Truman, stated that the fourth objective of his foreign policy was to make the benefits of that country's scientific advances and industrial progress available for the improvement and growth of 'underdeveloped' areas. According to Sachs (2010: xvii), it was the rising influence of the Soviet Union that forced Truman to come up with a vision of 'development' that would engage the loyalty of the decolonising countries in order to sustain the struggle against communism. Since then, the usage of the word 'development' for human societies was popularised to describe the process through which the former colonies were to be transformed into modern nations (from what their colonisers saw as backward, primitive and underdeveloped societies) (Reddock, 2000). In the 1950s, a new sub-discipline of 'development economics' provided a set of analytical and policy tools that responded to the political need for the development of the 'underdeveloped' countries, in the context of the post Second World War era, decolonisation and the Cold War. The development economists theorised simplistically about the stages of development that societies had to pass through to become 'developed' and coined the triad: Underdeveloped » Developing » Developed (Girvan, 2005).

Since then, Esteva (2010: 2) notes that billions of people ceased being what they were, in all their diversity, and were transmogrified into an inverted mirror of others' reality, in the terms of a homogenising and narrow minority. Rist (2008) argues that by defining 'underdevelopment' as a lack rather than the result of historical circumstances, the 'underdeveloped' were simply treated as poor without seeking the reasons for their destitution. He further observes that this new identity was accepted by those who headed the independent states, because it was a way of asserting their claim to benefit from the aid that was supposed to lead to 'development'. In gaining political independence, they forfeited their identity and economic autonomy, and were forced to travel the 'development path' mapped out for them by others.

In the 1950s and early 1960s, the work in development economics was complemented by political scientists and public administration theorists who addressed the difficulties involved in building democratic states and modern bureaucracies, and by anthropologists and sociologists concerned with tensions generated by the interaction between traditional and modern value and knowledge systems. The *modernisation theorists* assumed that these transitions would be relatively rapid and painless, as these societies imported Western capital, technology and organisational systems (Brett, 2009). They, too, developed a triad: Traditional » Transitional » Modern (Girvan, 2005). These theories implied a covertly Western-centred evolutionism insofar as they assumed that poor countries had stagnated on a relatively low level of development and could develop, or modernise, in the direction of a Western-type society. This development discourse was Eurocentric in the sense that it was not just the economies but also the indigenous people who had to be modernised, by adopting the values of the white race (Kennet, 2001).

Rahnema (2010) notes that the modern economy has reduced everyone to becoming the agent of an invisible national or world economy, geared only to producing things for whoever can pay for them. In most developing countries, neither the production of economic resources and commodities nor the extension of social services has ultimately served the poor. More often than not, both have resulted in further diminishing poor people's capacity to meet their real needs, which they used to do in the context of their vernacular livelihood. Aid, as an approach to poverty alleviation, only forces people in poverty to work for others rather than for themselves. Rist (2008) argues that it is in the nature of 'development' to produce inequality and exclusion as sacrifices are demanded of many to guarantee the prosperity of few.

Based on Marxist critique of Western capitalism for its explanations of Third World poverty, the *dependency theorists* turned modernisation theory upside down. They argued that the capitalist system benefited from a dependent, peripheral Third World and that the capitalist system was designed to perpetuate this dependency. They called for a critical attitude toward Western technology, and a commitment to Third World self-reliance. The dependency theorists argued that the perpetuation of these unequal relations is managed by a clientele class in the South that collaborates with the dominant capitalist class in the North. To overcome this, they called for the overthrow of this clientele class, an end to links with the North, and a focus on self-reliant development (Connelly et al., 2000).

Subsequently, *world systems theory* has gained importance in the analysis of (under-) development. According to Wallerstein, the world economy is constituted through one capitalist world system, consisting of countries falling into the core (the industrialised countries), the semi-periphery (the newly industrialised countries) and the periphery (agricultural export countries). He saw little prospect for Third World countries to exit the global system. However, the fluidity of global capital provides national governments with opportunities to influence capital flows, so that a peripheral country could move to the semi-periphery and then to the core (Kennett, 2001).

DEVELOPMENT AID

For decades, Development Aid was the main strategy by which the capitalistic countries sought to 'develop' the 'underdeveloped' countries in the context of the Cold War. However, in some cases, this has led to an increase in underdevelopment rather than the contrary, for a variety of reasons now summarised.

The US government was the first to initiate *tied aid* schemes. Bilateral aid programmes established by the US redistributed dollars which enabled recipient countries to buy US exports and to purchase military, political and economic advantages for the US. Aid-tying by the US eventually resulted in European and Japanese adoption of the practice. As a proxy for the US, the International Monetary Fund (IMF) was given a key role to play in this tied aid strategy. Developing countries found that their debt kept them tied to their creditors and the IMF ordered them like debt slaves. If they remained within the system, the debtor countries were doomed to perpetual underdevelopment, or rather to development of their exports at the service of multinational enterprises, at the expense of development for the needs of their own citizens (Payer, 1974).

The 1980s saw the rise of neo-liberal Structural Adjustment Programmes (SAPs). The Reagan–Thatcher era was characterised by the ideology of neoliberalism, promoting minimum government interference and making the market responsible for social regulation. In this context, the World Bank (WB) and the IMF argued that Third World debt was a result of inward-oriented, statist, development strategies of the 1950s and 1960s. They promoted the SAPs through which

developing countries, as a condition of loans, were required to cut public spending to balance their books and enable the development of their private economies, often through a strategy of export-led growth. This marginalised and dismissed developmental theories and policies. As a result, many countries in the global South suffered a reversal of previous gains (Girvan, 2005), giving rise to the notion of the 1980s as the lost decade.

There are a number of problems associated with foreign aid agencies. In a comparative study of multilateral foreign aid agencies (comprising all the UN organisations and bilateral foreign aid agencies based in individual countries), Easterly and Pfutze (2008) found that aid agencies are typically not transparent about their operating costs and expenditure of aid money. The worldwide aid budget is split among a multitude of small bureaucracies; and even small agencies fragment their efforts across different countries and sectors. Fragmentation creates coordination problems and high overhead costs for both donors and recipients. Aid practices such as money going to corrupt autocrats and aid spent through ineffective channels, like tied aid, food aid, and technical assistance, also continue to be a problem despite decades of criticism.

The need for an *alternative development model* has led to a *paradigm shift* from economic growth-based development to more comprehensive models of social development based on people-centred ideologies. Important perspectives derive from postcolonialism, post-modernism, multiculturalism and participatory values. *Post-colonial theory* has emerged as a conceptual reorientation towards the perspectives of knowledges, as well as needs, developed in the former colonies. It seeks to intervene, to force its alternative knowledges into power structures of the West as well as the non-West (Young, 2003). Meanwhile, post-modernism drew attention to social and cultural diversity and the primacy of localised experiences that replaced the grand narratives with the colonial roots of post-development perspectives (Lewis and Kanji, 2009). Multi-culturalism is one of the offshoots of post-colonialism as it sought to challenge and overturn the cultural dimensions of imperial rule by establishing the legitimacy of non-Western religions, ideas and philosophies. It implies a positive endorsement of communal diversity, identity politics and minority rights (Heywood, 2007). Participation emerged as the central concept of people-centred ideologies. According to a Human Development Report (HDR) (United Nations Development Programme, UNDP, 1993), participation means that people have direct or indirect access to decision making and power in the economic, social, cultural and political processes that affect their lives. These perspectives have often also been influenced by feminist thinking. According to Bhasin and Khan (1986), anyone who recognises the existence of sexism, male domination or patriarchy, in society, and who takes some action to change the situation, is a feminist. They emphasised that feminists not only ask and fight for equality, dignity and freedom of choice to control their lives and bodies, but for a just society for women and men, both.

THE ROLE OF THE UN

As the key international development system that shapes the international governance of social policy, the UN comprises three distinct parts: the UN of governments; of staff members; and of the closely associated non-governmental organisations (NGOs), experts and consultants (Jolly et al., 2009; see also Appendix 4). The interactions between the three have led to the shift from economic to social development reflected in its four 'decades' of development and two decades of poverty eradication. The First Decade of Development (1960–1970) was based on the hypothesis that injections of capital into the economies of developing nations would trickle down to those placed low in the economic scale. By the mid-1960s, the UN

reassessed its original commitment and advocated that the social programmes should be fully integrated with economic planning in an effort to enhance social welfare. In 1969, the UN *Declaration on Social Progress and Development* was proclaimed by the UN General Assembly as a common basis for social development policies.

In the Second Decade of Development (1970–1980), the International Labour Organization (ILO) introduced the idea of basic needs as the objective of development policy with the acknowledgement that the 'trickle down' approach to development had failed. However, the influence of neo-liberalism led to the collapse of the near-consensus on addressing basic needs as a policy objective (Jolly, 2010). The Third Decade of Development (1981–1990 – the lost decade) saw publication of landmark reports, namely, *Development with a Human Face*, (by UNICEF) and *Our Common Future* (by UN World Commission on Environment and Development). These led to the paradigm of sustainable development and the first HDR by the UNDP.

The period 1991–2000 (Fourth Decade of Development) was marked by significant UN world summits – on women and gender, the environment, human rights, and, appropriately for this chapter, social development. The First Social Development Summit resulted in the Copenhagen *Declaration on Social Development and the Programme of Action* (1995) indicating a collective determination to treat social development as one of the highest priorities of national and international policies, with human beings at the centre of development. The economic and social initiatives of the 1990s highlighted that neither economic growth nor development aid had eliminated poverty and, in 1997, the UN launched the first UN Decade for the Eradication of Poverty. A Second World Summit for Social Development (in Geneva, 2000) resulted in the UN *Millennium Declaration*, making a major commitment to Development and Poverty Eradication. Eight goals, the Millennium Development

Goals (MDGs), were identified to be met by the year 2015 (see Appendix 6). A Second Decade for the Eradication of Poverty (2008–2017) has the theme 'Full employment and decent work for all'.

SOCIAL DEVELOPMENT POLICY DIRECTIONS AND MEASUREMENTS

Major policy directions

Based on the people-centred ideologies, several international policy directions for social development have emerged through development studies, interventions and conferences, coordinated by the UN development systems together with the global civil society and measures have been developed to assess effectiveness. Poverty measurement will be considered after a summary of the main policy directions.

The increased influence of civil society and emphasis on 'user participation' has also been evident in the growth of *participatory development*. Social activists, who attributed the failures of development projects to the fact that the populations concerned were kept out of all the processes of the projects, advocated an end to 'top-down' strategies of action and the inclusion of participatory methods of interaction as an essential dimension of development (Rahnema, 2010). Participatory development therefore emphasises 'bottom-up' approaches, empowerment for marginal strata, and valuing of 'local people's knowledge' over bureaucratic expertise (Przeworski, 2006).

Alongside this, the *gender and development (GAD)* approach has emerged from the grass-roots organisational experiences and writings of Third World feminists. Within the GAD perspective, a distinction is drawn between practical and strategic gender needs. Practical gender needs arise from concrete conditions: they are immediate perceived needs, e.g. food, shelter, education, health care. Strategic gender interests arise out of an analysis of women's subordination and require changes in the structures of gender, class, and race that define women's position in any given culture. The politicisation of practical needs and their transformation into strategic interests constitute central aspects of the GAD approach (Connelly et al., 2000).

Additionally, increased emphasis has been placed on the need for developments to be sustainable. According to a 1987 UN World Commission on Environment and Development's Report:

> *Sustainable development* is development that meets the needs of the present without compromising the ability of future generations to meet their own needs .... the goals of economic and social development must be defined in terms of sustainability in all countries – developed or developing, market-oriented or centrally planned (UNWCED, 1987).

Other policy perspectives include the Human Development and Social Protection strands. Sen and others have provided the conceptual foundation for the *human development* approach, defined as a process of enlarging people's choices and enhancing human capabilities and freedoms. Components include enabling people to live healthy lives, with access to knowledge and able to participate in community life and decisions affecting them. Annual Human Development Reports published by the UNDP have addressed different themes (Deneulin, 2009). The *social protection* strand refers to long term policies aiming to protect and promote the economic and social security of poor people (Cook et al., 2003). Devereux and Sabates-Wheeler (2007) have identified two broad ideologies informing approaches to social protection, one related to social risk management (based on instrumental ideology) and the other, transformative social protection, based on activist ideology. The latter aims at universal social protection with a minimum level of income or consumption granted as a right by the state to all citizens and residents of a country, thus treating every one with equal consideration and respect.

A major concern in relation to social development (including in the implementation and monitoring of aid programmes) is the issue of governance. A UNDP (1997) policy document on *Governance for Sustainable Human Development* states that there is a growing international consensus that good governance and sustainable human development are indivisible and that developing the capacity for good governance should be the primary way to eliminate poverty. A decade later, the UN report (2007) on governance for the MDGs identified critical dimensions of good governance needed for their achievement: a pro-poor policy framework, public administration and civil services, accountability and transparency, rule of law, human rights, decentralisation and delivery of services and role of civil society. Finally, the UN policy directions on development aid cover commitment to human priority areas; a peace dividend through cuts in military spending in donor countries and freeze in developing countries; development cooperation through global partnership and global taxation; aid as an investment and a moral imperative (streamlining conditionality); ending tied aid; and donor coordination in place of disparate projects, priorities and programmes.

Measures of social development

In 1990, concerned to establish a basis for the development of 'objective', comparative data, the UNDP formulated the Human Development Index (HDI). Its three key components are 'longevity'; knowledge; and the real gross domestic product (GDP). These three dimensions are standardised to values between 0 and 1, and the simple average is taken to arrive at the overall HDI value in the range 0–1. The HDRs annually report progress of countries globally according to human development indicators.

The 2011 HDR (UNDP, 2011) provides data on the number of countries and the average of HDIs by level of development (Table 5.1). The 2010 HDR (UNDP, 2010) also provides the data by region, showing significant inequalities in development levels between different regions (Table 5.2).

The 2010 HDR introduced the Multi-dimensional Poverty Index (MPI), which complements money-based measures by considering multiple deprivations and their overlap. The index identifies deprivations across the same three dimensions as the HDI and shows the number of people who are poor (suffering a given number of deprivations) and the number of deprivations with which poor households typically contend. It can be deconstructed by region, ethnicity and other groupings as well as by dimension, making it an important tool for policymakers. The 2010 HDR shows that the regional rates of multidimensional poverty vary from around 3 percent in Europe and Central Asia to 65 percent in sub-Saharan Africa.

- Sub-Saharan Africa has the highest incidence of multidimensional poverty, with considerable variation across the 37 African countries in the sample, from a low of 3 percent in South Africa to a massive 93 percent in Niger.

Table 5.1   Average Human Development Index Values by Level of Human Development

Level of Human Development	Average HDI Values in 2011
World	0.682
Very High Human Development	0.889
High Human Development	0.741
Medium Human Development	0.630
Low Human Development	0.456
Least Developed Countries	0.456

Table 5.2   Average HDI values per region

Region	HDI values in 2010
World	0.68
Developed countries	0.89
Developing countries	0.64
• Latin America and the Caribbean	0.77
• Europe and Central Asia	0.75
• East Asia and the Pacific	0.71
• Arab States	0.66
• South Asia	0.57
• Sub-Saharan Africa	0.43

- The intensity and incidence of multidimensional poverty in South Asia is greater than in any other region.
- In Latin America and the Caribbean multidimensional poverty affects 2 percent of the population in Uruguay to 57 percent in Haiti.
- The Arab States constitute a highly heterogeneous group of countries: the incidence of multidimensional poverty is generally below 7 percent, for example, in the United Arab Emirates and Tunisia, but the rate rises to 81 percent in Somalia.
- In Europe and Central Asia, the rates are close to zero in several countries, with the highest estimated rate in Tajikistan (17 percent).
- In most of East Asia and the Pacific, rates of multidimensional poverty are relatively low.

As mentioned, a target of the MDGs is eradication of extreme poverty and hunger and MDG-1 proposes the halving, between 1990 and 2015, of the proportion of people whose income is less than one US dollar a day. The 2011 MDG Report (UN, 2011) shows that robust growth in the first half of the decade reduced the number of people in developing countries living on less than $1.25 a day from about 1.8 billion in 1990 to 1.4 billion in 2005. At the same time, the corresponding poverty rate dropped from 46 percent to 27 percent. The economic and financial crisis that began in the advanced countries of North America and Europe in 2008 sparked declines in commodity prices, trade and investment, resulting in slower growth globally. Despite these declines,

current trends suggest that the momentum of growth in the developing world remains strong enough to sustain the progress needed to reach the global poverty-reduction target. Based on recently updated projections from WB, the overall poverty rate is still expected to fall below 15 percent by 2015, indicating that the MDG target can be met. By 2015, the number of people in developing countries living on less than $1.25 a day is projected to fall below 900 million. The Report further notes that the fastest growth and sharpest reductions in poverty continue to be found in East Asia. In China and India combined, the number of people living in extreme poverty between 1990 and 2005 declined by about 455 million, and an additional 320 million people are expected to join their ranks by 2015. Projections for sub-Saharan Africa are slightly more upbeat than previously estimated. Based on recent economic growth performance and forecasted trends, the extreme poverty rate in the region is expected to fall below 36 percent (UN, 2011).

HUMAN RIGHTS, SOCIAL JUSTICE, SOCIAL WORK AND DEVELOPMENT

Triggered by the world conference on human rights in 1993, the rights-based approach to development developed in this century in the context of neo-liberal globalisation and democracy in many formerly authoritarian countries. The importance of rights-based development lies in its contention that development is not a charity but is legally enforceable. In this approach, human rights is seen as an intrinsic part of development and development as a means of realising human rights. It returns the role of the state to the forefront of development debates.

Although closely allied to the notions of human rights and equal rights, the term 'social justice' does not appear in the UN Charter, nor in the Universal Declaration, nor the two International Covenants on Human Rights. It first appeared in UN texts during the second half of the 1960s. At the initiative of the Soviet Union, and with the support of developing countries, the term was used in the *Declaration on Social Progress and Development*, adopted in 1969. However, it is frequently referred to in the Copenhagen Declaration and Programme of Action adopted by the 1995 World Summit for Social Development. The Declaration states:

> We share the conviction that social development and social justice are indispensable for the achievement and maintenance of peace and security within and among our nations....We also recognise that broad-based and sustained economic growth in the context of sustainable development is necessary to sustain social development and social justice.

Social justice was scarcely mentioned in the United Nations Millennium Declaration, but the HDR on *Human Rights and Human Development* (UNDP, 2000) shows how human rights bring principles of accountability and social justice to the process of human development.

As the preceding sections indicate, the circumstances in which people live have been the object of significant international investigation, often motivated by the pursuit of social justice. Social work has been one profession which has taken a keen interest in matters of justice, and it can be said to be one of its most distinguishing features. Indeed, social workers' responsibility to promote

social justice, in relation to society generally, and in relation to the people with whom they work, is a cardinal value in the IFSW's *Code of Ethics* (2005). The quest for justice has produced a number of theories. While the notion of justice has been the subject of enduring thought and discussion, social as opposed to formal (legal) justice is a relatively recent innovation (Barry, 2005). In the Western world, conceptions of social justice received particular attention and gained their strongest momentum during the European Enlightenment in the 18th and 19th centuries (Sen, 2009). Two basic and divergent lines of reasoning about social justice emerged from the political climate of change and social and economic revolutions taking place in Europe and America during the Enlightenment period which have continued to influence the course of events since.

There are significant differences separating these two traditions. On the one hand, approaches stemming from the work of the 17th-century political philosopher, Thomas Hobbes (1651/1991), concentrated on identifying just (fair) institutional arrangements for a society, since termed 'transcendental institutionalism' (Sen, 2009: 5) because of their utopian quality. This tradition has two distinct features. First, it concentrates its attention on what it identifies as perfect justice. It tries only to identify social characteristics that cannot be transcended in terms of justice. Second, in searching for perfection, transcendental institutionalism concentrates primarily on getting the institutions right, and it is not directly focused on the actual societies that would ultimately emerge (Sen, 2009: 5–6). Both features converge in what has come to be known as 'contractarianism' (Rawls, 1971).

In contrast are approaches deriving their understanding of justice from comparisons of existing institutions as well as attendant non-institutional features, such as people's actual behaviour and their social interactions. Members of the comparative school of thought range across the political spectrum from Adam Smith (1790/1976), through John Stuart Mill (1859/1974) to Karl Marx

(1875/1938), and currently, Amartya Sen (1993) and Martha Nussbaum (2006). These approaches to justice are forged by 'realization-focused comparison' (Sen, 2009: 7). Although they advance quite disparate ways of making comparisons, they all focus on the removal of manifest injustice, rather than confining their analyses to the search for a perfectly just society which, they assert, would transcend those that others would dismiss as irremediably unrealistic.

So there is no shortage of theories about social justice – and any synthesis seems unlikely – and the question posed by MacIntyre (1988) 'which should we choose?' can usefully be asked in relation to social work and development. The characterisation of perfectly just institutions has become the central exercise in modern theories of justice (Sen, 2009). However, it has been some variant of utilitarianism rather than contractualism which has held sway in practice (Rawls, 1971). In its simplest form, utilitarianism strives to attain the greatest good for the greatest number. The major reason for its popularity as a basis for justice is that 'good', interpreted in terms of utility in the form of overall happiness, welfare or desire, appears amenable to quantification. The idea of maximising the good has a deep intuitive appeal; it seems both comprehensive and eminently rational. It is 'tempting to suppose that it is self-evident that things should be arranged so as to lead to the most good' (Rawls, 1971: 25). Indeed, social work has long subscribed to this view of justice (Solas, 2008). Yet, utilitarianism is arguably neither just nor good enough. The problem is that it does not matter, except indirectly, how the greatest good is distributed among individuals over time. The aim is simply maximisation. Utilitarian theories of justice promise only equity, not equality, and even equity is not guaranteed, since calculations of 'the good', however defined, have proven to be illusive (Sen, 1980). The point is, however, that in a finite world, everything that anyone has is something that others cannot have.

It is also the case that there is no correspondence between what is good and what is right. The separation between good and right makes it possible for aggregations to arise, which a minority of the population finds offensive, or worse: an example is the preference for maximising the utility of racial purity and superiority. The question, then, is 'can deprivation and sacrifice be sanctioned by the claim that it is for the greater good?' It is not the realisation that the world falls short of being perfectly just, that moves those who think not, but that there are injustices which can (with concerted effort) be remedied and even eliminated. This is no less evident in our personal lives than it is in our view of the state of the world in which we live. As Sen remarks:

> …Gandhi would not have challenged the empire on which the sun used not to set, Martin Luther King would not have fought white supremacy in the 'land of the free and the home of the brave', without their sense of manifest injustices that could be overcome. They were not trying to achieve a perfectly just world (even if there were any agreement on what that would be like), but they did want to remove clear injustices to the extent they could. (2009: vii)

In 1651, Hobbes observed that the lives of people were notoriously 'solitary, poor, nasty, brutish and short' – a view that still applies to the lives of so many people across the globe today, despite substantial material progress. Unlike individuals, institutions are not ends in themselves; they are merely the means to ends. Those who consider that people are ends in themselves seek an alternative to conventional means-focused approaches to justice. The capability approach developed by Sen and Nussbaum (1992) offers such an alternative. This approach focuses on a person's capability to do the things he or she has reason to value, and not just on the distribution of means such as income or wealth: it 'proposes a serious departure from the means of living to the actual opportunities of living' (Sen, 2009: 233).

Nussbaum (2006) has developed a list of broadly defined central human capabilities, refined over a number of years and derived from extensive cross-cultural discussion. The latest version of the list identifies ten capabilities under the headings: life; bodily health; bodily integrity; senses, imagination, and thought; emotions; practical reason; affiliation; other species; play; and control over one's environment. These capabilities are held to be important for all citizens, in all nations, and each person is to be treated as an end. All individuals, provided with the right educational and material support, can become fully capable of all of them and the state's role is to do all it can to remedy unequal starting points due to natural endowment, luck and power. In general, the state must enable people to function in all these ways, leaving them free to determine their own course. These ways of functioning are, moreover, irreducibly plural: the need for one cannot be satisfied by giving a larger amount of another. There is a limit to the extent to which they can be subjected to trade-offs.

According to the IASSW/IFSW international definition, the social work profession (2004) has an important role to play towards preventing social exclusion and promoting social justice and human rights-based sustainable and gender-aware social policies and programmes for social development. It can do so through contribution to development studies, advocacy for social policy, developmental interventions and promoting regional cooperation. Schools of social work need to promote the social development paradigm in preparing professional social workers. However, the developed countries generally focus on clinical social work or welfare policy approaches – and not all schools in the developing countries offer courses in social development. Schools of social work need to develop teaching and training programmes on social development which are rooted in the values of social justice, since the task for social work locally, regionally and globally, is to advance, rather than

perfect, social justice. This is a fundamentally important task. A basic understanding of the theories and principles of social justice serves as the starting point for solidarity and ultimately forms the basis for value-based practice, not least in the field of social development.

IMPLICATIONS FOR INTERNATIONAL SOCIAL WORK AND CONCLUSIONS

The forgoing raises a number of important implications for social work at micro, mezzo and macro levels. Historically, and currently, social workers have played a significant role in many countries in addressing privations wrought by poverty, exploitation and dispossession (sometimes at risk to themselves). However, an assessment of the progress in human development and poverty eradication in the world shows continuing substantial inequalities, internationally and within regions and countries. This chapter provides a critical understanding of how poverty and development are both social constructs, affecting huge populations. Social work is one of a minority of professions dedicated to anti-oppressive practice and remains a driving force for global partnership, regional co-operation and local engagement. In making choices about where to direct its efforts and assets, social work needs to be conscious of the moral presuppositions that govern what people aspire to and actually do. At the very least, such reflection on and in action can add to the struggle for inclusion, justice and development. In developing global strategies for the development of economic, political, intellectual and social capital, social workers must advocate for social development policies that are gender-aware, sustainable and rights-based.

In assessing the level of social development, social workers need to take full account of measures directed at the eradication of poverty and expansion of capabilities, not simply increments of GDP. Finally, social work needs to place equal emphasis on both the enhancement and perfection of social justice. Perfect justice is an end, but it is one end of a process. That is to say, we must contend with realities – things as they are – as we strive towards utopian (consensual) notions of justice – things as they ought to be. Utopian proposals cannot on their own address questions about advancing justice. Indeed, they are bound to give answers which are quite distinct and distant from those that concern people engaged in discussions about justice in an unjust world.

In much development work, the profession collaborates with government agencies, NGOs, such as the UN, and aid agencies with a common interest. The profession has played a part in promoting and defending human rights, providing aid and nurturing the self-determining and emancipating efforts of indigenous peoples. While the battle lines are often distinguishable, it is not always clear how bad things can happen to good people, as has been shown in definition and allocation of development grants and utilitarian approaches to justice. The ideals of growth and development and the pursuit of happiness have been the motives of good deeds but also the common pretext for the worst atrocities. Social work serves the cause of freedom and justice in recognising, exposing and challenging hidden agendas. In so doing, it must be vigilant about the danger of becoming complicit in the intrigues that sometimes accompany the quest for peace, security and development. But, to what extent can social work resist the opportunity for gain which entails pragmatism and compromise? What is the benefit of occupying the moral high ground if it serves no common purpose? None of the approaches to social justice outlined above prevent social workers from having to contend with this dilemma. Such theories, however, together with an understanding of the myriad influences on international efforts in relation to social development, do offer a firm guide to praxis.

NOTE

1. In some countries the term 'discrimination' would be used instead of 'negative discrimination'. The word 'negative' is used here because in some countries the term 'positive discrimination' is also used. Positive discrimination is also known as 'affirmative action'. Positive discrimination or affirmative action means positive steps taken to redress the effects of historical discrimination against specific groups.

REFERENCES

Barry, B. (2005) *Why Social Justice Matters*. Cambridge: Polity.

Bhasin, K. and Khan, N.S. (1986) *Some Questions on Feminism and its Relevance in South Asia*. New Delhi: Kali for Women.

Brett, E.A. (2009) *Reconstructing Development Theory: International Inequality, Institutional Reform and Social Emancipation*. London: Palgrave Macmillan.

Connelly, P., Li, T.M., MacDonald, M. and Parpart, J.L. (2000) 'Feminism and development: theoretical perspectives', in J.L. Parpart, M.P. Connelly and V.E. Barriteau (eds), *Theoretical Perspectives on Gender and Development*. http://www.idrc.ca/es/ev-27444-201-1-DO_TOPIC.html, accessed 8 December 2009.

Cook, S., Kabeer, N. and Suwannarat, G. (2003) 'Introduction', in S. Cook, N. Kabeer and G. Suwannarat (eds), *Social Protection in Asia*. New Delhi: Har-Anand Publications. pp. 13–56.

Deneulin, S. (2009) 'Ideas related to human development', in S. Deneulin and L. Shahani (eds), *An Introduction to the Human Development and Capability Approach: Freedom and Agency*. London: Earthscan. pp. 49–70.

Desai, M. (2002) *Ideologies and Social Work: Historical and Contemporary Ideologies*. Jaipur: Rawat Publishers.

Devereux, S. and Sabates-Wheeler, R. (2007) 'Editorial introduction: debating social protection'. *IDS Bulletin: Debating Social Protection*, 38(3). http://www.ids.ac.uk/go/idspublication/debating-social-protection, accessed 12th May, 2010.

DFID (Department for International Development) (2005) *Reducing Poverty by Tackling Social Exclusion: A DFID Policy Paper*. http://webarchive.nationalarchives.gov.uk/+/http://www.dfid.gov.uk/Documents/publications/social-exclusion.pdf, accessed 21 February 2011.

Easterly, W. and Pfutze, T. (2008) 'Where does the money go? Best and Worst Practices in Foreign Aid', *Journal of Economic Perspectives,* 22(2): 29–52.

Esteva, G. (2010) 'Development', in W. Sachs (ed.), *The Development Dictionary: A Guide to Knowledge as Power,* 2nd edn. New York: Zed Books. pp. 1–23.

Freire, P. (1972) *Pedagogy of the Oppressed.* London: Penguin Books.

Girvan, N. (2005) *The Search for Policy Autonomy in the South.* Geneva: United Nations Research Institute for Social Development.

Grusky, D.B. and Takata, A.A. (1992) 'Social stratification', in E.F. Borgatta (ed.), *Encyclopedia of Sociology* (vol. 4). New York: Macmillan. pp. 1955–70.

Heywood, A. (2007) *Political Ideologies: an Introduction* (4th edn). New York: Palgrave Macmillan.

Hobbes, T. (1651/1991) *Leviathan.* Cambridge: Cambridge University Press.

IFSW and IASSW (International Federation of Social Workers and the International Association of Schools of Social Work) (2000) *Definition of Social Work,* http://www.ifsw.org/p38000208.html, accessed 22 July 2010.

IFSW and IASSW (International Federation of Social Workers and the International Association of Schools of Social Work) (2004) *The Global Standards for the Education and Training of the Social Work Profession.* http://www.ifsw.org/cm_data/Global-SocialWorkStandards2005.pdf, accessed 23 July 2010.

IFSW (International Federation of Social Workers) (2005) *Code of Ethics.* Canberra: AASW.

Jolly, R. (2010) *UN Intellectual History Project.* http://www.unhistory.org/briefing/7UNandDevStrategies.pdf, accessed 17 December 2010.

Jolly, R., Emmerij, L. and Weiss, T.G. (2009) *UN Ideas that Changed the* World. Bloomington: Indiana University Press.

Kennett, P. (2001) *Comparative Social Policy: Theory and Research.* Philadelphia: Open University Press.

Leiby, J. (1987) 'History of social welfare', in *Encyclopaedia of Social Work.* Silver Spring, MA: National Association of Social Workers. pp. 755–77.

Lewis, D. and Kanji, N. (2009) *Non-Governmental Organisations and Development.* London: Routledge.

MacIntyre, A. (1988) *Whose Justice? Which Rationality?* Notre Dame, IN: University of Notre Dame Press.

Marx, K. (1875/1947) *Critique of the Gotha Program.* Moscow: Foreign Languages Publishing House.

Mill, J. (1859/1974) *On Liberty.* Harmondsworth: Penguin Books.

Newman, M. (2005) *Socialism: A Very Short Introduction.* New York: Oxford University Press.

Nussbaum, M. (2006) *Frontiers of Justice: Disability, Nationality, Species Membership.* Cambridge: Harvard University Press.

Payer, C. (1974) *The Debt Trap: The International Monetary Fund and the Third World.* New York: Monthly Review Press.

Przeworski, A. (2006) 'Democracy, social inclusion, and development', in *Participatory Governance and the Millennium Development Goals (MDGs).* New York: United Nations. http://unpan1.un.org/intradoc/groups/public/documents/un/unpan028359.pdf, accessed 12 November 2009.

Rahnema, M. (2010) 'Poverty', in W. Sachs (ed.), *The Development Dictionary: A Guide to Knowledge as Power,* 2nd edn. New York: Zed Books. pp. 174–94.

Rawls, J. (1971) *A Theory of Justice.* Cambridge: Harvard University Press.

Reddock, R. (2000) 'Why Gender? Why Development?', in J.L. Parpart, M.P. Connelly and V.E. Barriteau (eds) *Theoretical Perspectives on Gender and Development.* http://www.idrc.ca/es/ev-27443-201-1-DO_TOPIC.html, accessed 8 December 2009.

Rist, G. (2008) *The History of Development: From Western Origins to Global Faith,* 3rd edn. New York: Zed Books.

Sachs, W. (2010) 'Preface', in W. Sachs (ed.), *The Development Dictionary: a Guide to Knowledge as Power,* 2nd edn. New York: Zed Books. pp. vi–xiv.

Schaull, R. (1972) 'Foreword', in P. Freire, *Pedagogy of the Oppressed.* London: Penguin Books. pp. 9–14.

Sen, A. (1980) *Levels of Poverty: Policy and Change: A Background Study for World Development Report.* Washington, DC: World Bank.

Sen, A. (1999) *Development as Freedom.* New York: Random House.

Sen, A. (2009) *The Idea of Justice.* Cambridge: Harvard University Press.

Sen, A. and Nussbaum, M. (eds) (1992) *The Quality of Life.* New York: Oxford University Press.

Smith, A. (1790/1976) *An Inquiry into the Nature and Causes of the Wealth of Nations.* Chicago: University of Chicago Press.

Solas, J. (2008) 'What kind of social justice does social work seek?', *International Social Work,* 51(6): 813–22.

UN (United Nations) (1995) *Copenhagen Declaration on Social Development.* http://www.un-documents.net/cope-dec.htm, accessed 23 May 2010.

UN (United Nations) (2007) *Governance for the Millennium Development Goals: Core Issues and Good Practices.* http://unpan1.un.org/intradoc/groups/public/documents/un/unpan025110.pdf, accessed 24 May 2010.

UN (United Nations) (2010) *Report on the World Social Situation 2010 'Rethinking Poverty'.* http://social.un.org/index/ReportontheWorldSocialSituation/2010/MediaKit.aspx, accessed 15 July 2010.

UN (United Nations) (2011) *Millennium Development Goals Report 2011.* New York. http://www.un.org/millenniumgoals/pdf/(2011_E)%20MDG%20Report%202011_Book%20LR.pdf, accessed 11 August, 2011.

UNDP (United Nations Development Program) (1993) *Human Development Report: People's Participation.* New York: Oxford University Press.

UNDP (United Nations Development Program) (1997) *Governance for Sustainable Human Development: a UNDP Policy Document.* http://mirror.undp.org/magnet/policy/chapter1.htm, accessed 19 December 2009.

UNDP (United Nations Development Program) (2000) *Human Development Report: Human Rights and Human Development.* New York: Oxford University Press.

UNDP (United Nations Development Program) (2010) *Human Development Report: The Real Wealth of Nations: Pathways to Human Development.* New York: Oxford University Press.

UNDP (United Nations Development Program) (2011) *Human Development Report: The Real Wealth of Nations: Pathways to Human Development.* New York: Oxford University Press.

UNWCED (United Nations World Commission on Environment and Development) (1987) *Our Common Future.* Oxford: Oxford University Press.

Young, R.J.C. (2003) *Postcolonialism: a Very Short Introduction.* New York: Oxford University Press.

6

Migration, Minorities and Citizenship

Uma A. Segal and Gerda Heck

INTRODUCTION

As nations around the globe seek to assess the implications of human migration, news reports and general perceptions imply massive international population movement. While the overall number of people living outside their country of origin has grown from 150 million in the year 2000 to 214 million in 2008, at 3.1 percent of the world's people (UN, 2009), this is still a relatively small share of the total population. Nevertheless, there has been a sharp increase in international migration in the last 50 years. At the same time, citizenship, nationhood, and migration regulations have recently become intensely disputed issues in global politics. Since Europe had been the birthplace of the nation state and modern nationalism at the end of the eighteenth century and was prophesised to be the 'graveyard' of these concepts at the end of the last century (Brubaker, 2004), there will be particular focus on developments in Europe in the first part of this chapter. At a time of financial and cultural globalisation, the emerging of supra-national political institutions (like the European Union or the North American Free Trade Agreement) and last but not least also the increase of human mobility, the nation state itself seems to lose importance. However, despite the increased levels of international integration, corresponding forms of global government or formal global citizenship have yet to evolve, leaving the nation state a major regulating force in terms of migration (Torpey, 2000).

This chapter presents an overview of historical perspectives on population mobility, theories of migration, and varying host country debates regarding immigrant inclusion and integration. While nations continue to struggle with migration issues, human migration persists, and the chapter offers a view into current migration patterns and the contributing factors of economic disparities, internal and international conflicts, as well as the attraction of better opportunities elsewhere. The chapter concludes with a discussion of the implications of migration for social work.

HISTORICAL PERSPECTIVES ON MIGRATION, CITIZENSHIP AND THE NATION STATE

Historically, approaches to immigration and migrants themselves have been subject to intense changes, which have been closely related to the shifting role and function of the nation state and its borders. In the early modern era, Europe was already governed by lordships with customs and juridical borders, but these had a different character. For example, customs borders were not necessarily at the same time as territorial or juridical borders. The 'de facto' impact of a frontier depended on who wanted to cross it. While craftsmen or students, for instance, had the right to cross from one territory to the other the unemployed usually did not. Neither systematic border controls nor a comprehensive bureaucratic apparatus to enforce them existed in the eighteenth century (Fahrmeir, 2007).

Following the French Revolution and the Napoleonic Wars, the concept of the modern nation state spread globally. The former French colony of Haiti was founded in 1804 after a successful slave revolution as the first black-led republic; nation states emerged in Latin America, Asia and Eastern Europe throughout the nineteenth and early twentieth century following the collapse of absolutist empires (e.g. the Hispanic, Chinese, Ottoman, Habsburg and Tsarist regimes) and the decline of colonialist powers in Africa and Asia (Meabe et al., 2008).

The emergence of sovereign nation states in eighteenth- and nineteenth-century Europe created societies of citizens, equal before the law. Unlike in previous feudal-absolutist states, the most significant juridical differentiation was no longer between aristocrats and citizens, but between (national) citizens and foreigners (Meabe et al., 2008). As the nation state defined 'the foreigner', passport and border control systems emerged addressing questions of citizenship and nationality (Torpey, 2000). The regulation of migratory movements was directly linked to two essential requirements of the burgeoning modern state: the need for human labour and for army recruits.

For example, in the states of the German Confederation, the introduction of passports went along with the systematic differentiation of 'natives' and 'foreigners'. This was simultaneously accompanied by a shift in responsibility from local authorities to the state (Dohse, 1985). Passport obligations were also implemented to control travellers who were suspected of spreading revolutionary ideas (Fahrmeir, 2000). In the United States of America (US), immigrants were counted from the 1830s onwards. With arrivals from Europe subject to controls, unwanted migrants could be excluded, although overall, until the beginning of the twentieth century, the US borders remained highly porous and in parts unguarded. The relatively open immigration policy and large-scale absence of controls can be seen in the context of demographic policy considerations: the US was until then thinly populated and needed immigrants for labour and to secure its territory. In addition, in Canada, Australia and Latin America, with the increasing need for a steady supply of labour and with economic expansion, immigration policies remained on the whole liberal until the Chinese Exclusion Act of 1882 in the US. Countries such as Argentina set up immigration agencies in European countries to recruit immigrants, with the expressed purpose of attracting and facilitating the entry of foreigners.

Passport systems, definitions of citizenship, and the structure of governmental migration policies have been crucial for the development of the modern nation state and, with it, the emergence of the juridical category of the 'illegal resident'. With the concept of the modern nation all other connections that united a community, for example, estate ownership or religion, became secondary to national membership (Landshut, 1969). The nation state, representing the unity of rulers and governed subjects, required the definition of territorial boundaries. Although the concept of the nation state was established only in the nineteenth century, it seems to have become an almost exclusive political framework for countries around the world today. Linked to the formation of nation states are usually issues such as equal rights, individual freedoms, democratization, technical progress, the general increase of wealth and, associated with these, questions of social (in)equality.

Foucault (1976) suggests in his reflections on the history of modernity that at the end of this period is not freedom for people, but their submission and classification as 'regular' and 'non-regular' subjects. The power of states is based, among other beliefs, on the identification of minorities and 'deviant population groups'. Foucault describes a disciplined society, in which individuals are controlled via specific techniques of power. The 'places of discipline' in modern states (such as the police, factories, the military, schools, or the uncountable institutions of welfare and charity) represent a structure in which vulnerable or 'needy' individuals have to conform to specific expectations and be integrated into the social structure (Reuter, 2002). Separating the regular from the non-regular keeps both in check. This allows the extensive control of specific population groups and at the same time 'normalises' the majority of the population that voluntarily accommodates the system. The nationalisation of states was implemented through judicial, linguistic, cultural and ideological homogenisation of a population within each territory. Those who do not belong to this 'entity' and lack the required state permits are described as 'illegal'.

Following World War I, the system of the nation state was consolidated in Europe and modern borders developed as clearly marked lines, by which (as much as possible) all travellers were controlled. There are three major motives for this development: first, the presence of refugees, whose numbers had assumed new proportions in Europe between the two World Wars; second, new definitions of 'belonging' for citizens of Western states;

and third, the construction of systems of national social insurance, which required precise definitions of eligibility among citizens (Torpey, 2000).

Economic slowdown following World War I, economic instability, and political turbulence led also to increasingly restrictive migration policies in countries such as the US, which enacted quotas for immigrants in 1921 and 1924 (Heck, 2008). Migrants then began moving instead to Brazil or Argentina (Chiswick and Hatton, 2003).

In the 1930s, the spread of German National Socialism led to thousands of people fleeing European countries in search of security; this proved futile for many. Several refugees were stranded on 'paper walls', lacking required documents, which prevented their journey forward. They often found themselves in a neighbouring 'safe' country, but caught in a trap, unable to truly enter that nation (Torpey, 2000; Arendt, 1951; Marrus, 1985).

After World War II, with economic growth, the US loosened its border controls for some immigrants using a broad quota system. Western European states, such as France, the UK and Germany recruited migrant workers through 'guest worker' programmes or postcolonial immigration. The more significant transformation of immigration has occurred in the last 50 years and has been both accompanied by – and a product of – globalisation processes. The internationalisation of production, the development of cities as coordination and management hubs of a global economy, and local conditions, in which the Western metropolis was faced by competition from production facilities in the global South are significant processes, which affected the entry and status of migrants (Sassen, 1998). The demand for migrant labour in the formal and informal economy is closely linked to the hierachisation of the status of migrants. As a result of the oil crisis at the beginning of the 1970s, West European countries terminated guest worker programmes and opportunities for legal immigration became limited. Nevertheless, migrants continued to move, but their immigration was unauthorised and/or undocumented. In the beginning of the 1990s all Western countries established measures to decrease undocumented immigration, and currently, the control of immigration has become an important focus of policy. The borders between countries of the global North and less rich countries have become fortified, and increasingly sophisticated tools are used to control them. Ostentatious examples are the border fences between the Spanish exclaves Ceuta and Melilla (on the African continent) and Morocco,[1] which surrounds them. Governments in the global North, but increasingly also the South expect the sealing of exterior borders and the exclusion of migrants within countries to reduce undocumented immigration. However, migration is a phenomenon that is significantly determined by a series of factors outside governmental control including family expectations and responsibilities, community relationships or support, as well as historical patterns and economic opportunities. Awareness of this lack in influence has also led to a modification of border regimes: unable to prevent the entry of unwanted or 'undesirable' migrants, the state allocates them different hierarchical positions, classifying them as legal, tolerated or undocumented immigrants.

MIGRANT GROUPS AND POPULATIONS

An overarching question in immigration literature, then, is why people leave their homelands. Moving to another country is arduous, even under optimum circumstances, usually requiring elaborate preparation, great financial costs, loss of social and family ties, acquisition of a new language, and adapting to an alien culture. With increasing globalisation and ease of transportation and transnational relocation, migration will continue to rise. While the configuration of events leading to migration may differ among individuals,

there appears to be an interplay of two phenomena that is the catalyst for migration: a 'push' from the country of origin, and a 'pull' to the country of destination.

Despite the development of a range of sociological, economic, and psychological theories, the 'push–pull' factors suggested in early migration theories continue to persist. In addition, most of the literature suggests two types of immigrants: those who plan to leave their countries indefinitely and those who intend to return after accomplishing specific goals. However, some of those who expect to leave permanently do return, while others who plan to migrate only temporarily often make their final residence in the host country. Migrants may fall into two further categories: those who are voluntary (authorised or unauthorised) or involuntary (forced from their homelands). Tables 6.1–6.4 present 2010 mid-year summaries of worldwide and regional migration numbers (UN, 2009), revealing, as expected, that although voluntary migrants are found in large numbers in the more developed areas of the globe, a substantial movement, particularly of refugee groups, but also of voluntary migrants, is seen in less developed areas. It is not uncommon for international migrants to seek economic, social, and political opportunity and asylum in bordering nations that may not be substantially more developed than countries of origin but may offer somewhat improved living conditions.

Motivations for emigration are myriad, and personal choices are rarely clear. No single cause serves as impetus for so dramatic a change as leaving one's homeland, one's roots, and all that is familiar. Whether the move is voluntary or not, whether it is the result of careful planning, the effects of war, the aftermath of a natural disaster, or enforced political exile, it still requires personal choice. Not all who are discontented with their lives in their homelands, those who are afflicted by the ravages of war, forced from their houses because of disasters such as earthquakes and floods, or even people whose lives are threatened by those with political

Table 6.1   Numbers of international migrants

Year	World	Africa	Asia	Europe	Latin America & Caribbean	North America	Oceania
1990	155,518,065	15,972,502	50,875,665	49,400,661	7,130,326	27,773,888	4,365,023
2000	178,498,563	17,062,143	51,915,384	57,639,114	6,470,622	40,395,432	5,015,868
2010	213,943,812	19,263,183	61,323,979	69,819,282	7,480,267	50,042,408	6,014,693

Table 6.2   Mid-year numbers of refugees

Year	World	Africa	Asia	Europe	Latin America & Caribbean	North America	Oceania
1990	18,481,171	5,350,411	9,922,102	1,317,766	1,197,445	583,450	109,997
2000	15,645,933	3,575,274	8,820,204	2,487,214	49,695	639,837	73,709
2010	16,345,740	2,567,719	10,869,688	1,593,350	529,365	726,143	59,475

Table 6.3   Mid-year numbers of international migrants by development status of regions

Year	More developed regions	Less developed regions
1990	82,354,728	73,163,337
2000	104,433,692	74,064,871
2010	127,711,471	86,232,341

Note: The categories of 'More developed regions' and 'Less developed regions' are listed by the UN (2009) and can be accessed through the website http://esa.un.org/migration/index.asp?panel=3. 'The more developed regions comprise Australia, Europe, Japan, New Zealand and North America', with 'the less developed regions Africa, Asia (excluding Japan), Latin America and the Caribbean, Melanesia, Micronesia and Polynesia'.

Table 6.4   Mid-year numbers of refugees by developed region

Year	More developed regions	Less developed regions
1990	2,010,446	16,470,725
2000	3,198,489	12,447,444
2010	2,370,691	13,975,049

power either choose to leave or truly have the option of leaving. Rarely are those in the most dire circumstances and extreme distress able to leave. Such a drastic step requires that one must have, at the very least, the personal and internal resources, including self-confidence and hope, to risk all that is known. Furthermore, it is not always the oppressed or those without resources who leave their native lands. Several leave in order to further enhance their already comfortable lives or to achieve educational, professional, and other personal objectives that cannot be met in their homelands. What binds all emigrants is the awareness that certain needs of importance to them can be better fulfilled outside their countries of origin. It is evident that over the last half century, with improvements in cross-national communication and transportation, migration is an increasingly complex phenomenon, and migration patterns are rarely simple.

POLITICAL CONFLICT AND COMPLEX HUMAN EMERGENCIES

While all migration results in the disruption of familiar lifestyles, the face of voluntary, or planned, migration is different from that of forced migration. Primary causes for forced migration may be inter- or intra-country conflict and ecological or environmental disasters. Both conflict and natural disasters force movement of domicile, and while both conflict and natural or man-made disasters may result in the internal displacement of people, often they force people out of their homelands.

Current sites of conflict

On going socio-political turbulence is evidenced across the world, and conflicts involving arms are evident in all regions, with substantial and grave implications for residents of afflicted areas. Uppsala Universitet's Conflict Data Program (UCDP, 2011) has since 1979 recorded on going organised world conflicts and reported that in 2009 there were 29 intrastate and seven internationalised conflicts. In the events of 2011, now known as the 'Arab Spring', the Middle East saw the results of political unrest and changes as dictatorships were, and continued to be, challenged, country-by-country – Tunisia, Yemen, Egypt, Bahrain, Iran, Libya, and Syria. March 2011 witnessed the results of the Libyan uprising against Colonel Muammar el-Qaddafi, the dictator who was in power for 42 years. This has drawn in international forces and news reports indicated mass migrations to Italy of Somali, Eritrean, and Ethiopian workers from Libya. The longest lasting, on going, dangerous, and often forgotten internal conflict is occurring in India with the Nexalite–Maoists, whose insurgency began in 1967. On 9 March 2011, the *Times of India* reported that 2680 civilians and security force personnel were killed by Maoists between 2008 and 2010. At the time of writing continued conflicts are evident, among other places, in Afghanistan, Iraq, Sudan, Somalia, Côte d'Ivoire, Israel – Palestine, Mexico, Myanmar, the Philippines, Colombia, and Peru (UCDP, 2010).

Natural and man-made disasters

Natural disasters and the depletion and degradation of the environment and its resources can impact levels of poverty, food and water insecurity, conflict and inequality (Stojanov, 2009) leading to increased population movements. While relatively little attention was placed on the impact of these disasters on migration, media coverage of natural disasters in recent years (e.g. of the Indonesian tsunami of 2004 and 2005 hurricane Katrina in the US) has raised awareness of this phenomenon (Stojanov and Kavanová, 2009). The 2010 earthquake (Richter Scale 7.0) in Haiti devastated the nation and claimed close to a quarter of a million lives, and earthquakes in that year in Chile and New Zealand, along with heat waves in Russia caused substantial economic and social damages. The major 2010 man-made disaster caused by the Deepwater Horizon rig explosion in the Gulf of Mexico affected an area already reeling from previous disasters. On 11 March 2011, a 9.0 earthquake in northern Japan set in motion a series of events that have unfathomable consequences; the earthquake was followed by over a hundred aftershocks, a tsunami of unprecedented proportions and impact, and explosions in three nuclear plants. With the focus on clean-up, there was, at the time of writing, little information regarding migration in this area.

IMPACT OF IMMIGRATION ON HOST AND SENDING COUNTRIES

While emigration is often a result of a combination of the historical socio-politico-economic conditions in home countries and current personal opportunities and choices, immigration is circumscribed by the contemporary socio-politico-economic climate in the receiving country and its nationals' perceptions of newcomers in general and newcomers from particular origins. The major voluntary movements of people are perceived to be to the developed world. The International Organization for Migration (IOM, 2010) reports that migration is distributed across several more nations with the top 10 receiving countries attracting a smaller share than they did in 2000 and emerging economies attracting a large segment of the migrating population. Immigration is an important and often unrecognised ingredient in the economy of developed nations. In the first half of the twenty-first century, the native-born populations of the most developed nations are projected to decline and age as a result of below-replacement fertility and increasing longevity, and, in the absence of a young immigrant pool, the workforce will deteriorate and reductions in population size will be even greater than projected (UN, 2009).

There are several advantages to migration which may include: (1) the new opportunities available for individuals and families, easing the effect of unemployment on economies that send migrants; (2) the transfer of technology; (3) investments from the Diaspora; (4) increased trade; and (5) the use of remittances which are substantial and increasing. Although the percentage of international migrants increased only by 0.2 percent in the last decade (IOM, 2010), remittances rose from 132 billion US$ in 2000 to 414 billion US$ in 2009 (UN, 2009). The majority (316 billion US$) went to developing countries, and it is believed that if formal and informal remittances could be identified, this number could well increase threefold (IOM, 2010). Remittances are important to the micro-economics of the family in the home country, supplementing their assets and affording them subsistence or luxury items, but they are also significant in affecting the economy of the nation receiving the remittances.

Despite these advantages, approximately 25 percent of all countries, both developed and developing, in 2001, reported that immigration and its impact were too high (UN, 2002). Disadvantages appear to be at the forefront, with immigrants being seen as a drain on resources, as well as a threat to the native workforce in receiving countries, and as emigrants being viewed as a part of the 'brain drain' by sending countries (Elliott et al., 2010). The latter indicates the loss of trained professionals from developing countries to countries with more economic and social opportunities (which experience a 'brain gain'). International migration is no longer unidirectional or as permanent as it once was presumed. It is clear that migration, for many, involves 'brain circulation' (Saxenian, 2005) or 'brain rotation' suggesting a cyclical pattern of migration (Baldacchino, 2006).

SELECTED EXPLANATORY THEORIES OF MIGRATION

Theories of migration have emerged in several disciplines and reflect discipline dependence, focusing on a limited knowledge base or a particular academic field (see Elliott et al., 2010). Clearly the study of immigration is interdisciplinary: human geography, economics, demography, anthropology, political science, and social work are just some of the disciplines from which immigration theory may emerge, and each may address different aspects of human migration. Castles and Miller (2009) discuss migration not as an individual's decision or experience, but as collective action arising out of social change and resulting in further change that affects both sending and receiving nations.

As described by Elliott et al. (2010), Portes (1999) proposed that a grand theory of immigration is of little value because of the degree of high level generalisation necessary, and, instead, the best explanations come from mid-level theories. However, mid-level theories tend to become discipline-dependent, and draw from a limited range of knowledge, focusing on the knowledge base of the particular academic discipline. In Massey and colleagues' 2005 review of explanatory theories of human migration, the authors present six theory groups, and the influence of a disciplinary frame of reference is apparent in each group. However, these authors also present and discuss a synthesis approach to these theories as a seventh possible theory group which assists in transcending some of the academic discipline restrictions, while stopping short of grand theory. Massey et al.'s review includes: *neoclassical economics; the new economics of migration, segmented labour market theory, world systems theory, social capital theory, cumulative causation* and the above-mentioned *synthesis approach.*

Labour supply and demand is the focus of the *neoclassical economics* approaches. It is argued, at the macro-economic level, that labour will move from a country with a plentiful labour supply and therefore low wages, to a country with a low supply and high wages. A parallel micro-economic process also occurs in this case, argue Massey et al. (2005), where individuals and families make a cost-benefit analysis of migration which informs and motivates their decision to migrate or not. The *new economics approach* moves away from income as a measure of success or satisfaction and focuses more on relative deprivation (Kubursi, 2006). This involves comparing with others in the full range of the socio-economic structure of a society. It is argued that as countries get richer, the sense of relative deprivation increases, and the more likely are individuals or representatives of the family to migrate. Remittances support the family in the homeland (Nyame and Grant, 2007). The neoclassical economics model and the new economics model both involve individual decision making in the immigration process. *Segmented labour market* theory (Vilalta-Bufi, 2007) moves to a more structural explanation of human migration. The need for a

class of low wage earners in an advanced industrial economy, and the inability or unwillingness of the economic system to provide a higher level of minimum wage because of the need to preserve status and hierarchy in the social structure, offers opportunity to immigrants who see the low wages as an improvement in their condition in their native country: mobility also offers the opportunity for increased status because of the remittances that can be returned to the family in the home country. *World systems theory,* which recognises the economic interdependence (and inequality) of nations (Goldfrank et al., 1999), provides yet another predominantly structural explanation of migration as opposed to individual and family decisions proposed by the neoclassical and new economics models. World systems theory suggests that in the process of becoming involved in a developing country, capitalist countries dislodge the equilibrium through new economic, social, cultural, and political influences and create motivation for migration through contact with capitalist products and lifestyles. This theory, it may be argued, is evidenced by the fact that migrants do not come from the poorest regions but from countries that have had contact with global capital systems.

Furthermore, this system perpetuates the poverty of the poorer countries, because the system is arranged in favour of the rich countries. *Social capital theory* accepts the individual nature of the migration decision, but proposes that as a result of successive migrations, institutions, social welfare agencies and entrepreneurs in the host country help develop social capital in the new homeland, facilitating the journey and making less risky the settlement of later migrants. With lowered risk and increased assistance in the receiving country, others are likely to be motivated to migrate (Akcapar, 2006). The final group of explanations reviewed by Massey et al. (2005) is *cumulative causation* developed by Myrdal (1957) and further applied by Massey and his colleagues. Similar to social capital theory, cumulative causation theory argues that successive immigrations make the process easier for those who follow, but in this case, in a broader context than the single variable of social capital. Variables considered by cumulative causation theorists include migrant networks, income equality, land distribution, agrarian production, and culture.

TYPES OF MIGRATION

While migration theories may focus on the economic aspects of labour migration, the face of migration is also affected by numerous additional economic factors that can give rise to the exploitation of the vulnerable. Thus, in addition to the voluntary (both legal and unauthorised) and involuntary (refugee) migrants, additional pools of migrants are found among the individuals who may migrate under a range of circumstances that may neither be identified as entirely voluntary nor as completely involuntary. Child migration, human trafficking, female domestic labour migration, and return migration (particularly of rejected asylum seekers and temporary workers) are frequently hidden from public view or policy and programme intervention.

Child migration

When children begin contributing to the family income at a very young age, sometimes as young as four or five years, they quickly assume the economic roles thrust upon them. While the assumptions of these roles are not always conflict free and parental authority and punitive measures are frequently applied (Hashim, 2006), children frequently find the attainment of their personal goals can also be achieved by working. O'Connell Davidson et al. (2007) propose that the international community with its views on children's rights should reassess perceptions that child migration and labour

are inevitable risks and that the perception of risk is socially and culturally constructed. The Development Research Center on Migration, Globalisation and Poverty (DRCMGP, 2003) reports that while there is usually a focus on those children who cross national borders, the independent migration of children within a country is the norm in many nations. On the other hand, the United Nations Children's Fund (UNICEF, no date) estimates that the lucrative and illegal activity of child trafficking processes 1.2 million children annually for cheap labour or sexual exploitation.

Human trafficking, not smuggling

Human trafficking and human smuggling are often grouped together as they are both clandestine and dangerous activities. However, the very significant difference between the two is the element of consent. In instances of human smuggling, the person being smuggled usually initiates the contact and pays the smuggler for transportation, while in human trafficking, the individual being transported either is taken unwillingly or is duped into the reason for the travel (Bhabha, 2005). In addition, in the latter instance, payment is made after arrival as trafficked individuals find themselves in virtual servitude, or as bonded to the person who transports them (Touzenis, 2010).

Migrant domestic workers

Known as a contemporary female labour diaspora (Parreáas, 2001), Filipina women are found across the globe occupied in domestic work and separated from their families (Lan, 2003). Women from poorer Asian countries are found in domestic occupations in more affluent Asian nations, and women from Central and South America leave their families for the more affluent economies of the United States and Canada. Here, ironically, their function is to *mother* the children of their employers (Parreáas, 2001). Although female domestic workers have dominated the global market (some particularly because of their English language capabilities; Lan, 2006), a review of media reports suggests that the employment, and frequent exploitation, of migrant women from diverse nations is on the rise.

Return migration

The International Labour Organization (ILO, 2009) reports that few countries have programmes to address the issues faced by returning migrants. While several may return with adequate resources, they may be unable to reintegrate into the communities they left. In addition, women who return may find it difficult to acquire employment, may find little left of their remittances, and experience conflict with their families. Nevertheless, there is a dearth of literature on voluntary returnees (Zlotnik, 2006), but the few studies focusing on repatriated refugees indicate that reintegration is traumatic and may result in substantial mental health concerns (Fu and Vanlandingham, 2010; von Lersner et al., 2008).

COSMOPOLITAN CITIZENSHIP

In a globalised world, which is increasingly affected by the mobility of people and by the reality that people have, simultaneously, multiple nation states as points of reference, migration cannot be regarded anymore from a single nation state perspective. Through the ease of global mobility, it is possible today to be born in one country, to work in another and to spend one's retirement in yet another country. According to the philosophy of human rights, individuals are protected on the basis of personhood, not of nationality or citizenship. However, our social and political rights are still for the most part linked to the membership of a nation state. Furthermore, human rights still remain often without any legally binding criteria, particularly when they are not recognised in all states.

With the background of a rising group of people who live as migrant workers, as unauthorised migrants or as asylum seekers and refugees outside their country of origin and who have often no or limited access to basic and fundamental rights, there are growing debates on the right to mobility, how to secure or reinvent citizenship and how to organise migrant participation within the nation state. This intensified discussion raises questions for governments, societies and in the social sciences.

The Universal Declaration of Human Rights (1948) recognises the right to freedom of movement across borders, a right to leave a country, but not a right to enter a country. There exists an apparent conflict between the right of emigration and the state claim of sovereignty, both to control its borders and to define the number and the criteria for the admission of immigrants (Benhabib, 2004, 2006). Developing Hannah Arendt's notion about the right to have rights, Seyla Benhabib elaborates the idea of cosmopolitan rights (a cosmopolitan citizenship). According to Benhabib (2004), there should be a redefinition in the context of transnationalism, as well as the decoupling of the right to have rights from the rights emanating from the status of citizenship. From an ethical perspective, she argues for active, participative citizenship. In other words, all people should gain civil rights in the respective community in which they live, work, and are participating socially. Within the European Union (EU), for example, this is already realised to some extent (Soysal, 1994; Sassen, 2007). However, there exists a striking contradiction between the cosmopolitan handling of the EU citizen and the exclusion of a citizen of a 'third' state. This gap is increasingly difficult to justify judicially, politically, and ethically. Democratic societies cannot be closed; according to Benhabib (1996) the permeability of its borders is a necessary condition for a democratic state.

The case of the EU shows that mobility has become a privilege that is unevenly distributed globally. While citizens from developed countries may travel and establish themselves almost anywhere in the world, citizens from less developed or emerging economies depend upon the uncertain issuance of visas and residence permits to migrate. As a result, border controls also play a role in reinforcing inequalities between countries. Etienne Balibar (1998) demands a democratisation of global borders, or rather border crossings. But here appears the question, how can an institution such as the border be democratised without redesigning the international legal order and the understanding of sovereignty? There is no doubt that the modern nation state is in transformation. According to Sassen (1998, 2007) the nation state, in this role as the only enforcer and guarantor of rights, is challenged by supranational organisations, multinational financial corporations and relations, and also through transnational non-governmental organisations (NGOs), people in social movements, migrants and minorities.

To claim their rights, social movements as well as migrants are linking together and doing so even internationally and beyond the nation state. Sassen indicates that clandestine migrants, especially, practice post-national self-determination by accessing rights that they are officially denied by immigrating clandestinely into the nation state. Through their daily presence in the metropolises of the global North and their permanent border crossings, they undermine the idea of the controlled nation state and assume their right to mobility. Their daily participation in local communities – working, raising families, participating in everyday routines – are civic practices, through which an informal social contract emerges between undocumented migrants and the respective communities. As a result, even unauthorised migrants gain political importance (Sassen, 2007). Given current levels of global mobility, the debates on cosmopolitan, global or transnationalcitizenship as well as the right to

mobility have to be broadened in the social sciences.

IMPLICATIONS FOR SOCIAL WORK

Despite its increasing recognition of the impact of the global economy on individuals' lives and on international social work, the profession has still paid relatively little heed to the implications of cross-border movements. With the impact on sending, receiving, and transit countries, as well as on the migrants themselves and their families, the failure of social work to attend more to this dimension of human life is of concern.

While social workers have long worked with refugees (Harrison and Melville, 2010), the profession has focused only incidental attention on migration-related issues. In addition, despite a 'person-in-environment' orientation and the international definition of social work as agreed upon by International Association of Schools of Social Work (IASSW) and the International Federation of Social Workers (IFSW) (Hare, 2004), there is a tendency to address immigrant and refugee issues from a micro-perspective. It behoves service providers to also assess whether mezzo-level changes are needed in existing organisations to provide adequate services, within ethnic communities, or at the macro-level of public policy implementation. Policies on social and family welfare, housing, education, health/mental health, and criminal justice all substantially colour the daily lives of immigrants, as they do for all citizens of a nation.

Country policies towards international migrants

Often erroneously juxtaposed are discussions regarding 'immigration' and 'immigrant' policies. The former are frequently exclusionary, determining who may enter a nation, the conditions under which they may enter, and how those who are not welcome can be kept out. Immigrant policies, on the other hand, describe immigrant access to host country opportunities. Social workers are often engaged in policy implementation, particularly once migrants are in the country. However, they may also find themselves participating in policy-making discussions and advocacy efforts in balancing the needs of a country with those of the immigrant, all the while working towards enhancing the social and economic integration of newcomers. Since governmental policy may preclude immigrants and refugees from access to certain (or most) services, social workers may find themselves struggling with the ethical dilemmas of implementing existing policy while attempting to advocate for, or provide humanitarian aid to, groups ineligible for the available resources (Humphries, 2004).

Practice in communities

As population groups from sending countries establish communities and, oftentimes, ethnic enclaves in host countries, their increasing visibility may pose unintended challenges to local residents. By facilitating dialogue between native-born residents and immigrant groups, community social workers can enhance social and economic integration efforts. Xenophobia, which may be a reaction of self-preservation in relationship to those who are different, could embody concerns about loss of identity, culture, norms, and values. Diversity training aims at increasing individuals' knowledge about the 'other' and can be used effectively also in community practice. Often trained in working with those who are different, community social workers can tap their knowledge to address intercultural fears and promote cross-cultural understanding.

Administration and programme development

Implementation of immigrant policies and integration efforts are the purview of administrators and programme developers at the local level. When these groups are knowledgeable about the immigrant experience, they will effectively implement directives of policy makers regarding immigration, and, in addition, they will implement mainstream programmes with sensitivity to the unique concerns of immigrants and refugees. Collaboration and cooperation within communities can improve awareness of needs unique to migrant populations, enabling organizations to adapt or develop services to address, at the very least, the most serious. Sufficient literature has indicated that migrant populations indicate a disproportionately low rate of use of mainstream social work services. The resulting perception, then, is that either immigrant communities take care of their own people, or that these individuals are able to navigate life's difficulties using their own resources; neither of these may be accurate. As such, social work organizations may be failing to fulfil their responsibility of helping people and environments to adapt to each other. As administrators become increasingly cognizant of the several economic, social, and psychological issues arising from translocation, they can help design a milieu that reaches migrants in need. With globalization, the demographic landscape in most countries is in flux. Social work organizations must continually apprise themselves of the environment in which they function and be aware of the resulting effects of new populations.

Direct services

Professional awareness and competence with immigrant populations require both an understanding of the social, political, economic, and cultural contexts of the country of origin as well as a knowledge of the immigrant experience (Chan, 2003), and reasons leading to departure from the homeland. Regardless of the circumstances under which people migrate, whether it is voluntarily or not, the decision to leave all that is familiar is monumental. Likewise, a nation's decision to accept newcomers is usually not a universally accepted choice of the general population. With this backdrop, new immigrants may find that, in the absence of traditional support systems, they are struggling alone with new and bewildering social environment, systems, and expectations.

It would be erroneous to state that all immigrants require the services of social workers. When individuals have the resources for migrating, including appropriate levels of education, exposure to other cultures in their homelands, language competence, and psychological capabilities, their adaptation is likely to be relatively smooth. In the absence of economic access and personal support, the immigration experience may exacerbate difficulties in adjusting to the host country. Lum's (2003) framework for cultural competence provides practitioners with basic tools in working with diverse populations. This framework, of four components, requires practitioners be culturally self-aware, focus on learning as much as possible about other populations, adapting traditional social work practice skills for congruence with another culture, and training others with this new knowledge and self-awareness that they have acquired.

Academia

The often mentioned 'gap' between academia and service provision appears to be endemic to many disciplines. The increases in migrant populations in all countries have influenced policy makers and practitioners across professions, and although social workers may have been slow in recognizing the impact of immigrants on their practice, social work academia has been even slower. Human migration will continue to grow as the demand for workers in developed countries is answered by those in developing countries where there is a population surplus. Transnational movement is essential and social work academics must educate themselves and prepare practitioners and the discipline for the inevitability of working with changing demographic profiles in their communities. Lyons and Huegler (2012), furthermore, indicate that social workers, themselves, are increasingly mobile

as they travel to assist in disaster relief efforts, seek work outside their home countries or engage in other forms of international social work.

CONCLUDING COMMENTS

There exists a tendency among several immigrant and refugee groups to rely only on themselves and their own resources and minimise the use of the supportive services that are available in mainstream society. When their resources are sufficient to cope with their own difficulties, drawing on these rather than turning to professional support services is appropriate and may be considered a personal strength. However, because of the tendency to protect privacy, an emphasis on family loyalty and group sense, and issues of shame, for many immigrants, there is an aversion to turning to outsiders for assistance. Some may even avoid accessing the services offered by their own communities. Since problems are not visible to them, mainstream social services often are insensitive to immigrants' concerns (which may or may not be associated with migration) and they fail to educate themselves or reach out to inform these populations of available support options.

Though grouped together, immigrants around the world are extremely diverse, and xenophobia often underlies the behaviour of those who migrate as well as those living in the host country. The former group is bewildered by the latter, and the latter struggles to find equilibrium as its environment is changed. As migrants adapt to their new home, they bring with them their traditions, foods, languages, religions, and families, and these influence the lives of native residents. As each views the other with curiosity or with wariness, society's increasing interest in identifying variations has often camouflaged the reality that human beings are more similar than they are different. There is much people have in common, regardless of their countries of origin, their traditions, and their languages; all seek health, happiness, and the ability to support their families.

For immigrants, as for all people, much is dependent on their personal resources, but, for them, the receptiveness of the host country is paramount. While immigration policies that admit only certain groups of people, reflecting the host country's preferences, daily opportunities and obstacles encountered by immigrants affect adjustment and integration. International migration is expected to continue to increase, and both immigrants and hosts must make efforts to learn about each other. Many professions may help mediate, but social workers, with their unique focus on the intersection of the individual and the environment, should assume the task of being brokers across this divide.

NOTE

1   The fences around the two Spanish exclaves Ceuta and Melilla were fortified in 2005. They are now 6 m high, topped with NATO wire, and with watchtowers every 40 m. In between the fences directional microphones and headlights have been installed, as well as a tear gas plant (Heck, 2008).

REFERENCES

Akcapar, S.K. (2006) 'Conversion as a migration strategy in a transit country: Iranian Shiites becoming Christians in Turkey', *International Migration Review*, 40(4), 817–853.

Arendt, H. (1951) *The Origins of Totalitarianism*. New York: Schocken Books.

Baldacchino, G. (2006) 'The brain rotation and brain diffusion strategies of small islanders: considering "movement" in lieu of "place"', *Globalisation, Societies and Education,* 4(1): 143–54.

Balibar, E. (1998) 'The borders of Europe', in P. Chea and B. Robbins (eds), *Cosmopolitics. Thinking and Feeling beyond the Nation.* Minneapolis: University of Minnsesota Press. pp. 216–29.

Benhabib, S. (1996) *Democracy and Difference.* Princeton, NJ: Princeton University Press.

Benhabib, S. (2004) *The Rights of Others.* Cambridge, UK: Cambridge University Press.

Benhabib, S. (2006) *Another Cosmopolitanism.* New York, NY: Oxford University Press.

Bhabha, J. (2005) *Migration Fundamentals: Trafficking, Smuggling, and Human Rights.* Migration Information Source, Migration Policy Institute (MPI). http://www.migrationinformation.org/feature/display.cfm?ID=294, accessed 2 December 2010.

Brubaker, R. (2004) 'In the name of the nation: reflections on nationalism and patriotism', *Citizenship Studies*, 8(2): 115–27.

Castles, S. and Miller, M.J. (2009) *The Age of Migration,* 4th edn. New York, NY: Guilford Press.

Chan, S. (2003) 'Psychological issues of Asian Americans', in P. Bronstein and K. Quina (eds), *Teaching Gender and Multicultural Awareness: Resources for the Psychology Classroom.* Washington, DC: American Psychological Association. pp. 179–93.

Chiswick, B. & Hatton, T.J. (2003) International Migration and the Integration of Labor Markets. In Bordo, MD, Taylor, AM and Williamson, JG (eds). In Globalization in Historical Perspective, Chicago, IL: University of Chicago Press, pp. 65–120.

Dohse, K. (1985) *Ausländische Arbeiter und bürgerlicher Staat. Genese und Funktion von staatlicher Ausländerpolitik und Ausländerrecht. Vom Kaiserreich bis zur Bundesrepublik Deutschland.* Berlin: Express Edition.

DRCMGP (Development Research Center on Migration, Globalisation and Poverty) (2003) *Child Migration.* http://www.migrationdrc.org/research/typesofmigration/child_migration.html, accessed 2 December 2010.

Elliott, D., Mayadas, N.S. and Segal, U.A. (2010) 'Immigration worldwide: trends and analysis', in U.A. Segal, N.S. Mayadas and D. Elliott (eds), *Immigration Worldwide.* New York, NY: Oxford University Press. pp. 17–26.

Fahrmeir, A. (2000) 'Paßwesen und Staatsbildung im Deutschland des 19. Jahrhunderts', *Historische Zeitschrift* 271(1): 57–91.

Fahrmeir, A. (2007) *The Rise and Fall of a Modern Concept.* New Haven/London: Yale University Press.

Foucault, M. (1976) *Überwachen und Strafen. Die Geburt des Gefängnisses.* Frankfurt/Main: Suhrkamp Taschenbuch Verlag.

Fu, H. and Vanlandingham, M.J. (2010) 'Mental and physical health consequences of repatriation for Vietnamese returnees: a natural experiment approach', *Journal of Refugee Studies*, 23(2): 160–82.

Goldfrank, W.L., Goodman, D. and Szasz, A. (eds) (1999) *Ecology and the World System.* Westport, CT: Greenwood Press.

Hare, I. (2004) 'Defining social work for the 21st century: the International Federation of Social Workers' revised definition of social work', *International Social Work,* 47(3): 407–24.

Harrison, G. and Melville, R. (2010) *Rethinking social work in a global world.* New York, NY: Palgrave Macmillan.

Hashim, I.M. (2006) *The Positive and Negatives of Children's Independent Migration: Assessing the Evidence and the Debates.* Working Paper T16, Development Research Centre on Migration, Globalisation and Poverty, University of Sussex, Brighton, UK.

Heck, G. (2008). "Managing Migration" vor den Grenzen Europas: Das Beispiel Marokko. Paper presented at the conference on 'Migration(s) and Development(s): Transformation of Paradigms, Organisations and Gender', Center for Interdisciplinary Research, Bielefeld, Germany, July 10–11, 2008, Website: http://www.uni-bielefeld.de/tdrc/ag_comcad/downloads/workingpaper_45_heck.pdf, accessed April 4, 2012.

Humphries, B. (2004) 'An unacceptable role for social work: implementing immigration policy', *British Journal of Social Work,* 34(1): 93–107.

ILO (International Labour Organization) (2009) *Return Migration.* http://pstalker.com/ilo/o-return.html, accessed 3 December 2010.

IOM (International Organization for Migration). (2010) *World Migration Report 2010.* http://publications.iom.int/bookstore/free/WMR_2010_ENGLISH.pdf, accessed 19 December 2011.

Kubursi, A. (2006) *The Economics of Migration and Remittances Under Globalization.* http://www.un.org/docs/ecosoc/meetings/2006/hls2006/Preparatory/Statements/Kubursi_RT6.pdf, accessed 3 December 2010.

Landshut, S. (1969) 'Nation und Nationalismus', in W. Bernsdorf (ed.), *Wörterbuch der Soziologie.* Stuttgart: Enke. pp. 736–8.

Lan P-C. (2003) 'Negotiating social boundaries and private zones: the micropolitics of employing migrant domestic workers', *Social Problems,* 50(4): 525–49.

Lan, P-C. (2006) *Global Cinderellas: Migrant Domestics and Newly Rich Employers in Taiwan.* Durham, NC: Duke University Press.

Lum, D. (2003) *Culturally Competent Practice: a Framework for Understanding Diverse Groups and Justice Issues.* Pacific Grove, CA: Brooks/Cole.

Lyons, K. and Huegler, N. (2012) 'International labor mobility in social work', in L.M. Healy and R.J. Link (eds), *Handbook on International Social Work.* New York, NY: Oxford University Press. pp. 487–492.

Marrus, M. (1985) *The Unwanted. European Refugees in the Twentieth Century.* Oxford, NY: Oxford University Press.

Massey, D.S., Arango, J., Hugo, G. Kouaouci, A. Pellegrino, A. and Taylor, J. (2005) *Worlds in Motion.* Oxford, UK: Oxford University Press.

Meabe, J., Paredes, J. and Saguier, E. (2008) *The Universalization of the Nation-State and the Historical Crisis of its Institutive Order. Origin and Legitimating Function of the Founding Fathers in the Modern Sociopolitical Itinerary of Nations (1808–1989).* http://www.crisisyestado-nacion.org/archivo/Obra-Prologo-Ingles-I.pdf.

Myrdal, G. (1957) 'The principle of circular and cumulative causation', in G. Myrdal (ed.), *Rich Lands and Poor: the Road to World Prosperity.* New York, NY: Harper. pp. 11–22.

Nyame, F.K. and Grant, J.A. (2007) Implications of migration patterns associated with the mining and minerals industry in Ghana. http://www.imi.ox.ac.uk/pdfs/Nyame%20Grant%20Ghana%2007.pdf, accessed 3 December 2010.

O'Connell Davidson, J. and Farrow, C. (2007) *Child Migration and the Construction of Vulnerability.* Sweden: Save the Children. http://gipuzkoagazteria.net/admingazteria/dokumentuak/Childmigration and%20theconstruction%20ofvulnerability150208.pdf, accessed 21 March 2011.

Parreáas, R.S. (2001) *Servants of Globalization: Women, Migration and Domestic Work.* Stanford, CA: Stanford University Press.

Portes, A. (1999) 'Immigration theory for a new century: some problems and opportunities', in C. Hirschman, P. Kasinitz, and J. DeWind (eds), *The Handbook of International Migration: The American Experience.* New York, NY: Russell Sage Foundation.

Reuter, J. (2002) *Ordnungen des Anderen. Zum Problem des Eigenen in der Soziologie des Fremden.* Bielefeld.

Sassen, S. (1998) *Globalization and its Discontents. Essays on the New Mobility of People and Money.* New York: New Press.

Sassen, S. (2007) 'Die Re-Positionierung von Bürgerschaft', in M. Pieper, T. Atzert, S. Karakayalı and V. Tsianos (eds), *Empire und die biopolitische Wende. Die internationale Diskussion im Anschluss an Hardt und Negri.* Frankfurt am Main: Campus. pp. 143–68.

Saxenian, A. (2005) 'From brain drain to brain circulation: transnational communities and regional upgrading in India and China', *Studies in Comparative International Development*, 40(2): 35–61.

Segal, U.A. (2002) *A Framework for Immigration: Asians in the United States*. New York, NY: Columbia University Press.

Stojanov, R. (2009) *Environmentally-induced Migration in the World*. Dissertation thesis, University of Ostrava, Ostrava.

Stojanov, R. and Kavanová, K. (2009) 'El concepto de migrantes medioambientales (Comentarios introductorios)', *Estudios Migratorios Latinoamericanos*, 23(68): 39–54.

Soysal, Y. (1994) *Limits of Citizenship: Migrants and Postnational Membership in Europe*. Chicago: University of Chicago Press.

The Times of India. (2011) *Maoist Violence Claims 2,680 Lives in 2008–10*. 9 March 2011. www.timesofindia.indiatimes.com/india/Maoist-violence-claims-2680-lives-in-2008-10/articleshow/765 9524.cms.

Torpey, J. (2000) *The Invention of the Passport. Surveillance, Citizenship and the State*. Cambridge: Cambridge University Press.

Touzenis, K. (2010) *Trafficking in Human Beings*. Paris, France: United Nations Educational, Scientific and Cultural Organization (UNESCO).

UCDP (Uppsala Conflict Data Program). (2010) *Countries with One or More Conflicts*. http://www.ucdp.uu.se/gpdatabase/search.php, accessed 29 August 2011.

UCDP (Uppsala Conflict Data Program). (2011) *Department of Peace and Conflict Research*. www.pcr.uu.se/research/UCDP/, accessed 29 August 2011.

UN (United Nations). (2002) *International Migration Report*, New York, NY: United Nations, Department of Economic and Social Affairs Population Division. http://www.un.org/esa/population/publications/ittmig2002/2002ITTMIGTEXT22-11.pdf, accessed 21 March 2011.

UN (United Nations). (2009) *International Migration Stock: The 2008 Revision*, Department of Economic and Social Affairs, Population Division. http://esa.un.org/migration/, accessed 22 November 2010.

UNICEF (United Nations Children's Fund). (no date) *Child Protection from Violence, Exploitation and Abuse*. http://www.unicef.org/protection/index_exploitation.html, accessed 2 December 2010.

Vilalta-Bufi, M. (2007) *Labor Mobility and Inter-industry Wage Variation*, DEGIT Conference Papers c012_024, DEGIT, Dynamics, Economic Growth, and International Trade.

Von Lersner, U., Elbert, T. and Neuner, F. (2008) 'Mental health of refugees following state-sponsored repatriation from Germany', *BMC Psychiatry*, 8(88): 1–16.

Zlotnik, H. (2006) *The Complexity of International Migration Reviewed*. United Nations: Population Division, Department of Economic and Social Affairs. http://www.un.org/esa/population/migration/turin/Turin_Statements/ZLOTNIK2.pdf, accessed 3 December 2010.

Professional Contexts

Nigel Hall

INTRODUCTION TO SECTION 2: PROFESSIONAL CONTEXTS

Chapters in this section either locate social work as a professional activity in different contexts or analyse particular aspects of the profession. In Chapter 7, Malcolm Payne considers different political, organisational and professional discourses, which have created different forms of 'social works' in various countries, affected by local cultural and political values. These values – traditional, neo-liberal, socialist and social democrat – influence and shape social work identity and the value-base of the profession. To complicate this further, professional concerns based on biomedical, economic, legal, psychological and sociological discourses lead to further differentiation and emphases within social work. Consequently today the profession presents a range of perspectives around the world, including the generally accepted practice of social work itself, to social assistance, social pedagogy and social development. Also affected by these discourses are the particular managerial and organisational arrangements and the regulatory environment in which social work practice is incorporated into more formal social service. These are mediated by powerful international forces such as globalisation, the influence of neoliberalism and other national, regional and local factors.

This historical and thematic overview is also evident in Chapter 8, where Badwall and Razack consider social work theories, methods and practices. The authors investigate structural social work perspectives and in particular provide a critical analysis of post-structuralism and anti-racist discourse. Embedded within this is a critique of social work's genesis – its colonial influence and 'whiteness' which have resonance today and which continue to bias the profession. Critical reflexivity is a vital ingredient to ensure that we are constantly on guard and able to interrogate our assumptions that may inevitably be influenced by previous historical relationships – which favour dominant Northern perspectives. Commonly accepted social work values such as individualism and self-determination may not be ideal approaches for working in a global society – especially in the global South where the collective is prioritised over the individual. Critical social work has the potential to widen our range of perspectives, including those that are structural, radical and progressive as well as multi-cultural, anti-discriminatory and anti-oppressive.

These concerns also feature in any consideration of social work values, ethics and professional regulation, which Hugman and Bowles in Chapter 9 take us to. The authors describe the relationship between these, with ethical codes providing the bedrock of social work practice and setting out the value base of the profession. In several countries or regions of the world they form part of the statutory regulatory regime, while in others where social work is not distinctly regulated this is not the case. However in all situations they do provide guidance on what should be expected from social workers and may, where the profession is regulated, be used to hold workers accountable. Previous versions of the (IFSW) Code were more prescriptive but this has now changed to an aspirational and ethical vision stressing the central importance of human rights and social justice.

Taking inspiration from the universal Bill of Human Rights the jointly agreed IFSW/ IASSW (2004) ethical *Statement of Principles* was framed in a pluralistic sense and able to accommodate different ethical and rights-based priorities, although the challenge still remains for social workers to make judgements based on these values in the diverse circumstances they find themselves in. In particular there is need to provide greater recognition to values held in the global South where family or community 'communal' (macro) values may take precedence over 'Northern' (micro) values of individual freedom, although where the connections between these two are evident social work values are more sustainable. The authors ask whether a single (global) statement of ethics is plausible, and conclude that shared conversations about values and ethics in social work internationally are important. We are given the challenge as academics and practitioners to develop the common ground from which the diverse priorities within 'contextualised' or

locally based social work can be identified and nourished.

Hokenstad considers some of these factors in relation to social work education in Chapter 10 and provides an overview of how international trends are directing the shape of social work education in the future. The *Global Standards* (for the education and training of the social work profession) have been developed out of this, and these in turn provide a broad universal framework that can be adapted to local contexts and conditions. Several issues arise out of this, including the balance between the global and the local in curriculum development, the usefulness of universal models for social work practice, and the role of comparative research in building the social work knowledge base. Exchange programmes have helped contribute to better informed international courses and curricula, but there are concerns that international content is not infused sufficiently into social work courses, even though an international perspective is encouraged by many academic institutions. Where this has been encouraged more of a regional emphasis has been emphasised. However there are some useful examples of joint programmes between academics from different countries offering a course that may be jointly validated, or validated through one institution. There are generally minimal global standards of education (3-year undergraduate degrees), although there is also emphasis on masters level courses. While increasing academisation of social work programmes may be a concern, certainly higher degrees are generally considered necessary for teaching, including doctoral level studies, although access to these may be difficult from the less developed world.

There are however other opportunities for gaining comparative and international experience: projects and placements abroad, exchange programmes, and the development of communities of practice using the Internet have helped in bringing international themes into the curriculum. As noted elsewhere in this chapter and indeed as a theme that runs through this section of the *Handbook*, having global standards raises questions about the universality of values (such as individual versus family or communal values), and also raises questions over the need for social change versus consensus and questions related to diversity and human rights generally.

The final chapter (Chapter 11) by Orme and Karvinen-Niinikoski in this section looks at the issue of social work research from an international perspective. The authors note that the *Global Standards* emphasise the significance of research for social work practice internationally, including an appreciation and knowledge of key findings relevant to practice. In the situation where many social issues facing practitioners require global solutions, then international social work research becomes crucial to the development of theory and the improvement of practice. The expansion of social work knowledge and the research underpinning it are – or should be – integrally linked to social work education. Good quality research needs to be rigorous and provide carefully researched evidence to back up and complement teaching and practice, but this also needs to reflect diversity and avoid the charge of professional imperialism. Even with good intentions this is not necessarily straightforward as even international research projects may well be limited by use of a particular language, requiring presentation in formats that are preset in advance, and publication in specified respected international journals. There are opportunities however that can be harnessed as well to ensure that social work research becomes a progressive and useful means of transforming practice.

Overall this section points the way forward for social work and reminds us that the profession needs both to be rooted in the realities and concerns of the situation where it is practised, while learning from experience elsewhere – yet taking a critical stance in respect of the value assumptions that may prejudice or distort the professional response.

7

Political and Organisational Contexts of Social Work Internationally

Malcolm Payne

INTRODUCTION

Social work is a bottom-up profession, so its organisational and political context in any particular country is formed by the interaction of the needs, history, culture and political assumptions of that nation. Across the world, a range of social works has therefore emerged, produced by many different histories. While there is no international template, countries face similar issues and trends in social need. International interchange influences social policy and the development and organisation of social work services. In this way, the social works of different nations influence each other in a broad stream of development. Moreover, political and organisational systems are influenced by overarching political philosophies and organisational needs. So, we can identify the political values and organisational principles that underlie any national or international system.

This chapter therefore examines how practitioners may understand the political and organisational contexts of each national social work, starting from political, organisational and professional discourses that create national social works and social works that may be identified in the international context. Six main issues stand out:

- How political values influence the role of social work services and contribute to a political and social discourse that creates a welfare regime within which a national organisation of social work services develops and national social works emerge.
- How these factors create professional discourses from which emerge four main different social works in different welfare regimes: social work; social assistance and social care; social pedagogy; and social development practices.
- How important issues in managerial and organisational discourse have influenced recent change in the role of social work as a profession within welfare regimes.
- How relationships between national, regional and local structures and between social work and connected services influence the organisation and regulation of social work.

- How the mixed economy of welfare developed from the increasing impact of neoliberal values on welfare regimes through the impact of managerialism and globalisation.
- How social work is incorporated into and represented by a variety of international organisations.

POLITICAL VALUES AND SOCIAL WORK

Politics is about how power is divided among different social groups in a society. Four main sets of political values influence most political systems and the social work that emerges from those systems. No present-day society is wholly defined by one of these political value systems, but we can see how they interact to provide the underlying principles of different forms of social work across the world.

Table 7.1 sets out these four sets of political values. *Traditional authority* comes from a political elite or religious tradition. In countries like Saudi Arabia today, a royal family, allied with the influence of a dominant religion, Islam, maintains formal and significant power over people's lives and most economic and political decisions. Other authoritarian countries are ruled by a military dictator. Citizens have some political mechanisms for democratic participation and some economic freedom to pursue personal and family interests, but important decisions are mainly held by the ruling elite, religious leaders or dictators.

The main principle in such systems is respect for authority, which maintains the power of social groups who have traditionally held power and influence. Authoritarian regimes may provide welfare services to facilitate people's adaptation to the traditional social order. They respond to social problems such as youth offending and deal with personal difficulties arising from factors such as poverty, physical and mental ill-health, disability or old age.

Liberalism is a political philosophy based on the principle of individualism, that individuals should be free from the constraints of traditional authority to pursue their own interests, as part of personal social institutions, such as their family and community. Their actions are informed by their rational assessment of those interests. This encourages economic and social development, because individuals pursuing their own interests (or the interests of people close to them) are likely to achieve more than when they are directed by some external authority. In the economy, markets liberate people's interests. They can choose from alternative suppliers and are free to contribute their labour and resources to supporting themselves and creating economic growth, which benefits everyone by improving the general quality of life.

Government in liberal regimes operates by consent to stimulate an environment that provides basic protections, regulating behaviour in the market. Maintaining national and international social order facilitates markets and individual freedom. In countries like Korea or Singapore, today, democratic and state institutions give a strong priority to economic growth and development. The role of welfare is to maintain stability and develop the human resources to contribute to that development. Social work aims to resolve problems and conflicts for individuals and contribute to empowering individual capacity to contribute to society. Dealing with social problems is, therefore, not just about providing stability for the economy to flourish, but also to enable people to deal with problems, such as disabilities, that prevent them from having the freedom to further their own interests by contributing to the economy.

Neoliberalism is currently influential in the USA and across the world. This philosophy espouses liberal values, but developed in opposition to socialism and social democracy, so it is assertive in pursuing individualism to counter some of the problems of these other, non-individualistic philosophies.

Socialism argues that government represents people's collective interests, sanctioning

Table 7.1   Political values that influence social work

Political values	Principle	General aims	Aim of welfare	Social work
Traditional authority	Authoritarianism	Maintaining the power of traditional social groups	Social control	Facilitate adaptation to social order
(Neo)Liberalism	Individualism	Fostering individuals' freedoms to pursue their own interests will benefit everyone through economic growth	Social order	Empower freedom and capacity to contribute to society; problem-solving
Socialism	Collectivism	Planning participation of people in cooperative endeavours	Social change	Mutual support, collective (state) provision
Social democracy	Humanistic, reformist	State limits adverse impacts by maintaining democracy and human rights	Social reform	Service delivery from a variety of providers; state coordination

governance and law for the common good. The guiding principle is collectivism, with people participating in planning and organising society to benefit everyone, rather than pursuing only their own interests. Socialism identifies a conflict of interest between elites with economic and social power, often inherited from traditions that gave them unjustified influence, and others who may be oppressed by that power. The role of the state is to plan and organise cooperative endeavours, and to regulate conflicts of interest in the economy and society by promoting equality in the use of resources and facilitating oppressed people to secure their interests against the interests of elites, through cooperative and mutual support mechanisms such as trade unions. During the period 1950–1980, communist states in central and eastern Europe followed these policies. Many saw the main instruments of welfare as being state provision and mutual cooperation through state-organised trade unions, rather than a social work that helped individuals.

Social democracy developed as a response to liberalism and socialism. It accepts that individual freedom within a market system is the best way to achieve the benefits of economic growth, but sees the state as responsible for limiting the adverse consequences of extreme individualism. It does this by providing a democratic process for participation in governing the economy and society. Social reform aims to deal with social problems and maintains individual and collective human rights against any tendency towards oppression. The state is therefore responsible for the well-being of its citizens, and social work provision becomes part of state provision. Most European countries pursue a broadly social democratic value system, and most social work in Europe is provided by the state. However, alternatives from private companies and not-for-profit organisations create a 'mixed economy of care' in which services may come from a variety of organisations.

Most of these political philosophies are present to some degree in every country. For example, until the 1990s, the Republic of Ireland, although a conventional European social democracy in most respects, had extensive social provision by the (historically) influential Roman Catholic church. There was less state social work than in many European countries as a result, but this changed as the Church lost influence and state provision became more important. This and many other cultural and historical factors are important in how social work is provided in any country.

DISCOURSES WITHIN THE WELFARE REGIME CREATE SOCIAL WORKS

Political values are not the only influence on social work and social work services. The political and organisational context of social provision in each country creates a 'welfare regime', that is, the combination of social, political and economic arrangements that creates the organisation of welfare provision in that country (Esping-Andersen, 1990). Welfare regimes are important factors in how countries incorporate social work into systems of welfare provision. As it develops, social work in turn influences the development of the welfare regime in which it operates.

Discourse within the cultural and value traditions of any society influence the creation of the welfare regime and social work services within it. Discourses include political and public debates and professional and political writing: discourse is also represented by how people within society carry out actions, or how social institutions and relationships themselves operate. So social work discourses are not only what is debated, but also how practitioners and others involved in social work services act and the impact of social welfare institutions on the society in which they operate.

Three arenas of interaction are important in establishing the role and nature of social work services:

- Political and social debate in the formation of policy and governance of social work organisations, governance being the process by which the actions of organisations are authorised and managed.
- Interaction between professionals and the managers of social work agencies about the management and practice of their work.
- Interactions between the users of services and social work professionals in which needs and demands from users are interpreted by practitioners to influence the nature and outcomes of services provided (Payne, 2006).

The organisation of social work and the agencies within which it is practised,

therefore, respond to general political and social ideas circulating in a society; the practicalities of negotiating and managing agencies employing professionals; and the demands generated by service users' needs. This process may most easily be seen when a major change occurs in political and cultural assumptions. For example, until 1994, social work services in South Africa were dominated by a therapy-centred approach, based on models of practice derived from economically developed Western countries. After the election of an African National Congress government, when a focus on economic and social development for poor black populations became a priority, the emphasis began to shift towards delivering community development services using community work techniques (Weyers and van den Berg, 2006). Thus, professional priorities in social work shifted as a result of political change.

DOMINANT AND PROFESSIONAL DISCOURSES

Healy (2005) suggests that the dominant discourses about health and welfare, internationally, are biomedical, economic and legal. Her analysis is that these discourses are crucial in many societies in deciding the ways in which social work is understood and its organisations governed and managed.

Biomedical discourses are important for three reasons. First, healthcare services and medicine form well-established, socially influential organisations, professions and bodies of knowledge with wide public acceptance. Second, many welfare services are provided in conjunction with or as a supplement to healthcare. Third, social work often operates by analogy with a medical model of seeking to assess and resolve personal and social problems in the same way that a doctor or nurse would diagnose and provide treatment to address symptoms of ill-health. So, in political and social discourse, people understand social work as 'personal problem-solving' by this analogy with medical diagnosis and treatment.

Economic discourses are important because state services are supported by the productive capacity of a society and social services both benefit and draw on that productive capacity. For example, social services contribute to social resilience and solidarity, important sources of the stability needed by business to achieve economic growth, but, on the other hand, services are supported though taxation, a cost to business and potentially a drag on economic growth.

Legal discourses are important because much social provision is by the state, and thus directed by political decision-making implemented through legislation. Consequently how social services are organised and what social workers do are strongly influenced by legal mandates. Satka (1995) shows how the importance of law as a basis for public services in Finland has influenced the development of social work. She also shows how current practice, influenced by American attempts to introduce social casework across Europe in the 1950s, has contended with and eventually balanced this emphasis on legal and administrative expertise in Finland.

However, Healy (2005) goes on to suggest that much of the discourse within social work is based on psychological and sociological ideas and these compete with dominant discourses. For example, in palliative care services for dying people, social workers might argue that it is important to improve social resilience by helping people deal with the social impact of dying and of bereavement on families, workplaces and communities and the psychological effects of grief. A biomedical view might focus on pain and symptom management and physical care to ensure comfort for a dying person. Because palliative care is seen as a medical specialty providing healthcare for people with advanced illnesses, the model in social work discourse has difficulty in overcoming a dominant biomedical discourse. Therefore, the primary service is for people dying of advanced

diagnosed illnesses, and experience in this field has been slow to transfer to care for wider groups of people dying through the frailties of old age (Reith and Payne, 2009).

There are also, in Healy's (2005) model, alternative discourses vying for influence. For example, some discourses see people's rights and interests as consumers of a service as a priority. Accepting such discourses would lead a welfare regime to give priority in social work to advocacy for people's rights, or to the incorporation of social work as an important element of social security services. Local government social work in Denmark and Finland is engaged with providing discretionary social security benefits. Clients for interpersonal social work in those countries are often referred in the first instance through these social security responsibilities. The legal and administrative discourse on social security thus forms an important element in understanding the role and nature of social work in those countries and the concerns of social work practice.

At any time and in any society, there is a social and political settlement of the role of social work services in a welfare regime. This changes over time and therefore so does the role of social work. For example, Chenoweth (2008) describes welfare reform in Australia between 1990 and 2010. Change in welfare policies reveal similarities of strategy in Australia and the US. Both countries sought to reduce the size and cost of welfare provision, assuming that the underlying cause of social problems such as poverty, unemployment and, in the USA, single parenthood, was individual behaviour rather than social factors. Such policies reflect a shift in favour of liberal political values. In Australia, the 'job network' experiment required welfare recipients to engage in active job-seeking behaviour, and replaced a national network of public sector labour exchanges with a network of smaller services provided by charities, local non-governmental organisations (NGOs) and for-profit providers which contracted with the government. The 'job network' services provide basic computerised job vacancies services for recently unemployed people. Other people, unemployed for more than twelve months, receive more intensive case management to prepare them for work. Non-participation leads to negative reports, fines and cuts in benefits. Staff, who include some social workers, are subject to performance targets, which leads to decreased professional autonomy in making decisions and a casualised workforce. A separate organisation, Centrelink, provides services to a range of government departments deciding, using a highly computerised system, who is eligible for a variety of government benefits and referring people to the job network. Policies are founded on obligations to work rather than rights to security and may contribute to social polarisation between people who are in work and others who are seen as on the margins of society. Social work help to disabled people, people with mental illnesses and people experiencing long-term unemployment for reasons such as single parenthood is mainly on the outside of the welfare system, advocating for exceptions for people needing help, rather than seeking entitlements on behalf of people with serious personal problems.

This Australian experience illustrates some of the consequences of welfare regime changes that derive from changes in the public perception of and the organisation of social services in different sectors of the economy.

FOUR DIFFERENT SOCIAL WORKS

We have been exploring a range of political factors that lead to variations in the political and organisational context of social work services in different nations; those variations have created across the world four main types of social work. Each of these social works emphasises different aspects of the social work role described in the international definition of social work: 'The social

work profession promotes social change, problem solving in human relationships and the empowerment and liberation of people to enhance well-being' (IFSW, 2000).

- *Social work*: a practice where interpersonal skills are used with individuals, families and small groups to resolve interpersonal and social relationship problems, with a 'liberation for well-being' objective.

Examples are found in clinical social work in healthcare settings or social work in schools. Social work is strong in the USA, where its practice has developed into 'clinical social work', a complex relationship-based practice. The theories and skills that underlie clinical social work contribute to the interpersonal elements of social assistance and social care in developed countries. It may also be used in particular services in less developed countries, for example adoption, healthcare or to respond to the personal effects of social dislocation.

- *Social assistance, social care*: services where social work disciplines lead in providing services focusing on the problem-solving objective of social work, often as part of public welfare provision.

This may include adult and child safeguarding, arranging packages of social care services or access to care homes where people need help with everyday living. In some countries, social work is involved in providing social security and housing welfare. Social assistance and social care is an important part of social provision in most developed countries, where the state usually accepts wide responsibility for social provision. Examples are found in European welfare regimes pursuing the European social model where the state takes wide responsibility for interpersonal support and management of welfare provision. The 'problem-solving' objective is about the delivery of care services. Alternatively, in resource-poor countries, this model is often concerned with basic disaster relief, health improvement or poverty-reduction initiatives. In recent years, for example, devastation caused by a tsunami, floods or war have led to this kind of response. One problem for countries where international aid organisations and specialist charities, often based in the West, are active is that meeting organisations' objectives, may not always support the policies or priorities of the nation in which they operate (see Chapter 18).

- *Social pedagogy, social education, cultural education*: social work disciplines that focus on the education and personal development of people who are disadvantaged or oppressed by social injustice to achieve the 'liberation through well-being' objective (through an educative rather than therapeutic approach); clients are seen as developing within a supportive social milieu.

In some countries, examples of social pedagogy are found mainly in services for young people and/or in group care settings such as residential, day and after school care. This personal social development becomes part of informal education to improve social solidarity. Social pedagogy and similar practice is particularly strong in mainland Europe (Kornbeck and Jensen, 2009).

- *Social development*: concentrates on the social change objective of social work: it encourages people affected by economic development to come together in groups to identify and take action on issues of shared concern and is aimed at enhancing social solidarity and resilience in responding to social change.

Most social development takes place in resource-poor countries or regions, particularly in the global South. Its practice interacts with community work carried out with less-well-developed regions or problematic communities in Western countries (Midgley, 1995; Dominelli, 2007; Midgley and Conley, 2010). In some resource-poor countries, mainly in Africa, Asia and South America, this is the main form of social work. Examples might be helping communities organise to provide a community well to obtain water, or assisting rural people with business or agricultural skills to enhance family incomes. These actions connect increasing economic growth in poor regions with strengthening capacity to plan and manage facilities in the community. Hence, they improve social resilience. In economically developed countries, community development is dissociated from economic development and focuses more on tackling deprivation by improving community or welfare facilities.

We can see aspects of these forms of social work in most countries. Bon (2010), for example, describes four main forms of intervention in France: help through practical assistance (social assistance and social care) and interpersonal casework (social work); specialised education, child care and youth work (social pedagogy); animation that stimulates personal development through organising activities in institutions (a mixture of social pedagogy and social development); and home care provision, such as foster care, day care, personal care and domiciliary help (social assistance and social care).

MANAGERIAL AND ORGANISATIONAL DISCOURSES IN SOCIAL WORK SERVICES

The welfare regime incorporates social work into social services through particular managerial and organisational arrangements, and these arrangements are also affected by political and social discourses. Four issues have had an important impact: professionalisation; managerialism; globalisation; and risk management.

The role of social work as a profession

Although social work has sought to become recognised as a profession along the lines of medicine or the law, this objective has always been debated, because the organisation of social work primarily in state agencies (in the global North) has led some to suggest that it is, at best, a 'semi-profession' (Toren, 1972) because it can never attain similar autonomy of decision making through social control of an established evidence or knowledge base.

Thus, social workers were seen as 'bureau-professionals' whose discretion has been limited by the top-down political authority of democratically elected government through the machinery of managerial control of social agencies. This is why the political and social discourse is an important arena of influence on social work practice. However, research suggests that professionals often balance this influence with the demands of service users in the professional-service user discourse, functioning as 'street-level bureau-crats' (Lipsky, 1983) whose decisions are not always observable or controllable by managers. Also, policy may not provide for rational management of practice, reflecting instead an approach of 'muddling through' (Lindblom, 1959). Recent trends in three areas have contested this basic model of management and led to further concerns that social work may be in a process of deprofessionalisation.

Managerialism and new public management

Part of the deprofessionalisation came from the rise of managerialism, a neoliberal response to economic changes in the 1980s, resulting from a rapid rise in the price of oil. Neoliberal theorists argued that extensive welfare provision along the lines of the European social model was unaffordable. However, such services have strong public support, so new public management (NPM) seeks to manage them so that they are more economically efficient. This involves dispersing managerial power from the centre and using managers with generalist (rather than professional) skills and setting numerical activity targets (rather than using processes like professional supervision and

consultation). We can see this process going on in the Australian example, above. In addition to this, there is a greater focus on managing the culture of organisations, rather than permitting groups including professions such as social work, to develop their own professional culture (Hughes and Wearing, 2007)

Globalisation

One of the pressures towards NPM is globalisation, a series of structural changes affecting human institutions in the later 1990s and early 2000s (Payne and Askeland, 2008). Global markets in banking, insurance and transport developed, displacing the influence of national markets under the control of national political discourse. New institutions acting internationally emerged, including multinational corporations integrating production and marketing in many different countries. To manage the consequences of these changes, new rules and norms grew up, with international regulation by market economic policies, human rights and environment conventions and multilateral trade agreements becoming influential on national welfare regimes. New communication tools such as the Internet, email and mobile phones and cheaper air travel linked people and countries simultaneously. These led to political, economic and cultural changes, bringing people closer together but also preventing countries from pursuing independent social policies.

Risk management

The greater speed of communication, enhanced international interdependence and loss of national control of economic and social policy meant that economic and social policy actors faced an environment of greater risk. Greater efforts were made to reduce professional discretion in order to manage risk factors such as economic and political pressures, and reputational risks, such as the risk of scandal due to events such as child safeguarding failures (Webb, 2006; Hughes and Wearing, 2007).

SOCIAL WORK PROVISION IN DIFFERENT SECTORS OF THE ECONOMY

Since welfare regimes derive partly from the position of welfare services within the economic system of any country, how the elements of welfare provision is divided between different economic sectors affects how social work is provided. The main sectors involved are the public; private; not for profit; informal; and social enterprise sectors.

In the *public sector* model, organisations are controlled and financed by the state and authorised to act by legislation enacted by the parliament of a country. Most states accept some responsibility for the social well-being of their population and in many developed economies, this includes extensive service provision. The implications of competing value systems (socialist; liberal; social democrat) have been referred to above. In the European context, social democrats seek to balance the need to maintain economic growth through energetic markets with a strong responsibility for social well-being and this approach has influenced the development of a (Western) European 'social model' of balancing policies that aim at market efficiencies with policies that seek to provide social protection and equality. Scharpf (2002) argues that one of the problems of the European Union is that free market policies are the main focus of the European level of government, while national governments are the main providers of welfare. Thus, the different levels of government constrain each other in the pursuit of their objectives.

In the *private* or *for-profit sector*, organisations controlled by non-state bodies are established to provide goods and services in return for profits that provide an income for the individuals or corporations that finance them. Social work is provided by for-profit organisations in two ways. First, some social workers operate in private practice, either as individuals or in groups. Mostly, these organisations offer counselling-style help or training and consultancy in social work management, policy and practice. Individual clients or organisations provided with training or consultancy pay the practitioner directly. The second pattern is for companies to provide services, for which some individual clients may pay directly. More typically, however, the service is provided by contract to a public body. Most such services are fairly concrete provision of residential or day care centres and agencies providing care workers for residential, day or domiciliary care. There are now examples of international companies providing social care services.

The voluntary, not-for-profit or *third sector* is controlled by non-state bodies, often referred to as NGOs. These are established to provide goods and services for the benefit of the community or individuals in need, and in which any financial surpluses earned in the process are returned to improve the service provided. The not-for-profit sector is present in most countries, extending from very small informal organisations responding to a local issue (e.g. a local support group for carers of older people with dementia) to large national organisations providing services across the country. Some NGOs have been established for a century or more and some have developed 'branches' or related agencies in other countries. Third sector agencies may cover a range of functions: engaging participation in providing local services; making services responsive to local opinion; campaigning on behalf of social groups or raising concern about social issues that have not achieved public or government support; developing new ideas for services to show that they are worthwhile; or providing extensive services through contracts with government agencies or supported by charitable funding. Countries where socialist and social democratic values are strong, such as the Nordic countries, often have only a small-scale not-for-profit sector, with most provision being by state organisations.

The *informal sector*, provides goods and services through individuals and communities because they have a personal or social relationship with the recipients of the goods and services, whether as family, friends, neighbours or participants in a community of shared interest. This sector is universal, since most care everywhere is provided by families, neighbours and friends of people in need. In developed economies, where formal social work services are extensive, provisions are often interwoven with informal care, and social workers operate in partnership with informal carers. This requires a degree of humility and responsiveness to the needs and wishes of carers in the way in which services are organised. In less developed-countries, there may be very little support for informal carers, and what support is available comes from local sources rather than formal services.

Lastly, the *social enterprise* sector is a recently developed hybrid sector in which private, for-profit organisations provide goods and services for social and community benefit, with any profits being returned to provide benefits for the community in which they were generated. It is not clear what role social enterprises will play in social work. Germak and Singh (2010) argue that social work has not played a strong role in developing social enterprise, partly because their training has often not fitted practitioners for a business planning role, and also because many social enterprise developments have been in economic rather than social development. The classic example is the Nobel prize-award-winning Grameen Bank, which gives very small loans of money to enable Bangladeshi families to develop businesses that support their family and personal development. However, there is also some evidence that social workers are engaging with social enterprise ventures in Hong Kong, for example, in the field of work integration (Ho and Chan, 2010).

These sectors overlap. For example, both private and social enterprise organisations make profits, but for different objectives and stakeholders. Social enterprises provide goods and services to achieve social purposes and their profits do not benefit the organisation and its financiers themselves, but the community it serves. Another example is that voluntary and informal organisations often look rather similar, but voluntary organisations usually have a more formal legal structure, while informal organisations rely on mainly interpersonal relationships and personal connections. Voluntary organisations are often legally structured as companies, like private and social enterprise organisations, but they have a stronger emphasis on social purposes, and cannot distribute profits to the people who finance them. Private, voluntary, informal and social enterprise organisations are often financed by public authorities to provide services in partnership with them or on their behalf, but the public authority retains public accountability for the services it finances and directs.

Different political values lead to different points of view on the mixed economy of care. Liberal and neoliberal philosophies actively favour the availability of alternatives to the state, while socialist values favour state provision. Social democratic values are open to a mixed economy or primarily state provision. It is this openness in many Western societies that have led to debate about the role of the state in welfare regimes and in social work. The influence of neoliberal ideas since the 1980s has led to an increase in the role of the private and not-for-profit sectors and a shift in the role of the state from being the primary provider to being part of a mixed economy, as we saw in the Australian example above.

Social work may be provided in any of these types of organisation, and is often provided through partnerships between organisations in different sectors. In many countries, the state takes primary responsibility for social work services, mainly because social work is provided to people in practical and financial difficulties, who cannot afford to pay for services, and therefore cannot generate a profit for a private company. In most countries, organisations from other sectors may contract with the state to provide elements of the service. Where the political history or ideological or cultural tradition of a country means that welfare provision is mainly by charities in the voluntary sector, the state supports charitable endeavour by giving tax advantages and contracting services to voluntary providers. Many important social work organisations in the USA operate in this way, although public sector services are also important in providing basic care provision. Normally, however, the state holds a coordinating and planning role, commissioning and financing services, especially for service users who are unable to pay for the costs of their services.

However, some countries have a significant sector, variously described, of industrial social work, in which large companies provide social welfare services for their employees and sometimes their families. In Japan, this is an extension of the historic paternalistic role of important local political leaders: with industrialisation, this role naturally extended to employers. Sweden and the USA, among developed countries, also have significant employer welfare provision, and in some resource-poor countries, private welfare and health provision is economically important to large companies in maintaining a stable workforce and in contributing to the total available welfare provision in a country.

NATIONAL, REGIONAL AND LOCAL RESPONSIBILITIES

An important organisational consideration is the relationship between national, regional and local responsibility for social work and related services. In many countries, social work and social services are delegated to local responsibility. Subsidiarity in European policy aims to place all state action at the lowest possible level of state organisation. This is partly influenced by the Catholic church, which resisted state involvement in family policy, but tradition in many other countries, for example, Japan, gives priority to family and community in providing personal and social help (Payne, 2005). Very centralised countries, like the UK, develop policy nationally on the role of locally provided social services. Most countries are less centralised and may provide services at each tier of government. For example, in Poland, very local municipalities and communes provide social assistance centres, districts (poviats) provide family aid centres and regions (voivodships) have social policy centres (Ministry of Labour and Social Policy, 2011). In such cases, there may be uncertainty, overlap or conflict over responsibility for a particular service and control of central and local government agencies may lie with different political parties.

This also raises the role of regulation. Where there is an extensive mixed economy, government manages and supervises non-state services, and this regulation must be independent of competitive services that the government itself provides. This is sometimes a requirement even where services are primarily in the public sector. For example, in Poland, regional social policy centres have a role in coordinating and ensuring quality and appropriateness of local services. In the UK, with a large mixed economy, a regulator, the Care Quality Commission, sets standards and inspects care homes and hospitals. However, where the state retains only a regulatory role, this sometimes leads to difficulties because if government agencies provide no alternative service, they do not retain the expertise to take over if something goes wrong and a major non-state provider ceases to operate. There is a recent example of this in the UK, where a provider of more than 30,000 residential home places for mainly older people went out of business, almost no public provision to substitute for this loss remains in many parts of the country and there are no public sector staff to take over the service.

For similar reasons, regulating social work as a profession has also become important. Bibus and Boutté-Queen's (2011) comparative study of different national processes for licensing and registration of social work practice shows that government, professional and education organisations play a role. The focus is on selection for, education of and regulation of appropriate practice, but the interactions between different interests vary in different countries. Bibus and Boutté-Queen (2011) suggest that how regulation of both professional practice and, to some degree, the private lives of professionals takes place also has implications for the kinds of social work practised, with important consequences also for the context in which practitioners do their work. Weiss and Welbourne's (2007) comparative study demonstrates marked differences in the autonomy and prestige of social work across the world which affects the influence of social work discourses on the political and cultural discourse of particular countries.

In mixed economies of care, therefore, social work is often divided. Practitioners may have roles in regulating services, providing them and in providing social work, either separately or as part of wider social services. Another division may occur between provision and case/care management, in which the decisions are made to commission the services required by individual people in need. As a consequence, the impact of social work interests in political and cultural discourse varies according to its representation. Most countries have a professional association of social workers, but its role may be less influential than local government or agency managers in identifying and forming the role of social work. Another factor is the position of the professional association in relation to trades unions. In the Nordic countries, the professional association of social workers is a specialised part of larger local

government trade unions, and therefore plays a role in trade union representation, whereas in the UK legal requirements force a separation of trade union and professional association structures, while in the USA trade unions are not influential in representing professional interests (Payne, 2005: chapter 8).

The relationship between central and local government finance and policy also need careful analysis, because management and regulation may become separate from finance. In the UK, for example, the National Health Service is an agency of central government, with finance and management being part of the same organisational structure. However, the social services are part of local government, with finance coming from the central government Department for Communities and Local Government. Guidance and policy-making for social work functions is carried out in the Department for Education (for children's services) and the Department of Health (for adult services), so policy-making may become divorced from financing.

SOCIAL WORK AND OTHER FIELDS OF PRACTICE

Social work is practised as part of or in connection with other social services. Kamerman (2002) identifies a number of fields of practice that social work services are often connected with: education; employment and unemployment; health and mental health; housing and homelessness; justice (both civil and criminal); and social security and poverty. The organisation of social work services may incorporate social work within specialist services, as in the Australian social security and employment services discussed above, or develop a range of forms of interaction between social work, social work services and these connected fields of practice.

There are four main models of partnership between social work organisations and other fields of practice, ranging from social work taking a leading role to having a subsidiary position. Alternatively, social workers may operate primarily as referral agents or advocates: in the *advocacy model* social work agencies assist clients to get appropriate services from another agency.

Where *social work has a leading role in a social service organisation,* social work has a primary role and less formalised relationships with other professionals. For example, in some Nordic countries such as Denmark and Finland, social work is the leading profession in local government agencies organising discretionary social security provision. Referrals for social work help therefore sometimes come from these social security responsibilities, rather than from, for example, doctors, nurses or teachers.

Alternatively, social work sometimes has a *secondary role in agencies in other fields.* A common example is hospital social work. Hospitals focus mainly on medical and other healthcare issues. Many larger hospitals also employ social workers, who work as part of teams of doctors, nurses and other healthcare professionals, but are also often organised as a social work team for mutual support. A sports analogy is relevant. The multiprofessional ward team is like a football team during a match: they all work together, sharing interventions and taking roles according to professional expertise. The social work team is like a tennis team playing separate matches on behalf of a club: they all carry out social work, but do so in relation to different wards and clinics.

In a *conglomerate model,* social workers provide specialist services but are part of a department providing a range of services. An example is the typical structure of children's services in England, which are usually part of an education department in local government. Schools support and administration forms the main division and children's services provide social work services mainly for deprived, vulnerable, abused or neglected children. An education welfare (or social work in education) function is concerned with ensuring that poverty and family problems do not interfere with children's attendance at school. Counselling and personal help to young people in schools is usually not a social work function, being handled by teachers trained in 'pastoral care'. In the US, on the other hand, there is a strong workforce of social workers practising in schools with a significant counselling role (see also Chapter 14). This example shows how different welfare regimes draw the boundaries between professional skills and official roles and responsibilities differently. However, some overarching professional roles are universal. For example, in England and the US, social workers, counsellors, education welfare workers and pastoral care teachers would all take professional responsibility for identifying signs of – and taking action on – parental abuse and neglect.

INTERNATIONAL STRUCTURES

Most cooperation at international or (continental) regional levels, for example, in the United Nations or the European Union, focuses strongly on economic and peacekeeping issues. However, international actions on these issues often have social implications. Therefore, social policy and social service implications often flow from economic and other policies, particularly as globalisation has encouraged sharing of policy and organisational goals among different nations. For example, the European Union has funded a number of projects to coordinate education for social work professions, as part of a wider policy of assisting mobility of the European workforce (Chytil and Seibel, 1999; Warzywoda-Krusyńska and Krystzkowski, 2000).

Four types of international organisations exist, in which social work plays a part (Payne and Askeland, 2008):

- *Development agencies* in the South, where people from developed countries work to assist less-developed countries. Examples are organisations such as Save the Children, Caritas and *Médecin Sans Frontiéres*.

- *Official international organisations*, including representative organisations, often connected with the United Nations, or with structures covering continental regions, such as Europe or south-east Asia, or continental sub-regions, such as the Nordic group of countries.
- *Organisations dealing with transnational issues* that transcend national boundaries. Common issues include cross-country adoption, transmigration, family disputes leading to abduction of children, and trafficking of women and children (e.g. for prostitution or domestic servitude). Increasingly, technology is an important means of communication within formal organisations, networks or movements. While concerns arise about its misuse, such as for the international transmission of images of child abuse and sexual offences, it also provides opportunities for those who wish to intervene in shared issues, such as environmental issues and climate change. Many of the organisations engaged in this work are governmental agencies, but alongside them there are also organisations that assist individuals in difficulty or requiring support (Negi and Furman, 2010). International organisations addressing transnational social issues (including related to refugees and disasters) are an important locus for international social work practice.
- *International organisations for social workers and agencies*, include the main international membership and representative organisations, including the International Association of Schools of Social Work (IASSW, also known in the French and Spanish abbreviation as AIETS), the International Council on Social Welfare (ICSW) and the International Federation of Social Workers (IFSW). World conferences (in even-numbered years) and conferences based in continental regions (odd-numbered years) alternate and provide an important opportunity for international exchange and discourse. These organisations also run or finance development projects reflecting their interests; bring together groups around particular topics (e.g. to devise policy statements) and represent social work with other international and continental regional organisations, not least the UN.

Recent studies (Ramon, 2008; Lavalette and Ioakimidis, 2011) suggest that in areas where political conflict dominates daily life, or in the context of major disasters, social work becomes a more basic matter of relief to displaced and disrupted communities, help with survival, rescue and reconstruction. There may also be trauma and stress of dealing with extreme situations. In the longer term, ways of achieving reconciliation and helping people deal with the memory of disaster is also important (see also Chapters 18 and 19).

CONCLUSION

I have argued in this chapter that the organisation of social work emerges from national political and cultural discourses interacting with discourses within the profession of social work. Each of these discourses is in turn affected by cultural and political change and the social pressures of continuing need, as well as the more spontaneous needs associated with disasters, affecting people within any society. Practitioners can understand their role within the national organisational context of social work by exploring international comparators and being aware of the impact of globalisation in creating a strong international influence for neoliberal political values within the organisation and political context of many different social works across the world.

REFERENCES

Bibus, A.A. and Boutté-Queen, N. (eds) (2011) *Regulating Social Work: A Primer on Licensing Practice*. Chicago: Lyceum.

Bon, C. (2010) 'Elements of knowledge about social work in France: the position of social work and the social workers', *European Journal of Social Work*, 13 (3): 415–20.

Chenoweth, L. (2008) 'Redefining welfare: Australian social policy and practice', *Asian Social Work and Policy Review*, 2 (1): 53–60.

Chytil, O. and Seibel, F. (eds) (1999) *European Dimensions in Training and Practice of Social Professions*. Boskovice: Verlag Albert.

Dominelli, L. (ed.) (2007) *Revitalising Communities in a Globalising World*. Farnham: Ashgate.

Esping-Andersen, G. (1990) *The Three Worlds of Welfare Capitalism*. Cambridge: Polity.

Germak, A.J. and Singh, K.K. (2010) 'Social entrepreneurship: changing the way social workers do business', *Administration in Social Work*, 34: 79–95.

Healy, K. (2005) *Social Work Theories in Context: Creating Frameworks for Practice*. Basingstoke: Palgrave Macmillan.

Ho, A.P. and Chan, K. (2010) 'The social impact of work-integration social enterprise in Hong Kong', *International Social Work*, 53(1): 33–45.

Hughes, M. and Wearing, M. (2007) *Organisations and Management in Social Work*. Los Angeles: Sage.

IFSW (International Federation of Social Workers), (2000) *International Federation of Social Workers: Definition of Social Work*, http://www.ifsw.org/f38000138.html, accessed 6 August 2005.

Kamerman, S.B. (2004) 'Fields of practice', in M.A. Mattaini, C.T. Lowery, and C.H. Meyer (eds), *Foundations of Social Work Practice: a Graduate Text*. Washington DC: NASW Press. pp: 319–39.

Kornbeck, J. and Jensen, N.R. (eds) (2009) *The Diversity of Social Pedagogy in Europe*. Bremen: Europäischer Hochschulverlag.

Lavalette, M. and Ioakimidis, V. (eds) (2011) *Social Work* In Extremis*: Lessons for Social Work Internationally*. Bristol: Policy Press.

Lindblom, C.E. (1959) 'The science of "muddling through"', *Public Administration Review*, 19: 79–88.

Lipsky, M. (1983) *Street Level Bureaucracy: Dilemmas of the Individual in Public Services*. New York: Russell Sage Foundation.

Midgley, J. (1995) *Social Development: the Developmental Perspective in Social Welfare*. London: Sage.

Midgley, J. and Conley, A. (eds) (2010) *Social Work and Social Development: Theories and Skills for Developmental Social Work*. New York: Oxford University Press.

Ministry of Labour and Social Policy (2011) *Social Assistance*. http://www.mpips.gov.pl/en/social-assistance/, accessed 3 August 2011.

Negi, N.J. and Furman, R. (2010) *Transnational Social Work Practice*. New York: Columbia University Press.

Payne, M. (2005) *The Origins of Social Work: Change and Continuity*. Basingstoke: Palgrave Macmillan.

Payne, M. (2006) *What is Professional Social Work?* 2nd edn. Bristol: Policy Press.

Payne, M. and Askeland, G.A. (2008) *Globalization and International Social Work: Postmodern Change and Challenge*. Aldershot: Ashgate.

Ramon, S. (ed.) (2008) *Social Work in the Context of Political Conflict*. Birmingham: Venture.

Reith, M. and Payne, M. (2009) *Social Work in End-of-life and Palliative Care*. Bristol: Policy Press.

Satka, M. (1995) *Making Social Citizenship: Conceptual Practices from the Finnish Poor Law to Professional Social Work*. Jyväskylä: SoPhi.

Scharpf, F.W. (2002) 'The European social model: coping with the challenges of diversity', *Journal of Common Market Studies*, 40(4): 645–70.

Toren, N. (1972) *Social Work: The Case of a Semi-Profession*. Beverly Hills, CA: Sage.

Warzywoda-Krusyńska, W. and Krystzkowski, J. (eds) (2000) *Education of Social Workers on the Eve of the European Union's Enlargement*. Łodz: Instiytut Socjologii, Universitet Łodz.

Webb, S.A. (2006) *Social Work in a Risk Society: Social and Political Perspectives*. Basingstoke: Palgrave Macmillan.

Weiss, I. and Welbourne, P. (eds) (2007) *Social Work as a Profession: A Comparative Cross-National Perspective*. Birmingham: Venture.

Weyers, M.L. and van den Berg, A.M. (2006) 'The success factors in community work services: a critical incident survey', *International Social Work*, 49(2): 177–87.

8

Social Work Theories, Research/ Methods and Practices: Critical Perspectives and New Challenges

Harjeet Badwall and Narda Razack

INTRODUCTION

The spread of social work has been histori-cally mired in colonisation and whiteness. This situation is still evident through the ways in which the exportation of knowledge and practice continues alongside the perpetu-ation and dominance of Western knowledge production and consumption. Developing an understanding of the origins of social work theory allows us to be critical, informed and creative in the project of transforming and applying critical concepts, ideas and methods in our work within our different contexts (Healy, 2005). In this chapter we seek to contribute to the crucial project that the profession of social work is currently undertaking – that of focusing on the devel-opment of a more expansive, critical knowl-edge base from which to sustain critique of theoretical and practice approaches.

Pease and Fook (1999) state that social work itself is a discourse built on dominant and subjugated knowledge about what con-stitutes good practice. Practice norms in critical social work are broadly situated within goals for social justice (Dominelli, 2002; Lundy, 2004). As the literature demon-strates, practices range from empowerment to consciousness-raising, to anti-oppressive practice. The common thread running through these practices is social work's commitment to social justice, empathy and helping. In this chapter, these grounding principles are criti-cally analysed. It is our argument that these practices continue to perpetuate colonial practices, irrespective of how 'critical' the theoretical framework may be. Critical per-spectives for theory, research and practice – particularly those foregrounding analyses of critical race theory and whiteness – emerge as pivotal in the profession's ongoing commitment to social justice, empathy and caring as well as being critical in upholding the profession.

In this chapter, we begin with an overview of structural social work perspectives and how they have contributed to the project of social justice. This then turns to the critical contributions of contemporary perspectives such as poststructuralism and anti-racist discourse. These perspectives challenge dominant perspectives and the practices flowing from them, offering critique and transformative potential for the field of social work. The last part seeks to connect these critical insights to the historical development of social work theory, practice and research. This analysis begins the work of connecting the colonialism underpinning the historical development of social work beginning with the Charity Organization Society in the UK and the Settlement project in North America.

STRUCTURAL/POSTSTRUCTURAL SOCIAL WORK PERSPECTIVES

A central and organizing principle of critical social work is the value of social justice. Knowledge production within social work is designed to support social justice efforts to create a better world through changing current social relations (Hick and Pozzuto, 2005). The relationship between the person and their environment (family, systems, and social structures) is the site in which social justice is explored. The term 'critical' is often explored through multiple meanings and entry points of analysis. Richard Pozzuto captures this complexity as follows:

> Critical is a concept that blends meanings. It has to do with looking at something and not taking it solely as a given but also imagining what it could be. In this sense critical work is not work that duplicates the present but work that imagines possible alternative futures, and strives for them. Marx has taught us to look at economic structures. The Frankfurt School has highlighted the significance of ideology. Antonio Gramsci sensitized us to hegemony and Michel Foucault pointed out the inseparability of knowledge and power. To be critical is to draw upon these lessons. (2000: 1)

Pozzuto weaves for the reader the various threads of theoretical analysis that have contributed to the development of critical theory. He highlights the roles of social structures, domination, power and knowledge in critical analysis. However, the role of power, structural domination, and knowledge production unfolds in multiple directions and as a result, there is 'no single conception of critical social work' (Hick and Pozzuto, 2005: ix). As Hick and Pozzuto (2005) suggest, critical social work encompasses a wide range of perspectives and emerged, in particular, from structural, radical and progressive as well as anti-oppressive practices.

In the contemporary juncture, poststructural influences in social work have, in turn, developed out of these earlier perspectives – prompting reflection upon and critical questioning of the ideals of emancipation, consciousness-raising and empowerment practices embodied in earlier perspectives (Healy, 2000). Poststructural influences highlight significant contradictions in social work's social justice project, focusing on the micro-politics of power and rejecting fixed notions of oppression in the world (Healy, 2000, 2005; Napier and Fook, 2000). Structural and poststructural influences in social work have created key debates within the profession about what constitutes critical practice.

Structural social work

Bob Mullaly (2000: 122) states, 'much of the developmental work of structural social work has been carried out in Canada, where it is now assuming increasing importance as a major social work perspective'. A key figure in the movement towards radical or structural social work was Maurice Moreau, whose work in the late 1980s pioneered the structural perspective in Canada, at Ottawa's Carleton University (Lundy, 2004; Mullaly, 2000). Carleton University was the first school in Canada to develop a radical perspective, leaving behind the individualist ego-psychology approach of psychoanalysis (Lundy, 2004: 37).

The goals of structural social work are, first, to alleviate the effects that an exploitive and alienating social order has on populations and, second, to transform the conditions and social structures of society (Lundy, 2004; Mullaly, 2000). Structural social work includes major radical themes from Marxism, feminism, radical humanism, and radical structuralism (Mullaly, 2000). The literature also points to structural theory as a means to address the role of the dialectic in social work – a movement towards abandoning the false dichotomy of the person and the environment, and to recognise the ways in which both need to be addressed for meaningful social change to occur (Healy, 2000; Lundy, 2004; Mullaly, 2000).

Marxist theory greatly influenced a conflict perspective of society, in which the world is split into the powerful elite of society, and the oppressed (Healy, 2000; Ife, 2001; Lundy, 2004; Mullaly, 2000). Marxist theory points to social structures (primarily capitalism) and the role of these structures in producing alienation in both thought and action (Healy, 2000: 15). In this perspective, alienation produced by structural oppression requires interventions based on empowerment strategies and consciousness-raising to support the oppressed in their liberation (Ife, 2001; Lundy, 2004; Mullaly, 2000). A widely held belief by critical social workers is that 'through reason and action people can fundamentally reorder their private and collective life circumstances' (Fay, 1987, as cited in Healy, 2000: 18).

Anti-oppressive social work practice has become a dominant framework within the structuralist paradigm of social work (Dominelli, 2002; Healy, 2005; Lundy, 2004; Mullaly, 2000). Millar (2008: 364) states that anti-oppressive discourse is a 'multi-faceted

social phenomenon' which demands ongoing interrogation and less focus on definitions. The social worker has a very specific role within this practice: to change the social system and to work with clients to minimise the negative effects of a defective social system (Mullaly, 2000: 124). The overarching social justice goals of the profession are sought through the creation of 'new, non-oppressive social relations' (Dominelli, 2002: 39). Karen Healy (2005: 183–7) summarises anti-oppressive practice as follows:

1 Critical reflection on self in practice. Workers are to engage in critical reflection about their own biographies and membership in social divisions. The goal is to examine how one's social location may shape practice relationships.
2 Critical assessment of service users' experiences. Service users' lived experiences are understood as truth. Therefore, workers engage in empowerment strategies to support change in clients' lives.
3 Empowerment of and consciousness-raising of service users.
4 Working in partnership with service users.
5 Minimal intervention – to reduce the oppressive dimensions of social work intervention.

Social workers' professional status automatically places them in a privileged position to the client. Hence, workers engage in their practice to minimize the effects of unequal power relations between the worker and the client (Healy, 2005). The worker identity is constituted as having more power than the client, 'even when the social worker shares certain experiences of oppression with the client (such as gender oppression)' (Healy, 2000: 23). Workers and clients are positioned as opposites and the inequities in the clinical relationship 'replicate and reinforce broader processes of oppression' (Moreau, 1971: 81, as cited in Healy, 2000: 22).

Postmodern/poststructural social work

Many scholars have turned to postmodern and/or poststructural theories to address the limitations of structural social work practices (Healy, 2000; Hick and Pozzuto, 2005). Poststructural concepts are used to disrupt modern or structural conceptualisations of power as fixed and possessed. The poststructural concept of self is one that is historicised and rejects discourses on the naturalisation of identities (Healy, 2000: 58). Healy (2005) highlights the strength of Foucault's ideas in social work, particularly his conceptions of power as exercised and not possessed; power as productive; and an analysis of power as produced at local levels. Power is not possessed by any individual or group, but is produced relationally (Chambon et al., 1999; Healy, 2000; Pozzuto, 2000). Using postmodern and poststructural approaches 'involves a shift and moving beyond the notion of dichotomies; it challenges the very notions of certainty, objectivity, and worldviews, stripping away the notion of grand narratives which attempt to develop general, abstract and timeless axioms' (Fook, 1995, as referenced in Camilleri, 1999: 27). Fixed identities and the grand truths of modernity are critically explored as contextual, rule-dependent and the effects of discourse (Flax, 1992: 452).

As Karen Healy (2005: 196) observes, 'Foucault's work urges us to be cautious in our claims to "help", "empower" and "emancipate" as he shows us that these practices can also be associated with the "will to power" over others'. Poststructuralist social workers are thus concerned with the power/knowledge axis in opposition to modernist/structural perspectives which 'situate power in overarching social structures' (Healy, 2000: 63). 'Post' theories in social work engage in the use of discourse analysis and critical reflexivity to examine the ways in which power and knowledge constitute particular practices for the profession (Napier and Fook, 2000; Rossiter, 2005) offering a critical means to confront and complicate the power and control embedded in practices of helping and empathy (Rossiter, 2001). Contemporary critical practices need to be interrogated to reveal the ways in which they continue to engage in practices of social

control even while striving towards social justice. This involves critical attention to the colonial history from which social work emerged as a 'helping' profession in many countries.

Critical race theory – another critical contemporary perspective – holds significance for social work and builds on anti-oppression discourse and practice. However, critical race analysis as a focal point for research, theory and practice has not held a significant place in social work as it is promoted erroneously as privileging one marginalised group (namely racialised minorities) over others who occupy the margins of society. Critical race analysis helps to construct meanings for minorities and whites in particularly significant ways. Critical race theory, which includes analyses of whiteness, shifts the discourse of race and racism from the black –white dynamic, to one that includes multiple voices and experiences (Solorzano and Yosso, 2002). It also gives voice to those who are on the margins of society to recognise their knowledge, histories and experiences (Delgado Bernal, 2002: 106). Critical race theory helps us to understand how privilege is enacted; how, for example, 'identities that move' from North to South and country to country become unsettled in the process, and how whiteness is then configured in postcolonial terrain. These arguments are especially critical for migration in and across continents and are not limited to a North–South dynamic.

Anti-racist discourse has been taken up quite forcefully by a few in the profession (Dominelli, 1988; Razack and Jeffery, 2002; Jeffery, 2005) but momentum has not been maintained primarily because of the unsettling spaces produced by these discussions and also, as we will discuss below, the challenge they present to the construction of the social worker's professional identity. Thus, although globalisation and international social work are gaining prominence, inclusion of critical race analysis is lacking. It is our contention that anti-racist pedagogy, research and practice perspectives can and should inform structural theoretical and practice perspectives. Jeffery (2005: 409) maintains that anti-racist pedagogies, including self-reflexivity and the examination of white privilege, are necessary to understand the 'benevolence' in our work with those who are marginalised in society. It is to these concerns that we now turn.

Production of the 'white' subject

Social work scholar June Jing Yee argues that by remaining unnamed and unmarked, whiteness attains power (2005: 93). Yee states:

> Whiteness can be defined as a complex social process that perpetuates and maintains the dominant and/or majority group's power within social service organizations and is the primary mechanism that prevents anti-racist workers from changing today's societal and institutional arrangements.

Goldberg (1993: 1) asserts that our understanding of social subjects takes place in 'racial terms' through processes of normalisation and naturalisation, founded on liberal ideals of individualism. The goals of modernity during industrialisation constituted a subject who was 'abstract and atomistic, general and universal, divorced from the contingencies of historicity' (Goldberg, 1993: 4). The virtuous, moral subject remains raceless, unmarked, universal, and representative of all humanity (Dyer, 1997), in relationship to a racialised subject, who is marked by difference (Fellows and Razack, 1998). The white subject is 'taught to believe that all that she or he does, good or ill, all that they achieve, is to be accounted for in terms of our individuality' (Macintosh, as cited in Dyer, 1997: 9). Therefore, whiteness becomes the norm against which all *Others* are measured (Frankenberg, 1993, as cited in Jeffery, 2002: 184). Racialised populations are constituted as deviant, to affirm the power of the dominant group (Fellows and Razack, 1998). As Dyer powerfully communicates:

> White discourse implacably reduces the non-white subject to being a function of the white subject,

not allowing her/him space or autonomy, permitting neither the recognition of similarities nor the acceptance of differences except as a means for knowing the white self. (1997: 13)

Theorisation about social work practice must examine the operation of whiteness throughout educational and practice discourses. To explore the ways in which white dominance shapes social work, we argue that the white subject relies on knowing itself as a virtuous, moral and free subject (Fellows and Razack, 1998; Goldberg, 1993). Goldberg (1993: 14–15) states that 'virtue' is central to the making of social identity, and being a virtuous subject means 'nothing less than being a good citizen'. He suggests that the good citizen embodies virtues such as 'temperance or self-restraint, generosity, courage, justice (lawfulness or fairness) and mildness' and that being virtuous can only be achieved by 'following the example of virtuous citizens' (Goldberg, 1993: 15). The constitution of the virtuous subject is thus implicitly developed against a subject who embodies difference and who requires direction and management (Goldberg, 1993; Jeffery, 2002). As will be discussed below, early Canadian social workers, for example, operationalised this dichotomy by making their primary focus the management of difference – primarily the poor, Aboriginal communities and immigrants (Margolin, 1997; Lynn, 1999).

As a site of virtue, social work is celebrated for fostering an understanding of community in which individuals came together to cultivate 'responsibility, love and duty, and caring and sharing' (Lieby, as cited in Bisman, 2004: 111). As our discussion of early social work practitioners and organisations in the UK and North America reveals, helping disadvantaged populations constituted early social workers as virtuous subjects. Indeed, social work as an imagined site of virtue continued into the contemporary period through structural practices claiming to empower and emancipate oppressed groups (Margolin, 1997; Todd, 2005).

Building on Goldberg's (1993) analysis, Donna Jeffery suggests the contemporary move in social work is to be inclusive and acquire skills to better understand populations that are disadvantaged by difference (2002: 73). Practices designed to empower marginalised communities also operate to centralise the white worker and secure her identity as innocent and good (Todd, 2005). Practices such as cultural sensitivity, multiculturalism, and diversity training (Yee, 2005) serve to mark racialised bodies and make invisible racist practices that have emerged out of colonialism. The focus on cultural or diversity training keeps intact the desire to understand and know populations of difference, while at the same time securing the white subject as the subject/agent of knowledge production. People of colour are the targets of knowledge – the populations to be administered. Yee (2005) asserts that these practices were not created by people of colour, but by white social workers that struggled with their practice across different cultures (Yee, 2005: 89).

Todd (2005: 146) suggests that modern-day heroic narratives present in structural discourses about resisting oppression and developing allied relations with the oppressed are directly linked to 'the necessity of moral citizenry' leading to the possibility of being a virtuous subject. She states that the imagined autonomy of feminist movements produces a feminist organiser who is a 'self-regulated, moral citizen who does not require supervision' (p. 145) but instead works to help vulnerable segments of society. This position stabilises a professional identity that is innocent within oppressive social relations (p. 141). Within this constitution of feminist identity the contributions of women of colour remain marginal or entirely forgotten (Gutierrez and Lewis, 1995, as cited in Todd, 2005: 144) as 'their lives are not signified in terms of white middle-class feminism' (p. 145). She argues that white women's sense of self greatly relies on helping 'needy' racialised populations (p. 129). For example, historically, social service workers in Canada would list incidents of abuse amongst immigrant families to classify and contrast the immigrant family as different from Canadian families (Lacovetta, 1992, as cited in Roger, 1998: 106).

APPLYING CRITICAL PERSPECTIVES TO CONTEMPORARY PRACTICES

In contemporary social work education, students and workers are taught to be 'critical' of social work's history of helping (Healy, 2000; Hick, 2005; Rossiter, 2001). Skepticism about social work's heroic past invites students to question notions about 'helping' and their own investments within the worker/client relationship (Rossiter, 2001). Critical social work education aims to support students in melding personal, political and professional intentions in an effort to challenge oppressive systems and create equitable social relations (Dominelli, 2002; Healy, 2005; Ife, 2001; Mullally, 2000; Rossiter, 2005), while continuing to place social justice ideals at the centre of social work practice. Social workers are trained to turn their lens onto their own subject positions as a means to minimise power imbalances between the worker and the client (Heron, 2005; Healy, 2000; Napier and Fook, 2000). However, we argue that the white subject remains dominant and centred within social work education and practice through social work's continued construction of itself as a site of virtue. Below we explore the saliency of critical race analyses for social work especially in a globalised world and begin by complicating the principles of caring and empathy which underpin social work history and subjectivity.

Helping, caring and empathy

Helping, caring and empathy are core values of the social work profession locally, nationally and globally. Roger (1998: 148) suggests that within helping professions, whiteness is reproduced through the professionalisation of empathy and kindness. Empathic practice is used to facilitate kindness and effect change within client populations. Empathy functions to create a more aware worker who can understand another person's experience. Clients are invited to examine the difficulties within their lives with the use of empathy. Successful practice depends on clients feeling heard. Roger (1998) suggests that empathy as a tool for practice shapes the worker's respectability within the profession.

Jeffery (2002) states that in the Northern context, 'discourses of "helping" are enmeshed in raced, classed and gendered discourses of imperialism' (p. 99). These traditional ideals of helping in social work are being challenged by various social work academics discussed above who advocate for structural approaches (Mullaly, 2000); post-modernism (Healy, 2000; Leonard, 1994); multicultural (Al-Krewani and Graham, 2002); and anti-racist (Dominelli, 1988; Razack and Jeffery, 2002) perspectives for social work. Euro-Western helpers working in Southern contexts may reproduce, through their benevolence, acts of imperialism if there is lack of attention to history and power in their work. Western concepts of helping may not be culturally relevant or appropriate when working in urban and rural contexts in the South, and also in many Euro-Western countries, where the population is diverse. Individualism and self-determination, the traditional goals of helping in many countries of the North, may not be ideal approaches for working in a global society – especially in the global South where the collective is prioritised over the individual.

Historically, individual reform was understood as the mechanism that could lead to better management of life challenges, helping individuals to cope more effectively (Berlin, 2005: 489). Current narratives of helping are embedded in acts of 'doing good' – but helping can also be viewed as a 'vehicle for promoting neo colonialism' (Mahrouse, 2010: 170). Mahrouse contends

that uncritical and un-reflexive social justice activism, for example, can keep us from becoming aware of our complicity 'in current power imbalances and allows us to conceive of ourselves as innocent' (p. 183). Critical analysis of caring, helping and empathy is required if we are to understand how racialised power is enacted.

Critical empathy

As noted above, empathy is an enduring principle of social work since it allows workers to empathise with the suffering, pain and concerns faced by the client, group or community. However, Delgado (1996) claims that this is false empathy – the experiences of the other is felt in a very superficial way. Delgado believes genuine empathy is only possible when there is some form of egalitarianism in situations regarding culture, economics, personal and social values. In other words, true empathy can only occur when there are mutual benefits and the possibility for reciprocity. Empathy becomes problematic when there is social and economic apartheid – indeed, false empathy can produce or reproduce structurally unjust situations (Duncan, 2005: 90).

S. Razack (2007) uses Hartman's work to discuss the 'slipperiness of empathy' where the stories of the pain of others unwittingly become stories about us and not about the other. Razack's (2007: 387–8) depiction of Hartman's essays on slavery illustrates how black bodies provide whites with a form of 'race pleasure', confirming white superiority through images of black suffering. Navigating empathy is difficult because we engage in a 'process of consumption' and do not feel outrage thereby confirming white superiority (p. 380). N. Razack (2009) describes how classrooms can produce colonising spaces when we in the North 'imagine' the pain of others in the South and proceed to invoke acts of benevolence, empathy and caring without questioning our own implications in colonisation and imperialism.

Sakamoto and Pitner (2005) state that the first step in 'developing critical consciousness requires an examination of one's various identities, locations and standpoints'. Our particular intersectionalities, especially with reference to race, class, gender and ability, help us to perceive how we see ourselves, how we see others and how we see ourselves in others. Todd (2005: 150), for example, encourages a move towards ambiguity in the analysis of power relations. Contradictory, as opposed to knowable, subject positions may offer a useful conceptual vehicle through which social workers and academics can seek to explore new terrains in the future.

It is therefore critical to begin the project of tracing through how the social work principles of helping, caring and empathy, based around particular constructions of whiteness, have historically influenced social work practice perspectives. Exploring this history will help social workers to understand how particular relations of power and subject positions within those relations have been produced in particular spaces. This project of exploration will also enable us to re-think how we continue to reproduce and sustain dominance in our interactions with the 'other' including marginalised workers and clients.

HISTORICAL CONSTITUTION (CONSTRUCTION) OF SOCIAL WORK

The history of social work in the United Kingdom and North America is mired in colonisation. From a postcolonial perspective, one major antecedent of social work is the history of missionary activity carried out by Christian churches in conjunction with the spread of European imperialism and colonisation. Looked at from the point of view of the metropolis, it emerged 'out of philanthropic activities directed at poor people living in the slums of the rapidly industrialising cities of North America and Europe' (Midgley, 1997: 162). Lorenz (1994: 44) states that churches had a direct influence on

social work training in almost all European countries. Social work developed simultaneously in the US and Europe (Rodgers, 2004). During World War II several schools of social work in Europe were closed (Healy, 2008). However, at the end of the war many global projects and opportunities emerged (Kendall, 1978). The nature and development of social work in Europe was significantly influenced by the history of social politics and was driven by four ideological frameworks: Christianity, philanthropy, feminism and socialism (Kendall, 1978: 41).

Given the political history of Europe, social work in Europe has endured as a 'highly complex and diverse phenomenon' (Lorenz, 2008: 626). The core of social work resulted from ideological underpinnings of the women's movement where bourgeois women helped to lay the foundation to be aligned with dominant government policies to appear to be politically neutral (p. 54). However the rise to power of Fascism changed the landscape of social work as it was difficult to resist the current social conditions and policies under this regime. Lorenz (1994) identified the struggle for renewal after the Second World War and social pedagogy became a dominant ideology to bring about 'better social adjustment' (p. 93). Social pedagogy has emerged as a powerful alternative to case work and has historical significance for social work as it encompasses all social activity including theoretical considerations and reflexivity. Social pedagogy has been incorporated as a framework for teaching, research and practice. Lorenz (1994: 97) states that:

> ... social pedagogy defines the task and the process of all 'social activity' from theoretical positions beyond any distinct institutional setting and instrumental interest, and thereby safeguards the autonomy of the profession and appeals to the reflective and communicative abilities of the worker as the key to competence.

Social pedagogues rely on theories from other disciplines which are not too far removed from our current attempts to theorise and practice social work in a globalised society.

During the 19th and 20th centuries, the industrial revolution radically transformed social, economic and political relations both within and among countries (Haug, 2004: 129). Two social movements in social welfare emerged at that time that helped to shape the profession of social work, the Charity Organization Societies (COS), led by Mary Richmond and the settlement house establishment led by social reformer, Jane Addams (Lynn, 1999). Both movements were based on philanthropic models of care and friendly visiting (Berlin, 2005: 486), and they both held different philosophies (Van Wormer, 1997: 162). Helping activities were carried out typically by middle and upper class single white women whose desire was to engage in charity work (Jeffery, 2002: 59). These women began by providing aid in the settlement of recent immigrants. The gendered nature of caring is still endemic to the profession (Baines et al., 1999). The role and function of social workers was to serve as 'friendly visitors', who expressed acceptance towards the poor and the vulnerable (p. 487). However, Berlin (2005) suggests that these early expressions of acceptance were shaped by 'visitors' view that clients' problems could be traced to poor personal choices, indulgent habits, and unfortunate family backgrounds. It was also coloured by the belief that clients could significantly reduce their problems by submitting to the advice and example of the visitors.

Mary Richmond's influence during the COS movement was key in establishing a 'science of caring' (Lynn, 1999: 943) through the development of assessment processes.

The ideology of individualism resulted in requests for help being judged on responsible citizenship. The COS functioned within a moral code based on helping the 'genuine' unemployed and the 'deserving poor'. The overarching belief was that individuals of good character and resolve could be helped to surmount their plight and pull themselves out of the poverty trap. Thus the division of the poor into 'deserving and undeserving' became

a key concept within Personal Caring, forming the basis of assessment schemes for the first volunteer workers of the movement, the first social workers (Lynn, 1999).

This 'science of caring' was carried out through particular social investigations, which rapidly increased due to urban growth and industrialisation (Lynn, 1999; Margolin, 1997). Through the use of psychoanalytic theory, casework approaches to caring and acceptance became linked to medical perspectives, paving the way to the professionalisation of social work. Mary Richmond's influence during the COS movement was key in establishing a 'science of caring' (Lynn, 1999: 944).

In adopting the tenets of psychoanalysis, UK educators set social work on a trajectory that laid the foundations for dependency on an American model of practice, consolidated social work education's position within the dominant ideology of Personal Caring, and marginalized theories associated with Social Justice.

Alternatively, the mission of the Settlement House Movements differed greatly from the Charity Organization Societies. Its central figure, Jane Addams, was less concerned with reforming the individual and more focused on reforming society. Addams' early work is a reference point for social activism in contemporary practice (Healy, 2000: 12). Many authors have linked Addams' early work as a key emergence in radical practice (Berlin, 2005; Healy, 2000; Lundy, 2004). Addams' goals were not to fix people, but to provide them with opportunities that created possibilities (Berlin, 2005: 489). In addition, the social reform movement in North America was greatly influenced by the social gospel movement (Berlin, 2005; Lundy, 2004), consisting of African-American reformers concerned with uplifting societies through their dedication to service and acceptance of others (Berlin, 2005: 491). Social reformers rejected the professionalisation of social work instead advocating for changes in social welfare, housing, and working conditions

(Lundy, 2004: 23). Whereas individual reform efforts looked to psychoanalysis (Lynn, 1999) as an entry point to investigate problems, social reformers 'looked to sociology, economics, and political economy, as well as social gospel, for a conceptual and theoretical framework to inform their activities' (Lundy, 2004: 23).

The early beginnings of social work illuminate the influence of both psychological and sociological discourses in practice (Healy, 2005). Some scholars argue that these two threads in social work's history in North America and the UK constituted the traditional and critical split in social work. Traditional perspectives such as psychodynamic theory continued to influence direct clinical practice in social work till the 1950s (Healy, 2005; Lundy, 2004; Pozzuto, 2000). However, 'there was a growing interest in putting the "social" back into social work theory' (Stein as cited in Healy, 2005: 51). Functional systems theory emerged as a generalist practice, attempting to make connections between the individual and society split. Systems theory worked from the premise that individuals depended on various systems (family, school and workplace) and problems arose when there was a breakdown between individuals and various systems (Healy, 2005; Lundy, 2004). The emergence of systems theory was an attempt to 'unify the profession and integrate the methods of casework, group work, and community practice with a focus on both the individual and society' (Lundy, 2004: 35). Systems theory was a welcomed shift in social work knowledge production, however, some 'scholars felt there was a lack of recognition of the political and economic power that produced unequal social relations (Lundy, 2004: 36). Hence, the 1970s saw a shift back to social justice concerns, particularly in the development of structural social work, poststructural perspectives and the emergence of critical theories for practice as discussed at the onset of the chapter.

The historical analysis above illustrates the shifts in ideology which help to shape social work education, research and practice. However a brief synopsis of the spread of social work to countries outside of North America and Europe is necessary in order to frame current contexts for postcolonial and critical race theoretical frameworks.

Within a Canadian context, a concrete example of managing populations of difference was during early civilising missions (Valverde, 1991). New immigrants, Aboriginal populations and the poor were constituted as sexually deviant, savage and unable to control their sexual desires (Valverde, 1991: 104–5). Control was exercised through practices of binary differentiation, used to maintain civilised order amongst primitive societies (Goldberg, 1993: 156). Aboriginal populations and the increasing presence of immigrants did not reflect the morals and values of the British, and posed a threat to Canada as a nation (Roger, 1998: 66). For example, as cited in Valverde (1991), Dr Bryce of the Canadian Purity Education Association (CPEA) argued against immigration as new immigrants were viewed as a threat to the nation's health and purity (p. 49). Moral reform efforts reflected a 'dual process of infusing "foreigners" with moral values and asserting the autonomy of Canada by finding distinctly Canadian cultural traits' (p. 107).

The spread of social work internationally

> I do not know of any developing country in which social work education was an original product of national development; the origins can always be traced back to strong foreign influences [mainly the US, Britain and other European countries] (de Jongh, 1972: 23).

It is important to know how colonisation and imperialism influence social work theory and practice. The spread of social work to different parts of the world helps us to understand the pervasiveness of Western influences. However, although the West has greatly influenced social work's beginning, indigenising of social work in different contexts helps to decolonise these early influences (Razack, 2009).

Social work began to spread to other countries with the international transfer of its values and ideologies. The establishment of the welfare state in these countries was organised in response to the industrial revolution which catapulted large portions of the metropolitan population into poverty and unemployment. Simultaneously, imperial powers were inflicting violence and genocide on colonised populations. At the same time, intellectual forms of dominance by the North on the South were taking shape (Said, 1978). In its origins, international social work grew out of the imperial West's conception of its civilising mission to spread Western/European knowledge throughout the world (see, Razack, 2009). Later, the dominant Western ideals of social work were spread to other countries (Midgley, 1981). After the Second World War, the United Nations (UN) and United Nations Children's Fund (UNICEF) helped to introduce social work to countries like Jordan and the Sudan (Healy, 2001). Clearly the West has dominated the field through exportation, management and control over theoretical and practice approaches. Northern countries are heavily implicated in relations of power with their Southern counterparts, and processes of dominance continue to influence modern day practices. Although efforts are made to be inclusive in associations (e.g. International Association of Schools of Social Work) clearly the West dominates as the major language at conferences and board meetings continue to be conducted in English even when held in countries where English is not the dominant language.

A Chilean doctor visited a school of social studies in Brussels, which led to the first school of social work in Chile in 1925 (Kendall, 2000). Other South American countries soon followed pattern. Social work training in Africa began around 1924 in order to address the problems of 'poor whites' (Mazibuko et al., 1992). The theoretical base

consisted of material borrowed from the US and Europe. Ntusi (1995) explained that joint programs were developed in other African countries with the focus on whites only. A South African philanthropist who believed in equal opportunity founded the first school of social work for non-whites in 1941 (Kendall, 2000: 85).

The first school of social work in the Middle East/North Africa began in 1936 where the American model was adopted in Egypt (Ragab, 1995: 281). An American missionary introduced a settlement house/agency into Bombay, India which led to the opening of the first school of social work in Tata, Bombay, in 1936 (Manshardt, 1941: 15). It is important to heed the way in which social work began to spread throughout the world. The introduction of social work to India, Africa and to other countries, 'was not the product of indigenous inspiration' on the part of the country's inhabitants (Kudchodkar, 1963: 96), but rather, social work was brought to these countries from missionaries and other white Northerners.

Social work in China was established in Beijing in 1921 by an American social worker and American missionaries, whose focus was on urban clinical practice which was unsuitable for the services needed in China (Leung, 1995). The UN was responsible for the spread of social work to a number of developing countries (Healy, 2001: 34). As islands in the Caribbean gained independence in the 1950s and 1960s, social work was identified as being critical to self-government and in 1937 community development programs were established (Maxwell, 1993).

At the world meeting of the International Council on Social Welfare in 1972, social work entered a phase of indigenisation where Western models were beginning to be rejected in order to carve out new directions based on the needs and resources of the particular country (Stein, 1972: 161). These indigenous trends have continued, albeit at times in limited ways, to affect the way in which social work is taught and practiced in most countries. The hegemony of the North inherent in the early beginning and the spread of social work still continues in the South through exportation of Western knowledge through texts and other media (Razack, 2009; Gray et al., 2008). Given the history of the early beginnings of social work and the concomitant spread to different corners of the globe, it is critical to re-conceptualise how current forces of globalisation and transnationalisation have come to affect social work education, research and practice. It is also critical to examine how this history of colonisation helped to secure the white subject.

CONCLUSION

In this chapter, we began with an overview of structural social work perspectives and critical analyses of poststructuralism and anti-racist discourse. We also provided a critique of the history of social work theory, practice and research. Within this analysis it was important to capture the colonial underpinning of the history and development of social work beginning with the Charity Organization Society and the Settlement project in North America and the UK. The spread of social work was mired in colonisation and whiteness, a project, which is still evident in the ways in which the exportation of knowledge continues apace with the Western perpetuation and dominance of knowledge production and consumption. Knowing and understanding the origins of theory allows us to be critical, informed and creative as we transform and apply our ideas in our work within our different contexts (Healy, 2005). It is therefore crucial that the profession of social work focus on a more expansive critical knowledge base from which to sustain critiques of theoretical and practice approaches.

Pease and Fook (1999) state that social work itself is a discourse built on dominant and subjugated knowledge about what constitutes good practice. Practice norms in critical social work are situated within goals for social justice (Dominelli, 2002; Lundy, 2004). As the literature demonstrates, practices range from empowerment, to consciousness-raising, anti-oppressive practice, and critical reflexivity ranging across a number of perspectives – feminist, anti-racist, anti-oppressive practice. The common thread running through these practices are social work's commitments to social justice, empathy and helping. In this chapter, these principles were critically analysed because these are the grounding principles of social work. It is our argument, however, that these practices continue to perpetuate colonial practices, irrespective of how 'critical' the theoretical framework may be. Critical perspectives for theory, research and practice, including analyses of critical race theory and whiteness, are vital to uphold for the profession.

REFERENCES

Al-Krenawi, A. and Graham, J.R. (2002) *Multicultural Social Work in Canada: Working with Diverse Ethnoracial Communities.* Toronto: Oxford.

Baines, D. (2002) 'Storylines in racialized times: racism and anti-racism in Toronto's social services', *British Journal of Social Work,* 32: 185–99.

Baines, C.T., Evans, P.M. and Neysmith, S. (eds.) (1999). *Women's Caring: Feminist Perspectives on Social Welfare.* Toronto: Oxford University Press.

Berlin, S. (2005) 'The value of acceptance in social work direct practice: a historical and contemporaryview', *The Social Service Review,* 79(3): 482–510.

Bisman, C. (2004) 'Social work values: the moral core of the profession', *British Journal of Social Work,* 34: 109–23.

Chambon, A., Irving, A. and Epstein, L. (eds) (1999) *Reading Foucault for Social Work.* New York: Columbia University Press.

Camilleri, P. (1999) 'Social ork and its search for meaning: theories, narratives and practices', in B. Pease and J. Fook (eds), *Transforming Social Work Practice: Postmodern Critical Perspectives.* London: Routledge.

Delgado Bernal, D. (2002) 'Critical race theory, Latino critical theory, and critical raced-gendered epistemologies: recognizing students of color as holders and creators of knowledge'. *Qualitative Inquiry*, 8(1): 105–26.

Delgado, R. (1996) *The Coming Race War? And other Apocalyptic Tales of America after Affirmative Action and Welfare.* New York: New York University Press.

De Jongh, J.F. (1972) 'A retrospective view of social work education', in International Association of Schools of Social Work (IASSW), *New Themes in Social Work Education.* XVIth International Congress of Schools of Social Work, The Hague, Netherlands, 8–11 August 1972. New York: IASSW. pp. 22–6.

Dominelli, L. (1988) *Anti Racist Social Work: A Challenge for White Practitioners and Educators.* Philadelphia: Temple University Press.

Dominelli, L. (2002) *Anti-Oppressive Social Work Practice.* London: Palgrave.

Duncan, G.A. (2005) 'Critical race ethnography in education: narrative, inequality and the problem of epistemology', *Race Ethnicity and Education,* 8(1): 93–114.

Dyer, R. (1997) 'The matter of whiteness', in *White.* London: Routledge. pp. 1–40.

Fellows, M. and Razack, S. (1998) 'The race to innocence: confronting hierarchical relations among women', *The Journal of Gender, Race & Justice,* 335–52.

Flax, J. (1992) 'The end of innocence', in J. Butler and J.W. Scott (eds), *Feminists Theorize the Political.* New York: Routledge.

Goldberg, D.T. (1993) *Racist culture: philosophy and the politics of meaning.* Oxford: Blackwell.

Gray, M., Coates, J. and Yellow Bird M. (eds) (2008) *Indigenous Social Work Around the World.* Burlington, VT: Ashgate.

Haug, E. (2004) 'Critical reflection on the emerging discourse of international social work', *International Social Work,* 48(2): 126–35.

Healy, K. (2000) *Social Work Practices: Contemporary Perspectives on Change.* London: Sage Publications.

Healy, L. (2001) *International Social Work: Professional Action in an Interdependent World.* 2nd edn. New York: Oxford.

Healy, K. (2005) *Social Work Theories in Practice.* New York: Palgrave Macmillan.

Healy, L. (2008) *International Social Work.* New York, NY: Oxford University Press.

Heron, B. (2005) 'Self reflection in critical social work practice: subjectivity and the possibilities of resistance', *Reflective Practice,* 6(3): 341–51.

Hick, S. (2005) 'Reconceptualizing critical social work', in S. Hick, J. Fook and R. Pozzuto (eds), *Social Work:*

a Critical Turn. Toronto: Thompson Educational Publishing Inc.

Hick, S. and Pozzuto, R. (eds) (2005) *Social Work: a Critical Turn.* Toronto: Thompson Educational Publishing.

Ife, J. (2001) *Human Rights and Social Work: Towards Rights-Based Practice.* Singapore: Cambridge University Press.

Jeffery, D. (2002) *A Terrain of Struggle: Reading Race in Social Work Education.* Doctoral Dissertation, Ontario Institute for Studies in Education.

Jeffery, D. (2005) '"What good is anti-racist social work if you can't master it?": exploring a paradox in anti-racist social work education', *Race, Ethnicity and Education,* 8(4): 409–25.

Kendall, K. (1978) 'The IASSW from 1928-1978', in K. Kendall (ed.), *Reflections on Social Work Education 1950–1978.* New York, NY: IASSW. pp. ix–xii.

Kendall, K. (2000) *Social Work Education: Its Origins in Europe.* Alexandria, VA: Council on Social Work Education.

Kudchodkar, L.S. (1963) 'Observations', *Indian Journal of Social Work* 24(2): 96.

Leonard, P. (1994) 'Knowledge/power and postmodernism: implications for the practice of a critical social work education', *Canadian Social Work Review,* 11(1): 11–26.

Leung, J. (1995) 'China', in T.D. Watts, D. Elliott and N.S. Mayadas (eds), *International Handbook of Social Work Education.* Westport, CT: Greenwood Press. pp. 403–19.

Lorenz, W. (1994) *Social Work in a Changing Europe.* New York: Routledge.

Lorenz, W. (2008) 'Paradigms and politics: understanding methods paradigms in an historical context: the case of social pedagogy', *British Journal of Social Work,* 38(4): 625–44.

Lynn, E. (1999) 'Value bases in social work education', *British Journal of Social Work,* 29: 939–53.

Lundy, C. (2004) *Social Work and Social Justice: A Structural Approach to Practice.* Toronto: Broadview Press.

Mahrouse, G. (2010) 'Questioning efforts that seek to "do good": insights from transnational solidarity activism and socially responsible tourism', in S. Razack, M. Smith and S. Thobani (eds), *States of Race: Critical Race Feminism for the 21st Century.* Toronto: Between the Lines. Chapter 8, pp. 169–90.

Manshardt, C. (1941) 'Education for social work', *Indian Journal for Social Work,* 11(1): 12–22.

Margolin, L. (1997) *Under the Cover of Kindness: the Invention of Social Work.* London: University Press of Virginia.

Maxwell, J.A. (1993) *Caribbean Social Work: its Historical Development and Current Challenges.* Paper presented at the Caribbean Regional Social Work Conference, St Michaels, Barbados.

Mazibuko, F., McKendrick, B. and Patel, L. (1992) 'Social work in South Africa: coping with apartheid and change', in M.C. Hokenstad, S.K. Khinduka and J. Midgley (eds), *Profiles in International Social Work.* Washington, DC: NASW Press.

Midgley, J. (1981) *Professional Imperialism: Social Work in the Third World.* London: Heineman.

Midgley, J. (1997) *Social Welfare in a Global Context.* California: Sage.

Millar, M. (2008) 'Anti-oppressiveness: critical comments on a discourse and its context', *British Journal of Social Work*, 38: 362–75.

Mullaly, B. (2000) *Structural Social Work: Ideology, Theory, and Practice.* 3rd edn. Toronto: Oxford University Press.

Napier, L. and Fook, J. (2000) *Breakthroughs in Practice: Theorizing Critical Moments in Social Work.* London: Whiting & Birch.

Ntusi, T. (1995) 'South Africa', in T.D. Watts, D. Elliott and N.S. Mayadas (eds), *International Handbook of Social Work Education.* Westport, CT: Greenwood Press. pp. 261–79.

Pease, B. and Fook, J. (eds) (1999) *Transforming Social Work Practice: Postmodern Critical Perspectives.* London: Routledge.

Pozzuto, R. (2000) 'Notes on a possible critical social work', *Critical Social Work*, 1(2): 1–3.

Ragab, I.A. (1995) 'Middle East and Egypt', in T.D. Watts, D. Elliott, and N.S. Mayadas (eds), *International Handbook of Social Work Education.* Westport, CT: Greenwood Press. pp. 281–304.

Razack, N. (2009) 'Decolonizing the pedagogy and practice of international work', *International Social Work*, 52(1): 7–19.

Razack, N. and Jeffery, D. (2002) Critical race discourse and tenets for social work. *Canadian Social Work Review*, 19(2): 257–61.

Razack, S. (2007) 'Stealing the pain of others: reflections on Canadian humanitarian responses', *Review of Education, Pedagogy, and Cultural Studies,* 29: 375–94.

Rodgers, M. (2004) 'The Christian context of international social work practice', *Social Work & Christianity,* 31(2): 209–31.

Roger, K. (1998) *'Fairy Fictions': White Women as Helping Professionals.* Doctoral Dissertation, Ontario Institute for Studies in Education.

Rossiter, A. (2001) 'Innocence lost and suspicion found: do we educate for or against social work'? *Critical Social Work,* 2(1): 30–7.

Rossiter, A. (2005) 'Discourse analysis in social work: from apology to question', *Critical Social Work,* 6(1): 1–10.

Said, E.W. (1978) *Orientalism.* New York: Routledge.

Sakamoto, I. and Pitner, R.O. (2005) 'Use of critical consciousness in anti-oppressive social work practice: disentangling power dynamics at personal and structural levels', *British Journal of Social Work,* 135(4): 435–52.

Solorzano, D. and Yosso, T.J. (2002) 'Critical Race Methodology: Counter-Storytelling as an Analytical Framework for Education Research', *Qualitative Inquiry,* (1): 23–44.

Stein, H.D. (1972) 'Cross-national themes in social work education: a commentary on the sixteenth IASSW Congress', in IASSW, *New Themes in Social Work Education.* New York: IASSW. pp. 155–64.

Todd, S. (2005) 'Becoming and unbecoming feminist community organizers', in S. Hick, J. Fook and R. Pozzuto (eds), *Social Work: a Critical Turn.* Toronto: Thompson Educational Publishing Inc. pp.137–52.

Valverde, M. (1991) *The Age of Light, Soap, and Water: Moral Reform in English Canada, 1885–1925.* Toronto: McClelland & Stewart.

Van Wormer, K. (1997) *Social Welfare: a World View.* Chicago: Nelson-Hall.

Yee, J.Y. (2005) 'Critical anti-racism praxis: the concept of whiteness implicated', in S. Hick, J. Fook and R. Pozzuto (eds), *Social Work: a Critical Turn.* Toronto: Thompson Educational Publishing Inc. pp. 87–103.

9

Social Work Values, Ethics and Professional Regulation

Richard Hugman and Wendy Bowles

INTRODUCTION: ETHICS AND PROFESSIONALISATION IN SOCIAL WORK

In this chapter, we first examine the international statement on social work ethics (IFSW/IASSW, 2004) that forms a common frame of reference for all the countries in which professional social work is recognised. From there we explore some of the questions that are posed by cultural and social differences between countries. Recent debates have raised the question of whether social work can be said to have an internationally common set of values and ethical principles, so this aspect must be addressed. Then, finally, we describe some of the main features of some selected examples of different regulatory systems in order to see how ethics plays a central role.

All professions make some statement about ethics, in which they set out the principles that are intended to guide the interactions between practitioners and service users (Congress, 2010). Indeed, many sociological analyses of the professions have identified a formal ethical statement or code as one of the defining characteristics of professions (Hugman, 1991; Freidson, 1994; Macdonald, 1995; Bowles et al., 2006). A brief review of such codes across professions in our own country, Australia, shows that these can vary in their structure and detail, from a short list of statements defining 'good practice' (for example, hospital pharmacy (SHPA, 1996)) through to extensive documents that set out the underlying moral values and the ethical principles that are used to consider these for practice before then turning to specific statements about areas of practice (for example, nursing, occupational therapy and medicine [ANC et al., 2001; OTA, 2001; AMA, 2003]) (Hugman, 2005: 143–6; compare with AASW, 2010).

To understand the importance that professions afford ethics it is necessary to consider the relationship between the profession (both collectively and in the form of individual practitioners) and the wider society. The nature of most professional work is such that good practice requires *trust* in the practitioner on the part of the service user (Freidson,

1994; Koehn, 1994; Oakley and Cocking, 2001). Professions deal with matters that can affect the very lives of service users in a variety of ways, including physical, psychological, social, emotional and spiritual well-being. This in turn requires that the members of professions are *trustworthy*. Codes or other statements of ethics thus provide the basis for service users to be able to understand what they might expect of professionals and so create a foundation for trust to be developed. At the extreme, when trust breaks down, a formal code of ethics can be used to hold professionals accountable (for example, in the form of seeking redress from, or a sanction being applied to, a practitioner who is seen as having broken trust in some way).

The importance of ethics can be understood by looking at the nature and purpose of social work. The things with which social work is concerned are centred on aspects of our lives concerning which we hold strong moral values (Bowles et al., 2006). Social work is concerned with well-being in our communities, our families and other relationships and even, at times within our very 'selves'. Consequently the objectives, the theories and the methods of social work are highly contested. The extent to which members of the wider society consider that 'anyone could do this' influences the degree to which a profession's claims to knowledge and skills are likely actually to be subject to such a challenge (Hugman, 1991: 12). So for this reason the contested nature of professionalism is perhaps more the case with social work than other similar occupations, although the same situation can be observed with regard to some aspects of nursing, of occupational therapy and of school teaching (especially at the primary level).

The ethical core of social work can be considered in more detail by examining the international definition of social work, which was accepted by the International Federation of Social Workers (IFSW) and the International Association of Schools of Social Work (IASSW) following debate at their meeting in Montréal in 2000:

> The social work profession promotes social change, problem solving in human relationships and the empowerment and liberation of people to enhance well-being. Utilising theories of human behaviour and social systems, social work intervenes at the points where people interact with their environments. Principles of human rights and social justice are fundamental to social work (IFSW/IASSW, 2000/2001).

Notwithstanding the current (as in 2010) review of this definition, occurring because it too is contested, it offers an inclusive view of social work from the macro-level (social change) to the micro-level (problem solving in human relationships). Of particular significance for this discussion is the final sentence, which is a statement of ethical principles. While it would be implausible for social work to claim these principles as distinctive to itself (as a brief review of other professions' codes would show, see above) it has been thought to be crucial in the international arena to make explicit that they apply in social work.

It should not be thought that these two principles are the only ethics that are relevant to social work. As we discuss below, it is often necessary to think about other principles (and the values that underpin them) and at the national level we can find a variety of statements that draw more widely on a range of other ideas in addition to the principles of human rights and social justice (Banks, 2006). Nevertheless, these two principles are the ones that find international agreement in that they are recognised in all the member countries of the two peak bodies as central to good social work. As such, these principles guide consideration of the broader goals and purposes of social work around the world, as well as the more concrete ways in which individual practitioners might be expected to act in specific situations.

It is this combination of the way in which this value base can be used to understand social work as a whole and create a framework for particular instances of practice that give ethics a key role in the recognition and regulation of social work as a profession.

In many countries, but especially those in which social work is a regulated profession, ethics becomes a central element of formal professional structures. As we will see later in this chapter, ethics is a core component in most (if not all) of the regulatory systems that have developed in various parts of the world because it can be used to form a set of quasi-legal rules through which the wider society can be offered accountability. In the same way, it can also play a similar important role in the 'self-regulation' processes that apply in some other countries. Looking at the ways in which this aspect of ethics is used differently in various countries provides one dimension in consideration of professionalisation in social work around the world.

CORE CONCEPTUAL ISSUES: THE INTERNATIONAL STATEMENT OF ETHICAL PRINCIPLES

Internationally, the framework for social work ethics has been set by the IFSW and the IASSW in a joint 'statement' of ethical principles (IFSW/IASSW, 2004). The current document replaced an earlier 'international code of ethics' that was originally accepted in 1976 and subsequently modified in 1994 (IFSW, 1994). This present statement is deliberately shorter than the earlier documents and focuses explicitly on the core principles of 'human rights' (grounded in 'human dignity and worth') and 'social justice' (although it does also contain a short section on the application of these principles). The earlier documents were more detailed, specifying in great detail the expected standards of social work practice in relation to a very wide range of roles and tasks. These documents had increasingly been criticised within international social work circles as too prescriptive, given national differences of emphasis in the functions of social workers, and in addition that this reflected a tendency for the moral values

contained within it to be representative of global Northern cultures to the exclusion of the global South. It was also thought that a 'code' of ethics was no longer credible in circumstances where the organisations in question cannot exert any direct influence on or hold to account practitioners in a way that is implied by the notion of a code or, indeed, of the way that document was itself written (personal communications).

There are two major influences on this shift towards a document that has a more explicit focus on two core principles. The first of these is in the contemporary scholarship of ethics generally and specifically the debates and writing about human rights and social justice in social work. The second concerns a growing conversation about the extent to which the formulation of ethics ought to be one that can be consciously embraced by social workers from all parts of the world. We address the first of these points here and return to the second below in a discussion of key trends and issues.

Human rights has increasingly been seen as a major concern of social work internationally, as a value (something that is pursued because it is regarded as 'good'), as a principle (a way of organising our ideas about this 'good') and as a practice (a way of acting to create and sustain this 'good') (Reichert, 2003; Ife, 2008). Indeed, it can be argued that both IFSW and IASSW exercise leadership within the profession and in the wider international community, through their explicit attention to human rights in such joint activities as education and advocacy work, including the production of training materials, dialogue and lobbying with national governments and a focus on human rights issues in the use of special reporting status at the UN (Wood Wetzel, 2007).

The concept of human rights has a long history, emerging in its modern form through the Enlightenment period in Europe, from the work of philosophers such as Locke and Paine (MacIntyre, 2002). From a social work perspective, Ife (2008) follows Wronka's (1992) 'three generations' model of rights, beginning first with 'civil and political rights'. These include the right to have a say in who governs one's country, the right to freedom from arbitrary arrest and to a fair trial, and the right to own property. The second generation of rights concerns economic, social and cultural aspects of life. These include matters such as employment, health, education, housing and so on. Then the third generation rights 'only make sense if they are defined at a collective level' (Ife, 2008: 33). They include rights to clean water and clean air, to live peacefully and to have one's culture recognised, as well as the right to social and economic development.

A crucial point of the 'three generation' model is that the historical recognition of these rights has followed sequentially in the global North, while in many traditional global Southern cultures, collective rights have had fundamental importance for centuries. In some instances in these cultures collective rights take priority over first or second generation rights. In the global North, however, each successive 'generation' is more contested than the previous one. Of particular note for our later discussion is Ife's comment (2008: 33) that the liberal individualism of first generation rights is often the basis of criticisms that the idea of rights is culturally biased, which in turn is an expression of claims to third generation rights.

The significant external point of reference to conceptualisations of human rights in social work is the *Universal Declaration of Human Rights* (UN, 1948; see Appendix 5). This forms the basis of Wronka's (1992) model. It is also explicitly stated as a primary point of reference in the international social work ethical statement, along with several other international instruments that have refined and applied the principle of human rights, such as the *Convention on the Rights of the Child* (IFSW/IASSW, 2004: §3; UN, 1989). For the international social work ethics statement, human rights is seen as interconnected with the value of human dignity and worth, from which it originates philosophically. The approach to ethics

known as *deontology*, which is largely derived from the work of the German philosopher, Kant, argues that every human being has an equal moral worth, which is grounded in our facility for reason that in turn underpins our capacity to be moral agents. Thus we each owe to each other, without exception, the duty of acting in such a way as to respect the dignity and moral worth that is inherent in all people. So the rights stated in the *Universal Declaration* and other international instruments, as well as much subsequent discussion of human rights within social work, can be said to derive from what it is to be fully human. These are things without which it is difficult or even impossible to think about our lives as truly reflecting our humanity. Therefore, as Lundy (2006) argues, these are things that are necessities and cannot be simply seen as 'needs' as if relative to desert or availability.

The IFSW/IASSW (2004: §4.1) statement of principles includes four different dimensions in its definition of human rights and human dignity. These include the rights to self-determination, participation, treating each person as a whole (taking their family, community, societal and natural contexts into account), and taking a strengths-based or empowering approach. Framing social work's approach to human rights in this way, which incorporates an understanding of people within their contexts, thus includes first, second and third generations of human rights as the province of social work (Bowles et al., 2006).

The foundations of the idea of social justice lie in a different philosophical tradition. The concept of justice goes back to the ancient thinkers of Greece (Plato) and of China (Confucius), but the modern understanding of *social* justice has its roots in the European Enlightenment period. Here the argument rests on understanding that because human life occurs in conditions of limitation (to natural resources, to time and so on) decisions always have to be made about the balance of claims that each person makes on the world. Thus, determinations of what is good are based on the consequences of actions. The best-known consequential approach to ethics is *utilitarianism*, in which the notion of 'utility' refers to the balance between good and bad outcomes for all who are affected by an action (MacIntyre, 2002). An example of utilitarianism in operation that has practical significance for many social workers is that of taxation-based public services, including health and education services, income maintenance, public housing and other social services. The balance in this situation is between the costs to those who pay tax because they are required to do so (not a free choice) and the benefits to those who use tax-funded services (irrespective of whether or not they have paid tax).

Another way of understanding social justice would be to regard it as the pursuit of 'fairness', to correct moral imbalances, for example, in situations where some people have more than they need of the world's resources while others lack the basic requirements of a human life (Singer, 2002). Thus, as with the human rights principle, there is a range of meanings within the term 'social justice', from ideas of procedural fairness, first expressed by Rawls (1972), to notions of distributive justice as in the taxation example above, to freedom from domination and oppression (Young, 1990; Valentine, 2005). Included in the notion of freedom from domination and oppression is the positive imperative for social workers to incorporate an understanding of cultural and minority rights into their understanding of social justice (Craig, 2002: 671). A further moral imperative associated with this understanding of social justice is that social workers need to shift to a 'professionalism based on partnership' (Hugman, 1991; Thompson, 2002: 717). This idea, that social workers should work in solidarity, or as colleagues, with those with whom they work, rather than from the position of superiority that was embedded in previous forms of professionalism, is a central theme of anti-racist social work (Dominelli, 2008) and critical social work practice (Allan et al., 2009).

For some social workers, social justice must be regarded as the primary value, that which is paramount in defining good practice (for example, Jordan, 1991). Solas (2008) argues that social work fails when it does not make social justice its central aim, which he defines in terms of the pursuit of radical equality. Other advocates of the importance of social justice as core to social work suggest a slightly more nuanced understanding, in that they recognise and respond to the ways in which our understanding of what is 'just' (or 'fair') has shifted between contexts and over time (for example: Reisch, 2002; Bowles et al., 2006). Thus the way in which social justice is presented in the international statement on ethics for social work (IFSW/ IASSW, 2004: §4.2) includes challenging negative discrimination, recognising diversity, distributing resources equitably, challenging injustice and working in solidarity. These five elements incorporate the range of meanings associated with social justice described above.

It is possible to read these two major principles as potentially in conflict. For example, it has been argued that, in a world in which the starting point of life chances are often extremely unequal, social arrangements that support the unearned advantage of some at the expense of the misery of others cannot be seen as acceptable – this is not liberty but simply self-interest (Rawls, 1972; Jordan, 1991; Singer, 2002). So, holding the two ideas of human rights and social justice together can prove to be a major challenge to social work. Where the focus of practice is on a situation that is well understood in terms of a breach of human rights or one in which the unjust distribution of resources is the concern, then understanding ethical choices for action might be more straightforward. But very often we do not face such clear-cut situations. So we need to have a framework for holding these values and principles in creative tension and finding ways to reconcile them in practice.

Banks (2006) argues that in most situations this need to find a resolution of competing values is part of everyday life, not only the special challenge to professionals. Banks points to the concept of 'common morality' as a way of thinking about this process. This refers to the way in which people develop judgement between competing values, giving precedence to different aspects of their values in different circumstances. Moreover, from within the same occupation it is possible for people to disagree about the precedence of particular values or principles based on competing analyses of the surrounding society, of the cause of social problems and the avenues for their solution and so on (Banks, 2006: 445).

What Banks (2006) is suggesting here is that social work requires a *pluralist* approach (compare with Hinman, 2008). Pluralism recognises that it may be entirely reasonable to hold competing, and sometimes even incompatible, values without giving up the capacity to make clear ethical choices. Thus, it seeks to avoid the extremes of a universalism that claims one value as paramount, always over-riding all others, and a relativism which argues that it is not possible to make clear ethical choices. Looked at in this way, it should not be seen as a problem that social work holds values of human rights and social justice, even though these may come from competing philosophical approaches and present different principles for deciding how to act. The challenge is for social workers consciously to develop a shared wisdom about making judgements on the basis of these values in the diverse circumstances of our various practices.

In an extensive survey of formal social work ethical instruments from different countries, Banks (2006) shows from a sample of 31 countries that the ideas discussed above are very widely shared. While it should be observed that only five out of 31 countries surveyed are global Southern, it is also the case that global Northern countries do not all share the same social welfare structures or a prevailing ethos regarding values such as individual freedom as against family or community responsibilities.

Some critics of social work ethics (Jordan, 1999; Solas, 2008) have argued that the way in which the idea of human rights is interpreted places too much emphasis on individual claims and, as a consequence, insufficient scope for social work to address social justice through challenging inequalities. For example, Jordan (1991: 6) has castigated social work for an emphasis on 'self-determination, individualisation and confidentiality' that leads to a limitation on the right of the state to protect the needs and interests of those who are less well-off. Almost two decades later, Solas (2008) asserts that nothing much has changed and that social work effectively accepts an inequitable social order in the name of autonomy and independence. Drucker (2003) and Mohan (2008) make the same argument specifically about *international* social work.

Yet, during the first decade of the 21st century it can be seen that there has also been a considerable effort to consider the relationship between these two ethical claims of social work in a more positive way. Not only is it the case that appropriate attention by social workers to human rights *ought* not to be considered as if it was a distraction from a focus on social justice, but it does not *have* to be looked at in this way. Indeed, many other commentators (Reisch, 2002; Reichert, 2003; Lundy, 2006; Ife, 2008) address these ideas as closely and inevitably interlinked. Lundy (2006), for example, actually speaks of human-rights-*and*-social justice, as a single perspective, in such a way that it is not possible to achieve the one without the other. Recent work by Baldry (2010) puts this very well. She suggests that in a world in which exact material equality is probably neither desirable nor feasible, the relationship between social justice and human rights is dynamic. The underlying concern of social justice is that everyone achieves human rights: above all else, it is access to human rights that social justice seeks to have equally distributed. So, in an unequal world, social justice demands that human rights are pursued. Such a view has much to say not only to social work in specific national contexts but also to international social work practice.

KEY TRENDS AND ISSUES IN INTERNATIONAL SOCIAL WORK ETHICS

Interest in social work ethics is growing internationally. Banks documents an 'ethics boom' in social work (Banks, 2008: 1240). With such increasing interest and as we become ever more interdependent in our globalising postmodern world (Bauman, 1999), it is inevitable that social work ethics is highly contested – between countries and cultures and between different political and religious commitments. In discussing trends in international social work ethics, it is important to recognise the historical background; that in those countries where social work is relatively new, the people introducing the profession have either trained in or come from the global North. Similarly most textbooks used to educate social workers around the world are written from a global Northern perspective (especially from an English-language background).

At governmental level, which established the background to social work practice and policy, Bowring (2002) argues that neither the USA nor the UK extend their notion of human rights to social and economic rights (also see Staub-Bernasconi, 2007; Wood Wetzel, 2007). Pakulski (2004) agrees that in general the affluent nations of the global North tend to emphasise first generation human rights of individual liberty and political rights while countries in the global South focus on the 'survival' second and third generation human rights. In this context of differing interpretations, and with no international body able to enforce human rights, Pakulski warns that the interpretation of the powerful (the global North) will dominate. Although there are some limited instances where such rights are recognised in law and

policy, such as the *Convention on the Rights of the Child* (UN, 1989), it can also be noted that many global Northern countries attach 'reservations' to aspects of human rights while some global Southern countries do not; and the USA is a notable non-signatory of this UN instrument. Reichert (2003: 225) notes that National Association of Social Workers' (NASW) policy calls for social workers to promote these conventions and to argue for their country's ratification of them.

Ife (2008), arguing that community development is the main expression of third generation rights in social work, points out that community work is often undervalued in social work in the global North just as third generation human rights are undervalued in global Northern countries. More recent analysis argues that, rather than seeing micro and macro approaches to social work as being in conflict (and thus first generation rights being in conflict with third generation human rights), some global Southern countries, especially in Africa and Asia, are developing their own 'authentic' approaches to social work that emphasise the connections between the micro and macro levels rather than seeing them as separate or opposed (Hugman, 2010: 80–2). Examples of this include programmes with literacy for girls and women in Nepal (Acharya and Koirala, 2006), women's health in El Salvador (Juliá and Kondreit, 2005) and HIV/AIDS in South Africa (Demmer and Burhart, 2008), as in each case methods of working with individuals, including counselling, with families and with communities are combined to great effect. A common feature is in the affirmation of local knowledge and strengths, which in all these examples appears to be a major factor in their success.

If we are to understand how different approaches to complex notions such as human rights drive differing priorities in social work, we must incorporate an understanding of the context in which they are used (Bowles et al., 2006). Indeed Banks (2008: 1244), in acknowledging the importance of social work ethics being seen as situated within cultural, social and political contexts, pleads for stronger links between social work ethics, moral philosophy and politics.

The question remains: if we accept that social work must be understood as a situated practice, can it be said that social work has an international identity through a commonly held set of values and principles? Or are the questions posed by cultural and social differences between the global North and South so fundamental that even the IFSW statement, with its deliberate level of generality, cannot be consciously embraced by social workers from all parts of the world?

On one hand, there are social work writers from the global Southern regions of Africa (Silavwe, 1995), China (Yip, 2004) and the Pacific Islands (Mafile'o, 2006) who accuse global Northern social work of 'professional imperialism' (compare with Midgely, 1981). These authors claim that imported, individualistic global Northern social work approaches are often imposed unthinkingly on cultures and contexts which prioritise a more relational or collective approach. They discuss how social work practice that honours the ethics of their countries' cultures might be constructed.

On the other hand, there are signs that beyond 'professional imperialism' the groundwork for real conversations between different approaches can be laid. For example, we have discussed in relation to the 'macro versus micro social work' debate above, how some global Southern social work approaches offer new perspectives for what has previously been seen as irresolvable dichotomies between social justice and human rights in the global North. Similarly, elsewhere (Hugman, 2010: 69–70) it has been argued recently that a broader understanding of social work – one that encompasses global Southern social work priorities – is necessary if social work is to be relevant and seen as able to address international issues such as those raised by the UN Millennium Development Goals (UN, 2000). Actively engaging in 'cultural exchange' between global Northern and Southern social work perspectives as advocated by Yip (2004), Mafile'o (2006) and others (for example, see Hugman, 2008, 2010; Banks, 2008) opens possibilities for renewal and reinvigoration of social work not only at the international level, but also within global Northern social work.

REGULATORY SYSTEMS

It is noted above that ethics plays an important part in processes of professionalisation. This occurs through the formulation of 'codes of ethics', in which the values and principles that are used to understand good practice can be turned into standards of action to which practitioners can be held accountable (Reamer and Shardlow, 2009). This is a matter of ensuring, first, that those outside the profession know what to expect from its members and, second, that when the necessary trust between professionals and the wider community is breached that there is a strong basis for accountability to take place (Congress, 2010). At an extreme, it is about the possibility of redress. How ethics actually plays this role in particular forms of professionalisation differs according to the history and the institutions of each country. These vary from examples where social work is highly regulated to those in which social work is not so clearly differentiated as a distinct profession.

The major examples of social work as a highly regulated profession are to be found in the global North. The most obvious of these is North America, where social work is regulated in all states of the United States of America (USA) and most provinces of Canada, either through registration or licensing. In recent years formal regulation has been introduced also in countries such as Aotearoa-New Zealand, Ireland and the United Kingdom (UK) (Orme and Rennie, 2006). Similar structures have also been developed in global Southern countries, often drawing on USA or UK systems, such as the Philippines and Hong Kong.

While there are technical differences between individual jurisdictions each system produces the same result: if found to have practised in an unacceptable way a practitioner can be barred from working as a social worker. The two grounds for being barred from practice are incompetence (it is shown that the practitioner has acted in a wrong way technically) or ethics (the practitioner is shown to have acted in a wrong way morally). Indeed, acting competently in itself may be regarded as an ethical matter (NASW, 2008). Under these circumstances it is necessary to have a formal code of ethics, one that is explicit, clear and publicly available (Reamer, 2001).

However, these processes depend on legislation. In other words, for this type of regulation to occur it is necessary to get state support. This in turn requires governments not only to recognise social work as a distinct profession but also that it is one that needs statutory regulation in order to ensure public accountability. When such regulatory mechanisms are established they are, therefore, bodies that derive their powers from and act on behalf of the state. That they use ethics as a primary vehicle for determining acceptable practice means that they must have a close relationship with the profession, but this gives the profession the power of influence rather than of direct control (Hugman, 1991). It is also important to observe that as professional associations are separate from state regulatory bodies, it is necessary for the professional organisations to maintain their own ethical review processes and sanctions (Reamer and Shardlow, 2009).

At the same time, each country that has formal statutory regulation has distinct aspects of professionalisation that arise from the specific issues they face. A particular example can be seen in Aotearoa-New Zealand where the process of reconciliation between Maori and those of European descent has led to a bicultural code of ethics, in which the influence of the different cultures on values is explicitly incorporated alongside a recognition of the special place of Maori as the indigenous people within Aotearoa-New Zealand society (ANZASW, 2008). This code is a document of reference for the registration board for social work and so the practice of social workers in that country is appraised against these distinctive ethical requirements. While some other societies that have indigenous populations might also gain from similar developments (the Australian Association of Social Workers is undertaking such work as we write) there are many others for whom there are different localised issues that must be taken into account both in formulating professional ethics and in regulatory systems.

But not all countries have statutory regulatory mechanisms. In some others, such as Australia, professional bodies have a different relationship with the state through which forms of 'self-regulation' occur. In this approach the profession exerts a strong influence over who should be regarded as a member of the profession, for example, through accreditation of educational programmes that are then accepted for membership. Within this model the role of a code of ethics has great similarities to that in statutory regulation systems, but ultimately the sanction is that an individual who breaches a code is deemed to be 'not eligible for membership' of the profession compared to losing registration or a license to practice. This is a weaker response, in that it depends on employing organisations and others recognising such 'eligibility' as the basis for someone being able to continue practising as a professional social worker.

Finally there are the many countries in which there is a professional association, for example, as defined by membership of the IFSW, but in which there is limited recognition by either employing organisations or the state that might lead to formal regulation. Many of these are in the global South. In some circumstances it is the case that the profession is not sufficiently developed or else the general place of professions in the society is not structured in this way. In other cases, however, social workers may actually keep a distance from the state because they regard their role as necessarily requiring such separation. In these sorts of situations the role of a code of ethics can be seen much more in terms of a means by which the profession can communicate its core values to its own members and to the surrounding society. There may even be use of the IFSW/ IASSW ethical documents either in place of a national code or as a point of reference to advocate for the role of social workers in promoting human rights and seeking social justice (personal communications).

Some commentators (such as Reamer, 2001) regard a strong, detailed code of ethics that is sanctioned by law and upheld by the state to be a mature stage of professionalisation. In these circumstances, he suggests, the profession has clear boundaries and is accountable. (In the American system on which Reamer is basing his remarks this includes the capacity of aggrieved service users to sue or seek some other legal redress for bad practice.) However, in other places, a contrary view is proposed. For example, Yu (2006) argues that in the Philippines this type of corporate relationship between the profession and the state has led to social work forming too close an accommodation with a repressive regime, such that the cost of professionalisation has been to participate in a system that is totally at odds with the values of human rights and social justice.

We also have to consider carefully those situations in which ethical evaluations are undertaken *by* a body that is external to the profession itself. Examples of this are found in the UK, where the regulatory bodies not only exercise the power of registration but also create codes of *practice* (UK) or *conduct* (Aotearoa-New Zealand) by which social workers are to be evaluated (Orme and Rennie, 2006: 336). These are distinct from the codes of ethics of the British Association of Social Workers or the Aotearoa-New Zealand Association of Social Workers. Such systems are quite different from those instances in the USA or Canada where the statutory registration bodies refer to the

profession's code of ethics in such matters (although in both cases the UK and Aotearoa-New Zealand structures seem to reflect wider approaches that apply to other professions also).

The point here is that ethics potentially becomes used as a set of sanctions for what is 'bad' rather than a framework for defining and pursuing that which is 'good'. In contrast again, in countries where social work is not regulated the codes of ethics of professional associations themselves may be used as a moral point of reference, but will only affect an individual's practice if used by an employer as the basis for evaluating practice (Orme and Rennie, 2006; Reamer and Shardlow, 2009). These differences point to a central question for the practical implications of a code of ethics. Namely, the potential for a code to be used in the way described by Reamer (2001) is dependent in many ways on the social system in which social workers live and work.

Whatever the detailed operation of particular types of regulatory structures, where political and legal systems are open and democratic, at least in broad terms, then a code of ethics can be seen as a tool to support good practice. However, in other circumstances a code of ethics might be seen more accurately as a point of reference for struggle or a set of moral claims that can be used to defend social workers against expectations that they engage in oppressive actions.

Finally, in relation to regulation, the possession of a code of ethics should not be seen as a technocratic 'fix' for the possibility of inappropriate action on the part of social workers. We are not suggesting that anyone actually makes the claim that it is or ought to be, but it is necessary to be overt about this point. What we wish to be clear about is that professional ethics can become reduced to a list of specific conducts or it can hold on to its meaning as moral discourse that enables social workers to understand and live up to the core values that are claimed. The 2004 statement of the IFSW and IASSW is intended to be the latter.

FUTURE DIRECTIONS AND CONCLUSION

Mirroring the current state of social work values, ethics and professional regulation, this chapter has addressed two entirely different sets of issues: international debates about ethics and the national concerns with functional codes and the processes of regulation.

At a national level, one of the key challenges for the future is whether social work in different countries will be able to use codes of ethics to define and promote 'good' practice, and to defend social workers against expectations that they engage in oppressive actions. A further challenge is whether such codes can be presented so that they are accessible and able to be used by general populations as benchmarks for good social work practice and to hold social workers accountable.

At the international level, we have argued that it is useful for social work to acknowledge its pluralist approach to ethics; that pluralism offers a way forward between universalist and relativist approaches in which both human rights and social justice can be maintained as core values. We have further argued that pluralism is inherent in the multidimensional understandings of human rights and social justice expressed in the IFSW/IASSW (2004) *Statement of Principles*. Some common ground is needed however, to facilitate the developing conversations between global Southern and Northern social work, especially so that the voice of the global South is heard.

Social workers need to explore further this common ground. Already there are some signs that this is beginning. For example, commentators such as Yip (2004), Healy (2007) and Suarez et al. (2008) have demonstrated how social work approaches that acknowledge and work with the different cultural contexts and ethical perspectives of all the people concerned can be effective in challenging violence in families. These diverse writings not only demonstrate the importance of seeing social work as

contextualised, but also show how social work from very different cultural and ethical assumptions can share common ethical ground – in this case agreement about the capability of 'being secure against assault' (Nussbaum, 2000: 78). All three papers discuss interventions that are recognisably 'social work' to address violence within families (Yip, 2004; Healy, 2007; Suarez et al., 2008).

We have argued that future directions for international social work ethics need to include more robust conversations to identify parameters for a framework that is inclusive of the global Southern and Northern perspectives. We have identified some instances in which contributions from global Southern social work are beginning to be recognised and valued. There is also evidence that the current IFSW/IASSW (2004) statement encompasses a pluralist approach that offers an inclusive platform from which to develop such negotiations. The challenge for social work theorists and practitioners is to articulate the common ground from which diverse priorities within contextualised 'social work' can be identified and nourished.

REFERENCES

AASW (Australian Association of Social Workers). (2010) *Code of Ethics (1999)*. Hawker ACT: AASW.

Acharya, S. and Koirala, B.N. (2006) *A Comprehensive Review of the Practices of Literacy and Non-Formal Education in Nepal*. Working Paper #11. Kathmandu: UNESCO.

Allan, J., Briskman, L. and Pease, B. (eds) (2009) *Critical Social Work Theories and Practices for a Socially Just World*. Crows Nest, NSW: Allen & Unwin.

AMA (Australian Medical Association) (2003) *Position Statement: AMA Code of Ethics*. Sydney: AMA.

ANC/RCNA/ANF (Australian Nursing Council/Royal College of Nursing Australia/Australian Nursing Federation) (2001) *Code of Ethics for Nurses in Australia*. Canberra: ANC/RCNA/ANF.

ANZASW (Aotearoa-New Zealand Association of Social Workers) (2008) *Code of Ethics*. Christchurch: ANZASW.

Baldry, E. (2010) *Mental Health Disorders and Cognitive Disability in the Criminal Justice System.* Keynote address to the Community Legal Centres NSW Conference, Sydney, 6 May.

Banks, S. (2006) *Ethics and Values in Social Work.* 3rd edn. Basingstoke: Palgrave Macmillan.

Banks, S. (2008) 'Critical commentary: social work ethics', *British Journal of Social Work*, 38(6): 1238–49.

Bauman, Z. (1999) *Globalisation: The Human Consequences.* Cambridge: Polity Press.

Bowles, W., Collingridge, M., Curry, S. and Valentine, B. (2006) *Ethical Practice in Social Work: An Applied Approach.* St. Leonards, NSW: Allen & Unwin.

Bowring, W. (2002) 'Forbidden relations? The UK's discourse of human rights and the struggle for social justice', *Social Justice and Global Development Journal*, 1, retrieved from http://www2.warwick.ac.uk/fac/soc/law/elj/lgd/2002_1/bowring/.

Congress, E. (2010) 'Codes of ethics', in M. Gray and S.A. Webb (eds), *Ethics and Value Perspectives in Social Work.* Basingstoke: Palgrave-Macmillan.

Craig, G. (2002) 'Poverty, social work and social justice', *British Journal of Social Work*, 32(6): 669–82.

Demmer, C. and Burghart, G. (2008) 'Experiences of AIDS related bereavement in the USA and South Africa', *International Social Work*, 51(3): 360–70.

Dominelli, L. (2008). *Anti-Racist Social Work* 3rd edn. Basingstoke: Palgrave Macmillan.

Drucker, D. (2003) 'Whither international social work? A reflection', *International Social Work*, 46(1): 53–61.

Freidson, E. (1994) *Professionalism Reborn: Theory, Prophecy and Policy.* Chicago: University of Chicago Press.

Healy, L. (2007) 'Universalism and cultural relativism in social work ethics', *International Social Work*, 50(1): 11–26.

Hinman, L.M. (2008) *Ethics: A Pluralistic Approach.* Belmont, CA: Wadsworth-Thompson.

Hugman, R. (1991) *Power in Caring Professions.* London: Macmillan.

Hugman, R. (2005) *New Approaches in Ethics for the Caring Professions.* Basingstoke: Palgrave-Macmillan.

Hugman, R. (2008) 'Ethics in a world of difference', *Ethics and Social Welfare*, 2(2): 118–32.

Hugman, R. (2010) *Understanding International Social Work: A Critical Analysis.* Basingstoke: Palgrave-Macmillan.

Ife, J. (2008) *Human Rights in Social Work: Towards Rights-Based Practice*, revised edition. Port Melbourne, VIC: Cambridge University Press.

IFSW (International Federation of Social Workers). (1994) *The Ethics of Social Work: Principles and Standards.* Berne: IFSW. http://www.ifsw.org/p38000020.html, downloaded 6 July 2010.

IFSW/IASSW (International Federation of Social Workers/International Association of Schools of Social Work). (2000/2001) *Definition of Social Work.* Berne: IFSW/IASSW. http://www.ifsw.org/f38000138.html, downloaded 6 July 2010.

IFSW/IASSW (International Federation of Social Workers/International Association of Schools of Social Work). (2004) *Ethics in Social Work: Statement of Principles.* Berne: IFSW/IASSW.

Jordan, B. (1991) 'Competencies and values', *Social Work Education*, 10(1): 5–11.

Juliá, M. and Kondreit, M.E. (2005) 'Health care in the social development context', *International Social Work*, 48(5): 537–52.

Koehn, D. (1994) *The Ground of Professional Ethics.* London: Routledge.

Lundy, C. (2006) 'Social work's commitment to social and economic justice: a challenge to the profession', in N. Hall (ed.), *Social Work: Making a Difference. Social Work Around the World IV.* Berne/Oslo: IFSW/FAFO. pp. 115–28.

Macdonald, K. (1995) *The Sociology of the Professions.* London: Sage.

MacIntyre, A. (2002) *A Brief History of Ethics.* London: Routledge.

Mafile'o, T. (2006) 'Matakinga (behaving like family): the social worker-client relationship in Pasifika social work', *Social Work Review/Tu Mau*, 18(1): 31–6.

Midgley, J. (1981) *Professional Imperialism: Social Work in the Third World.* London: Heinemann.

Mohan, B. (2008) 'Rethinking international social work', *International Social Work*, 51(1): 11–24.

NASW (National Association of Social Workers). (2008) *Code of Ethics of the National Association of Social Workers.* Washington, DC: NASW. http://www.socialworkers.org/pubs/code/code.asp, downloaded 8 July 2010.

Nussbaum, M. (2000) *Women and Human Development.* New York: Cambridge University Press.

Oakley, J. and Cocking, D. (2001) *Virtue Ethics and Professional Roles.* Cambridge: Cambridge University Press.

OTA (Occupational Therapy Australia). (2001) *Code of Ethics.* Fitzroy, VIC: OTA.

Orme, J. and Rennie, G. (2006) 'The role of registration in ensuring ethical practice', *International Social Work*, 49(3): 333–44.

Pakulski, J. (2004) *Globalising Inequalities: New Patterns of Social Privilege and disadvantage.* St Leonards, NSW: Allen & Unwin.

Rawls, J. (1972) *A Theory of Justice*. Oxford: The Clarendon Press.

Reamer, F. G. (2001) *Ethics Education in Social Work*. Alexandria, VA: Council on Social Work Education.

Reamer, F.G. and Shardlow, S. (2009) 'Ethical codes of practice in the US and UK: one profession, two standards', *Journal of Social Work Values and Ethics*, 6(2): http://www.socialworker.com/jswve/content/view/120/68/, downloaded on 9 July 2010.

Reichert, E. (2003) *Social Work and Human Rights*. New York: Columbia University Press.

Reisch, M. (2002) 'Defining social justice in a socially unjust world', *Families in Society: The Journal of Contemporary Social Services*, 83(4): 343–54.

Silavwe, G. (1995) 'The need for a new social work perspective in an African setting: the case of social casework in Zambia', *British Journal of Social Work*, 25(1): 71–84.

Singer, P. (2002) *One World: the Ethics of Globalisation*. Melbourne: Text Publishing.

SHPA (Society of Hospital Pharmacists of Australia). (1996) *Code of Ethics*. South Melbourne: SHPA.

Solas, J. (2008) 'Social work and social justice: what are we fighting for?', *Australian Social Work*, 61(2): 124–36.

Staub-Bernasconi, S. (2007) 'Economic and social rights: the neglected human rights', in E. Reichert (ed.), *Challenges in Human Rights: a Social Work Perspective*. New York: Columbia University Press. pp. 138–61.

Suárez, Z.E., Newman, P.A. and Glover Reed, B. (2008) 'Critical consciousness and cross-cultural/ intersectional social work practice: a case analysis', *Families in Society: The Journal of Contemporary Social Services*, 89(3): 407–17.

Thompson, N. (2002) 'Social movements, social justice and social work', *British Journal of Social Work*, 32(6): 711–22.

UN (United Nations). (1948) *Universal Declaration of Human Rights*. New York: UN.

UN (United Nations). (1989) *Convention on the Rights of the Child*. New York: UN.

UN (United Nations) (2000) *United Nations Millennium Declaration*. Resolution 55/2. New York: UN.

Valentine, B. (2005) *An Exploration of the Constructs of Social Justice in the Australian Social Work Discourse*. Unpublished PhD Thesis, Wagga Wagga, NSW: Charles Sturt University.

Wood Wetzel, J. (2007) 'Human rights and women: a work in progress', in E. Reichert (ed.), *Challenges in Human Rights: A Social Work Perspective*. New York: Columbia University Press. pp. 162–87.

Wronka, J. (1992) *Human Rights and Social Policy in the 21st Century*. Lanham, MD: University Press of America.

Young, I. (1990). *Justice and the Politics of Difference*. Princeton New Jersey: Princeton University Press.

Yip, K-S. (2004) 'A Chinese cultural critique of the global qualifying standards for social work education', *Social Work Education*, 23(5): 597–12.

Yu, N.G. (2006) 'Interrogating professional social work', *International Journal of Social Welfare*, 15(3), 257–63.

10

Social Work Education: The International Dimension

Terry Hokenstad

INTRODUCTION

Social work education today reflects the realities of global interdependence. Both economic and technological globalisations have impacted professional education for social workers. As a contextual profession, social work is influenced by both the societal and organisational environments in which it is practised. This is equally true for the educational programmes providing professional training. The development and focus of social work education around the world, thus, is increasingly impacted by international trends and issues.

This chapter will first give attention to the global scene and its effect on social work education. It will then examine the current structure and status of social work's international dimension, with particular emphasis on the International Association of Schools of Social Work (IASSW). A historical chronology will be followed by an in-depth examination of several issues for social work education that have an international dimension.

Finally, current challenges and future directions for the internationalisation of social work education will be considered.

In the 21st century, social work education is increasingly influenced by a globalised environment. The global shapes the local where social work is practiced. Economic globalisation directly effects country wealth and individual wellbeing. Communications technology offers instantaneous contact across time zones. It is no longer possible to simply 'think globally and act locally', as human problems and their solutions often require international action.

International organisations ranging from the United Nations (UN) to the European Union to thousands of international non-governmental organisations (INGOs) are a growing part of the social service structure in this environment of problems and programmes extending beyond one country. They address the challenges and victims of human trafficking and civil conflicts, including refugees and asylum seekers as well as other migrant populations. Disaster response and recovery also is increasingly international in scope and involves action by agencies without borders (Elliott, 2008; Healy, 2008).

A growing number of social workers are employed by these international organisations, in addition to national organisations with international mandates. Often these social workers gain their international experience and expertise on the job rather than through their professional education. They compete with other disciplines for these positions and bring generalised but not specialised knowledge and skills to the job. Now, social work education is giving more attention to courses and specialisations in international problems and programmes that better prepare students for employment in these organisations. While such specialised education remains a challenge, employment opportunities are mandating further curriculum development with an international dimension (Hokenstad and Midgley, 1997; Healy, 2008).

Communications technology is another key influence on the international dimension of social work education. Both the increased ease and decreased cost of communicating across countries and continents have resulted in a rapidly increasing sharing of ideas, information, and experiences by social work educators and students. This factor along with faster and more convenient international travel has ushered in an era of growing contacts and collaboration among social work educators and educational programmes around the world. Knowledge development and dissemination as well as student learning have benefitted from this international interaction.

A variety of collaborative models have evolved to enhance the international dimension of social work education. These range from email and internet exchange to international video conferences and from short-term study visits to semester- or year-long study abroad projects. Many of these projects involve one-way travel, but a growing number involve reciprocity across nations. Social joint degree programmes by educational organisations in different nations have also resulted from such interaction. In some cases, international courses and curriculum modules have been built on these exchange experiences. Thus, the realities of global interdependence have already had a major impact on social work education around the world. There is a growing response, but full internationalisation of the discipline and the profession remains a goal for the future (Healy et al., 2003; Hokenstad and Midgley, 1997, 2004; Lyons et al., 2006).

INTERNATIONAL ASSOCIATION OF SCHOOLS OF SOCIAL WORK

The major international organisation for social work education is the IASSW. IASSW describes itself as the worldwide association of schools of social work, other tertiary level social work programmes and social work educators (IASSW, 2009). With its affiliated regional organisations in Africa, Asia and the Pacific, Europe, Latin America and North America, it serves about 1700 educational programmes around the world. Its functions, as described on its website, include programme development, the encouragement of international exchange, the sponsorship of forums for sharing research and scholarships, and the promotion of human rights through policy and advocacy activities. Another key function, the development of standards to enhance the quality of social work education internationally, will be considered later in this chapter.

In terms of professional staff, IASSW is a small and rather fragile organisation with a secretariat that moves in accordance with the residence of the current president. Volunteer officers and board members carry major responsibilities for the operationalisation of its functions. It has sponsored or co-sponsored a biennial International Conference (now World Conference) since its founding at the First International Conference of Social Work held in Paris in 1928. Periodic and current co-sponsors of these biennial meetings are the International Federation of Social Workers (IFSW) and the International Council of Social Welfare (ICSW). The same three organisations co-sponsor the scholarly journal *International Social Work*, which is published by SAGE. Articles about the international dimension of social work education including those discussing curriculum models, comparative research projects, and the balance between the international and the local, are regularly featured in the journal. IASSW also has cooperative projects with the International Consortium for Social Development, another international organisation composed mostly of social work educators (Hokenstad and Kendall, 1995; Hokenstad, 2008).

One major role and responsibility of IASSW is representing social work education at the international level through consultative status at the UN. Consultative status with the Economic and Social Council (ECOSOC) of the UN provides the opportunity to give written or oral testimony during deliberations on issues in areas of social work expertise. It also provides membership in non-governmental organisation (NGO) committees focused on subjects of social work interest. Current IASSW representatives at UN headquarters in New York participate in NGO Committees on Ageing, Mental Health, Migration, Status of Women, and Social Development. In Geneva, a social work educator is active with the NGO Committee on Human Rights. In addition to NGO committee involvement, IASSW representatives have been asked to provide expert consultation as members of UN Technical Committees, which work with the Secretariat in the drafting of major policy documents. For example, a social work educator was appointed to the Technical Committee assisting the Department of Social and Economic Affairs in the initial draft of the *Madrid International Plan of Action on Aging* in 2002.

Another IASSW-IFSW programmatic function is co-sponsorship of the annual Social Work Day at the UN. From 600 to 800 social work educators, practitioners, and students assemble at the UN headquarters in New York to hear UN officials and social work representatives address current international issues and programme responses. The 25th anniversary of this event was celebrated 3 years ago. Recently, a Global Student Conference at a social work school in New York has been initiated on the day prior to the event.

Growing student interest and involvement in both events are evidence of the increasing international focus on social work education (IASSW, 2009).

HISTORICAL DEVELOPMENT OF SOCIAL WORK EDUCATION

Social work education originated in Europe and North America at the end of the 19th century and the beginning of the 20th century. Its emergence can be traced to a period of history when the social sciences were evolving and social reformers worked to remodel charity as scientific philanthropy. They focused on the use of knowledge from social surveys and social theory to develop a more scientific base for addressing social problems and helping the poor and other vulnerable groups in the society. The focus on scientific knowledge was coupled with the establishment of formal training programmes for charity workers. This training in the beginning usually consisted of summer courses with supervised field work for agency staff (Hokenstad and Kendall, 1995).

Britain led the way in the 1890s. Lectures and field work were included in training programmes provided by the Charity Organization Society and the Women's University Settlement in London. In Germany, courses were started as an outgrowth of the embryonic women's movement, but the credit for establishing the first training programme identified as a school of social work goes to a group of reformers in the Netherlands. In 1899, they founded the Institute for Social Work Training in Amsterdam. At approximately the same time and for similar reasons, social work training was underway in North America. The Charity Organization Society in New York and Hull House Settlement in Chicago initiated short summer courses, which were expanded into more formal agency-based training programmes at the beginning of the new century (UN, 1959; Kendall, 2000).

The first two decades of the 20th century marked a rapid growth in educational programmes for the emerging profession of social work. Fourteen diploma programmes had been established in Europe and the United States by 1920. These programmes were initially either agency affiliated or independent institutes. However, it was not until the second decade of the century that some existing and some new training programmes became affiliated with universities. In the United States and elsewhere, there were major debates over the preferred location for social work education. Agency proponents argued that it should be located where practice took place, while university proponents maintained that it should be located where knowledge was produced and transmitted. University-based professional education prevailed, but with a major field learning component included (Kendall, 2000; Leininger, 2000).

Professional training for social workers came to other continents and countries at later dates. In 1920, the first school in Latin America was opened in Santiago, Chile. The Tata Institute of Social Sciences was established in Bombay, India, in 1936, and served as a pioneer for social work education in Asia. Other early programmes were initiated in South Africa, in 1924, and Egypt, in 1936. However, most African countries did not open schools or departments of social work until the 1960s (Hokenstad and Kendall, 1995).

Following the early decades of the century, the next period of major growth for social work education came after World War II. At this time, the UN was established and it became a major motivating force for the development of social welfare services and the establishment of social work education in the developing world. The Commission for Social Development in the Economic and Social Council (ECOSOC) gave attention to the preparation of social welfare personnel beginning in 1947. An international survey of social work training was completed in 1949 (UN, 1950). Two years later, an ECOSOC resolution cited social work as an emerging profession with distinguishable functions and educational requirements. Social work education now had international presence and recognition (UN, 1951).

The UN continued to support the development of social work training internationally during the 1950s and 1960s. It assisted national governments in staff training for newly established social welfare programmes and contributed to the growth of social work schools throughout the developing world. Its contributions included expert working groups, international and regional seminars, and international exchange and fellowship opportunities. International survey results were included in UN reports on social work and social work education. An international survey of training for social work in 1959 explored the nature of social work and its relationship to emerging fields such as community development. It examined curriculum content and methods of teaching in social work education around the world, as well as the training of non-professional personnel in the social welfare field (UN, 1959).

Regional Associations of Social Work Education affiliated with IASSW were established during this post-war period. The first of these regional groupings were set up in Latin America, Asia, and Africa, in the late 1960s and 1970s. An IASSW initiative emphasising indigenous curriculum development played a seminal role in this process of regionalisation. This programme supported by the UN included seminars and workshops for faculty from different regions and countries to explore the possibilities for and models of curriculum focused on local needs and emphasising local cultures (Hokenstad and Kendall, 1995).

Regional development came later in Europe and North America. By 1980, the European Regional Group for Social Work Education was established. A Regional Association for North American and Caribbean Schools of Social Work inaugurated in 1992, after several years of planning and negotiation by social work educators in the region. All five regions now run their own conferences and work with the UN agencies and other international organisations in their region. They are also closely affiliated with IASSW, including a structure of regional presidents serving as vice presidents of the global organisation. Several subregional affiliates have also been established to focus on the common interests of schools and educators in contiguous geographical areas (Hokenstad, 2008).

In the 1990s, the social transition in the former communist bloc countries led to another period of rapid expansion for social work and its educational programmes. World events coupled with technical innovations provided the context and the momentum for both establishment of new schools of social work and an increased educational exchange. The social, political, and economic transition in Central and Eastern Europe created an environment conducive to the redevelopment and then expansion of professional social work education. Many countries where social work education existed prior to World War II and the following communist takeover re-established and modernised social work education. Both undergraduate and graduate programmes in social work became part of the system of higher education in those countries.

Social work education was also initiated in the countries of the former Soviet Union, which, contrary to Central and Eastern Europe, had no professional social work prior to World War II. Russia, in particular, experienced an explosion of courses and programmes in the 1990s. Associations of social workers and social work educators were organised to provide an organisational framework for this rapid programmatic growth. Social workers from the West were invited to their meetings to share information about programme structure and curriculum models. Other countries in the newly formed Commonwealth of Independent States also established training programmes for social workers during this timeframe (Hokenstad, 2008).

This period of social transition witnessed a sharp increase in international exchanges. The growth was centered in East–West exchange, reflecting the above discussed social transition. Still, technology, transportation, and growing globalisation also served to facilitate increased South–North exchange. A general growth in university exchange and study abroad programmes encouraged and supported the educational exchange in social work. In Europe, the ERASMUS scheme established in 1987, by the European Commission (EC) to promote mobility and exchange in higher education and its successors SOCRATES and Tempus, in the next two decades, funded and facilitated networks of European schools of social work. The latter schemes enabled inclusion of schools from Central and Eastern Europe (Ginsburg and Lawrence, 2006). In the United States, the University Affiliations programmes in the US State Department provided some funding, but more came from non-governmental sources, such as foundations, faith-based organisations, and the universities themselves. The Open Society Institute (Soros Foundation), whose programmes were primarily focused on the social transition in former Soviet Bloc Nations, was one major source of support (Healy et al., 2003).

International models of educational exchange in social work education vary from a single programme between two countries to programme consortia involving several programmes and sometimes several countries.

Some are faculty-only exchanges while others include students or are for students only. Those dependent on government or foundation grants have been time limited, but the growing number funded by universities have generally involved more long-term interaction.

In addition to exchanges focused on training and curriculum development, an increased number have emphasised or included joint research projects with visiting scholars. The research includes analyses of social welfare programmes and social work practice in different parts of the world. Models of international collaboration in social work education have been examined by scholars in both Europe and North America. One criterion for evaluation is reciprocity, the degree that there is mutuality of contribution and benefit in the programme. Another is sustainability, the long-term impact of the exchange. A final criterion of success is ripple effect, the impact of the exchange on students, faculty, and programmes not directly involved. While the exchanges have had mixed results on these criteria, they clearly have been a major factor in the increasing internationalisation of social work education (Dominelli and Thomas Bernard, 2003; Healy et al., 2003).

The final historical chapter in the expansion of social work education internationally has occurred in China. The People's Republic of China, while continuing its communist regime, has revived and rapidly expanded social work programmes that were established in 10 Chinese universities prior to 1948. The social work revival in China started slowly but accelerated after the formation of the China Association of Social Work Education in 1994. Now the country with the largest population in the world has a goal of producing the largest number of social workers in the second decade of the 21st century. Hong Kong universities and their social work programmes and educators are playing a major role supporting the development of schools within mainland China. They also have special short-term training programmes for Chinese professors with social science backgrounds, who are assuming the teaching roles in these schools. Social work educators from the rest of the world are now also providing consultation and support for the rapid buildup of social work education in this part of the world. The rapid buildup of social work education presents challenges such as suitable practice learning opportunities, but it is clear that China now has an important role in the internationalisation of social work education (Yip, 2007; Yuen-Tsang and Ip, 2009).

COMPARATIVE PERSPECTIVES ON SOCIAL WORK EDUCATION

Globally social work education is framed by *political, professional, academic and cultural forces* and the relative influence of each varies over time and geography.

Political forces have sometimes subverted or completely obliterated social work and its associated educational provisions. During the second half of the 20th century, examples of 'deletion' of social work occurred in Russia, China and Ethiopia under Communism and in various Latin American countries under Fascist dictatorships. In democratic states in Europe in the 1990s the role of national governments in determining the shape of social work and its impact on social work education was evident (Henkel, 1994), as it still is in some countries (Welbourne, 2011). Economic forces constitute a specific factor impacting on social work education – poorer states have less money to spend on welfare services and the training of personnel – but the values of national political systems are significant in determining how available money is spent. The disastrous consequences for social work and education of close association between political ideology and economic misfortune have been illustrated in Zimbabwe (Mupedziswa and Ushamba, 2006) while Vietnam affords an example of positive political support (Hugman, 2010).

Professional and academic forces operate at the institutional level, where the tensions between agencies and academia are reflected in the extent to which social work education is shaped by field practices or the policies of higher education. Sometimes this results in differences between vocational training (offered in some countries) and professional education (in others). The former stresses skills training for specific practice roles while the latter stresses the scientific bases for social work. The differences in emphasis have been noted even within a sub-region, such as the Nordic countries, which politically, economically and in welfare terms show many similarities (Juliusdottir and Petersson, 2004).

Cultural forces are closely related to values: both operate at macro, mezzo and micro levels with profound implications for social work education. The culture and values of a society contribute to the expectations of social workers and attitudes towards their professional roles. Social work education has to prepare students to undertake work in diverse settings and there may be public misunderstanding or even negative perceptions of social work roles and values, including in the US (Clark and Woods-Waller, 2006) and Europe (Radulescu, 2006). At the mezzo-level there may be a clash between the culture and values of social work in the field compared to those in higher education. For example, co-operative efforts may be the norm in professional settings while individual efforts are a more likely reality in universities. The emphasis placed on anti-oppressive values, policies and practices in social work programmes in some countries may be at variance with more traditional attitudes prevalent in higher education institutions. This can be a source of tension and even conflict between social work educators and their academic employers (Lavalette, 2011).

At the micro level, culture is a significant variable between and within countries and important in shaping social work education. In many countries the culture gap between social workers and clients is long-standing, related to class or caste (e.g. in Argentina or India). Education requires resources not available to the poorest members of society who are likely to be the 'targets' of social work interventions. Class/caste distinctions may also be related to ethnic differences, present in most countries (e.g. Thailand or Peru). In countries with sizable immigration, racial, ethnic and cultural difference pose particular challenges, sometimes leading to national policies addressing diversity but also requiring social work education to prepare students for practice with new minority communities. This has led to an emphasis at the qualifying stage on students developing cultural competence (e.g. USA) or anti-oppressive values (e.g. UK) or engaging in inter-cultural learning (e.g. Germany) (Lyons and Lawrence, 2006).

Social work education can also be compared internationally in terms of *structure* and *content*. The first includes the *location, length* and *level* of programmes. These structural variables have implications for the recruitment of students and are significantly related to professional recognition, status and salaries of graduates. Minimally, education for the social professions is *located* in the upper levels of secondary education (with an emphasis on vocational training) but worldwide it is more likely to be located within higher education. In many countries this sector is not limited to universities and social work education outside universities may have implications for future career options. In some countries (e.g. Greece) professional education is not available within the university sector while in others (e.g. Germany) different qualifications are offered in universities (degrees in social pedagogy) as compared to *Fachhochschulen* (Universities of Applied Science) which are more likely to offer both social work and social pedagogy or combined qualifications.

The *length* of courses offered at certificate or diploma level (e.g. in some African countries) is likely to be of only one or two years' duration, relative to three- or four-year degrees in higher education institutions (e.g. Canada and US, respectively). Latin American countries offer programmes over four or five years leading to the award of *licenciado* although in Mexico the majority of programmes are based in technical schools/ colleges (Hokenstad, 2008). Lengths of qualifying programmes have varied in the European region from 2-year diploma courses e.g. in France, to 5-year degree courses, e.g. in Belgium. The Bologna accord, requiring EU countries to harmonise their higher education awards at first degree and masters level (and subsequently agreed) doctoral level, affords both opportunities and disadvantages in terms of the length of courses in the region – with implications for structure and content (Lyons and Lawrence, 2006).

Length is also influenced by the status of social work as vocational training or professional education which includes practice or fieldwork/placements. Placements are virtually a universal requirement of social work education, but their length and pattern varies across (and sometimes also within) countries. While placements are often integrated into the overall course structure they also may constitute a unit/module at the end of a programme. Comparative material on the practice component of social work education is scattered and has not been the focus of a text since the mid-1990s (Doel and Shardlow, 1996). Length is also affected by whether programmes are undertaken on a full- or part-time basis, with 'practice placements' sometimes being within the student's employing agency.

The main factor determining the length of programmes is the *level* at which they are offered. While the minimum professional qualification at undergraduate degree level is now widespread internationally, there are also countries where courses are available predominantly at masters level (e.g. India). Masters programmes are likely to be of 2-years duration (students having already gained a first degree in a 'relevant subject'

and perhaps also experience). In the US students who have gained a social work generalist degree might complete a more specialised masters degree in 1-year–18 months. Establishment of generalist masters degrees is particularly the pattern when social work education is being newly established and when qualified social workers are not available to take on teaching roles and leadership in newly established social service organisations. This pattern was evidenced in the expansion of social work education in the post-1989 expansion in East European countries and now in China. In these countries (and also Ethiopia) the establishment of undergraduate programmes has usually followed relatively quickly, giving rise to a two-tier award system paralleling those evident in the UK in which social workers might qualify at either level.

International comparisons of the *content* of social work education include the taught courses (modules/units) offered in the individual *curricula* of social work programmes, the field work, and the relationship with other disciplines and professions. Taken together these reflect the *theoretical orientation* of the programme and the relative emphasis given to knowledge, values and skills. The main goal in curriculum design is that resulting courses should prepare students for practice in national and local settings. Comparison of the curricula of social work progammes internationally shows some similarities as well as some striking differences. Almost all programmes include reference to social science theories and knowledge, whether taught as discrete courses by disciplinary specialists or integrated into 'social work' courses. All have core courses in 'social work theory and methods' (variously titled) and many have separate courses in social work skills. Frequently there are courses focusing on interventions with children and families and/or older people and/or people with disabilities; and some courses may focus on 'social problems' (e.g. HIV/AIDS). Some programmes focus on individual/case work, group work and community work, respectively; and a social development focus is more apparent in many countries. Teaching about social policy and law is variable; as are courses about social work history, research methods, inter-professional work or values and ethics. There is no comprehensive data about the extent to which social work curricula include regular courses about international social work although anecdotal evidence suggests an increased number of courses with international and comparative content.

INTERNATIONALISING SOCIAL WORK EDUCATION

The notion of 'international social work education' describes a variety of models and possibilities. Earlier in the new millennium, Johnson (2004) drew on a continuum suggested by Healy (1986) to advocate for strategic development of the international dimension of social work education. Healy had suggested that attitudes and resulting activities ranged from *'tolerance'* (isolated efforts by individual social work educators and the presence of international students) through *'responsiveness'* (to the wishes of students by offering an elective or providing placements abroad; and/or supervision for international doctoral research); to *'commitment'* (a well-articulated programme of international study, practice opportunities and research). Johnson (2004) argued that most schools were at the 'tolerance' stage of 'internationalisation', with only a very small minority of schools globally implementing a commitment to international social work education through a specialisation and/or infusing generic courses with an international dimension. Some standard-setting bodies (e.g. in US and UK) have given 'official recognition' to the need to acknowledge the global context and the possibility of international research contributing to practice

skills and interventions. Additionally, there is increasing recognition of the international dimension of social problems and the need for transnational social work (e.g. Lyons, 2006a). Educators have also argued that opportunities for exposure to social work in different national contexts increases students' critical awareness of their own systems, practices and values; and contributes to their personal and professional development (Lyons and Ramanthan, 1999; Dominelli and Thomas Bernard, 2003).

Examples of models and opportunities

Models and opportunities for international social work education include 'infusion' through regular courses; specialist options and degree-bearing programmes; and student and faculty exchange.

It is difficult to gauge the extent of infusion of international content into international programmes globally. At a national level, Powell and Robinson (2007) estimated that about 40 percent of English 3-year degree programmes have some international dimension in their curricula. This includes content on the impact of globalisation and the social consequences of interdependence; reference to international and regional conventions; and comparative examples of the social, economic, and political conditions shaping welfare systems and social work/development practices. The increase in 'transnational work' requires knowledge about social welfare systems in other countries. While there is no expectation that the majority of students in social work will work or study abroad, course content can provide an international perspective and contribute to better informed practice locally. International specialisations (at the masters level) contain a similar range of material and also include more in-depth analysis of human rights instruments and social justice theories as well as topics such as migration and disasters.

There are indications that efforts to internationalise the curriculum have a strong regional focus, usually related to funding opportunities (Powell and Robinson, 2007). For instance, in Europe an evaluation of the impact of the ERASMUS scheme on education for the social professions identified three main approaches to the development of the European dimension, summarised as short, 'intensive seminars'; common modules/courses; and longer courses/progammes leading to certificates or degrees. These classroom activities were in addition to the opportunities for supervised practice placements or combinations of course attendance and project work abroad undertaken by a minority of individual students (Lyons, 1999; Ginsburg and Lawrence, 2006). The aims, content and parameters of these models were determined by criteria set by the EC.

Common courses (modules), jointly developed but separately delivered by faculty in a given network, were seen as enhancing the curriculum of participating schools. These modules were usually integrated into programmes. In another model, faculty teams from different schools of social work developed curricula which were validated by a particular institution and offered in the same or different locations. Other programmes had their origins in European networks, but were established later without funding and have persisted as international courses validated and run at the same institution (Lawrence, 2006). Such programmes have developed their separate characteristics and cultures but commonly experience similar challenges, related to the different educational traditions and social work experiences brought by international students.

Similar opportunities have been developed in North America. International models of educational exchange vary from a single programme between two countries to consortia involving several programmes and sometimes several countries. Some are 'faculty-only' exchanges while others include students or are for students only. Those dependent on government or foundation grants have been time-limited, but university-funded programmes generally involve long-term interactions (Hokenstad, 2008). Some of the bilateral and consortia programmes operate on a North–South axis with schools from the US and/or Canada partnering with schools in Central and South America, although there are also examples of agreements between schools in North America and in other regions (Barlow, 2007).

Some understandings of international social work are rooted in the idea of individual social work students taking the opportunity to visit, work or study abroad. While the students involved generally benefit, the cost of such individually focused efforts has been one factor making this a less favoured option for some programmes. Alternatively, a few postgraduate programmes include the requirement that students undertake part of their programme abroad with the responsibility of making their own arrangements and bearing most of the cost (e.g. UEL, 2010).

Models of international collaboration involving mobility have been examined by scholars in both Europe and North America. Criteria for evaluation include reciprocity (mutuality of contribution and benefit in the programme) and the long-term impact of the exchange. A final criterion of success is the ripple effect, the impact of exchanges on students, staff and programmes not directly involved. While many exchanges have had mixed results on these criteria, they have been a significant factor in the increasing internationalisation of social work education (Dominelli and Thomas Bernard, 2003; Healy et al., 2003).

Critiques of international social work education

Some concerns have been raised about either the aims of international social work education or the specific means by which they might be realised. One of the criticisms is that international social work education perpetuates cultural and intellectual imperialism and discourages development or valuing of indigenous models by promoting dominant western ideas and practices. There is a growing body of literature which identifies the need for indigenisation of social work education and practices in Africa (Rankopo and Osie Hwedie, 2011) and Asia (Yunong and Xiang, 2008) and which advocates inclusion of minority Indigenous populations (e.g. Gray et al., 2010). Such movements can be seen partly as a response to the effects of globalisation, including the continued neglect or exploitation of minority groups and the pressures on professional staff in developing countries to accept western ideas and values. Clearly these are concerns which must be addressed by international social work education.

Another criticism is associated with equity since specific opportunities for international education are currently only available to a minority of students mainly from wealthier countries. Even within specific countries opportunities are not evenly spread and various constraints prevent some students from participating. In addition, if students from the developed world undertake placements/ projects in a developing country, they run the risk of either being perceived as 'experts' or themselves assuming a sense of superiority or judging the experience to be irrelevant to their own learning needs. Student mobility therefore requires careful preparation and plans for support, as well as attention to the power imbalances inherent in existing global structures and interpersonal relationships (Lyons and Ramanathan, 1999; Barlow, 2007). The risk of professional imperialism is even more real if international social work education takes the form of faculty mobility aimed at contributing to course development. Dean reflects on the experiences of expatriate academics when teaching in host countries and offers 'some strategies for mutual learning' (2007: 136). These include mainstreaming international perspectives, making them available to all students and employing additional modes of cross-national communication.

INTERNATIONAL ISSUES FOR SOCIAL WORK EDUCATION

Three broad issues of international relevance currently challenge social work education. These include the academisation of social work education (with particular reference to doctoral study); the role of information and communications technology (ICT) in curriculum development for international social work; and regulation and the role of international and regional associations, including the articulation of global standards for social work education.

Social work education and disciplinary development

Information from around the world suggests that in many countries social work education is a marginalised activity in the context of higher education. In these countries, social work faces the issue of whether it is a form of vocational training or of professional education – and, if the latter, what are the implications for disciplinary development? Some responses to those questions involve increasing the scientific content of the subject, the level at which it is taught and placing emphasis on research. This in turn leads to concerns about the 'academisation' of the subject (Zavirsek, 2009). While some see academisation as threatening the relevance of education for practice others see it as affording opportunities including determining the research agenda and contributing to the knowledge base available to the profession.

Doctoral studies provide opportunities for professional development; extending the research capacity of the profession; and providing a research base for professional policies and practices. Social work is a demanding profession which requires personnel with critical and analytical skills. In some countries there are long established expectations that the faculty responsible for educating social workers should hold higher degrees and be involved in research in and for the profession. However, internationally, the opportunities for research training vary significantly and doctoral programmes designed for social workers are not generally available.

Doctoral research can take different forms as illustrated by a French-led regional research initiative, the CERTS project, funded by the European Community from the late 1990s through 2004. Initially it proved difficult to establish a comprehensive data base of the topics being researched in the 10 different countries. However, the data showed that students in South European countries needed to register for research degrees under the auspices of traditional disciplines (e.g. sociology or psychology) whereas students in some North European countries were more likely to be studying in a school of social work and/or to have social work qualified supervisors. This had implications for the theoretical orientation of theses and the social research paradigm and methods used, with a greater likelihood of qualitative approaches being used in Northern countries. Students in Northern Europe were more likely to gain their higher degree through part-time research; on a professional doctoral programme (with a 'taught' element); or through publication (Laot, 2000). The 'PhD by publication' route recognises the relatively recent emphasis placed on the need for European faculty to hold a PhD and builds on faculty's pre-existing research and publications (Lyons, 2006b).

Social workers/educators in developing countries most often need to enrol in a PhD programme abroad. However, the development of doctoral opportunities has been the focus of some bilateral or less formal relationships and is an important strategy in reestablishing social work education (e.g. Ethiopia, the Czech Republic). There are also the beginnings of 'international doctoral programmes', as in the case of INDOSOW, involving five schools from four European countries (Finland, Germany, Slovenia and UK) with associate members in Israel and Sri Lanka (Zavirsek, 2009).

Information and communications technology (ICT) and curriculum development

As indicated in the introduction to this chapter, communication technology is having a growing influence on social work internationally. Modern systems – e-mail, the web, Skype and video-conferencing – are contributing to the development of more accessible and inclusive forms of social work education. Open and distance learning for delivering courses already exist in a number of countries, sometimes providing programmes which have been validated by an institution in another country. For example, an Australian university runs an educational programme including face-to-face and distance education to students in Singapore (Brydon, 2011). Social work educators are also using ICT to engage their students in cross-national partnerships aimed at learning about comparative social work. For example, Bozalek and Matthews (2009) describe a project in which adult learners from one institution in the US and another in South Africa are paired and use e-mail exchanges to explore how cultural and economic factors impact on personal and professional identities.

Information technology is also enabling social work faculty to engage with and learn from colleagues abroad with potential spin-off for their teaching and research. Plummer and Nyang'au (2009) provide an example of exchanges between an academic in the USA and a Director of an NGO in Kenya; while Williams (2010) established and researched a 'virtual community of practice' as a medium for exchange between social work academics at schools in England and India. Undoubtedly, there is greater scope for using technology notwithstanding the inequalities which exist internationally in terms of access. While the use of ICT may be less effective than face to face contact in meeting the goals of 'inter- or cross-cultural' learning, the benefits of wider access and less cost make its increased use an important tool for developing international social work education.

GLOBAL STANDARDS AND PROFESSIONAL ASSOCIATIONS IN SOCIAL WORK EDUCATION

Variations in the structure and content of professional education across different regions of the world are paralleled by variations in regulation. Also, there are different roles which national professional associations play in providing leadership and ensuring standards. At the international level, the IASSW has also given attention to standards for professional education. A major initiative of the new millennium was the establishment of a working group, also including representatives from the IFSW, which devised the *Global Standards for the Education and Training of the Social Work Profession* in 2004. While there have been heated debates about the appropriateness of articulating global standards, the initiative has been well received by many, including countries where there is effectively no national regulation. Individual standards cover programme mission, objectives and outcomes, as well as curriculum content and field work. There are also standards covering the qualifications of professional staff; cultural and ethnic diversity and ethical codes of conduct (Hokenstad, 2008). The aims in creating the *Global Standards* were that the profession should take responsibility for establishing its own standards and move closer to a situation where the qualifications gained by social workers in one country are accepted as broadly comparable with those achieved elsewhere. This initiative recognised both the increase in regulation of social work education in many countries and the international mobility of social workers (Sewpaul and Jones, 2004). There is anecdotal evidence and some data to demonstrate that there is increasing mobility of social workers within and between continental regions (Lyons and Hanna, 2011).

National and regional associations of social work education have varied involvement in standard setting and professional development.

- In *Africa* regulatory frameworks are in little evidence but social work programmes in some countries (e.g. South Africa) are working to develop national professional structures. In addition, the recently re-established (2005) Association of Schools of Social Work in Africa (ASSWA) aims to provide focus and leadership, including in the processes of indigenisation (Mwansa, 2011).

- In the *Asia Pacific regions*, there are relatively few examples of national regulation. Accreditation standards have been implemented in Hong Kong and Japan; in Australia the Australian Association of Social Workers is responsible for accrediting social work programmes; and in New Zealand newly qualified social workers are assessed for recognition by the Social Workers Registration Board. In addition, the Asian and Pacific Association for Social Work Education (APASWE) has a broad and growing membership with an active agenda of conferences and consultation contributing to the development of social work education regionally (Noble, 2004).

- In *Europe* a mixed picture reflects diverse traditions in both higher education and welfare services, and the regulation of social work and its associated educational programmes is patchy. For example, in Britain and Italy there are frameworks for approval of social work programmes and/or the registration of newly qualified social workers. Elsewhere, programmes have been impacted by national responses to the European Union effort to standardise European academic awards through the Bologna Agreement although this does not regulate professional education. The European Association of Schools of Social Work (EASSW) was active in supporting the expansion of social work education beyond the 27 member states of the EU: it offers member schools a range of services including funding for projects aimed at curriculum development, research and (sub-regional) seminars.

- In *Latin America* national regulation is not widespread but the Latin American Association for Social Work Teaching and Research (ALAIETS) provides coordination and development functions for programmes and educators in the region. This regional body was established in 2006 to replace earlier regional organisations and to meet 21st-century demands for social work education and practice, attuned to regional socio-economic and cultural realities. Its objectives include knowledge building and continuing education, as well as agreement on basic approaches at the academic degree and post-degree levels. Associations of

Schools of Social Work in a number of Latin American countries are participants in the new organisation see chapter 29).

- In *North America* the North American and Caribbean Association of Schools of Social Work (NACASSW) was established in 1992, when a newly formed Caribbean sub-region joined with the US-based Council on Social Work Education (CSWE) and the Canadian Association of Schools of Social Work (CASSW). NACASSW is active in promoting opportunities for shared learning and staff development. Regulation of social work education remains a national concern. In Canada, CASSW is the accreditation agency for educational programmes: documentation and processes reflect the bilingual policy (French/English) of the country as a whole and its work includes the accreditation of First Nation focused programmes (Healy, 2004). The CSWE is the educational policy and standard setting body for social work programmes in the US but almost all US states also have licensing or registration processes for social workers (Hoffman, 2008). There is increasing attention to interdependence in social work education in the region and, although programmes in the Caribbean region may not be formally accredited, NACASSW is active in promoting opportunities for shared learning and staff development.

CONCLUSION

An increased emphasis on the international dimension of social work education is both necessary and inevitable in our globalised society. This chapter has examined some of the trends and issues facing the educational component of the social work profession as its international dimension evolves. It has placed these trends and issues in a historical and organisational context with particular emphasis on the IASSW and its affiliate regional associations. National and regional variations in the structure and content of social work education have been considered and the debate over the appropriate role of global standards has been highlighted. In sum, the chapter provides a moving picture of past developments, current issues, and future challenges in the internationalisation of educational programmes across the world.

ACKNOWLEDGMENT

Thanks are due to Karen Lyons for contributing some of the material on which this chapter is based.

REFERENCES

Barlow, C. (2007). 'In the third space: A case study of Canadian students in a social work practicum in India', *International Social Work*, 50(2), 243–54.

Bozalek, V., and Matthews, L. (2009). 'E-learning: A cross-institutional forum for sharing socio-cultural influences on personal and professional identity', *International Social Work*, 52(2), 235–46.

Brydon, K. (2011) 'Offering social work education in an offshore context: a case study of an Australian programme delivered in Singapore', *International Social Work*, 54(5), 681–700.

Clark, E.J. and Woods Waller, G. (2006). 'Improving the profession. Changing perceptions – Social work in the USA', in N. Hall (ed.), *Social Work: Making a world of difference*. Oslo: IFSW and Fafo.

Dean, Y. (2007) 'Finding common ground: Can the teaching of social work transcend cultural and geographic borders?' in S. Boorman, M. Klassen, and C. Spatscheck (eds), *International Social Work: Social Problems, Cultural Issues and Social Work education*. Opladen: Barbara Budrich Publishers.

Doel, M. and Shardlow, S. (eds) (1996) *Social Work in a Changing World: An International Perspective on Practice Learning*. Aldershot: Arena Publishing.

Dominelli, L. and Bernard, W.T. (eds). (2003) *Broadening horizons: International exchanges in social work*. Aldershot, England: Ashgate Publishing.

Elliott, D. (2008) *Encyclopedia of Social Work* (20th edition, Vol. 2, pp. 480–482). New York, NY: Oxford University Press.

Ginsburg, N. and Lawrence, S. (2006) A changing Europe, In K. Lyons and S. Lawrence (eds.), *Social work in Europe: Educating for change* (pp. 17–36). Birmingham: BASW/IASSW.

Gray, M., Coates, J. and Yellow Bird, M. (eds). (2010) *Indigenous social work around the world: Towards culturally relevant education and practice*. Aldershot: Ashgate Publishing.

Healy, L. M. (1986) The international dimension in social work education: Current efforts, future challenges. *International Social Work,* 29, 135–147.

Healy, L. M. (2004) Social work education in the North American and Caribbean region: Current realities, future issues. *Social Work Education,* 23(5), 581–595.

Healy, L. M. (2008). *International social work: Professional action in an interdependent world.* New York, NY: Oxford University Press.

Healy, L. M., Asamoah, Y. and Hokenstad, M. C. (eds). (2003) *Models of international collaboration in social work education.* Alexandria, VA: Council on Social Work Education.

Henkel, M. (1994) Social Work: An incorrigibly marginal profession. In T. Becher (ed.) *Governments and professional education.* Buckingham, SRHE/Open University Press.

Hoffman, K. (2008) Social work education. In T. Mizrahi & L. E. Davis (eds.), *Encyclopedia of Social Work* (20th edition, Vol. 4, pp. 107–114). New York, NY: Oxford University Press.

Hokenstad, M. C. (2008) International social work education. In T. Mizrahi & L. E. Davis (eds.), *Encyclopedia of Social Work* (20th edition, Vol. 2, pp.488–493). New York, NY: Oxford University Press.

Hokenstad, M. C. and Kendall, K. A. (1995) International social work education. In R. L. Edwards (ed.), *Encyclopedia of Social Work* (19th ed., vol. 2, pp. 1511–1520). Washington, DC: National Association of Social Workers Press.

Hokenstad, M. C. and Midgley, J. (eds). (1997) *Issues in international social work: Global challenges for a new century.* Washington, DC: National Association of Social Workers Press.

Hokenstad, M. C., & Midley, J. (eds). (2004) *Lessons from abroad: Adapting international social welfare innovations.* Washington, DC: National Association of Social Workers Press.

Hugman, R. (2011) *Understanding international social work: A critical analysis.* Basingstoke, Palgrave Macmillan.

International Association of Schools of Social Work (2009). *About IASSW.* Retrieved from http://www.iassw-aiets.org/

International Association of Schools of Social Work and International Federation of Social Work (2004) *Global standards for the education and training of the social work profession.* Retrieved from http://www.ifsw.org/cm_data/GlobalSocialWorkStandards2005.pdf

Johnson, A. (2004) Increasing internationalisation in social work programmes. Healy's continuum as a strategic planning guide. *International Social Work,* 47(1), 7–23.

Juliusdottir, S., & Petersson, J. (2004) Nordic standards revisited. *Social Work Education,* 23(5), 567–580.

Kendall, K. A. (2000) *Social work education: Its origins in Europe.* Alexandria, VA: Council on Social Work Education.

Laot, F. (2000) Doctoral work in the social work field in Europe, *Social Work in Europe,* 7(2), 2–7.

Lavalette, M. (ed.) (2011) *Radical social work today: Social work at the crossroads.* Bristol: The Policy Press.

Lawrence, S. (2006) Post-graduate provision in Europe. In Lyons and Lawrence (eds.), *Social work in Europe: Educating for change.* Birmingham, England: Ashgate Publishing.

Leininger, L. (2000) *Creating a new profession: The beginnings of social work education in the United States.* Alexandria, VA: Council on Social Work Education.

Lyons, K. (1999) European dimensions in the training of the social professions – Synthesis report. In O. Chytil and F. W. Seibel (eds.), *European dimensions in training and practice of social professions.* Blansko, Czech Republic: ALBERT.

Lyons, K. (2006a). Globalization and social work: International and local implications. *British Journal of Social Work,* 36, 365–380.

Lyons, K. (2006b). Research and professional education. In K. Lyons and S. Lawrence (eds), *Social work in Europe: Educating for change* (pp. 59–80). Birmingham, England: Ashgate Publishing.

Lyons, K. and Hanna, S. (2011) European social workers in England: Exploring international labour mobility. *Social Work Review,* 10(3), 185–196.

Lyons, K. and Lawrence, S. (eds), (2006) *Social work in Europe: Educating for change.* Birmingham: BASW/IASSW.

Lyons, K. and Ramanathan, C. S. (1999) Models of field practice in global settings. In C.S. Ramanathan and R. Link (eds.). *All our futures: Principles and resources for social work practice in a global era.* Belmont, CA: Wadsworth.

Lyons, K., Manion, K. and Carsen, M. (2006) *International perspectives on social work: Global conditions and local practice.* New York: Palgrave MacMillian.

Mupedziswa, R. and Ushamba, A. (2006) Challenges and prospects: Social work practice in Zimbabwe in an environment of economic meltdown. In N. Hall (ed.), *Social Work: Making a world of difference.* Oslo: IFSW and Fafo.

Mwansa, L. K. (2011). Social work education in Africa: Whence and whither? *Social Work Education,* 30(1), 4–16.

Noble, C. (2004). Social work education, training, and standards in the Asian-Pacific region. *Social Work Education,* 23(5), 527–536.

Plummer, C. and Nyang'au, T. O. (2009). Reciprocal e-mentoring: Accessible international exchanges. *International Social Work,* 52(6), 811–823.

Powell, J. and Robinson, J. (2007) The 'international dimension' in social work education: Current developments in England. *European Journal of Social Work,* 10(3), 383–400.

Radulescu, A. (2006) Shaping the role and public image of social workers in Europe. In N. Hall (ed), *Social Work: Making a world of difference.* Oslo: IFSW and Fafo.

Sewpaul, V. and Jones, D. (2004) Global Standards for social work education and training, *Social Work Education,* 23(5), 493–513.

Sewpaul, S. and Lombard, A. (2004) Social work education, training, and standards in Africa. *Social Work Education,* 23(5), 537–554.

University of East London (2010) Course information: MA International Social Work with Refugee Studies. Retrieved from www.uel.ac.uk/programmes/hss/postgraduate/summary/intsocialrefugee.htm

United Nations (1950) *Training for social work: An international survey* (United Nations Publication No. 50, IV.II). New York, NY: Author.

United Nations (1951) *Report of the social commission: Economic and social council official records* (13th session, Supplement 12). New York, NY: Author.

United Nations (1959) *Training for social work: Third international survey* (United Nations Publication No. 59 IV.I). New York, NY: Author.

Welbourne, P. (2011) 21st century social work: The influence of political context on public service provision in social work education and service delivery. *European Journal of Social Work,* 14(3), 403–420.

Williams, I. (2010) The virtual community of practice involving social work lecturers in the UK and India: Themes and issues arising from sharing knowledge and learning in different societal contexts. Unpublished PhD thesis. Chelmsford, UK: Anglia Ruskin University.

Yip, K-S. (2007) Tensions and dilemmas in social work education in China, *International Social Work,* 50(1), 93–105.

Yuen-Tsang, A. and Ip, D. (2009) Indigenising social work education: Experiences of People's Republic of China students in Hong Kong. In S. Ramon and D. Zaviršek (eds.), *Critical edge issues in social work and social policy: Comparative research perspectives.* Ljubljana: Faculty of Social Work, University of Ljubljana.

Zaviršek, D. (2009) Social work with adults with disabilities: An international perspective, *British Journal of Social Work,* 39(7), 1393–1405.

11

Social Work Research

Joan Orme and Synnove Karvinen-Niinikoski

INTRODUCTION

This chapter provides an overview of the development of social work research globally. In doing so it identifies the different and shared issues when considering who undertakes social work research; what is researched and how research is undertaken. It considers debates about what international social work research involves and what needs to be done to facilitate it.

The significance of research for social work practice internationally is reflected in the *Global Standards for the Education and Training of the Social Work Profession* (IASSW, 2004a). The section on 'Methods of social work practice' states that all social work education should include knowledge of social work research and skills in the use of research methods, including ethical use of relevant research paradigms, and critical appreciation of the use of research and different sources of knowledge about social work practice.

This requirement clearly links practice and research but puts the onus for undertaking research on social work educators. Practitioners are expected to be able to understand the implications of extant research for their practice but not necessarily undertake it. Different arrangements for social work education suggest that the first imperative is unrealistic but we argue that the requirements for good practice globally mean that knowledge of social work research findings, an understanding of the results of research and their implications for practice are minimum requirements of good social work.

The challenge is to realise this in an international context. Traditions in social work research mean that both the methodological expertise and infrastructure for research vary widely. In view of this there can be difficulties in global access to research, complicated by both language and the relevance of commonly accepted or dominant research methods to some societies and communities. While it is easy to suggest that international social work research has to respond to the diversity of social work internationally, the debates about what is meant by international social work have implications for research.

Lorenz's (2006) suggestion that the roots of social work are in nation states is also true for social work research. However, international approaches can bring enhanced knowledge about shared social problems.

As Tripodi and Potocky-Tripodi (2007) argue, social work research is vital for international social work practitioners to enable them to make decisions based on previous studies and to contribute to future research. In addition, the growing acknowledgement that a number of social issues facing practitioners (e.g. refugees, child trafficking, pandemics) require global solutions; then the development of international social work research becomes crucial to the development of theory and the improvement of practice.

DEFINITIONS

Such assertions raise the question of what constitutes international social work research. A very basic definition of international social work research is that it is research that is relevant to international social work (Tripodi and Potocky-Tripodi, 2007: 18); although this is complicated by the various understandings of international social work discussed elsewhere in this volume and in other major publications (e.g. Healy, 2001; Cox and Pawar, 2006; Lyons et al., 2006). The more detailed analysis of international social work research provided by Tripodi and Potocky-Tripodi (2007) and based on a threefold description is more helpful:

Supranational: alternatively described as 'beyond borders' involves research and research participants from one country but draws on literature from two or more countries and discusses the implications for two or more countries.
Intranational: alternatively described as 'within borders' involves a population from one country being studied within another and includes consideration of literature from and implications for both countries.
Transnational: alternatively described as 'across borders' involves comparative research between the populations of two or more countries.

However, even such a detailed definition can be challenged, not least because it comes

from a Western perspective. In the following sections we explore the implications of a wider international perspective.

TRADITIONS IN RESEARCHING SOCIAL WORK: HISTORICAL AND CURRENT ASPECTS

The development of social work knowledge and research underpinning it are integrally linked to the development of social work education (Mäntysaari and Weatherley, 2010). As Payne and Askeland point out; 'as social work becomes more academic the contribution of more and better knowledge has been emphasised' (2008: 34). It is therefore necessary to briefly identify how trends in social work education have impinged on research.

Prior to World War II research in the social sciences generally was dominated by Europe and the United States. In both England and the US social work education had its origins in the first decade of the 20th century. However, it was the commitment of the Chicago School of Sociology to research that initiated a long tradition of 'scientific' social work research (Shaw, 2008) and contributed to the dominance of the US in social work research.

Initially research in the US was associated with the pragmatic approach which aims to provide answers to questions. This was evident in the work of Jane Addams who in the late 19th century introduced a tradition of community based studies in the Hull House Neighbourhood in Chicago. However, in the early 20th century the role of psychoanalysis in the development of practice in the US also led to a focus on clinical practice or 'intervention research' where the outcomes of research should be made directly relevant to practice. Such research depended on systematic procedures for designing, testing and evaluating social work interventions based on a scientific approach. As evidence of the continuation of this scientific approach in the

US the editorial for the journal *Qualitative Social Work,* in June 2010, made the observation that at the Society of Social Work Research (SSWR) conference that year the majority of papers were quantitative in methods and orientation.

In the UK and Europe philosophical developments associated with social democratic movements meant that social work research was influenced by other social sciences disciplines including sociology and political theory. The influence of Alice Salomon (Kuhlman, 2000), an economist by background, in Germany, is one example of such traditions. In former Czechoslovakia the impact of the Prague Spring in 1968 caused graduates in for example economics and sociology to resign from their professions and become social workers (Chytil and Popelká, 2000). Developments in the Nordic countries were closely aligned with both sociology and social policy in Finland while in Sweden and Norway psychological and psychodynamic orientations were influential.

The founding the International Association of Schools of Social Work (IASSW) in 1928 could be seen to be the defining movement towards international social work. Although 42 countries were represented this did not necessarily constitute a global movement; most of the activities were headed by representatives from the US and Europe. It was not until 1956 that the board of directors included members from Australia, Guatemala, Japan and India and membership began to include schools of social work developed in the newly independent countries in Asia and Africa (Healy, 2008).

Nor did the formation of IASSW necessarily mean a burgeoning of social work research at either the national or international level because until recently the emphasis was on education rather than research. The relevance of research for practice in this context was problematic. For example, debates in the Nordic countries about the academisation processes of social work education related to the relationship between research and

practice and were echoed in other countries. In post-socialist countries the development of social work has been strongly supported by the European Union (EU). Starting from the post cold war situation where such subjects as social work and social policy were hardly known (Hering, 2009), EU projects such as PHARE, INTAS and EU-Leonardo and Tempus[1] have had a huge impact on the establishment of social work education up to masters and advanced levels (Friesenhahn et al., 2008). They have also been instrumental in linking social work education with research. Such funds have supported the production of educational materials based on research (e.g. biographical methods/ Leonardo-Invite), helped establish research institutes and scientific communities (e.g. Udmurtia-institute) and publications (e.g. *Social Policy and Social Work in Transition,* a peer-reviewed scientific journal).

However, differences in levels of social work education have implications for social work research. For example, Sweden and Finland have well-established university-based training with responsive professors emphasising the importance of research while Norway and Denmark have only recently (as a result of the Bologna process in 2008) established academic social work education in universities (see Chapter 10). This has led to a remarkable increase in research (e.g. Mäntysaari and Weatherley, 2010). Similar developments have occurred in the Netherlands where a national review advised professional schools to put more effort into research (van der Laan, 2000), and in the UK with the introduction of a national research strategy linked to raising academic standards for social work education (Orme and Powell, 2008). There is a developing pattern that research-orientation and activities are regarded as being of high importance in those countries where social work education has been affiliated to the universities (Campanini, 2007; Powell and Robinson, 2007). Such developments have consequences for the relationship between research and practice.

DEVELOPMENTS IN INTERNATIONAL SOCIAL WORK RESEARCH

Publications such as the special edition of the *European Journal of Social Work* (2005, 8(3); 'Towards research-oriented social work education in Europe') and IASSW funding of projects (e.g. Powell, 2007) as well as the Global Standards, reflect an international acceptance that social work education and research are interdependent. Despite these developments, there are still tensions – especially concerning the issue of research – between the older, more traditional universities and the higher education institutions, such as universities of applied sciences, in which social workers in many European countries are trained (e.g. Labonté-Roset, 2007). Such debates are also relevant to the development of social work research outside Europe and North America when course development and approval (including higher degrees) might involve an 'expert' from one of those regions.

The growing emphasis on social work research globally is further evidenced by the growing number of descriptions of the development of research at a national level in, for example, Australia (Crisp, 2000), Finland (Karvinen et al., 1999), Israel (Auslander, 2000) and the UK (Orme and Powell, 2008). However, there are few comparative descriptions of the development of research. Powell's (2007) case studies of research teaching on four social work programmes is based on the link between education and research development and identifies both similarities and differences between programmes and countries. While she focuses on content and process of research teaching she points out that differences in activity and approach to learning reflect differences in national requirements for professional education and training and the varying degrees of regulation of social work practice.

Also Powell (2007) observes that national differences between the emphasis placed on either quantitative *or* qualitative approaches, reflect the different traditions between scientific, pragmatic approaches of the US and the more philosophical epistemological explorations of European traditions (Gredig and Marsh, 2010). However, she also identifies an emphasis on participatory approaches to research in the curriculum in South Africa which she links to the political culture of schools in that country. Ryan and Sheehan's (2000) survey of all the schools of social work in Australia found that Australian programmes had a more varied curriculum that included basic methods such as statistics, alongside qualitative and feminist approaches, and the inclusion of the politics of research. Fook (2003) has suggested that this 'traditional/progressive' approach can be claimed as distinctive, particularly given recent developments in indigenous research movements in Australia, alongside a growing interest in the exploration of more complex forms of practice research.

The influence of indigenous communities on research in countries such as Australia, New Zealand and Canada has begun to impact on social work practice education and research globally (e.g. Gray et al., 2008). These developments have implications for the understandings and definitions of international social work research. If there is no uniform approach how can country-specific research be integrated? Also, to have influence and to inform practice globally, research methods and results need to be accepted globally and be accessible, with implications for dissemination. However, theoretical development of culturally appropriate social work practice also needs to be conducted within an indigenous research paradigm (Kee, 2004). From the perspective of researching in Malaysia Kee argues that there is an inextricable relationship between research methodology, ways of knowing and culture.

CURRENT ISSUES OF SOCIAL WORK RESEARCH

With globalisation there is an expectation that knowledge from research should increasingly be universal (Payne and Askeland, 2008) but the accessibility of knowledge based on research is a complex issue. Peer-reviewed social work journals have emerged in India, China and the Asia Pacific region more generally and in Africa and South America (see chapters in Section 5) reflecting research undertaken in these areas. However, this does not necessarily lead to international recognition of published research studies as these journals are not always accessible globally. The problem is compounded because journals which describe themselves as 'international' still tend to have a national focus.[2] Additionally, content analysis of articles in seven social work journals over a 10-year period showed that international social work research apparently decreased while domestic research showed an increase (Young Jung and Tripodi, 2007).

Some journals launched in the last decade have made a more concerted effort to include international contributions.[3] But even then, barriers to dissemination remain, due to expectations about language (most require articles to be submitted in English); format; and the nature of the research undertaken (Munford et al., 2009). The dominant traditions from Europe and the US, while competing and contrasting with each other, have tended to influence criteria for what constitutes rigorous and appropriate social work research and these are used in assessing quality by journal editors and assessors. Such criteria can render important messages from research inaccessible to practitioners.

The issues concerning dissemination are further compounded by pressure on social work research from a number of sources. In the global climate of university rankings and research evaluations 'international impact' is becoming a requirement of social work research. An international reputation is also required to secure research funding and academic career promotion. In many 'Western' countries social work academics are now under similar pressures to those experienced in the UK to produce high –quality research in order to secure funding (Orme and Powell, 2008). Definitions of

quality are externally imposed and often include a hierarchy of publications which has implications for publishing outlets. Payne and Askeland (2008) give the example of the professor from Bergen who undertook a joint project between Bergen and Nepal. He came under pressure from his institution to publish in Norwegian or in an international publication either of which would disadvantage the Nepalese collaborators. On the other hand, developing international research in North America is challenged by pressures from legislature and policy makers to undertake intervention research that demonstrates which social work interventions are effective (see *Social Work Research,* 2008, 32 [4]). This encourages a focus on local/national boundaries rather than on international collaboration and dissemination.

In Nordic countries governments adopted a policy of governing by information and knowledge in the field of social welfare which aroused debate about the extent to which services and social work practice are research-informed and oriented. A positive outcome was the establishment of funded projects for promoting dissemination of research, research on research, research-utilisation and evaluation research (e.g. Bergmark and Lundström, 2010; Soydan, 2010; Mäntysaari and Weatherley, 2010). However, it is not clear what emphasis there is on international research in such schemes. Similarly, the UK Research Strategy (JUC SWEC, 2005) only mentions internationalising research in the context of building networks while the investigation into the kinds and quality of social work research (Shaw and Norton, 2008) takes into account international impact and esteem but has little discussion of undertaking international research (however defined).

It may be that funding sources influence the nature of social work research. Different governments have different priorities based on both social problems and governmental philosophies. They are unlikely to fund cross-national studies, although there may be an expectation that researchers draw on best practice in other countries. Similarly, independent research councils and other funding bodies tend to fund either national priorities or research that relates to the mission of the organisation (e.g. children's charities). At the level of European (e.g. Goethe[4]) or United Nations funding, this relates either to shared or comparative regional or global issues, or is used to recruit researchers from several countries to research a major international problem. For example, comparative research is an international agenda in itself. Some organisations, e.g. the Organisation for Economic Co-operation and Development (OECD), provide member states with comparative data to steer policy development. Statistical data and documented materials provide highly respected comparisons of the impact of policy (Kangas, 2010). However, the criteria used for allocation of funding often mean that social work researchers have little success in competitive bids.

A further issue is the range of views about what constitutes good quality social work research. Regarding international research, Tripodi and Potocky-Tripodi (2007) quote Lane's (1990) assertion that good international research is based on good social science theory, but this begs a lot of questions, not least related to diversity. There are dangers in adopting an uncritical approach to 'the quest for a universal social work' (Gray and Fook, 2004) – or social work research. Issues of Westernisation, localisation and indigenisation have to be considered. For example, Payne and Askeland (2008) argue that cross-national activities in social work reveal modernist and universalising assumptions: this is also true of social work research. As Shaw and Norton observe, international frameworks of quality for social work research could unintentionally become the vehicle to limit rather than strengthen national and regionally diverse modes of social work research (2007: 61).

One danger is that some form of standardised, uniform and universal approach is seen as the goal as opposed to the need to recognise and learn from difference. On the other hand, post-modern interpretations of a global world permit many different social works emerging from many different cultures framed by social and historical contexts (Payne and Askeland, 2008: 64). For example, globalisation has increased the scale and complexity of migration, which influences social problems everywhere. Social workers require cross-cultural knowledge based on research to engage at all levels from the personal to the societal. Hence Payne and Askeland (2008) suggest that, in a post-colonial world, there is a need for caution in assuming all cross-national research is worthwhile. International social work involves both working in international settings and incorporating international perspectives into local practice (Lyons et al., 2006). International research therefore has to provide knowledge as a resource to inform the professional decisions of practitioners rather than a definitive set of normative guidelines about how social work research should be undertaken or how social work should be practiced. As Shaw acknowledges, 'Internationalisation need not mean lowest common denominator globalisation. Indeed it opens up new scope for addressing issues of methodology and culture' (2003: 111).

METHODOLOGICAL AND ETHICAL ISSUES

Three themes dominate methodological discussions globally: methodological approaches; evidence-based practice and policy development; and participatory and emancipatory approaches. They are subject to debate and what follows highlights the debates, but does not necessarily provide solutions.

Methodological approaches

The dominance of US and European approaches in social work research have not been without tensions. The pragmatic relative to the more philosophical approaches developed into what are called 'the paradigm debates' in social work research (Orme and Shemmings, 2010). These permeate international social work research and relate to how, where and by whom decisions about social work research methods are made (Munford et al., 2009).

In many countries outside North America there has been enthusiasm for qualitative methodologies as being more appropriate to the topics that social work researches, to the point where Shaw cautions against the danger that qualitative approaches become the 'uncritical method of choice' in social work research, potentially leading to a lack of methodological imagination (Shaw, 2003: 110). The presence of particular research methods in countries which are academically isolated or marginalised (e.g. in South America or Africa) may be because of their dependence on researchers from other countries who have the resources to travel and influence the research methods to be used. The outreach work by schools of social work into, for example, South America, or the attraction for social work academics from countries with less well developed academic infrastructures of undertaking doctoral studies in North America have also helped disseminate *particular* approaches globally. In the Asia Pacific region Mumford et al. (2009) have identified the predominance of qualitative approaches in research and they suggest that geographic and linguistic marginality means there are few opportunities for researchers in this region to debate and advance ideas about social work research.

EVIDENCE-BASED PRACTICE AND POLICY DEVELOPMENT (E-BP)

The influence of E-BP in social work seems global if we accept the 'world' definition which highlights the significance of research for practice: 'Social work bases its methodology on a systematic body of evidence-based knowledge derived from research and practice evaluation' (IASSW/IFSW, 2001).

Thyer and Kazi (2004) assert that the subject of international research cannot be addressed without addressing evidence-based practice arguing that disparate initiatives promoting E-BP are occurring in most countries. The fact that contributions to their text on the subject come from 10 countries representing most continents would seem to illustrate this claim. However, contributions from the US and the UK predominate with examples from only six other countries suggesting that the 'dominance' of the approach is not necessarily widespread.

Also E-BP is contentious even in those areas where it predominates (e.g. see Gambrill, 2007 for debates in North America). Many of the contributors to the *Sage Handbook of Social Work Research* (Shaw et al., 2010) engage critically with E-BP. The approach raises questions about what counts as evidence in that quantitative approaches, large scale data sets and random control trails are seen as 'the gold standard' for social work research. Social work cannot argue with the need to have the best possible evidence for practice *but* there are different views about what constitutes rigorous research and there is no agreement that this requires particular approaches. While some suggest that evidence of effective interventions has to be 'tested' across diverse populations, others argue that global approaches to research have to recognise different ways of producing evidence and acknowledge the diversity of methodological approaches reflected in, for example, narrative research (Munford et al., 2009).

These debates have also been informed by the growth of 'emancipatory approaches' in social work research, that is, approaches that recognise different stakeholders in knowledge production including practitioners and service users.

Participatory and Emancipatory approaches

In mainstream research the assumption is that research is carried out by academic, government or private researchers who have expertise (see the descriptions of research in Tripodi and Potocky-Tripody, 2007, as examples), but epistemological approaches influenced by feminism, indigenisation and the disability movement have led to alternative approaches in social work research to the organisation of research and who undertakes it. The recognition that 'objective' researchers need to have a particular perspective was initially associated with what Tripodi and Potocky-Tripodi (2007) call cultural competence. Such competence in aspects of international research is vital in order to avoid cultural imperialism, when researchers from one country impose their interpretations on another. Minimal approaches to avoid this often use a notion of participatory research that 'includes' certain groups either as research 'subjects' or as token representatives involved at some point in the research (see Gellis, 2001, cited in Tripodi and Potocky-Tripody, 2007). However, as Kee (2008) points out, such competence in an international context has to include not only knowledge of language but also understanding of cultural norms, sensitivities and taboos in both the content and process of communication and these understandings have to permeate research processes and practices.

Emancipatory approaches to research have taken this further and argued for the need for 'standpoint' research, that is, research undertaken by particular groups on behalf of their members. This is based on assumptions that only those 'in' the situation can understand it. In the UK this has led to the recognition of both social work practitioners and service users as potential researchers (Fisher, 2002; Shaw, 2005) and has implications for all aspects of the research process. However, as with E-BP, such approaches are not without controversy (see Orme, 2004; Hammersley, 2003). For international social work the implications are complicated: does it mean only those in a country can research its social problems? If so: how can researchers collaborate across geographic boundaries? What are the messages for practice globally if only country-specific perspectives are privileged?

Emancipatory approaches to practice drawn on by social workers involved in rural development, community development and/or developmental social work provides some directions. Participatory rural approaches or a rapid rural approach (RRA) to development is based on systematic but semi-structured activity 'in the field' by a multidisciplinary team and is designed to obtain new information and formulate new hypotheses about rural life based on information directly from those involved (Crawford, 1997). A core concept of RRA is that the team carrying out the research should comprise members drawn from a variety of appropriate disciplines, some with relevant technical backgrounds and others with social science skills. Such approaches are particularly pertinent to social development practiced across geo-political borders and at different levels of social, political, and economic organisation and, according to Estes (1998), falls within the remit of international social work. This distinctive form of social work could include academics (from different countries), practitioners, non-governmental agency representatives, community representatives and those to whom services are to be delivered.

However, even when expertise and cultural competence are to the fore there can still be ethical problems. For instance, Askeland and Bradley, discussing their research on the use of critical reflection in an African country, describe themselves as 'coming from the outside' and recognise that they might not fully understand that different political backgrounds and perspectives might put people involved in research projects at risk (Askeland and Bradley, 2007: 681).

Ethical issues

This highlights that established ethical approaches need to be reconsidered in the context of international social work research.

First, there are issues of power associated with knowledge transference. Assuming that knowledge from research in 'Western countries' should influence practice in the rest of the world has been identified as professional imperialism (e.g. Hall and Midgley, 2004; Nimagadda and Cowger, 1999). It is a legitimate question whether knowledge and social work methods developed from research in western countries can be useful in non-Western countries (Askeland and Bradley, 2007).

Indigenisation and understandings of cultural competence both have significant implications for ethical considerations in social work research (Askeland and Bradley, 2007; Munford et al., 2009; Briskman, 2010). Codes of ethics that have been devised for social work research based on European philosophy (see Butler, 2002; Hugman, 2010a) are not always appropriate to other cultures and religions. Briskman (2010), for example, identifies how the position and status of aboriginal people and asylum seekers requires researchers to challenge more traditional ethical approaches to research in order to gain access. Research with Maori people in New Zealand (Pere and Barnes, 2009) and Asian people in east-Africa (Ryen, 2008) illustrates how acknowledging different philosophical traditions gives different perspectives on ethical approaches, including who 'owns' the research. However, this should not necessarily lead to differences in approaches to ethics. Acknowledging the strictly contextual nature of ethical choices could be an internationally unifying base for international social work as illustrated by the process of establishing the professional codes for ethics and the ongoing critical review (IASSW, 2004b).

RESEARCH STUDIES IN DIFFERENT FIELDS

Ethical considerations in research therefore inform the development of knowledge of and for social work. Other ways in which international social work research has done this can be illustrated by examples of research studies in different fields.

Intervention research

Reid and Shyne's (1969) early empirically based study led to wide ranging changes in both social work practice and organisation related to adoption of their task centred casework model. Other examples of research informing intervention are associated with the continued emphasis in the US on E-BP discussed above. One consequence of an E-BP approach in the UK has been the increased use of cognitive behavioural methods of intervention (Sheldon, 2000). The tradition of the early scientific approach by Fischer (1973) in the US on the effectiveness of intervention has not been developed globally; the emphasis is more often on evaluation. Therefore globally few research studies have led to the development of new methods of intervention that have been adopted internationally, although Saleebey's (1997) strengths perspective appears to have initiated intervention research worldwide.

Child care

The area of child care has been a fruitful source of 'internationalising' social work research. Research on resilience across cultures (Ungar, 2008) involving data from 14 sites across five continents (chosen on the basis of maximising variability) is an example of research to ascertain the global, cultural and contextually specific aspects of resilience in children. Significantly, in the light of the ethical discussions above, Ungar recognises that 'resilience' is a Eurocentric concept using Western social science concepts to describe a phenomenon (2008: 22). Nevertheless, the research aims to 'test out' the global relevance of the concept.

Examples also exist of research methodology that has informed practice in one country, the UK (Ward, 2000), being translated and tested in others, for example Australia (Fernandez and Romeo, 2003) and Finland (Hall et al., 2003). Other studies published in international journals have provided analysis of national arrangements (Satka and Harrikari, 2008) and international comparisons of child welfare (Thoburn, 2007). These approaches have led to networking around research in the area of child care, which include the International Association of Outcome Based Evaluation and Research on Family and Children's Services (IOBER) and the European Scientific Association for Residential and Foster Care for Children and Adolescents (EUSARF) (Ruffolo et al., 2010).

Health inequalities

Internationalising of research has also taken place around health inequalities. Many facets of health, illness and disease are shared globally but some, for example the impact of HIV/AIDS, have a more significant impact in certain countries and among certain populations (Palattiyil and Chakrabarti, 2008). However, even in a subject area that is so obviously global, Bywaters and Ungar (2010) recognise the dominance of the UK and US in research, mainly because attendance at conferences and seminars to discuss research is influenced by the choice of expensive venues skewing participation towards those from wealthy developed countries (Bywaters and Ungar, 2010: 394). To redress this bias the Social Work and Health Inequalities Network[5] was established. But with members mainly from 12 countries it is acknowledged that even this does not constitute extensive coverage and the organisers recognise that very little social work research in the area of health has addressed issues associated with the processes of globalisation (Bywaters, 2009).

Societies in conflict

A third example of international research based on shared interest in global issues is

the work around societies in conflict (Ramon et al., 2006). To date the focus has been mainly on countries experiencing conflict in Europe but in a volatile world there is the potential to widen collaboration to include other areas in conflict, although this will bring its own level of methodological and ethical complexity.

ORGANISATION FOR INTERNATIONAL RESEARCH

In addition to networks described above (developed around specific issues such as children or health inequalities) regional and international networks also exist based on methods or methodological approaches and ethical commitments. For example, an early network, the Toronto Group, was established in Canada in 1997 based on a common commitment to the empowerment of service users in research (Beresford and Evans, 1999).

The Inter-Centre Network for the Evaluation of Social Work Practice (Insoceval[6]) was established as a collaborative international network made up of autonomous research units attached to government or universities from Denmark, England, Finland, the Netherlands, Scotland, Sweden and Switzerland, as well as incorporating a North American perspective. Members recognise the benefits of international exchange on issues of common interest in European social theory and share a core interest in the development of productive research and practice relationships in social work and social care (Mäntysaari and Weatherley, 2010).

There are also examples of national or regional networks or organisations that have widened their focus. The regional organisation, Forsa,[7] was originally established in individual Scandinavian countries to promote social work research and help the discipline achieve academic credibility (e.g. in Finland the Forsa-Finland is a member of the National Delegation for Scientific Societies). In 2008 a Nordic Forsa[8] was developed and has established a *Nordic Journal of Social Work Research* in order to reach an international audience and to offer Nordic researchers an international publication forum. Debates between the five participating countries have focused on the relationship of the professions to research, especially the research-practice or theory-practice gap. Here the practitioners represented by their labour unions have shared the interests for the profession to establish its own knowledge base and knowledge production. There is also an international discourse on practice research which argues that research needs to be democratised, involving practitioners throughout the research process to ensure that research is relevant to operational priorities and is useful in practice (Evans, 2011; Fisher, 2011).

Elsewhere in Europe, a different collaboration has led to the formation of the European Research Institute for Social Work (ERIS), an institute of the University of Ostrava (in Czech republic) involving formal cooperation agreements with six European universities in Finland, France, Germany, Britain and Slovakia and other associated member universities across Europe. Collaboration involving dialogue on epistemological issues in social work research, initiated by European Resource Centre for Research in Social Work (ERCSW), has led to a network to establish a European Database of Social Work Research and more recently to work on a shared understanding of methodological issues in social work and on the theme of participative research (www.certs-europe.com).

One form of promoting international social work research around comparative social work is to produce networks of comparative research through international research and exchange with an interest in comparing both forms of services (e.g. child care, elder care, home care, etc.; see e.g. Kröger, 2001; Powell and Hendrics, 2009; Melin Emilsson, 2009) and social work practitioners' attitudes and values or interpretations of different phenomena (e.g. Blomberg et al., 2010). The *Journal of Comparative Social Work*[9] aims to recognise different perspectives of a practice

focused international model for social work and social work research. Its premise is that comparative social work is a research discipline which emphasises comparative studies of social work between different countries and cultures.

A further mechanism for promoting international social work research is the promotion of doctoral training in and through international networks. International funding is available from bodies such as Leverhulme to study in the US, but opportunities for social work are limited. However, there are signs in some countries that funding for individual applications at national level encourages internationalisation and includes schemes to promote academic and practitioner exchange to undertake doctoral level programmes. This not only widens the agenda but also facilitates dialogue between representatives of different countries. Initiatives such as the first joint European doctoral programme, the International Doctoral Studies in Social Work (INDOSOW)[10], offer postgraduate students the opportunity to take part in an international interdisciplinary study of social work, welfare systems and social policies. The partnership between social work faculties in Finland, Germany, Slovenia and the UK provides the chance for comparative study of similarities and differences of welfare regimes in the EU countries and beyond. A goal of the programme is to establish an academic network while the main focus of the doctoral study is on research work, interdisciplinary study, and cooperation with internationally renowned local and foreign experts. In some countries this has been accompanied by efforts to encourage practitioners to undertake doctoral studies (Orme, 2003; Juliusdottir and Karlsson, 2007; Julkunen 2011).

RESOURCES FOR INTERNATIONAL RESEARCH

One possible implication of the different aspects of international social work research is that generic databases are constructed that can be accessible to researchers and practitioners for reference and determining the effectiveness of evidence about interventions in different countries and with different communities. Research resources such as the Campbell collaboration[11] and (in health research) the Cochrane collaboration[12] are examples of on-line resources of extant research. However, they illustrate some of the complexities already outlined. For example, in order to construct such databases there has to be agreement about the methodological integrity of the studies to be included. The emphasis on E-BP in some countries discussed above could lead to the exclusion of research results based on certain methodological approaches. Also the analysis is not always practitioner-friendly.

The work of the Social Care Institute for Excellence[13] (SCIE) in the UK is an example of a more inclusive approach. The mission of SCIE is to identify and disseminate the knowledge base for good practice in all aspects of social care throughout the UK. The philosophy is that services can be improved only by understanding what works in practice. While SCIE's primary targets are practitioners, managers and others with responsibility for service delivery in adults' and children's services in the UK, their resources, which include databases of research and systematic reviews, are accessed globally.

These examples illustrate how the compilation of national and/or international resources and databases for global access via the internet can be vital for comparative research. However, they also raise concerns about who compiles, maintains and monitors such databases. The internationalising of social work research can involve assumptions of uniformity which would run counter to the developments in methodological and ethical approaches described earlier that have been stimulated by diversity.

A second concern about international databases is accessibility. The availability of on-line resources is linked to the growth in the role of the internet in internationalisation of

the social work research community (Shaw, 2003). It can provide access to international data bases and wider dissemination of research through changes in publishing (see Chambon and Ruckdeschel, 2010) as well as facilitating communication between researchers in international collaborative projects (Tripodi and Potocky-Tripodi, 2007). However, without opportunity for ethical and methodological debate at international events the existence of databases will be of limited use (Mumford et al., 2009).

INDICATIONS FOR FUTURE RESEARCH INTERNATIONALLY

There is general agreement in the literature about the themes and issues that influence the international social work research agenda. Cox and Pawar (2006) suggest that understanding many local situations and developing constructive analysis of causal factors requires a global perspective with practice informed by research. The topics they identify include indigenous minorities; rural poverty; the HIV/AIDS pandemic; isolated elderly; and various forms of drug addiction. Others list poverty; disease; forced migration; impact of conflict and natural disasters (Mäntysaari and Weatherley, 2010). Lyons et al. (2006) argue that there is less empirically based material about how globalisation has impacted on the activities of social workers in, for example, working with communities in conflict; people caught up in forced migration; child exploitation; and pandemics.

In addition to topic areas, Tripodi and Potocky-Tripodi (2007) recognise that international collaboration over methods is of major importance and identify the need for methodological developments, such as the cross validation of instruments for collecting data in international social work research. They also advocate the sharing of social work knowledge about interventions education and policy development between countries (2007: 231).

It is difficult to produce definitive lists of what will or should be researched: the agenda will grow and change as the nature of societies and the interactions within and between nations change. The very process of researching at any level will continue to reveal personal and social issues that could become the topic of wider research and dissemination. Perhaps it is more useful to acknowledge that international social work research should contribute to good social work practice and to efforts to achieve consensus on human rights and the rights of marginalised/oppressed groups (Mäntysaari and Weatherley, 2010). As has been indicated, this will require appropriate recognition of both local issues as significant topics for international attention as well as diverse methodological approaches. Only then will social work research be seen to be truly addressing 'the person in their environment'.

Finally, for research to be useful and relevant at an international level it has to address the implications of international social work practice. While this notion is beginning to be addressed (Hugman, 2010b), the development of international social work practice itself is an area for future research.

CONCLUSION

This chapter has provided an overview of some of the challenges to and achievements in international social work research. The main challenge is to ensure that international social work research is rigorous and provides sound evidence for best social work practice but at the same time reflects and recognises the diversity present in global social issues. While issues of social exclusion and health and social policy are recognised at a global level, solutions and practice implications for social work are often played out at the national and local level. Social work has to meet these challenges by becoming a research based discipline and sharing that research to develop a global research base.

The chapter has indicated that there is a great deal of international collaboration but also highlighted the dangers of intellectual imperialism in the emerging arrangements. Developing research approaches that are participatory and inclusive is challenging in an international context. While there may be a temptation to establish global databases these provide ethical and practical challenges in that, to date, they have tended towards methodological uniformity and have not reflected the innovation and theoretical developments represented by diverse approaches to research methods sensitive to cultural diversity. Truly international research has to address such issues of power and dominance.

The chapter has highlighted other challenges. While the establishment of networks, conferences and seminars can provide opportunities for exchange of views and knowledge they can also be exclusionary as they require funding, are conducted in limited languages and demand particular format for presentations. As such they provide limited opportunity for methodological debates or discussing the implications of the research for different national contexts.

The other main opportunity for exchanging ideas about methods or implications of findings and analysis internationally is by publication in international journals. However, similar problems are created by the criteria for the inclusion of research papers in international publications where both methodological approaches and language requirements can prove to be barriers for emerging social work researchers in different regions. This means that certain geographic regions and methodological approaches maintain their privileged status.

However, such challenges are being addressed. International projects are being established that are funded to support collaboration of researchers and/or research students. Although technology can have a negative impact if used only to provide standardised information, it can also be harnessed to support collaborations and communication. Above all, work is being undertaken to ensure that research to inform social work knowledge and practice is available to practitioners and those who require their services. Hence, there is evidence to suggest that social work research will not merely transfer knowledge globally but also transform it.

NOTES

1　PHARE: Pologne–Hungarie assistance à la restruction des économies 1989–2006 involving the Balticum; INTAS: The International Association for the promotion of co-operation with scientists from the New Independent States of the former Soviet Union 1993–2006; EU-Tempus IB_JEP-22016-2001 *A Centre for Social Policy at the Udmurt State University.*

2　The aim here is not to name and shame but examples include *Social Work Research* (the journal of the National Association of Social Work) which is almost exclusively US-focused while *Social Work and Social Science Review: an International Journal* is almost exclusively British.

3　See for example *Journal of Social Work Research and Evaluation: An International Publication and Qualitative Social Work; Research and Practice,* but even in these journals the balance of articles is in favour of authors from the US and the UK although there are a growing number from Australia, Europe and New Zealand.

4　Goethe (Governance of Educational Trajectories in Europe). www.goethe.eu.

5　www.warwick.ac.uk/go/swhin.

6　www.intsoceval.org.

7　See www.forsa.dk/english/presentation.asp for information about FORSA as a strong Nordic linking organization.

8　www.forsa-norge,no/ForsaNorden1.htm.

9　www.jcsw.no.

10　www.indosow.net.

11　www.campbellcollaboration.org/.

12　www.cochrane.org/.

13　http://www.scie.org.uk/about/index.asp.

REFERENCES

Askeland G.A. and Bradley, G. (2007) 'Linking critical reflection and qualitative research on an African social work master's programme', *International Social Work*, 50: 671–85.

Auslander, G.K. (2000) 'Social work research and evaluation in Israel', *Journal of Social Work Research and Evaluation: An International Publication*, 1: 17–34.

Bergmark, A. and Lundström, T. (2011) 'Guided or independent? Social workers, central bureaucracy and evidence-based practice', *European Journal of Social Work*, 14: 3, 323–7.

Beresford, P. and Evans, C. (1999) 'Research note: research and empowerment', *British Journal of Social Work*, 29(5): 671–7.

Bergmark, A. and Lundström, T. (2010) 'Guided or independent? Social workers, central bureaucracy and evidence-based practice', *European Journal of Social Work*, 1–15.

Blomberg, H., Corander, C., Meeuwisse, A., Scaramuzzino, R. and Swärd, H. (2010) 'Social work and child welfare politics through Nordic lences', in H. Forsberg and T. Kröger (eds), *Social Work and Child Welfare Politics Through Nordic Lenses*. Bristol: Polity Press. pp. 29–45.

Briskman, L. (2010) 'Nations', in I. Shaw, K. Briar-Lawson, J. Orme and R. Ruckdeschel (eds), *The Handbook of Social Work Research*. London: Sage.

Butler, I. (2002) 'A code of ethics for social work and social care research', *British Journal of Social Work*, 32(2): 239–48.

Bywaters, P. (2009) 'Tackling inequalities in health: a global challenge for social work', *British Journal of Social Work*, 39(2): 353–67.

Bywaters, P. and Ungar, M. (2010) 'Health and well being', in I. Shaw, K. Briar-Lawson, J. Orme and R. Ruckdeschel (eds), *The Handbook of Social Work Research*. London: Sage.

Campanini, A. (2007) 'Social work in Italy', *European Journal of Social Work*, 10(1): 107–16.

Chambon, A. and Ruckdeschel, R. (2010) 'The uses of social work research', in I. Shaw, K. Briar-Lawson, J. Orme and R. Ruckdeschel (eds), *The Sage Handbook of Social Work Research*. London: Sage.

Chytil, O. and Popelká, R. (2000) 'Social policy and social work in the Czech Republic', in A. Adams, P. Erath and S. Shardlow (eds), *Fundamentals in Social Work in Selected European Countries*. Lyme Regis: Russell House Publishing.

Cox, D. and Pawar, M. (eds) (2006) *International Social Work Issues, Strategies and Programs*. Thousand Oaks, CA: Sage.

Crawford, I.M. (1997) *Marketing Research and Information Systems*. (Marketing and Agribusiness Texts - 4) Rome, Food and Agriculture Organization of the United Nations. http://www.fao.org/docrep/

W3241E/w3241e00.htm#Contents, accessed 29 April 2011.

Crisp, B.R. (2000) 'A history of Australian social work practice research', *Research on Social Work Practice*, 10: 179–94.

Estes, R.J. (1998) Developmental Social Work: a New Paradigm for a New Century, paper presented to 10th International Symposium of the Inter-University Consortium for International Social Development (IUCISD) Cairo, Egypt. http://www.sp2.upenn.edu/restes/Estes%20Papers/Developmental%20SW_1998.pdf, accessed 29 April 2011.

Evans, T. (2011) 'Editorial', *Social Work and Society*, 9 (1), special issue on Practice Research. http://www.socwork.net/sws/article/view/1/9, accessed 19 May 2011.

Fernandez, E. and Romeo, R. (2003) *Implementation of the Framework for the Assessment of Children and their Families: the Experience of Barnardos Australia*. Australia: University of New South Wales. Report to the UK Department of Health.

Fischer, J. (1973) 'Is casework effective? A review', *Social Work*, 18: 5–20.

Fisher, M. (2002) 'The role of service users in problem formulation and technical aspects of research', *Social Work Education*, 21(3): 305–12.

Fisher, M. (2011) 'Practice literate research: turning the tables', *Social Work and Society*, 9 (1) http://www.socwork.net/sws/article/view/4/16, accessed 19 May 2011.

Fook, J. (2003) 'Social work research in Australia', *Social Work Education*, 22(1): 45–57.

Friesenhahn, G. Lorenz, W. and Seibel, F. (2008) 'Ausbildung für eine europäische Sozial Arbeit', in *Bielefelder Arbeitsgruppe 8* (Hrsg., 2008). Soziale Arbeit in Gesellschaft. Wiesbaden: VS Verlag für Sozialwissenschaften. pp. 96–104.

Gambrill, E. (2007) 'Views of evidence-based practice: social workers' codes of ethics and accreditation standards as guides for choice', *Journal of Social Work Education*, 43(3): 447–62.

Gellis, Z. (2001) 'Using a participatory approach to mobilize immigrant minority family caregivers', *Journal of Social Work Research and Evaluation: An International Publication*, 2: 267–82.

Gray, M. and Fook, J. (2004) 'The quest for a universal social work: some issues and implications', *Social Work Education*, 23(5): 625–44.

Gray, M., Coates, J. and Yellow Bird, M.Y. (eds) (2008) *Indigenous Social Work around the World: Towards Culturally Relevant Education and Practice*. Aldershot: Ashgate.

Gredig, D. and Marsh, J. (2010) 'Improving intervention and practice', in C. Hall, K. Juhila, N. Parton and

T. Pösö, T. (2003) *Identities and Practices*. London: Jessica Kingsley.

Hall, C., Juhila, K., Parton, N. & Pösö, T. (eds.) (2003) 'Constructing Clienthood in Social Work and Human Services'. *Interaction, Identities and Practices*. London: Jessica Kingsley.

Hall A. and Midgley, J. (2004) 'Social Policy for Development', *Journal of Social Policy*, 34(2): 311–19.

Hammersley, M. (2003) 'Social research today: some dilemmas and distinctions', *Qualitative Social Work*, 2(1): 25–44.

Healy, L.M. (2001) *International Social Work: Professional Action in an Interdependent World*. New York: Oxford University Press.

Healy, L.M. (2008) 'Introduction: a brief journey through the 80 year history of the International Association of Schools of Social Work', *Social Work & Society*, 6 (1). http://www.socwork.net/sws/article/view/98/387 accessed 29 April 2011.

Hering, S. (ed.) (2009) *Social Care under State Socialism (1945–1989): Ambitions, Ambiguities, and Mismanagement*. Opladen & Farmington Hills, MI: Barbara Budrich Publishers.

Hugman, R. (2010a) *Understanding International Social Work. a Critical Analysis*. New York: Palgrave Macmillan.

Hugman, R. (2010b) 'Social work research and ethics' in I. Shaw, K. Briar-Lawson, J. Orme and R. Ruckdeschel (eds), *The Sage Handbook of Social Work Research*. London, Sage.

IASSW/IFSW (International Association of Schools of Social Work/International Federation of Social Workers) (2001) *Joint International Definition of Social Work*, adopted at Copenhagen. http://www.iassw-aiets.org/index.php?option=com_content&task=blogcategory&id=26&Itemid=51.

IASSW (International Association of Schools of Social Work) (2004a) *Global Standards for Social Work Education and Training*, adopted by IASSW and IFSW at their General Assemblies in Adelaide, Australia, October 2004. http://www.iassw-aiets.org/index.php?option=com_content&task=blogcategory&id=28&Itemid=49.

IASSW (International Association of Schools of Social Work) (2004b) *Ethics in Social Work, Statement of Principles*, approved at the General Meetings of the International Federation of Social Workers and the International Association of Schools of Social Work in Adelaide, Australia, October 2004. http://www.iassw-aiets.org/index.php?option=com_content&task=blogcategory&id=27&Itemid=50.

Jergeby, U. and Soydan, H. (2002). 'Assessment processes in social work practice when children are at risk:

a comparative cross-national vignette study', *Journal of Social Work Research and Evaluation*, (3)2, 127–144.

Juliusdottir, S. and Karlsson, T. (2007) 'Some indications for professional development in social work: a study of theoretical interest and attitudes towards research among Icelandic social workers', *European Journal of Social Work,* 10(1): 21–37.

Julkunen, I. (2011) 'Knowledge-production processes in practice research – outcomes and critical elements', *Social Work and Society,* 9(1): http://www.socwork.net/sws/article/view/7.

JUC SWEC (The Joint University Council. Social Work Education Committee) (2005) *A Social Work Research Strategy in Higher Education 2006–2020.*

Karvinen, S., Pösö, T. and Satka, M. (eds) (1999) *Reconstructing Social Work Research.* University of Jyväskylä, SoPhi.

Kangas, O. (2010) 'One hundred years of money, welfare and death; mortality, economic growth and the development of welfare state in 17 OECD countries 1900–2000', *International journal of Welfare 2010* (Issue Supplement S1) July 2010, 42–49.

Kee, L.H. (2004) 'The search from within: research issues in relation to developing culturally appropriate social work practice', *International Social Work,* 47(3): 336–45.

Kee, L.H. (2008) 'The development of culturally appropriate social work practice in Sarawak', in M. Gray, J. Coates and M. Yellow Bird (eds), *Indigenous Social Work around the World: towards Culturally Relevant Education and Practice.* Aldershot: Ashgate.

Kröger, T. (2001) *Comparative Research on Social Care: The State of the Art.* Luxembourg: European Communities.

Kuhlmann, C. (2000) *Alice Salomon. Ihr Lebenswerk als Beitrag zur Entwicklung der Theorie und Praxis Sozialer Arbeit.* Weinheim: Deutsche Studien Verlag.

Labonté-Roset, C. (2007) 'Status and special features of social work research within the canon of the social sciences and humanities: open and hidden asymmetries', *European Journal of Social Work,* 10(3): 417–21.

Lane, J.-E. (1990) 'Data archives as an instrument for co-operative research', in E. Oyen (ed.), *Comparartive Methodology: Theory and Practice in International Research.* Newbury Park, CA: Sage.

Lorenz, W. (2006) *Perspectives on European social work – from the Birth of Nation State to the Impact of Globalization.* Oplagen and Farmington Hills: Barbara Budrich Publishers.

Lyons, K., Manion, K.H. and Carlsen, M. (2006*) International Perspectives on Social Work: Global Conditions and Local Practice.* Basingstoke: Palgrave.

Mäntysaari, M. and Weatherley, R. (2010) 'Theory and theorizing: intellectual contexts of social work research', in I. Shaw, K. Briar-Lawson, J. Orme and R. Ruckdeschel (eds), *The Sage Handbook of Social Work Research.* London: Sage.

Melin Emilsson, U. (2009) 'Health care, social care or both? A qualitative explorative study of different focuses in long-term care of older people in France, Portugal and Sweden', *European Journal of Social Work,* 12(4): 419–34.

Munford, R., Tomofumi, O. and Desai, M. (2009) 'Qualitative social work research in the Asia-Pacific region', *Qualitative Social Work,* 8(4): 419–26.

Nimagadda, J. and Cowger, C.D. (1999) 'Cross cultural practice: social worker integrity in the indiganisation of practice knowledge', *International Social Work,* 42(3): 261–76.

Orme, J. (2003) 'Why does social work need doctors?', *Social Work Education,* 22(6): 541–54.

Orme, J. (2004) 'It's feminist because I say so: Feminism, social work and critical practice in the UK', *Qualitative Social Work,* 2(2): 131–54.

Orme, J. and Powell, J. (2008) 'Building research capacity in social work: process and issues', *British Journal of Social Work,* 38(5): 988–1008.

Orme, J. and Shemmings, D. (2010) *Developing Research Based Social Work Practice.* Basingstoke: Palgrave.

Palattiyil, G. and Chakrabarti, M. (2008) 'Coping strategies of families in HIV/AIDS care: some exploratory data from two developmental contexts', *AIDS Care,* (7): 881–5.

Payne, M. and Askeland, G.A. (2008) *Globalization and International Social Work.* Aldershot: Ashgate.

Pere, L. and Barnes, A. (2009) 'New learning from old understandings', *Qualitative Social Work,* 8(4): 449–67.

Powell, J. (2007) *Social Work Research in a Global Context.* Final report of IASSW funded project. http://www.iassw-aiets.org/images/Documents/Project_Reports/final_report_gswr_july_2007%2C_jackie_powel.doc.

Powell, J. and Hendrics, J. (eds) (2009) *The Welfare State in Post-Industrial Society: A Global Perspective.* New York: Springer.

Powell, J. and Robinson, J. (2007) 'The "international dimension" in social work education: current developments in England', *European Journal of Social Work,* 10(3): 383–99.

Ramon, S., Campbell, J., Lindsay, J., McCrystal, P. and Baidoun, N. (2006) 'The impact of political conflict on social work: experiences from Northern Ireland,

Israel and Palestine', *British Journal of Social Work,* 36(3): 435–50.

Reid, W. and Shyne, A. (1969) *Brief and Extended Casework.* New York: Columbia University Press.

Ruffolo, M.C., Thoburn, J. and Allen-Meares, P. (2010) 'Children, young people and families', in I. Shaw, K. Briar-Lawson, J. Orme and R. Ruckdeschel (eds), *The Sage Handbook of Social Work Research.* London: Sage.

Ryan, M. and Sheehan, R. (2000) 'Research education in Australian BSW programs', *Advances in Social Work and Welfare Education,* 3(1): 136–51.

Ryen, A. (2008) 'Trust in cross-cultural research; the puzzle of epistemology, research ethics and context', *Qualitative Social Work,* 7(4): 448–65.

Saleebey, D. (1997) *The Strengths Perspective in Social Work Practice.* New York: Longman.

Satka, M. and Harrikari, T. (2008) 'The present Finnish formation of child welfare and history', *British Journal of Social Work,* 38(4): 645–61.

Shaw, I. (2003) 'Cutting edges in social work research', *British Journal of Social Work,* 33, 107–20.

Shaw, I. (2005) 'Practitioner research: evidence or critique?', *British Journal of Social Work,* 35: 1231–48.

Shaw, I. (2008) 'Merely experts? Reflections on the history of social work, science and research', *Research, Policy and Planning,* 26(1): 57–65.

Shaw, I. and Norton, M. (2007) *The kinds and quality of Social Work Research in UK Universities,* London: Social Care Institute for Excellence (Scie).

Shaw, I. and Norton, M. (2008) 'Kinds and quality of social work research', *British Journal of Social Work,* 38(5): 953–70.

Shaw, I., Briar-Lawson, K., Orme, J. and Ruckdeschel, R. (eds) (2010) *The Sage Handbook of Social Work Research.* London: Sage.

Sheldon, B. (2000) 'Cognitive behavioural methods in social care: a look at the evidence', in P. Stepney and D. Ford (eds), *Social Work Models, Methods and Theories.* Lyme Regis: Russel House Publishing.

Soydan, H. (2010) 'Evidence and policy: the case of social care services in Sweden', *Evidence and Policy,* 6(2): 179–93.

Thoburn, J. (2007) *Globalisation and Child welfare: Some Lessons from a Cross National Study of Children in Out-of-Home Care.* Norwich: UEA Social Work Monographs.

Thyer, B.A. and Kazi, M.A.F. (eds) (2004) *International Perspectives on Evidence-based Practice in Social Work.* Birmingham: Venture Press.

Tripodi, T. and Potocky-Tripodi, M. (2007) *International Social Work Research: Issues and Prospects.* New York, Oxford University Press.

Ungar, M. (2008) 'Resilience across cultures', *British Journal of Social Work,* 38: 218–35.

van der Laan, G. (2000) 'Social work in the Netherlands,' in A. Adams, P. Erath and S. Shardlow (eds), *Fundamentals in Social Work in Selected European Countries.* Lyme Regis, Russell House Publishing.

Young Jung, S. and Tripodi, T. (2007) 'Trends in international social work research', *International Social Work,* 50(5): 691–8.

Ward, H. (2000) *The Development Needs of Children: Implications for Assessment.* London: Department of Health.

Key Issues for Social Work Internationally

Nigel Hall

INTRODUCTION TO SECTION 3: KEY ISSUES FOR SOCIAL WORK INTERNATIONALLY

These eight chapters constitute the core of this handbook and cover key issues for social work internationally, presenting analyses of social work theories, policies and practices in relation to the different aspects of welfare in which social workers are engaged. As such, they cover a wide range of areas concerning poverty, health, education, social justice, environmental concerns, spirituality, disasters and political conflict.

Akimoto and Sungkawan (Chapter 12) consider the connections between social work, economic conditions and livelihoods. The protection and promotion of people's livelihood is a key issue for social work – including, crucially, improving the economic conditions of the very poor – although in practice this has been mainly limited to involvement in income maintenance programmes, particularly in developed countries. An understanding of the international macroeconomic situation, globalisation, industrialisation and their consequences on the social and cultural fabric of societies will provide useful information for social workers. The neo-liberal agenda with government disengagement from welfare impacts poverty alleviation strategies; however, new opportunities for greater involvement of social and development workers in this field arise with more initiatives and projects undertaken by non-government organisations (NGOs) and social enterprises.

In Chapter 13 Bywaters and Davis consider health issues from a human rights perspective as a fundamental concern for international social work. Poverty and other inequalities are exacerbated by the lack of access in many parts of the world to basic facilities such as health care, schools and education. Inequality in health care provision is a major cause for concern, particularly as there are social determinants which create this situation. The International Federation of Social Workers (IFSW) *International Policy on Health* stresses that health is a fundamental human right that is primarily determined by social, economic, environmental and political conditions. Serious global infectious diseases such as HIV/AIDS, TB and malaria cause untold suffering around the world and although the means to relieve much of this is available, political commitment often falls far short of what is required. It is very important that social workers engage in this arena more than they have to date, advocate for improved access to health care and reduction of health inequalities, and do this through making alliances with other professionals and activists who share these common aims and values.

Huxtable, Sottie and Ulziitungalag in Chapter 14 suggest that social workers can make a vital contribution to education around the world and presently play important roles as school social workers. The authors give various examples of school social work, particularly in Ghana and Mongolia, and identify some challenges and changes in this field. Outside of the formal educational system social workers also play a significant role in promoting opportunities for informal education and social pedagogy, while continued advocacy is required on the part of international social work organisations with educational bodies to promote human development goals, particularly where groups are disadvantaged by poverty, disability, gender or ethnicity.

In Chapter 15 Preston-Shoot and Höjer focus on social work, justice and protection systems. Social work is a value-laden activity and its commitment to social justice is enshrined in the *International Definition of Social Work* which states that principles of human rights and social justice are 'fundamental' to social work. The authors describe social work as a moral activity with a mandate to protect adults and children at risk of abuse or neglect. While there are international declarations and conventions guaranteeing respect for human rights, some nations may not subscribe to these, while others are either slow in responding to evident abuses, or complicit in carrying them out.

A variety of factors however may inhibit social workers from speaking up on some of these issues, from lack of formal recognition as a profession in some countries to concerns for personal safety. To ensure human dignity and social inclusion social workers will need to engage more constructively in well researched and informed interventions.

Social justice is also an important consideration when it comes to the environment and it is vital that social workers develop practice models that take into account questions of sustainability and ecological cost. In Chapter 16, McKinnon explores social work and changing environments, commenting on the ways in which environmental, social and economic environments are inter related. Social justice is also an important consideration and it is vital that social workers develop practice models that take into account questions of sustainability and ecological cost. Relevant to social work are issues concerning depletion of natural resources, conflict over access to resources, desertification and climate change, in a situation where world population is rapidly increasing and human-created natural disasters occur more frequently. Although social workers have often recognised the relevance of 'environment' and ecological approaches, this now needs to be extended to the non-human and natural world, where concern for sustainability and equilibrium is critical to social well-being. While environmental concerns broaden the scope of social work considerations, social workers are challenged to think holistically about the living situations of their clients.

Social workers practising in an international or locally diverse context need to be aware of and take into account cultural considerations, which may include concepts of spirituality and religious faith. Shier and Graham in Chapter 17 examine religion and spirituality as significant to the well-being of individuals and communities and central in some cultures. This is an important consideration in social work where it is increasingly felt necessary to respect and acknowledge local culture and belief systems. In addition, faith-based organisations are often vital in bringing services to communities, particularly when formal service provision is unable to cope, such as in the event of natural disasters.

In Chapter 18 Mathbor and Bourassa discuss disaster management and note that this requires social workers who understand and know how to access disaster response mechanisms, at a pre-disaster or preparedness stage and at post-disaster relief and recovery stages. An environmental analysis or understanding the PIE ('person interacting with the environment') perspective – the *social* dimension of practice – is very relevant as this is where social workers can make their best professional contribution, added to work at the more individual level of post traumatic stress disorder (PTSD). A practice wisdom is developing through social workers' contribution to relief, recovery and rehabilitation initiatives in a wide range of disasters around the world. The authors stress the importance of participatory techniques and the inclusion of survivors in all phases of the recovery processes.

Ramon and Maglajlic in Chapter 19 focus on social work, conflict and displacement and suggest that this is an important area for social work involvement, given the increase in political conflicts around the world. Social work from its own definition is committed to the liberation and empowerment of people who are marginalised and facing oppression, including those affected by political conflicts. Social action is at the core of our profession and this is highlighted in the concerned response of social workers and social work educators to human rights abuses, war and political conflict. The profession needs to have in place both short and long term training within social work education and practice settings to deal with some of the severe consequences of human conflict. The chapter concludes with an overview of the social work response to the impact of political conflict, and how this is aligned with the radical tradition within our profession.

Overall, this section covers a broad swathe of social concerns, but all are relevant to the social work frame of reference, which at all times needs to encompass a wide range of initiatives and responses. In an international context, it is even more urgent that social work engages at a variety of levels, and in particular that the profession considers its response at a macro-level and in alliance with others in tackling some of these issues.

12

Social Work, Economic Conditions and Livelihood

Tatsuru Akimoto and Decha Sungkawan

INTRODUCTION

The protection and promotion of livelihood and employment is one of the core missions of social work and this chapter presents a basic framework to understand the present situation and structure of this internationally. There are two major parts to this. First are the *meanings* and current scenarios behind industrialisation and globalisation, particularly under the prevailing capitalist economy, which are core factors that can explain social change, the existence of nation states, the gap between 'developing' and 'developed', employment differentials and working conditions, including the growth of the informal sector.

Second are the *strategies* to alleviate poverty, improve livelihood and promote employment, together with some topical issues – the limitations of the market economy, the weakening government programmes and new ways of working with social enterprises. Finally, the work of social workers in this arena is examined.

MACRO DETERMINANTS – INDUSTRIALISATION AND GLOBALISATION

We are now in a capitalist era, or euphemistically (free) market economy, which historically replaced feudalism and other forms of economic organisation. Although Marxists predicted the rise of socialism and communism this seems now to be uncertain, especially after the collapse of the USSR, and a framework of 'modified' capitalism which incorporates social democratic ideals seems much more likely at least for the time being. Additionally the development of our global society is generally explained by the progress of industrialisation and globalisation together with other factors such as rapid population increase, new technologies and economies, the aging population, and the feminised labour market.

The industrial structure of a society shifts from the primary industries (agriculture, fishery and forestry) to secondary industries (mining, construction, manufacturing, and transportation, communication and utilities), and to tertiary industries, with some deviations and exceptions. Industrialisation, and economic development, generally also feature social and cultural changes. Along with the shift from an agrarian to industrial society, people migrated from farm areas to towns and cities and their work and life changed from being nature- and weather-oriented to time- and clock-oriented. Wages were low, working hours long, safety and health, fringe benefits, and other working conditions were neglected or inhumane, and living quarters poor and unsanitary. Although this should not be idealised, previous traditional lifestyles were lost, while crime, drugs, and alcoholism prevailed, family, kinship, and communal ties were loosened, and the environment destroyed. In a post-industrial society, the sense of belonging and identity were often further destroyed, while the stress and insecurity prevailed. Although income may increase, competition may also become fierce, while life is oriented not to production but to consumption. These negative losses pose the question: 'What is development?' and this raises questions of quality of life.

The post-industrial era in major leading 'developed' countries overlaps with globalisation and means the transference of primary and secondary industries to less 'developed' countries, while value-added tertiary industry remains in the 'developed' part of the world. Once this division of work is made, it is often difficult for the poorer parts of the world to develop further, while the majority of workers in 'developed' countries are now liberated from the hardship of labour and someone else must shoulder the work to produce their daily necessities. Meanwhile workers in 'developing' countries migrate into urban areas to be engaged in such labour, either in their own countries and/or to other post-industrial countries, to find very similar working and living conditions which their predecessors in the present post-industrial countries once experienced in the late 19th or the early 20th centuries (Seabrook, 2002).

The commonplace description of globalisation is the 'easy' crossing of goods, people, money, and information across borders, with countries and regions becoming interdependent and the world becoming one. The core element of globalisation is, however, the market/capitalist economy, which started out in 15th century Europe (Wallerstein, 1983). This process continued in succeeding centuries, almost covering the globe by the end of the 19th century, while by the end of World War II the division of the world market was almost complete. Globalisation in the modern usage is defined as the era since the 1960s, and in particular, since the respective collapse of the Berlin Wall and the USSR in 1989 and 1991, respectively, that integrated the communist/socialist economies into a market economy. The remaining 'communist/socialist' countries have now also introduced a market economy and are part of this process.

Globalisation does not mean the disappearance of nation states (see Chapter 6), which have formed layers among themselves with a central core and a periphery. Some have even insisted on a unipolar world, where the centre is seen to be superior, and everything else is then transmitted from the centre to the periphery (e.g. Krauthammer, 2004). Economic globalisation engenders social and cultural globalisation, transmitting not only deregulation, competition and privatisation but also human relations, customs, religions, views of the world, and even a sense of beauty. Values and systems generally are then transferred to other countries, and the consequence for the periphery is that 'globalisation is invasion of forceful foreign extraneous objects, and the balance and protective walls are destroyed and the power to transform systems is infused from outside without choice', – with or without being forced (Ohno, 2000: iv).

Multi-national corporations and international organisations are major promoters of globalisation in addition to nation states. The sales of many multinational corporations are bigger than the gross domestic product (GDPs) of many countries – for example,

Royal Dutch Shell ranked 24th and Walmart 29th from the top in a combined country and multinational corporation list, while 44 of the world's top 100 companies are multi-corporations (Fortune Magazine, 20 July 2009; IMF, 2009). Multi-national corpora-tions are not nationality-free – they act on the basis of nation states and also expect states to work for them (Kinoshita, 2007). In a similar way there are international organisations which both represent and structure the global community. The most representative interna-tional organisations are the United Nations, the World Trade Organisation (WTO), International Monetary Fund (IMF)/World Bank, and regional banks, which are places for nation states to cooperate, compete, fight and oppress. This has relevance for social work, explored in a later section.

NATIONAL WEALTH AND STANDARD OF LIVING

People's lives and livelihood are largely determined by the place where they are born, the particular country or region of their birth and the class/income stratum they find them-selves in. The most basic statistics to repre-sent the size of national economies are GDP or GNI (gross national income),[1] which includes income from abroad. They signify not only economic power but also political and social power, and they also remind us of the importance of nation states in the era of globalisation.

The total GDP in the world today is roughly 60 trillion US$ (figures are for 2008, hereinafter the same in this chapter unless otherwise specified). The highest GDP, that of the United States of America (US$14,441 billion, is more than 100,000 times as big as the smallest, which is that of Kiribati (US$0.14 billion), an island country. The United States alone claims 24 percent of the total GDP of the world, the largest five countries (the US, Japan, China, Germany and France) total roughly 50 percent, while

33 'advanced economies' named by the IMF comprise more than 70 percent (IMF, 2010a).

GDP or GNI per capita is often used as an indicator to show the standard of living of peoples. Sixty countries/regions exceeded $10,000 per capita – including most Western countries, several Asian countries, several Arabic oil-producing countries, and some Latin American countries. Fifty-nine coun-tries, nearly a third of the all countries/regions, are below $1825, twenty-nine African and Asian countries are below $730, while eight African countries are below $365 (IMF, 2010a). Although these figures do not reflect the fluctuation of exchange rates among currencies and the differences in commodity prices among countries/regions, they roughly show the absolute and relative levels of the standard of living of peoples. For reference, see the data recalculated with purchasing power parity (PPP), which have been published by the IMF, World Bank and Central Intelligence Agency (CIA) and also the Organization for Economic Co-operation and Development (OECD) (e.g. see CIA, 2010).

Using GDP or GNI per capita, interna-tional organisations classify countries into 'developed countries' and 'developing coun-tries'. The World Bank names countries with a GNI per capita of US$11,116 and more as 'countries with high income'. OECD DAC (Organization for Economic Co-operation and Development Assistance Committee) names countries eligible for aid using a GNI per capita of less than US$9206 in the 2003 list. The UN ECOSOC (Economic and Social Council) classifies 50 countries (as of August 2007) as 'least developed countries' (LDCs) using GDP per capita combined with other factors on the standard of living and the economic indices.

The significance of money may, however, differ in each society. As an extreme exam-ple, in a self-sufficient economy, 'a dollar per day' income may not necessarily mean abso-lute poverty, conceptually. The UNDP (United Nations Development Programme)

has published a Human Development Index (HDI) to show the quality of life and the degree of development. The index is comprised of average life expectancy, education (adult literacy and total secondary level school entrance), and the GDP per capita based on PPP. A hundred and eighty-two countries/regions have been ranked under four classes, which indicate that 38 and 24 fall under the classification 'very high human development' and 'low human development', respectively.[2]

Another footnote to these figures above is that all figures regard the averages of populations and do not refer to the income distribution in each society. Some people in a rich country are poorer than some people in a poor country, and vice versa. Here class issues enter into consideration.

EMPLOYMENT

People's livelihood primarily rests on their economic conditions or mainly their employment which generates their income; those who can rely on wealth are limited.

Unemployment and employment structure

The first question is whether there are formal 'jobs' or not; many people cannot find jobs even in 'developed' countries. The unemployment rates are 11.3 percent in Spain, 7.4–7.5 in France and Germany, 6.7 percent in Italy and 4.0–6.5 percent in most other 'developed' countries while those of Norway, The Netherlands, Korea, and Switzerland are 2.6–3.4 percent – relatively low (ILO, 2010). The rates may fluctuate year by year. What the unemployment rate means is not necessarily clear even if a standardised measurement methodology is adopted (ILO-OECD). Suppose each full time job is divided into two part time jobs: then the unemployment rate would reduce by half! The hardships of

unemployment also differ depending on family and community support as well as social support such as insurance, entitlements and services. Under the unemployment definition of 'without work' (or 'not in paid employment or self-employment'), 'currently available for work,' and 'seeking work',[3] people could not technically be unemployed, for example, in urban slums in a very poor society. They just have to work for a dollar a day or so in whatever capacity they can in order to survive.

Once there are jobs, they widely vary in form, kind, content and condition. There are self-employers, family workers and employees, and various occupations – farming, casual labour, production work, sales, office work, technical work, professional work, administrative work, etc. There are jobs in tiny shops and huge corporations, full time work and part time work, and regular work and non-regular work.

The distribution of workers between or among sub-categories above changes significantly over time and among countries. As with industrial structure, employment structure follows a certain pattern, for example, a society shifts from a 'self-employment' society to an 'employees' society and from an 'agricultural' society to a 'blue-collar' society to a 'white-collar' society. In Sierra Leone, 92 percent of employment is broadly self-employed, while only 8 percent is 'employee-based' (in 2004). The ratios are 87:13 in Cambodia (2004), 57:43 in Thailand, 31:69 in Korea, 14:86 in Finland and 8:92 in the United States (ILO, 2010). In terms of occupational distribution, 'legislators, senior officials and managers', 'professionals', 'technicians and associate professionals', and 'clerks' ('white-collar jobs') increase while 'skilled agricultural and fishery workers' decrease.[4]

Within each country, this same shift is also observed in both employment status distribution and occupational distribution. These categorical shifts at macro level may be regarded as an improvement toward the jobs with higher earnings and/or better working conditions for a society, but may bring hardship to individual workers and their families who are in diminishing categories.

Recently, insecure employment – part-timers and 'irregular workers', which include contracted workers, dispatched workers, on-call workers, seasonal workers, day workers, and temporary workers, as well as layoffs and unemployment – has been increasing, particularly in 'developed' countries. The percentage of part-time workers (i.e. working less than 30 hours a week) among the employed has recently reached 36.1 percent in The Netherlands, 25.9 percent in Switzerland, and 20–24 percent in Australia, the United Kingdom, New Zealand, Germany, Iceland and Norway (OECD, 2009).

Wage differentials among countries are large, reflecting the employment structures as well as other factors such as consumer prices, although an accurate international comparison of the wage level is not easy to make. While the minimum wages of France and the UK were US$13 and $9.4 per hour as of 2009, those of Thailand and the Philippines were about $4.5–6.1 and $2.6–3.6 per day. The monthly minimum wage of Luxembourg was US$2423, while those of Indonesia (Jakarta) and China (Beijing) were about US$112 and US$117[5] (JPC, 2011).

Working conditions and core labour standards

Concerns which affect the livelihood of working people and their families (sometimes more than wages) also exist in relation to hours, occupational safety and health, and other working conditions; as well as with discrimination and neglect of human and civil rights (e.g. according to race, ethnicity, disability, gender, religion, language, education).

Not only must there be work but the work must be decent, a concept which is the International Labour Organization's (ILO) key policy objective, introduced by Juan Somavia, Director-General, to lead

organisational goals, policy frameworks and programme approaches – work must be decent and productive 'in conditions of freedom, equity, security, and human dignity' (ILO, 1999).

The list of problems and attempts at their resolution can be found extensively in the records of some 400 conventions and recommendations of the ILO covering the entire spectrum of working conditions. Owing to impatience with the slow ratification of conventions by many countries, in 1998 the ILO adopted the *Declaration on Fundamental Principles and Rights at Work*, requiring member states to uphold a set of core labour standards regardless of whether or not they had ratified the relevant conventions. These standards specify eight[6] conventions in four fields: (1) the freedom of association and collective bargaining; (2) elimination of forced and compulsory labour; (3) elimination of discrimination with respect to employment and occupation; and (4) abolition of child labour. Still, 5–20 percent of all countries, including 'developed' countries, have not ratified some of them. The United States has not ratified six out of eight, Korea four, Qatar and Canada three, and Japan, New Zealand and Singapore two. In addition ratification does not guarantee their observation or implementation. Poverty alleviation/income generation is a core mission of the ILO and the philosophy behind its mission is noted as '[P]overty anywhere constitutes a danger to prosperity everywhere' (*Declaration concerning the aims and purposes of the International Labour Organisation*, ILO Declaration of Philadelphia, 1944).

Informal work

The above description of employment has been skewed towards 'developed' countries in a sense. In 'developing' countries, many people work in the informal sector, which is often not covered by formal statistics of employment. In 'developing' countries, the number of informal workers is estimated at about 30–80 percent of the working population, whereas in industrial countries this is at 2–15 per cent. Research points out that the informal economy has expanded across the world – for instance, in Latin America nine out of 10 workers participate in informal services such as domestic service, self-employment and micro-enterprise (Devas, 2004: 146).

Informal work is found in various occupations ranging from small manufacturing shops, small scale retailing, transport, building labour, barbering, and car repairing, to domestic service. There are common characteristics such as unstable employment, legal avoidance (e.g. labour law and taxation law), and lack of legal contracts and licensing. Informal workers face countless difficulties such as lack of protection; insecurity; vulnerability; difficulties in exercising the right to freedom of association; the short lifespan of business; long working hours; low wages; loss of overtime and bonus; loss of sickness and social benefit; loss of national insurance benefit; no formal contract; loss of holidays; loss of maternity leave; and loss of sick pay and pension; which all cause stressful and unhappy working conditions. In addition, informal workers, particularly urban informal workers, are at risk of being charged with crime, corruption, abuse and exploitation due to lack of effective legal safeguards.

There is no standard definition of informal work, and the concept is used in different categories in each country. In some countries, even the unemployed, informal and service sectors are overlapped and undifferentiated (Devas, 2004).

An ILO report on Kenya in 1972 identified the informal sector as being characterised by ease of entry; reliance on indigenous resources; family ownership of enterprise; small scale of operation, labour-intensive methods of production and adapted technology; using skills acquired outside the formal system; unregulated and competitive markets; and, the most important feature,

avoiding state regulations (ILO, 1972; Devas, 2004). On the other hand, the informal economy is sometimes also well known for the following characteristics: invisible, shadow, underground, clandestine, undeclared, unreported, black, irregular, submerged, subterranean, sometimes including drug dealing robbery and money-laundering, which are socially and legally unacceptable (Ratner, 2000).

The informal sector plays a crucial role in a survival strategy for the poor; although it does not mean that all the poor work in the informal sector, nor does it mean that all workers in the informal sector are poor. In order to enhance economic development, countries may encourage the informal sector to integrate into the mainstream formal sector economy to reduce uncertainty and mistrust, and to ensure opportunities for livelihoods and entrepreneurship. The overall trend for sustaining economic development in a country is to enhance flexibility in the labour market, both in formal and informal sectors. Munck has clearly pointed out that the new international labour studies came under the rubric of 'social movement' in which capital accumulation occurred on a global scale and all workers, both in formal and informal sectors, came under its sway albeit through different regimes (Munck, 2010). There are growing numbers of international companies that subcontract out into the informal sector to enhance flexibility of their workforce, which leads to the benefit of cost reduction.

Furthermore, the adoption of effective national policies to deal with the informal economy requires participation of informal economy organisations to represent the concerns and ambition of informal workers and business in national policy making, to ensure that small enterprises receive flexibility, legal recognition, security and fair treatment. Formal and informal economies are interrelated and complement each other. It is impossible to sustain the formal economy without a thriving informal economy.

POVERTY AND ANTI-POVERTY STRATEGIES

Persistence of poverty

Regardless of the existence of jobs, poverty is found both in 'developed' and 'developing' countries. Although the number of people living on less than $1.25 a day is estimated to drop from 918 million to 883 million in 2015 (as projected by the World Bank), mass poverty has still persisted in some part of the world and the gap between rich and poor countries has been even widened (World Bank, 2011).

In the 'third world', there has been some development in both economic and social dimensions but the overall trends are varied. The United Nations designates the poorest countries of world as LDCs, which in the late 1990s numbered some 44–55, depending on the classification criteria used (Cox and Pawar, 2006). A high proportion of the population of LDCs receives no monetary income and lives in absolute poverty with high illiteracy rates and no access to health services. Thus, life expectancy is generally less than 60 years. On one hand, there are some 'least developed' and developing countries in East and SE Asia, which have recently had some success in economic development and social progress. On the other hand, several countries in Africa have experienced little achievement in economic and social development (Midgley, 1997). These countries still face economic problems due to indebtedness and inability to diversify their economies.

While the poverty line is commonly used to estimate the level and the number of the population in a certain area living at this level, there are some other measurements which indicate the state of affairs concerning poverty. A well known example is the United Nations' For example, the UNs Millenium Development Goals (MDGs) constitute a multi-dimensional approach to defining and measuring poverty (see Appendix 6). The MDGs include eight broad goals, each with specific targets for improving the level of misery and suffering experienced around the world. The eight goals are: eradicate extreme poverty and hunger; achieve universal primary education; promote gender equality; reduce child mortality; improve maternal health; combat diseases such as HIV/AIDS and malaria; ensure environmental sustainability; and develop a global partnership for development (ILO, 2003). Although the United Nations had adopted the eight MDGs as a clear-cut strategic goal to poverty alleviation in third-world countries, the MDGs have not been universally accepted as a positive innovation and it is unlikely that all nations will be able to achieve the goals by the target date of 2015 (Mapp, 2008). While some countries will miss their targets by a small margin, others are struggling even to maintain such progress as has been made.

Anti-poverty countermeasures

The primary responsibility to tackle poverty resides with each nation state, usually through economic growth and income maintenance. The former is usually targeted through macroeconomic policies, mainly fiscal and monetary policies, with growth typically measured by GDP and/or GDP per capita, with the hope that benefits would 'trickle down' to the bottom eventually, for example, if the rate exceeds 3 per cent,[7] (cf. Akimoto, 2001: 110). Sometimes, or even usually, little or no benefit filters to the bottom, and the 'rich get richer and the poor get the poorer', which widens the gap.

Some contend that if the intervention started at the bottom or with the people in most need, then the benefit would 'soak up' to the top and the contribution to the macro-economy could be measured (Akimoto, 2001). There are various social policies and forms of pro-poor interventions, but income maintenance programmes are the most typical: livelihood protection benefits (public assistance); unemployment insurance; workers' accident compensation insurance; medical insurance; old-age and disability pension;

child allowance; care insurance; and others. In 'developed' countries, these measures are in place, creating 'welfare states', while 'developing' countries have much less in the way of formal protection systems in place.

Though, in general, poverty reduction relies on local and national governments, external assistance is also important. Foreign governments, international organisations, NGOs and individuals provide various types of assistance. Supposing the cause of poverty largely rests in international relations and structure, the solution necessitates international support and co-operation.

Forms and strategies of assistance vary. Various forms of assistance on multilateral and bilateral bases lead to awarding of grants, loans, and technical assistance; macroeconomic, social policy and service approaches at various levels parallel those provided by nation states. Both their positive and negative effects have been extensively pointed out. Several examples of the strategies ... and NGOs can be identified as follows.

Macroeconomic development

Construction of large macroinfrastructures to improve economic growth, such as roads, ports, airports, trains, power plants, waterworks, sewerage and irrigation schemes are typical of assistance through official development assistance (ODA) and international financial organisations. 'Advice' and 'proposals' are sometimes given in the context of technical assistance regarding macroeconomic and social policies and programmes for growth and/or reconstruction of national economies. Sometimes virtual coercion may accompany this 'help'.

'Aid for Trade'

'Aid for trade' programmes are intended to help enhance a country's capacity and remove domestic constraints to boost economic growth and alleviate poverty.

'Aid for Trade' is a complement to the Doha Development Agenda[8] and aims to help developing countries, and the least developed countries in particular, to implement and enjoy benefits from WTO agreements (WTO, 2006). Aid for Trade can take several shapes and forms, but includes technical assistance to help countries develop trade strategies, negotiate more effectively and implement the outcomes; strengthen national and regional institutions in relation to development trade policy and regulation; and help enterprises to be more competitive and productive, paying attention to domestic barriers, infrastructure and border costs (IDS, 2009).

Supervisory functions

Some international organisations perform certain supervisory functions, and the ILO is a good example. It is not a funding institution but provides advice regarding international labour standards, reducing uncertainty and insecurity in people's lives. The values that inspire the work of the ILO, expressed in its *Constitution and the Declaration on Fundamental Principles and Rights at Work*, are a strong foundation for countries to build institutional frameworks for the governance of labour markets that meet the twin imperatives of fairness and efficiency (ILO, 2003). Supervisory mechanisms of the ILO have been developed with the argument that improving the governance of labour markets is central to increasing social cohesion and sustainable growth, and thus the reduction of poverty.

Governance

Governance and public management reform is another strategy, where training and capacity building, empowering NGOs, community-based organisations and civil societies, and strengthening democratic mechanisms are provided. UNDP has been variously involved in this activity with its core mandate, one of sustainable human development, building national capacity for people-centred, environmentally sustainable development and aid collaboration, national planning, and execution. The involvement of the government sector, public sector and civil society is said to be a key to success.

Micro projects

Numerous micro projects have been carried out in the field of poverty alleviation, income generation and employment promotion by various players such as international agencies, ODA agencies and, most typically, NGOs. Craft work, weaving and other traditional work utilising indigenous skills are typical projects and the designing and marketing of these products are found to be critical to their success. Unless essential core elements of projects are conceptualised and generalised, and then successful projects are replicated to other sites, the criticism of 'a drop in the ocean' is unavoidable if direct project participants are to benefit. Rare successful examples are projects utilising a labour intensive approach (e.g. road construction/maintenance with few machines but much human power) and micro-credit (e.g. Grameen Bank).

Comprehensive approach

The comprehensive approach is a type of 'one package strategy' which is inclusive of various levels of assistance from hardware infrastructures to software social programmes. In the Mekong sub-regional countries, for example, Official Development Assistance (ODA) Japan has played a key role in poverty alleviation and accelerating economic and social development. Its basic policy is to support self-help in developing countries, promote human security, assure fairness, share the donor country's own experience and expertise, create partnership and collaborate with the international community. A priority issue is poverty reduction, especially in remote areas. Its assistance ranges from the construction, renovation and improvement of highway routes, bridges, water supply systems, electric systems, and school buildings equipped with materials, to the assistance to core institutions of medical and health care, the provision of loans to support the development of social and economic infrastructure and the development of individuals as the base of the country's development (Wajjwalku, 2005).

Some topical issues

The following are just a few examples of recent issues and topics which have been discussed related to anti-poverty strategies. The first two pertain mainly to 'developed' countries and the second two mainly to 'developing' countries.

Shrinkage of income maintenance programmes and free market

In most 'developed' countries, income maintenance systems (social security) exist, but appear to have shrunk due to the impact of 'neo-classic' school ideology and neo-liberal governments. This not only affects income maintenance, but also social programmes and services generally which are now geared towards free markets, competition, deregulation, privatisation, self-reliance and small government.

Recent public attitudes on welfare has impacted on social work and community services as it reduces government involvement in service delivery, government expenditure and government service. In this context government only has a limited role as a supporter to provide welfare, whereas civil societies and NGOs actively participate in social and economic programmes as directive providers.

Australia's new social policy, for example, took this partnership approach. It aimed at the creation of a self-reliant community as an effective safety net, as well as the development of good partnerships among key stakeholders in order to improve effective services and develop appropriate policy responses. Proponents insist on the need to change from a passive welfare system to an active economic and social participation in society via providing access and promoting opportunities. Opponents however offer the critique that this social policy is rooted in government's attempt to escape from social welfare responsibilities and leave charity affairs to NGOs (Alston and McKinnon, 2001).

Although most of the social work community tends to be critical of the 'neo-classic school' and free market ideas, it may not have to be overly pessimistic. First, in some countries, the transfer of governmental function and responsibility to non-governmental sectors may have a positive effect. Governments may develop a broader and more inclusive approach in collaborating with private and other related agencies in order to deliver assistance, alleviate poverty and maintain social services (Rodger, 2000). In the past, political intervention was a problem for social workers since governments often would prevent or be unsympathetic to social developmental goals, but this new approach may gain more governmental co-operation.

Secondly, the concept of market economy has had a long history with a variety of models ranging from the 'government-monopoly market' in socialist parts of the world (such as Eastern Europe) in the post-World War II period, the 'free market' in capitalist countries (such as those in Western Europe), to the 'third way' or 'welfare-state' markets of modern European countries (such as France, The Netherlands and Germany since the 1960s). The pure 'laissez faire' market economy has not existed from the early days of capitalist society as various state interventions have always been made, including labour regulations, antitrust laws, and various other facilitative social policies and legislation.

The present dominant trend is towards welfare states, as the idea of a 100 percent free-market system without regulations could never be attainable. In the beginning of the 21st century especially, policy makers faced difficulties in setting up social policies due to the vast range of human needs encountered, yet social policies have to address specific social needs, often reflected through particular ethnic, cultural, sexual and gender concerns. For example, the number of non-Western resident persons in Denmark increased by 520 per cent between 1980 and 2005 and these residents had access to a universalistic welfare state based on high levels of public services such as health care and

education provided for citizens as well as residents in the country (Hedetoft, 2006). Therefore, a recent key welfare objective laid down in an inclusive-rights based approach is to integrate excluded groups into a common national community in order to let them enjoy the same opportunities, resulting hopefully in social justice. Currently the idea of participatory economic processes is to strengthen civil society while not abandoning the state's role, as well as ensuring social co-operation among stakeholders. This process leads to a new idea of the 'stakeholder economy', in which everyone has the opportunity to succeed and the responsibility to contribute, with the vision of building a common and integrated society to meet universal human needs (Rodger, 2000).

Social enterprises

A tug of war has always been played behind the market economy between the concepts of economic development and social development. Although economic development has often taken precedence over social goals, more recently social development has acted as a brake or checking factor on the reckless driver of economic development. Taking this further, social development can become the goal with economic development as the tool and the market economy can be used to achieve a social goal.

Beyond the notions of charity and welfare, the idea of social enterprise,[9] a social-purpose organisation that applies business culture, management and structure but aims to achieve the goals of social or environmental change has emerged with the creation of 'value-centred market economics' with recognition of the complexity of values (Frances, 2008). Unlike in the past, it refers to a broader range of social and moral values such as accessibility, quality education, accessible health care systems, available employment, clean water, sustainable energy, democratic government, etc. In the value-centred economic market, the market itself is not changed but business is driven by purpose rather than profit. Value-centred market economics believe that business is not only about value of money but also related to the value of human beings and social justice. Each sector, in the value-centred market, will focus on particular areas of concern, for example, income maintenance and better livelihood.

The social business idea developed over time, depending upon each specific context. Initially, there was an increase in the number of companies which included social responsibility in their business objectives, e.g. Westpac, Toyota, Rio Tinto, ANZ and BHP Billiton (Frances, 2008). However, this type of business does not result in real change. Therefore, the idea of social enterprise developed through linking social goals to consumer-based goals in a socially responsible way. In other words, the key feature of the social enterprise is to marry the business and social goals. The important feature of social enterprise is to ensure that all shareholders have opportunities to participate in the business market as well as being involved in social and environmental change, and a good partnership should lead to effective implementation and achievement of the desired outcomes. Nic Frances Furniture Resource Centre (FRC). This distributes furniture to people on low incomes, including by selling to landlords, and provides job training to homeless people. The project results in … and training homeless people (Frances, 2008).

Another example of social enterprise established by non-government welfare agencies in Hong Kong where the work-integration social enterprises (WISEs) programmes managed by social workers aim to provide disadvantaged groups with an opportunity for employment and training in income generation skills and expansion of their social networks. The programmes are found to improve the participants' psychosocial well-being as well as contributing to the labour market and to poverty alleviation and social capital building (Po-ying Ho and Chan, 2010).

Social enterprises are different from other businesses because their social and environmental purpose remains central to their operation. The structure of these social enterprises can be varied, ranging from small businesses to large companies. On the one hand, social enterprise can be considered as a way to reduce the dependence on charitable donations and grants; on the other hand, social enterprise itself is a vehicle for social change.

Corruption and governance

The following are two issues of concern in any discussion on foreign aid.

Corruption is defined as the abuse of public office for private gain and results in a number of negative impacts. Examples of corruption are bribery to win the bidding for government procurement contracts, payment to accelerate one's place in the queue (to gain access to officials, etc.), and payment to get investment licenses (Bardhan, 2005). Corruption usually is associated with the rise of organised crime, arms smuggling, money laundering, or human and drug trafficking, which corrupt governments either ignore, or are complicit with. Corruption and human rights are often related. Countries that have a high level of corruption usually also have a high level of human rights violations, since the corruption often obstructs people's access to the basic and fundamental needs such as clean water and sanitation, education and health, as well as freedom of information and press. Principles of good *governance* apply in this context as control of corruption requires public integrity via a 'checks and balances' system, free and democratic elections, reliable and impartial judiciary, free proactive media and NGOs, and a well trained and professionally regulated civil service (Sano and Alfredson, 2003).

Certain countries or regions are sometimes referred to as examples of poor governance because of high-level corrupt bureaucrats, politicians and businessmen. The fact that the governments of these countries are generally not able to deal with these problems reflects weaknesses in administrative services, police, military, intelligence, as well as the collapse of democracy. These countries thus need greater transparency, access to information and oversight mechanisms to regulate the functioning of the state's machinery, and this is fundamental to reversing this decline (Thakur and Newman, 2004). A radical reform in governance across the country or the region is essential and this reform is only possible if the people assert themselves and demand transparency, representation and accountability.

Debt relief policies

The debt of, and debt relief to, 'developing' countries have been discussed widely at various points in history, often related to financial or currency crises and development emergencies; 'Jubilee 2000' was one of the recent major campaigns to cancel debt.

Debt relief policies can take various forms. Many countries adopt belt-tightening measures in coping with debt crisis such as reducing demand for imported goods while supporting domestic production to encourage exports (Lairson and Skidmore, 1993).

During economic crises, IMF plays an important role as it is a multilateral lending agency directly involved in a debt crisis. Its main objective is to lend money to countries experiencing shortfalls in their current accounts (Lairson and Skidmore, 1993). The IMF may set conditions for the borrower country, particularly economic policy reform ranging from abolishing or liberalising foreign exchange and import controls; reducing growth in domestic money supply; raising interest rates; increasing taxes; reducing government wages; and seeking wage restraint from labour unions; privatising publicly owned companies; reducing restrictions on foreign investment; devaluing the local currency and cutting social benefits. 'Conditionality', as it is commonly termed, usually means a heavy human burden for local people. In the 1990s, that debt problem was greatly reduced by debt restructuring –

allowing repayment of debt over extended periods of time – and a fall in the world interest rate. The joint IMF–World Bank's comprehensive approach to debt reduction is also designed to ensure that no country faces a debt burden it cannot manage. In 2010, the debt reduction packages under the Heavily Indebted Poor Countries (HIPC) Initiative were approved for 36 countries, 32 of them in Africa, providing US$72 billion in debt-service relief over time. Four additional countries are potentially eligible for HIPC Initiative assistance. The HIPC Initiative on debt restructuring provision was supplemented by the Multilateral Debt Relief Initiative (MDRI) which provides for 100 per cent relief on eligible debt by three multilateral institutions – the IMF, the World Bank, and the African Development Fund – for countries completing the HIPC Initiative process (IMF, 2010b; World Bank, 2010). The initiative is intended to help those heavily indebted poor countries advance toward the United Nations' MDGs, which are focused on halving poverty by 2015.

SOCIAL WORKERS ROLE IN IMPROVING ECONOMIC CONDITIONS AND LIVELIHOOD

Assuming social workers are well equipped with the capacity to be leaders, lobbyists, awareness-raisers, advocates, moderators and change agents, with sensitivity to anti-oppressive and anti-discriminatory practice, and with a good understanding of the international and national economy and the present position of nation states. Social Work intervention would be called for and wanted – at the macro and the micro level, both in research and practice, by governments, international organisations and NGOs.

However, the actual involvement of professional social workers has been limited mainly to the fields of poverty/livelihood and such employment issues as 'welfare to work' and typical income maintenance (social security) schemes in 'developed' countries. Some professional social workers facilitate income maintenance by becoming part of the system because, as government employees, they administer the system.

In other words, social work involvement has been limited to (1) the work/employment/labour field closely related to, but with some distance from, the livelihood/poverty issue in 'developed' countries; (2) livelihood/economic conditions fields in 'developing' countries; and (3) international organisations such as ILO, ODA agencies and international NGOs (INGOs).

Today in 'developed' countries, the interest of social workers in the field of work and labour has been shifted towards 'industrial social work', 'occupational social work', and Employee Assistance Programs (EAP) with emphasis on mental health. However, a few decades ago there was more interest in 'workforce' policies and programmes and 'social work in the world of work' which covered all aspects of labour market, work place, community life, and labour unions, for example in the United States.

'Developing' countries, depending on their stage of industrialisation have suffered from the same and similar social problems which their predecessors once experienced, as well as some different and unique problems. Vast poverty, conflict and other 'livelihood' difficulties exist. A problem is that, in many and most 'developing' countries, there are few or professional social workers available to engage with these issues. In countries with low elementary school entrance rates, those who study social work at the post-secondary school level, which leads to degrees or diplomas (cf. IASSW's Constitution) are very limited in number. They are the elite, and many would not work in the field, or they may emigrate to greener pastures. In any case, there may be few or no social workers in some countries.

However, problems are being dealt with in these countries, by someone with or without the name of 'social workers' who may not necessarily be accepted as (or use the title of) 'professional social worker' in 'developed' countries. There are not a few 'social workers', for example, in Sri Lanka, who are trained and working in social development NGOs and even a social work agency. But the story was the same as with 'developed' countries. In the process of industrialisation of the present 'developed' countries – or previously 'developing' countries as they were – social workers worked in a similar way, tackling problems of poverty caused by industrialisation, both at an individual and policy level. In a sense social work was born in that process. 'Do-gooders', philanthropists, friendly visitors and settlement workers worked for migrants from rural areas, children, the poor, the unemployed, and workers, on issues concerning their low wages, long working conditions, occupational safety and health and housing, and labour and social security legislations. They were not necessarily 'professional social workers', but their role and activity have been well-documented in social work textbooks.

The biggest difference between the present and past 'developing' countries is the existence today of *globalisation*, and thus the type of approach and intervention of social work. Many problems which 'developing' countries have today are internationally rooted and the contribution of social workers must be to think through the implications of this. There are some professional social workers mostly from 'developed' countries who work in the projects and programmes of international organisations, ODA agencies and NGOs in developing countries: they work both at macro and micro levels, although the number is very limited. They have been engaged most typically in the fields of poverty alleviation, income generation, employment promotion, HIV, disabilities, children, refugees and human rights. An example of this was a professional social worker working in the ILO to design and implement a research project entitled '*Shrinkage of Urban Slums in Asia and their Employment Aspects'* and an experimental project for employment promotion and income generation (Akimoto, 1994, 1998: 1994) These social workers can be promoters of the well-being of people in the 'developing' countries, but might also be guilty of social work imperialism. Professional social workers have to recognise and address the negative forces of globalisation.

CONCLUSION

The major determinant of people's livelihood and employment conditions is their birth – where they are born, in which country and which particular social class. Macro trends such as industrialisation, the transition from primary industry to secondary and tertiary, and then globalisation, the diffusion of economy, political power and cultural values from the centre to the periphery in capitalist economies, need to be understood. It is also important to understand the present position of nation states in world history, particularly with regard to to the struggle for improvement in people's livelihoods.

Employment for income, job itself or decent work, is often not available. The informal sector is crucial for many, or sometimes most people in 'developing' countries to survive. Still poverty has persisted both in 'developed' and 'developing' countries. The need is usually twofold: for macroeconomic growth, and for income maintenance, and the primary responsibility rests on each nation state to promote both.

The priority concern is still the situation of mass poverty in 'the two-thirds world'. Although assistance from outside is called for, from other nation states, international organisations and NGOs, the cause of the poverty today largely rests in international relations and global structures. The solution necessitates international support and cooperation. The recent relaxation of social protection due to the 'neo-classic' school and neoliberal governments, the persistence of

corruption and the need for improved governance, and accumulated debt, offer a challenge to social workers, through, for example, the idea of social enterprises.

The protection and promotion of livelihoods and need to improve economic conditions, particularly of less privileged populations in the world, is the core mission for social workers. Actual involvement in this vision, however, has been very limited, except for their involvement in income maintenance programmes, particularly in 'developed' countries, while few social workers are involved in 'developing' countries. As long as social workers are defined as *professional* social workers defined by 'developed' country standards this situation will persist. Can only international social workers from 'developed' countries work in the midst of mass poverty? The answer is clearly no. The chapter also advocates that an understanding of the international macroeconomic situation is indispensable for social workers involved in research and practice.

NOTES

1   Previously GNP (gross national product).
2   Two other classes are 'high human development' (45) and 'medium human development' (75).
3   The resolution concerning statistics of the economically active population – employment, unemployment and underemployment – adopted by the Thirteenth International Conference of Labour Statistics (Geneva, 1982).
4   In Indonesia, 11 per cent of jobs are 'white collar jobs', that is, 'legislators, senior officials and managers', 'professionals', 'technicians and associate professionals', and 'clerks', and 35 per cent are 'skilled agricultural and fishery workers' among all occupations. The percentage of 'white collar jobs' increases in to 19 per cent in Paraguay, 25 per cent in Mexico, 40 per cent in Poland, 50 per cent in the United States, and 59 per cent in the Netherlands, where only 1.3 per cent is in the category of 'skilled agricultural and fishery workers'.
5   The coverage of France, UK, Luxembourg were national minimum wage and Thailand, the Philippines, and China were local minimum wage, and Indonesia was local and industrial minimum wage. The numbers were calculated from the currency of each

country into Japanese yen and recalculated into US dollar.

6 Originally seven conventions in 1998 and another added in 1999.

7 US economist Barry Bluestone in *The trend of US economy and the state of employment & work today* (Workshop) held on 17 December 1999, Japan Institute of Labour, Tokyo.

8 The Doha Development Agenda is the round of trade negotiations within the World Trade Organisation (WTO). It attempts to redefine the earlier agreements on global trade to make them fit the current political reality more closely, and to bring greater agreement among the constituents of the WTO.

9 Social enterprise is defined as a social organisation that applies market-based strategies to achieve a social change. Social enterprise can be either non-profits or for-profits business but the primary aim is to generate profit to achieve social and environmental goals. However, best model for social enterprise is a for-profit model because it allows risk, growth and activity on large scale while maintaining social values in market economy.

REFERENCES

Akimoto, T. (1994) '*Bangkok Congested Community Employment Promotion Project*. Bangkok: ILO/ROAP. 1994. (A revised version) From Arrogant Model to Lazy Model – Developmental Aid Project Design: The Bangkok Slum Employment Project', *Social Welfare*. pp. 65–84.

Akimoto, T. (ed.) (1998) *Shrinkage of Urban Slums in Asia and Their Employment Aspects*. Bangkok: ILO/ROAP.

Akimoto, T. (2001) 'Can the US model be a model for Japan? The refusal of "trickle down theory" and "venture business", in *Shade and Light of the United States – Exploration into the Trend of US Economy and the State of Employment & Work Today*. Tokyo: Japan Institute of Labour. pp. 80–118.

Alston, M. and McKinnon, J. (eds) (2001) *Social Work: Fields of Practice*. Oxford University Press.

Bardhan, P. (2005) *Scarcity, Conflicts, and Cooperation: Essays in the Political and Institutional Economics of Development*. London: MIT Press.

CIA (Central Intelligence Agency) (2010) *The World Factbook*. Guide to country comparison. (April) https://www.cia.gov/library/publications/the-world-factbook/rankorder/rankorderguide.html.

Cox, D. and Pawar, M. (2006) *International Social Work: Issues, Strategies, and Programs*. London: SAGE Publications.

Devas, N. (2004) *Urban Governance, Voice and Poverty in the Developing World*. James & James Science Publisher.

Fortune Magazine, 20 July 2009.

Frances, N. (2008) *The End of Charity: Time for Social Enterprise*. Allen & Unwin.

Hedetoft, U. (2006) *Denmark: Integrating Immigrants into a Homogeneous Welfare State*. Migration Information Source. Washington, D.C.: Migration Policy Institute. Washington, D.C.

Ho, P-y. A. and Chan, K. (2010) 'The social impact of work-integration social enterprise in Hong Kong', *International Social Work*, 53: 33–45.

IDS (Institute of Development Studies) (2009) 'Changing the aid for trade debate towards content', *IDS In Focus Policy Briefing*, issue 6, March, from www.ids.ac.uk/go/publications/in-focus.

ILO (International Labour Organisation) (1972) *Employment Income and Equality: A Strategy for Increasing Productive Employment in Kenya*. Geneva: ILO.

ILO (International Labour Organisation) (1999) *Decent Work*. Report of the Director-General in the International Labour Conference definition, 87th Session, Geneva.

ILO (International Labour Organisation) (2003) *Working out of Poverty*. International Labour Conference 91st Session, Geneva.

ILO (International Labour Organisation) (2010) *LABORSTA*. Internet retrieved on 8–29 September 2010. http://laborsta.ilo.org.

IMF (International Monetary Fund) (2009) *World Economic Outlook Database*. (October).

IMF (International Monetary Fund) (2010a) *World Economic Outlook Database*. (April).

IMF (International Monetary Fund) (2010b) *International Monetary Fund Factsheet*. http://www.imf.org/external/np/exr/facts/hipc.htm.

JPC (Japan Productivity Center) (2011) *Katsuyo Rodo Tokei 2011*.

Kinoshita, T. (2007) 'Unions challenging differential societies', *Preferences in Industrialized Countries: Finding the Balance,* 2004. Tokyo: Kaden-sha.

Krauthammer, C. (2004) *Democratic Realism: An American Foreign Policy for a Unipolar World*. Washington, D.C.: AEI Press.

Lairson, T.D. and Skidmore, D. (1997) *International Political Economy: The Struggle for Power and Wealth*. Cengage Learning Publishers.

Mapp, S.C. (2008) *Human Rights and Social Justice in a Global Perspective: An Introduction to International Social Work*. Oxford University Press.

Midgley, J. (1997) *Social Welfare in Global Context*. London: SAGE Publications.

Munck, R. (2010) 'Globalisation, labour and development: a view from the south', *Transformation: Critical Perspectives on South Africa*, 72/73: 205–24.

OECD (Organisation for Economic Co-operation and Development) (2009) *National Account of OECD Countries: Main Aggregate* (vol. 1) 1996–2007.

Ohno, K. (2000) *Globalization of Developing Countries*. Toyo-keizai-shinpo-sha.

Ratner, S. (2000) *The informal economy in rural community economic development*. February. http://www.rural.org/publications/Ratner00-03.pdf.

Rodger, J.J. (2000) *From a Welfare State to a Welfare Society*. Palgrave Macmillan.

Seabrook, J. (2002) *The No-nonsense Guide to Class, Caste & Hierarchies*. London: New Internationalist; Verso.

Sano, H.-O. and Alfredson, G. (eds) (2003) *Human Rights and Good Governance: Building Bridges*. Martinus Nijhoff Publishers.

Thakur, R. and Newman, E. (eds) (2004) *Broadening Asia's Security Discourse and Agenda: Political, Social, and Environmental Perspectives*. United Nations University Press.

Wajjwalku, S. (ed.) (2005) *Japan's Policy and Contributions to Human Development in Southeast Asia*. Thammasat University Press.

Wallerstein, I.M. (1983) *Historical Capitalism*. London: Verso.

World Bank (2010) *World Development Indicators Database* 2009. July.

World Bank (2011) *The World Bank Global Monitoring Report* 2011.

WTO (World Trade Organisation) (2006) *Recommendations of the Task Force on Aid for Trade, Aid for Trade Task Force*, WT/AFT/1, 27 July C.

13

Social Work and Health

Paul Bywaters and Cindy Davis

INTRODUCTION

The IFSW's international policy on health opens with the assertion that

> ... health is an issue of fundamental human rights and social justice and binds social work to apply these principles in policy, education, research and practice. All people have an equal right to enjoy the basic conditions which underpin human health. These conditions include a minimum standard of living to support health and a sustainable and health promoting environment. All people have an equal right to access resources and services that promote health and address illness, injury and impairment, including social services. (IFSW, 2008)

In this summary statement, health social work is placed unequivocally within the international context of human rights, reflecting the UN Universal Declaration of Human Rights adopted in 1948, and is distanced from a *primary* concern with medicine or healthcare services. Social work's contribution to health has come a long way since one early writer stated that

> It is essential to make it clear from the outset that the social worker is part of the medical organisation. She (sic) is one means of diagnosis and treatment. She is not to pursue independent sociological or statistical enquiries. She is not to be the agent of any other non-medical society (Cabot 1919, quoted in Bywaters, 1986: 663).

These shifts in focus, from the medical to the social, from the technical to the ethical, from illness to health, from treatment to rights, from individual to policy intervention are echoed in this chapter on the internationalisation of health social work since its emergence in the hospitals of USA and European urban areas at the end of the 19th century (Bell, 1961; Bywaters et al., 2009).

We begin the chapter by setting the context and exploring the key concepts in international health and social work. In the core of the chapter, we exemplify these themes through the discussion of four key global health issues: illnesses, people, providers and activism.[1]

SETTING THE CONTEXT

A brief recent history of international health concerns

The establishment of the World Health Organization (WHO) in 1946 marked a key point of development for health policy. Embedded in the constitution of the WHO were statements which have framed thinking about health in the period since the Second World War and which have established the international context of health policy and practice. First, the constitution created a definition of health which has become widely used, including in a recent International Federation of Social Workers (IFSW) policy (see later). While it is not immune from criticism, the idea that 'health is a state of complete physical, mental and social well-being and not merely the absence of disease or infirmity' (WHO, 1946: 1) was crucial in three key respects: it emphasised positive health rather than the relief of illness; it recognised that physical and mental health were inextricably connected; and it saw that health had a central social component. Second, the constitution declared that the 'enjoyment of the highest attainable standard of health is one of the fundamental rights of every human being without distinction of race, religion, political belief, economic or social condition'. By agreeing that health was a fundamental right, signatory countries accepted – separately and together – an obligation to act to protect and promote population health. Moreover, the benchmark for success was set at the 'highest attainable' level not merely a minimum standard. And, third, by explicitly rejecting the idea that anyone should be discriminated against because of their identity or social circumstances, the Constitution established the importance of inequities in health between and within populations.[2]

In 1978, the Alma Ata Declaration called for 'Health For All' by the year 2000 and both re-affirmed and significantly developed the principles of the original WHO constitution. The central feature of the Declaration was that it called for primary healthcare to be at the heart of healthcare systems, 'bringing healthcare as close as possible to where people live and work, and constitut(ing) the first element of a continuing healthcare process'(WHO, 1978: 1). The current Director General of the WHO, Margaret

Chan, recently called for a return to this vision (*Lancet*, 2008). The Declaration explicitly castigated the 'gross inequality' in health between and within countries and named a range of social and economic determinants only implied in 1948. For example, it linked expenditure on armaments and warfare with a call for governments to make resources available for health. Although influential in public health thinking, the Declaration's call for a new economic order actually coincided with the start of a period of over 20 years when neo-liberal economic policies held sway as globalisation accelerated (Labonte and Schrecker, 2007a).

In the 1980s and 1990s, it was another institution formed in the post-war years, the World Bank, which seemed to dominate international health policy making, in alliance with the International Monetary Fund (Labonte and Schrecker, 2007a,b,c; Global Health Watch, 2005). Pushing policies which required economic liberalization of developing countries' markets as the price of aid, the World Bank was responsible for the dismantling or erosion of already fragile public sector services in health and social care in many developing countries, and for the promotion of the role of profit-making transnational companies selling a variety of health-related products, including healthcare services, health insurance and pharmaceutical and other treatments. But, as became increasingly clear by 2000, neo-liberal economics had an even more damaging effect on the wider social determinants of health, creating widening inequities in health outcomes across the globe (Commission on the Social Determinants of Health, 2008). Poverty, food insecurity and environmental degradation went hand in hand with a failure to secure improved educational outcomes, water, sanitation and other elements of an infrastructure for health. For instance, the liberalization of the economy of the former Soviet Union saw a rapid deterioration in life expectancy (Bloom and Canning, 2000) and it also became clear that HIV/ AIDS thrived under conditions of neo-liberal globalization, with devastating results for millions of people (see later) (Altman, 1999; Bancroft, 2001).

The end of the 20th century saw evidence of growing political pressure to reverse these health-damaging policies, leading to the formation of the Millennium Development Goals (UN, 2000 and see Appendix 6) and the start of a period in which contradictory ideologies have rivalled each other for power. So, to give a few examples of issues with wide international resonance:

- There have been extended struggles over the power and autonomy of pharmaceutical companies, their control over patents, their desire to restrict the production of 'generic' rather than branded preparations and their pricing policies.
- New large global charitable trusts, such as the Gates Foundation, have entered the political and health arenas, often focusing on single diseases, with different commentators drawing different conclusions about whether their impact was positive or provided a smoke screen for 'business as usual'.
- Popular social and health movements have increasingly acted to protest against the impact of globalization on health.
- The WHO established the Commission on the Social Determinants of Health which boldly asserted that 'social justice is a matter of life and death' (CSDH, 2008: Preface) and that global health inequities were immoral as well as economically inefficient.
- The global financial crisis of 2008 plunged many people into poverty and contributed to instability in food security, while other health damaging social trends – many forms of migration; war, terrorism and violence; climate change; the promotion of private healthcare services and insurance – continued without effective international intervention.

Global economics and globalized health systems exert both a direct and indirect impact on health social work today. Social workers find themselves dealing with the consequences of migration; of environmental degradation; of health tourism, human and organ trafficking; of war and political conflict, as well as poverty (Bywaters et al., 2009). Financial pressures – to cut costs and make profits – threaten the capacity of social workers to act in the interests of service users' health in health settings (Sulman et al., 2001) and non-health settings alike (Ferguson, 2008). However, the emergence of new social movements, such as the People's Health Movement (http://www.phmovement.org/en) and AIDS activism in the health arena; and service user, mental health survivor and disability activism in the social sphere offer scope for new alliances for social workers working for health, locally and internationally.

Current health outcomes and determinants

As Mary Robinson has argued in founding the global 'Realizing Rights' organization (www.realizingrights.org) the right to life is the most fundamental human right. Mortality rates are also the starkest markers of health outcomes. In the lifetime of the WHO, life expectancy has substantially increased in most countries of the world. As Table 13.1 shows, average life expectancy at birth in developed countries has increased by over 10 years in the last 50 and continues to do so. In these countries it now stands at around 80 years, with countries enjoying greater social equality doing better than those which are more unequal (Wilkinson and

Table 13.1   Average life expectancy at birth 1960–65 and 2005–10

	1960–65	2005–10
Angola	34	47
Australia	71	82
Brazil	56	72
China	50	73
Costa Rica	63	79
Japan	69	83
South Africa	50	52
USA	70	79
Zimbabwe	52	44

Source: United Nations Department of Economic and Social Affairs, Population Division, World Population Prospects: The 2008 Revision, New York, 2009.

Pickett, 2009). China, with a rapidly expanding but managed economy, is one of the mid-range countries in terms of development which have tended to show larger increases but from a low base. China, Brazil and Costa Rice all have experienced an increase in average life expectancy of over 15 years in the last 50. But while some amongst the poorer countries have kept pace, others, especially those in sub-Saharan Africa, and also war-torn countries like Afghanistan, have failed to do so. In the worst cases, such as Zimbabwe, life expectancy has actually fallen so that inequalities in life expectancy between the most and least advantaged countries have grown. In summary, there are immense differences in the length and quality of people's lives largely – but not exclusively – a product of the wealth of the country in which you happen to be born and how that wealth is distributed.

Table 13.2 demonstrates even greater levels of inequality between countries. In the most developed countries only around five children in a thousand will die before they reach their fifth birthday. In the least developed countries, usually again those where structural poverty is combined with internal conflict or war, one in five will die; 40 times

as many. Maternal mortality rates vary even more alarmingly from under 10 deaths per 100,000 births in most developed countries in 2005, to over 1500 in the worst places to have a child, according to WHO data (UN data, 2010). These statistics raise significant issues of children and women's rights not just in the countries affected but also globally in terms of international economic and development policies and practices.

Table 13.2 also shows the big differences in survival rates between boys and girls in different countries. In some countries, the differential risks which boys are exposed to result in greater male mortality, but in others, where girls are less valued, their lives are also at risk. In China, for example, girls have a 40 percent higher under-five mortality rate. Other inequities in health outcomes within countries are also great, and in many cases growing, even in the global north. As the Commission on the Social Determinants of Health (CSDH, 2008) highlighted, the poorest district in a city in Scotland (Glasgow) has an average male life expectancy in the mid-50s, while in nearby districts it is in the high 70s. The sometimes grossly negative outcomes for indigenous peoples and disadvantaged ethnic or other minorities, even in countries with universal health services such as Canada and Australia, also reinforce the argument that it is social, economic, environmental and political factors rather than healthcare services that determine these health outcomes (Bywaters et al., 2009).

It is not only that there is a gap between rich and poor, every step up the ladder of income and wealth is reflected in better average health outcomes as Marmot's (2004) research demonstrated. This gradient in health means that equalizing health outcomes cannot be achieved by only targeting those in the worst economic circumstances, as the problem is not one of a gap but of a slope.

The WHO Commission on the Social Determinants of Health, after an exhaustive examination of the evidence, was very clear about the causes of these distressing inequalities.

Table 13.2   Estimated mortality under five per 1000 live births, 2005–10

	2005–10	2005–10	2005–10
	Both sexes combined	Males	Females
Angola	205.0	220.4	189.2
Australia	5.6	5.9	5.2
Brazil	29.1	33.1	24.9
China	29.3	24.6	34.9
Costa Rica	11.4	12.8	9.9
India	81.5	77.3	86.0
Japan	4.3	4.6	3.9
South Africa	71.7	79.5	63.8
USA	7.3	7.2	7.6
Zimbabwe	94.2	99.8	88.5

Source: United Nations, Department of Economic and Social Affairs, Population Division, World Population Prospects: The 2008 Revision, New York, 2009.

The poor health of the poor, the social gradient in health within countries, and the marked health inequities between countries are caused by the unequal distribution of power, income, goods, and services, globally and nationally, the consequent unfairness in the immediate, visible circumstances of people's lives – their access to healthcare, schools, and education, their conditions of work and leisure, their homes, communities, towns, or cities – and their chances of leading a flourishing life. This unequal distribution of health-damaging experiences is not in any sense a 'natural' phenomenon but is the result of a toxic combination of poor social policies and programmes, unfair economic arrangements, and bad politics. Together, the structural determinants and conditions of daily life constitute the social determinants of health and are responsible for a major part of health inequities between and within countries

(CSDH, 2008: 1).

It is the official recognition of social determinants worldwide which opens up the potential for social work to build alliances with other professions and other actors. The recent Strategic Review of Health Inequities in England Post-2010 (Marmot, 2010: 159), for the first time in a quasi-official document, made the link between the disadvantaged lives of most service users and their poor health and acknowledged the potential of social workers to 'make a significant contribution to health and to health inequalities'.

We turn next to the efforts being made within social work to address health issues at the international level, starting with the IFSW policy statement.

INTERNATIONAL HEALTH SOCIAL WORK

International Federation of Social Workers Policy on Health

The major initiative in recent years to create the basis for international action on health issues by social workers is the policy statement on health of the IFSW (2008; http://

www.ifsw.org/p38000081.html), summarized in seven key propositions:

1 Health is a key aspect of all fields of social work – practice, education, research and policy making – and in all settings.
2 Health is not merely the absence of disease, it encompasses physical, mental, emotional and social wellbeing.
3 Health is a central dimension of people's lives.
4 Health is an issue of fundamental human rights.
5 Health status is primarily determined by social, economic, environmental and political conditions and is an issue of social equality and justice.
6 Securing and sustaining health depends on local, national and global health and social policies and practices.
7 Securing and sustaining health depends on the concerted actions of international institutions, governments, civil society and peoples.

The full version of the policy contains a statement of the main issues for social work's role in health and a background analysis, as well as an extended account of these seven key points.

The origins of the statement can be seen in the WHO constitution discussed earlier, in that it adopts the holistic definition of health and asserts that health is an issue of human rights and social justice. It also endorses the thrust of the CSDH in focusing attention on the social determinants of health: 'the circumstances in which people grow, live, work, and age, and the systems put in place to deal with illness' (CSDH, 2008: Preface). A number of other key points follow from these central planks of the policy.

The first is that health is *all* social workers' business, whatever setting or organization they work in, because social work addresses the social determinants of health. Almost all those who use social work services – in all work settings and all countries – are either those whose physical and/or mental health is already poor or whose future health is threatened by the poor social and environmental conditions in which they live, and have lived across their lifecourse (McLeod and Bywaters, 2000). Many social workers, moreover, specifically work in the international health sphere. Front line social workers in U.N. agencies (e.g. UNICEF) and in international non-governmental organizations (INGOs; e.g. Oxfam, Project Hope, International Red Cross) are faced with providing direct services around the globe to those most in need (Jones, 2000; NASW, 2011).

Second, by arguing that health is a central dimension of people's lives, the policy is not only saying that health matters a great deal to people – which, of course, it does – it is saying that, whenever possible, people work for their own health on a daily basis. Stacey (1988) suggested that everyone is a lay health worker, in terms of choices about what to eat and drink, whether to take medication or exercise, working to get health back after illness or hospitalization, and balancing work and leisure. Many people also manage the health of children, partners, parents, relatives and friends at the same time. This lay health work – work people do for their own health and as informal carers of others – is the majority of health work and without it the healthcare professionals' work would be much less effective. Social professionals and development workers in both the global North and South often recognize the importance of lay health work and that lay health workers are experts on their own lives and their own health. However, social workers in some settings fail to recognize the health dimensions of their work or perceive health-related social work only as a specialist role. In the global North, informal carers, including children, are often relied on by welfare systems and the commitment of social care staff is exploited (Becker, 2007) while in the global South, informal care is likely to be the norm in the absence of well-developed health and social work services.

Third, the right to health includes the right to the resources which underpin health, to universal affordable basic healthcare, and the right to participate in decision making about health at the individual and policy levels. That is why IFSW opposes unregulated,

market-driven economic policies which convert health from a right to a commercial opportunity. When health is a commodity, unnecessary treatments are sold, people put their own lives at risk to make money from their bodies and the quality of the healthcare they can receive becomes a function of how much money they earn or how much wealth they can command (Blyth, 2009). That is why the policy states that it is governments, rather than the market, which must lead health policy making and why social workers should intervene in policy making processes at every level as well as through direct practice with individuals, groups and communities.

Fourth, securing and sustaining health depends on concerted international action. Because the context for health social work is increasingly global, responses must be global too. So the policy argues that social workers must hold governments to account for the commitments they have already made to the universal right to health in collaboration with others who share social work's values and objectives. Central also must be alliances with those who use health services, or who would if they could afford them, and with the global and local popular health movements. However, the capacity of IFSW to pursue this policy internationally is very limited and it has no permanent official standing with the WHO.

Other international structures and opportunities

Since the mid-1990s, a series of conferences under the title of 'Social Work in Health and Mental Health' have been held in various parts of the world. These have provided a major platform for discussion and debate across national boundaries with over 200 papers being given at the conference in Dublin (in 2010). The impetus for these conferences came from social workers in Australia, Israel and the USA who met at the pioneering Mount Sinai Leadership

Enhancement Programme initiated by Helen Rehr (Nilsson and Wellington-Boyd, 2006) which has itself been a powerful medium for exchanges albeit mainly between staff from the same three countries. One by-product of these conferences has been the establishment of the Social Work and Health Inequalities Network (www.warwick.ac.uk/go/swhin), with over 250 members in 25 countries in 2012. The Network aims to promote discussion and action by social work practitioners, managers, educators and researchers to combat the causes and consequences of unjust and damaging socially created inequalities in health. It has produced books and special issues of journals, run international seminars, had a significant presence at conferences and led the re-writing of the IFSW policy. There are other international health related social work associations, notably the Association of Oncology Social Work (http://www.aosw.org/html/about.php) with over 1000 members, (mainly in the USA). Another example is the Academic Network of European Disability experts (ANED) created by the European Commission in December 2007 with the aim of establishing and maintaining a pan-European academic network in the disability field that will support policy development in collaboration with the Commission's Disability Unit (http://www.disability-europe.net/en/about%20us).

There are two major US journals with a specific focus on health social work, *Social Work in Healthcare* and *Health and Social Work*, which accept a few international articles in English. But there is little exchange, for example, between social workers in South America and those in developed, western nations, and few published accounts of health social work in Africa where health outcomes are so markedly poor.

KEY ISSUES

We now explore the themes discussed above through the discussion of four key global health issues: illnesses, people, providers and activism. These four issues were selected because they cross national boundaries and impact health on a global level. Although it is possible to discuss any given health topic on a national or regional level, it is appropriate here to give examples of these topics from the vantage point of their impact on a global level.

Illnesses

The spread of infectious diseases is probably one of the most recognizable global health issues attributable to diseases such as HIV/AIDS, malaria, TB, SARS, swine flu, and West Nile virus. Social workers around the globe are involved in the treatment and impact of these illnesses on individuals, families, communities, and nations. The mobility of today's society elevates epidemic risks as diseases rapidly spread across borders (Lyons et al., 2006). To take one example, the AIDS epidemic is unparalleled in its effects on the global community. Since the beginning of the epidemic, almost 60 million people have been infected with HIV and 25 million people have died from HIV-related causes (UNAIDS, 2009). Despite available global resources to fight this epidemic, HIV and AIDS have an impact worldwide, as illustrated in Table 13.3.

There are several trends that shape the global epidemiological curve, including factors such as geographical region, an increasingly mobile global population, gender inequality, age, and access to antiretroviral medications (UNAIDS, 2009; Coovadia and Hadingham, 2005). Gender plays a key role in the prevention and transmission of HIV. Early in the epidemic, HIV infection and AIDS were primarily diagnosed in men, but today, the HIV/AIDS epidemic represents a growing and persistent health threat to women around the globe (UNAIDS/UNFPA/UNIFEM, 2004). Women now represent half of all adults living with HIV/AIDS, with the percentage as high as 60 percent among

Table 13.3   Regional statistics for HIV and AIDS, end of 2008

Region	Adults and children living with HIV/AIDS	Adults and children newly infected	Adult prevalence*	Deaths of adults and children
Sub-Saharan Africa	22.4 million	1.9 million	5.2%	1.4 million
North Africa and Middle East	310,000	35,000	0.2%	20,000
South and South-East Asia	3.8 million	280,000	0.3%	270,000
East Asia	850,000	75,000	<0.1%	59,000
Oceania	59,000	3900	0.3%	2000
Latin America	2.0 million	170,000	0.6%	77,000
Caribbean	240,000	20,000	1.0%	12,000
Eastern Europe and Central Asia	1.5 million	110,000	0.7%	87,000
North America	1.4 million	55,000	0.4%	25,000
Western and Central Europe	850,000	30,000	0.3%	13,000
Total	33.4 million	2.7 million	0.8%	2.0 million

*Proportion of adults aged 15–49 living with HIV/AIDS.
Source: UNAIDS (2009) AIDS Epidemic Update: Global Facts and Figures. World Health Organization.

young women between the ages of 15 and 24. Due to a combination of gender inequality, power theory and socioeconomic factors, some women may be unaware of their male partners' sexual behaviour or feel powerless to insist on condom use or negotiate safe-sex practices due to fear of repercussions to the relationship including abuse or abandonment (MacMaster et al., 2008). The problem is further compounded by the fact that infected women can pass the infection to a baby during pregnancy, delivery or breastfeeding. In 2008, approximately 430,000 children were born with HIV, the total estimate of children under 15 living with HIV increasing to over 2 million (UNAIDS, 2009). It is essential to address these factors when implementing HIV and other health prevention programmes for women around the globe.

The last decade has witnessed an unprecedented increase in access to HIV treatment through antiretroviral therapies (ART). Between 2003 and 2008, access to antiretroviral drugs in low and middle income countries rose 10-fold, helping to decrease the number of HIV-related deaths (UNAIDS, 2009). However, although industrialized countries have been reaping the benefits of ART for many years, results are only recently beginning to emerge in resource-limited

countries. For example, Africa is experiencing significant public health benefits associated with improved treatment access. In the Western Cape Province of South Africa, six-month mortality among patients at an HIV treatment centre fell by roughly half (from 12.7 percent to 6.6 percent) following the introduction of ART (Boulle et al., 2008), and northern Malawi witnessed a population-level reduction in mortality of 35 percent among adults following the introduction of ART (Jahn et al., 2008). But, despite considerable progress, global coverage remains low with only 42% of people in need of treatment having access to ART. Furthermore, only 38% of children from developing countries in need of treatment received ART in 2008 (UNAIDS, 2009).

Notwithstanding some positive gains, there is a significant shortfall in the resources and funds available to fight various infectious and non-infectious diseases and the future outlook is grim. The global economic downturn has resulted in a flatline for contributions (UN News Centre, 2010). The lack of funds and resources to fight these epidemics is resulting in millions of people being denied access to prevention and treatment, including women, young people and children. Health systems in developing countries are often unable to cope with the demands being placed on them to distribute funds, while single-disease funding can result in distortions in health systems and a lack of aid being delivered effectively to those most in need (Coovadia and Hadingham, 2005).

Social workers are trained to address human rights issues and are uniquely placed within a wide variety of health and welfare settings to make an effective contribution to the global effort to address infectious diseases, such as HIV/AIDS, malaria and TB (IFSW, 2007). Rather than an illness specific approach, they can contribute to capacity building and systematic strengthening of health systems aimed at reducing the inequities in healthcare delivery between resource-rich and -poor countries (Coovadia and Hadingham, 2005). In many countries, social professionals partner with allied health and mental health providers to build a continuum of care for those individuals, families and communities attempting to cope with the impact of both infectious and non-infectious diseases. Globally, social work must engage increasingly in advocacy to ensure that health issues are recognized by service providers and policy makers so that development efforts take into account awareness, prevention and treatment as priority areas in national and international systems and policies (IFSW, 2007).

People

The increased mobility of people has significant implications for health issues and health systems. The cross-border exchange of health workers and health services are changing the dynamics of health delivery systems around the world. One of many aspects of these processes is health tourism (Blyth, 2009). Health tourism is on the rise as national borders become more open and as healthcare cost and availability continue to vary between countries around the globe. Wealthy patients from developing countries have long travelled to developed countries for high quality

medical care, and a growing number of less-affluent patients from developed countries are now travelling to regions once characteried as 'third world', seeking high quality medical care at affordable prices (Herrick, 2007). Reports on the number of patients travelling abroad for healthcare are scattered. It is estimated, however, that approximately 250,000 foreign patients sought care in Singapore, 500,000 in India and as many as 1 million in Thailand during 2005 (Herrick, 2007). Healthcare tourism travels all ways, not simply rich to poor, but also rich to rich, and poor to rich for specialised treatments. Generally, social and economic determinants of health have to do with money but also with belief systems. For example, in some developed countries such as Hong Kong, disability and mental health are greatly stigmatized, resulting in people hiding or seeking care outside the country.

Health tourism could be viewed as a benefit to host countries and consumers in many ways. First and foremost, health tourism can be very financially rewarding for less-developed countries. In 2006, the medical tourism industry grossed about US$60 billion worldwide, and it is estimated to reach US$100 billion by 2012 (Herrick, 2007). As a major draw for and benefit to consumers, prices for treatment are lower in foreign hospitals, for a number of reasons, including lower labour costs; third parties (insurance and government) being uninvolved or less involved; increased price transparency with package pricing; fewer attempts to shift the cost of charity care to paying patients; fewer regulations limiting collaborative arrangements between healthcare facilities and physicians; and lower litigation costs (Herrick, 2007). However, health tourism often comes at a cost for the local population and creates issues of staff poaching. For example, in Thailand, the resources used to service one foreigner may be equivalent to those used to service four or five local Thai patients, which can result in lack of services provided to local patients (Labonte et al., 2010). Some countries (e.g. Thailand, India, Philippines and South Korea) are building private high-end hospitals partially staffed with medical personnel, particularly nurses, from more wealthy countries to cater to health tourism (Labonte et al., 2010).

Another issue is that medical tourism is often related to new technologies, moral values, or controversial treatments, such as end of life options, stem cell transplants, surrogacy or the international organ trade. For example, the most common form of international organ trade is 'transplant tourism', where potential recipients travel abroad to undergo an organ transplant. Several websites offer all-inclusive 'transplant packages' for a variety of organs, including liver, kidney, heart, and pancreas (Shimazono, 2007). These, like many other global health issues, are a consequence of global inequities and can be categorized as human rights issues. Social workers need to work with other professions and non-governmental organizations on health issues that can be characterized as human rights issues and advocate against inequalities in health and health practices (IFSW, 2005).

As social workers, it is important to advocate for equality in access to healthcare regardless of income or ability to seek treatment outside one's own country. The long-term implications of this new trend in global healthcare for health service delivery to local patients, staffing of medical services, quality of care and social work roles are yet to be fully understood. Additionally, the effects of healthcare tourism on the healthcare industry in tourists' countries of origin have yet to be fully studied, and may have unknown consequences in care available. Staff poaching is taking place across health and related fields resulting in staff shortages, including of social workers, in many countries, not least those of the global south (IFSW, 2008). The lack of social workers has significant implications for provision of services and care for the most vulnerable populations. Front line social professionals in UN organizations and INGOs are regularly confronted with these issues often without the financial resources

and institutional capacity necessary to address them at an international level.

Providers

The past several decades have seen radical changes in economic paradigms, promoting deregulation of developing countries' markets and new international agreements on international trade and finances, which have contributed to inconsistent outcomes in global health status and had significant implications for the provision of social work services. Two examples of global trade agreements that have direct health effects are the General Agreement on Trade in Services (GATS) and the Agreement on Trade Related Intellectual Property Rights (TRIPS). TRIPS introduced global minimum standards for the protection of patents, trademarks, copyrights and other intellectual property rights. The main impact of this agreement has been to increase drug prices in countries introducing drug patents and restricting the possibility of producing or importing essential drugs in developing countries (Labonte et al., 2010). Due to the risks involved in new trade agreements such as TRIPS, the World Health Assembly in May 1999 mandated WHO to monitor the health consequences of international trade agreements (Cornia, 2001).

These global economic changes have sparked profound alterations in the actors that exert influence in global health as well as the roles and norms within these global health systems. Traditional players in global health, such as the WHO, are now being joined and/or challenged by a variety of UN organizations, INGOs, low- and middle-income national governments, private firms, and private philanthropists (Szlezak et al., 2010). This increase in health providers, policy makers, and lobbying bodies creates new challenges regarding the roles and norms of various stakeholders. Moon and colleagues (2010) argue that a successful global health system in the current economic climate must undertake five core functions: agenda-setting;

financing and resource allocation; research and development; implementation and delivery; and monitoring, evaluation, and learning. They further contend that global partnership is essential to the success of an effective global health system and that no single stakeholder can or should set the agenda for action. However, for an efficient global health system, these stakeholders must strive to work in concert. Lessons from the fight against HIV/AIDS and malaria are two examples of the importance of global partnerships and the importance of taking into account the cultural and political climate of local communities and health systems (Moon, et al., 2010; Keusch, et al., 2010). In order to be successful in future health endeavours, global health systems must devise mechanisms for finding and targeting health consumers who suffer from specific illnesses; partners who contribute to research and development; and health practitioners and organizations that ultimately deliver interventions (Keusch et al., 2010). It is essential that long-term investments in education and training are provided at multiple levels to ensure the success of global health systems (Frenk, 2010; Moon, et al., 2010).

These global trends affect access to frontline social work services around the globe, particularly personnel working in UN organizations and INGOs. The IFSW (2008) argues that the right to social services is an inseparable part of health and healthcare along with interventions in formal medical settings. Social workers need to advocate for the social understanding of health and the roles social work can play in working for better health for individuals, families, communities, and populations. There is a substantial gap in the availability of frontline social work services to meet individual and collective needs across the range of community, clinic and hospital settings, resulting in many individuals and families being unable to access social work services (IFSW, 2008). A core objective of IFSW policy is to extend the availability of health social work services across the range of work settings, but this requires a commitment to train and resource frontline social workers. As globalization continues to impact people's access to healthcare and health outcomes, social workers need to engage more effectively at a policy level with international institutions with responsibilities for influencing healthcare and/or with non-governmental organisations working for health-related development (IFSW, 2008).

Activism

Over the past several decades, there have been significant changes in the role of consumers and advocates in the healthcare arena. A variety of movements across the globe (e.g. People's Health Movement and survivor/service user movements, consumer empowerment movements) have fostered the ability of consumers to take an active role in decisions and policies related to their health issues and the delivery of health services. An example of this trend is provided by the disability rights movement.

Before the development of the International Classification of Impairment, Disability and Handicap (ICIDH), there was no international organized disability rights movement (WHO, 2001). In fact, it was not until the 1980s that people with disabilities united in a recognised international force. Initially, scholars noted that the ICIDH model of impairment was the fundamental cause of the segregation of disabled people into institutions, inaccessible homes, and separate communities. People with disabilities also realized that 'unless they could live fully participating lives, their innate humanity – and the rights that pertain to that humanity – would never be recognised' (Hurst, 2003: 573). As a result, over the next several years, during the writing of the *International Classification of Function, Disability and Health* (ICF) (WHO, 2001), the rights of people with disabilities moved to the forefront of public debate. People with disabilities argued that disability is the outcome of environmental barriers and attitudes that discriminate against people with impairments (Hahn, 1985; Hurst, 2003).

However, the ICIDH had a lasting negative effect on the rights of such people because it perpetuated the idea that able-bodied people were normal while people with disabilities were not. This idea amplified the concept of disability, equating it with incapacity, impairment, and a lack of functioning (Hurst, 2003). As a result (during the revision of the ICIDH to the ICF) disability rights advocates proposed a social model of disability that identified the environment and its inherent barriers as causes of disability. With the new revisions introduced in 2001, the ICF has moved away from simply noting the consequences of disease and disablement to classifying components of health rather than impairment. This represented a change from labelling individuals by 'disability', 'impairments', and 'handicaps' to more neutral or positive terms, such as 'body functions and structures', 'activity', and 'participation'. Additionally, the ICF was created to measure more than the diagnosed condition by also including the consequences of the condition. The ICF (WHO, 2001) describes disability as the intersection between the biological body and the social and institutional structures surrounding it (Hurst, 2003; Imrie, 2004; Ueda and Okawa, 2003).

While the ICF embraces a model of empowering the minority group, the healthcare systems of many countries continue to operate under the bio-medical models of disease and disorder definition. Social workers who embrace or practice in a bio-medical model may find it difficult to view individuals with physical disabilities as healthy, self-determined beings. The social model, shifting attention away from the functional limitation of a person, focuses on the social environments that impose restrictions upon people with disabilities (Fine and Asch, 1988; Hahn, 1985) and mirrors social work ethical principles of social justice and service. Social workers are expected to address social problems and injustices and to pursue social

change on behalf of vulnerable and oppressed people. Empowerment social work embraces the social justice contract between individuals and society. It is incumbent on social workers to emphasize empowerment objectives rather than mere compliance with medically prescribed treatment plans or psychosocial clinical interventions (Beaulaurier and Taylor, 2001).

CONCLUSION

What will the future look like for international health social work? We have argued that health is a central battle ground for global policy making. International economic, social, environmental, and political arrangements affecting income and wealth, food, water, employment, and living conditions impact profoundly on people's health and the provision of healthcare is increasingly a globalized industry with overlapping elements affecting health insurance and other payments systems, health and social care services, pharmaceuticals and technology, staffing and regulation. Powerful tensions exist between liberalizing economic forces on the one hand and the movements for human rights, social justice and user empowerment on the other.

Social work's international bodies have clearly aligned themselves with the latter of these two approaches but are in a weak position to influence developments in an unequal world. Practitioners will be increasingly affected by global forces influencing who they serve, who employs them, how they are trained, and what they do. In this context, there is a continuing need to:

- develop the research base to underpin social work education and practice for health;
- articulate and make the case for social work's contribution to people's health and to reducing health inequity;
- make alliances with those professionals and activists who share common aims and values.

These three objectives can be enacted wherever social workers operate: on the front line of practice, in inter-professional and policy making forums within countries, and where opportunities present themselves for international action.

NOTES

1 Different approaches to the possible content of a chapter about social work and health in a global context reflect varied perspectives on the notion of international social work. Other authors have chosen to compare and contrast the different forms which medical or health-related social work takes in different countries (Heinonen and Metteri 2005; Berkman and D'Ambruoso, 2006). We have chosen rather to focus on a major aspect of healthcare – inequalities related in part to processes of globalization – and some of the concomitant challenges and opportunities facing social workers, internationally, whether they specialize in health social work or in the course of their daily practice.

2 The Commission on the Social Determinants of Health (CSDH, 2008: Preface) defines health inequity as 'avoidable health inequalities (which) arise because of the circumstances in which people grow, live, work, and age, and the systems put in place to deal with illness. The conditions in which people live and die are, in turn, shaped by political, social, and economic forces'.

REFERENCES

Altman, D. (1999) 'Globalization, political economy and HIV/AIDS', *Theory and Society*, 28: 559–84.

Bancroft, A. (2001) 'Globalisation and HIV/AIDS: inequality and the boundaries of a symbolic epidemic, *Health, Risk & Society*, 3(1): 89–98.

Bell, E.M. (1961) *The Story of Hospital Almoners*. London: Faber and Faber.

Beaulaurier, R. and Taylor, S. (2001) 'Social work practice with people with disabilities in the era of disability rights', *Social Work in Healthcare*, 32: 67–91.

Becker, S. (2007) 'Global perspectives on children's unpaid caregiving in the family research and policy on 'young carers' in the UK, Australia, the USA and sub-Saharan Africa', *Global Social Policy*, 7(1): 23–50.

Berkman, B. and D'Ambruoso, S. (eds) (2006) *Handbook of Social Work in Health and Ageing.* New York: Oxford University Press.

Bloom, D.E. and Canning, D. (2000) 'The health and wealth of nations', *Science*, 287: 1207–9.

Blyth, E. (2009) 'Reproduction in the global marketplace', in P. Bywaters, E. McLeod, and L. Napier (eds) *Social Work and Global Health Inequalities*. Bristol: Policy Press.

Boulle, A., Bock, P., Osler, M., Cohen, K., Channing, L., Hilderbrand, K., Mothibi, E., Zweigenthal, V., Slingers, N., Cloete, K. and Abdullah, F. (2008) 'Antiretroviral therapy and early mortality in South Africa', *Bulletin of the World Health Organization*, 86: 678–87.

Bywaters, P. (1986) 'Social work and the medical profession – arguments against unconditional collaboration', *British Journal of Social Work*, 16(6): 661–77.

Bywaters, P., McLeod, E. and Napier, L. (eds.) (2009) *Social Work and Global Health Inequalities*. Bristol: Policy Press.

Commission on the Social Determinants of Health. (2008) 'Closing the gap in a generation: health equity through action on the social determinants of health', *Final Report of the Commission on Social Determinants of Health*. Geneva: World Health Organization.

Coovadia, H.M. and Hadingham, J. (2005) 'HIV/AIDS: global trends, global funds and delivery bottlenecks', *Globalization and Health*, 1(13). Available at http://www.globalizationandhealth.com/content/1/1/13, accessed 25 August 2010.

Cornia, G.A. (2001) 'Globalization and health: results and options', *Bulletin of the World Health Organization*, 79: 9, available through http://www.scielosp.org/scielo.php?script=sci_arttext&pid=S0042-96862001000900008&lng=en&nrm=iso, accessed 25 August 2010.

Ferguson, I. (2008) *Reclaiming Social Work: Challenging Neo-Liberalism And Promoting Social Justice.* London: SAGE.

Fine, M. and Asch, A. (1988) 'Beyond disability and stigma: social interaction, discrimination, and activism', *Journal of Social Issues*, 44: 3–21.

Frenk, J. (2010) 'The global health system: strengthening national health systems as the next step for global progress', *PLoS Medicine*, 7(1): e1000089, doi:10.1371/journal.pmed.1000089.

Global Health Watch (2005) *Global Health Watch 2005–2006. An Alternative World Health Report.* London/New York: Zed Books.

Hahn, H. (1985) 'Toward a politics of disability: definitions, disciplines and policies', *Social Science*, 22: 87–105.

Heinonen, T. and Metteri, A. (eds) (2005) *Social Work In Health And Mental Health: Issues, Developments And Actions*. Toronto, ON: Canadian Scholars' Press.

Herrick, D.M. (2007) *Medical Tourism: Global Competition in Healthcare*. Policy Report 304, available at: http://www.unf.edu/brooks/center/pdfs/Medical%20Tourism%20Herrick.pdf, accessed 30 August 2010.

Hurst, R. (2003) 'The international disability rights movement', *Disability and Rehabilitation, 25*: 572–6.

Imrie, R. (2004) 'Demystifying disability: a review of the International Classification of Functioning, Disability and Health', *Sociology of Health and Illness, 3*: 287–305.

IFSW (International Federation of Social Workers) (2005) *International Policy on Human Rights*, available at: http://www.ifsw.org/p38000212.html, accessed 7 September 2010.

IFSW (International Federation of Social Workers) (2007) *International Policy on HIV/AIDS*, available at http://www.ifsw.org/p38001031.html, accessed 7 September 2010.

IFSW (International Federation of Social Workers) (2008) *International Policy on Health*, available at http://www.ifsw.org/p38000081.html, accessed 25 August 2010.

Jahn, A., Floyd, S., Crampin, A.C., Mwaungulu, F., Mvula, H., Munthall, F., McGrath, N., Mwafilaso, J., Mwinuka, V., Mangongo, B., Fine, P., Zaba, B. and Glynn, J.R. (2008) 'Population-level effect of HIV on adult mortality and early evidence of reversal after introduction of antiretroviral therapy in Malawi', *Lancet, 371*: 1603–11.

Jones, M. (2000) 'Hope and despair at the front line: observations on integrity and change in the human services', *International Social Work*, 43(3): 365–80.

Keusch, G.T., Kilama, W.L., Moon, S., Szlezak, N.A. and Michaud, C.M. (2010) 'The global health system: linking knowledge with action—learning from malaria', *PLoS Medicine* 7(1): e1000179, doi:10.1371/journal.pmed.1000179.

Labonte, R. and Schrecker, T. (2007a) 'Globalization and social determinants of health: introduction and methodological background', *Globalization and Health*, 3, article 5.

Labonte, R. and Schrecker, T. (2007b) 'Globalization and social determinants of health: the role of the gobal marketplace', *Globalization and Health, 3*, article 6.

Labonte, R. and Schrecker, T. (2007c) 'Globalization and social determinants of health: promoting health equity in global governance' *Globalization and Health*, 3, article 7.

Labonte, R., Blouin, C. and Forman, L. (2010) 'Trade, growth and population health: an introductory review', *Transdisciplinary Studies in Population Health Series*, 2(1). Institute of Population Health, Ottawa, Canada.

Lancet (2008) 'Margaret Chan puts primary health-care centre stage at WHO', *Lancet*, 371(9627): 1811.

Lyons, K., Manion K. and Carlsen, M. (2006) *International Perspectives on Social Work: Global Conditions and Local Practice*. Basingstoke, Palgrave Macmillan.

MacMaster, S., Bride, B., Davis, C. and Docktor, L. (2008) 'International perspectives on women and HIV: an overview', *Human Behavior in the Social Environment*, 17(3/4): 231–5.

Marmot, M. (2004) *The Status Syndrome: How Your Social Standing Affects Your Health And Life Expectancy*. London: Bloomsbury.

Marmot, M. (2010) *Fair Society, Healthy Lives: a Strategic Review of Health Inequalities in England Post-2010*. London: The Marmot Review.

McLeod, E. and Bywaters, P. (2000) *Social Work, Equality and Health*. London: Routledge.

Moon, S., Szlezák, N.A., Michaud, C.M., Jamison, D.T., Keusch, G.T., Clark, W.C. and Bloom, B.R. (2010) 'The global health system: lessons for a stronger institutional framework', *PLoS Medicine*, 7(1): e1000193, doi:10.1371/journal.pmed.1000193.

NASW (National Association of Social Workers). (2011) *Choices*, available at: www.socialworkers.org/pubs/choices/choices2.asp, accessed 5 August 2011.

Nilsson, D. and Wellington-Boyd, A. (2006) 'Outcomes from the Mount Sinai Social Work Leadership Enhancement Program: evaluation and extrapolation', *Social Work in Healthcare*, 43(2–3): 163–72.

Shimazono, Y. (2007) 'The state of the international organ trade: a provisional picture based on the intergration of available information' *Bulletin of the World Health Organization*, 85: 955–62.

Stacey, M. (1988) *The Sociology of Health and Healing*. London: Unwin Hyman.

Sulman, J., Savage, D. and Way, S. (2001) 'Retooling social work practice for high volume short stay', *Social Work in Healthcare,* 34(3–4): 315–32.

Szlezak, N.A., Bloom, B.R., Jamison, D.T., Keusch, G.T., Michaud, C.M., Moon, S. and Clark, W.C. (2010) 'The global health system: actors, norms, and expectations in transition', *PLoS Medicine* 7(1): e1000183, doi:10.1371/journal.pmed.1000183.

Ueda, S. and Okawa, Y. (2003) 'The subjective dimension of functioning and disability: what is it and what is it for?' *Disability and Rehabilitation,* 25(11–12): 596–601.

UN (United Nations). (2000) *United Nations Millennium Declaration* A/RES/55/2, available at: http://www.undemocracy.com/A-RES-55-2.pdf, accessed 15 September 2010.

UNAIDS (2009) *Global Facts and Figures 2009,* available at: http://data.unaids.org/pub/FactSheet/2009/20091124_FS_global_en.pdf, accessed 27 August 2010.

UNAIDS/UNFPA/UNIFEM (Joint United Nations Program on HIV/AIDS United Nations Population Fund/United Nations Development Fund for Women) (2004) *Women and HIV/AIDS: Confronting the Crisis.* Geneva: Author.

UN data. (2010) *Maternal Mortality Ratio (per 100,000 Live Births),* available at: http://data.un.org/Data.aspx?q=maternal+mortality+ratio&d=MDG&f=seriesRowID%3a553, accessed 15 August 2010.

UN News Centre. (19 July 2010) *UN Records Massive Rise in Number of People Receiving HIV Treatment,* available at: http://www.un.org/apps/news/story.asp?NewsID=35355&Cr=UNAIDS&Cr1=, accessed 31 August 2010.

Wilkinson, R. and Pickett, K. (2009) *The Spirit Level.* London: Allen Lane.

WHO (World Health Organization). (1946) *Constitution of the World Health Organization,* available at: http://apps.who.int/gb/bd/PDF/bd47/EN/constitution-en.pdf, accessed 25 August 2010.

WHO (World Health Organization). (1978) *Declaration of Alma Ata,* available at: http://www.who.int/hpr/NPH/docs/declaration_almaata.pdf, accessed 25 August 2010.

WHO (World Health Organization). (2001) *World Health Assembly Resolution 54.21,* available at: http://www.who.int/classifications/icf/wha-en.pdf, accessed 14 September 2010.

14

Social Work and Education

Marion Huxtable, Cynthia A. Sottie
and Khuajin Ulziitungalag

INTRODUCTION

Social work and education are complementary professions. The purpose of social work is to promote human wellbeing, human rights and social justice, with special attention to those who are marginalised by society, experiencing oppression, poverty or disability. Education is dedicated to developing human potential through transmitting knowledge, skills and values. Social work, using ecological systems theory to mobilize the strengths of school, family and community, is well-suited to supporting education by helping learners (from pre-school through tertiary education, including informal education and adult literacy) to overcome obstacles to educational success.

With the fast pace of social change, schools are increasingly recognizing that they cannot handle alone the issues that prevent the success of their students, and that they must tackle these problems as interdisciplinary teams using expert knowledge and skills of various support personnel, including, in some countries, school social workers. Where formal school social work services exist, the mission is to help school systems meet various performance goals and mandates for

inclusion by reducing personal and systemic barriers. School social workers may work with students individually or in groups, with their families and with whole communities to tackle problems that affect school attendance and performance. However, in many developing countries, access to education is still out of reach for portions of the population, social workers may be in short supply and specialist school social work may not exist. Responsibilities for addressing the educational needs of young people and adults may rest with other social professionals, for example, those working on community development programmes. The guiding principles for all social workers working with school populations are the right to education that respects the dignity, worth and culture of the individual and the goal of helping all learners reach their potential. There are commonalities regarding the basic social work methods, plus variations suited to local situations and cultures.

Although many of the problems faced by education systems are similar around the world, most social professionals dealing with these issues have little professional contact beyond the local school system or professional association. As the world becomes increasingly connected and awareness of the interdependence of national economies and societies grows, social workers are starting to reach out to colleagues outside of their immediate work area. For example, school social workers have developed an international network (http://internationalnetwork-schoolsocialwork.htmlplanet.com/) that has fostered wider communication and enabled school social workers to expand their vision of the role.

This chapter presents education as the basis for positive individual, community and societal development, including sustainable development of the global economy. It describes the Education for All (EFA) initiatives (United Nations Education, Scientific and Cultural Organization, hereafter UNESCO, 1990a, b). It presents the role of social professionals (school social workers and social pedagogues) in helping reduce obstacles to success in educational institutions, together with a summary of the development of school social work, its current status and international commonalities and variations, with some reference to national professional associations, training, licensing and texts. Case studies of the development of school social work in Ghana and Mongolia illustrate issues accompanying the introduction of social work into the school system. Future challenges and opportunities for the intersection of education and social work are described, including the use of information and communication technology as a tool for advancing educational opportunities and for enhancing social work practice. In conclusion, the authors call for the social work profession to become an international advocate for the right to education and for support services in educational institutions.

EDUCATION AS A UNIVERSAL RIGHT AND BARRIERS TO EDUCATIONAL SUCCESS

Since the *Universal Declaration of Human Rights* was adopted by the United Nations

General Assembly in 1948 (UN, 1948a), the international community has refined *Article 26, The Right to Education* (UN, 1948b), in an ongoing series of declarations and conventions. In 1976, in the *International Covenant on Economic, Social and Cultural Rights* (UN, 1976), and in 1990, with the *Convention on the Rights of the Child* (UNICEF, 1990), the international community affirmed that primary education shall be free and compulsory and that secondary and higher education be made available to all (Appendix 5).

In 1990, the World Conference on Education for All, with delegates from 155 countries, established a framework for child, family and adult education with goals and specific targets (UNESCO, 1990a, b): the Millennium Development Goals (MDGs see Appendix 6) for primary education and gender equity parallel the EFA goals. In 2000, the EFA assessment found that progress had been uneven and slow: less than a third of children of pre-school age had any pre-school education, 113 million children (60 percent of them girls) had no access to primary education and 800 million adults (mostly women) were illiterate. New targets were set for 2015, with specific objectives for early childhood education, free and compulsory primary education, youth and adult education programmes, eliminating gender disparity in primary and secondary education and improving the quality of education with measurable outcomes (UNESCO, 2000).

UNESCO's *EFA Global Monitoring Report* of 2010 (UNESCO, 2010a) provides information about significant progress towards each of these goals. For example, the number of primary school children out of school had dropped from 113 million to 72 million, with less gender disparity. However, it warned that the global financial crisis could erode the gains as education budgets are cut, while unemployment and poverty levels rise. For example, current trends would leave 56 million children out of school by 2015.

Enrolling and retaining all children in school is the first step needed for effective education worldwide. UNESCO and UNICEF have different ways of estimating the percentage of children not in school, but produced a joint estimate in 2005 that showed that 18% of children of primary-school age were out of school (UNESCO, 2005: 18). The average number of years spent in formal primary, secondary and tertiary schooling is another measure of the goal to enrol and retain children in school. The *EFA Global Monitoring Report* of 2010 shows 16 years of schooling on average in North America and Western Europe; at least 11 years in most other regions with the exception of South and West Asia (9.6 years) and sub-Saharan Africa (8.6 years). Sub-Saharan Africa shows the greatest gender disparity with females averaging 7.9 years of schooling compared with 9.3 years for males (Education for All, 2010: 339). However, there have also been increases in literacy in most countries over a 20-year period, including in sub-Saharan Africa (UNESCO, 2010a: 416).

The progress in educating girls has produced a corresponding improvement in child health. Gakidou et al.'s study (2010) found that 'The rapid progress in educational attainment of women has resulted in significant reductions in the gender gap in education. The effect of educational expansion on child health has been enormous. 4.2 million deaths averted can be attributed to the increase in women's education'. They further suggest that rapid progress in MDG 4 ('Reduce by two thirds the mortality rate among children under five') might be possible.

Even while progress is being made, wide disparities remain in access to education between countries and between specific groups. Among the various disadvantaged groups, children living in poverty, working children, children with disabilities and children in states engaged in armed conflict stand out as needing extraordinary educational supports.

World Bank data show 26 percent of the world's population living at a poverty level of less than US$1.25 a day (Chen and Ravallion,

2008). The EFA Global Monitoring Report declares:

> Poverty is one of the most pervasive sources of disadvantage in education. Globally, there are 1.4 billion people surviving on less than $1.25 a day. For these households, the cost of schooling competes with spending on other basic needs such as healthcare and food. Parents' inability to afford education is one of the major reasons why children are not in school, even in countries that have abolished formal school fees, since the cost of uniforms, books and pencils creates barriers to school entry. (UNESCO, 2010a: 25)

The international community has focused on the rights of working children. The participating governments at the International Conference on Child Labour (Oslo, 1997) declared all work that interferes with the child's education unacceptable, and agreed on goals for universal and compulsory basic education, with a particular emphasis on the education of girls (ILO, 1999). The International Labour Organization (ILO) reports that there has been a reduction in child labour, especially among girls and among children working in hazardous conditions, but that the pace of change has slowed since 2008 with the global economic crisis. The ILO's message is, '...we will not eliminate child labour without universal education and, conversely, we will not ensure every child is in school unless we bring an end to child labour, in particular its worst forms' (ILO, 2010: xiv).

UNESCO's Primary Education Web Portal estimates that:

> 40 million out-of-school children have some form of disability. This number is growing due to increasing poverty, armed conflict, child labour, violence and HIV/AIDS. The number of children under the age of 18 with disabilities around the world has been estimated to be between 120 and 150 million. Recent data shows that children with disabilities in developing countries are significantly less likely than their peers to be enrolled in primary school. (UN, 2011, page 206)

In 1993, the General Assembly adopted the *United Nations Standard Rules on the Equalization of Opportunities for Persons with Disabilities*, including the right to equal educational opportunities. The World Conference on Special Needs Education (organized by UNESCO in 1994) set out a framework for action on special needs education endorsing inclusion of children with special needs in regular schools (UNESCO, 1994: 9). This long-standing goal is only feasible if physical and attitudinal barriers are removed and with appropriate educational supports.

One of the most difficult obstacles to providing education is conflict. Save the Children estimates that 43 million out-of-school children live in states experiencing armed conflict (Save the Children UK, 2007). When children and youth are recruited to participate in combat, schooling becomes impossible. Once demobilized, education can help restore youth to community life. Psychosocial support is essential in restoring socialization and self-esteem while students develop literacy and skills to reintegrate into the community (USAID, 2007).

Despite this progress in each of the five EFA goals, it is slow and uneven. The EFA Development Index (a composite measure of the EFA goals) shows that 62 countries, including many developing countries, have achieved or are close to achieving the goals. Thirty-six countries have made some progress and 30 countries (17 of them from sub-Saharan Africa) have low enrolment, gender disparity, and low literacy. Many children, especially from socially marginalized groups, do not reach a satisfactory level of literacy or numeracy, even if enrolled. The *Global Monitoring Report* of 2010 makes the case that education is essential to building productive societies, eliminating inequality and escaping the hardships of poverty but concludes that the global economic slowdown threatens the attainment of the 2015 EFA targets: it issues a call for honouring international aid commitments in a . continued effort to reach marginalized populations (UNESCO, 2010a).

Reaching the EFA goals is the basic challenge but, even if met, much work remains for schools (in both developing and developed countries) to remove further barriers to educational achievement. Rapid social change presents obstacles that prevent children from successfully completing their schooling, including personal and family problems, as well as systemic problems in schools. Personal obstacles include disabilities, physical and mental health problems, drug abuse and teenage pregnancy. Family problems, such as domestic violence, poverty, divorce, child abuse and homelessness, affect significant numbers of children at some point in their education. Systemic school problems, such as inadequate teaching, poor facilities, ineffective classroom management, bullying and prejudice, also affect large numbers of children. Females encounter additional problems in secondary schools (such as lack of toilet facilities and sanitary supplies, sexual harassment and pressure for early marriage) while youths with alternative sexual orientation often also need protection and social support to continue in the school system. Many of the problems that affect children's progress are remarkably similar all over the world, and education systems are searching for ways to reduce the impact they have on children's learning. School staff everywhere have to contend (to varying degrees) with problems of poor attendance or dropout, limited attainment, and behavioural problems. Some schools seek the assistance of other professionals, including social workers (possibly working in multi-disciplinary teams), to assess and address problems reflecting external stresses on individuals, families and communities.

SCHOOL SOCIAL WORK AS A SPECIALISM

Origins and current roles

School social work is a relatively well-defined and researched specialism now found in at least 46 countries around the world. It had its origins in the UK in the late 19th century (Blyth and Cooper, 2002) and in the US early in the 20th century (Costin, 1969), as part of national universal education movements. The initial role of establishing and maintaining school attendance has evolved into wider roles in support of student attainment. The history of school social work shows that roles and methods have been imported and shared internationally, with independent pathways based on national cultures and education traditions.

Between the 1940s and 1970s, social professionals developed specialist roles in schools in 14 countries (including the Nordic states, Germany, Canada, Argentina, UAE and Hong Kong) and in the following period (up to 2007) it has extended to 22 more (Australia, Korea, Japan, Austria, Switzerland, New Zealand, Russia, Latvia, Hungary, Lithuania, Estonia, Saudi Arabia, Luxembourg, Sri Lanka, Taiwan, Mongolia, China, India, Singapore, Pakistan and Liechtenstein.). Most recently, school social work has been introduced as part of social work education in three central European countries: Bulgaria, the Czech Republic and Slovakia (*International Network Newsletters*, December 2007, October 2007, July 2007). There is little information about social work services in schools in many African, Asian and Latin American countries (but see case examples from Ghana and Mongolia later).

School systems around the world are experiencing difficulty meeting educational goals without addressing a wide range of complex human factors that interfere with learning and are not resolved by teaching methods, educational resources and good school management alone. Consequently, schools in many countries work (to varying degrees) with social workers, social pedagogues, and other human service professionals (e.g. nurses, psychologists and counsellors) to address these factors.

A major role for social work in countries where widespread poverty and the accompanying child labour contributes to under-enrolment in school is to support EFA targets by encouraging families to enrol children, providing for basic needs (e.g. school meals) and maintaining school attendance. Few of the countries where a significant percentage of the population lives below the World Bank's poverty level (US\$1.25 per day) have school social work programmes, but international aid programmes can help fund social workers to serve school populations (see the Mongolia case study below; Save the Children UK, 2007).

Where education is universal and compulsory and where poverty is relative and child labour less common, there are, nevertheless, many issues in schools that call for the expertise of social professionals. Ideally their roles are broad and flexible, using a systems approach with school, family and community on a wide range of changing problems.

Schools are charged not only with resolving the problems that interfere with learning, but also with providing preventive programmes to address various social and health problems, such as child abuse, bullying, drug abuse, teenage pregnancy, and discrimination of all kinds: social professionals are well-placed to develop and run such programmes.

Social pedagogy is a holistic child development profession, closely associated with education, and focusing on social development through extensive use of group work. It is unknown in North America, but is well-established in schools in many European countries (e.g. Belgium, Denmark, Spain and some of the former Soviet Union countries). In Germany, the professions of social pedagogy and social work have become more integrated (Wulfers, 2002) and in many of the German *Länder* school social workers are providing both typical social work services for troubled youth and extra-curricular and leisure activities more usually associated with social pedagogy (Terner and Rademacker, 2010).

Organization of school social workers varies between countries. For example, in the United States, Sweden and Finland (Allen-Meares, 2009; Anderson et al., 2002), social work services are an integral part of the school system and practitioners are typically part of a multi-disciplinary team, while elsewhere, for example, Hong Kong (Chiu and Wong, 2002), the service is provided through non-governmental organizations. In Germany (Wulfers, 2002), school social work is often provided through collaboration between youth welfare agencies and the school system. Working within the school system (especially if the social worker is assigned to a single school) provides opportunities for close working relationships with school staff, long-term initiatives, efforts to improve school culture and developing partnerships with community agencies: where it is customary to provide the service through an outside agency, advantages include greater independence and closer relationships with other agency services.

Variations in the job titles used by social professionals working with schools reflect different emphases in their roles. In the Nordic countries, for example, the title *school curator* (Latin: *cura* meaning care) projects a sense of supporting and helping (Anderson et al., 2002), while in the UK, the terms education welfare officer and education social worker are both used, reflecting the dual role of attendance enforcement and a wider, more therapeutic social work role (Blyth and Cooper, 2002). In Canada, the title can be school social worker or school social worker/ attendance counsellor (Loughborough et al., 2002), while in the United States, the title is usually school social worker. (However many social workers hold alternative positions in schools depending on the programme they are assigned to.)

Training, standards, literature, professional associations and international communication

An international 2006 survey found that the most common educational requirements for school social work are a bachelor's or master's degree (International Network for School Social Work). (The field of social pedagogy similarly requires a higher education award at bachelor's or master's degree level.) In some countries state licensing as well as national professional qualifications are required to practice as a school social worker and in the USA each of the 50 states has distinct licensing and certification requirements. This complexity can be multiplied many times regarding the professional standards of school social work around the world, including in many countries where education is locally controlled at the state or provincial level.

School social work literature has grown rapidly in many countries supporting a growing and sometimes only recently established speciality. Huxtable and Blyth (2002) provide information about school social work programmes in 10 countries and two regions, including descriptions of well-developed services (such as those in the US and Scandinavia) and of more recent service developments (e.g. in Eastern Europe and Japan). The monthly electronic newsletter of the International Network for School Social Work provides brief articles and news for distribution through national school social work associations while the recently established *International Journal of School Social Work* (a free online journal) will offer qualitative and quantitative research to support evidence-based practice. Many countries now have textbooks and peer-reviewed journals dedicated to social work in education settings.[1]

The continuing expansion of social work services in schools throughout the world shows widespread recognition of the value of bringing support into schools for both learners and the school community. However, introducing and maintaining education social work services has required extensive groundwork and advocacy, especially as governments increasingly introduce austere budgets with reduced budgets for both education and social services. The experience in countries with large, well-established school social work services, e.g. the USA, Sweden and the

UK shows that a speciality association facilitates lobbying for services, often jointly with other associations representing school support staff, such as school nurses and psychologists. The example of the USA shows that each of these professional support services has its own national and state speciality associations separate from the generalist professional association; and have not relied on the latter for advocacy or resources for their members. Countries with young school social work services have followed suit by forming speciality associations for school social workers, sometimes developing websites that provide extensive resources.

However, most of these professional associations do not function as unions, and in their absence, school social workers have turned to either teachers' unions (e.g. in the US) or public service trade unions (in the UK and Norway) for help with negotiating salaries and handling workplace grievances.[2] However, poor recompense, lack of employment security, inadequate or unsafe working conditions and workplace discrimination continue to make it difficult for many social professionals to reach their potential and at times to even function effectively in a hostile work setting without the protection of union representation.

Mutual support, communication and exchange of information are central to the practice of social work. Although social work is organized to address local problems, it is clear that globalization and urbanization increase the similarity of the issues faced by school social workers in differing cultures and across the world, so that exposure to methods and skills used in other countries can be useful. Also, the many products of information communications technology (ICT) have made it possible for school social workers to participate in international networks, retrieve information from the Internet and use social work resources from many countries to improve their practice. Language barriers limit some exchange of information but the growing international use of English may be sufficient for effective communication and free online services provide approximate translations. While English is a useful tool for international communication, it highlights that social work is largely a Western invention and is a poor channel for conveying indigenous understanding of issues and developing culturally appropriate models. In spite of possible drawbacks in this exchange, increasing access to knowledge is empowering in any worldview, as is sharing information about how social workers support education.

The International Network for School Social Work is one gateway to international communication, providing access to school social work programmes and professional associations in about 46 countries. Monthly electronic newsletters and periodic studies of the status of school social work globally have provided information and support to new school social work programmes and helped to strengthen those that are well-established. The Network offers opportunities for cultural learning for social workers providing services to increasingly diverse client groups.

International conferences are an important focus for exchange, and specialist school social work conferences have been hosted in North America (Chicago, 1999), Europe (Stockholm, 2003), Asia (Busan, 2006) and Australasia (Auckland, 2009); one in Ghana in 2012 will complete a cycle of meetings in each continent and provide a focus for new developments in African countries largely lacking education social work services. One disadvantage of international conferences is that they reach only a small number of professionals, with only limited mechanisms to extend the knowledge shared more widely. It is also difficult to measure the benefits of international conferences for a profession that functions primarily at a local level. However, it is clear that international conferences (like newsletters and journals) are a catalyst for knowledge development while offering mutual support, international communication and unique cultural experiences. Opportunities for participation in international conferences through online distance learning with minimal cost to participants would allow participation by many more who are unable or unwilling to travel, while avoiding the environmental impact of air travel.

DEVELOPING SCHOOL SOCIAL WORK IN LESS DEVELOPED COUNTRIES: TWO CASE STUDIES

While development of specialist forms of social work may not be feasible or desired in some less developed countries, the importance of formal and informal education in capacity building and developing national economies and civil societies suggests that investing in providing social work services to schools can be a useful strategy. The following case examples illustrate the issues facing the service, in Ghana and Mongolia, respectively.

Ghana's experience within the African context

Ghana is located on the west coast of Africa and was the first sub-Saharan African country to gain independence from British colonial rule in 1957.[3] Northern Ghana has the lowest literacy rates in Ghana, reflecting higher poverty and underdevelopment in the region. About 43 percent of children aged between 6 and 14 years in Northern Ghana have never attended school compared to 5 percent in the Greater Accra Region (Akyeampong et al., 2007; Casely-Hayford and Gartey, 2007).

In Ghana, family circumstances, school quality, community and cultural influences impact on the educational outcomes of both boys and girls (Sottie, 2011). Female education is influenced by poverty; gender discrimination; cultural practices; child fostering, domestic work and slavery (Tuwor and Sossou, 2008); and early marriage (in Northern Ghana). The patriarchal nature of

African societies further limits female education, which is not seen as crucial to performing traditional gender roles. Furthermore, poverty, unemployment and high food prices render education of secondary importance to many families. In 2003, 40 percent of children between the ages of 5 and 17 were reported to be economically active (GSS, 2003). Some of these children work to supplement family incomes, while others leave school to work to earn a living independent of the family. Poverty interacts with gender, disability, family structure and ethnicity to further decrease children's educational chances. The 2000 Population and Housing Census indicated that 52.8 percent of primary-school-aged children were not in school.

The educational system in Ghana has gone through several reforms in attempts to make it accessible to all. Among the most recent are the Free Compulsory Universal Basic Education (FCUBE) in 1996, the School Capitation Grant (SCG) in 2004, and the Ghana School Feeding Programme (GSFP) in 2005. These initiatives reduced the cost of education by removing school levies, providing children in primary school with at least one nutritious meal a day, free books and improved infrastructure and facilities (see GES, 2005; Ministry of Education, 1996; UNICEF, 2007). The UN, through its MDGs on education and its monitoring body, EFA, provided impetus for these reforms. The government also took initiatives to close the gender gap in education through the establishment of a Girls' Education Unit within the Ghana Education Service. Improvements have resulted from these reforms in terms of enrolment, net admission rate and gender parity index (UNICEF, 2007). By 2008, the primary school net enrolment ratio had increased to 72 percent and the female net enrolment ratio had risen to 71 percent in 2007 from 59 percent in 2000 (UNESCO, 2009), although maintaining enrolment remains a challenge.

In Ghana, school social work developed out of the need to improve educational outcomes by addressing attendance problems and increasing access to education. Social workers, referred to as welfare officers, are responsible for the Staff and Students' Welfare Unit and have roles in guidance and counselling, special education and school health education. School welfare officers are instrumental in informing individuals, families and communities about educational initiatives and play a vital role in maintaining enrolment, access and retention successes.

Generally, the specialized role of social workers in schools and in Ghanaian society is not fully understood, in part due to cultural factors. There is still considerable reliance on the extended family, the church and friends to provide counselling and welfare services. Few people choose to make use of the services of a professional given a reserve of readily accessible informal support. Furthermore, mystical construal is often given to personal difficulties and spiritual remedies are thus sought through religious leaders to rectify problems.

However, as Ghanaian society experiences social change, the need for social workers is becoming more apparent. Socio-economic circumstances, migration and the nucleation of families, have diminished the extended family's reputation as social security and a buffer in times of need (Apt, 2002). Increasing numbers of poor families and orphaned children have to survive on their own with no government safety net (such as might exist in Western countries). Consequently, when families are unable to meet basic needs, education becomes a luxury they cannot afford.

School social workers and other education workers have the challenging task of convincing parents to keep their children in school (despite their limited resources); and to participate in their children's education through maintaining links with their schools. The opportunity cost of children being in school is income loss to the family, both as a result of the child not working, and from paying for the child's educational needs. Where the child is concerned, choosing to remain in school means having to

sometimes go to school hungry or in torn uniforms (Sottie, 2011). Consequently, the child and family must be convinced that the future benefits of education outweigh current costs.

The main issue affecting the school social workers' goal (to ensure basic education for children) is limited economic and personnel resources, resulting in limited or no actual visits to schools. Instead, school social workers in Ghana are more involved in addressing common problems through providing workshops for a number of schools at a time and educating students on social issues affecting their education. Individual interactions with students and identification of personal and unique problems are often limited to emergency situations. Although social workers (employed by the Department of Social Welfare) are found in every community in Ghana, their efforts are supplemented by local and international government and humanitarian organizations (such as UNICEF, UNESCO, Save the Children, ILO and USAID) running projects in urban and rural communities. Together, social workers are involved in various activities to address individual, family and community problems that block children's access to education.

Strategies for success in Mongolia

Mongolia, in north-east Asia, is bordered to the south by China and to the north by the Russian Federation.[4] Universal compulsory education in Mongolia resulted in a 98% adult literacy rate for both males and females despite a low per capita income and a large nomadic population in isolated areas (UNESCO, 2006). Education has been one of the key drivers in Mongolia, both under communism and since democratization and transition to a market-driven economy in the 1990s. Starting in 2008, formal schooling was extended to 11 years and the entry age lowered from 7 to 6 years. A system of boarding schools and *ger* (mobile tent) schools provide regular access to education for children who would otherwise not be in school (UN, 2010).

Economic pressures associated with the shift to a market economy have resulted in diminishing resources for education. Social, political and economic changes accompanying the economic reforms created additional social problems both for pastoralists leading a traditional lifestyle and the 40 percent of the population living in the capital city, Ulaanbaatar. The combination of diminishing resources for schools and new social problems has resulted in increased dropout rates. Since education has remained a high priority, the government recognized the need for interventions aimed at both recovering its former educational standard and resolving new social problems in schools. School social work was therefore launched in Mongolia in 1997 as a strategy that could both support education and protect children's rights.

Initially, social workers were placed in secondary schools when Save the Children UK, in collaboration with the Mongolian Child Rights Centre, piloted a school social work project in Ulaanbaatar schools. The programme was expanded with the help of Save the Children UK, Save the Children Norway, and the Social Work Training and Research Centre at the Mongolia State University of Education. By 2010, an estimated 623 school social workers were employed throughout Mongolia, including in every secondary school. The title *surguuliin niigmiin ajiltan,* literally *school social worker* is used in Khalkha Mongolian (personal communication with Erdenetsetseg Tserenpuu, 2010). The first legislative provision for school social work was included in the Law on Child Protection when it was amended in 2003. Ongoing legislative activity relating to training materials, staff training, a job description and school social work standards has accompanied progress in this field (Save the Children UK, 2007).

In pursuit of an official job description that would enable school social workers to focus their efforts and avoid being diverted into administrative and supervisory duties, the 2009 National Forum for Education Social Workers worked with the Ministry of Science, Education and Culture to secure an improved job description and licensing. The job description outlines the four main purposes of providing a child-friendly environment, ensuring child protection, promoting the full participation of the child in school life and networking with parents, teachers and other local organizations that work for children.

Since 2000, the Social Work Department of the Mongolian State University of Education has provided a range of training programmes including tailor-made training to prepare social workers to work in schools, a 4-year full-time bachelor's degree and a master's programme. Textbooks, journals and research papers have contributed to further development of the field. About 79 percent of the 623 school social workers are members of the Mongolian Association of School Social Work, dedicated to supporting the newly trained workers, providing professional development and helping them to lobby for their role in schools (Ulziitungalag et al., 2009).

Collaboration between the University, Save the Children, State Ministries and a fledgling professional association has succeeded in providing social work services in secondary schools throughout the country in little more than a decade. Social workers have pursued legislation that accurately describes their role and have negotiated a suitable job description that makes it possible for them to fulfill their mission. Early initiation of a professional association and encouragement of full membership has provided a strong base for a young profession. The Association's international contacts with older school social work associations helped to move this new profession forward by tapping the experience of school social workers overseas (e.g. Batkhishig, 2001). Social work educators researched and developed curricula and textbooks, published journals and have engaged with practitioners to provide professional education and continuing training needed to build knowledge and confidence.[5] It still remains to provide professional-level training for most of the workers, so that they can fulfill the promise of promoting child-friendly school environments where every child feels safe and is a full participant in learning.

OPPORTUNITIES AND CHALLENGES

Integrating educational goals as a routine part of social work practice is the challenge with all clients and in all settings. Promoting educational access and success is a major route to human development whether the client is a patient in a psychiatric setting, a foster child, a recent immigrant, a member of a marginalized group or an entire community. School social workers and social pedagogues have the advantage of ready access to schools, while other social workers and helping professionals must establish working relationships which enable advocacy and planning for the client in partnership with the school.

New roles for social work develop as education evolves to meet changing needs. In higher education, social workers may already be providing mental health services for students, coordinating services for students with disabilities and conducting outreach to underserved populations in some places, and such services need to be extended. Outside of formal learning institutions, there are opportunities for social workers to innovate in partnership with governments and agencies such as UNESCO in developing informal learning opportunities. Social workers can promote lifelong learning for clients through vehicles such as mentoring, on-the-job training, and other activities. One example is distance learning using radio, television and online courses, particularly needed in remote rural areas.[6]

Access to the Internet and other ICT is increasing rapidly, theoretically offering learning opportunities to many under-served populations such as those living in remote areas or where subject matter has not been developed. For example, the percentage of the population in Mongolia with Internet access increased from 1 to 11 percent in the last decade. In Ghana, the change was from 0.2 to 4.2 percent. In many European Union countries, North America, Japan, Korea and other developed countries, over 75 percent of the population use the Internet (Internet World Stats). While the major digital divide is still between the haves and have-nots (in terms of Internet access), for many, the divide is now in the availability of broadband networks providing high speed, effective and reliable services. The United Nations has twice sponsored a World Summit on the Information Society (2003, 2005) to address the disparity in access. The resulting Plan of Action, designed to build an inclusive information society, set out a goal of bringing 50 percent of the world's population online by 2015. One of the plan's objectives was to connect schools to provide students with the tools and skills for the information society. The stocktaking process is ongoing as governments, business and organizations work to catch up. For example, the mission of the non-profit organization One Laptop per Child is 'to create educational opportunities for the world's poorest children by providing each child with a rugged, low-cost, low-power, connected laptop with content and software designed for collaborative, joyful, self-empowered learning' (http://laptop.org/en/vision/). The challenge for social professionals is to facilitate access to these new means of learning.

Lindsey and White (2007) describe ICT applications available for social professionals working with school populations. For example, software scoring for data collection, such as adaptive behaviour scales, helps social workers conduct standardized assessments; interactive software is useful for engaging pupils in therapeutic activities (such as narrative therapy); and digital cameras and PowerPoint presentations help to motivate media-wise learners for behavioural change and social skills. Additionally, data management systems are a powerful tool for educational institutions in tracking educational needs, designing programmes and evaluating them. For example, computer applications that allow school systems to organize and track daily pupil attendance are a vital tool for school social workers employed in the traditional role of improving school attendance (Huxtable, 2000).

Technology also has a negative side for schools and youth, stemming from the powerful influence that electronic media exercise over youth through their widespread use of social websites, email and text messaging. An example is cyberbullying, defined by the Cyberbullying Research Center as 'willful and repeated harm inflicted through the use of computers, cell phones, and other electronic devices' (www.cyberbullying.us). Teaching responsible use of technology, such as dealing with the consequences of cyberbullying, is a new focus for schools and social workers (Hinduja and Patchin, 2010).

Another challenge for the social work profession is to foster education among the indigenous peoples of the Americas, Australia, New Zealand and Africa who are still suffering from the after-effects of European imperialism. The Roma have experienced similar outcomes of culture loss and marginalization throughout their centuries of migration. Education for the modern world is both liberating and essential to survival in the world where global problems impact all, regardless of culture. Additional educational efforts are also needed to prevent loss of cultures and languages resulting from colonization and now globalization. There is much room for policy-makers, social work educators, school social workers and others, e.g. international non-governmental organizations (INGOs) to advocate for and support educational programmes that include indigenous worldviews that revitalize and empower threatened cultures.

The unprecedented pace of change in the first decade of the 21st century (e.g. the rate of climate change and the changes produced by the global financial crisis of 2008–9) points to the challenges that both education and social work will continue to face, and the difficulty of adapting to as yet unknown situations. The global financial crisis and recession of 2008–9 continues to affect public sectors in many countries with budget cuts in education and social services. International aid to education in developing countries is lagging behind planned targets as donor countries find their own economies have become precarious (Chang, 2010), while rises in unemployment and poverty make it harder for households to meet school costs.

In the 21st century, the world is interconnected in ways that continue to principally benefit developed countries, while poor countries and marginalized people experience decreasing access to a limited supply of resources such as water, land, energy and even food. Globalization draws attention to the fact that resources are finite. Consequently as portions of the developing world improve educational standards and more people acquire the means to improve their living standards, there is greater pressure on resources, leaving less for those left behind. Climate change caused by burning of fossil fuels and deforestation is an example of how excess consumption by wealthy countries will impact the most vulnerable over the next few decades.

One resource that will continue to increase is knowledge, and this provides hope for human development. In his millennium report *We the Peoples*, Kofi Annan, the then Secretary-General of the United Nations, stated, 'Education is the key to the new global economy' (Annan, 2000: para 97). However, education itself needs to change to prepare citizens to develop a new sustainable global economy, and a society that respects human rights and can manage conflicts for a more equitable world. This view of education for a sustainable future is part of a paradigm shift needed in 21st-century education. Schools must change to develop learners' knowledge, critical thinking, social responsibility, culture and ethical values, while preparing learners for rapid change. Children entering school in 2010 will live through more social, technological and global changes than any previous generation. Teachers and learners will increasingly use research, technology and media in newly constructed curricula to develop innovative 21st-century skills.

Social professionals in schools have a strong supporting role to play in this vision of education and must innovate to deliver services effectively. Initial and continuing training must prepare them to handle ever-changing situations with new skills and technologies, based on research that supports evidence-based practice. The International Council on Social Welfare, the International Federation of Social Workers and the International Association of Schools of Social Work are latent sources of support, research and curriculum development for the intersection of education and social work, internationally.

CONCLUSION

Social professionals such as school social workers and social pedagogues are needed in all countries to support full access to education for the development of human potential and the wellbeing of the world community. Social workers have a crucial role in helping educational establishments from pre-school to tertiary education cope with learners' diverse problems especially for those who are marginalized by poverty, disability, gender or ethnic group. School social work is a speciality with expertise in working with school systems, yet in many countries that need the most help to reach the goals of EFA, it does not exist. In countries where school social work has not been implemented, other social professionals have the responsibility of promoting school enrolment, inclusive education and support services for learners to enable them to complete their education. For social workers outside the formal education system, there are countless opportunities to promote the wellbeing of clients by both consistently engaging with formal educational institutions on behalf of the client and in promoting opportunities for capacity building through informal education. To fulfill the promise of social work in education, the profession must build trust and credibility with all levels of the education system (from classroom teachers to ministries of education) to achieve shared goals. Social workers, together with educators and other professionals, need to influence state ministries of education, decision makers, legislators and the public to shape policies that ensure sustainable and empowering education. Continued advocacy by international social work bodies is needed to promote recognition in civil society of the unique potential of social work joined with education to reach global goals of human development and social justice.

USEFUL WEBSITES

Association for School Social Workers in Switzerland: http://www.ssav.ch/.

Canadian Association of School Social Workers and Attendance Counsellors: http://www.casswac.ca/.

Cyberbullying Research Center: http://www.cyberbullying.us/.

International Network for School Social Work: http://internationalnetwork-schoolsocialwork.htmlplanet.com/.

Internet World Stats: Usage and Population Statistics: www.internetworldstats.com.

National Association of Social Workers in Education: http://www.naswe.org.uk.

Norwegian Union of Social Educators and Social Workers: http://www.epsu.org/a/280.

Save the Children. Re-write the Future: http://www.savethechildren.org/site/c.8rKLIXMGIpI4E/b.6148051/k.BB46/Rewrite_the_Future.htm

School Social Work Association of America: http://www.sswaa.org/.

School Social Work Association of Finland: http://www.talentia.fi/koulukuraattorit/

School Social Work Association of Japan: http://sswaj.org/index2.html.

Schulsozialarbeit Liechtenstein: http://www.schulsozialarbeit.li/.

The Hungarian School Social Workers Association: http://www.miszme.hu/.

The Swedish School Social Workers Association: http://www.skolkurator.nu/.

World Summit on the Information Society (2003, 2005): http://www.itu.int/wsis/index.html

NOTES

1   Literature on school social work has increased around the world in recent years, reflecting the growth of social work services in education in several countries. There are speciality school social work journals in the United States, Sweden, Finland, the United Kingdom, Mongolia and Japan and textbooks published in the United States (Rippey Massat et al., 2009; Bye and Alvarez, 2006; Dupper, 2003; Franklin et al., 2006; Allen-Meares, 2009; Openshaw, 2008; Kelly et al., 2010), in Germany (Speck, 2006, 2007; Kersten and Wulfers, 1999; Rademacker, 1992), in Austria (Vyslouzil and Weissensteiner, 2001), in Sweden (Wester, 2005), and in Japan (Yamashita, 2003; Kadota, 2010; School Social Work Association of Japan et al., 2008). In Korea, Professor Min-Sun Sung and several colleagues published a translation of Dr Paula Allen-Meares' 5th edition of Social Work Services in Schools (2008).

2   In the United States, the National Education Association, in the UK, Unison and in Norway, the Norwegian Union of Social Educators and Social Workers (Fellesorganisasjonen for Barnevernpedagoger, Sosionomer og Vernepleiere) provide representation (such as help with negotiating salaries and handling workplace grievances) for many social workers who work in schools as well as for other school employees.

3   Ghana covers approximately 238.5 thousand square kilometres and has an estimated population of 23.95 million as of 2010 (GSS, 2010). Ghana is divided into 10 regions and is highly multi-ethnic and multi-lingual. English is the official language of Ghana. The predominant religions are Christianity (69 percent), followed by Muslim (15.5 percent) and traditional religion (8.5 percent) (GSS, 2002). The Ghanaian economy is relatively stable compared to that of other countries in sub-Saharan Africa, and the discovery of oil in the Gulf of Guinea should further boost the economy. Agriculture is the mainstay of the Ghanaian economy, employing about

60 percent of the workforce and contributing to about 46 percent of GDP (A-engyuure and Adamtey, 2005). Ghana is rich in natural resources but relies heavily on technical and financial assistance from the international community. Ghana is a leading exporter of cocoa and also exports gold and lumber.

4   Mongolia has approximately 2,736,764 people scattered over a vast territory of 1.5 million km^2, making it the least densely populated and the 18th largest country in the world. About 40 percent of the population, or 1.08 million, live in the capital city Ulaanbaatar, while many still follow a nomadic life-style with herds of livestock and horses. A breakdown of the population shows that 29 percent of the population is 0–15 years old, similar to many Central Asian countries and higher than European countries. Average life expectancy has risen to 66.8 years, which is 1.5 years longer than in 2004. About *94 percent* of the population is Tibetan Buddhist, 4 percent Muslim, and 2 percent other religions. The official language is Khalkha Mongol and the principal ethnic groups are Khalkha (86 percent), Kazakh (6 percent), Bouriate (2 percent) and other ethnic groups (6 percent).

5   The School Social Workers Association of Mongolia publishes the journal *Mongolia School Social Work* Practice four times a year. In the United States, *The School Social Work Journal* has been produced by the Illinois Association of School Social Workers since the 1970s, and NASW's *Social Work in Education* (now called *Children and Schools*) has been in existence for over three decades. The entire January 2010 issue of the magazine *Sozialarbeit in Österreich* (entitled *Schulsozialarbeit Boom*) was dedicated to school social work, and reported rapid progress in introducing social work into the schools in Austria. Sweden has an online quarterly magazine *Skolkuratorn* for all members of the Swedish School Social Workers Association. In the UK, The National Association of Social Workers in Education also publishes its journal online for its members. The *Japanese Journal of School Social Work* was started in 2006.

6   Through the National Centre for Non-Formal and Distance Education (NFDE), the Mongolian Ministry of Education, Culture and Science provides curriculum and training for non-formal Education for Sustainable Development to promote quality of life and to cope with severe economic and environmental problems.

REFERENCES

A-engyuure, P.A. and Adamtey, N. (2005) *Analyses of Progress Towards the MDGs in Ghana – A Civil Society Perspective.* Community Partnerships for

Health and Development (CPDH). Accra: Commonwealth Foundation.

Akyeampong, K., Djangmah, J., Oduro, A., Seidu, A., Hunt, F. (2007) *Access to Basic Education in Ghana, the Evidence and the Issues.* Country Analytic Report, The Consortium for Research on Educational Access, Transitions and Equity (CREATE), Centre for International Education; University of Sussex.

Allen-Meares. P. (2009) *Social Work Services in Schools,* (6th edn). Englewood Cliffs, NJ: Prentice Hall.

Anderson, G., Pösö. P., Väisänen, E. and Wallin, A. (2002) 'School social work in Finland and other Nordic countries: cooperative professionalism in schools', in M. Huxtable and E. Blyth (eds). *School Social Work Worldwide.* NASW Press: Washington, DC.

Annan, K. (2002) *We the Peoples: the Role of the United Nations in the 21st Century.* Millennium Report of the Secretary-General of the United Nations, http://www.un.org/millennium/sg/report/ch2.pdf.

Apt, N. (2002) 'Ageing and the changing role of the family and the community: an African perspective', *International Social Security Review,* 55: 39–47, doi:10.1111/1468-246X.00113.

Batkhishig, A. (2001) *Development of Social Work Education of Mongolia – Lessons from American Social Work Education.* Ulaanbaatar.

Blyth, E. and Cooper, H. (2002) 'School social work in the United Kingdom: a key role in social inclusion', in M. Huxtable, and E. Blyth, (eds). *School Social Work Worldwide.* NASW Press: Washington, DC.

Bye, L. and Alvarez, M. (2006) *School Social Work: Theory to Practice.* Belmont, CA: Thomson Wadsworth.

Casely-Hayford, L. and Gartey, A.B. (2007) *The Leap to Literacy and Life Change in Northern Ghana: an Impact Assessment of School for Life (SFL),* Retrieved from: http://www.web.net/~afc/download2/Education/complimentary_edu_pamphlet.pdf.

Chang, G. (2010) 'Monitoring the effects of the global crisis on education provision', *Current Issues in Comparative Education,* 12 (2): 14–20.

Chen, S. and Ravallion, M. (2008) *The Developing World is Poorer than we Thought, but no less Successful in the Fight Against Poverty.* http://siteresources.worldbank.org/DEC/Resources/Poverty-Brief-in-English.pdf.

Chiu, S. and Wong, V. (2002) 'School social work in Hong Kong: constraints and challenges for the special administrative region', in M. Huxtable and E. Blyth, (eds). *School Social Work Worldwide.* NASW Press: Washington, DC.

Costin, L. (1969) 'A historical review of school social work', *Social Casework,* 50: 439–53.

Dupper, D. (2003) *School Social Work: Skills and Interventions for Effective Practice.* Hoboken, NJ: John Wiley & Sons.

Education For All (2010) *Reaching the Marginalized.* Global Monitoring Report. France: UNESCO Publishing. Retrieved from: http://unesdoc.unesco.org/images/0018/001866/186606e.pdf.

Franklin, C., Harris, M.B. and Allen-Meares, P. (eds) (2006) *The School Services Sourcebook: A Guide for School-Based Professionals.* USA: Oxford University Press.

Gakidou, E., Cowling, K., Lozano, R. and Murray, C. (2010), Increased educational attainment and its effect on child mortality in 175 countries between 1970 and 2009: a systematic analysis', *Lancet I,* 376: 959–74.

GES (Ghana Education Service) (2005) *Guidelines for the Distribution and Utilization of Capitation Grants to Basic Schools.* Accra: GES.

GSS (Ghana Statistical Service) (2002) *2000 Housing and Population Census.* GSS: Accra.

GSS (Ghana Statistical Service) (2003) *Child Labour Survey.* Accra: Ghana.

GSS (Ghana Statistical Service) (2010) *Population Statistics.* http://www.citypopulation.de/Ghana.html.

Hinduja, S. and Patchin, J. (2010) *Activities for Teens: Ten Ideas for Youth to Educate their Community about Cyberbullying.* http://www.cyberbullying.us/teens_cyberbullying_prevention_activities_tips.pdf

Huxtable, M. (2000) 'A reachable goal: an attendance program that works for school social workers with too little time and too much to do', *School Social Work Journal,* 25 (1): 45–58.

Huxtable, M. and Blyth, E. (2002) *School Social Work Worldwide.* Washington, DC: NASW Press.

ILO (International Labour Organization) (1999) *Convention Concerning the Prohibition and Immediate Action for the Elimination of the Worst Forms of Child Labour.* http://www.un-documents.net/c182.htm.

ILO (International Labour Organization) (2010) *Accelerating Action Against Child Labour.* http://www.ilo.org/global/resources/WCMS_126752/lang--it/index.htm.

International Network Newsletter (July, October, December 2007).

Kadota, K. (2010) *Social Work Practice in Schools: International Trends and the Development in Japan.* Tokyo: Chuohoki Publishing Co. Ltd.

Kelly, M., Raines, J., Stone, S. and Frey, A. (2010) *School Social Work: an Evidence-Informed Framework for Practice*. Oxford: Oxford University Press.

Kersten, B. and Wulfers, W. (1999) 'Wenn wir die nicht hätten: Schulsozialarbeit heute und was sie in Wiesbaden bewirkte', *Pädagogisches Forum,* 27: 92–6.

Lindsey, B. and White, M. (2007) 'Technology and school social work', in L. Bye and M. Alvarez, *School Social Work: Theory to Practice*. Belmont, CA: Thomson Wadsworth. pp. 288–97.

Loughborough, J., Shera, W. and Wilhelm, J. (2002) 'School social work in Canada: historical themes and current challenges', in M. Huxtable and E. Blyth (eds), *School Social Work Worldwide*. NASW Press: Washington, DC.

Ministry of Education. (1996) *Free Compulsory Universal Basic Education in Ghana by the Year 2005*. Basic Education Sector Implementation Programme Policy Document. Government of Ghana Vol. 1, April 1996.

Openshaw, L. (2008) *Social Work in Schools: Principles and Practice*. New York: Guilford Press.

Rademacker, H. (1992) 'Schulsozialarbeit: Was ist das?', *Erziehung und Wissenschaft*, 44 (12): 14–15.

Rippey Massat, C., Constable, R., McDonald, S. and Flynn, J. (2009) *School Social Work: Practice, Policy, and Research*. 7th edn. Chicago. IL: Lyceum Books.

Save the Children UK (2007) *Situation Analysis on School Social Work in Mongolia*. Summary of a Research Report.

School Social Work Association of Japan and Yamashita, E. (translator) (2001) *Social Work Services in schools*. Paula Allen-Meares (ed.). Tokyo: Gakuensha.

School Social Association of Japan and Yamashita, E., Hanba, R. and Uchida, H. (eds) (2008) *School Social Work – History, Theory & Practice*. Tokyo: Gakuensha.

Sottie, C. A. (2011) *Stemming the Tide: School Dropout in Ghana*, A Resource for School Social Workers, Educationists and Policy Makers. Lambert Academic Publishing.

Speck, K. (2006) *Qualität und Evaluation in der Schulsozialarbeit. Konzepte, Rahmenbedingungen und Wirkungen*. München: Reinhardt-Verlag.

Speck, K. (2007) *Schulsozialarbeit. Eine Einführung*. München: Reinhardt-Verlag. Statistical Service.

Terner, A. and Rademacker, H. (2010) 'School social work (*Schulsozialarbeit*) in Germany', *Newsletter of the International Network for School Social Work*, September.

Tuwor, T. and Sossou, M. (2008) 'Gender discrimination and education in West Africa: strategies for maintaining girls in school', *International Journal of Inclusive Education,* 12(4): 363–79.

Ulziitungalag, K., Erdenetsetseg, T., Munkhjargal, B. (2009) *Current Situation of School Social Work Services in Mongolia*.

UN (United Nations) (1948a) *Universal Declaration of Human Rights*. http://www.un.org/en/documents/udhr/.

UN (United Nations) (1948b) *Universal Declaration of Human Rights. Article 26*. http://www.un.org/en/documents/udhr/index.shtml#a26.

UN (United Nations) (1976) *International Covenant on Economic, Social and Cultural Rights*. http://www2.ohchr.org/english/law/cescr.htm.

UN (United Nations) (2010) We Can End Poverty: 2015 Millennium Development Goals. http://www.un.org/millenniumgoals/pdf/MDG_FS_2_EN.pdf.

UN (United Nations) (2011) *World Report on Disabilities*. http://whqlibdoc.who.int/publications/2011/9789240685215_eng.pdf.

UNESCO (United Nations Education, Scientific and Cultural Organization) *Primary Education*. http://portal.unesco.org/education/en/ev.php-URL_ID=32969&URL_DO=DO_TOPIC&URL_SECTION=201.html.

UNESCO (United Nations Education, Scientific and Cultural Organization) (1994) *The Salamanca Statement And Framework For Action On Special Needs Education*. http://unesdoc.unesco.org/images/0009/000984/098427eo.pdf.

UNESCO (United Nations Education, Scientific and Cultural Organization) (1990a) *World Declaration on Education For All*. http://www.unesco.org/education/pdf/JOMTIE_E.PDF.

UNESCO (United Nations Education, Scientific and Cultural Organization) (1990b) *The World Conference on Education for All*. http://www.unesco.org/education/efa/ed_for_all/background/world_conference_jomtien.shtml.

UNESCO (United Nations Education, Scientific and Cultural Organization) (2000) *Education for All 2000 Assessment*. http://unesdoc.unesco.org/images/0012/001200/120058e.pdf.

UNESCO (United Nations Education, Scientific and Cultural Organization) (2005) *Children out of School: Measuring Exclusion from Primary School*. http://www.uis.unesco.org/template/pdf/educgeneral/OOSC_EN_WEB_FINAL.pdf.

UNESCO (United Nations Education, Scientific and Cultural Organization) (2006) *Literacy Country Study: Mongolia*. United Nations Education, Scientific and Cultural Organization. http://unesdoc.unesco.org/images/0014/001462/ 146207e.pdf.

UNESCO (United Nations Educational, Scientific, and Cultural Organization) Institute for Statistics (2009) *World Education Indicators.* Paris: UNESCO. Retrieved from: http://www.uis.unesco.org/ev.php?URL_ID= 5263&URL_DO=DO_TOPIC&URL_SECTION=201.

UNESCO (United Nations Education, Scientific and Cultural Organization) (2010a) *EFA Global Monitoring Report: Reaching the Marginalized.* http://www.unesco.org/en/efareport/reports/2010-marginalization/.

UNESCO (United Nations Education, Scientific and Cultural Organization) (2010b) *Children with Disabilities.* http://www.unesco.org/en/inclusive-education/children-with-disabilities/.

UNICEF (United Nations Children's Fund) (1990) *Convention on the Rights of the Child.* http://www2.ohchr.org/english/law/crc.htm.

UNICEF (United Nations Children's Fund) (2007) *Achieving Universal Primary Education in Ghana by 2015: A Reality or a Dream?* UNICEF: Division of Policy and Planning.

UNIRIN (United Nations Integrated Regional Information Networks) (2006) *Ghana: Surging Enrolment Presents Challenges,* United Nations Office for Coordination of Humanitarian Affairs. http://www.irinnews.org/report.aspx?reportid=61308.

USAID (United States Agency International Development) (2007) *Role of Education and the Demobilization of Child Soldiers – Aspects of an Appropriate Education Program for Child Soldiers.* http://pdf.usaid.gov/pdf_docs/PNADI663.pdf.

Vyslouzil, M. and Weissensteiner, M. (2001) *Schulsozialarbeit in Österreich.* Wien: Verlag des Österreichishen Gewerkschaftsbundes GmbH.

Wester, Y. (2005) *Socionomen i Skolan.* Stockholm: Gothia.

Wulfers, W. (2002) 'School social work in Germany: help for youth in a changing society', in M. Huxtable and E. Blyth (eds) *School Social Work Worldwide.* NASW Press: Washington, DC.

Yamashita, E. (2003) *School Social Work: New Support System in Schools.* Tokyo: Gakuensha.

15

Social Work, Social Justice and Protection: A Reflective Review

Michael Preston-Shoot and Staffan Höjer

INTRODUCTION

International conventions address much of the subject matter of this chapter where the focus is on national and transnational systems for the protection of children and adults from abuse and neglect, young people within the criminal justice system, and the use of law by nation states in respect of individuals and communities. To varying degrees, these international pronouncements concern civil, political, and socioeconomic rights, and increasingly recognise global concerns such as sexual exploitation and drug trafficking.

Social work has boldly claimed part ownership of responsibility for delivering the aspirations expressed in these declarations. It has declared that principles of human rights and social justice form a fundamental part of its *raison d'être*, underpinning and shaping its role in promoting social and individual change, and in empowering and liberating people to enhance their well-being (IFSW/IASSW, 2001; Appendix 1). Social work asserts itself as a moral activity founded on values of care, honesty, social change and justice (Butler, 2002; Mansbach and

Kaufman, 2003), a practical profession with a strong value system (Lyons et al., 2006). Its ethical commitments (IFSW, 2006; see also Appendix 2) require practitioners to promote values-inspired debate and reflection. Equally, they commit social workers to drawing the attention of policy-makers, politicians and the public to situations where nation states, and the organizations they support, promote practices that are oppressive, inhumane, unfair and/or harmful (Hölscher and Berhane, 2008). However, as Healy (2008) somewhat ironically observes, social work has not been noted for its leadership within the human rights movement. Similarly, social work's engagement in practice has varied with respect to promoting social change, enhancing people's well-being and advocating human rights and social justice (Laird, 2007). Moreover, its capacity for engaging with cross-border and supranational issues, often related to globalization, has been questioned (Nikku, 2010; Sasaki, 2010).

The purpose of this chapter is less to critique the declarations themselves than to explore their impact on how nation states have taken forward people's rights to social justice and protection. Its purpose is also to review systems of protection and justice, and to reflect upon the challenges that social work has encountered in this field of activity.

HUMAN RIGHTS DECLARATIONS

Declarations about human rights abound. Some have global ambitions, such as the UN Convention on the Rights of the Child (UNCRC) (1989), the International Covenant on Economic, Social and Cultural Rights (1966), the International Convention on the Elimination of all forms of Racial Discrimination (1969), the Convention on the Elimination of all forms of Discrimination Against Women (CEDAW) (1979), and the Convention on the Rights of Persons with Disabilities (2006) (see also Appendix 5). Others focus on particular continents. These include the European Convention on Human Rights and Fundamental Freedoms (ECHR) (1950), the African Charter on Human and People's Rights (1981), the African Charter on the Rights and Welfare of the Child (1999) and the American Declaration on Human Rights (1969).

For this chapter's purposes, four critical questions arise immediately. First, how the principles within the various declarations are reflected in national legislation and subsequent policy and practice building. Second, the degree to which signatory states submit reservations, that is specifying those principles to which they will not adhere. Third, the arguable gaps that exist within this framework of human rights, including the absence of an international convention dealing with sexual and reproductive rights, or an explicit formulation of the right to recognition of one's own sexuality. And finally, how social work nationally and internationally is configured within, and itself interfaces with, and seeks to realize, these declaratory principles.

Some countries may choose to legislate in order to translate some if not all international

obligations into national law. Almost all European countries have signed the European Convention but have variously incorporated its civil and political rights into national legislation. The Human Rights Act 1998 has integrated the ECHR into UK law. However, the UK government has, to date, resisted advocacy that the UNCRC should also be so integrated. Others may decide to express human rights through cultural and religious traditions rather than legislation (Skegg, 2005). Still others resist using national legislation to accommodate or advance international declarations of human rights. Tang (2003) notes, for example, that both Norway and Canada have yet to incorporate the UNCRC into legislative systems despite a commitment to do so, perhaps partly because of fiscal constraints and opposition from family organizations. Canada and the UK have not made illegal all forms of corporal punishment of children, as required by the UNCRC and, arguably, also by the European Court of Human Rights which oversees how states observe the ECHR (A v UK [1998] 27 EHRR 611). Tang (2003) concludes, when analysing how Canada has taken forward the UNCRC, that the rights contained within it will remain soft until hardened by national legislation.

Declarations may be more honoured in the breach than the observance. The African Charter aims to eliminate all forms of discrimination and to provide equal protection under the law. However, across various African countries (as also among Middle East, Asia/Pacific, Caribbean and Central American nations) homosexuality remains illegal. Elsewhere, jurisdictions may not offer formal legal recognition of lawful same-sex unions. The ECHR has enshrined the right to live free of inhuman and degrading treatment and prohibits discrimination on any ground. However, France has sought to deport Roma people, arguably also in contravention of its European Union responsibilities in relation to freedom of movement, and the European Court of Human Rights has not infrequently judged that states have failed to guarantee these rights.

TOWARDS EQUALITY?

There is nothing inevitable about the legal rules that nation states promulgate; rather they reflect the society, and its law-makers, in which they are generated. One illustrative example is the extent to which nations pass laws that define hate-motivated crimes. Many states have enacted legislation that recognizes crime motivated by racial and/or religious hatred, and that permits enhanced penalties – Austria, Belgium and Armenia, for example. However, other countries either have not enacted legislation – Slovenia and Croatia, for example – or recognize the phenomenon but do not regard it as an aggravating factor when courts pass sentence. Some countries have broadened the categories to recognize in law crimes motivated by perceptions of age, disability, sexuality and gender – Spain, France, UK, New Zealand and Canada being examples. Whilst some countries include sexuality, others take the opposite view – Iran and Uganda being two examples. Proponents of hate-crime legislation argue that it indicates that such behaviour will not be tolerated. Those opposed argue that additional protection should not be necessary since a crime has already been committed and that enacting legislation may mask the need for society to do more through education and social programmes to address hate (Pollack, 2009).

Pollack (2009) also notes in respect of hate crime, variations in police enforcement, illustrating the observation that the law-in-theory (Jenness and Grattet, 2005) can prove insufficient to achieve the aims of policy-makers. The following examples invite a critique of the degree to which legal rules can achieve cultural change. Such evidence suggests that, in respect of counteracting discrimination and promoting social change, sustained examination is needed at three levels – the law-in-theory (what legal rules are (not) made), the law-in-between (how governmental and non-governmental agencies translate legal rules into organizational procedures), and the law-in-practice (how practitioners implement the legal rules in their day-to-day work).

Discrimination is often endemic and the pursuit of equality is made more difficult by how entrenched it is (Lyons et al., 2006). This has been evident in the UK where legislation requires public bodies to counteract discrimination and promote equality of opportunity (Equality Act, 2010). Nonetheless, courts have sometimes found that both central and local government has paid insufficient regard to these duties (R (Chavda) v Harrow LBC [2008] 11 CCLR 187; R (Equality and Human Rights Commission) v Secretary of State for Justice [2010] EWHC 147 (Admin)). Moreover, inspections (CSCI, 2008, 2009) have found that social welfare organizations need to give more attention to reviewing their equality strategies, policies and practices, to offering positive leadership, and to providing training that challenges discriminatory attitudes.

The African Charter on Human and People's Rights (1981) urges the elimination of discrimination, especially that which is rooted in race, ethnicity, sex and religion. However, Noyoo (2004) argues that racist attitudes have not been sufficiently challenged by the new legal system in South Africa and that newer legal norms have not reached far enough to stem racist practices. In Nigeria (Zumve, personal communication) laws have been designed to counteract all forms of discrimination but progress in providing equality of opportunity for women and for disabled people has been very slow. Same-sex relationships remain unlawful in some African countries.

Similarly, in India, Oommen (2002) offers evidence of racial and religious discrimination, notwithstanding the existence of legal rules. Legislation exists to protect women from domestic violence and gender inequality, for example, in Vietnam and Taiwan (Lin and Wang, 2010; Thi Thai Lan et al., 2010), but injustices continue because of the patchy nature of services, the scale of the problems, and the lack of integration between different legal initiatives and agencies. Johnson and

Marriott (2009) review progress in Australia relating to the deinstitutionalization of people with learning disabilities and provision of citizenship and community living rights. They note that practice commitment has not always fully met the policy drive, even though that has been supported by disability discrimination legislation and legal rules relating to service delivery. Rights can be compromised by limited resources and the absence of strong advocacy. A similar story could be told in the UK, US and Scandinavia. For instance, Preston-Shoot (2010) has documented the conclusions of judicial reviews, ombudsman investigations and inquiries, all of which have sometimes been critical of the attitudes and values expressed by central and local government, and by healthcare organizations, towards learning disabled and physically disabled people.

The over-representation of indigenous young people in criminal justice procedures has been noted in Australia (Chui, 2009). Certain groups from black and minority ethnic communities in the UK are also over-represented (Braye and Preston-Shoot, 2009) at each stage of the process from the exercise of police powers in the street, through decisions about diversion away from court appearances, to sentencing by magistrates and judges. Equalities legislation and anti-discriminatory values, even where (as in the UK) criminal justice legislation itself requires that those working within the system counteract discrimination, have yet to reach the attitudes of many of those who influence how criminality is constructed and rules relating to how offending is enforced (Braye and Preston-Shoot, 2009; Chui, 2009).

Attitudes and policies towards Roma people in France and elsewhere in Europe represent another example of the need for professionals to uphold the legal rules and professional commitments to counter discrimination. Finally, Healy (2007) has noted that CEDAW has attracted more reservations from member states than any other UN convention. The principle of counteracting discrimination against women appears far from unequivocally accepted, even though women are widely recognized as being especially vulnerable in situations of political, economic and social instability (Nikku, 2010; Sasaki, 2010; Zaviršek and Herath, 2010). Nonetheless, where political will is manifest, supported by strong social acceptance and participation, social change may follow. Guilarte (2005) documents this in respect of Cuban social policy towards disadvantaged social groups, designed *inter alia* to eliminate sexual and racial discrimination and to improve the health and well-being of older people, disabled people and neglected children.

ACCOUNTABILITY AND REDRESS

Equally, there is nothing guaranteed about how the 'rule of law' balances the needs and rights of individuals with the role of, and power exercised by, government. If nation states carry responsibility for protecting individuals and communities, they also exercise power with and over individuals and communities. Therefore, how such power is exercised should be scrutinized, alongside the ease or difficulty with which individual citizens may hold the state, and its organizations, accountable and seek redress for alleged failures.

Declarations also vary regarding whether they provide individuals with the means to challenge decisions by governments and organizations to which statutory powers and duties are delegated. The European Convention on Human Rights and Fundamental Freedoms (1951) provides individuals with the right to challenge the use and abuse of power by states directly and as represented through the organizations that exercise delegated authority. The American Convention on Human Rights (1969) has established an Inter-American Court of Human Rights but not all countries have endorsed the Convention. By contrast, the African Charter on Human and People's Rights (1981) created a commission, designed to promote the rights within it, but not a court of law. This is not just a semantic point. The European Court of Human Rights has criticized several states for the lack of care given to offenders and people with severe mental distress, deprived of their liberty (Keenan v UK [2001] 33 EHRR 913; Winterwerp v Netherlands [1979] 2 EHRR 387). Deaths in custody may be the result of inhuman and degrading treatment. If individual citizens cannot hold their national government accountable, they have no meaningful form of redress for failures in a duty of care.

In some countries, such as the UK and Germany, when individuals believe that national governments or local municipalities have misapplied the legal rules, abused their powers or neglected their duties, they may seek a judicial review or petition the ombudsman to investigate. Fairgrieve and Green (2004) illustrate the varying extent to which contrasting legal systems, such as those in Australia, New Zealand, Canada and the US, have enabled young people and their families to hold state agencies accountable for their role in failing to protect children from abuse and neglect, and families from unreasonable intrusion or poor standards of social work practice surrounding child protection. Their review concludes that Canada and New Zealand have been in the forefront of allowing civil actions to hold public authorities accountable for omissions and abuses in respect of children in public care. Elsewhere, only slowly have courts been allowed to consider claims of negligence against public authorities. In the UK and Ireland, negligence claims have been pursued through the courts against local health and/or social services organizations, covering such issues as abuse of children in residential care and foster care, failure to assess allegations by young people of neglect and abuse by parents and other care-givers, and failure to provide services to disabled people following assessment. In Sweden, a redress process has recently started through which the stories of neglect and abuse of over a thousand people

are being collected. In other countries, such as Holland and South Africa, use of the legal system may be rare, not because children are not neglected by their families or by the state, but due to standards surrounding the burden of proof, fragmentation of responsibilities across government departments at local and national levels, and the involvement of the judiciary in initial decision-making of whether and how abused or neglected children should be protected.

YOUTH JUSTICE

The UNCRC requires that the best interests of the child should be the primary consideration in all matters concerning young people. Similarly, the UN Standard Minimum Rules for the Administration of Juvenile Justice (Beijing Rules) (1985), together with UN Guidelines for the Prevention of Juvenile Delinquency (1990), offer guidance on the protection of children's rights through the development of a separate juvenile justice system. Key principles include fair and humane treatment, the promotion of young people's well-being and diversion away from the criminal justice system. Detention should be a measure of last resort, sentencing should be proportionate to the nature of the offence, and the age of criminal responsibility should not be low. Staff working with young offenders should receive specialist training. There should be procedural safeguards, such as the right to maintain silence and to have legal representation.

The reality is somewhat different from the rhetoric. Not all nation states have juvenile justice systems, the operation of which is separate from adult criminal courts, or legislation which focuses specifically on the needs of young offenders. In some countries where legislation does specify that young offenders should be treated separately from adults, with their welfare needs central, as in Nigeria, Nepal and the Philippines, the provisions are not always enforced (Zumve, personal communication; Boele, 2005; CLRRD, 2002). In Nepal, for instance, there is evidence of child maltreatment in police custody, failure to enforce legislation, poor training for staff, and lack of understanding of children's rights (CLRRD, 2002). In the Philippines (Boele, 2005), there is evidence that the existing legal rules are misapplied in practice, for example, in failing to separate young people from adults in custodial settings. Countries also differ quite markedly with where they set the age of criminal responsibility. Within Europe the span ranges from 7 to 18. Some countries have retained *doli incapax* (for example, Australia), where children below a certain age can only be held responsible for their offences if they can be shown to be able to distinguish between right and wrong. Others, for example, the UK, have abandoned this principle in favour of holding all children above a certain age liable to prosecution. The UK has been strongly criticized (UN, 2008) regarding its compliance with the UNCRC in respect of where it has set the age of criminal responsibility and for deciding that the principal aim of the youth justice system is to prevent offending rather than to meet the child's welfare. Similar criticisms have been made of other nation states, for example, the Philippines (Boele, 2005).

Whilst an increasingly punitive orientation can be detected across countries (Junger-Tas and Decker, 2006), a continuum continues to exist between welfare and justice approaches to youth offending, with community-based responses in, say, Canada and Ireland, contrasted with educational measures in France and greater use of custodial penalties in Nigeria and the UK. Incarceration of young offenders has grown steadily in the UK, in contrast to France, Spain, Norway and Sweden. However, this may mask more subtle differences. In some countries, such as the UK, youth justice is clearly differentiated from systems of child care and child protection. In other countries, such as Finland (Pitts and Kuula, 2005), the opposite applies. In Finland, youth offending is seen as a symptom, for example, of depression or family violence. A variety of responses may follow, including the use of foster care, children's homes and psychiatric care. Young people may therefore experience institutional living but for a differently defined reason. Social work may not be the prominent profession within residential and custodial settings and, as in Sweden, the daily care of young people presenting the most pressing problems may become the responsibility of staff with little, if any professional education, contrary to the requirements of the UNCRC.

Political, media and public responses also vary when confronted with rising levels of youth crime. Such responses are mediated by the degree to which professionals have retained control of policy-making. They may also reflect contrasts in the relationship between the state and the individual, perhaps more adversarial and antagonistic in the US and UK than other countries in Europe (Pitts and Kuula, 2005).

Desai (2009) contrasts the approach of Goa and Singapore regarding children who offend. A wider range of non-custodial options appears available in Singapore alongside institutional provision. A restorative justice approach seeks to balance rehabilitation, social inclusion and deterrence, and to promote dialogue between victims and offenders but, significantly and contrary to the UNCRC, corporal punishment and solitary confinement are also used. A wider range of multi-agency programmes, responding to perceived roots of youth offending in poverty, class conflict, mental distress and educational difficulties, appears available in Singapore. If social work is not prominent in these youth justice systems, it has been instrumental in their creation and subsequent operation elsewhere, including Australia and the UK. In these jurisdictions, social workers play key roles in young people's interrogations by the police, and then in pre-sentence reports for the courts and supervision of community penalties (Braye and Preston-Shoot, 2009; Chui, 2009). Coincidentally, it is in these jurisdictions also where questions are posed about the effectiveness of a welfare approach in preventing youth crime and diverting young people with criminal records away from offending. Restorative justice models have also been explored, therefore, but not without questions surrounding whether they assist young people to reintegrate into their communities or encourage further stigmatization.

CHILD PROTECTION

Child abuse and neglect, including trafficking, does not distinguish between nation states, although the prominence of different forms may vary. It is difficult to establish the scale of trafficking and child labour (Lyons et al., 2006) but the figure has been estimated at 4 million each year (UN, 2000). Besides the UN Trafficking Protocol (2000), some countries have enacted legislation on child trafficking, such as Nigeria, the Philippines and the UK. Others have yet to do so, for example, Uganda. Social policies protecting children's rights may be modest, as in Mongolia, or more extensive. Legal systems vary in the degree to which children are seen as the holders of legal rights as opposed to recipients of welfare-based interventions and their interests conflated with those of their families (Tang, 2003; Braye and Preston-Shoot, 2009). Countries with emerging and longer established social work systems have legislated to protect and promote the welfare of children in need, such as Taiwan (Lin and Wang, 2010), Nepal (Nikku, 2010), Vietnam (Thi Thai Lan et al., 2010), Japan (Sasaki, 2010), Mongolia (Namdaldagva et al., 2010), Sri Lanka (Zaviršek and Herath (2010), UK (Braye and Preston-Shoot, 2009) and Australia (Swain and Rice, 2009). However, these same countries report developing and/or variable practice standards in child protection services, limitations in provision, with social workers' caseloads high and working conditions poor. Children's rights and perspectives may be insufficiently embedded in practice, with training for working with young people restricted. Social work may or may not be prominent and effective in intervening in situations of abuse and neglect, for instance, with children on the street (sent by families) or of the street (escaping from violence). Costa Rica, Nepal and Mongolia provide, to some degree, contrasting pictures relating to social work intervention (Tice and Long, 2009).

The law-in-theory may also not be reflected in practice. Although Nigeria, Nepal and the Philippines, for example, have enacted legislation to protect the rights of children and prohibit trafficking, these do not appear to be consistently enforced (Zumve, personal communication; Boele, 2005; CLRRD, 2002). Moreover, when countries have acknowledged their responsibility to protect children from abuse, they have not always been safe. In the UK, Sweden, Malawi and Romania, for example, practice and the monitoring of provision have been inadequate and children have been abused or neglected (Tice and Long, 2009; Preston-Shoot, 2010). Sometimes social workers have exposed these abuses, and experienced hostility from their employers as a result (Preston-Shoot and Kline, 2009). Sometimes non-governmental agencies, advocacy organizations, and service users have voiced concerns.

Responses to child abuse and trafficking may emphasize procedures by tightening legal controls, or seek to tackle underlying causes, for example, family poverty, by providing specialist services, such as microcredit schemes, housing, refuges, and support. They may adopt an advocacy and lobbying role. Three features stand out: firstly, the importance of involving children and young people in the design, decision-making and implementation of services; secondly, engaging with communities and kinship networks rather than just remedial casework (Lyons et al., 2006; Laird, 2007); and thirdly, building capacity by sharing practice models, such as family group conferences, and moulding them into specific social and cultural contexts (Nikku, 2010).

ABUSE OF VULNERABLE ADULTS

Similarly, variable responses appear in respect of protecting vulnerable adults, and particularly older people, from abuse. Some estimates of elder abuse, for example, in community settings, hover between 4 and 6 percent of the population (Krug et al., 2002; Oh et al., 2006) in the USA, UK, Canada, Korea, Finland and the Netherlands. Daichman (2005) has estimated elder abuse of between 4 and 7 percent in developed nations but suggests that levels, for instance, of psychological abuse, may be upwards of between 25 and 45 per cent in some parts of the world, such as South America. An Israeli study concluded that the figure there was approximately 18 per cent (Siegel-Itzkovich, 2005). In Vietnam and Mongolia (Thi Thai Lan et al., 2010; Namdaldagva et al., 2010), increasing numbers of vulnerable older people and disabled people have been noted.

Zaviršek and Herath (2010) document cases of violence against disabled people in Sri Lanka. Mba (2007) identifies reports of elder abuse from Kenya, Ghana and Zimbabwe, and recommends employment, social protection and education as preventive measures and responses to individual cases. The rise in elder abuse, both in the community and within nursing homes and residential care, appears linked to the breakdown of traditional social welfare systems, organized around the extended family, and to structural inequalities, including gender discrimination, lack of educational opportunities, high unemployment and poor health services (Daichman, 2005; Mba, 2007; Thi Thai Lan et al., 2010). Daichman (2005) also notes the exclusion of women from decision making and the risk to them of sexual violence and physical abuse. She observes that in developing countries legal frameworks remain inadequate and, even where legal rules do exist to protect vulnerable adults, they can be neglected or misunderstood. This may be the result of missing structures and facilities, the impact of bureaucracy on social welfare departments, patriarchal attitudes, lack of information and awareness, and fragmented social networks. However, misunderstanding of adult protection legal rules among social workers has also been found in the UK (Preston-Shoot, 2010).

A number of countries have legislated to protect adults, and especially older people, from abuse, including Japan, South Africa, Australia, the USA and the UK. The degree to which social work is central to adult protection systems varies. Neither Mba (2007) nor Daichman (2005) refer to social work in respect of elder abuse in developing countries. Poor working conditions and escalating workloads, uncertainty about role, and variable practice standards may limit social workers' responses (Sasaki, 2010; Thi Thai Lan et al., 2010; Namdaldagva et al., 2010). In Australia (Ozanne, 2009) social workers are involved in assessment of people's needs and decision-making capacity, the provision of advice, and the coordination of care services and multi-agency interventions. Where adults do not have decision-making capacity, the least restrictive intervention that meets someone's needs is sought. Similar approaches apply in the UK (Braye and Preston-Shoot, 2009) and the US (Daly and Jogerst, 2001). The US adult protection system requires the mandatory reporting of abuse and neglect to adult protection services. In Sweden too, all employees in the public and private sectors working with older people and disabled people must report to the local welfare board evidence of unsatisfactory care given by service providers. Parallel requirements exist with respect to health care settings. In some national jurisdictions, such as the UK, US and Australia, court orders are available to protect victims from abuse and violence, for instance, restricting the behaviour and movements of offenders. There are also judicial systems to resolve questions relating to an individual's decision-making competence and to allocate responsibility in such cases for looking after someone's finances, health and welfare. Nonetheless, concerns exist about under-reporting and lack of recognition of physical, sexual, financial and psychological abuse, and whether existing legal rules are sufficient to empower and protect victims by means of an effective multi-agency response (Braye and Preston-Shoot, 2009; Ozanne, 2009).

ENGAGEMENT WITH HUMAN RIGHTS

Social work's concern with social justice requires practitioners to reflect consistently on whether or not they have become complicit in legitimizing inequalities (Yu, 2006). Such reflection may well conclude that social work has perhaps a mixed track record in respect of advocating for social justice and human rights. In South Africa, during apartheid, social work organizations were heavily involved in challenging dehumanizing practices which denied people their human rights (Noyoo, 2004). However, South Africa faces ongoing challenges of poverty, racism, violence against women and children, and high crime levels. Noyoo (2004) argues that social work, which should play a leading role in identifying and rectifying current oppressive patterns in South Africa, may be in danger of becoming an instrument of exclusion and injustice because it has changed its focus from macro issues, such as conflicts of interest between classes, genders and races, to preoccupation with caseloads.

Similarly, Oommen (2002) accuses social workers in India of being driven by power and weakened by a process of bureaucratization. Zaviršek and Herath (2010) note how social work's concern for social justice may have been neutralized by politicians working for their own goals. Humphries (2004) has accused social workers in the UK of complicity in implementing inhumane government policies on asylum seekers. In the US, social work's commitment to social justice has been questioned, alongside whether human rights feature in its work with individuals, their families and communities

(Lowe and Reid, 1999). Weiss and colleagues (2002) have suggested that in Israel and the US, in contrast to the UK, social workers have distanced themselves from disadvantaged groups. However, UK social workers practising in statutory health and social care agencies are also constrained by bureaucratization in their organizational context when seeking to empower and advocate for their clients (Braye and Preston-Shoot, 2009).

Partly in contrast, Yu (2006) is heavily critical of how social work organizations responded in the Philippines during the Marcos era. Although some practitioners chose to work in non-governmental organizations in order to avoid co-option by the state and to protest against human rights abuses, an unequivocally critical response from the professional community did not materialize. Indeed, official social work publications overlooked repression and inequalities and did not question government directly. Yu (2006) also questions the degree to which, subsequent to the Marcos regime, social workers have taken a categorical stand against neo-liberal policies.

Healy (2008) comments approvingly on social work's record in anti-apartheid and in children's rights movements. She notes the record of involvement in human rights of early social work leaders but contrasts this with the limited early references to human rights in journals and conferences, and also with periods of invisibility. She charts International Federation of Social Worker (IFSW) statements to governments on human rights violations and advocacy for individual social workers who have been abused or harassed for their work, in countries as diverse as East Timor, Chile, Malaysia, USA, Israel and Columbia. However, as with Noyoo (2004), she observes that social work is perhaps more comfortable when engaging with cases rather than macro issues.

Like Healy (2008), Hölscher and Berhane (2008) also note that IFSW has challenged human rights violations and concerns in Australia, Canada, Kuwait, Grenada, Zimbabwe, Sudan and East Timor. However, they accuse IFSW of responding unevenly and use Eritrea as a case study. Here social work education has been curtailed and only government-controlled organizations allowed. Civil and political rights have been violated and large-scale displacements, increased disability and growing numbers of orphans have increased the need for social work at a time when the political situation has made it arguably impossible to practise in line with international definitions. However, they argue, public expression of solidarity and condemnation of human rights violations have not been forthcoming.

How power is configured and exercised within organizations can nullify individual appreciation of right and wrong (Lyons et al., 2006). This may be because, across diverse South American, Central American, North American and European countries (Weiss-Gal and Welbourne, 2008), social work does not have a monopoly over specified tasks and functions. A cultural bias towards individual rights rather than a collective perspective, for example, in the US and Australia (Congress and McAuliffe, 2006), may also be implicated. Nonetheless, this does not fully account for when practitioners decide to adopt or shun a rights-centred approach to their work. In an Australian context, Kennedy and Richards (2007) express concern regarding how individual workers comply with, filter or defy agency expectations, and of how agencies attempt to resist, influence or mediate the requirements of legal rules. In a UK context, Preston-Shoot (2010) has identified how social welfare agencies have disregarded the legal rules when assessing and providing services for children and their families and for adults requiring provision of care in the community. From a US context, Madden (2007) argues that managers must know the law in order to use discretion appropriately in practice. Research from Australia (Lonne et al., 2004), the US (Strom-Gottfried, 2000), and Europe (Musil et al., 2004; Papadaki and Papadaki, 2008) reports unsettling evidence about the impact of organizational procedures on workers and the erosion of

ethical practice. In the Czech Republic, social workers appear to avoid dilemmas rather than to challenge the working conditions that provoked them (Musil et al., 2004). In Greece (Papadaki and Papadaki, 2008), social workers practise within the constraints they encounter rather than challenge agency practices and policies or develop activities to improve inadequately resourced services. Australian (Murray and Swain, 1999; Lonne et al., 2004), US (Strom-Gottfried, 2000) and UK (Preston-Shoot, 2010) studies also document concerns about employees' relationships with their employing agencies, including lack of adequate supervision and poor case management, and about how organizations appear to struggle to discuss ethical concerns about practice.

Law is a feature of some but not all social work curricula. Even where featured (as in the UK (Braye and Preston-Shoot, 2009), Australia, (Swain and Rice, 2009), Nepal (Nikku, 2010), Vietnam (Thi Thai Lan, 2010) and India (Menoa, 2002)), the limited time devoted to it may be insufficient for students to develop and maintain competence in their legal knowledge and skills, and confidence in their understanding of welfare and human rights law to challenge agency practice and decision making. Equally, social work courses will vary, as will individual practitioners, in the degree to which they emphasize rights-based practice as opposed, say, to technical competence or clinical skills (Braye and Preston-Shoot, 2009; Nikku, 2010). Finally, social workers may be excluded from settings, such as criminal justice institutions, where legal and other kinds of advocacy are most needed.

This evidence questions the image of social work as a morally active and legally literate profession. Standards are clearly vulnerable to compromise. Just as the law-in-action may differ from the law-in-theory, so too values-in-theory may not automatically transfer to values-in-practice. Arguably too, social work has been too protective of the organizations in which it has been practised, especially welfare bureaucracies and particularly when they have denied benefits to individuals eligible for help. Welfare department cultures have meant that social workers have often found themselves in a corrupted world of service where many feel powerless to assert social work's values (Lowe and Reid, 1999; Preston-Shoot, 2010). Perhaps this uncovers a process of acculturation and institutionalization fostered in social work organizations, which require employees to limit their vision to agency procedures. The end result is a practice configured quite differently from that envisaged in social work's ethical codes.

STRENGTHENING SOCIAL WORK

What makes social work vulnerable? Social workers' organizations do not make ethical decisions in a vacuum but rather at the confluence of organizational, political and cultural dynamics in which there are internal and external influences (Mansbach and Kaufman, 2003). Internal influences include the organization's own needs, whilst external influences centre around the location and distribution of political and cultural power. Their interplay will affect the ability of social work organizations to promote and support the ethical behaviour of practitioners and managers in the field. They will also influence the response to whistle blowers. In many countries, social work practice operates under considerable pressure. Very often social workers complain about a culture of silence in human service organizations, where they do not dare to speak up against malpractice or mismanagement. The following factors may have constrained social work in its assertion of human rights and social justice:

- close political links and dependence on government funding;
- social work being an emergent profession in some countries whilst under threat in others;
- lack of formal recognition by government and absence of national social work associations;

- variable quality and standards of social work education;
- concern for personal safety, for instance, when contemplating whistle-blowing;
- protection of the profession, to maintain its legitimacy;
- high workloads and poor working conditions, including erratic supervision, within agencies which are bureaucratic and functional in organization rather than rights-based or values-oriented;
- low regard; variable and often ambivalent public image; public sector location; low status of service users; lack of specific definition of social work;
- social justice and human need seen as technical rather than social or political problems;
- inadequate theoretical orientation and lack of identification with human rights, suggesting there may not be a common professional project in respect of social justice;
- knowledge about how to address social problems may be imported rather than developed alongside local conditions.

(See for example, Yu, 2006; Hölscher and Berhane, 2008; Weiss-Gal and Welbourne, 2008; Nikku, 2010; Thi Thai Lan et al., 2010; Sasaki, 2010; Zaviršek and Herath, 2010).

In a survey across 10 countries, only three had licensing procedures and one (India) did not have a code of ethics (Weiss-Gal and Welbourne, 2008). Not all countries with ethical codes had included sanctions to enforce compliance. Indeed, the picture is very variable. Japan (Sasaki, 2010) and Taiwan (Lin and Wang, 2010) have statute-based social work licensing and certification systems. Mongolia has yet to develop a social work code of ethics (Namdaldagva et al., 2010) Nepal lacks a national social work association (Nikku, 2010). Arguments for social worker registration and licensing systems propose that such procedures help to ensure that social workers are trained, committed to high standards and accountable for their work, and that service users will have guarantees of what practice standards to expect and be better protected. Counter-arguments question how codes of ethics can guarantee sound professional practice when expressing general principles and not supported by sanctions (Preston-Shoot, 2010). Since social workers practise in hierarchical organizations and also alongside other professionals, it may additionally prove difficult to pinpoint responsibility. Social work associations may depend on government funding and have close political ties, which may weaken the supposed protection, for practitioners and service users alike, of professional licence to practise (Yu, 2006).

Mansbach and Bachner (2009) surveyed social work students in Israel for their readiness to whistle blow. Students recognized the tension between loyalty to employers or colleagues and a moral or legal duty to report serious unlawful or unethical behaviours. Israeli social work students expressed a readiness to whistle blow. However, self-reported willingness to challenge does not mean that practitioners will actually report poor practice. It takes place against a backdrop where social work organizations may respond self-protectively and where loyalty to colleagues is, implicitly at least, stressed above that to clients. This type of organizational response is not unique to Israel, having also been seen in the UK (Preston-Shoot and Kline, 2009), Australia (Kennedy and Richards, 2007) and Sweden (Hedin and Månsson, 2011), for instance.

In an Australian study of practitioners, over half feared the consequences of complaining or whistle blowing (Lonne et al., 2004). Some evidence existed of organizations downplaying ethical breaches by staff or ethical concerns raised by them, although there were also formal responses to both such scenarios. The researchers concluded that welfare organizations cannot be relied upon to promote social work's moral mission or to be ethically responsive. Similar evidence exists in the UK of strong pressures on practitioners to accept what is professionally unethical and to remain silent. The number of social work whistle blowers remains low (Preston-Shoot and Kline, 2009), arguably because protective legislation is too weak

and the organizational response is often one of anger and retaliation. An overdue reform may be to provide a contractual right for practitioners to raise concerns safely with an organization responsible for inspection or regulation without fear of repercussions from their employers. However, the capacity and competence of the inspectorate to act in response to reported concerns is then crucial and, as experience in the UK has shown, by no means guaranteed.

Ethical and behavioural codes assign responsibility to individual practitioners to be accountable for their own work and work within agreed standards of best practice. However, social workers, especially those employed by state-funded municipalities, may not be autonomous agents in their practice, independent of the organizational context in which they are situated (Lonne et al., 2004; Papadaki and Papadaki, 2008; Weiss-Gal and Welbourne, 2008). Critical reflection, ethical orientation and professional autonomy may, therefore, be circumscribed by organizational procedures, conditions of employment and managerial practices. Across jurisdictions, practitioners have sought guidance about work conditions adverse to competent practice (Murray and Swain, 1999; Strom-Gottfried, 2000).

Against powerful employer imperatives the codes provide insufficient protection for other reasons too. The first problem is their ambiguity about how to practise. The Greek code of ethics does not offer specific guidance to social workers who feel constrained to challenge unjust policies and practices (Papadaki and Papadaki, 2008). Codes can be overly general, difficult to apply or enforce, and unrealistic when contrasted with the challenges that practitioners face (Strom-Gottfried, 2000). A second ambiguity concerns when principles have been breached and what may constitute incompetent practice (Murray and Swain, 1999; Strom-Gottfried, 2000). Moreover, as in the UK, employer responsibilities for adequate supervision and management of practice lack statutory force (Preston-Shoot, 2010).

CONCLUDING DISCUSSION

Three themes emerge from this chapter which have great importance for addressing social justice and social protection issues in social work. They concern the difference between rights- and needs-based systems, the difference between policies and practice in relation to the defence of human rights, and the visibility of and role for (international) social work.

It is not easy to detect a clear line between rights-based and needs-based models in different countries in social work. In countries like the UK and Sweden where (perhaps) the belief in the welfare state and its representatives remains quite high, people expect the state to take care of children in need, to organize safe settings for older people and to promote social inclusion of disabled people. In such countries, a needs-based system of laws has been implemented. However, in other countries, including those emerging from a colonial past or where the state or its professionals have been accused of being corrupt, there is a stronger tendency to have a rights-based system. Here it may be considered an advantage to specify different rights.

A needs-based system may hold out the promise of interventions that meet people's needs. However, the challenges of a needs-based system include its vagueness, the interface between need and available resources, the risk of an abuse of power and the difficulties for professionals when handling professional discretion. A rights-based system, by contrast, may extend the promise of predictability and clarity, but may sometimes prove rigid, or deny particular rights, the complexity of different social divisions, and resource constraints.

The presence of legislation and policies, whether expressed in a language of needs or rights, does not guarantee a beneficial outcome. There remains the problem of translation – from the law-in-theory to the law-in-practice, and values-in-theory to values-in-practice. For instance, social workers express uncertainty about how to implement some of the legal rules, for instance, concerning human rights or the sharing of information, and social work education may not always provide a secure legal knowledge and skills base (Braye and Preston-Shoot, 2009). Contributing to this uncertainty is how social workers should respond when law and ethics collide. Some possible actions may be lawful but unethical. Others may be unlawful but ethical. Should it be the case that law made by a body with legislative power should be obeyed, even if its moral content is contrary to social work values? Or should social workers prioritize their ethical commitments? Moreover, how should social workers balance doing things right, in terms of law and ethics, with doing right things and rights-thinking (Braye and Preston-Shoot, 2009)? A human rights- and social justice-based practice has the potential to enrich needs-based and rights-based approaches to people's welfare (Skegg, 2005) but only if such questions are openly debated.

Undoubtedly, when social workers raise concerns about, and advocate for, people's human rights and social justice, including for the need for an international convention on sexual and reproductive rights, they may encounter hostility from some communities, employers and government agencies. Social work education may require an enhanced focus on helping to build social workers' capacity and resilience for undertaking this responsibility.

Finally, in the international context, social work operates along a continuum. At one end, its role is clearly outlined, for instance in many jurisdictions being centrally located in child protection. At the other end, social work appears to have been given or to have assumed for itself little part to play in meeting people's needs. Action in respect of hate crime might be one example here. In the space between individuals and the state, social work might do more to identify where it sees its primary territory and where it has a supporting role alongside other professions and non-governmental organizations.

To ensure that people's lives are characterized by human dignity and social inclusion, with economic security, access to education and health care, affordable housing and services to meet needs arising from daily living, social work may have to articulate more clearly, and then deliver, research-informed and evidenced interventions that ensure social protection.

REFERENCES

Boele, F. (2005) *Rights of the Child in the Philippines*. Geneva: OMCT.

Braye, S. and Preston-Shoot, M. (2009) *Practising Social Work Law*, (3rd edn). Basingstoke: Palgrave Macmillan.

Butler, I. (2002) 'A code of ethics for social work and social care research', *British Journal of Social Work*, 32 (2): 239–48.

Chui, W.H. (2009) 'Juvenile justice', in P. Swain and S. Rice (eds), *In the Shadow of the Law. The Legal Context of Social Work Practice*, (3rd edn). Sydney: The Federation Press.

CLRRD (Centre for Legal Research and Resource Development) (2002) *Baseline Survey on Criminal Justice in Nepal*. CLRRD: Bhaktapur.

Congress, E. and McAuliffe, D. (2006) 'Social work ethics: professional codes in Australia and the United States', *International Social Work*, 49(2): 151–64.

CSCI (Commission for Social Care Inspection) (2008) *Putting People First: Equality and Diversity Matters 1. Providing Appropriate Services for Lesbian, Gay and Bisexual and Transgender People*. London: Commission for Social Care Inspection.

CSCI (Commission for Social Care Inspection) (2009) *Putting People First: Equality and Diversity Matters. Achieving Disability Equality in Social Care Services*. London: Commission for Social Care Inspection.

Daichman, L.S. (2005) 'Elder abuse in developing nations', in M.L. Johnson (ed.), *Cambridge Handbook of Age and Ageing*. Cambridge: Cambridge University Press.

Daly, J. and Jogerst, G. (2001) 'Statute definitions of elder abuse', *Journal of Elder Abuse and Neglect*, 13 (4): 39–57.

Desai, M. (2009) 'A comparative study of measures for children in conflict with the law in Goa and Singapore', *International Social Work*, 52(3): 313–26.

Fairgrieve, D. and Green, S. (eds) (2004) *Child Abuse Tort Claims against Public Bodies: A Comparative Law View*. Aldershot: Ashgate.

Guilarte, E. (2005) 'Cuban social policy and disadvantaged social groups', in S.-A. Månsson and C.P. Cervantes (eds), *Social Work in Cuba and Sweden. Achievements and Prospects*. Gothenburg University and Havana University.

Healy, L. (2007) 'Universalism and cultural relativism in social work ethics', *International Social Work*, 50(1), 11–26.

Healy, L. (2008) 'Exploring the history of social work as a human rights profession', *International Social Work*, 51(6): 735–48.

Hedin, U-C. and Månsson, S-A. (2011) 'Whistleblowing processes in Swedish public organizations – complaints and consequences', *European Journal of Social Work*, doi. 10.1080/13691457.2010.543890.

Hölscher, D. and Berhane, S. (2008) 'Reflections on human rights and professional solidarity: a case study of Eritrea', *International Social Work*, 51(3): 311–23.

Humphries, B. (2004) 'An unacceptable role for social work: implementing immigration policy', *British Journal of Social Work*, 34(1): 93–107.

IFSW (International Federation of Social Workers). (2006) *Ethics in Social Work, Statement of Principles*. Bern: International Federation of Social Workers/ International Association of Schools of Social Work.

IFSW/IASSW (International Federation of Social Workers/International Association of Schools of Social Work). (2001) *International Definition of Social Work*. Copenhagen: International Association of Schools of Social Work and the International Federation of Social Workers.

Jenness, V. and Grattet, R. (2005) 'The law-in-between: the effects of organizational perversity on the policing of hate crime', *Social Problems*, 52(3): 337–59.

Johnson, K. and Marriott, A. (2009) 'The never ending story: deinstitutionalisation and people with intellectual disability', in P. Swain and S. Rice (eds), *In the Shadow of the Law. The Legal Context of Social Work Practice*, (3rd edn). Sydney: The Federation Press.

Junger-Tas, J. and Decker, S. (2006) *International Handbook of Juvenile Justice*. New York: Springer.

Kennedy, R. with Richards, J. (2007) *Integrating Human Service Law and Practice*, (2nd edn). Victoria: Oxford University Press.

Krug, E.G., Dahlberg, L.L., Mercy, J.A., Zwi, A.B. and Lozano, R. (eds) (2002) *World Report on Violence and Health*. Geneva: World Health Organisation.

Laird, S. (2007) 'The application of African practice models to the social problems of emergent democracies', in S. Borrmann, M. Klassen and C. Spatscheck (eds), *International Social Work. Social Problems, Cultural Issues and Social Work Education*. Opladen: Barbara Budrich Publishers.

Lin, W-I. and Wang, Y-T. (2010) 'What does professionalization mean? Tracing the trajectory of social work education in Taiwan', *Social Work Education*, 29(8): 869–81.

Lonne, B., McDonald, C. and Fox, T. (2004) 'Ethical practice in the contemporary human services', *Journal of Social Work*, 4(3): 345–67.

Lowe, G. and Reid, P.N. (1999) *The Professionalization of Poverty. Social Work and the Poor in the Twentieth Century*. New York: Aldine.

Lyons, K., Manion, K. and Carlsen, M. (2006) *International Perspectives on Social Work. Global Conditions and Local Practice*. Basingstoke: Palgrave Macmillan.

Madden, R. (2007) 'Liability and safety issues in human services management', in J. Aldgate, L. Healy, B. Malcolm, B. Pine, W. Rose and J. Seden (eds), *Enhancing Social Work Management. Theory and Best Practice from the UK and USA*. London: Jessica Kingsley.

Mansbach, A. and Kaufman, R. (2003) 'Ethical decision-making of social workers' associations: a case study of the Israeli Association of Social Workers' responses to whistle-blowing', *International Social Work*, 46(3): 303–12.

Mansbach, A. and Bachner, Y. (2009) 'Self-reported likelihood of whistleblowing by social work students', *Social Work Education*, 28(1): 18–28.

Mba, C. (2007) 'Elder abuse in parts of Africa and the way forward', *Gerontechnology*, 6(4): 230–5.

Menoa, N. (2002) 'Law and social work: an emerging partnership?', in P. Visvesvaran (ed.), *Social Work Today. Present Realities and Future Prospects*. Madras School of Social Work.

Murray, H. and Swain P. (1999) 'Queries and complaints: the maintenance of ethically justifiable standards of conduct', *Australian Social Work*, 52(1): 9–16.

Musil, L., Kubalčíková, K., Hubíková, O. and Nečasová, M. (2004) 'Do social workers avoid the dilemmas of work with clients?', *European Journal of Social Work*, 7(3): 305–19.

Namdaldagva, O.-E., Myagmarjav, S. and Burnette, D. (2010) 'Professional social work education in Mongolia: achievements, lessons learned and future direction.,' *Social Work Education*, 29(8): 882–95.

Nikku, B.R. (2010) 'Social work education in Nepal: major opportunities and abundant challenges', *Social Work Education*, 29(8): 818–30.

Noyoo, N. (2004) 'Human rights and social work in a transforming society: South Africa', *International Social Work*, 47(3): 359–69.

Oh, J., Kim, H.S., Martins, D. and Kim, H. (2006) 'A study of elder abuse in Korea', *International Journal of Nursing Studies*, 43: 203–14.

Oommen, T. (2002) 'Social work and human rights: for a feasible linkage', in P. Visvesvaran (ed.), *Social Work Today. Present Realities and Future Prospects*. Madras School of Social Work.

Ozanne, E. (2009) 'Elder abuse and the law', in P. Swain and S. Rice (eds), *In the Shadow of the Law. the Legal Context of Social Work Practice* (3rd edn). Sydney: The Federation Press.

Papadaki, E. and Papadaki, V. (2008) 'Ethically difficult situations related to organizational conditions: social workers' experiences in Crete', *Journal of Social Work*, 8(2): 163–80.

Pitts, J. and Kuula, T. (2005) 'Incarcerating young people: an Anglo-Finnish comparison', *Youth Justice*, 5(3): 147–64.

Pollack, D. (2009) 'Hate crimes and social work: an international perspective', *International Social Work*, 52(3): 409–15.

Preston-Shoot, M. (2010) 'On the evidence for viruses in social work systems: law, ethics and practice', *European Journal of Social Work*, 13(4): 465–82.

Preston-Shoot, M. and Kline, R. (2009) 'Memorandum of written evidence', in House of Commons Children, Schools and Families Committee, *Training of Children and Families Social Workers. Seventh Report of Session 2008–09. Volume II*. London: The Stationery Office.

Sasaki, A. (2010) 'Social work education in Japan: future challenges', *Social Work Education*, 29(8): 855–68.

Siegel-Itzkovich, J. (2005) 'A fifth of elderly people in Israel are abused', *British Medical Journal*, 330: 498.

Skegg, A.-M. (2005) 'Human rights and social work. A Western imposition or empowerment to the people?', *International Social Work*, 48(5): 667–72.

Strom-Gottfried, K. (2000) 'Ensuring ethical practice: an examination of NASW Code Violations, 1986–97', *Social Work*, 45(3): 251–61.

Swain, P. and Rice, S (eds) (2009) *In the Shadow of the Law. The Legal Context of Social Work Practice* (3rd edn). Sydney: The Federation Press.

Tang, K.-L. (2003) 'Implementing the United Nations Convention on the Rights of the Child. The Canadian experience', *International Social Work*, 46(3): 277–88.

Thi Thai Lan, N., Hugman, R. and Briscoe, C. (2010) 'Moving towards an "indigenous" social work education in Vietnam', *Social Work Education*, 29(8): 843–54.

Tice, C. and Long, D. (eds) (2009) *International Social Work Policy and Practice*. New Jersey: Wiley.

UN (United Nations). (2000) *Economic and Social Council Report: Report of the Special Rapporteur on Violence against Women, its Causes and Consequences*. E/CN.4/2000/68. February.

UN (United Nations). (2008) *Convention on the Rights of the Child. Consideration of Reports Submitted by State Parties under Article 44 of the Convention: Concluding Observations – United Kingdom of Great Britain and Northern Ireland. CRC/C/GBR/CO/4. UN Committee on the Rights of the Child.*

Weiss-Gal, I. and Welbourne, P. (2008) 'The professionalisation of social work', *International Journal of Social Welfare*, 17: 281–90.

Weiss, I., Gal, J., Cnaan, R. and Maglajlic, R. (2002) 'Where does it begin? A comparative perspective on the professional preferences of first year social work students', *British Journal of Social Work*, 32(5): 589–608.

Yu, N. (2006) 'Interrogating social work: Philippine social work and human rights under martial law', *International Journal of Social Welfare*, 15: 257–63.

Zaviršek, D. and Herath, S. (2010) '"I want to have my future, I have a dialogue": social work in Sri Lanka between neo-capitalism and human rights', *Social Work Education*, 29(8): 831–42.

16

Social Work and Changing Environments

Jennifer McKinnon

INTRODUCTION

Awareness of nature as something more than an infinite resource for human exploitation has been in the public consciousness ever since the publication of Rachel Carson's groundbreaking book, *Silent Spring*, in 1962. Although public interest has varied in the ensuing period, widespread awareness of the impact of human activity on the environment was raised in 2006/2007 as several events converged and momentum was gained. Release of the Stern Review in Britain (Stern, 2006), Al Gore's (2006) documentary film *'An Inconvenient Truth'*, and the most recent Intergovernmental Panel on Climate Change (IPCC, 2007) report, all confirming that human intervention makes an undoubted contribution to global warming, together with a range of other events around the same time, led to a period of unprecedented public awareness and alarm at the perceived environmental crisis.

Awareness is also developing about the ways in which human wellbeing is linked to a healthy environmental context (Low and Gleeson, 1999; McMichael, 2003; World Resources Institute, 2003). In more recent years, some countries have moved to introduce carbon pollution reduction schemes and other measures designed to reduce human-induced impacts on the environment and to deal with global warming (Owen, 2007; Sherrard and Tate, 2007). A worldwide agreement on emission reduction targets was not reached at the much-vaunted Copenhagen Summit in 2010; hence action could only be taken at the individual country level (Parks and Roberts, 2010). The actions of various countries have been taken under the duress imposed by a strong campaign questioning the validity of the science that identified human-induced climate change (UNEP, 2007). Meanwhile widespread and regular reports appear in the media of climate-related natural disasters, and ever-increasing rates of species extinction, loss of habitat and biodiversity.

While these events have taken place in the public arena, there has not thus far been a substantial debate about environmental issues in the social work literature as we struggle to elicit the implications of the environmental crisis for social work theory and practice.

Such a debate would go to the very heart of the way social work as a profession is defined, as well as the boundaries of its professional domain.

Perhaps it is the case that social workers generally agree that their expertise is in matters social, and therefore natural environmental factors are not germane to a debate on social work's professional interests. I argue that there is a clear connection for social work with matters environmental, particularly in the links between social justice and environmental justice, and that social work's established expertise can aid ongoing relevance of the profession if a clear focus on environmental sustainability is incorporated into the social work curriculum and into continuing professional development programmes.

The nexus of 'social justice', which is commonly regarded as having a legitimate place in social work's professional arena, and 'environmental justice', which is not always regarded as a legitimate aspect of social work, is a broad one, and these two fields are linked in a number of ways. Most notably, it is becoming increasingly obvious that negative environmental consequences are experienced disproportionately by the most vulnerable members of society, the very people with whom social workers most often work (Warren, 2000; Plumwood, 2002; Coates, 2003a; Zapf, 2009). Such effects can be observed around the world in phenomena such as individuals and families who cannot afford to move away from polluted neighbourhoods (Warren 2000); indigenous peoples who have been driven from their ancestral lands as a result of the cutting and burning of rainforest; placement of heavily polluting industries and waste sites in areas occupied by people on low incomes – most notably people who are poor and non-white; and fishers and indigenous peoples whose livelihoods have been impacted, if not destroyed, by depletion of fish stocks (Coates, 2003a). Climate change in the form of global warming is the outstanding threat for human societies in the current environmental crisis (Owen, 2007), but I also argue that social workers should be aware of the impact of an ever-increasing world population, depletion of natural resources, intensification of political and ethnic conflicts, and soil desertification.

At the heart of this chapter is the notion that the environmental crisis is a social justice issue. For Beck, climate change is a potent example of the links between social justice and environmental issues:

> Social inequalities and climate change are two sides of the same coin. One cannot conceptualize inequalities and power any longer without taking the consequences of climate change into account, and one cannot conceptualize climate change without taking its impacts on social inequalities and power into account. (Beck, 2010: 257)

Dialetachi points out that the direct consequences from climate change will be more dramatic for the most economically disadvantaged populations:

> The most fragile, most unprotected, those who have less resource, who have less survival alternatives will be affected intensely: they are small farmers without agricultural insurance when crops fail, residents of the stream's edge who face flooding, slum-dwellers leaning on the hills, victims of tropical diseases spread to new areas, crab catchers covered by the elevation of ocean level and so on. (Dialetachi, 2009: 246)

For the social work profession, which has had a long-standing focus on social justice, the goal will be to recognise the dangers for society of ignoring the ecological crisis; recognise the irrational thinking that has led to the current ecological crisis; recognise the ecological impacts of current social forces such as globalisation and consumerism and work with individuals, groups and communities to counter these forces; and work towards development of a place-sensitive culture.

The main objectives of this chapter are to:

- canvass the range of issues relevant to social workers as they are confronted by changing environments;
- demonstrate links between social justice and environmental justice; and
- provide examples of social work practices that address issues related to changing environments.

HISTORY OF SOCIAL WORK AS IT RELATES TO CHANGING ENVIRONMENTS

Poverty has been a key focus of theory and practice since social work's inception as a profession. Jones (2001) points out that poverty remains the most common problem confronting social work's diverse client population. This focus on poverty reflects in some ways the fact that social work, in most countries where it is practised, arose out of concerns for urban slum-dwellers. For example, interest in the health of children living in such conditions, especially in regard to the need for 'fresh air', drove social interest in taking a systematic approach to ensuring that the environment was amenable to health. Many children affected by tuberculosis and asthma were sent to attend 'special schools' with access to the aforementioned 'fresh air'. The Charity Organisation Society (COS) in Britain is often quoted as a driving force in child welfare in late-Victorian Britain, though Taylor (2008) makes the point that there were many other forms of organised charity (including those specifically related to child care). Taylor (2008: 687) notes the overall 'coalescence of anxieties around dirt, boundaries and pollution' in the child-protection discourse of the time.

There is also historical evidence of practising social workers in the US who viewed the environment as intrinsically important and incorporated nature into their work. For example, Jane Addams '…never separated the human need for beauty, art and nature from the need for social reform' (Bartlett, 2003: 116). Addams was a health advocate, social reformer, and one-time garbage collector, and understood well the relationship between sanitation and health. She also established the first parks and recreation centres in the city of Chicago. Addams advocated and worked for the creation of public green spaces primarily for workers and their families to find respite from the restrictions of the factories and the harsh working conditions of the slaughterhouses.

Early in the 20th century Mary Richmond acknowledged the physical environment as an important contextual consideration for practice when she was laying the conceptual foundations for the new profession of social work. However, Richmond (1922: 99) perceived the importance of the physical environment to be related to its social aspects, asserting that the physical environment 'becomes part of the social environment' insofar as it 'frequently has its social aspects'. Zapf (2009) claims that, from the outset, the social work profession has been more comfortable using social science lenses to view the environment rather than perspectives from the physical or natural sciences. Yet at a later point, social work did adopt an ecological perspective taken from the natural sciences. For instance, the ecosystems perspective provided social work with an outlook closely related to biological science , and encouraged a 'simultaneous focus on person and environment' (Suppes and Wells, 2009: 58). But this model, derived as it was from the basic assumptions of systems theory, was also based on assumptions that the person would be interpreted from psychological theory, and the environment could be interpreted by sociological and economic theory (Zapf, 2009). Thus, while 'the environment' is acknowledged in social work literature since the early days of the profession, it is generally conceptualised in socio-cultural terms. The environment is rarely conceived in the social work literature as being about the physical/natural environment.

Over the past decade or so, the social work literature has reflected a slowly increasing interest in environmental factors as they relate to social work. Indeed, in 2001 a survey of members of the Australian Association of Social Workers (AASW) found that some eleven percent of members identified ecological sustainability as one of the top ten policy issues on which they would like the AASW to focus (AASW, 2001). Soon after, the AASW made a change to the code of ethics that introduced the concept of 'social development and environmental management in the interests of human welfare' as an expressed value for social workers (AASW, 2002), and this change was further developed in changes made to the AASW code of ethics in 2010.

The International Federation of Social Workers (IFSW), United States National Association of Social Workers (NASW), British Association of Social Workers (BASW) and Canadian Association of Social Workers (CASW) have now incorporated statements about social workers' responsibilities toward the environment into their codes of ethics/policy statements as discussed later in this chapter.

INTERNATIONAL CONTEXT

This chapter is written at a time of intense international pressures. The combined effects of globalisation, climate change, and a number of conflict zones – most particularly in the Middle East – have contributed to the mass movement of people on a major scale. In addition to the refugee movements arising from war and repressive regimes, there is evidence of movement of peoples due to rising sea levels and other effects of climate change, and also due to economic pressures created by loss of arable land. War zones around the world are not all related to political/ideological conflict as one might assume – some major conflicts are related to food and water shortages. Access to water resources, especially good-quality potable freshwater, and disputes over fishing rights in saltwater environments are expected to provide an ongoing and increasing source of settlement tension. Recent humanitarian crises, such as those in Sudanese Darfur and the genocide in Rwanda have been linked to conflict over water (Tulloch, 2009). There is currently an identified lack of adequate drinking water for some 1.1 billion people around the world, thus increasing future potential for water conflict (Delli Priscoli and Wolf, 2007).

Low-lying Pacific and Indian Ocean islands are identified as being particularly vulnerable to sea-level rises associated with global warming, and people of the Carteret Islands have already experienced loss of villages due to sea-incursion. Some residents, who had to leave the Carterets due to loss of homes and villages as water-levels rose, have been referred to as the 'first climate change refugees' (*The Age*, 2009). Tuvalu and the Seychelles are also both acknowledged as potentially needing to shift entire populations from the islands if sea levels rise as predicted (IPCC, 2007).

Extreme weather events, such as storms, floods, droughts, and hurricanes are expected by the IPCC to increase in number and severity due to global warming. The implications for social work of such events are clear: large-scale movements of people, resultant trauma due to permanent or temporary loss of homes, and the health effects of extreme weather will bring a different focus to social work at individual and community levels in affected areas.

Some human-created disasters are also having an impact on large population groups. In Japan in 2011, for example, two natural disasters – an earthquake and the resultant tsunami – were combined with the disastrous effects of the earthquake upon a nuclear power reactor. This situation left the people of Japan dealing with the uncertainties associated with potential radiation leaks and conflicting information about whether or not they were in danger, and eventually resulted in the large-scale movement of people away from residential areas near the nuclear reactor. At the same time, the country was dealing with the grief and trauma associated with the loss of thousands of lives, homes, jobs and industries, as whole villages were swept away by the tsunami. In this instance, the human-created disaster associated with the nuclear power plant was a complicating factor in the country's attempts to recover from the natural disaster. At the time, NASW aimed to lend support to their colleagues in

Japan in the belief that social workers were well-placed to assist the population:

> In this complex and developing disaster, our colleagues in the Japanese professional social work association are uniquely suited to assess the disaster environment in a culturally competent manner and to provide leadership in promoting effective disaster relief and recovery efforts. (NASW, 2011)

While we can hope that social workers already possess the skills needed to deal with the humanitarian effects of natural disasters, if the Intergovernmental Panel on Climate Change (IPCC) prediction that increasing numbers of natural disasters associated with global warming is correct, then social workers will need:

- specific education in dealing with large-scale human movements associated with natural disasters;
- education in regard to dealing with large-scale community trauma;
- to be involved in community-based approaches to preventing the disasters by leading values-based discussions on carbon-emissions reductions.

An integrated approach to consideration of the environment means that economic and social realities must be considered at the same time. On a worldwide basis, this process began in 1992 with the United Nations Conference on Environment and Development in Rio de Janiero, Brazil. For social workers, an important point that emerged from this conference was Agenda 21, a blueprint for action by governments at all levels to address human impact upon the environment (United Nations, 2011). The Rio conference was followed a decade later by a World Summit on Sustainable Development in Johannesburg, South Africa, to further address the intersection of social, environmental and economic issues.

A yearly conference is also sponsored by the UNFCCC (2011) and one of its most important meetings was in Japan in 1997, from which the Kyoto Protocol was developed. Among other goals, this conference set agreed limits on greenhouse gas emissions as well as targets for reductions in emissions to be achieved by 2012. The 2011 Conference of Parts (CoP) meeting, held in Durban, South Africa, received mixed reports about progress on achievements toward the 2012 goals. 2012 is the Rio+20 year, and the CoP meeting is again scheduled to be held in Rio de Janiero. Commentators and analysts will be interested to see if governments can achieve a unified approach to greenhouse gas emission reductions and carbon trading, at a time when the needs and interests of both developing and developed nations are not necessarily compatible.

SUSTAINABILITY

'Sustainability' is an over-used term that has lost some of its significance as a result. There is no single accepted definition of sustainability, and it can be considered a complex and contested term (Cocklin and Alston, 2003). Nevertheless, it is an important concept for social workers as we develop ideas about how social work can assist individuals, groups and societies in their quest for sustainability (See also Chapter 3). Cocklin and Alston (2003) suggest that sustainability involves balance and compromise as social, economic and environmental priorities are set, as well as a sense of progress toward preferred futures. Social aspects of sustainability (a focus on social sustainability) must be recognised as interconnected to the economic and environmental agenda.

The interdependence of social, economic and environmental systems is the underpinning ideology of sustainable development (WCED, 1987), as manifested in official documents such as Agenda 21. Agenda 21 provides a guide to balancing the weight of economic, social and environmental factors in each country. However it is difficult to find such balance in modern industrialised nations, controlled as they are largely by the productivist interests of capital (Bauman, 2004).

As social workers consider how they might work towards sustainability in their professional role, it is perhaps salutary to review the ways in which some entire societies have fared historically as they grapple with environmental problems. The American social geographer, Jared Diamond, and Canadian historian, Reginald Wright, have each examined historical cases of a range of societies, some of which lasted for thousands of years, which have eventually collapsed. Such cases can provide some guidance as we look for clues to help us deal with contemporary issues of social sustainability. Diamond (2005), for example, has examined the historical records of a number of major societies, including the Anasazi people of North America, the Rapanui people of Easter Island, the Roman Empire, the Angkor Wat civilization in Cambodia, and Norwegian settlers in Greenland. Diamond found that there are five general predictors of sustainability for any given society. These are relations with friendly neighbours, relations with unfriendly neighbours, ability to adapt to changing climatic conditions, the environmental damage they cause, and cultural response.

Drawing on historical evidence, Diamond postulates that, when any one of the five factors is a problem for the civilization, even a major one, the civilization can generally cope. However, when the civilization is overstretched by having to cope with any two or more of the factors at the same time, it is usually just a matter of time before its eventual collapse. Although Diamond's work has been criticised on the basis of environmental determinism (Gladwell, 2005), he presents strong evidence from the historical record that societies can die out, either slowly or spectacularly, because of a lack of response to impending environmental disaster.

Wright also reviews the history of society on Easter Island, as well as civilizations such as Sumeria and Ur. He found a common pattern among these collapsed civilizations, a pattern that he speculates could possibly

have been used in advance to predict their downfall: a tradition of 'sticking to entrenched beliefs and practices, robbing the future to pay the present, and spending the last reserves of natural capital on a reckless binge of excessive wealth and glory' (2004: 79). While in the present period there is a clear political focus on terrorism, Wright identifies this focus as a diversion from the truly important issues, as

> terrorism is a small threat compared with hunger, disease, or climate change...[when] 25,000 die every day in the world from contaminated water alone. Each year 20 million children are mentally impaired by malnourishment. Each year, an area greater than Scotland is lost to erosion and urban sprawl, much of it in Asia. (Wright, 2004: 126)

The factors identified by both Wright and Diamond underscore the need for civilizations to learn from the lessons of the past. Their analysis speaks to the importance of attitudes of adaptability and flexibility, of being willing to examine the interplay of social, economic and environmental issues as they are (not as we might want them to be) and of devising solutions based on the response that is needed – rather than continuing to do things in the way they have always been done. The picture they each present also reinforces the importance for contemporary societies of the interplay between social, economic and environmental systems and the need to view these systems as interdependent rather than as separate structures.

SOCIAL WORK AND THE ENVIRONMENT

What does the mounting evidence of environmental decline mean for the domain and boundaries of social work theory and practice? Professional boundaries established rigidly in the past that did not recognise the importance and relevance of the natural environment to human relations can be questioned. Higgs and Cherry (2009: 8) argue that

'Climate change is an example of a universal practice challenge that demands serious study of the very different ways in which people develop understanding, make decisions, communicate, act and, above all, learn to change the way they behave'. That universal practice challenge is equally applicable to the social work profession.

Social workers have engaged with the concept of 'the environment' for many years, yet within the social work literature 'the environment' refers almost exclusively to the socio-cultural or psycho-social environment (Coates, 2003a; Alston and McKinnon, 2005; McKinnon, 2008; Zapf, 2009). Potential links between the natural environment, as characterised by ecological systems, and social work theory and practice have been left relatively unexplored. For example, although there has been extensive use of Bronfenbrenner's (1979, 2005) ecological systems theory in social work, as well as eco-maps to plot the interactions between various social actors and systems, the focus of such theories and methods of analysis has been on the interplay of family, economic, cultural, and political structures – not on the interplay between humans and the rest of the natural world.

Likewise, the person-in-environment concept has been an important element in social work practice theory for many years, and the 'ecological approach' has gained favour as a practice model more recently, though each can be seen to have a substantially psycho-social focus (Healy, 2005). Payne (2005: 91) for example, describes the person-in-environment (or situation) approach as 'focusing on current situations and relationships and seeking better understanding of others, insight into reasons for the clients' and others' behaviour; evaluation of feelings associated with the situation and behaviour'. Such frameworks are not predicated upon social workers' understanding of the links between non-human and human environments.

The IFSW, through its International Policy Statement on Globalisation and the Environment (IFSW, no date) recognises that both natural and built environments have a direct impact on people's potential to develop and to achieve their potential, and that the earth's resources should be shared in a sustainable way. The policy also supports vigorous enforcement of existing environmental protection laws and standards, and urges social workers to work towards a healthier environment and to ensure that environmental issues gain an increased presence in social work education. However the sentiments implicit in this policy statement are still not greatly evident in the social work literature in the form of practice models, though some recent international social work and community development texts have attempted to include it (e.g. Cox and Pawar, 2006; Ife and Tesoriero, 2006).

Social work ethics and the environment

In recent years, social work associations in some countries have moved to incorporate into their respective national code of ethics a requirement for awareness of environmental issues among practicing social workers. One example is the series of changes made by the Australian Association of Social Workers (AASW). In 1999 a change to the code of ethics required Australian social workers to incorporate awareness of 'social development and environmental management in the interests of human welfare' into their practice. Further revisions to the AASW code of ethics in 2010 removed the anthropocentric features of environmental awareness for social workers, and included the notion that the social work profession 'promotes protection of the natural environment as inherent to social wellbeing' (AASW, 2010: 13).

Changes in social policy in recent decades have seen increasing levels of deregulation and competition in welfare contexts, which can present ethical challenges for social workers. Organisational contexts have a substantial impact on professional ethics.

Ethical principles are not absolute, but vary according to the context of practice and the client group. For example, social work education and literature generally pays scant attention to the complex issues involved in working with involuntary clients. As a result, social workers must translate social work theory and value for themselves in order to fit with the context in which they work.

Social workers can find themselves in a similar situation with regard to environmental imperatives because there is little direction in the various codes of ethics to help them address the ethical conflicts that arise when human need or desire is in direct (or sometimes indirect) divergence with non-human needs. Such a conflict might arise, for example, in relation to housing development needed for an increasing population where the proposed location involves the destruction of a forest area that provides valuable wildlife habitat. In times past, there may have been no contest: human needs were always assumed to over-ride non-human needs (Plumwood, 2002). Efforts to save a forest, for instance might have depended on existing residents' views or considerations about catchment management, for example: the needs of local or migratory wildlife would not have provided a reason to over-ride human needs. However, there is increasing recognition that ever-expanding human settlements have negative effects on the natural environment that, in turn, can have multiple negative effects on humans (McMichael, 2003; IPCC, 2007; ABS, 2006). There is also increasing recognition that the non-human (or more-than-human) world is entitled to recognition of dignity and worth for its own intrinsic sake, and not simply for its instrumental value to humans (Warren, 2000; Plumwood, 2002). Such a position raises equity considerations in regard to environmental costs imposed on people who can ill afford to pay them. Social work can take a leadership role in facilitating discussions about such value-issues in the community.

Social work practice and the environment

Coates argues that 'Social work developed and functions within modernity and has been, as a result, limited by its assumptions and boundaries', and like so many professions, social work shares the underpinning values of modernity – individualism, dualism, materialism and domination. In order to achieve its place and status as a profession within the social welfare paradigm, social work 'embraced the scientific method and endorsed reductionist efforts toward seeking individual clarity' (2003a: 58), thus leading to the development of specific intervention methodologies. For this reason, Coates claims that modernity has an ideological stranglehold on social work that gets in the way of our accord with nature, affecting even the so-called 'radical' traditions within social work. Changes to codes of ethics in recent decades are seen as a promising way forward for social workers, providing legitimation for considering environmental issues as part of professional practice.

A major criticism of social work has been that, while social work has promoted human wellbeing, it has neglected to connect the exploitation of nature with the exploitation of people. In the context of a debate over modernist and postmodernist ideology, Walker argues for an interpretive approach to social work practice – one that emphasises the local and specific, while at the same time aspiring to broader political action in the pursuit of 'social and eco-centric justice' (2001: 36).

The processes of industrialisation are closely associated with the phenomenon of globalisation, and include the multiplicity of social and economic factors associated with the movement of people, technology, commerce, and cultures across national borders. In early industrial society, the side effects of modernisation were accepted because of the rewards it offered in the struggle against scarcity (Wallace and Wolf, 2006). Hunger, however, is no longer the major problem it was for most people in industrial or post-industrial societies, yet people face hazards and risks that are 'a wholesale product of industrialisation and are systematically intensified as it becomes global' (Giddens, 1994: 21). Beck (2010) argues that risk in modern society is, above all, associated with chemical and nuclear production forces and the effects of global warming.

Zapf's (2009) concept of 'person as place' provides the conceptual bridge that would provide a theoretical basis for legitimation of social work practice that incorporates nature and understanding of the environmental context more generally. 'Person as place' provides a conceptual foundation for incorporation of sustainability and protection of the environment as an essential aspect of social work practice. There are some existing bodies of social work literature that touch on the importance of place. Rural and remote social work in particular emphasises the relevance of context, and extends practice to include sensitivity to the environment and as being embedded in the community. Zapf (2009: 181) argues that this recognition of attachment to place in rural and remote area social work offers an appreciation that 'geography affects both where and how people live', and with that comes a sense of responsibility for maintaining a healthy physical environment, and a sense of stewardship.

ENVIRONMENTAL ISSUES, AGRIBUSINESS AND THE PALM OIL INDUSTRY

As social workers consider how they might make a personal and/or professional stand on environmental issues, it is pertinent to consider the interconnection of rural and urban dilemmas. For example, a city social worker in any part of the world who is trying to reduce their own carbon footprint may be choosing to use biofuels (such as ethanol) in their own vehicle in an effort to cut greenhouse gas emissions. While this approach is laudable, the choice is not as straightforward as it may first appear, and a case in point becomes evident through examination of the Indonesian palm oil industry.

Palm oil production is growing exponentially; it is used in a wide range of food products, but its role in the bio-fuels industry is the focus of this example. Various studies have observed that palm oil production in Indonesia is associated with environmental degradation such as deforestation, habitat destruction, soil erosion, loss of biodiversity, and water pollution (Mol 2007; McCarthy et al., 2011). Much of this degradation is associated with the sale of small landholdings that are subsequently taken over by investment companies for consolidated monocultural palm oil plantations.

Much of the palm oil development around the world, as in Indonesia, is supported by all levels of government because of the envisaged potential for jobs and investment opportunities, particularly into new export markets, and as a way of bringing poor rural farmers out of poverty (Mol, 2007). Tropical regions of the world are seen as having a great advantage, in terms of climate and soils, for biofuel production. Outcomes for vulnerable poor people in most palm oil production areas have not been as positive, though, as first imagined.

Positive outcomes have been achieved for urban dwellers through lower emissions from traffic, but having sold their land for palm oil production it is difficult to see any positive outcomes for the rural dwellers. The risks to locals in palm oil areas are related to: reduced space for local food production (combined with reduced forest areas from which nuts, seeds, fruit and building materials were previously obtained), water degradation (associated with disease and with long journeys for fresh water), and loss of agency in regard to decision-making about traditional lands (Mol, 2007).

Palm oil production is associated with the international commodities market, and as such is product of globalisation. Indonesia is the world's largest exporter of crude palm oil (McCarthy et al., 2011) and palm oil production is a growing industry, however it is clear that potential pathways out of poverty can be associated with the creation of environmental and social problems. Social workers will need to weigh up the implications of this sort of agribusiness development for their own personal choices and for their professional practice.

SOCIAL JUSTICE, THE ENVIRONMENT AND SOCIAL WORK

Social justice is defined as a core value for social workers, encompassing satisfaction of basic human needs, equitable distribution of resources, fair access, recognition of individual and community rights and duties, equal legal treatment and protection, and social development and environmental management in the interests of human welfare (AASW, 2002: 4). Social workers are understood to have an obligation to promote social justice, particularly for people or groups of people who are 'oppressed or victimised by discrimination' (Zastrow, 1999: 51). In fact, Zastrow (2007) couples the promotion of social justice by social workers with the obligation to promote economic justice, recognising that oppression related to ethnicity, gender, culture, age, class, religion, or disability is generally tied to economic deprivation. Links between social and economic justice are widely accepted in the social work literature, where economic justice is commonly related to issues of employment access, income security, and income parity (Ife, 2002).

Environmental justice, also known as eco-justice, is not so well known in social work. The environmental justice movement is described as a confluence of three great challenges: the struggle against racism and poverty; the effort to conserve and improve the natural environment; and the need to change social institutions away from class division and environmental depletion toward social unity and global sustainability (National People of Color Environmental Leadership Summit, in Matsuoka, 2003).

This concept incorporates the idea that 'the environment' has its own intrinsic value, separate from the instrumental value of nature insofar as it provides for the needs of human beings. Harm to the environment, also known as eco-harm, is viewed from within the environmental justice framework as needing attention in the same way that vulnerable human populations need attention, because the environment has few defences against harmful human interventions (Plumwood, 2002).

The concepts of social justice and environmental justice can be seen to overlap in many examples of injustice toward both people and the environment. Following are three examples taken from both economically developing and developed countries; Bangladesh, the UK and the US.

In Bangladesh devastating floods have seen the need for entire coastal villages to be relocated as homes and village common land are lost when land subsides due to the combined effects of river flooding and sea-level rises. The flooding is, in part at least, related to damage to the environment beyond the state boundaries, and Parks and Roberts (2010) make the point that nations facing rising oceans and other disasters are often those least responsible for the problem and with the least resources to manage these issues.

In the UK, Walker and Burningham (2011) have outlined patterns of social inequality in relation to both flood risk exposure and vulnerability of populations to the diverse impacts of flooding. Their concerns are related to the framing of flood risk and flood impacts, which is directly linked to the level of risk deemed acceptable by government authorities. They conclude that there is evidence of significant inequalities and grounds on which claims of injustice might be made.

Lastly in the US, Rainey and Johnson (2009: 146) document the activist role of people of colour against environmental injustices, and they identify that 'If you are poor, a person of color and female, you are more likely to be a victim of all sorts of environmental dangers and degradation that are life threatening'. Rainey and Johnson detail examples such as 'Chemical Alley' – an 85- mile stretch of the Mississippi River that is home to a quarter of all US chemical plants that also happens to be co-located with primarily black communities. Living near Chemical Alley is associated with a range of health problems, and a population without the resources to relocate to an area associated with better health outcomes.

These examples illustrate that there is a distinct link between large-scale environmental problems and the individuals who are affected by those problems. Social justice and environmental justice are both of interest to social work because they represent a confluence of personal troubles and public issues among the very vulnerable populations with whom social work seeks to make a difference.

Social workers enacting environmental values

Jasanoff claims that

> The interpretive social sciences have a very particular role to play in relation to climate change. It is to restore to public view, and offer a framework in which to think about, the human and the social in a climate that renders obsolete important prior categories of solidarity and experience. It is to make us more aware, less comfortable, and hence more reflective about how we intervene, in word or deed, in the changing order of things (Jasanoff, 2010: 249).

It may be open to debate whether social work can claim to be an interpretive social science. However, the relevance of Jasanoff's message for social work is clear. Social workers through their professional role intervene in the lives of individuals, groups and communities, and they are doing so at a time of unprecedented environmental crisis. Social workers can choose to do so in a way that is

'more aware, less comfortable, and … more reflective', as advocated by Jasanoff (2010).

If Urry (2010: 8) is correct, climate change entails 'the total reorganization of social life, nothing more and nothing less'. What does, and will, this mean for social workers? Shove (2010) alerts us to suggestions that transitions towards sustainability require social innovations in which 'the contemporary rules of the game are eroded, in which the status quo is called into question and in which less resource-intensive regimes, routines, forms of know-how, conventions, markets and expectations take root'. Processes of fracture and dissolution are also predicted to result from transitional processes that move societies toward more sustainable ways of life (Shove, 2010) and resource-intensive social systems can be expected to yield to less demanding types. There is an expected need for facilitation and legitimation of more sustainable patterns of demand – away from what Urry (2010) refers to as 'excess' and from what Beck (2010: 256) refers to as an 'insatiable appetite for natural resources'.

Ward (2005, as cited in Shove, 2010: 282) concludes that the majority of environmentally impactful consumption is undertaken 'not for its own sake but as part of the ordinary accomplishment of everyday life'. Social workers will be interested in understanding how such social practices emerge, are facilitated to persist, and in how they wane. Changing patterns of food consumption and mobility, heating and cooling, water and energy consumption will need to be understood in order to specify and promote social transitions toward more sustainable lifestyles.

Zapf's (2009) notion of 'person as place', understandings about social sustainability, and Coates' (2003a) suggestion regarding place-sensitive culture are all relevant concepts that provide a way forward for social work. The next step will be to expand current social work practice models to include these concepts. Education is identified as the most important mechanism for developing ecological thinking in social workers due to its role not only for learning technical skills, but also as a mechanism for developing an accompanying general culture (Bourdieu, 1990). Such a change would help social work to move attention beyond minor adjustments or improvements to capital markets and growth-dominated social structures, and enable a critique beyond purely social matters (Coates, 2003b).

There are many examples of how practitioners and communities are taking environmental matters into account and seeking different outcomes for affected individuals and groups. In such cases social, environmental, and economic factors have provided an integrated basis for assessment, decision-making and action. The following are just a few of the examples of such practice integration in Australia, Europe and India.

In Australia, social workers at Kildonen Care in Victoria are using energy audits as part of their practice and they highlight the relevance of natural environmental issues for social work practice (Borrell et al., 2010). The authors make the point that the overlap between energy audit and social work practice applies to both service user issues and the professional skill base of social workers. There are examples in Europe of the introduction of an eco-social approach to tackling disadvantage by members of a network. This was primarily a Finnish-led social work project aimed at analysing the significance of the eco-social environment and citizen participation in disadvantaged residential areas. At the same time the group has worked on developing new kinds of action models and research methods (Matthies et al., 2000). Finally in India, social workers in a small non-governmental organisation (NGO) have developed approaches to harvesting water to boost agricultural productivity, in a project aimed at reducing poverty in the remote tribal drylands of western India. The authors see this grassroots social work and development model as having the potential to 'increase agricultural output, guarantee food security in villages, prevent farmers' suicides, protect natural resources, and above all, eliminate rural poverty' (Agoramoorthy et al., 2009).

CONCLUSION

At the present time, all people on earth are part of an unfolding debate with regard to the natural environment. Population growth and more than two hundred years of industrialisation have resulted in varying levels of pollution of land, oceans, and air, habitat destruction, exponential extinction rates of non-human species, and now global warming as a result of carbon in the atmosphere. This situation is classed as an environmental crisis by most commentators, yet social work is still developing its response. Leadership is a critical role for all professional groups, and never more so than in regard to the environmental issues that face everyone globally at present. Social work has an opportunity to gear its professional practice, theory and education toward making a difference on these important issues.

This chapter has shown how critical it is for social workers to develop practice models that incorporate an understanding of sustainability. Such models must incorporate the recognition that environmental, social and economic systems are intertwined, and all need to be taken into account if sustainability is to be achieved. There are many isolated examples of ways in which social workers are incorporating understandings of the changing environment into their practice. The challenge now is for such practice and understandings to become commonplace for social workers and for social work education and theory-building to expand the foundation for consistent social work practice in this regard. Social work that is environmentally-aware is a step toward sustainability.

REFERENCES

AASW (Australian Association of Social Workers) (2001) Member's policy interests. *National Bulletin*. Canberra: AASW.

AASW (Australian Association of Social Workers) (2002) *Code of Ethics*. Canberra: AASW.

AASW (Australian Association of Social Workers). (2010) *Code of Ethics.* Canberra: AASW.

ABS (Australian Bureau of Statistics). (2006) *Measures of Australia's Progress 2006.* Canberra: ABS.

Agoramoorthy, G., Chaudhary S. and Hsu M. (2009) 'Sustainable development using small dams: an approach to avert social conflict and relive poverty in India's semi-arid regions', *Asia Pacific Journal of Social Work and Development*, 9(2): 52–69.

Alston, M. and McKinnon, J. (eds) (2005) *Social Work: Fields of Practice.* 2nd edn. Melbourne: Oxford University Press.

Bartlett, M. (2003) 'Two movements that shaped a nation: a course in the convergence of professional values and environmental struggles', *Critical Social Work*, 3(1): 108–29.

Bauman, Z. (2004) *Wasted Lives: Modernity and its Outcasts.* Cambridge: Polity Press.

Beck, U. (2010) 'Climate for change, or how to create green modernity?', *Theory, Culture and Society*, 27(2–3): 254–66.

Borrell J., Lane S. and Fraser S. (2010) 'Integrating environmental issues into social work practice: lessons learnt from domestic energy auditing', *Australian Social Work*, 63(3): 315–28.

Bourdieu, P. (1990) *The Logic of Practice* (R. Nice, Trans.) Cambridge: Polity Press.

Bronfenbrenner, U. (1979) *The Ecology of Human Development: Experiments by Nature and Design.* Cambridge, MA: Harvard University Press.

Bronfenbrenner, U. (2005) *Making Human Beings Human: Biological Perspectives on Human Development.* Thousand Oaks: SAGE.

Carson, R. (1962) *Silent Spring.* New York: Houghton Mifflin.

Coates, J. (2003a) *Ecology and Social Work: Toward a New Paradigm.* Halifax: Fernwood.

Coates, J. (2003b) 'Exploring the roots of the environmental crisis', *Critical Social Work*, 3(1): 44–66.

Cocklin, C. and Alston, M. (2003) 'Introduction', in C. Cocklin (ed.), *Community Sustainability in Rural Australia: a Question of Capital?* Wagga Wagga: Centre for Rural Social Research. pp. 1–9.

Cox, D. and Pawar, M. (2006) *International Social Work: Issues Strategies and Programs.* California: SAGE.

Dialetachi, S. (2009) 'o tempo e o clima', *Direitos Humanos no Brasil*. São Paulo, Relatório da Rede Social de Justiça e Direitos Humano. p. 246.

Delli Priscoli, L. and Wolf, A. (2007) *Managing Water Conflicts: Dispute Resolution, Public Participation, and Institutional Capacity-Building.* Cambridge: Cambridge University Press.

Diamond, J. (2005) *Collapse: How Societies Choose to Fail or Survive.* Camberwell, Victoria: Penguin.

Giddens, A. (1994) 'Living in a post-traditional society', in U. Beck, A. Giddens and S. Lash (eds.), *Reflexive Modernization: Politics, Tradition and Aesthetics in the Modern Social Order.* Cambridge: Polity Press.

Gladwell, M. (2005) 'The vanishing', in *The New Yorker*, 3 January 2005.

Healy, K. (2005) *Social Work Theories in Context: Creating Frameworks for Practice.* Basingstoke: Palgrave MacMillan.

Higgs, J. and Cherry, N. (2009) 'Doing qualitative research on practice', in J. Higgs, D. Horsfall and S. Grace (eds), *Writing Qualitative Research on Practice.* Rotterdam: Sense Publishers.

Ife, J. (2002) *Community Development: Community-Based Alternatives in an Age of Globalisation.* 2nd edn. Sydney: Pearson Education Australia.

Ife, J. and Tesoriero, F. (2006) *Community Development: Community-Based Alternatives an Age of Globalisation.* 3rd edn. Sydney: Pearson Education Australia.

IFSW (International Federation of Social Workers). (no date) *International Policy Statement on Globalisation and the Environment*, http://www.ifsw.org, retrieved 18 April 2011.

IPCC (Intergovernmental Panel on Climate Change). (2007) 'Summary for policymakers', in M.L. Parry, O.F. Canziani, J.P. Palutikof, P.J. van der Linden and C.E. Hanson (eds), *Climate Change 2007: Impacts, Adaptation and Vulnerability. Contribution of Working Group II to the Fourth Assessment Report of the Intergovernmental Panel on Climate Change.* Cambridge: Cambridge University Press.

Jasanoff, S. (2010) 'A new climate for society', *Theory, Culture and Society*, 27(2–3): 233–53.

Jones, C. (2001) 'Voices from the frontline', *British Journal of Social Work*, 31(4): 547–62.

Low, N. and Gleeson, B. (1999) *One Earth: Social and Environmental Justice*: Tela.

McCarthy, J., Gillespie, P., and Zen, Z. (2011) 'Swimming upstream: local Indonesian production networks in "globalized" palm oil production'. *World Development 2011.*

McKinnon, J. (2008) 'Exploring the nexus between social work and the environment', *Australian Social Work*, 61(3): 256–68.

McMichael, A. (2003) *Keynote Paper on Sustainability, Health and Wellbeing.* Paper presented at the In Search of Sustainability Conference.

Matthies, A., Turunen, P., Albers, S., Boeck, T. and Narhi, K. (2000) 'An eco-social approach to tackling social exclusion in European cities: a new comparative research project in progress', *European Journal of Social Work*, 3(1): 43–52.

Mol, A. (2007) 'Boundless Biofuels? Between environmental sustainability and vulnerability', *European Journal for Rural Sociology*, 47(4): 297–315.

NASW (National Association of Social Workers). (2011) *Social Workers Prepared to Help Victims of Devastating Earthquake and Tsunami in Japan*. http://www.naswil.org/news/chapter-update/social-workers-prepared-to-help-victims-of-devastating-earthquake-and-tsunami-in-japan/, retrieved 5 May 2011.

Owen, G. (2007) *Equity and Climate Change – UK and EU Experience*. Paper presented at the Equity in Response to Climate Change Roundtable.

Parks, B.C. and Roberts J.T. (2010) 'Climate change, social theory and justice', *Theory, Culture and Society*, 27(2–3): 134–66.

Payne, M. (2005) *Modern Social Work Theory*. Basingstoke: Palgrave MacMillan.

Plumwood, V. (2002) *Environmental Culture: the Ecological Crisis of Reason*. London: Routledge.

Rainey, S. and Johnson, G. (2009) 'Grassroots activism: an exploration of women of color's role in the environmental justice movement', *Race, Gender & Class*, 16(3/4): 144–73.

Richmond, M. (1922). *What is Social Work?* New York: Russel Sage Foundation.

Sherrard, J. and Tate, A. (2007) *An Australian Snapshot*. Paper presented at the Equity in Response to Climate Change Roundtable.

Shove, E. (2010) 'Social theory and climate change: questions often, sometimes and not yet asked', *Theory, Culture and Society*, 27(2–3): 277–88.

Stern, N. (2006) *Stern Review: the Economics of Climate Change*. HM Treasury, http://www.hm-treasury.gov.uk/d/Executive_Summary.pdf.

Suppes, M.A. and Wells, C.C. (2009) *The Social Work Experience: an Introduction to Social Work and Social Welfare*. Boston: Ally & Bacon.

Taylor, C. (2008) 'Humanitarian narratives: bodies and detail in late-Victorian social work', *British Journal of Social Work*, 38: 680–96.

The Age. (2009) 'First climate refugees start move to new island home'. http://www.theage.com.au/

national/first-climate-refugees-start-move-to-new-island-home-20090728-e06x.html.

Tulloch, J. (2009) 'Water conflicts: fight or flight', *Allianz Knowledge*. http://knowledge.allianz.com/health/?303/water-conflicts.

UN. (2011) *Aenda 21*. http://www.un.org/esa/dsd/agenda 21, accessed 12 January 2012.

UNFCCC. (2011) *United Nations Framework Convention on Climate Change*. http://unfccc.int/essential_background/convention/items/2627.php, accessed 4 July 2011.

UNEP (United Nations Environment Program). (2007) *Global Environmental Outlook (GEO$_4$): Environment for Development: Summary for Decision Makers*. Malta: Progress Press Company Ltd.

Urry, J. (2010) 'Consuming the planet to excess', *Theory, Culture and Society*, 27(23): 191–212.

Walker, S. (2001) 'Tracing the contours of postmodern social work', *British Journal of Social Work*, 31: 29–39.

Walker, G. and Burningham, K. (2011) 'Flood risk, vulnerability and environmental justice: evidence and evaluation of inequality in a UK context', *Critical Social Policy*, 31(2): 216–40.

Wallace, R.A., and Wolf, A. (2006) *Contemporary Sociological Theory: Expanding the Classical Tradition*. New Jersey: Pearson Prentice Hall.

Warren, K. (2000) *Ecofeminist Philosophy: a Western Perspective on What it is and Why it Matters*. Lanham: Rowman & Littlefield.

WCED (United Nations World Commission on Environment and Development). (1987) *Our Common Future*. New York: United Nations.

World Resources Institute. (2003) *Ecosystems and Human Wellbeing: a Framework for Assessment*. Washington: Island Press.

Wright, R. (2004) *A Short History of Progress*. Melbourne: Text Publishing.

Zapf, M.K. (2009) *Social Work and the Environment: Understanding People and Place*. Toronto: Canadian Scholars' Press Inc.

Zastrow, C. (1999) *The Practice of Social Work*. Pacific Grove, CA: Brooks/Cole.

Zastrow, C. (2007) *The Practice of Social Work: a Comprehensive Worktext*. Belmont, CA: Thompson Brooks Cole.

17

Social Work, Religion, Culture and Spirituality

Micheal L. Shier and John R. Graham

INTRODUCTION

At present, most social work scholarship on religion and spirituality is in relation to specific cultural groups, or national contexts; less frequently do we see these topics as distinct subjects of international social work (taken here to mean primarily, social work practice in environments outside one's country, of citizenship, or specialist forms of trans national practice). Thus, early in the chapter, we provide the reader with an overview of the concepts of religion, spirituality, and culture in broader scholarship, and then in social work.

First, we provide the reader with definitions of the way the terms religion, spirituality and culture are used in this chapter and the way in which each is connected to the others. We emphasise the overlapping nature of spirituality and religion, but also their differences as analytical concepts. Following this, we describe the way in which social work historically has been connected to religion and the more recent emergence of spirituality in social work literature. Next, an overview section describes the contemporary

context and debate within the social work scholarship on religion, spirituality, and culture; within these discussions the role of religion and spirituality for human development, personal well-being, and human relationships at individual and community levels is apparent. The final section provides examples that highlight implications for international social work practice and education.

We recognize two fundamental things about religion and spirituality for social work (whether internationally or nationally focused). The first is that religion and spirituality occur among populations across the world. While spirituality may be growing in popular and academic usage, religion is a long-standing concept that (like its spiritual counterpart) continues to have significance in the lives of many individuals and communities. Mainstream social science disciplines in the early- to mid-20th century argued that the presence and influence of religion was diminishing (Lynd and Lynd, 1929, cited in Swatos and Christiano, 2000: 7; Weber, 1946, cited in Swatos and Christiano, 2000: 4). Today many scholars challenge these previous views of secularism, pointing out the predominance of religious culture, practices, values, and beliefs worldwide (Berger, 1997; Beyer, 2000; Derezotes, 2009; Martin, 2005; Stark, 1999). Many social work scholars, likewise, write about the influential role of religion and spirituality in the lives of service users (Graham, 2006; Hodge and Roby, 2010) and of some social work practitioners themselves (Todd, 2007).

Our second assertion therefore is that religion and spirituality are important to some clients with which social workers come in contact. For instance, Graham et al. (2008, 2009a, 2009b) found Islam to be vitally important for social work clients of Muslim background in Canada (see also: Ashencaen Crabtree et al., 2008). An emerging social work scholarship – based on data from many countries – explores how people around the world are adhering to their faith traditions and spiritual beliefs, and are using them as a means of understanding themselves, their identities, their communities, and the worlds in which they live; some of this research will be described later (Al-Krenawi and Graham, 2009; Beattie, 2007; Beyer, 2000; Jenkins, 2002; Taylor, 2007; Cnaan et al., 1999).

DEFINING RELIGION, SPIRITUALITY, AND CULTURE

Social science has defined, extensively, the terms religion, spirituality, and culture. We prefer general, holistic definitions which could be inclusive of multiple understandings throughout the world. In a previous article we pointed out the following qualities about religion, religiosity, and faith traditions:

> ...[Following] Durkheim's definition...religion is: 'a unified set of beliefs and practices relative to sacred things, that is to say, things set apart and forbidden, beliefs and practices which unite into one single moral community ... all those who adhere to them' (Durkheim, 1915: 62), a concept that considers dimensions associated with both

actions and beliefs but acknowledges the collective nature of religions. Religiosity has been defined by dimensions that assess the degree to which a person or group are religious (Cornwall et al., 1986). 'Faith', 'faith tradition', and 'religious tradition' are used interchangeably, and each refers to specific religions that have emerged over time (Smith, 1998). (Graham and Shier, 2009: 218)

These definitions describe religion as being based on both individual and collective relationships, belief systems, and practices. Religion is often referenced to formal doctrines, institutions, and collective identities. Spirituality, on the other hand, can include religion, but does not necessarily do so in all instances. Religious people may be spiritual; but, the argument continues, spiritual people may not be religious. While the following pages discuss both religion and spirituality, it is important, at the outset, to appreciate the distinctions between these two terms.

Some social work definitions see spirituality in relation to individual experiences or cognition. For example, Canda and Furman see it as 'a universal quality of human beings and their cultures related to the quest for meaning, purpose, morality, transcendence, well-being, and profound relationships with ourselves, others, and ultimate reality' (2010: 5). Likewise, 'spiritual relationships are defined as relationships to self, others, a higher power, or the environment that brings forth a sense of inner strength, peace, harmonious interconnectedness, and meaning in life' (Walton, cited in Laurence, 2000: 233). In any case, religion and spirituality, together or separately, are important for a profession that is concerned with individuals and communities, and the internal dynamics of the human psyche in relation to individual self-determination and collective, socio-cultural interactions. While religion and spirituality can be mutually reinforcing or overlapping they can also be very distinct concepts for some people. Religion and spirituality are intertwined with culture. Indeed, some people of particular faith traditions see their religion as a major marker for their cultural identity. And for international social work, culture is an important concept in understanding ethno-racial differences (Al-Krenawi and Graham, 2003), and as such can be defined as: 'the totality of ideas, beliefs, values, knowledge, and way of life of a group of people who share a certain historical, religious, racial, linguistic, ethnic, or social background' (Henry et al., 1995: 326). While definitions of culture vary throughout the social sciences, we prefer a generalized definition such as this one in relation to international social work as it allows for consideration of multiple aspects of diversity.

Religion and spirituality are inter-related with culture, gender, socioeconomic class, and other forms of social identity; and social work practitioners are therefore challenged to understand these identities and to appreciate how they intersect with religion and spirituality. Also, some social work scholars have considered spirituality as a process in which people make sense of their experiences. Carroll (1998), for example, identifies two dimensions of spirituality that are important to social work intervention: (1) the essence of individual existence and the underlying motivation for personal development and fulfillment; and (2) the behaviours and actions that contribute to how people develop meaning in life and their relationship to some higher being. The first dimension could be considered as spirituality, as it has been articulated by some social work scholars.

The second could include such religious practices as chanting, meditation, or prayer, but in other instances may not involve formal religious practices.

There are several dominant religions throughout the world. Table 17.1 provides a demographic breakdown of the most prominent of these.

Of course other less dominant religious or faith traditions not included in Table 17.1 exist; consider, for example, myriad Aboriginal and Indigenous spiritual practices and beliefs. While these faith traditions are not considered prominent religions, they could likewise contribute to a specific cultural identity (with regard to familial relationships, individual perceptions and outlooks, and organisation and structure of communities, among others) to be considered by social workers.

While religion and culture may seem obviously interconnected, spirituality may less frequently be seen as a cultural marker. Nonetheless, social work scholars call for a profession that is both spiritually and religiously sensitive to its own history, and the practices and values of its professionals, its clients and the communities the profession serves (Canda and Furman, 2010; Graham and Shier, 2009). And, as we argue later in this chapter, spirituality could usefully be a more explicit term in international social work scholarship, as, to some extent, religion has become in relation to culture.

Table 17.1 Prominent world religions

Religion	Date of origin	Estimated number of followers
Baha'i	19th century	6,600,000
Buddhism	5th century BCE	396,000,000
Christianity	1st century CE	2,200,000,000
Confucianism	Between 1050 and 256 BCE	6,600,000
Druze	11th century CE	1,000,000
Hinduism	Before 3000 BCE	924,000,000
Islam	7th century CE	1,300,000,000
Judaism	circa 18th century BCE *(estimates vary)*	16,000,000
Sikhism	circa 15th century CE	20,000,000
Taoism	5th to 6th century CE	66,000,000
Zoroastrianism	circa 2nd century BCE	200,000

BCE: before common era; CE: common era.
Sources of data: Nissim, 2003; Riggs, 2006.

HISTORY OF RELIGION AND SPIRITUALITY IN SOCIAL WORK

A previous generation of historians tended to look at social work as a product of industrialisation, urbanisation, and transition from religiously inspired helping to secular, professional practice. The history of social work therefore tends to emphasize a teleology of progress – of replacing religious sentiment with emergent social science theory; faith-based practice with professional and deliberate skills of the emerging field of social casework, community development, and policy practice; and later, after World War II, of empirically based practice dominating social work (Coates et al., 2007). The establishment of schools of social work began in the early years of the 20th century. Over the course of the interwar period, Freudian (i.e. psychoanalytic) and later Rankian (i.e. functional) theories held sway in an emerging social casework (see Turner, 2011), and a variety of community development and group work theories paralleled (and were often influenced by) a growing corpus of behavioural and social scientific thought.

During colonial periods Anglo-European approaches to charitable activities that included Christian – predominantly Roman Catholic and Protestant – institutions, were transplanted throughout the world. The religious roots of social work in colonized parts of the world certainly preceded European contact to the extent that Aboriginal or indigenous peoples had spiritual orientations, too, and one of the tragedies of colonialism resulted in that spiritual tradition being disrespected. For example, in North America, by the mid-19th century, there was an elaborate system of social care frequently anchored to religious traditions of colonial society. But these social welfare structures would change over the course of the next 100 years and have implications for the newly emerging profession of social work in Africa, South America, and Asia where colonialism had taken root.

Several social work scholars began to pay more attention to religion and spirituality for the profession of social work, at least in North America and Israel, in the 1970s and 1980s (Canda, 1983, 1988; Loewenberg, 1988), such that religion has become an aspect of diversity in emerging models of anti-oppressive, culturally respectful, and spiritually sensitive social work practice (Al-Krenawi and Graham, 2003). In the 1990s a further shift occurred: in geopolitically northern countries (such as Canada, Great Britain, and the United States) more emphasis began to be placed on the concept of spirituality (Barker, 2007; Graham, 2006). One reason for such a renewed interest in spirituality, as Canda and Furman (1999) have argued, is because, through these discussions, multiple religions and those spiritually based thoughts, processes, and actions that have no formal connection to a specific faith tradition are considered together.

Much English language social work scholarship refers to the Christian foundations of the social work profession; but others have also received attention. Loewenberg (2001) notes that social work has been historically linked to Jewish social welfare organisations throughout the world, and in recent years growing academic attention has also been placed on the influence of Eastern faith traditions, such as Buddhism and Confucianism (Chan et al., 2001; Kissman and Maurer, 2002). In all, social work has been closely linked to religion and spirituality, and scholars are elaborating with greater depth how these concepts are important for social workers and the people with whom they engage in direct practice.

CURRENT SCHOLARSHIP ON RELIGION, SPIRITUALITY, AND CULTURE

The concepts of spirituality, religion, and culture need to be considered in combination with each other. Globally, cultural values and beliefs have often been intertwined with faith and spirituality. However, social work is only beginning to better understand the significance of religion and spirituality for people in a diversity of distinct cultural groups (however they are defined) throughout the world. Religion has been an influential socio-cultural factor impacting people and societies, but from an international perspective, the literature at present has substantial omissions. Two literature reviews conducted in recent years demonstrate this point.

A study conducted by Graham (2006) investigated literature content on spirituality in social work and found that the social work literature since the mid-1980s has focused primarily on spirituality in the global North, mainly North America. Almost 200 of the 227 articles published in *Social Work Abstracts* had first authors affiliated with the USA, followed by five in Canada and four in the United Kingdom. There were also some authors from the global South: 16 from Australia, two from Hong Kong, and one each from India and New Zealand; 15 of the 227 articles presented data or perspectives from populations in countries of the global South.

More promising results were uncovered after analysing content in the *Social Service Abstracts* database, where Graham (2006) found that first authors were affiliated with 14 different countries, but still with the overwhelming majority of first authors affiliated with the United States of America (307 of 354 articles), and only 44 of the articles reporting data or perspectives from countries of the global South. The usefulness of including more spirituality-based scholarship from the perspectives of those living in countries of the global South might seem obvious for some readers and practitioners of international social work. For others it might be less obvious. For Graham (2006), understanding spirituality from diverse cultures and contexts could provide a means of sharing social work knowledge from a multitude of unique

culturally based perspectives. To summarize, he states:

> The potential for social work innovations to be shared between the North and the South and for knowledge development to be truly reciprocal and emancipatory has always been, in my view, stunted. The humble argument I am asserting, and have asserted with Alean Al-Krenawi for 15 years, is that spirituality is a perfectly viable place to carry out this agenda (I would like to say continue it, but I am skeptical of our success, to date). This is not solely of immediate relevance to communities and social workers in the global South, although were it so, this would be sufficient imperative, as far as I am concerned. It also directly bears upon the global North, which is becoming increasingly diverse, and whose knowledge productions need to reflect accordingly (and have very poorly done so) its growing diversities and reciprocal demographic networks with the global South. (Graham, 2006: 69)

Scholars describe the increasing globalisation of life, as people move across national boundaries – in many cases with ease – and with the growing access to information from almost every place in the world (Naples, 2002). As part of this broader phenomenon, social work education and practice on a global scale could become less about transplanting ideas and practices from afar, focusing instead on the localized contexts in which social work is being practised. This is an ideal scenario, in our view, and in no way do we mean to imply it occurs well in all instances, and in many places it has not occurred (Rehmatullah, 2002). Understanding those spiritual aspects of a person from somewhere other than English-language countries, which have dominated the literature, is imperative to the further development of a localized and culturally aware profession of social work.

Similar findings for the topic of religion and social work were found in Graham and Shier's (2009) study, in which they analysed social work literature on 13 different faith traditions in *Social Work Abstracts* and *Social Service Abstracts* for the period 1966–2007. Using content analysis they analysed patterns and themes within 1205 abstracts. They found an increasing number of publications on faith traditions in each decade since the 1960s. First author affiliation was not so over-whelmingly from the United States; only 51 percent of authors were affiliated with a university or other organisation located in the USA. Other countries included Australia, Canada, China, England, France, India, Indonesia, Israel, Malaysia, Netherlands and Thailand.

Graham and Shier (2009) analysed the thematic content of the published articles. Through a process of inductive analysis, they found those journal articles related to discussion of (1) how religion impacts upon social work, (2) how religion and social work were interrelated, (3) how religion impacts upon social processes and issues, and (4) how considering religion could improve religious and cultural sensitivity and social workers' competency when practising with people from diverse religions and cultures. People move across national boundaries, and social locations are never static. The terms global North' and 'global South' are therefore fluid; but at the same time, Graham and Shier (2009), like Graham (2006) before them, argue that some utility can occur by analysing first author identity of social work scholarship relative to their institutional affiliation in the global North or global South. They go on to argue that international social work scholarship on spirituality is mostly written by people in the global North, and could usefully develop a more non-North author pool. But the research to date, particularly in recent years, has paid more attention to aspects of religious and cultural sensitivity, and (again) the majority of this has been written from a North American perspective with the intention of creating an improved multi-cultural framework for practice. In many parts of the world, though, specific religious identities may be major socio-cultural aspects of people, community, or place. Therefore, increased attention in international scholarship could usefully focus more on these locally dominant religious cultural perspectives and the implications for social work

practice and local communities. Issues regarding minority religious rights are also salient.

CULTURE, RELIGION AND SPIRITUALITY IN SOCIAL WORK EDUCATION INTERNATIONALLY

Social work practice is influenced in part by the socio-cultural underpinnings of our communities, distinctively defined from one national or local context to the next. When spirituality and religion are fundamental to that socio-cultural context of practice, omitting them from generic practice methods or tools, such as assessment or intervention, is highly problematic. One corrective is to improve social work educational curriculum by including coursework from a range of academic disciplines, including that of anthropology and religious studies. But given the limitations of social work scholarship, particularly in its application to diverse communities world-wide, it is not always easy to incorporate ideas of culture, religion, and spirituality in international social work education. English language scholarship on religion and spirituality in social work is primarily produced in the global North, just like most topic areas in the social work canon (Healy, 1999; Midgley, 1981). And so the top-heavy nature of global North authorship may limit how much attention has been paid to the range of cultural, religious, and/or spiritual communities around the world. International social work education and practice likewise remains relatively national in focus, with emphasis on teaching practitioners who will work in international settings to be culturally sensitive or aware.

Penna et al. (2000) provide a useful framework for thinking about the role of social work in an international context. They argue that social work is aligned with the culture of a particular nation state but at the same time social work incorporates concerns that might be global in perspective or rooted in the culture of another country. If social work is rooted in the dominant culture it is even more important to reflect critically on alternative cultural identities that exist. When thinking about religion and spirituality in social work this conceptual model helps to explain the reasons for such a central focus on things like religiously and culturally sensitive social work practice. Since much of the literature on religion and spirituality in social work in international contexts is coming from an outsider perspective it is difficult, therefore, for social workers to develop the level of understanding that is necessary in reflective social work practice with people from a different cultural identity than their own. To be effective at training social workers in cultural or religious contexts of practice that are distinct from their own – whether in their own country or abroad – social work education needs to adopt research and teaching practices that include perspectives from the population with whom the practitioners will be working.

Religion, spirituality, and culture impact upon many aspects of the help-seeking process, including from whom people seek help and their expectations while in a helping relationship with a professional social worker. Of course other things affect this help-seeking process, including locality, geography, social dynamics, and personal or cognitive functioning, among others. And all of these (spirituality included) are mutually intersecting categories. Social workers are challenged to think about the environment of their clients. To be effective, social workers must deconstruct their own existence and environments in relation to that of their clients (Wong and Vinsky, 2009). This, though, is not an easy task. How could we educate practitioners to be reflective and mindful in their practice to achieve such an outcome? One strategy might be to link these discussions of religion, spirituality, and culture with other parameters of our social environment which might impact practice and people. Some scholars have attempted this through discussions of indigenisation and localisation of social work

practice (Al-Krenawi and Graham, 2009; Gray et al., 2008) and through revamped theories of the person-in-environment (Canda and Furman, 2010; Zapf, 2005).

A core group of scholars has emerged within the social work discipline with a focus on investigating the role of spirituality and religion in direct social work practice; these scholars identify several areas where social work education could be more religiously and spiritually sensitive. These lessons are useful for educators of international social work as they can help in the development of a framework in which considerations of religion and spirituality can be better incorporated in curriculum content. For instance, some educators have pointed out the need to demonstrate how spirituality or religion for some people is a fundamental aspect of being human (Zahl and Furman, 2005), or an aspect of providing holistic treatment for service users (Gilbert, 2000). Others have pointed to religion and spirituality as components of culturally sensitive practice (Gilligan and Furness, 2006), entrenched in the lived experiences of service users and how they understand the world (Gotterer, 2001). These writings could usefully continue to grow, and the experiences of social workers practising in different national contexts with multicultural communities need to be considered in further research, too.

Religion and spirituality in national and cultural contexts

The International Federation of Social Workers' (IFSW) 'Global Standards for the Education and Training of the Social Work Profession' (2005), when referring to religion and culture specifically, states that social workers are to 'promote respect for traditions, cultures, ideologies, beliefs and religions amongst different ethnic groups and societies, insofar as these do not conflict with the fundamental human rights of people' (IFSW, 2005: 3, see also Appendix 3). The IFSW also states that social workers should have 'knowledge of how traditions, culture, beliefs, religions and customs influence human functioning and development at all levels, including how these might constitute resources and/or obstacles to growth and development' (2005: 6). With regard to core educational paradigms, the IFSW (2005) has determined that social workers should have 'an appreciation [of] and respect for diversity in relation to "race", culture, religion, ethnicity, linguistic origin, gender, sexual orientation and differential abilities' (IFSW, 2005: 8). How these fundamental principles are brought into the social work curriculum is less known. In fact, in North America and Europe some research has found that curriculum specifically about religion and spirituality is sparse (Canda and Furman, 2010; Whiting, 2008). If existent, these topics are presented generally in courses on diversity or offered as a special elective course (Rothman, 2009). This is consistent with other areas of diversity within social work curricula (Gray et al., 2008).

There have been some attempts to bring spirituality into social work writing on spiritually sensitive practice (Bullis, 1996; Canda and Furman, 1999; Derezotes, 2006). More recently, several studies have been conducted with social work practitioners who have identified aspects of spirituality incorporated into their own practice (Gilligan and Furness, 2006) and with distinct population groups. For example, Kvorfordt and Sheridan (2007) found that some social workers working with children and adolescents found it effective to utilize spiritually based interventions. A similar finding was uncovered with social workers practicing with elderly people (Murdock, 2005). Other research considers the topic of spirituality and religion when working with service users experiencing terminal illness, bereavement, adoption, decreased decision-making capacity, and foster care (Newberry and Pachet, 2008; Zahl, 2006), or when working with specific immigrant populations (Lee and Chan, 2009). A growing, and sophisticated corpus of research, principally led by David Hodge, considers spiritual

assessment as a worthy category of direct practice (Hodge, 2003).

Some have adapted practice interventions based on the spiritual or religious needs of clients (Graham et al., 2010; Hodge and Nadir, 2008). But the spiritual and religious needs of specific client groups may differ. This is an important consideration for social work education and any attempts made to create a single model of spiritually focused social work intervention. Most of this scholarship is written for an audience of social workers practising in North America and Europe. It can act as a framework for understanding how religion and spirituality impact upon demographic groups in a diversity of cultures, but research is definitely needed from other nation states. This research might act as a foundation for further comparative work between countries or differing cultures.

Likewise, location is a necessary consideration. The role of spirituality in social work practice is different from one international context to the next (Stirling et al., 2010; Zahl, 2003). For instance, social workers practising in the United Kingdom and the United States were found to be more accepting of religion and spirituality in their direct practice than their Norwegian counterparts, and United States social workers were found to be more accepting than those in the United Kingdom (Furman et al., 2005; Zahl et al., 2007). Further research and practice knowledge is needed to gain an improved understanding of how social workers practising in a more diverse range of countries are incorporating aspects of religion and spirituality into their practice.

There is scholarship on the question of what motivates social workers to follow a spiritually sensitive approach to practice. Stewart and Koeske (2006) found that the religious and spiritual beliefs of social work students along with the local culture helped to predict attitudes towards the use of spiritually based interventions (see also Mattison et al., 2000). This finding is important, especially for educators and students of international social work, because it suggests that social workers may not include the spirituality based needs of their clients while engaged in social work practice due to their personal beliefs, or due to the local environment and culture, or all of these things. If the inclusion of spirituality in more mainstream ways within the social work curriculum is useful – as some of the research on the subject suggests – understanding student, practitioner, professorial, institutional, and community perceptions of spirituality and religion in social work practice becomes even more important. It is likewise important to appreciate how attitudes and practices vary by country; future research, indeed, could profitably assess the perceptions of practitioners in many countries around the world.

Spirituality is a less explored concept in international social work. There have been a few books published in recent years on the topic of spirituality in social work generally. These books, though, have been developed in geo-politically global north countries such as Australia (Crisp, 2010), Canada (Coates et al., 2007), and the United States (Canda and Furman, 2010). Further research might contrast social work and spirituality in diverse parts of the world (as in Tan et al., 2004). Finding similarities and differences amongst specific cultural groups would contribute to increasing socio-cultural understanding within social work of people and places.

Scholars have also pointed out the role of spirituality in intervention with adverse life situations. For example, Hodge and Roby (2010) investigated the spiritually rooted coping mechanisms utilized by sub-Saharan African women with HIV and AIDS. Likewise, Wendt (2008) found that the Christian religion affected rural Australian women's perceptions of domestic violence. Other scholarship has focused on traditional, more culturally rooted models of therapy and how these might be incorporated into social work interventions (Al-Krenawi and Graham, 2009; Canda, 1983; Coates et al., 2006). A spiritually based helping practice considers how clients' cognition or psyche is intertwined with their inherent spirituality. Recently, for example, Cheon and Canda (2010) demonstrate how spirituality is a component of youth development and should be explored by practitioners working with this population group.

A number of articles in recent years have been written about specific cultural groups and aspects of some members' spiritual and religious needs to consider in social work practice. For example, Berthold (1989) highlighted the spiritual practices of some Puerto Ricans and the implications for help-seeking among this population. Rian and Hodge (2010) investigated the spiritual and religious aspects of the Mandaean cultural group. Al-Krenawi and Graham (2009) demonstrated the role of religious practices and traditional healing for the Bedouin Arab people. Roga (2004) described how to better incorporate concepts of spirituality in social work practice with Latvian families. Likewise, Ng (2003) identified the role of shamanic healing for Chinese people and implications for social work practice. Together, this scholarship demonstrates the value of research specifically about the cultural and spiritual aspects of service user groups, and the reality that no one method of intervention can be applied to every cultural group (Bushfield and Fitzpatrick, 2010).

Religious organisations and international social work

Religious organisations that offer some level of socially based services or are responding to the social welfare needs of people locally and globally are plentiful throughout the world; each with a mission, mandate, and set goals to achieve some outcome relating to human well-being. These organisations can be multinational, like the Salvation Army, though most are locally based – such as the work of Buddhist monks from temples in Thailand (Nye, 2008). In a further example, faith-based organisations (FBOs) in South Africa have been expected to provide some level of service or support within the struggles of poverty and in combating the HIV and AIDS pandemic in that country (Nieman, 2006; van der Merwe et al., 2009). In many parts of the world these local FBOs are remnants of a colonial era wherein Christian missions were established in Asia, Africa, and South America, challenging (and in many cases eradicating) local cultural, religious, and spiritual practices.

Religion-based organisations providing international social services and development proselytize in varying degrees, and some not at all. Consider the Salvation Army, founded in 1865 in the United Kingdom and providing a wide range of social and disaster services worldwide to persons of all faiths. The Salvation Army's mission anchors the organisation as an evangelical part of the Universal Christian Church, and ministry, carried out through various evangelistic and service activities, is central to its work (The Salvation Army, 2010). Another well-known Christian aid organisation is World Vision International, a humanitarian organisation established in 1950 to administer assistance to impoverished children. Over the last six decades World Vision International activities have expanded to community development, advocacy, and disaster relief programs. Although it may be best known for its child sponsorship programme, it also undertakes microloan and health and nutrition initiatives. Like the Salvation Army, World Vision provides services to people from all faith backgrounds. But, in contrast to the The Salvation Army, World Vision asserts that it does not proselytize (World Vision International, 2010).

There are myriad civil society groups, including the Muslim Brotherhood (established 1928 in Egypt) which has spawned similar movements in countries throughout the Arab Middle East, many of which have a reputation for developing systems of social aid from hospitals to charities, and responding to human need in times of natural catastrophes (Harmsen, 2008; Rahman and Nurullah, 2010). Of course, there are many

organisations beyond the ones we have discussed. It is important to recognize the prevalence of large international and regionally focused organisations that are linked to the religious traditions of Christianity. Other religious faiths have fared less well on the international landscape due to the political and culturally hegemonic position of Christianity globally.

Other international development organisations do not classify themselves as religious, but may have religious roots or operate according to religious values. For example, some activities that are now under the umbrella of the Aga Khan Development Network were established in the late 19th century to meet the needs of the Ismaili community in South Asia and East Africa. Today, while explicitly not a religious organisation, the Aga Khan Development Network is nonetheless described by its leaders as guided by the Islamic ethical principles of consultation, solidarity with the less fortunate, human dignity and self-reliance (Aga Khan Development Network, 2007).

Comparative research on faith-based social service organisations between countries is scarce, but some analysis has been done, linking practices from one local context to the next (see, for example, Ferguson et al., 2008). Further international research could lead to better understanding of the history, diverse roles, and scopes of social work in FBOs and likely differences between countries of the global North and South. While geopolitically Northern countries have histories or eras wherein welfare state models have resulted in (secular) national or local government operated or sponsored social welfare programmes, systems of social welfare have developed differently in many global South nations and FBOs are likely to assume greater importance in the overall provision of social work and care services.

The intersection between non-sectarian and religiously orientated social service organisations has long been of importance for internationally based social workers.

Religiously based organisations may well provide some level of social services. But overlapping roles and functions of non-sectarian and religiously oriented social service organisations may be missed in internationally based civil society classification systems. The International Classification of Non-Profit Organisations differentiates between social service providing organisations and religious organisations – bifurcating into mutually exclusive categories, where the real world of non-governmental organization (NGO) work is often more blended in collaborative practices, funding structures, and the like (Statistics Canada, 2005). While some work has been done to correct these separate categories (see Stone Tice and Salamon, 2006), comparative research could help us to better understand the socio-cultural roles of religious organisations throughout the world in meeting the social welfare needs of people in their local communities. The role of religion and religious organisations in addressing global issues remains an under-investigated area of research (Derezotes, 2009). Social workers employed in these internationally or locally based organisations might have different perspectives from others who work with (but outside) them: again, future research could explore these nuances. The direct practice of social work in international contexts and the implications of spirituality and religion tend to be overshadowed in generalist discussions of culture. Further in-depth research, specifically on experiences of practitioners with spirituality and religion in international social work practice, could be a fruitful focus.

CONCLUSION

This chapter provides an overview of the concepts of spirituality, religion and their intersection with culture. It considers them as they have influenced the development of social work throughout the world, and as they pertain to current issues within the international social work training curriculum and practice. While an increasing corpus of scholarship has emerged in the last two decades on the topics of religion and spirituality, further research on the direct practice contexts and experiences of practitioners worldwide is needed.

Largely absent from international social work scholarship is a focus specifically on the concept of spirituality (Gilchrist-James et al., 2009). Some scholars have criticised the Euro-centric focus on spirituality rather than religion in international scholarship (Henery, 2003; Gray, 2008; Wong and Vinsky, 2009). Indeed, many cultures worldwide have strong spiritual traditions tied to both faith and religiosity and also to personal practice, and each should be considered together. For example, in indigenous social work scholarship spirituality is presented as a fundamental cultural aspect of many Aboriginal cultural groups throughout the world (Gray et al., 2008). Gray et al. (2008) are also clear that social work, itself, is a cultural construction. However, as a scholarly account of religion and spirituality in social work, this chapter is based primarily on 'Western' literature which has paid less attention to Aboriginal spiritual traditions in the context of helping.

Finally, spirituality and religion are not always positive socio-cultural factors, nor are they always positively related (Dehan and Levi, 2009). As religion and culture have intersected historically (and currently in some contexts) the result has been the oppression of social groups identifiable by some common trait, such as gender, socio-economic class, ability, sexual orientation, health status, ethno-racial identity, spiritual beliefs, among many others. Religious, spiritual, and cultural beliefs likewise have implications for how social problems are perceived and for whom social welfare should be available. While our focus has been on religion and spirituality in the context of culture, many of the challenges that religion in some ways brings to anti-oppressive social work practice should be understood in relation to a discussion of cultural relativism – i.e. understanding social processes and experiences in relation to a particular culture, usually distinct from one's own. This later issue is important when educating social workers and dealing with those socially based issues – such as abortion, female genital mutilation, the sociopolitical rights of gay and lesbian people and other oppressed groups, voluntary euthanasia, contraception, among others – that result in conflict between the professional values and ethics and principles of practice of social work and the practices, values, and beliefs of diverse cultural groups. There is no easy answer here for how such issues are resolved in direct practice, and social work education has not been sufficiently adapted globally to address these challenges. One solution has been the adaptation of social work knowledge bases by social work practitioners when working in multicultural contexts. But, like service users, social workers' own behaviours, values, and beliefs are also tied to their own religion, spirituality, and culture. Social work practitioners in international settings, therefore, are challenged to consider all these aspects of religion, spirituality, and culture as they seek culturally and spiritually sensitive social work practices.

REFERENCES

Aga Khan Development Network (2007) *Frequently Asked Questions*. http://www.akdn.org/faq.asp, retrieved 8 September 2010.

Al-Krenawi, A. and Graham, J.R. (2003) *Multicultural Social Work with Diverse Ethno-Racial Communities in Canada*. Toronto, ON: Oxford University Press.

Al-Krenawi, A. and Graham, J.R. (2009) *Helping Professional Practice with Indigenous Peoples: the Bedouin-Arab Case*. Lanham, MD: University Press of America.

Ashencaen Crabtree, S., Husain, F. and Spalek, B. (2008) *Islam and Social Work: Debating Values, Transforming Practice*. Bristol, UK: The Policy Press.

Barker, S.L. (2007), The integration of spirituality and religion content in social work education: Where we've been, where we're going', *Social Work and Christianity*, 34(2): 146–66.

Beattie, T. (2007) *The New Atheists: the Twilight of Reason and the War on Religion*. London, UK: Darton, Longman & Todd.

Berger, P. (1997) 'Epistemological modesty: an interview with Peter Berger', *Christian Century*, 114 (30): 974.

Berthold, S. (1989) 'Spiritism as a form of psychotherapy: implications for social work practice', *Social Casework*, 70(8): 502–9.

Beyer, P. (2000) 'Secularization for the perspective of globalization', in W.H. Swatos and D.V.A. Olson (eds), *The Secularization Debate*. Lanham, MD: Rowman and Littlefield Publishers. pp. 81–94.

Bullis, R.K. (1996) *Spirituality in Social Work Practice*. Washington, D.C: Taylor & Francis.

Bushfield, S. and Fitzpatrick, T.R. (2010) 'Therapeutic interventions with immigrant Muslim families in the United States', *Journal of Religion & Spirituality in Social Work*, 29(2): 165–79.

Canda, E. (1983) 'General implications of shamanism for clinical social work', *International Social Work*, 26(4): 14–22.

Canda, E. (1988) 'Spirituality, religious diversity, and social work practice', *Social Casework*, 69(4), 238–47.

Canda, E.R., and Furman, L.D. (1999) *Spiritual Diversity in Social Work Practice: the Heart of Helping*. New York, NY: The Free Press.

Canda E.R. and Furman, L.D. (2010) *Spiritual Diversity in Social Work Practice: the Heart of Helping*, 2nd ed. New York, NY: Oxford University Press.

Carroll, M.M. (1998) 'Social work's conceptualization of spirituality', in E.R. Canda (ed.), *Spirituality in Social Work*. New York, NY: The Haworth Pastoral Press. pp. 1–13.

Chan, C., Ho, P.S.Y. and Chow, E. (2001) 'A body-mind-spirit model in health: an Eastern approach', *Social Work in Health Care*, 34(3/4): 261–82.

Cheon, J.W. and Canda, E.R. (2010) 'The meaning and engagement of spirituality for positive youth development in social work, *Families in Society*, 91(2): 121–6.

Cnaan, R.A., Winehurg, R.J . and Boddie, S.C. (1999) *The Newer Deal: Social Work and Religion in Partnership*. New York, NY: Columbia University Press.

Coates, J., Gray, M. and Hetherington, T. (2006) 'An "ecospiritual" perspective: finally, a place for indigenous approaches', *British Journal of Social Work*, 36: 381–99.

Coates, J., Graham, J.R. and Swartzentruber, B. with Ouellette, B. (eds) (2007) *Spirituality and Social*

Work: Selected Canadian Readings. Toronto, ON: Canadian Scholars' Press Inc.

Cornwall, M., Albrecht, S.L., Cunningham, P.H. and Pitcher, B.L. (1986) 'The dimensions of religiosity: a conceptual model with an empirical test', *Review of Religious Research*, 28(3): 226–44.

Crisp, B.R. (2010) *Spirituality and Social Work*. Surrey, UK: Ashgate Publishing.

Dehan, N. and Levi, Z. (2009) 'Spiritual abuse: additional dimension of abuse experienced by abused Haredi (ultraorthodox) Jewish women', *Violence Against Women*, 15(11): 1294–310.

Derezotes, D.S. (2006) *Spiritually Oriented Social Work Practice*. Boston, MA: Pearson.

Derezotes, D. (2009) 'Religious resurgence, human survival, and global religious social work', *Journal of Religion & Spirituality in Social Work: Social Thought*, 28(1): 63–81.

Durkheim, E. (1915) *The Elementary Forms of the Religious Life: a Study in Religious Sociology*. Trans. Joseph Ward Swain. New York: Macmillan.

Ferguson, K.M., Dortzbach, K., Dyrness, G.R., Dabir, N. and Spruijt-Metz, D. (2008) 'Faith-based programs and outcomes for street-living youth in Los Angeles, Mumbai and Nairobi: a comparative study', *International Social Work*, 51(2): 159–77.

Furman, L.D., Zahl, M.A., Benson, P.W., Canda, E.R. and Grimwood, C. (2005) 'A comparative international analysis of religion and spirituality in social work: a survey of UK and US social workers', *Social Work Education*, 24(8): 813–39.

Gilbert, M.C. (2000) 'Spirituality in social work groups: practitioners speak out', *Social Work with Groups*, 22(4): 67–84.

Gilchrist-James, G., Ramsay, R. and Drover, G. (eds) (2009) *International Social Work: Canadian Perspectives*. Toronto, ON: Thompson Educational Publishing.

Gilligan, P. and Furness, S. (2006) 'The role of religion and spirituality in social work practice: views and experiences of social workers and students', *The British Journal of Social Work*, 36(4): 617–37.

Gotterer, R. (2001) 'The spiritual dimension in clinical social work practice: a client perspective', *Families in Society*, 82(2): 187–93.

Graham, J.R. (2006) 'Spirituality and social work: a call for an international focus of research', *Arete*, 30 (1): 63–77.

Graham, J.R. and Shier, M.L. (2009) 'Religion and social work: an analysis of faith traditions, themes, and global north/south authorship', *Journal of Religion & Spirituality in Social Work*, 28(1/2): 215–33.

Graham, J.R., Bradshaw, C. and Trew, J. (2008) 'Social workers' understanding of the Muslim client's perspective', *Journal of Muslim Mental Health*, 3: 125–44.

Graham, J.R., Bradshaw, C. and Trew, J. (2009a) 'Adapting social work in working with Muslim clients: insights for education', *Social Work Education: The International Journal*, 28(5): 544–61.

Graham, J.R., Bradshaw, C. and Trew, J. (2009b) 'Addressing cultural barriers with Muslim clients: an agency perspective', *Administration in Social Work*, 33(4): 387–406.

Graham, J.R., Bradshaw, C. and Trew, J. (2010) 'Cultural considerations for social service agencies working with Muslim clients', *Social Work*, 55(4): 337–46.

Gray, M. (2008) 'Viewing spirituality in social work through the lens of contemporary social theory', *British Journal of Social Work*, 38(1): 175–96.

Gray, M., Coates, J. and Yellow Bird, M. (eds) (2008) *Indigenous Social Work Around the World: Towards Culturally Relevant Education and Practice*. Aldershot, UK: Ashgate.

Harmsen, E. (2008) *Islam, Civil Society, and Social Work: Muslim Voluntary Social Welfare Associations in Jordan Between Patronage and Empowerment*. Amsterdam: Amsterdam University Press.

Healy, L. (1999) 'International social work curriculum in historical perspective', in R.J. Link and C.S. Ramanathan (eds), *All our Futures: Principles and Resources for Social Work Practice in a Global Era*. New York, NY: Brooks/Cole. pp. 14–29.

Henery, N. (2003) 'The reality of visions: contemporary theories of spirituality in social work', *British Journal of Social Work*, 33: 1105–113.

Henry, F., Tator, C., Mattis, W. and Rees, T. (1995) *The Colour of Democracy: Racism in Canadian Society*. Toronto: Harcourt Brace.

Hodge, D. (2003) *Spiritual Assessment: Handbook for Helping Professionals*. Botsford, CT: North American Association for Christians in Social Work.

Hodge, D.R. and Nadir, A. (2008) 'Moving toward culturally competent practice with Muslims: modifying cognitive therapy with Islamic tenets', *Social Work*, 53(1): 31–41.

Hodge, D.R. and Roby, J.L. (2010) 'Sub-Saharan African women living with HIV/AIDS: an exploration of general and spiritual coping strategies', *Social Work*, 55 (1): 27–37.

IFSW (International Federation of Social Workers) (2005) *Global Standards for the Education and Training of the Social Work Profession*. http://www.iassw-aiets.org/index.php?option=com_content&ta

sk=blogcategory&id=28&Itemid=49, retrieved 22 August 2010.

Jenkins, P. (2002) *The Next Christendom: the Coming of Global Christianity*. New York, NY: Oxford University Press.

Kissman, K. and Maurer, L. (2002) 'East meets west: therapeutic aspects of spirituality in health, mental health, and addiction recovery', *International Social Work*, 45 (1): 35–43.

Kvarfordt, C.L. and Sheridan, M.J. (2007) 'The role of religion and spirituality with children and adolescents: results of a national survey', *Journal of Religion and Spirituality in Social Work*, 26(3): 1–23.

Laurence, P. (2000) 'Exploring spirituality', in J. Beversluis (ed.), *Sourcebook of the World's Religions: an Interfaith Guide to Religion and Spirituality*. Novata, CA: New World Library. pp. 232–5.

Lee, E.O. and Chan, K. (2009) 'Religious/spiritual and other adaptive coping strategies among Chinese American older immigrants', *Journal of Gerontological Social Work*, 37 (4): 517–33.

Loewenberg, F.M. (1988) *Religion and Social Work Practice in Contemporary American Society*. New York, NY: Columbia University Press.

Loewenberg, F.M. (2001) *From Charity to Social Justice: the Emergence of Communal Institutions for the Support of the Poor in Ancient Judaism*. New Brunswick, NJ: Transaction Publishers.

Martin, D. (2005) *On Secularization: Towards a Revised General Theory*. Aldershot, UK: Ashgate.

Mattison, D., Jayaratne, S. and Croxton, T. (2000) Social workers' religiosity and its impact on religious practice behaviours. *Advances in Social Work*, 1(1), 43–59.

Midgley, J. (1981) *Professional Imperialism: Social Work in the Third World*. London, UK: Heinemann.

Murdock, V. (2005) 'Guided by ethics: religion and spirituality in gerontological social work practice', *Journal of Gerontological Social Work*, 45(1/2): 131–54.

Naples, N.A. (2002) *Women's Activism and Globalization: Linking Local Struggles and Transnational Politics*. London: Routledge.

Newberry, A.M. and Pachet, A.K. (2008) 'An innovative framework for psychosocial assessment in complex mental capacity evaluations', *Psychology, Health, and Medicine*, 13(4): 438–9.

Ng, H. (2003) 'The "social" in social work practice: Shamans and social workers', *International Social Work*, 46(3): 289–301.

Nieman, A. (2006) 'Churches and social development: a South African perspective', *International Social Work*, 49(5): 595–604.

Nissim, D. (2003) *The Druze in the Middle East: Their Faith, Leadership, Identity and Status*. London, UK: Sussex Academic Press.

Nye, C. (2008) 'The delivery of social services in northern Thailand', *International Social Work*, 51(2): 193–205.

Penna, S., Paylor, I. and Washington, J. (2000) 'Globalization, social exclusion and the possibilities for global social work and welfare', *European Journal of Social Work*, 3(2): 110–22.

Rahman, S.A. and Nurullah, A.S. (2010) 'Islamic awakening and its role in Islamic solidarity in Egypt: contribution of the Muslim Brotherhood', *Journal of Islam in Asia*, 7(1): 109–22.

Rehmatullah, S. (2002) *Social Welfare in Pakistan*. London: Oxford University Press.

Rian, E. and Hodge, D.R. (2010) 'Developing cultural competency with Mandaean clients: synchronizing practice with the Light World', *International Social Work*, 53(4): 54–255.

Riggs, T. (ed.) (2006) *Worldmark Encyclopedia of Religious Practices* (Volume 1: *Religion and Denominations*). Farmington Hill, MI: Thomson-Gale.

Roga, V. (2004) 'Context of spirituality in social work practice with families in Latvia', *Social Work & Christianity*, 31(2): 177–89.

Rothman, J. (2009) 'Spirituality: what we can teach and how we can teach it', *Journal of Religion & Spirituality in Social Work*, 28(1): 161–84.

Smith, J.Z. (1998) 'Religion, religions, religious', in M.C. Taylor (ed.), *Critical Terms for Religious Studies*. Chicago: University of Chicago Press.

Stark, R. (1999) 'Secularization, R.I.P.', *Sociology of Religion*, 60(3): 249–73.

Statistics Canada. (2005) *The International Classification of Nonprofit Organizations (ICNPO)*. http://www.statcan.gc.ca/pub/13-015-x/2009000/sect13-eng.htm, retrieved 30 August 2010.

Stewart, C. and Koeske, G. (2006) 'Social work students' attitudes concerning the use of religion and spiritual interventions in social work practice', *Journal of Teaching in Social Work*, 26(1–2): 31–49.

Stirling, B., Furman, L.D., Benson, P.W., Canda, E.R. and Grimwood, C. (2010) 'A comparative survey of Aotearoa New Zealand and UK social workers on the role of religion and spiritualiy in practice', *The British Journal of Social Work*, 40(2): 602–21.

Stone Tice, H. and Salamon, L.M. (2006) 'The International Classification of Non-profit Organizations', *Classifications Newsletter*, 18: 5–6.

http://unstats.un.org/unsd/class/intercop/newsletter/newsletter_18e.pdf, retrieved 30 August 2010.

Swatos, W.H. and Christiano, K.J. (2000) 'Secularization theory: the course of a concept', in W.H. Swatos and D.V.A. Olson (eds), *The Secularization Debate.* Lanham, MD: Rowman and Littlefield Publishers. pp. 1–20.

Tan, P.P., Bowie, S. and Orpilla, G. (2004) 'A Caribbean perspective on spirituality in social work practice', *Caribbean Journal of Social Work*, 3(1): 74–88.

Taylor, C. (2007) *A Secular Age.* Cambridge, MA: Harvard University Press.

The Salvation Army. (2010) *About Us,* http://www.salvationarmy.org/ihq/www_sa.nsf/vw-dynamic-index/5F180AE9ED2270FE80256D4B0044DBA2?openDocument, retrieved 9 September 2010.

Todd, S. (2007) 'Feminist community organizing: the spectre of the sacred and the secular', in Coates, J., Graham, J.R., Swartzentruber, B. and Ouellette, B. (eds), *Spirituality and Social Work: Selected Canadian Readings.* Toronto, ON: Canadian Scholars' Press Inc. pp. 161–74.

Turner, F.J. (ed.) (2011) *Social Work Treatment: Interlocking Theoretical Approaches* (5th edn). New York: Oxford University Press.

van der Merwe, W., Swart, I. and Hendriks, J. (2009) 'Faith-based organizations in the context of social welfare and development in South Africa: towards conceptualization', *Maatskaplike Werk/Social Work*, 45(2): 125–39.

Wendt, S. (2008) 'Christianity and domestic violence: feminist poststructuralist perspectives', *Affilia*, 23(2): 144–55.

Whiting, R. (2008) 'For and against: the use of a debate to address the topic of religion and spirituality in social work education', *The Journal of Practice Teaching & Learning*, 8(3): 79–96.

Wong, Y. and Vinsky, J. (2009) 'Speaking from the margins: a critical reflection on the "spiritual-but-not-religious" discourse in social work', *British Journal of Social Work*, 39(7): 1343–59.

World Vision International. (2010) *Frequently Asked Questions,* http://www.wvi.org/wvi/wviweb.nsf/maindocs/B59C94637940E8B98825737800734A3C?opendocument, retrieved 9 September 2010.

Zahl, M.A. (2003) 'Spirituality and social work: a Norwegian reflection', *Social Thought: Journal of Religion in the Social Services*, 22(1): 77–90.

Zahl, M.A. (2006) 'Incorporating a spiritual dimension in social work practice', *Socialno Delo*, 45(3–5), 127–33.

Zahl, M.A. and Furman, L.D. (2005) 'The connection between work and religious and other worldviews: water under the bridge or part of a wider approach?', *Nordisk Sosialt Arbeid*, 25(2): 98–110.

Zahl, M.A., Furman, L.D., Benson, P.W. and Canda, E.R. (2007) 'Religion and spirituality in social work practice and education in a cross-cultural context: findings from a Norwegian and UK study', *European Journal of Social Work*, 10(3): 295–317.

Zapf, M. (2005) 'The spiritual dimension of person and environment: perspectives from social work and traditional knowledge', *International Social Work*, 48(5): 633–42.

18

Disaster Management and Humanitarian Action

Golam M. Mathbor and Jennifer A. Bourassa

INTRODUCTION

Disasters can occur at any time, with or without warning, and in any place. When a disaster strikes, national infrastructures and social systems often collapse and thousands of people are left amongst the ruins desperately trying to piece their lives back together. In 2010, mega-disasters such as the earthquake in Haiti or the floods in Pakistan were strong reminders of this level of destruction. The death toll for Haiti reached over 200,000 with an estimated 1 million people being displaced from their homes (Reuters, 2010). In Pakistan, the number of affected people reached a staggering 17.2 million with a death toll of more than 1500 people (USAID, 2010). Especially in mega-disasters such as these, alongside the loss of life (including the people who would deliver services), government buildings, schools, hospitals, clinics, markets, businesses as well as other community structures are destroyed, together with transport and communication systems. international non-governmental organisations (INGOs) and non-governmental organizations (NGOs) converge on the disaster zone in an effort to deliver life-sustaining services.

The *World Disaster Report: Focus on Public Health* (2000) indicated that 96 percent of deaths from natural disasters have occurred in developing countries. It suggests that some of the root causes of deaths from natural disasters are lack of resources, deforestation, global capitalism, global warming, and political agendas (IFRC, 2000). Given the immense loss of family, friends, livelihoods and communities, psychological and social (or psychosocial) interventions have to be included in international organizations' programming. How a community has handled disasters in the past, as well as the actors, are key issues. People who have been involved either in a disaster or in disaster management are essential to any discussion on how better to address disasters.

This chapter emphasizes the social worker's role in humanitarian action in conjunction with disaster management strategies needed during preparedness, relief, and recovery stages. Actors and organizations in the field of disaster management, particularly the United Nations (UN) and its work through national governments, intergovernmental organizations, international non-governmental agencies, and civil society organizations, are discussed. A framework for disaster management that emphasizes both pre- and post-disaster periods is presented, including reference to essential stages of disaster management, such as assessment, mitigation, preparedness, relief, and recovery. The chapter draws on examples from different locations to illustrate the vulnerability of particular communities and possible responses to human-caused and natural disasters.[1]

CHALLENGES RESULTING FROM HUMAN-CAUSED AND NATURAL DISASTERS

The number of disasters globally is increasing, as is the number of disaster victims (Zakour, 2010). Gillespie and Danso (2010) suggest that the increasing occurrence of disasters around the world, with their impact on the environment, property and services as well as populations, makes it imperative that social work educators, researchers, and practitioners become knowledgeable about disasters. Challenges resulting from recent human-caused and natural disasters, from terrorist attacks to tsunamis, earthquakes, hurricanes, and volcanic eruptions, have demonstrated the need for specialized training so that effective responses can be offered to those affected. Calls for more coordinated emergency planning to mitigate the devastating humanitarian catastrophes that follow naturally occurring disasters (such as floods, hurricanes, and earthquakes) are not new (e.g. Banerjee and Gillespie, 1994); and some scientists consider that the impact of natural disasters can be addressed and reduced with rigorous planning and the coordination of efforts among local, national, and international organizations (Soliman,

2010: 237). However, stronger local, national, regional, and international partnerships for effective interventions in disaster situations, both in the long and short terms, are still to be developed.

The literature on disaster management reveals that populations that are already vulnerable (e.g. due to poverty and associated factors) tend to be ones that suffer most. The efforts of social work as a profession are concentrated on the concerns of vulnerable populations, e.g. people who are economically disadvantaged, mentally challenged or medically frail, including older people and children (Mathbor, 2007: 358). Zakour (2010: 16) notes that demographic characteristics such as age and household income are also associated with different levels of biopsychosocial functioning, partly because of the impact of the social and physical environment on the well-being of the very young, the very old and impoverished populations. Populations whose disaster vulnerability is associated with social and demographic characteristics include low-income people, children and older individuals, socially marginalized populations, ethnic groups, and people of color (Gillespie and Danso, 2010: 16).

Newburn (1993) reported that social workers' skills in communications, networking, stress management, and therapeutic listening are important in both immediate and long-term responses to disasters. Disaster mental health services have become a specialized area within the crisis intervention field of practice. Social workers must be trained to assess, intervene and when necessary, treat persons who have survived disasters. Clinical social workers are aware of the necessity of the implementation of specific conceptual frameworks which improve outcomes with persons in crisis situations. Developing competency in identifying those persons in need of disaster mental health services, determining the level of intervention necessary, and the timing of the provision and type of services to be delivered requires knowledge and training not found in social work education in many parts of the world. In addition, more community-orientated skills and efforts are needed in many situations as will be discussed later.

THE FIELD OF DISASTER MANAGEMENT AND THE UNITED NATIONS

As the human population continues to grow, the impacts of disasters are likely to escalate causing enormous loss of life, livelihoods, and sense of security. Disaster management focuses on identifying risks and creating measures that will assist populations to respond and recover from the negative consequences of a disaster. Adopting approaches with a focus on reducing vulnerability, communities are able to analyse potential threats and calculate how likely their occurrence will be (Guzman, no date). The interpretation of this data is essential when formulating disaster preparedness and response plans.

Sovereign states (as recognized in UN Resolution 46/182) have the chief responsibility of ensuring the safety of their nation's people (OCHA-B, no date). By instituting emergency response policies and procedures, governments can sometimes mitigate the harmful outcomes generated by disasters. Unfortunately, some national governments are unable – or unwilling – to provide support, especially during mega-disasters or during times of civil conflict. Cohen and Werker warn that 'The existence of humanitarian aid produces a bailout effect; governments under-invest in disaster prevention when they know that they will be bailed out in the event of disaster' (2004: 4). This lack of government support results in significant barriers to accessing relief and recovery services for the affected communities and can leave thousands of people struggling for survival, sometimes resulting in additional loss of life.

Governments, inundated by local and international humanitarian organizations offering assistance, quickly discover that the coordination of the response is a daunting task. Humanitarian actors such as INGOs and NGOs are prevalent in most large-scale disaster events. The distinction between INGOs and NGOs is tricky. INGOs typically have members and financial support from at least three different countries, whereas NGOs have members from one or two nations but receive financial support from one nation only (Skjelsbaek, 1975). Keene (2003) estimates that 50,000 NGOs are operating at a global level. Coordination of services becomes more complicated when the impact has been spread across a wide geographical area; maintaining a coordinated effort becomes even more problematic especially if the disaster is associated with environmental degradation and/or civil unrest (e.g. as in 2010 Haiti and Pakistan disasters) (Save the Children, 2010). Social workers therefore have to use every skill available in their 'tool kit', with resourcefulness, coordination and networking being key features.

Disasters also have political dimensions. Governments can use disasters as a tool to redistribute power by attempting to funnel disaster aid into the more affluent communities rather than those that are oppressed and dissident, leaving impoverished communities even more vulnerable. Some experts claim that the best way to deal with this type of inequitable distribution of disaster aid is to work directly with the impacted communities, rather than negotiating with government entities (Cohen and Werker, 2004).

Conversely, the exclusion of government officials in relief and recovery efforts can produce adversarial relationships towards relief agencies and, in some cases, humanitarian actors have enlisted military or private security forces to secure the delivery of relief aid (Save the Children, 2010). However, this alliance blurs the lines between humanitarian actors and military interventions, sometimes resulting in relief workers becoming targets of violence. In 2008, 260 workers were severely injured, taken hostage or killed while working in insecure environments

(Stoddard et al., 2009). A Save the Children report (2010) asserts ' ... projects implemented through military structures in conflict zones are often poorly executed, being designed for a fast impact but lacking the community involvement required to make them sustainable'. Hence, employing approaches which advocate the participation of all voices, including government officials, is a far better engagement strategy and is less likely to provoke an antagonistic and obstructive stance towards humanitarian actors.

The foregoing points emphasize that, without formalized response structures to establish proper communication and networking strategies for humanitarian actors, relief efforts quickly become uncoordinated, causing duplication or critical gaps in services (Encyclopedia of the Nations, no date). As a result, in 1971, the UN assumed the leadership role of coordinating disaster response efforts. In the years following, the UN morphed its disaster management office from United Nations Disaster Relief Office (UNDRO) to Department of Humanitarian Affairs (DHA) to its current title of Office for the Coordination of Humanitarian Assistance (OCHA-A).

Initially, UNDRO established a databank and an independent telecommunications system, allowing response organizations to indentify needs and match them rapidly with potential relief resources (Encyclopedia of the Nations, no date). The DHA then made a major contribution when the UN General Assembly passed Resolution 46/182 (Encyclopedia of the Nations, no date) providing three key response mechanisms: the Inter-Agency Standing Committee (IASC), the Central Revolving Fund (CERF) and the Consolidated Inter-Agency Appeals Process (CAP). The IASC was established to formulate and coordinate humanitarian assistance policies. CERF is a US$50 million fund, which is earmarked for immediate distribution during large-scale disasters. The CAP is an assessment body comprised of UN and international organizations, its main

role being to calculate the needs arising from critical situations and to prepare a comprehensive interagency response strategy (Encyclopedia of the Nations, no date).

The current responsible body, the OCHA-A, is activated during the most difficult of circumstances. Its main role is to assess and coordinate humanitarian assistance regardless of security risk. OCHA is responsible for policy planning, humanitarian early warning systems (HEWS) and the coordination of disaster relief, support and mitigation efforts (Encyclopedia of the Nations, no date). OCHA operates 32 offices in various countries across the globe and has established the Relief Web database, which provides up-to-date information on responses. One of the more important features of this agency is the appointment (by the UN Secretary General) of the Emergency Relief Coordinator (ERC) (Encyclopedia of the Nations, no date) whose duties include chairing the IASC.

IASC is a unique forum involving key UN and non-UN humanitarian partners. The IASC is expected to convene immediately after a large-scale event in order to assess and coordinate response services. Since its inception, the IASC has established four subsidiary groups, six task forces, one reference group as well as five other groups. It has produced approximately 90 reports, which include work plans and response guidelines specifically designed for humanitarian actors engaged in disaster work (IASC, 2009).

All social workers working in this international milieu would benefit from understanding these disaster response mechanisms. This knowledge, coupled with disaster management training, can ensure that social workers conduct the most ethical, practical and appropriate strategies even in the midst of chaos. As there is no one social work programme or institution providing this basic information, the responsibility lies with individual social workers to seek it: information produced by the IASC and, more specifically, the IASC Reference Group on Mental Health and

Psychosocial Support in Emergency Settings, is a vital resource.

FRAMEWORK FOR DISASTER MANAGEMENT IN PRE- AND POST-DISASTER SITUATIONS

Pre-disaster

As part of the overall range of disaster management strategies, it is useful for organizations and communities to make a full *assessment of vulnerability* of the locality, and to undertake *disaster mitigation* and *preparedness programmes,* before any disaster occurs.

Assessment of vulnerability

Professor Mohan Munasinghe[2] has developed an innovative tool for assessing the vulnerability and adaptation of communities in natural disasters (MIND, 2006). He argues that the mechanism of identifying and analysing economic–environmental–social interactions plays a key role in the implementation of sustainable development goals, with a major impact on development goals under disaster conditions (including future climate change hazards). Unique features of the AIM (Action Impact Matrix) methodology include: determining the most important national goals and policies, which, in turn, help in determining vulnerability and adaptation (VA) in areas affected by climate change. Also, it determines the status of VA areas subject to only natural climate variability.

The methodology helps determine the impacts of climate change on VA areas and helps identify how VA areas might affect goals and policies. Using this methodology helps with prioritizing the most important interactions and determining appropriate remedial policies and measures; it includes more detailed studies and analysis of key interactions and policy options. These unique features can be factored in calculating the effects on development of specific

vulnerabilities, while the figures produced help in assessment of development effects on vulnerabilities. Items in these features can be expanded to include other issues and goals based on the unique circumstances of disaster prone communities (MIND, 2006).

Disaster mitigation

Some forms of natural disasters can be predicted – if not in terms of actual location and timing of occurrence, at least in terms of their likelihood under certain weather conditions. In the case of floods, hurricanes and tornadoes, emphasis should be placed on identifying the most frequent cause of disasters and agreeing the risk to be prioritized. For example, in the case of flooding, constructing permanent embankments/levies and developing a system of maintenance would be a priority. Constructing sufficient dams (and developing maintenance systems) can be the responsibility of an NGO or a 'for-profit' agency (e.g. fisheries). In addition, constructing or adapting buildings to be used as shelters during the disaster (e.g. schools, religious institutions, and community houses) with sufficient sanitary latrines and safe water supply, is a necessity. It is also important that effective river and water management systems are implemented including the negotiation of management of rivers crossing national borders. Eruption of volcanoes are less predictable and difficult to defend communities against (other than through relocation); and early warning with regard to earthquakes is also difficult, although use of appropriate construction techniques in vulnerable localities may prevent the destruction of some buildings and help reduce the numbers killed or injured. The exact timing and extent of effect of tsunamis are not impossible to predict although the early warning systems needed are expensive to put in place and/or have not been developed by some vulnerable countries (see later).

Disaster preparedness

In this phase, *plans of action* are prepared for the time when disaster strikes. Such plans

20

cover mobilization and coordination of emergency services in the response, rehabilitation and recovery stages. Disaster readiness includes provision of emergency warning systems, shelters, evacuation plans, and maintenance of resources and training of personnel. An effective model of readiness from Bangladesh is described below.

The idea of a Cyclone Preparedness Programme (CPP) started in 1965 when the national Red Cross society in Bangladesh (now the Bangladesh Red Crescent Society, BDRCS), requested the assistance of the International Federation of Red Cross/ Crescent (IFRC) to establish a warning system for the population living in the coastal belt. In 1966, the IFRC and the Swedish Red Cross implemented a pilot scheme for cyclone preparedness which consisted of both human and manufactured warning systems which was subsequently extended. In 2007, at an international seminar on disaster planning, Loane[3] reiterated that:

> Bangladesh has the most exposed and vulnerable coastline to flooding with the largest population presence of anywhere in the world. On an annual basis, thousands of persons are displaced and lives destroyed through flooding. Anticipation of floods in Bangladesh is thus somewhat straightforward and because of this a greater emphasis can be placed on preparation and response. Again it is not surprising that the country has one of the best prepared local capacities for disaster response and for anyone trying to draw lessons in relation to coping mechanisms, this case study provides fascinating insight into how societies manage their disaster response mechanism. (Loane, 2007: 14)

Experience from the CPP shows that proper guidance, transparency, and access to information at all stages of development initiatives (including project proposal, planning, implementation and evaluation) and recognition of people's worth is needed in projects seeking to manage disasters (Mathbor, 2007). Volunteers' commitment to the fundamental principles of humanity, impartiality, neutrality, independence, voluntary service, unity, and universality (as proclaimed in the

Red Cross/Red Crescent's mission), cultivated through a sustained training programme, has enhanced the effectiveness of CPP and saved many lives in recent disasters hitting the coastal areas of Bangladesh. It is suggested that many of the recent tsunami victims in South and South-East Asia could have been saved if there were similar kinds of preparedness programme in vulnerable areas.

CPP volunteers are well trained cadres in disaster management activities. They are familiar with the local community and its resources (e.g. location of safe shelters, relief and rehabilitation programmes), and the evacuation plan to be followed at the time of disaster. An on-going interaction among and between the members, as well as with the project leaders, helps avoid mistrust and misunderstanding in the development process. People come forward to join CPP on a voluntary basis. Round-the-year training fosters solidarity among and between the volunteers and generates leadership qualities and management skills, as well as reinforcing the motive to serve humanity. The volunteers are rewarded by the social recognition of their efforts in helping distressed people in their communities. CPP operates through a chain of command using a communication networking system which is quick to respond to the immediate needs of the coastal communities, utilizing both personal and technical means of communication. CPP sees its volunteers as magnetic catalysts to convey the programme's messages to local people, and community training and public awareness events are arranged by and with the volunteers, utilizing local folk media, drama, films and video shows.

Light (2005) reports that the limited level of preparedness at local level was a real weakness during Hurricane Katrina (*Boston Globe*, 4 September 2005). Smith (2007) noted that existing (technical) warning systems in some countries may not be sufficiently understood by some local cultures. For instance, in the 1991 Bangladesh cyclone, people heard the cyclone warning signals

3–6 hours before the storm surge, but they did not take refuge in shelters. A similar situation occurred in relation to Hurricane Katrina. People were not evacuated in time due to the lack of well-coordinated plans between and among the organizations involved. In contrast, no deaths occurred among the indigenous people of the Andaman Islands during the tsunami devastation because of their understanding of early warning systems. Tropical cyclone Sidr which hit low-lying coastal regions in November 2007 was the deadliest storm to strike Bangladesh in the last decade, killing more than 3100 people, but credit goes to the BDRCS for an effective early warning system and its volunteers who evacuated 3.5 million other people to shelter houses before the storm struck.

Before any disaster strikes, governments should undertake disaster mitigation and preparedness programmes, to include:

- creating more awareness through use of posters, billboards, advertising in mass media, and providing information about what to do at the time of disaster;
- upgrading and updating existing forecasting systems on a regular basis;
- maintenance of food stocks at regional centres for subsequent distribution;
- on-going training programmes for disaster responders, e.g. about search and rescue, evacuation, first aid, and logistics.

Post-disaster

Once disasters strike, governments should form a coalition with all community-based organizations (CBOs), including NGOs, to mobilize resources serving affected communities and people. It is evident from various disasters reported in the world news that communities characterized by higher levels of social cohesion, solidarity, collaboration, and networking are better prepared and more effective in responding to disasters (Mathbor, 2010). A stronger coalition among organizations and communities helps in reaching out

to international organizations for immediate help as the parties speak with one voice to address the aftermath of disasters. There are specific phases with associated tasks in responding to disasters, and the 'relief and recovery' phase is described below.

Disaster relief and recovery

In this phase, communities and organizations mobilize the first responders (fire fighters, police, army, doctors, engineers, social workers, and volunteers of CBOs, NGOs; but also helpers by circumstance) to expedite the following operations:

- search and rescue operation;
- evacuation to shelter houses;
- needs analysis in relation to food, safe water, first aid and medical services (e.g. establishing a mobile hospital);
- all relief efforts should be administered by an agreed coordinating agency (e.g. Red Cross/Red Crescent Society) or committee.

The response phase includes the mobilization of the *necessary emergency services* and *first responders* in the disaster - affected area. Necessary emergency services include search and rescue, evacuation, demand and resource analysis, emergency relief (food, water, sanitation, first aid, etc.), and logistics supply (e.g. tents).

Mathbor (2007) applied the model proposed in relation to developing social capital (e.g. Woolcock, 2001) to the rebuilding of communities in the post-disaster phase; as did Hawkins and Maurer (2010) subsequently in relation to Hurricane Katrina. This involves using the processes of bonding, bridging, and linking (Figure 18.1) to redevelop affected communities, including reintegration of the most vulnerable groups. The model suggests strong interrelations between and among social capital attributes such as integration, cohesion, solidarity, networking, communication, interaction, coordination, collaboration, social supports, leadership, and volunteerism.

The following section explains how steps noted in Figure 18.1 in building social capital

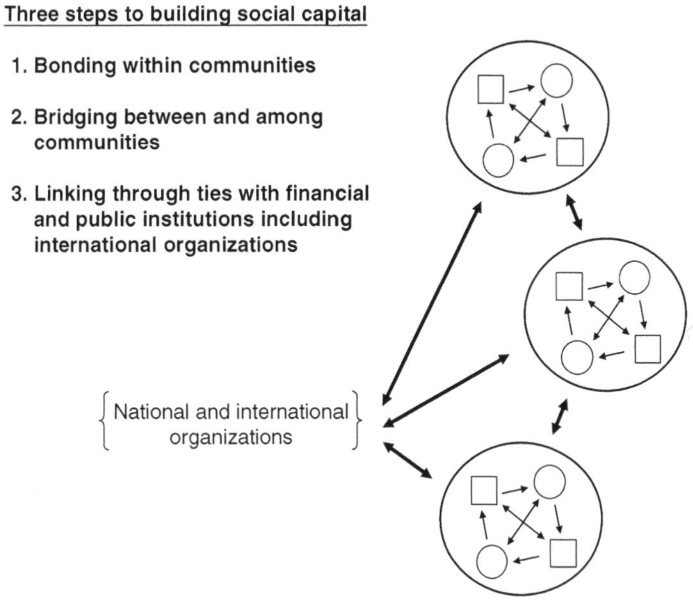

Three steps to building social capital

1. Bonding within communities

2. Bridging between and among communities

3. Linking through ties with financial and public institutions including international organizations

National and international organizations

Figure 18.1   Three steps to building social capital

can be harnessed in disaster relief and management.

1   Bonding within communities: (re)development of social capital starts with re-establishing bonds within the community. Effective coordination of community activities, collaboration and support of members' activities, fostering leadership qualities, and assisting other community members are all important steps in bonding which can be encouraged through re-establishment of recreational activities; religious and spiritual gatherings; political and institutional affiliations; economic and business activities; repair or replacement of physical infrastructure including buildings; and psychological and social supports.

2   Bridging between and among communities: at the next level, groups and interested citizenry from one community can reach out to other communities in the wider society to identify common needs and form coalitions to engage in collaborative ventures (e.g. devising more effective warning and preparation systems).

3   Linking communities through ties with financial and public institutions: the historic relationship developed between communities and the government, including financial institutions, can assist in mitigating the consequences of natural

disasters or may prove to be a hindrance. But (re) establishment of positive relationships is crucial in mobilizing a community's resources, expertise, professionals and volunteers, in the recovery work that takes place during and after a disaster (and before another one) (Mathbor, 2007).

SOCIAL WORK ROLES IN IMPROVING PRE-DISASTER PREPAREDNESS

Social workers need to be prepared in anticipation of disaster rather than wait until disaster strikes. Traditionally, social workers have been present at disaster sites to help in the response and recovery efforts, but their efforts may be too little and too late (Gillespie and Danso, 2010: xi). There is an expanding body of literature that demonstrates that much can be done before disasters strike to reduce and even eliminate some of the negative impacts from disasters (Weichselgartner, 2001), but as Gillespie and Danso (2010) remark, even in the multidisciplinary literature, there is very limited evidence of the involvement of social work researchers. Social work education needs to better prepare a new generation of social workers for involvement in disaster work at all stages and levels. In addition, training must also be developed for practicing social workers to be included before, during, and after disasters. Adger et al. (2005) note that social and ecological vulnerability to disasters and the outcomes of any extreme event are influenced by the buildup or erosion of resilience both before and after disasters. The authors further state that resilient social-ecological systems incorporate diverse mechanisms for living with, and learning from change and unexpected shocks. Social work is a discipline that originated from grassroots movements dealing with unexpected shocks and utilizing people's strengths. Mukhier (2006) reports that psychosocial support, previously considered 'soft' and not tangible in terms of assistance to those affected by disasters, is now a key component for any effective emergency response, following experience after the devastating earthquake that struck Bam, Iran (which killed 29,878 and injured 22,628 people).

In many locations, social workers are well connected to local communities: they are familiar with community resources and leadership potentials, and are equipped with knowledge and skills that can address issues at micro, mezzo, and macro levels. While other professionals have valuable skills for responding to disasters, the social work perspective takes into account the many factors that affect access – or lack of access – to services and resources (Stoesen, 2006: 5). It is evident from the aforementioned CPP case study and other citations that social workers with a community development orientation can play an important role in the pre-disaster preparedness stage in providing assistance in the following areas:

- public awareness campaigns;
- community capacity building;
- enhancement of community preparedness for disasters;

- educating people about mitigating the consequences of disasters;
- strengthening the capacities of existing civil society institutions;
- resource mobilization using social and human capital;
- communication, particularly utilizing interpersonal communication for disseminating warning signals;
- recruitment of local volunteers.

SOCIAL WORK ROLES IN DISASTER RELIEF

Historically, the social work professional has strong roots in psychosocial theory. The most rudimentary forms of this theory can be traced back to one of the original social work founders, Mary Ellen Richmond (Turner, 1979). She theorized that the 'maladjustment' of a person could be attributed to and analysed by their relationship with their social environment (Szymoniak, 2006). With the individual as the central focus, psychosocial casework can be adjusted and varied to meet the specialized needs of each client. The limitation of this traditional approach lies in its emphasis on interpersonal and intra-familial environments, interventions which lack a more macro focus. However, contemporary social work theorists have extended social work casework practice by placing more emphasis on the *relationships* that exist between the person and their (wider) environment (person-in-environment (PIE)). The PIE theory allows social workers to broaden their assessments and interventions beyond the intrapersonal realm to address more mezzo and macro levels. This perspective enables social workers to practice from a more viable framework when engaging with disaster populations within the international arena.

In comparison, psychosocial work in the international arena spans the last 25–30 years. International aid agencies have been drawn to psychosocial concepts due to their flexible and open nature in creating change with disaster populations (Bourassa, 2009). In fact, psychosocial practice has been considered essential when working with refugee or internally displaced populations in emergent environments such as conflicts or disasters (Ingleby, 2005; Strang and Ager, no date; Williamson and Robinson, 2006). In spite of this acknowledgement, there are still diverging views on how best to define the term 'psychosocial' and what subsequent practice methodologies are then considered to be efficacious. According to the Psychosocial Working Group, 'psychosocial is poorly integrated within humanitarian assistance … the reasons for this lack of integration include definitional problems, widely differing approaches to intervention, and a lack of coherence in practice development' (cited in Ager, 2004: 1). One of the causes of this inconsistency may derive from the fact that psychosocial professionals have various professional backgrounds and may or may not be affiliated with regulatory or licensing bodies. As a result, psychosocial programmes range in their focus from community development to direct clinical practice, including programmes with a human rights or child protection focus (Strange and Ager, no date).

This diverse range of interests highlights the challenge of establishing a standard set of practices for psychosocial work. Some practitioners prefer to focus on more clinical interventions (Ager, 2004), while others are steering towards other psychosocial methodologies due to concerns about the overuse and misuse of the post-traumatic stress disorder (PTSD) diagnosis (Becker, 2003; Miller, 2005; Van Ommeren et al., 2005; Pupavac, 2004; Summerfield, 2001; Wickramage, 2006). Mark Van Ommeren, a World Health Organization (WHO) specialist in disaster mental health, states 'It's not clear that this is the disorder [PTSD] that burdens people most … It's only one of many problems that arise after a disaster' (as cited in Miller, 2005: 1032). Galappatti (2005) suggests that the best interventions are those which centre on meeting social and material

needs, with 'talk therapy' representing a more supportive listening and 'befriending' role, particularly in the earlier stages of a disaster response.

This discussion suggests that we need to find a better balance between the clinical perspective and the 'social' aspects of the psychosocial equation (Bourassa, 2009). If responders are only viewing survivors through a PTSD lens, then the potential is high for other social or psychological needs of individuals or communities to be overlooked. The debate over the use of the PTSD diagnosis demonstrates a need for better research on the efficaciousness of psychosocial interventions and their application by humanitarian actors in disaster contexts.

Alongside this debate, cultural and language barriers are persistent hurdles for communication amongst international agencies and even more problematic when agencies attempt to interact with disaster communities. For instance, in developing countries, spiritual and mental health concerns are often addressed by local resources in the form of traditional healers, shamans, and other religious leaders (Carballo and Heal, 2005; Galappatti, 2005). During times of disasters, international organizations incorporate a more Westernized agenda towards mental health. As a consequence, local and traditional practices have a tendency to be underutilized or dismissed. Duncan and Arnston (2004: 9), representatives of the International Psychosocial Evaluation Committee, state 'to design cultural interventions, one must understand and truly respect relevant beliefs and practices in a given local setting'. Hence, as values informing psychosocial practice vary dramatically from one international organization to another, perhaps the best answer lies in building collaboration and mutual respect between all stakeholders.

On a more macro level, the issues listed above are evident in all facets of disaster response and not exclusively in psychosocial work. In fact, due to increasing concerns for coordination and communication amongst responding agencies, in 2005, the UN developed and implemented the Cluster Approach (OneResponse, no date). 'Humanitarian reform seeks to improve the effectiveness of humanitarian response by ensuring greater predictability, accountability and partnership' (OneResponse, no date). Clusters are comprised of professionals working in areas such as water and sanitation, shelter, health, etc. Clusters encourage networking and coordination of projects in an effort to reduce duplication or gaps within service delivery. During the 2010 Haiti earthquake response, there were 12 such clusters (Reuters, 2010).

The psychosocial cluster is typically a subsector of Health with the World Health Organization being designated as the cluster lead. It is not surprising to note that lack of coordination and networking have been a long-standing concern for agencies working in the psychosocial milieu (Ager, 2004; Bauman et al., no date; Couldry and Morris, 2005; Galappatti, 2005; Wickramage, 2006). However, if psychosocial organizations make a commitment to meet and network on a regular basis, then critical connections between mental health and community development practices can be established and the foundations for best practices laid (de Jong et al., 2005).

The advantage of incorporating evidence-based practices or lessons learned from previous experience can be easily lost when working in emergent environments. As Pupavac chides, 'since psycho-social approaches intrude into the most intimate aspects of individuals' belief systems and interpersonal relationships, international agencies should have strong evidence for the efficacy of their work' (2002: 9). As far back as 1979, Turner recommended that psychosocial personnel should acquire a solid understanding of both clinical and development theories, thereby forming powerful alliances for social action and social change. Even though social work has a long history in both clinical/case work and community development practices, the interweaving of these methodologies within social work education is far from widespread.

In response to complications arising from the field, IASC, in collaboration with mental health and psychosocial organizations, has published two key handbooks: *IASC Guidelines on Mental Health and Psychosocial Support in Emergency Settings* (2007) and *IASC Mental Health and Psychosocial Support in Humanitarian Emergencies: What Should Humanitarian Health Actors Know* (2010). These handbooks are essential for any psychosocial or social work professional working within the international disaster management field. Other sources of psychosocial information can be located within various organizations such as the International Federation of Red Cross Red Crescent Reference Center for Psychosocial Support; the Psychosocial Working Group; World Health Organization; Refugee Studies Centre; UN Relief Web; Save the Children; and International Society for Traumatic Stress Studies.

SOCIAL WORK ROLES IN DISASTER RECOVERY

When the immediate danger of the disaster has passed, the best recovery strategies are undertaken alongside relief efforts. In OCHA's cluster approach, the United Nations Development Programme (UNDP) country representative is engaged with relief efforts from the onset, linking recovery strategies with the in-country emergency response coordinator (ERC). The goal is to partner relief and recovery processes in a way which creates fluidity in addressing the reintegration challenges of refugees and internally displaced people (IDP). By linking these together, it is hoped that recovery programmes will improve the access to services of refugees and IDPs (especially during times of civil conflict), and also promote non-discriminatory practices (Kalin, no date). Key themes are the inclusion of survivors in all aspects of recovery processes; the protection of women and children against domestic violence and sexual exploitation; ensuring children's rights to access education; and establishing systems for the acquisition of critical documentation such as land titles and birth certificates (Kalin, no date). Supported by human rights and refugee laws as well as the guiding principles on internal displacement, OCHA's intention is to lead governments, international organizations and all other response actors to provide the most ethical and effective supports to impacted populations.

As mentioned earlier, disasters occur within political contexts, and this can produce significant barriers for societies nationally as well as for humanitarian actors. As Becker (2003) states, 'trauma work is a product to be sold, and its success simply depends on how much is being sold, not so much on what it does' (2003: 9). In terms of being labelled 'vulnerable' or 'traumatized', survivors are often deemed incapable of determining and pursuing their own recovery goals. Hence, the underlying interests of global capitalism can undermine humanitarian aid imperatives and encourage the submission of impacted populations for the gain of others (Pupavac, 2002). Consequently, some grassroots organizations and governments are now expressing opposition to global capitalism and are becoming sceptical and resistant to humanitarian aid.

As Williamson and Robinson (2006) proclaim, 'If we treat people as helpless victims, we undermine their prospects for future progress from relief to development' (2006: 12). With disasters causing an even greater divide between 'the haves and have-nots', international disaster organizations need to establish interventions that will address the concerns of the most vulnerable during all phases of response. Humanitarian aid which utilizes participatory methodologies has been lauded as one the best ways to enhance community capacity. Ager et al. (2006: 30) contend that the capacity of a community increases when changes can be reflected in 'increased knowledge, improved confidence,

greater sense of control, connection to social networks, [and] deeper awareness of human rights'. Utilizing a grassroots, bottom-up approach, communities are inspired to participate in the design, creation, coordination and implementation of programmes. Particularly if community development work utilizes empowerment processes and builds upon a community's strengths, capacities, and resources, then more culturally appropriate interventions will be established. As a result, this will increase a community's sense of control over their own reconstructive activities and produces more sustainable programming (Van der Veer, 2006).

Participatory approaches incorporating empowerment philosophies, similar to those found in social work praxis, are liberating communities to develop their own reconstruction goals (Parks et al., 2005). However, with little research to inform humanitarian actors in the efficaciousness of their interventions with developing countries, a pattern of haphazard and non-uniform delivery of interventions is perpetuated. As each aid agency struggles to figure out their own practice methodologies, critical knowledge is being lost amongst the confusion and miscommunication.

Incorporating evaluation processes within humanitarian organizations is essential for acquiring funding and will facilitate the creation of best practices. Conducting evaluations no longer becomes an option but rather a vital component for any international development work. Most importantly, research conducted utilizing participatory approaches encourages development programmes to utilize evaluation techniques with input generated from key stakeholders (Estrella and Gaventa, 1997). Participatory Research in Asia (1995) affirms, 'PE [participatory evaluation] is an attempt at redefining and reaffirming development as a "bottom-up", "people-centered", and "people-controlled" process and not a technocratic, top-down intervention' (as cited in Estrella and Gaventa, 1997: 21). Appropriate research and evaluation programmes could go a long way in ensuring that anti-oppressive practices are employed, even in the midst of chaos and upheaval caused by large scale disasters.

The concerns outlined above have stimulated a movement towards standardizing basic mental health and psychosocial guidelines and, as mentioned, IASC has published key documents to guide the practice of mental health and psychosocial professionals. In the *IASC Guidelines on Mental Health and Psychosocial Support in Emergency Settings,* a decision-making matrix has been developed to assist workers during planning, emergent, and recovery processes (2007). This document, with the use of action sheets, encourages empowerment or participatory methodology while encapsulating human rights and protection considerations (IASC, 2007). This is an essential platform from which primary interventions can be measured and evaluated.

The challenges that face international workers in the field of disaster work are comparable with the struggles found within the wider field of social work praxis. Guided by social work principles of people's right to self determination, adopting participatory and empowerment strategies should be a natural fit. Regardless of the role, social workers have a strong tradition of advocating for the equitable treatment of all people, especially those who are experiencing oppression, discrimination, or marginalization. During the recovery stage, the most vulnerable people are those who are internally displaced or refugee women and children. Social workers are likely to engage with communities to address reintegration issues for children by supporting or developing initiatives that focus on the rights to play, receive an education, and with their families. Incorporating initiatives such as these can protect orphans from military recruitment and human trafficking.[4] For women, focusing on systemic and community integration issues that reduce gender-based violence and discrimination is crucial. These strategies include: facilitating the inclusion of women's voices in reconstruction activities, advocating for land titles for female-headed households, creating access to micro-finance programmes to reduce social equities, facilitating safe access to services, and instilling safeguards within camp management to reduce domestic violence and sexual exploitation.

In general, all IDP and refugee groups require advocacy and networking with government and public service programmes. It is vital for IDPs and refugees to have support in the extrication of lost documents, property restitution or compensation, and access to health care and education (Reyes and Charles, 2010). But most importantly, social workers need to advocate and facilitate the inclusion of these members' voices in all decision-making processes, including camp layout, resettlement location, distribution of aid, and micro-finance opportunities.

Ideally, social workers will have training and experience in both international development and clinical approaches. This type of crossover training, in combination with disaster management preparation, will equip social workers with greater professional competence and encourage more ethical practice, while also generating more sustainable outcomes. Depending on the social worker's particular role, there is a plethora of additional information available from a variety of resources. For instance, a range of international conventions, charters, and standards relevant to international social work in other fields (not least, in relation to refugees and the rights of various groups) are as relevant to social workers in disaster work and such knowledge will enhance a social worker's ability to advocate, navigate, and coordinate with other critical services.

Lastly, working in disasters is undoubtedly stressful. The needs of the survivors are of an urgent and critical nature. Social workers are often working in multidisciplinary teams and are frequently called upon to be leaders in community engagement strategies. They can provide psychosocial interventions, connect with resources and mediate conflicts in all arenas. Nevertheless, their role is not exclusive to impacted population groups. Psychosocial workers and social workers alike are often called upon to provide emotional support for colleagues. Social workers need to incorporate good self care strategies and mentor this with colleagues. Establishing friendly and supportive relationships with co-workers can make all the difference to the emotional, physical, mental, and spiritual wellbeing of both the social worker(s) and colleagues. The sustainability of any programme can hinge on this very component.

CONCLUSION

As the global population increases and disasters continue to occur, nations throughout the world will need to be better prepared for the disasters and better able to deal with their consequences. Relief and developmental agencies strain to meet needs, with the psycho social needs of the survivors being among their primary concern. Experience has shown that the impacts of disasters can cause an even greater divide between the haves and have-nots. Therefore, international disaster organizations must establish interventions that address the concerns of the most vulnerable groups, such as IDP and refugee women, older people, and children, during all phases of preparation and response. The challenges of this work are significant but not insurmountable.

In this chapter, the disaster management framework has been presented in two segments: pre-disaster and post-disaster. The pre-disaster segment includes the assessment, mitigation, and preparedness phases, while the post-disaster division focuses on the relief and recovery phases. In an effort to coordinate large and growing numbers of response organizations, the UN has assumed a leadership role to establish effective communication during all disaster phases. With the adoption of the cluster approach, it is hoped that humanitarian actors will establish better accountability and partnerships.

The key goals are to encourage the implementation of more efficacious interventions and reduce duplication or gaps in services.

Following large-scale disasters, many people become IDPs or refugees and social work's long history of psychosocial and community development work has provided important insights and skills for working with such populations. Leaving aside the more pathologising tenets of PTSD, social workers operating in the PIE framework and applying social work principles and values (including as they relate to people's right to self determination) should promote participatory and empowerment strategies and thereby community capacities. Perhaps now is time for the International Council on Social Welfare (ICSW), the International Association of Schools of Social Work (IAASW) and the International Federation of Social Workers (IFSW) to encourage greater attention to the education of social workers for disaster work. In addition, encouraging the use of participatory research methodologies and establishing an enhanced body of knowledge in this field is vital to the development and integration of effective practices. Failure to equip social workers with skills and knowledge appropriate to work in this field detracts from the profession's ability to make an effective contribution internationally to populations affected by disasters, particularly those individual and communities most vulnerable to their impacts.

NOTES

1 Some of the issues are similar whether disasters are a result of natural causes or human activity (or inactivity) and the two are often interrelated as indicated in the report cited. This chapter focuses on the implications of (generally natural) disasters for social workers in international organizations. However, modern transport and communication systems have also enabled, or resulted in, significant disasters which have international dimensions: some of these are rooted in internal and international conflicts and are alluded to in Chapter 19.

2   Professor Munasinghe heads the Munasinghe Institute for Development in Sri Lanka.

3   In January 2007, the Katherine A. Kendall Institute (KAKI) of the Council on Social Work Education (CSWE) organized and sponsored the International Seminar on 'Disaster Planning, Management, and Relief: New Responsibilities for Social Work Education' held in St Michael, Barbados, at which Geoff Loane, Head of Delegation, North American and Canada of International Committee of the Red Cross, was the keynote speaker.

4   In relation to the risk of human trafficking faced by children orphaned by disasters, it has been estimated that, since the 2010 earthquake in Haiti, 7300 boys and girls have been smuggled across the Dominican Republic border for the purpose of trafficking. This is a significant increase from the 950 previously recorded in 2009 (Reyes and Charles, 2010).

REFERENCES

Adger, W.N., Hughes, T.P., Folke, C., Carpenter, S.R. and Rockstrom, J. (2005) 'Social-ecological resilience to coastal disasters', *Science Journal*, 309: 1036–9. Washington DC: American Association of the Advancement of Science.

Ager, A. (2004) *The Psychosocial Working Group, Integrating Psychosocial Response within Humanitarian Action in Complex Emergencies: A Proposal*. Available online at: http://www.forcedmigration.org/psychosocial/papers/PWGpapers.htm/integrating_response_proposal_paper_abs.pdf, accessed 16 December 2011.

Ager, A., Strang, A. and Wessells, M. (2006) 'Integrating psychosocial issues in humanitarian and development assistance: a response to Williamson and Robinson', *Intervention: International Journal on Mental Health Psychosocial Work and Counseling in areas of Conflict*, 4 (1): 29–31.

Banerjee, M. and Gillespie, D. (1994) 'Linking disaster preparedness and organisational response effectiveness', *Journal of Community Practice*, 1(3): 129–42.

Bauman, P., Paul, G. and Ayalew, M. (no date) *Comparative Analysis of the Impact of Tsunami and Tsunami Interventions on Conflicts in Sri Lanka and Aceh/Indonesia*. Available online at: http://web.mit.edu/cis/www/migration/pubs/rrwp/34_tsunami.htm, accessed 14 November 2006.

Becker, D. (2003) *Mental Health and Human Rights: Thinking about the Relatedness of Individual and Social Processes*. Available online at: http://www.medico-international.de/en/projects/social/ps_becker_en.pdf, accessed 16 December 2011.

Bourassa, J. (2009) 'Psychosocial interventions and mass populations: a social work perspective', *International Social Work*, 52(6): 743–55.

Carballo, M. and Heal, B. (2005) *The Public Health Response to the Tsunami*. Available online at: http://www.fmreview.org/FMRpdfs/Tsunami/04.pdf, accessed 14 November 2006.

Cohen, C. and Werker, E. (2004) *Towards an Understanding of the Root Causes of Forced Migration: The Political Economy of Natural Disasters*. Available online at: http://web.mit.edu/cis/www/migration/pubs/rrwp/25_towards.doc, accessed 14 November 2006.

Couldry, M. and Morris, T. (2005) 'UN assesses tsunami response', *Forced Migration Review Special Issue*. Available online at: http://www.fmreview.org/, accessed 3 November 2010.

De Jong, K., Prosser, S. and Ford, N. (2005) *Addressing the Psychosocial Needs in the Aftermath of the Tsunami*. Available online at: http://medicine.plosjournals.org/perlserv/?request=getdocument&doi=10.1371/journal.pmed.0020179, accessed 23 October 2006.

Duncan J. and Arnston, L. (2004) *Children in Crisis: Good Practices in Evaluating Psychosocial Programming*. Available online at: http://siteresources.worldbank.org/INTMH/Resources/Evaluating_Psychosocial_Programming.pdf, accessed 16 December 2011.

Encyclopedia of the Nations (no date) *Social and Humanitarian Assistance – International Disaster Relief*. Available online at: http://www.nationsencyclopedia.com/United-Nations/Social-and-Humanitarian-Assistance-INTERNATIONAL-DISASTER-RELIEF.html, accessed 15 October 2010.

Estrella, M. and Gaventa, J. (1997) *Who Counts Reality? Participatory Monitoring and Evaluation: A Literature Review*. Available online at: http://www.ids.ac.uk/files/Wp70.pdf, accessed 16 December 2011.

Galappatti, A. (2005) 'Reflections on post-tsunami psychosocial work', *Forced Migration Review Special Issue*. Available online at: http://www.fmreview.org/, accessed 3 November 2007.

Gillespie, D.F. and Danso, K. (2010) *Disaster Concepts and Issues: A Guide Book for Social Work Education and Practice*. Alexandria, VA: CSWE Press. p. 16.

Guzman, E. (no date) *Towards Total Disaster Risk Management Approach*. Available online at: http://unpan1.un.org/intradoc/groups/public/documents/

apcity/unpan009657.pdf, accessed 31 January 2011.

Hawkins, R. and Maurer, K. (2010) 'Bonding, bridging and linking: how social capital operated in New Orleans following Hurricane Katrina', *British Journal of Social Work*, 40: 1777–93.

IASC (Inter-Agency Standing Committee) (2007) *IASC Guidelines on Mental Health and Psychosocial Support in Emergency Settings*. Available online at: http://www.humanitarianinfo.org/iasc/pageloader. aspx?page=content-subsidi-tf_mhps-default, accessed 16 December 2011.

IASC (Inter-Agency Standing Committee) (2009) *Annual Report for 2009*. Available online at: http://www. humanitarianinfo.org/iasc/pageloader.aspx?page= content-documents-default&publish=0, accessed 15 October 2010.

IASC (Inter-Agency Standing Committee) (2010) *Psychosocial Support in Humanitarian Emergencies: What Should Humanitarian Health Actors Know*. Available online at: http://www.who.int/mental_ health/emergencies/what_humanitarian_health_ actors_should_know.pdf, accessed 26 February 2011.

IFRC (International Federation of Red Cross and Red Crescent Societies) (2000) *World Disasters Report 2000: Focus on Public Health*. Bellegarde-sur-Valserine (France): SADAG Imprimerie.

Ingleby, D. (ed.) (2005) *Forced Migration and Mental Health*. New York: Springer Science & Business Media.

Kalin, W. (no date) *Natural Disasters and IDPs' Rights*. Available online at: www.fmreview.org/textOnly-Content/FMR/Tsunami/03.doc, accessed 28 October 2010.

Keene, J. (2003) *Global Civil Society*. Available online at: http://www.johnkeane.net/pdf_docs/gcs_sample _chapter.pdf, accessed 01 November 2010.

Light, P. (2005) 'Lessons learned: Hurricanes Katrina and Wilma hit U.S. Gulf coastal states', *Boston Globe*, 4 September.

Loane, G. (2007) 'Multidimensional domains of disaster response for social work practice: preparedness, response, recovery, and mitigation', *Proceedings of the International Seminar on Disaster Planning, Management, and Relief: New Responsibilities for Social Work Education*. St Michael, Barbados: Council on Social Work Education. pp. 12–18.

Mathbor, G.M. (2007) 'Enhancement of community preparedness for natural disasters: the role of social work in building social capital for sustainable disaster relief and management', *International Social Work*, 50(3): 357–69.

Mathbor, G.M. (2010) 'Surviving disaster: the role of invisible assets of communities', in *Disaster Concepts and Issues: a Guide for Social Work Education and Practice*. Alexandria, VA: CSWE Press. pp. 145–62.

Miller, G. (2005) 'The tsunami's psychological aftermath', *Science Magazine*, 309: 1030–3.

MIND (Munasinghe Institute for Development) (2006) *Second International Conference on Sustainable Hazard Reduction, Rehabilitation, Reconstruction, and Long Term Development Report*, 11–12 January 2006. Colombo, Sri Lanka: MIND. pp. 7–8.

Mukhier, M. (2006) 'Surviving the Bam earthquake: psychosocial support helps people to heal', *Optimist: Looking Beyond the Horizon*. Available online at: http://www.optimistmag.org/gb/0014/one.php, retrieved 27 April 2006.

Newburn, T. (1993) *Disaster and After: Social Work in the Aftermath of Disaster*. London: Jessica Kingsley.

OCHA-A (United Nations Office for the Coordination of Humanitarian Affairs) (no date) *OCHA on Message: Humanitarian Access*. Available online at: http://ochaonline.un.org/OCHAonMessage/tabid/6702/language/en-US/Default.aspx, accessed 01 November 2010.

OCHA-B (United Nations Office for the Coordination of Humanitarian Affairs) (no date) *General Assembly Resolution 46/182: Strengthening of the Coordination of Humanitarian Emergency Assistance of the United Nations*. Available online at: http://www.ifrc.org/Docs/idrl/I270EN.pdf, accessed 16 December 2011.

OneResponse (no date) *Humanitarian Reform and Global Cluster Approach*. Available online at: http://oneresponse.info/Coordination/ClusterApproach/Pages/Cluster%20Approach.aspx, accessed 05 February 2011.

Parks, W., Gray-Felder, D., Hunt, J. and Byrne, A. (2005) *Who Measures Change? An Introduction to Participatory Monitoring and Evaluation of Communication for Social Change*. Available online at: http://www.communicationforsocialchange.org/, accessed 01 March 2007.

Pupavac, V. (2002) *Therapeutising Refugees, Pathologising Populations: International Psycho-Social Programmes in Kosovo*. Available online at: http://reliefweb.int/sites/reliefweb.int/files/resources /77E8853E90165CCDC1256C610035083E-hcr-ther apeurising-aug02.pdf, accessed 16 December 2011.

Pupavac, V. (2004) 'Psychosocial interventions and the demoralisation of humanitarianism', *Journal of Biosocial Science*, 36(4): 491–504.

Reuters AlertNet (2010) *'U.N. Aid Chief Chides Agencies on Haiti Relief'*. Available online at: http://www.reuters.com/article/idUSTRE61H3MM20100218, accessed 01 November 2010.

Reyes, G. and Charles, J. (2010) *Trafficking, Sexual Exploitation of Haitian Children in the Dominican Republic on the Rise*. Available online at: http://www.palmbeachpost.com/news/crime/trafficking-sexual-exploitation-of-haitian-children-in-the-992808.html, accessed 16 December 2011.

Save the Children (2010) *At a Crossroads: Humanitarianism for the Next Decade*. Available online at: http://www.savethechildren.org.uk/en/54_12550.htm, accessed 01 November 2010.

Skjelsbaek, K. (1975) *International Nongovernmental Organisations and their Functions*. Available online at: http://www.laetusinpraesens.org/docs/functun.php, accessed 31 January 2011.

Smith, M. (2007) 'A social justice framework for teaching disaster-related knowledge and skills', *Proceedings of the International Seminar on Disaster Planning, Management, and Relief: New Responsibilities for Social Work Education*. St Michael, Barbados: Council on Social Work Education. pp. 110–14.

Soliman, H. (2010) 'Ethical considerations in disasters: a social work framework', *Disaster Concepts and Issues: A Guide for Social Work Education and Practice*. Alexandria, VA: CSWE Press. pp. 223–40.

Stoddard, A., Harmer, A. and DiDomenico, V. (2009) *Providing Aid in Unsecure Environments: 2009 Update Trends in Violence against Aid Workers and the Operational Response*. Available online at: http://www.odi.org.uk/resources/download/3250.pdf, accessed 2 November 2010.

Stoesen, L. (2006) 'Experts examine disasters, disparities', *NASW News*, April 2006. Washington D.C: NASW. p. 5.

Strang, A. and Ager, A. (no date) *Building a Conceptual Framework for Psychosocial Intervention in Complex Emergencies: Reporting on the Work of the Psychosocial Working Group*. Available online at: http://www.ishr.org/conference/articles/strang.pdf, accessed 22 October 2006.

Summerfield, D. (2001) 'The invention of post-traumatic stress disorder and the social usefulness of a psychiatric category', *British Medical Journal*, 322: 95–8.

Szymoniak, S. (2006) *Richmond, Mary Ellen*. Available online at: http://www.learningtogive.org/papers/index.asp?bpid=119, accessed 19 November 2006.

Turner, F.J. (1979) *Social Work Treatment: Interlocking Theoretical Approaches*, 2nd edn. New York: Collier Macmillan.

USAID (United States Agency for International Development) (2010) *Pakistan Flood Relief: USAID Statistics*. Available online at: http://www.centcom.mil/pakistan-flood/pakistan-flood-relief-usaid-statistics, accessed 1 November 2010.

Van der Veer, G. (2006) 'Training trainers for counselors and psychosocial workers in areas of armed conflict: some basic principles', *Intervention: International Journal on Mental Health Psychosocial Work and Counseling in Areas of Conflict*, 4(2): 97–107.

Van Ommeren, M., Saxena, S. and Saraceno, B. (2005) 'Mental and social health during and after acute emergencies: emerging consensus?', *Bulletin of the World Health Organization*, 83: 71–6. Available online at: http://www.who.int/mental_health/media/mental_and_social_health_in_emergency.pdf, accessed 24 October 2006.

Weichselgartner, J. (2001) 'Disaster mitigation: the concept of mitigation revisited', *Disaster Prevention and Management*, 10(2): 85–95.

Wickramage, K. (2006) 'Sri Lanka's post-tsunami playground: lessons for future programming and interventions following disasters', *Intervention: International Journal on Mental Health Psychosocial Work and Counseling in Areas of Conflict*, 4(2): 163–8.

Williamson, J. and Robinson M. (2006) 'Psychosocial interventions, or integrated programming for well-being?', *Intervention: International Journal on Mental Health Psychosocial Work and Counseling in Areas of Conflict*, 4(1): 4–25.

Woolcock, M. (2001) 'The place of social capital in understanding social and economic outcomes', *Isuma: Canadian Journal of Policy Research*, 2(1): 1–17.

Zakour, M. (2010) 'Vulnerability and risk assessment: building community resilience', *Disaster Concepts and Issues: A Guide for Social Work Education and Practice*. Alexandria, VA: CSWE Press. pp. 15–33.

19

Social Work, Political Conflict and Displacement

Shulamit Ramon and Reima Ana Maglajlic

INTRODUCTION

At the 2010 conference of the International Association of Schools of Social Work (IASSW), the International Federation of Social Workers (IFSW) and the International Council of Social Welfare (ICSW), there were presentations from Australia, Azerbaijan, Bosnia and Herzegovina, Brazil, Cambodia, Israel, Palestine, Slovenia, South Africa, South Korea, United Kingdom, Uzbekistan and Zimbabwe. Each of these countries has either been directly involved in a recent political conflict and displacement resulting from it, or has been impacted by a conflict that has originated in another country. Yet in only two of these presentations were issues of political conflict and displacement identified as relevant to understanding the specific country and social work in that country.

The example illustrates the lack of attention to the need for social workers, be they practitioners, academics or students, to consider the manner in which political conflicts impact their current and future work contexts – particularly as the available literature indicates that social workers often tend to avoid

addressing and dealing with these issues (Baum, 2007). This chapter aims to explain why social work should understand better the impact of political conflicts on our identity and practice, based on relevant examples from the last decade of the 20th century and the first decade of the 21st century. The chapter concludes with an overview of an integrated and firmer understanding of the social work response to the impact of political conflict, and how this is aligned with the radical tradition within our profession.

EXPERIENCING POLITICAL CONFLICT AND ITS IMPACT

Existing evidence highlights the connections between violent political conflict and displacement either outside of one's country (as a refugee, UNHCR, 2001: 16–17) or inside one's own country (as an internally displaced person [IDP], UNHCR, 2007: 45). At the end of 2010, there were 43.7 million forcibly displaced people world-wide – 27.5 million IDPs, 15.4 million refugees and 983,000 asylum seekers (UNHCR, 2010). In Sri Lanka, a country that suffered from the effect of natural disaster in the tsunami of 2004 as well as from the civil war between the Sinhalese majority and the Tamil minority, two-thirds of those who were internally displaced had been uprooted by the political conflict. Yet in the world's media the tsunami and its victims received a lot more coverage than the victims of the political war (Amnesty International, 2009; UNOCHA, 2009). It is estimated that 4.7 million people became refugees abroad as a result of the most recent war in Iraq, while 1.6 million became IDPs with only less than 10 percent returning to their homes (Ferris, 2008). Of the 654,965 people who died in Iraq between 2003 and 2005, it has been estimated that 601,027 died a violent death (Burnham et al., 2006).

The figures on conflict and displacement themselves are invariably politicised because of their intense, yet differentiated, significance to the involved populations. For example, the population of Bosnia and Herzegovina prior to the 1992–1996 war was nearly 4.4 million. The figures available on war damage are varied, hard to properly reference and often tailored to various political purposes. Estimates on the number of people killed in the war range from a conservative figure of 100,000 to as high as 300,000. More than 10,000 people were killed in the capital Sarajevo alone and 50,000 were injured during the 3-year siege from 1992 to 1995. At least 16,000 children were killed and some 35,000 were injured. Of the total pre-war population, over one million people fled the country during the war, some 650,000 of whom were children. Since the signing of the General Framework Agreement for Peace in Bosnia and Herzegovina (GFAP, popularly known as the Dayton Agreement) in December 1995, more than one million civilians have returned, mainly to areas where they are now ethnic minorities (Wilkinson, 2005) in the context of the creation of two ethnicised entities (Bosniaks and Serbs). According to UNHCR data (2006), at the end of 2005, 182,700 people remained internally displaced. Despite the variations in the data presented, this indicates that nearly half of the pre-war population was either internally displaced or became refugees, while between one in fifteen or one in forty citizens were killed. Accurate figures on the current population of Bosnia and Herzegovina are unavailable in the absence of a post-war census. A census has not been organised due to political reasons, as it would reveal the true extent and effect of ethnic cleansing during the war.

At around the same time (1990–1993), the Hutu and Tutsi people, who had lived with each other relatively peacefully for generations in Rwanda, turned on each other with an astonishing degree of cruelty. The number of people killed is estimated at 950,000 (Melvern, 2004), earning the conflict the title the '*Rwandan genocide*'. Due to a shared colonial history and the movements of rebel armies, the war in Rwanda spilled also into the Democratic Republic of Congo (during the First Congo War from 1996 to 1997 and the Second Congo War from 1998 to 2003), destabilising the whole area.

In addition to localised historical and economic reasons, the causes of these conflicts and the responses to them by the international community include the impact of post-colonial legacies, economic vested interests of major power states, profit-led arms trade, racism, and their effect on international aid and conflict resolution policies (Goose and Smyth, 1994; Akhavan, 1997; Nanda et al., 1998; McNulty, 2000).

Becoming a refugee is already an end product of a journey that has often meant losing one's physical home, school or workplace, neighbourhood; losing or being separated from family members, friends, possessions, social status and identity documents. Moving away from one's region may have included days of malnutrition, lack of food, shelter, clean water or health services; sleeplessness; not having a safe place to stay, to cook, or to rest; being attacked, injured or raped on the way; family members disappearing or dying during the journey; not knowing where to go.

Arriving means facing the unknown: if you are a refugee you are confronted with people telling you what to do, possibly in a language you do not know, and keeping you in a confined area; waiting for decisions made by others about your fate; being taken to an unknown place and, at least initially, not being allowed to work or study; having to prove your identity when your documents have either been left behind in the escape process, taken away from you or destroyed during your displacement. You may need to cross not one but several borders, as many countries may not allow you to stay on their territory.

A number of Western host countries impose quotas for refugee resettlement that are frequently tightly prescribed and politicised (see, for example, Thielemann, 2005). However, the majority of refugees usually remain in the continent or region of their origin. Furthermore, in 2010, 4/5 of the world's refugees reside in developing countries, and 42 percent live in countries where the GDP per capita is less than 3000 per annum (UNHCR, 2010).

If you become internally displaced, you may experience the advantage of remaining within your own country; but you may be treated as a non-citizen: you have no right to choose where to live; may not have any entitlement to health and social welfare, schooling, work or housing; and often you are treated as the enemy or as the inferior, poor relative. Furthermore, depending on where you arrive, you may also fear being involved in further conflict or exposed to other threats to your life or limb.

On the border between Azerbaijan and Armenia, there are ghost settlements, consisting of brand new houses, empty of people. The houses were built by the UN for Azeri citizens who became IDPs during the conflict between the two countries that erupted violently at the end of the 1980s, but their government would not allow them to move to these permanent houses, as such a move

would weaken the political bargaining position of the Azeri government. Thus more than 20 years after the war between the two countries many IDPs continue to live in squalor, while Armenian churches in Baku (the capital of Azerbaijan) remain closed and empty. Churches are important symbols of ethnic and national identity in this case: their existence in the centre of Baku highlights how closely the two communities lived together for centuries; as long as these buildings remain intact there is hope for the return of the Armenians.

Some of the one and a half million people of the Gaza strip are the original refugees from the 1948 war between Jews and Arabs in Palestine (known as the *War of Independence* in Hebrew and the *Naqba* – the disaster – in Arabic), the rest are their children and their grandchildren. Most of these refugees continue to live in camps and to receive food, schooling, health and social care services funded by the UN and the EU, due to lack of agreement for more than 60 years between Israel and the seven Arab countries involved, preventing the establishment of the envisaged second state – that of the Palestinians – from becoming a reality. The cycles of violence and stagnation that followed since 1948 have added layers of despair, hatred and further devastation to the initial outcomes of the conflict.

In terms of asylum applications in industrialised countries during the 1980s and 1990s, the EU accounted for 68 percent of all applications while North America accounted for most of the remaining applications (Hatton and Williamson, 2006). The proportion of successful asylum status applications fell from 50 to 20 percent in the same two decades. While evidence suggests that the best way to address issues related to 'migration management and control' include those that address the root causes of such movements in the countries or regions of origin, such as poverty or political instability, these actions are both costly and require long-term commitments on behalf of the international community (Taylor, 2006). At the same time, these issues – particularly during times of economic crises such as those experienced in the late 2000s – become contested issues for current governments in the host countries, which may prefer to focus on the next election results rather than on long-term solutions (Taylor, 2006).

On the whole, political conflicts, whether between nations or within a country, lead to negative outcomes for the populations involved. The consequences can take generations to be put right, if ever; both for individuals and the collectives of which they are members. Deterioration of previously achieved health and social care standards is noticeable, leading to increased inequality (Ramon, 2009). Furthermore, the consequences impact also on populations in countries far from the actual conflict zones through the arrival of refugees and/or military involvement (e.g. in case of the UK, in Iraq and Afghanistan) (Guru, 2010).

However, there are examples of positive outcomes of violent political conflict, albeit mostly unintended. Wars lead to reconsideration of both individual and collective life priorities or to works of art and literature of previously unimagined depth of creativity and perception. Thus the development of many welfare states in Europe can be linked directly to the Second World War; Florence Nightingale's – largely unsuccessful – work as a nurse in the Crimean war led to the establishment of nursing as a profession; Polish social work continued to be taught within a Catholic monastery during the Second World War. The psychiatric hospitals bombed during the 1991–1996 war in Bosnia and Herzegovina were not re-built, but led to the establishment of a community mental health system. Social work students in Ljubljana continue to be involved in supporting the families of 'The Erased', 18,000 people, mainly ex-Yugoslav citizens, who became non-citizens in Slovenia when they failed to register as citizens in 2002 (although they had lived in the country for a long time) (Zorn and Lipovic-Cebron, 2008). Their case led to a recent decision (July 2010) by the

EU to call on the Slovenian government to give citizenship to all of The Erased.

A more controversial example is provided by research evidence that highlights professional growth (e.g. in relation to skills, professional identity and team cohesion) among Israeli Jewish social workers during the 2nd Intifada, and none of it among Israeli Arab social workers, some of whom reported an increased sense of exclusion and rejection by their Jewish colleagues (Baum and Ramon, 2010). This example illustrates the significance of the combined personal, social and professional identities social workers have, resulting in a differential impact a political conflict may have on them.

There are many examples of resilience and adversity-activated development. Defined as positive responses to adversity, resilience and adversity-activated development have been amply demonstrated by individuals within the context of political conflict in a range of activities from learning to live frugally to sheltering strangers even at a considerable risk to oneself just because they were human beings caught in adversity, discriminated due to prejudices (the true story of Anna Frank is only one such example of the many Jewish children rescued by non-Jewish people; Dr Yanush Korchak's march to death with the orphans he was responsible for as a social pedagogue during the Nazi occupation of Poland is another). All liberation movements in Africa, Asia, Europe, and South America in the 20th century also provide examples of adversity-activated action by people ready to risk their lives for the sake of a better society. Yet a number of the organisations involved in such movements have also killed innocent people, and some have engaged in a variety of cruel acts, perhaps as a result of the fact that participating in an armed struggle brutalises all involved.

Experiences of trauma following acute political conflict are equally typical as are instances of resilience. Trauma is usually defined as experiencing a highly adverse and often unexpected outcome that potentially or actually leads to a variety of losses

(Wessley, 2003; Williams, 2005). Within the psychiatric literature there is a focus on post-traumatic stress disorder (PTSD), recognised as a mental illness diagnosis since 1980 in the aftermath of the Vietnam War, both in the American DSM (Diagnostic Manual of Mental Disorders) and the World Health Organization (WHO) classification of mental and behavioural disorders (ICD-10). This type of trauma is characterised by reactions to the experience of an event that led to extreme fear, helplessness and threat, intense anxiety, confusion, depression, aggression (directed either at oneself and/or at others), often accompanied by unexpected re-living of aspects of the original experience.

Psychological models of trauma focus on dissociation, the distortion of the maturation process (e.g. in childhood, as a result of child abuse), and the re-formulation of world views. The latter is a cognitive-behavioural approach that assumes the need for re-formulation of the world by the individual (and the collective) following a major trauma as a way of finding meaning that enables people to assimilate the trauma to their world view, and/or accommodate their previous view (Janoff-Bulman and Friese, 1983).

PTSD as a label has been questioned in terms of its applicability and validity in non-Western cultures (Chemtob, 1996). While forms of traumatic stress reactions resemble each other in various cultural settings, there can be significant differences in the meaning attributed to these reactions (for example, the manner in which dreams or nightmares are awarded value and meaning in different cultures). Ways of coping and healing can be phrased in terms of communal rather than individual experience and space.

Psychosocial perspectives include the recognition that the perpetrators of a traumatic event have been influenced by a given social context, and that in the case of political violence such actions are often condoned within that specific context (Smail, 1993). Likewise, the significance given to the trauma depends in part on its social meaning and power, as does the healing process. For example,

women raped as part of a political conflict are often forbidden by their communities from discussing this trauma in public, as it casts a negative shadow on the ability of their male partners and the male community to defend them.

An increase in the prevalence of identified mental illness has been reported in most populations that have experienced acute political conflict, as well as among those experiencing an ongoing, non-acute conflict (Wessley, 2003). Depression, anxiety and PTSD are the most frequently diagnosed issues (Weaver and Burns, 2001). However, only a minority responds by developing a severe form of mental illness, estimated at 6.7 percent. While this is a small percentage, it is double the rate of the estimated prevalence of psychosis in most populations. Thus the likelihood of vulnerability to mental ill health has been proposed as an underlying factor in determining who will respond to the abnormal situation of acute political conflict and dislocation by developing a mental illness and who will not (Wessley, 2003). However, the rate of recovery is high if suitable intervention follows, such as early debriefing (Wessley et al., 2000), a variety of psychosocial interventions, and re-connecting people to supportive networks (Shalev et al., 2003; Ursano et al., 2003). In fact, the statistics beg the question as to why the rate of mental illness is so low, given the severity of the losses. If anything, it highlights the resilience capacity of ordinary people.

In this context it is important to note that the rate of mental illness among the population of the concentration camps during the Second World War was low, even though this group was much more deprived psychologically, socially and physically than most other local groups during the same period. This is explained as related to the ability of using mental dissociation as a defence mechanism while concentrating on actual physical survival. A number of people became mentally ill only after they left the camps, i.e. when they could 'afford' to become vulnerable (Barel et al., 2010).

However, we are aware of a higher prevalence of mental ill health among the children of survivors of concentration camps anywhere, perhaps due to unresolved psychological and social issues for their parents, coupled with the difficulty of sharing the emotional burden the parents must have experienced. Some survivors have responded by becoming driven towards economic success, being highly ambitious for their children, and no doubt burdening the second generation with the responsibility to overcome the disturbing legacy of the political conflict they have experienced (Danieli, 1982; Cassel and Shenfield, 2006).

For many refugees and displaced people post-acute conflict life is only a pale shadow of the life they had before, consisting of a lower social status, less personal and career satisfaction, the experience of economic hardship and of being a foreigner in exile, often disconnected from one's country of origin. These issues are a fertile ground for the development of low self esteem, depression and isolation. Grieving is likely to continue for a long time, casting a long shadow on the life of the individual and those sharing that life. The fear of re-occurrence of a violent conflict exacerbates the prevalence of mental ill health. Thus the losses include people, limbs, material possessions, hopes and dreams, and that of certainty. The grieving process becomes particularly complicated if the body of a loved one is not found, is not buried, and the mourning ceremony is not held. People also grieve to different degrees for different losses, and in individualised ways in addition to collective ways.

INTERNATIONAL REGULATION OF POLITICAL CONFLICT RELATED ISSUES

The above noted experiences suggest a number of violations of human rights, frequently occurring in the context where the state's governance is challenged and/or changing. A number of international regulations were set in the aftermath of the Second World War, which shaped the responses to political conflict. Internationally, conflict regulation comprises three elements – prevention, management and settlement (Wolff, 2009). These relate not solely to the relevant legislation and policies, but also to diplomatic interventions (e.g. mediation), international judicial measures, economic interventions (from assistance to embargos) and military interventions (e.g. peacekeeping forces).

There are four treaties and three additional protocols that comprise the Geneva Conventions, a set of standards in international law for humanitarian treatment of the victims of war, created in 1949. The use of weapons of war had been covered in separate previous documents of the Hague Conventions (1899 and 1907) and the 1925 Geneva Protocol. The conventions seek to protect people no longer taking part in a political conflict (e.g. wounded or sick soldiers, prisoners of war, civilians and medical or religious personnel). Three additional protocols were added in 1977 and 2005, relating to the protection of participants in international and non-international armed conflicts and the adoption of an additional distinctive emblem for medical services.

Grave breaches of the Conventions include wilful killing, torture or inhumane treatment, wilfully causing great suffering or serious injury to body or health, compelling people to serve in the forces of a hostile power, wilfully depriving people of the right to a fair trial, taking hostages, expensive destruction or appropriation of property that is not justified by military necessity and carried out unlawfully, and, finally, unlawful deportation, transfer or confinement. Hence the Geneva and the Hague Conventions have become cornerstones of the international humanitarian law.

The International Bill of Human Rights includes the Universal Declaration of Human Rights (1948); the Covenant on Civil and Political Rights (1966); the Covenant on

Economic, Social and Cultural Rights (1966); and the Optional Protocol to the International Covenant on Civil and Political Rights (1966). These form the foundation of many other important UN human rights instruments, such as the Convention on the Prevention and Punishment of the Crime of Genocide (1948); the Convention (1951) and Protocol (1967) regarding the Status of Refugees; the Convention on the Elimination of All Forms of Racial Discrimination (1965); the Convention Against Torture and Other Cruel, Inhuman or Degrading Treatment or Punishment (1984); and the Convention on the Rights of the Child (1989). These documents include non-derogable rights (rights from which no detraction is permitted, even in exceptional circumstances), such as the right to life, freedom from torture or inhuman treatment, the right not to be convicted or punished under retroactive laws, the right to recognition as a person before the law and the right to freedom of conscience, thought and religion.

While each state has the primary responsibility to monitor these human rights treaties, the UN General Assembly also created the post of High Commissioner for Human Rights in 1993 and bodies such as the Committee on Torture in 1989. This Committee has the unique power to investigate cases on its own initiative concerning information that torture is being systematically practiced in the territory of a state party.

As with many other international and local legislative contexts, the implementation of the international humanitarian law has been the subject of much scrutiny, particularly during the past decade. For example, the manner in which international peacekeeping was deployed during the conflict in Bosnia and Herzegovina, particularly through the creation of the Office of the High Representative with the ultimate decision-making powers above the state itself, has been seen by some as counter-productive and resulting in the marginalisation of locally accountable solutions (Chandler, 1999).

Equally, the outcomes of the International Criminal Tribunal for the former Yugoslavia attracted controversy over the manner in which those who faced charges were treated and supported to make fair representation to the actual weighing of punishments, depending on the particular judicial tradition of the Tribunal judges. However, others felt that the defendants were given a free, unlimited, stage in which to present their views, using endless delaying tactics, at the expense of the international community and the victims of that dispute.

The Truth and Reconciliation Commission (TRC) in South Africa (Doxtader and Salazar, 2008) has set in motion an alternative approach to that undertaken by the International Criminal Tribunal. It is one focused on attempting to have more in-depth knowledge about the South African conflict, as well as attempting to enable previous enemies to come to terms with what has happened and live better together as one society. Although the value of the TRC varies for different participants (Vora and Vora, 2004), it has led thus far to establishing eleven such commissions elsewhere, demonstrating the appeal of this approach. Whereas the international tribunal attempts to provide a closure to a difficult chapter, the TRCs aim at a closure that enables a new beginning.

SOCIAL WORK METHODS AND ROLES IN CONFLICT AND DISPLACEMENT SITUATIONS

The focus on the relationship between social work and political conflict raises a number of questions. Beginning with the wider context, the question is whether there is a recognised and distinctive role for social work in the societies affected by political conflict, as compared to other disciplines. Do the existing social work skills, values and knowledge have something new and different to contribute to the changing needs of the populations we work with in the societies affected by political conflict, either during or after the conflict? A related question is whether it matters if this work takes place in our own or in another country. Equally, what does the context of political conflict mean for the political dimension of our role, often unrecognised or silenced by many of our social work peers, even in societies that are relatively free of brutal political conflicts?

Over the past twenty years, development studies emerged as a distinctive field with claims to knowledge and skills of work in contexts that are transformed by poverty and/ or political conflict, often labelled as developing countries. Hence, the branding of the aforementioned IASSW/IFSW/ICSW 2010 World Conference as one on social work and social development is both intriguing and promising. The basic social work 'triplets' of work with individuals, groups and communities seem applicable and relevant. Individuals affected by war are likely to need tailor-made assistance materially, physically, psychologically and socially. Communities will require support in their physical and social rebuilding. However, as of yet, political conflict has not inspired approaches that can be labelled as social work's own when addressing the needs of populations affected by them. In many contexts (e.g. during the 1991–1995 war in Croatia) the majority of activities initiated to address the newly created needs can be subsumed under the labels of either 'humanitarian aid' or 'psycho-social support' (Pečnik and Stubbs, 1994). Neither of these is specific to social work, and they are more akin to local charitable or medicalised traditions. It is the dual focus on the social and the psychological which is unique to social work in general, and also to its contribution within the context of political conflict, of which ample examples are available (see Ramon, 2008).

In parallel, there is a distinct radical and politicised tradition within our profession, challenging the existing social, economic and political obstacles which lead to the marginalisation of its citizens. Its principles are also embodied in the international definition of social work, with its focus on the liberation of people who are marginalised within different societies, including those affected by political conflicts. Yet we frequently shy away from the political dimension within our day-to-day practice. A number of these approaches can be witnessed in societies affected by political conflict, with greater affinity to group and community work (e.g. working in refugee camps). However, the majority of such programmes have not been initiated by social workers themselves, though these projects embody some of the fundamental principles of our profession (Lavalette, 2010).

There are also differences in needs, threats and expectations in relation to the different phases of any given political conflict – either the build-up to it, its (often violent) process and the phase following its end, usually labelled as 'transitional'.

This leads us to the additional dimension of locality and space. Development studies, as a discipline that emerged and formed in Western European universities, implies work carried out in contexts other than those from where the development workers come from, requiring an international perspective to one's work. However, they do so alongside the many non-Western social workers in developing countries who are directly engaged in community development too.

The impact of political conflict on social workers

Social workers who live and work in contexts affected by political conflicts face additional challenges to those faced by all social workers. They themselves can become displaced people, refugees, lose family members, homes and/or become disabled (Wairire, 2008). They can also become either co-opted politically or face risks of retaliation (Campbell and McCrystal, 2005). As members of their respective societies, they too take sides in the ensuing conflict, and it then becomes extremely difficult for them to maintain a fully professional response towards clients identified as members of 'the enemy', or the minority group perceived as hostile to the majority. Research on this issue is still at its beginning (Ramon et al., 2006; Nuttman-Schwartz, 2008).

There are gaps and dilemmas in our understanding and ability to predict the roles of social workers in political conflict, including whether we should continue to borrow methodologies for work from other disciplines or focus more on developing our own. The examples below illustrate some of the dilemmas faced by social workers in their responses to political conflict and solutions they developed.

Examples of the dilemmas social workers may face in the context of political conflict

Working with asylum seekers

Social work with asylum seekers is often dictated by the regulations a particular government has stipulated for this client group. Often these regulations are aimed at finding reasons not to allow the person/family to remain in the new country, segregating them in 'reception centres' structured as semi-prisons, and disabling them from taking a productive and dignified role in life. Social workers are expected to participate in inquiries and decision-making processes predominately aimed at sending the person back to the country they have fled, while the decision whether they will be at risk if sent back is not taken by social workers. This is a particularly sensitive issue if the person/group felt threatened in their country of origin and refuses to go back. In today's world we have too many examples of asylum seekers who commit self-harm in protest of the decision to send them back, children separated from their parents, and returnees tortured upon return, all happening in countries perceived to be civilised and ruled by adherence to international law (e.g. Crawley, 2007).

This state of affairs has led Humphries (2004) to ask if supporting immigration control is an acceptable role for social workers. Yet clients helped by social workers in this context sing their praises (e.g. Kellaway, 2010), and it stands to reason to assume that having a social worker as an advocate for an asylum seekers may be helpful at times. Furthermore, this is an instance in which collective objection to the regulations and the way asylum seekers are treated can support legislative and policy change towards a more human rights led approach (Briskman and Cemlyn, 2005).

The treatment of asylum seekers is an international as well as a national issue, one that calls for international collaboration among social workers, and one that entails not only immigration control (Kohli, 2007).

Supporting immigrant workers in the aftermath of the 9/11 World Trade Centre explosion

Hill et al. (2008) have documented their work as social security social workers in New York, attempting to secure health care for legal immigrants who worked in cleaning the World Trade centre area after 9/11, and became ill in the process of doing so. As immigrants, they had no health insurance and were not insured by any of the existing federal insurance schemes. Initially no one wanted to either recognise that they became ill due to lack of supportive measures (e.g. suitable clothing) made available to them during the cleaning operation, or to pay the costs. They have also lost the right to work in the US due to being off work while ill for a long time.

The social workers at the Mount Sinai hospital in New York organised a public campaign to mount support for them, together with trade unions and immigration lawyers, which included lobbying in Washington and creating a non-government organisation (NGO). The campaign was successful in passing special legislation that enabled registered ill immigrants to receive funding covering their health care cost to the tune of

$5,000,000 distributed by the Red Cross to about 500 such workers. However, the campaign failed to get sufficient support for reinstating their right to work in the US, even though they had become ill in the process of supporting the US in one of its hours of greatest need.

Training needs and advocacy roles: positive diversity policies and conflict prevention

The above text has highlighted the centrality of social work intervention within an interdisciplinary team in the context of political conflict. While basic social work values and skills apply, most social workers are unprepared for this type of work either in their social work qualifying or post-qualifying training, as this type of work is not considered to be likely to take place.

The increase in the number of violent political conflicts even since the beginning of the 21st century alone, the ease with which such conflicts are transferred to other countries as part of the globalisation process and the prolonged period of dislocation of both refugees and IDPs, have all demonstrated that the above assumption does not fit current realities.

Given that political conflict is part of the 21st century reality, then the profession needs to have in place both short-term and long-term training within social work education and within social services settings. This should focus on the core issues of political conflict; its wide-ranging impact; the role of social workers in relation to it; the range of intervention methods; awareness and ways of responding to the ethical dilemmas embedded in social work's response.

Most of the training responses tend to concentrate on short-term programmes primarily earmarked to emergency situations of political conflict, resulting in the neglect of long-term training programmes. The short-term programmes are usually related to distinct, short-term projects aimed at changing a

particular aspect of welfare (e.g. development of community-based mental health services or introduction of case management).

There are, however, relevant and innovative examples of long term training. Queens University in Belfast has initiated the systematic involvement of service users who have experienced 'The Troubles' (the formal name of the thirty years of acute political conflict in Northern Ireland) as an integral part of teaching the introduction to social work, and in the module focusing on interventions (Duffy, 2006; Campbell and Duffy, 2008). Working with an NGO in the city, the service users have been prepared for their contribution and so have been the students. This example illustrates the value of direct involvement of social work clients (which is now a requirement of the UK General Social Care Council for all social work qualifying training programmes) and the value of learning from subjective and inter-subjective experiences of being a citizen and a recipient of social care during the acute political conflict in Northern Ireland. It is intended to include social workers too in this effective training model.

Similarly, the Israeli–Palestinian Parents Circle – Families Forum,[1] made up of several hundreds of families bereaved as a result of the violence in the region, has a helpline for family members and arranges visits to schools, universities, and prisons to talk in pairs of at least one Israeli Jewish and one Palestinian together about their experiences and the lessons learned.

Working at the University of Plymouth, Butler (2005) has established a project for refugees where social work students are undertaking one of their fieldwork placements. This opportunity enables the students to: become informed about policies and regulations related to refugees; get to know them as individuals and as a group, and their life stories; offer solidarity; offer welfare advice, casework and family work; and engage in advocacy.

An interesting example of training the trainers of those working with refugees in

New Zealand on mental health issues is provided by Reynolds and Shackman (1993). Experiencing loss, communicating emotions and assessments were the core areas, looked at primarily from the perspective of perceiving the refugees as survivors, rather than as victims. For example, this perspective has implications for including the community as a resource in assessments and in support around living with loss.

Nuttman-Schwartz and Dekel (2009), working in Israel, outline a project in which social work students befriended young people about to be dislocated from their homes to a new environment as a result of the government's decision to evacuate the Israeli Jewish population from the Gaza Strip in the summer of 2005. The training focused on the needs of the young people; what the students could offer towards meeting these needs and what they could not provide; the knowledge and skills required for this type of work; as well as supervision and opportunities for reflection. Thus this project offers training opportunities *in situ*.

In our view, all of these creative and useful projects cannot replace the basic training to understand what political conflict is about; the values, knowledge and skills that adequate responses to it require from social worker;, and the need for such training to be an integral part of social work education (Ramon, 2008). Harms et al. (2008) provide an important example as to how to go about re-constructing such a curriculum within the Australian social work education system, where the main issue is improving social work with the indigenous people of Australia.

CONCLUSION

Since its inception, our profession has been influenced by political conflicts. At the policy level, the birth of the welfare state following the Second World War is one such relevant example. In parallel, social work practice itself responded through alignment with other helping professions to face the new challenges. After the two World Wars of the 20th century, the borrowing of ideas from the neo-Freudian and ego-psychology could be observed, together with aspirations towards obtaining the status of a medical profession (Parton, 1994). These responses existed side by side with the provision of material and social support to individuals and communities through re-building responses in the context of political conflict. Presently, concepts such as globalisation, social exclusion, human rights – all related to the issues discussed in this chapter – are reaffirmed as a significant vernacular for our practice and understanding of our profession, related to social action as the core of social work practice (van Wormer, 2005; Sewpaul, 2006). This perspective highlights that within the context of political conflict 'the problems experienced by people with whom we work are, in large measure, linked to structural sources of oppression, exclusion and poverty' (Sewpaul, 2006: 430) globally and locally and require an identified and internalised political role for our profession. Thus the continuous challenge confronting social work is to combine the social with the individual perspectives in its understanding and response to the upheaval political conflict brings with it.

The global lack of attention to this issue, be it in training for social work, in practice or in research, makes this challenge all the more difficult to meet. Given this background, we – a group of social work lecturers from five countries – are attempting through a small scale IASSW-sponsored project to promote awareness pertaining to the need for putting political conflict on the global and local map of social work education for students and for qualified social workers. As a first step we embarked on a survey that focuses on building a curriculum on social work in the context of political conflict; the findings will be analysed, and will serve to construct such a teaching and learning educational module.[2] We hope that this modest development will be taken forward by the readers of this chapter.

NOTE

1   www.theparentscircle.org.
2   Contact shula.ramon@anglia.ac.uk for further information.

REFERENCES

Akhavan, P. (1997) 'Justice and reconciliation in the Great Lakes Region of Africa: the contribution of the International Criminal Court for Rwanda', *Duke Journal of Comparative and International Law*, 7: 325–48.

Amnesty International (2009) *Unlock the Camps in Sri Lanka: Safety and Dignity for the Displaced Now.* London: Amnesty International.

Barel, E., Sagi-Schwartz, A., Van Ijzendoorn, M. and Barermans-Kranenburg, M.J. (2010) 'Surviving the Holocaust: a meta analysis of the long term sequalue of a Genocide', *Psychological Bulletin*, 136(5): 677–98.

Baum, N. (2007) 'Social work practice in conflict-ridden areas: cultural sensitivity is not enough', *British Journal of Social Work*, 37: 873–91.

Baum, N. and Ramon, S. (2010) 'Professional growth in turbulent times', *Journal of Social Work*, 13: 163–82.

Briskman, L. and Cemlyn, S. (2005) 'Reclaiming humanity for asylum seekers: a social work response', *International Social Work*, 48: 714–24.

Burnham, G., Lafta, R., Doocy, S. and Roberts, L. (2006) Mortality after the 2003 Iraq invasion: a cross-sectional cluster survey. *The Lancet*, 11 October: 1–8, online. Retrieved 10 September 2011.

Butler, A. (2005) 'A strengths approach to building futures: UK students and refugees together', *Journal of Community Development*, 40(2): 147–57.

Campbell, J. and McCrystal, P. (2005) 'Mental health social work and The Troubles in Northern Ireland: a study of practitioners' experiences', *Journal of Social Work*, 5(2): 173–90.

Campbell, J. and Duffy, J. (2008) 'Social Work, political violence and citizenship in Northern Ireland', in S. Ramon (ed.), *Social Work in the Context of Political Conflict*. Birmingham: Venture Press. pp. 57–76.

Cassel, L. and Shenfeld, P. (2006) 'Salutogenic and autobiographical disclosure among Holocaust survivors', *Journal of Positive Psychology*, 1: 212–25.

Chandler, D. (1999) 'The limits of peacebuilding: international regulation and civil society development in Bosnia', *International Peacekeeping*, 6 (1): 109–25.

Chemtob, C.M. (1996) Posttraumatic Stress Disorder: Trauma and Culture. International Review of Psychiatry, (2): 254–288.

Crawley, H. (2007) *When is a Child not a Child? Asylum Age Disputes and the Process of Age Assessment.* London: ILPA.

Danieli, Y. (1982) 'Families of survivors and the Nazi Holocaust: some short and long-term effects', in C.D. Spielberger, I.G. Sarason, and N. Milgram (eds), *Stress and Anxiety*. New York: McGraw Hill/ Hemisphere. pp. 405–23.

Doxtader, E. and Salazar, P.J. (2008) *Truth and Reconciliation in South Africa: The Fundamental Documents.* Cape Town: New Africa Books.

Duffy, J. (2006) *Participating and Learning: Citizen Involvement in Social Work Education in the Northern Ireland Context.* London: SCIE (Social Work Institute of Excellence).

Ferris, E. (2008) *The Looming Crisis: Displacement and Security in Iraq.* Washington: The Brooking Institute.

Goose, S.D. and Smyth, F. (1994) 'Arming genocide in Rwanda', *Foreign Affairs*, 73 (5): 86–96.

Guru, S. (2010) 'Social work and the "War on Terror"', *British Journal of Social Work*, 40 (1): 272–89.

Harms, L., Douglas Whyte J. and Clark, A. (2008) 'Preparing social work students to work with indigenous Australian communities', in S. Ramon (ed.), *Social Work in the Context of Political Conflict*. Birmingham: Venture Press and IASSW. pp. 245–70.

Hatton, T.J. and Williamson, J.G. (2006) 'Refugees, asylum seekers and policy in Europe', in F. Foder and R.J. Langhammer (eds) *Labor Mobility and The Economy*. Heidelberg: Springer. pp. 250–84.

Hill, E., Mora, L. and Garcia, L. (2008) 'The role of social security social workers in the aftermath of 9/11', in S. Ramon (ed.), *Social Work in the Context of Political Conflict*. Birmingham: Venture Press and IASSW. pp. 169–88.

Humphries, B. (2004) 'An unacceptable role for social workers: implementing immigration policy', *British Journal of Social Work*, 34: 93–107.

Janoff-Bulman, R. and Friese, I.H. (1983) 'A theoretical perspective for understanding reactions to victimisation', *Journal of Social Issues*, 39: 1–17.

Kellaway, K. (2010) 'Real lives', *The Observer*, 20 June 10: 14, 17.

Kohli, R. (2007) *Social Work with Unaccompanied Asylum Seeking Children*. Basingstoke: Palgrave Macmillan.

Lavalette, M. (2010) 'Social work and popular resistance: examples from Palestine and Lebanon', presented at the *Joint World Conference on Social Work and Social Development*, Hong Kong, China, 10–14 June 2010.

Melvern, L. (2004) *Conspiracy to Murder: The Rwandan Genocide*. New York: Verso.

McNulty, M. (2000) 'French arms, war and genocide in Rwanda', *Crime, Law & Social Change*, 33: 105–29.

Nanda, V.P., Muther, T.F. and Eckert, A.E. (1998) 'Tragedies in Somalia, Yugoslavia, Haiti, Rwanda and Liberia: revisiting the validity of humanitarian intervention under international law: part 2', *Denver Journal of International Law and Policy*, 26(5): 827–69.

Nuttman-Schwartz, O. (2008) 'Working with "others" in a context of political conflict: is it possible to support clients whose views you disagree with?', in S. Ramon, (ed.), *Social Work in the Context of Political Conflict*. Birmingham: Venture Press: 35–56.

Nuttman-Schwartz, O. and Dekel, R. (2009) 'Challenges for students working in a shared traumatic reality', *British Journal of Social Work*, 39(3): 522–38.

Parton, N. (1994) '"Problematics of government", (post) modernity and social work', *British Journal of Social Work*, 24: 9–32.

Pečnik, N. and Stubbs, P. (1994) *Working with Refugees and Displaced Persons in Croatia: From Dependency to Development?* Available at: http://gaspp.stakes.fi/NR/rdonlyres/68A172BC-FD88-437A-828E-785061347F37/4866/Croatiafromdependencyto development.pdf, accessed 10 July 2010.

Ramon, S. (2008) 'Introduction: the issues that political conflict entails for social workers and their clients', in S. Ramon (ed.), *Social Work in the Context of Political Conflict*. Birmingham: Venture Press and IASSW. pp. 1–9.

Ramon, S. (2009) 'The health impacts of political conflict: new engagements for social work?', in P. Bywaters and L. Dyer (eds) *Social Work and Global Health Inequalities: Practice and Policy Developments*. Bristol: The Policy Press. pp. 63–74.

Ramon, S., Campbell, J., Lindsay, J., McCrystal, P. and Baidun, N. (2006) 'The impact of political conflict on social work: experiences from Northern Ireland, Israel and Palestine', *British Journal of Social Work*, 36: 1–26.

Reynolds, J. and Shackman, J. (1993) *Refugees and Mental Health: Issues for Training*. Wellington: Mental Health Foundation of New Zealand.

Sewpaul, V. (2006) 'The global–local dialogue: challenges for African scholarship and socialwork in a post-colonial world', *British Journal of Social Work*, 36: 419–34.

Shalev, A.Y., Adessky, R., Boker, R., Bargai, N., Cooper, R. and Freedman, S. (2003) 'Clinical interventions for survivors of prolonged adversities', in R.J. Ursano, C.S. Fullerton and A.F. Norwood (eds), *Terrorism and Disaster: Individual and Community Mental Health Interventions*. Cambridge: Cambridge University Press. pp.162–88.

Smail, D. (1993) *The Origins of Unhappiness*. London: HarperCollins.

Taylor, S. (2006) 'From border control to migration management: the case for a paradigm change in the Western response to transborder movement', *Social Policy and Administration*, 39 (6): 563–86.

Thielemann, E.R. (2005) 'Towards refugee burden-sharing in the European Union: state interests and policy options', *Ninth Biennial International Conference of the European Union Studies Association* (USA), 31 March–2 April 2005, Austin, Texas, USA.

Vora, J.A. and Vora, E. (2004) 'The effect of South Africa Truth and Reconciliation Commission: perceptions of Xhosa, Afrikaner and English South Africans', *African Journal of Black Studies*, 34 (3): 301–22.

UNHCR (United Nations High Commissioner for Refugees) (2001) *Refugees 50th Anniversary: the Wall Behind which Refugees Can Shelter: The 1951 Geneva Convention*. Geneva: UNHCR Public Information Service, 2(123).

UNHCR (United Nations High Commissioner for Refugees) (2007) *Internally Displaced Persons: Questions and Answers*. Geneva: UNHCR: Media relations and public information services.

UNHCR (United Nations High Commissioner for Refugees) (2010) *2009 Global Trends: Refugees, Asylum-seekers, Returnees, Internally Displaced and Stateless Persons*. Available at http://www.unhcr.org/statistics.html, accessed 13 December 2011.

UNOCHA (United Nations Office for the Co-ordination of Human Affairs) (2009) *Joint Humanitarian Update: North East Sri Lanka*. Geneva: UNOCHA, 10 September 2009.

Ursano, R.J., Fullerton, C.S. and Norwood, A.F. (2003) 'Terrorism and disasters: prevention, intervention and recovery', in R.J. Ursano, C.S. Fullerton and A.F. Norwood (eds), *Terrorism and Disaster: Individual and Community Mental Health Interventions.* Cambridge: Cambridge University Press. pp. 333–40.

Van Wormer, K. (2005) 'Concepts for contemporary social work: globalisation, oppression, social exclusion, human rights, etc.', *Social Work & Society*, 3 (1): 1–10.

Wairire, G. (2008) 'The challenge for social work in the Kenyan context of political conflict', in S. Ramon (ed.) *Social Work in the Context of Political Conflict.* Birmingham: Venture Press. pp. 101–22.

Weaver, H.N. and Burns, B.J. (2001) '"I shout with fear at night": understanding the traumatic experiences of refugees and asylum seekers', *Journal of Social Work*, 1(2): 147–64.

Wessley, S. (2003) 'The role of screening in the prevention of psychological disorders arising from major trauma: pros and cons', in R.J. Ursano, C.S. Fullerton and A.F. Norwood (eds) *Terrorism and Disaster: Individual and Community Mental Health Interventions.* Cambridge: Cambridge University Press. pp. 121–45.

Wessely, S., Bisson, J. and Rose, S. (2000) 'A systematic review of brief psychological interventions ("debriefing") for the treatment of immediate trauma related symptoms and the prevention of posttraumatic stress disorder', in M. Oakley-Browne, D. Churchill, M. Gill, M. Trivedi and S. Wessely (eds) *Depression, Anxiety, and Neurosis Module of the Cochrane Database of Systematic Reviews*, (2nd edn). Oxford: Update Software.

Wilkinson, R. (2005) 'After the war was over', *Refugees*, 3(140): 6–18.

Williams, J.E. (2005) 'Living with Trauma', in S. Ramon and J.E. Williams (eds), *Mental Health at the Crossroads: The Promise of the Psychosocial Approach.* Aldershot: Ashgate. pp. 171–85.

Wolff, S. (2009) 'The regional and international regulation of ethnic conflict: patterns of success and failure', 6th Asia Europe Roundtable *'Minority Conflicts – Towards an ASEM Framework for Conflict Management'* in Derry/Londonderry and Letterkenny, 10–12 June 2009.

Zorn, J. and Lipovic-Cebron, U. (eds) (2008) *Once Upon an Erasure: From Citizens to Illegal Residents in the Republic of Slovenia.* Ljubljana: Students Publishing House.

Life-course Perspectives

Nathalie Huegler

INTRODUCTION TO SECTION 4: LIFE-COURSE PERSPECTIVES

Chapters in this section consider the specific roles and challenges for social workers working with populations around the globe at different stages throughout the life course. The section is introduced by an in-depth perspective on the diversity of 'family' across different time, social, economic and cultural contexts. Following from this, the next chapters explore the different meanings, roles and dilemmas associated with three specific stages of the life course: childhood and youth; adulthood; and old age. Each chapter discusses the implications of changing global and local contexts for social work activities relating to the needs and characteristics of particular populations.

Life-course perspectives have interdisciplinary roots, particularly in developmental psychology and sociology. Elder et al. (2004) suggest that five general principles underlie a life course approach: the concept of *lifelong development* involving biological, psychological and social changes; a focus on *agency*, i.e. the notion that people make choices and act within the opportunities and constraints of their environment; *time and place*, i.e. the

fact that lives are shaped by and embedded in historical and geographical contexts; the significance of the *timing* of events and transitions within a person's life course; and the principle of *linked lives*, which acknowledges the role of social networks and the impact of macro-level events on individuals and communities. Many of these notions are likely to be familiar to social workers whose practice is informed by 'ecological' frameworks in a broad sense. At the same time, the principles also resonate with themes that have been identified in this handbook as particularly relevant to *international social work*, because they highlight how the 'global' and the 'local' are interlinked; acknowledge the importance of contexts (including time and place); and emphasise both the diversity and the commonalities of the human experience.

This diversity is evident in the first chapter (20) of this section, in which Desai considers different types of 'family' throughout pre-modern agricultural, modern industrial and post-modern post-industrial contexts. Cultural practices concerning family formation and family life vary, for example, according to whether 'traditional' social norms still hold true or are challenged by changes and influences on both local and global levels. An example is the increasing number of families who live their lives 'transnationally' across borders (often as a result of migration). Key issues for social workers in the different contexts include the exploitation and abuse of women and children within patriarchal systems or the commodification of relationships in increasingly consumerist societies. While social workers need to adapt their approaches according to the cultures, beliefs and practices of different families, Desai argues that a human rights orientation is fundamental in order to protect and promote the welfare of families worldwide.

The theme of 'agency' as opposed to powerlessness is particularly relevant to social work with children and young people, and this stage of the life course is addressed by Rock, Karabanow and Manion in Chapter 21. While there is widespread international acknowledgement that children are among the most vulnerable members of the world's societies, not least through the almost unanimous ratification status of the 1989 United Nations Convention on the Rights of the Child (with the exception of the United States and Somalia), significant differences exist regarding the cultural and social assumptions, legal boundaries and experiences of this life stage. Nearly half of the world's children live in poverty and national provisions for the welfare of all children – and those in need of care – vary enormously. Theories relating to child development have mainly emerged in Western contexts, and these have informed approaches to safeguarding and promoting their welfare at different times. As shown by the examples provided in this chapter (children affected by the global HIV/AIDS crisis; by natural disasters; and children on the street), children are often particularly at risk through global factors impacting on local conditions, but they can also demonstrate enormous resilience. Social workers need to be mindful of these ambiguities and the diversity of children's lived realities in order to effectively protect them from harm.

In the next chapter (22), Chau applies a life-course perspective to the stage of adulthood, using comparative and international perspectives to explore its contemporary meanings. Despite being (usually) the longest phase in the life course, adulthood as such has received relatively less attention in policy, research and practice. This might reflect the degree to which adults are affected by societal norms and role expectations, particularly concerning productivity in the contexts of 'family' and 'work'. As a result, the focus tends to be on adults who are considered particularly vulnerable and as a result of individual (and often assumed or constructed) attributes less capable of fulfilling such expectations, for example, adults with (mental) health problems or disabled adults. However, global changes and their local consequences have created risks for an ever wider range of adults in relation to their ability to sustain livelihoods and families. A variety of interconnected and contextual factors shape individual experiences of this life stage, as reflected in the notion of intersectionality (see, for example, Chapters 1 or 27 in this handbook). Drawing from 'social model' approaches which emerged particularly from disability movements around the world, and from the concept of 'active aging', Chau argues that welfare efforts should remove barriers to active participation in social, cultural and economic spheres – both through structural approaches which challenge the global capitalist hegemony and through more flexible and personalised support which takes on board the diversity of experiences of adulthood.

In the final chapter in this section (Chapter 23), Hokenstad and Roberts consider old age in a global context and summarise statistics relating to the increasing numbers of people over 60 (in both hemispheres) and increasing longevity (with some exceptions to both these trends). Importantly for social work there is also an increase in the numbers of 'frail elderly', presenting socio-economic and geopolitical challenges as well as issues for social workers and care providers. Noting the

International Federation of Social Workers (IFSW) International Policy on Aging and Older Persons, the authors suggest that there are three priority directions for social workers in this field, which can be headlined as poverty alleviation; promoting health and well-being; and creating supportive environments. In addition, social workers have special responsibilities in relation to elder abuse and neglect. Finally there is a need for more specialist education in social gerontology and greater attention to service and practice developments in relation to this user group.

REFERENCE

Elder, G.H. Jr, Kirkpatrick Johnson, M. and Crosnoe, R. (2003) 'The Emergence and Development of Life Course Theory', in J.T. Mortimer and M.J. Shanahan (eds), *Handbook of the Life Course*. New York: Springer. pp. 3–19.

20

The Life-course Perspective and Changing Contexts of Families

Murli Desai

INTRODUCTION

Families are an inseparable part of our identity, name, language, ethnicity, religion and nationality. What is this family? Has it always been the same or is it changing? Is it the same everywhere or does it vary in different parts of the world? Is family more important or community or individuals? Is family a source of nurturing and protection from the world's problems or is it a source of the problems?

The major theoretical frameworks that help understand family in an international context are the institutional, structural-functional and ecological frameworks developed by sociologists and anthropologists. Marxist and feminist family theories provide key frameworks that help a critical understanding of family. This chapter refers to all these frameworks, but uses the dynamic family life-course perspective to develop an overall contextual framework to study the diversity in families across the world, and lay

the foundation for the subsequent chapters on different life stages.

THE LIFE-COURSE PERSPECTIVE

The life-course framework emerged from the family development theory that focuses on the systematic and patterned changes experienced by nuclear families as they move through stages and events of their life (White and Klein, 2008). The development stages in such families depend on the life transitions of their members. Key stages in this model include: young people getting married and bearing children, also known as family formation; parenting children and adolescents or growing up in a family; and older couples whose children get married and bear their own children. The focus on the Western ideal of the nuclear family in this approach is less relevant for the rest of the world. It is also losing its relevance in the Western world where the nuclear family form has become less prevalent. Another limitation of developmental theories is that they are ontogenetic (i.e. focusing on biological processes) and dominated by certain psychological models as they look for universal, predictable events and pathways. Glen Elder Jr (1974, cited by Hutchison, 2008) proposed the life-course perspective which paid attention to how historical time, social location and culture affect individual experiences at each life stage. In the context of the life-course perspective, Dannefer (1984, cited by Bengtson and Allen, 1993) has advocated for the term 'sociogenesis' which emphasises the sociological aspects of development as a counterpart to the biologically dominated ontogenetic models.

According to Bengtson and Allen (1993), a life-course perspective emphasises the importance of time, context, process, and meaning on human development and family life. They note five specific points as central to life-course concepts and theories, especially as applied to studying families: (1) the first and central feature of life-course theories is the focus on the multiple temporal contexts of development: this includes ontogenetic time events in the unfolding biography of the individual that alter behavioural schemes or processes (e.g. the transition from childhood to adulthood through puberty); generational time-events or family transitions that alter interactions or selves (such as role changes occurring when parents become grandparents); and historical time-events in the broader social or societal context that alter roles or values of individuals and families; (2) the individual is viewed as an active agent in interaction with social contexts and structures, with reciprocal influence on familial and social contexts; (3) the focus of the perspective is on process and change, leading to a dynamic rather than static approach to the study of lives and families; (4) the emphasis of the perspective is not only on modal or average trends in development over time, but also diversity

across the range of patterns; (5) this approach emphasises the utility of multidisciplinary perspectives.

CONTEXTUAL FRAMEWORK TO STUDY FAMILY WORLDWIDE

The family life-course perspective, with its dynamic approach and emphasis on diversity, has enormous relevance in understanding family diversity and social change at the cross-cultural and international levels. Using a socio-historical approach, family characteristics are broadly classified in this chapter into those in the pre-modern pre-industrial context, the modern industrial context and finally the post-modern post-industrial context. Although this classification conveys change, the change is not linear. Since today's world consists of pre-industrial, industrial and post-industrial societies, all three categories of family characteristics exist worldwide in an overlapping manner. Modernisation is taken as a major reference point as the development of industrial modes of production has had significant effects on societies worldwide. According to Talcott Parsons, in domestic and agrarian economies, family members were an economic asset and extended kinship was quite functional. He suggested that modernisation in the form of industrialisation and urbanisation put pressure on the families by 'defunctionalising' large areas of family activity, especially in regard to extended kinship (White and Klein, 2008).

Social work as a profession emerged in the West in the modern age and therefore many training and education programmes focus on work with families in the context of modern industrialised societies. This chapter aims to discuss the diversity and characteristics families in the pre-modern, modern and post-modern contexts. It introduces the range of key family characteristics useful for identifying issues for cross-cultural and international social work with families.

FAMILIES IN PRE-MODERN CONTEXTS

Historical perspectives on the family

Engels (1884) attempted to explain the origin of family through Marx's historical materialist theory. He claimed that before the family had existed, there had been a situation of free sexual relationships and sharing of partners and children. Such group living gave way to a matrilineal system as children were biologically attached to their mothers. The development of weapons facilitated hunting for men which allowed surplus production of food and other goods. This situation created a system of private property on the one hand and a dominant role of men in the production process on the other. After that there was no longer any need for a joint economy, so clans broke down into families as independent economic units. Engels noted that through the domestication and breeding of animals, which was controlled by men, they understood the principle of impregnation. Men now wanted to pass on their property to their own children. To ensure this inheritance, women had to be domesticated and confined and their sexuality regulated and controlled (Newman, 2005). Subsequently, the introduction of marriage customs can be seen as an attempt to control women's sexuality. Similar theories suggest that the high female contribution to subsistence in agricultural societies favoured the development of patrilocal marriage practices where a woman left her parental family after marriage to stay with the husband's family (Pandhe, 1989).

Characteristics of families in the pre-modern context

The pre-modern family developed as a productive unit in the context of agriculture. The overall characteristics of this form of family are kinship orientation and familism, patriarchal roles and power and a strong influence of religion. According to Hamilton (2007), when resources are scarce, people are more likely to work together to survive and thrive. In collectivist societies, there tends to be greater adherence to religious and traditional conventions (Toth and Kemmelmeier, 2009). As a result, kinship orientation is particularly important for families in pre-modern contexts, where belonging to an ethnic community is an integral part of life. Rogers and Sebald (1962) define kinship orientation as the degree to which a family fulfils the role expectations of the kinship reference group. Familism describes the subordination of individual interest to those of the family group. The traditional reference to familism is best illustrated in literature by Confucius, the religious leader of China who influenced the whole of East Asia. In his teachings, five relationships make up the warp and woof of social life, three of which relate to the family: those between father and son (filial piety); between elder brother and younger brother; and between husband and wife (Smith, 1958).

Through male domination in the agrarian production process patriarchy emerged as a system of control and distribution of resources by hierarchies of age, gender and generation, leading to the strict determination of roles and responsibilities. The father or the eldest male is considered the patriarch or 'head of the household'. Control over marriage and child-bearing are important requirements of patriarchal families, while control over resources and the assumption of superiority give the patriarch the power to make decisions about his dependents, particularly women and children. Power has implication for a person's status within the family. Since men and (male) elders have more power in patriarchal families, they have a higher status than women and children. Arguably, there has never been a true matriarchal culture in existence. Even in matrilineal cultures, where women hold the title to property, patriarchy functions through financial decision-making power vested in brothers (Leslie and Korman, 1984).

Traditionally, marriage has been regarded as a private contract that could be dissolved at the will of either or both parties. When religions were institutionalised, marriage became an important matter of concern to religion and society. For example, Christianity, Islam and Hinduism (the three religions with the largest numbers of followers today) have promoted patriarchy, mainly by common presentation of God as male, by traditions of male religious leadership and by the exclusion of women from major rituals and religious texts. Christianity promoted patriarchy which influenced families in the West by promoting the division of labour between women (considered responsible for child rearing) and men (responsible for providing food) as well as legitimising the notion that husbands have power over their wives (Ingoldsby, 2006a). Based on ideas that women have a seductive nature, Islamic societies tend to consider that female family members need watching and protecting and therefore promote practices of gender separation where women occupy private rather than public spheres and often use veils in public. Although Hinduism has female deities as well as male deities, female ones are portrayed as dangerously passionate, capable of giving and taking life, and needing the control of male gods (Burn, 2000).

The most common method of selection in marriages in pre-modern collective societies has been that of arrangement by parents, who, with the aid of certain relatives or professional matchmakers, select the spouse for their child (Ingoldsby, 2006b). Arranged marriages generally observe the rules of endogamy and exogamy. Endogamy refers to rules in marriage that require partners to be chosen from within the religion, caste and sub-caste, social class, linguistic/regional group, race and nationality. All religions are strict about rules of religious endogamy. Inter-marriages or mixed marriages are violations of such rules. On the other hand, every society limits choices in marriage by requiring that one chooses a partner outside

some specified group, called exogamy. The prohibition usually applies to close blood relatives. While incestual taboos are universal, cousin marriages are common in some societies with clan systems.

After the Renaissance, love gradually became the principal criterion for selection in marriage in the Western nuclear family (Ingoldsby, 2006b). However, in communities where arranged marriages and strict practices concerning exogamy and endogamy persist, couples who want to select their marriage partner out of 'love' often face many obstacles and sometimes ostracism.

Diversity of pre-modern families

Pre-modern families are diverse in relation to various kinship systems, marriage forms, family forms and financial exchanges in marriage. Some of the diversity can be explained by socioeconomic class, and by the varying role of women in agriculture and religion. Matrilineal families that give primacy to lineage and inheritance from the mother's side are a historical form still prevalent today in Northeast India and other parts of Asia and in North Africa. These families are generally matrilocal, which means that after marriage the woman remains in her parental family and the husband may visit her or move to stay with her. Ingoldsby (2006c) analysed Murdoch's Ethnographic Atlas of 1157 societies in 1967 and found that only 20 percent of these societies were matrilineal. Patrilineal families that give primacy to lineage and inheritance from father to son were more prevalent, making up 42 percent of the societies surveyed by Murdoch. Taking one's surname from the father or the husband is a patrilineal concept. These families are generally patrilocal, that is after marriage the wife moves to stay with her husband's family.

Marriage systems can be divided into polygamous and monogamous forms, influenced by religions and socio-economic contexts.

Polygamous marriages involve more than one spouse at a time. Islamic traditions permit a Muslim man to take up to four wives. All wives are entitled to separate living quarters at the behest of the husband and if possible, all should receive equal attention, support, treatment and inheritance. Monogamy on the other hand was promoted by the early Catholic movement (Ingoldsby, 2006c). This, along with a focus on non-marital chastity and marital fidelity strengthened the prevalence of the nuclear family model in Western societies. While in extended families there is a focus on blood ties, marital relationships are at the centre of nuclear families (Leslie and Korman, 1984).

As discussed above, the original joint (or extended family) family became institutionalised as a self-sufficient economic unit to protect jointness of property, which historically was mainly agricultural land. It carried out the economic, educational, political and religious functions of society (Zimmerman, 2001). The link between families and the development of private property is reflected in the traditional role of marriage as a chiefly economic transaction. Examples of financial exchanges in the context of marriage include the practice of bride price, dowry or dower, still common in some communities in Thailand, China, Africa and Central Asia. Such practices often reflect the value placed on women's contributions to families: for example, dowry is an inducement for a man to marry a particular woman and thereby relieve her family of the financial burden of caring for her, indicating a low value placed on women and their contributions (Ingoldsby, 2006b). In Islam, dower is a sum of money or any other property that a wife is entitled to receive from her husband in consideration of marriage. It is an obligation imposed upon the husband as a mark of respect to the wife. The dower is a source of security for the wife at the time dissolution of the marriage or death of the husband, so women activists among Muslims are trying to strengthen this practice.

FAMILIES IN MODERN CONTEXTS

Context for the emergence of the modern family

With industrialisation, the economic, educational, political and religious functions carried out by the agricultural joint family were slowly relegated to non-familial institutions (Zimmerman, 2001). Goode had argued in 1964 that as societies became more modern, the joint family type would give way to the nuclear family type, and polygamy would be replaced by monogamy, as the latter is better suited to the consumption-based industrial economy (Ingoldsby, 2006c). As collective societies are gradually replaced by individualistic societies in many parts of the world, community orientation is loosened and kinship supports for families is weakened. Love has gradually become a principal criterion for selecting one's partner for the purpose of founding a nuclear family in the Western world (Ingoldsby, 2006b). These changes together with improvement in health services have led to demographic changes such as lower fertility rates, increased longevity and smaller households.

In industrial societies, children spend longer times in education, and therefore the average age for getting married has increased. This, together with an increased age of women at the birth of their first child, a higher survival rate of children beyond infancy, the more widespread use of contraceptives and increased rates of employment among mothers have led to lower fertility rates. The median level of contraceptive use rose from 30.9 percent in the 1970s to 61.1 percent around the year 2000. At the same time, the median level of fertility in developing countries fell by more than half, from 5.3 children per woman in the 1970s to 2.5 children at the turn of the Millennium (United Nations, 2007).

With better health conditions, more people live longer. With increased longevity and reduced fertility rates, the proportion of older people is increasing, leading to what is called population ageing or 'greying'. A population ages when the proportion of older people (meaning those aged 60 years or over) increases, while the proportions of children (under the age of 15) and of people of working age (15–59) decline. In the more developed regions, where population ageing is far advanced, the number of children dropped below that of older persons in 1998. At the global level, the number of older people is expected to exceed the number of children for the first time in 2045 (United Nations, 2009a).

In European countries as well as the United States and Canada there has been a dominant trend of steady decline in household size from around five members in the middle of the 19th century to between two and three in 1990. This decline reflects a trend away from the traditional more complex household structures of the past toward the simpler nuclear households that dominate in contemporary industrialised societies (Bongaarts, 2001). According to Bongaarts (2001), the average household size in 43 developing countries ranged from 5.6 in the Middle East/North Africa to 4.8 in Latin America, similar to levels observed in the second half of the 19th century in Europe and North America.

Trends in families in the modern context

According to Stacey (1996, cited by Appell, 2010), the 'modern' family refers generally to a 'nuclear household unit made up of a married heterosexual couple and their biological or adopted children'. We can expand this definition to 'an individualistic monogamous nuclear family as a consumer unit'. In this family type patriarchy has become more established through the 'housewifisation' (see below) of women. Other (negative) trends include growing consumerism and individualism, a higher incidence of family violence, an increase in marriage breakdown

(and with it, the emergence of reconstituted families), and the marginalisation of the elderly, all of which lead to more interventions by the state as discussed below.

While preindustrial productive work was carried out at home or in the fields by men, women and children (Haas 2006), industrialisation led to a separation of the work place from the home. Men joined industrial employment, while women lost their productive roles and stayed at home to look after the family and do household work. This process is referred to as the housewifisation of women (Zimmerman, 2001). The gender-based allocation of the major roles of the industrial family later came to be considered as 'natural'. Such allocation of roles resulted in gender differences concerning access to resources and therefore power and status (Haas, 2006). The advancement of women's education led to an increase in working women in waged employment and the phenomenon of dual career families. Supporting families in balancing work and family life is high on the policy agendas of many countries. The increase in female participation in the labour market calls for adjustment in the gender division of labour within the household and the sharing of family responsibilities. Among the policy instruments aimed at reconciling work and the family are parental leave, childcare services and child benefits (United Nations, 2009b).

Consumerism created a world of possessive individualism that became essential for economic growth but also meant that social values are considered secondary to the creation and satisfaction of wants (Pereira, 1997). Individualism has led to increased self-centredness and indifference and promoted the commodification of relationships. Since the 1950s, family has increasingly come to be seen as an impediment to individual self-fulfilment. During these years, the relationship between family values and values of individualism and personal autonomy has become more and more fragile (Zimmerman, 2001).

Patriarchal family systems bear an inherent risk of power leading to abuse of the less powerful. With the nuclearisation of families; the separation of private and public spheres; the increased commodification of relationships; and weak community supports, the vulnerability of the less powerful members in patriarchal families to domestic violence has increased. Family violence, occurring in the private sphere, often remains invisible, undiscussed and unchallenged (Bhasin, 2000). Levinson (1989, cited by Leeder, 2004) noted that the groups of women least abused worldwide are those who have a sense of support from other members of the community. Exclusive female work groups that are indicators of female solidarity or female economic power serve to prevent wife beating. Women (especially housewives), children and increasingly also the elderly (who are not considered productive) are often the least powerful members of a family, making them most vulnerable to abuse.

In tribal and rural societies, divorces were and are more easily obtainable through customary practices. Religious taboos and long legal procedures developed in urbanised areas have made divorces more difficult in industrialised societies. A Catholic marriage is considered indissoluble, however, the Protestant movement liberalised the grounds for divorce (Ingoldsby, 2006d). In Islam, a husband has an absolute and unilateral right to end the marriage at his will, while a Muslim wife has no such right. Traditionally, divorce was unknown in Hindu law until the legislation of the Hindu Marriage Act of 1955. However, a large number of Indian societies belonging to the lower castes and tribes have practised customary divorce, recognised by law. Cherlin (1996, cited by McKenry and Price, 2006) has divided access to divorce in the Western world into three periods: the era of restricted divorce, the era of divorce tolerance and the era of unrestricted divorce. These trends represent increased level of individualism in families (Toth and Kemmelmeier, 2009).

Increased divorce rates have led to an increased number of stepfamilies which are also known as reconstituted or blended families. Strong et al. (2008) note that these families have unique characteristics: almost all the members in the reconstituted family have lost an important primary relationship; one biological parent typically lives outside the current family; and the relationship between a parent and his or her children predates the relationship between the new partners.

The steady growth in the proportion of elderly people in the population was, at least until the 1980s, managed in Western societies through the emergence of retirement on the one hand and the provisions of the welfare state on the other. For the much of the 20th century, old people were viewed as a static population, constrained in the narrow range of cultural as well as geographical spaces. They were also regarded as a group locked into different forms of 'dependency' (Phillipson, 2006). In the modern family, the traditional male patriarch elder has lost his place of dominance to the main earner.

The state has played a prominent and controversial role in the modern age, including in matters concerning the welfare of the modern family. A prominent example of state intervention is the field of child welfare. According to Harding (1991), the juvenile justice system is an example of extensive state intervention that undervalues the child's biological family. It favours substitute care such as foster family care or adoption when the care of the natural family is found to be inadequate. He pointed out the class element of state care interventions when middle-class decision-makers pass judgement on working-class parents whose children are placed in somewhat better-off substitute families. Mason (1991) noted that adoption, especially international adoption, enhances the existing inequalities and promotes the transfer of children from the poor to the more affluent.

Harding (1991) notes that the defence of the birth family and parents' rights perspective encapsulates the idea that birth or biological families are important for both children and parents and should be maintained wherever possible. This perspective emphasises the rights of parents, and in looking at the causes of poor quality child care is sympathetic to parental difficulties. It sees the role of the state as being supportive of families, providing a range of services that they need to remain together and sees placing children in substitute care as generally undesirable and the last resort. According to this approach, where children do have to come into state care, considerable intervention should be devoted to helping their families and maintaining links with them so that the children can return home again if it is safe for them to do so. The United Nations Convention on the Rights of the Child (UNCRC) of 1989 stresses the child's rights to growing up in a family environment, including the right to family care and relations (Articles 5, 7.1 and 8.1); the right to being parented by both parents and the right of families to be supported in the process of child-rearing (Article 18); the right of children not to be separated from parents unless this is in their best interests (Article 9) and to be reunited with their parents in case of separations (Article 10).

The impact of modernisation on families worldwide

The colonisation of Asian and African countries by the European rulers led to the industrialisation, development and 'modernisation' of these countries. This led to the 'modern' type of family to be spread to countries throughout the world, with a tendency to homogenise existing diverse family systems. For example, British rulers considered the matrilineal practices and cousin marriages in parts of its colonies inferior to the 'modern' practices of patriliny and exogamy and tried to impose the latter. While women played significant roles in the agricultural countries, most of the Western-sponsored development programmes in these countries assumed that 'households' were following the model of an idealised 'Western nuclear family' with a male breadwinner and dependent women and children. This led

planners to focus mainstream development interventions on men, undermining women's economic opportunities and autonomy (Kabeer, 2003).

Advances in technology have led to increased migration together with increased unemployment among men whose labour is replaced by automatic machines. This has resulted in a major expansion of the unprotected, unorganised labour force. This force includes an increasing number of women, who were left out of development projects, and children. The unorganised sector does not provide social security or scope for unionisation, nor are anti-discrimination laws applied. This has led to increased poverty among female-headed families, a trend referred to as the feminisation of poverty. As Ilich (1983) put it, the higher labour force participation by women implies that more women have been incorporated into the population that is economically discriminated against on the grounds of sex.

In contrast to the individualistic culture of the Western colonisers, the cultural systems in the colonies were collectivistic. The rapid transition from an agricultural to an industrial society introduced by the colonisers was too abrupt for these countries; they have therefore remained more collectivistic than the Western countries (Triandis, 1988). Modernisation has brought individualism but not disturbed much of the collectivism in the former colonies. For example, although families in highly industrialised countries such as South Korea have become individualistic in some respects, they still emphasise kinship orientation and familism. Hamilton (1996, cited by Flynn, 1999) noted that even business in Asia is based on networks of relationships built around obligations other than those arising from short-term economic transactions.

Globalisation has brought about an unprecedented level of international migration for education, work and marriage, especially from developing to developed countries. This has led to a growing number of transnational families with family members across borders living in different cultural and economic contexts. As they stay in regular contact to maintain their bonds and responsibilities, new forms of and adaptations to family life are emerging (Orozco, 2006). Inter-country adoption also leads to transnational families of a sort as the children's biological and adoptive families live in two different countries. In the last two decades, inter-country adoption has progressively changed from its initial purpose of providing a family environment for children, to becoming more demand-driven. Increasingly in industrialised countries, inter-country adoption is viewed as an option for childless couples. To meet the demand for children, trafficking flourishes, for example through psychological pressure on vulnerable mothers to give up their children, adoptions organised before birth, false maternity or paternity certificates, abduction of children, and children being conceived for adoption (UNICEF, 2004).

FAMILIES IN POSTMODERN CONTEXTS

Context for the emergence of post-modern families

Bell (1974) describes post-industrial societies as being dominated by the service sectors and professional and technical occupations – in contrast to industrial societies which are dominated by manufacturing-based economies. It is marked by the centrality of human relationships and 'intellectual technology', based on information and computing technology. According to Manuel Castells (2001), the network society is the social structure which is characteristic of the information society or post-industrial society. He defines a network society as a society where the key social structures and activities are organised around electronically processed information networks. For example, in the last thirty years, women have changed the way they think about themselves. Women questioned the patriarchal family

system strove for gender equality and decided that they had to develop their own interests and culture, or have their own relationship to work. Once women have changed in these areas, everything changes. The family changes; therefore, the socialisation of children changes; therefore, identity changes, sexuality changes, and so on.

Post-modernism that has arisen in the post-industrial context recognises the highest ideals of modernity in the West as immanent to a specific historical time and geographical region and also associated with certain political baggage. Such baggage includes notions of the supremacy of the West, and the legitimacy of science (Nicholson, 1990). When applied to family, post-modernism challenges all the norms of the modern family and marriage. It reflects the disillusionment with the optimistic assumptions of human progress and with the universality and the regularity of the laws of science; hence, lack of faith in the previously established order (Zeitlin et al., 1995). In the 1970s, Shorter (1975, cited by Zeitlin et al., 1995) described the emerging post-modern family by noting three important characteristics: the indifference of adolescents to the family's identity; instability in the lives of couples, accompanied by rapidly increasing divorce rates; and destruction of the 'nest' notion of nuclear family life with the liberation of women.

Characteristics of families in the post-modern context

A key element of post-modernity is the immense increase in diversity as a result of the breakdown of 'conventional' forms and ideals of modernity. According to Stacy (1996, cited by Appell, 2010), the post-modern family is not as easily defined as the modern family. This family type can be characterised by a decline in paternal (and patriarchal) authority, marital instability in fact and in concept, and a less distinct division of labour outside the home between husband and wife. Some women and men prefer to focus on careers and deliberately prefer the single life to marriage and parenthood. There is also a trend in people wanting to marry and not have children or wanting to have children but not marry (Kelley and Byrne, 1992). Thus in this family type, either marriage or child-bearing or both are challenged.

Marriage is becoming less of a requirement for childbearing. In 62 countries with data on extramarital births, the median percentage of all births to non-married couples rose substantially, from 7.1 percent in the 1970s to 29.2 percent at the beginning of this century. The increase was similar in developed and developing countries where data was available (United Nations, 2007).

Single-parent families, cohabitation or consensual unions, and same-sex parents are some of the trends where families form without marriage. While a traditional cause for single parenthood was the death of one parent, there are now more single-parent families as a result of parental separation, divorce or because the parents are not in a relationship at the time of birth. Overall, a majority of single-parent families are female-headed as women are more likely to assume responsibility for child-rearing and legal custody is also typically awarded to women. The gay rights movement in the West has given greater visibility to gay and lesbian families. Like heterosexual couples, gay and lesbian couples also desire lifelong commitments to a loving partner and, in many cases, want to have children. Many have children from a previous heterosexual relationship and for others the child is brought into the family through adoption or surrogacy (Smith, 2006).

In post-modern families, several people may play a role in the bearing and parenting of a child. Technology has made it possible for women to get pregnant in ways other than through heterosexual intercourse, for example, through artificial insemination, *in vitro* fertilisation and surrogacy. These methods have opened up the possibility of parenthood for both couples with fertility problems and for same-sex couples. Foster family care and

adoption are not new forms of families but these are also being used today by same-sex couples or those wanting to bring up children without themselves having to bear them. The tension between biological and social ordering raises many questions regarding family formation, dissolution, constitution, rights, and responsibilities, including whether and to what extent biology should be the basis of parent–child relationships (and relatedly sibling and extended family relationships); what the balance should be between biological and social relationships; whether and how social relationships and individual intentions should establish family status; and whether physical intimacy is necessary for family status (Appell, 2010). Moreover, tensions have arisen between adult rights of secrecy and children's rights to know their biological parents in such families (Connolly and Ward, 2008).

Zeitlin et al. (1995) noted that the post-modern life appears to reverse, or de-differentiate, many characteristics of the modern family back to pre-modern lifestyles and values. For example, workplace and home are now often again the same; love can be contractual or consensual; parenting may be shared; mothers may work full time; children may become socially mature at an earlier age in full view of adult activities and so on. Nevertheless, they note that there remain quantum differences between pre- and post-modern lifestyles, for example in relation to the size of families; the level of dependence on kins; the relationship between physical and electronic influences on life; manual labour versus 'brain work'; local versus global contexts; low versus high levels of privacy and personal choice; predetermined versus optional social roles; and set rules of right and wrong versus pluralistic and relativistic values.

CONCLUSION AND IMPLICATIONS FOR FAMILY SOCIAL WORK INTERNATIONALLY

This chapter has outlined the characteristics of three different 'types' of families: the pre-modern family as a diverse production unit, the modern family as a homogenous consumer unit and the post-modern family as again a diverse family unit that challenges all social norms for marriage and child-bearing. The question that remains is whether there are any common characteristics of a family? The fact that there are roles and relationships between two or more people is probably the one common characteristic which defines a family against the backdrop of the diversity discussed in this chapter. It is also clear that family characteristics in the pre-modern, modern and post-modern contexts are overlapping and not exclusive monolithic concepts. Some pre-modern traits have continued to influence modern families, for example with respect to religion; and some modern characteristics continue to be relevant for post-modern families: for example, a family with egalitarian sex roles may still decide, out of choice, to get married and have children. In short, family is changing so fast that for most people the family they create as adults is not necessarily similar to the one they grew up in.

Social workers need to be mindful of the contexts in which they work with families. Social workers working with families in pre-modern agricultural contexts should use collectivism as a strength, balancing respect for cultural diversity with the prevention of patriarchal violations of human rights In modern industrialised contexts, social workers are faced with the implications of collectivism being replaced by individualism; the fact that patriarchal structures may be aggravated through the 'housewifisation' of women; the increase in family violence, marriage breakdown and the emergence of reconstituted families and dual career families; the marginalisation of the elderly; and an increase in interventions by the state. An emerging issue for social workers working with families in the post-modern context are negative perceptions and non-acceptance of these families by the mainstream society through labelling terms such as 'broken families', 'marital instability' and 'family instability'. In this context, the challenge is to formulate laws and intervention strategies that respect the emerging plurality of family forms and prevent their implications for human rights violations.

A core purpose of the social work profession comprises the promotion of respect for traditions, cultures, ideologies, beliefs and religions amongst different ethnic groups and societies, insofar as these do not conflict with the fundamental human rights of people (IASSW and IFSW, 2004). Social workers may be working with different religious or cultural groups or nationalities in one country or on cross-country issues such as inter-country adoption/ trafficking, refugees, transnational marriages and transnational family relationships. They need to prevent a Eurocentric or an ethnocentric approach that tends to discuss human behaviour in terms of norms or 'average' behaviours, leading to the concepts of normal and abnormal. Diversity is then confused with abnormality or deficiency. Multiculturalism seeks to challenge and overturn the cultural dimensions of imperial rule by establishing the legitimacy of non-Western and sometimes anti-Western political ideas and traditions. By challenging a predominant Eurocentric world view, it allows non-Western religions, ideas and philosophies to be taken more seriously (Heywood, 2007).

Cultural relativism is considered by some the only alternative to the dangers of ethnocentrism. However, Zechenter (1997) notes that cultural relativism has the potential of undermining the modern human rights law developed during the last fifty years. Social workers need to be concerned with the way culture can affect human rights through some religious practices, patterns of marriage selection and financial exchanges in marriage. They need to prevent the violation of human rights in these situations through laws and intervention. Family laws for marriage, lineage and residence, child bearing, childbirth, guardianship and custody of children, maintenance, death and inheritance and succession, are often based on religions.

They need to be gender-aware, child-centred and elderly-friendly, and based on a human rights perspective that is accepted as universal.

Principles of human rights and social justice are fundamental to social work, according to the international definition of social work (IFSW and IASSW, 2000). As far as the application of these principles to family is concerned, the profession can draw from the motto of the International Year of the Family (IYF) proclaimed by the UN General Assembly in 1994. The motto of IYF was 'Building the smallest democracy at the heart of society', identifying democratic principles in the family as the most important norm instead of norms for family forms, structure and functions. The principles of the IYF seek to promote the basic human rights and fundamental freedoms accorded to all individuals by the set of internationally agreed instruments, formulated under the aegis of the UN. The Convention on the Elimination of All Forms of Discrimination against Women (CEDAW) (1979), the Convention on the Rights of the Child (CRC) (1989) and the UN Principles for Older Persons are most important in this regard. Such a human rights-based approach to family would be necessary for protection of less powerful family members from exploitation and abuse, while promoting democracy and egalitarianism in the family, acceptance of the diversity of forms that are not always accepted by societies and for the protection of the rights of biological families from unnecessary state intervention.

Social workers in developed welfare states often work in the state systems, whereas social workers in developing countries work in a welfare mix setting where family plays an important role. State intervention has played a prominent role in family welfare in the modern age, which has now become controversial. An increase in dual-career families has made child day care and family-friendly employment policies a universal need aiming at achieving a better balance between work and family life, rather than a welfare provision. The role of the state in substituting family care is now being challenged by those who see the role of the state as supportive, providing various services that they need to remain together. There is an emphasis on birth or biological families as important for both children and parents and this should be maintained wherever possible.

Social work, in various parts of the world, is targeted at interventions for social support and for developmental, protective, preventive and/or therapeutic purposes (IASSW and IFSW, 2004). However, prevention has received a relatively lower priority in family social work. Family life education based on human rights and multiculturalism needs to be given importance to prevent social problems from developing. Such preventative programmes can be promoted through schools, colleges and community organisations, with individuals, couples, and families across the life span.

REFERENCES

Appell, A.R. (2010) *Ghosts in the Postmodern Family*, http://works.bepress.com/cgi/viewcontent.cgi?article=1002&context=annette_appell&sei-redir=1#search=%22postmodern+family%22, accessed 15 June 2011.

Bell, D. (1974) *The Coming of Post-Industrial Society: A Venture in Social Forecasting*. London: Heinemann.

Bengtson, V.L. and Allen, K.R. (1993) 'The life course perspective applied to families over time', in *Sourcebook of Family Theories and Methods: a Contextual Approach*, http://www.imamu.edu.sa/topics/IT/IT%206/The%20Life%20Course%20Perspective%20Applied%20to%20Families%20Over%20Time.pdf.

Bhasin, K. (2000) *Understanding Gender*. New Delhi: Kali for Women.

Bongaarts, J. (2001) *Household Size and Composition in the Developing World*. Viewed 14 June 2011, http://www.popcouncil.org/pdfs/wp/144.pdf, accessed 14 June 2011.

Burn, S.M. (2000) *Women across Cultures: a Global Perspective*. London: Mayfield Publishing Co.

Castells, M. (2001) *The Network Society and Organizational Change*. Regents of the University of California, http://globetrotter.berkeley.edu/people/Castells/castells-con4.html, accessed 24 June 2011.

Connolly, M. and Ward, T. (2008) 'Navigating human rights across the life course', *Child and Family Social Work*, 13: 348–56.

Engels, F. (1884) *The Origin of the Family, Private Property and the State*, http://www.marxists.org/archive/marx/works/1884/origin-family/index.htm, accessed 2 February 2011.

Flynn, N. (1999) *Miracle to Meltdown in Asia: Business, Government, and Society*. New York: Oxford University Press.

Goode, W.J. (1964) *The Family*. New Jersey: Prentice Hall, Inc.

Haas, L. (2006) 'Household division of labor in industrial societies', in B.B. Ingoldsby and S.D. Smith (eds), *Families in Global and Multicultural Perspective* (2nd edn). London: Sage Publications. pp. 351–78.

Hamilton, V.M. (2007) *Human Relations: the Art and Science of Building Effective Relationshi*. Upper Saddle River, NJ: Pearson Prentice Hall.

Harding, L.F. (1991) *Perspectives in Child Care Policy*. London: Longman.

Heywood, A. (2007) *Political Ideologies: an Introduction* (4th edn). New York: Palgrave Macmillan.

Hutchison, E.D. (2008) 'A life course perspective', in E.D. Hutchison (ed.), *Dimensions of Human Behavior* (3rd edn). Los Angeles: Sage Publications. pp. 1–38.

IASSW/IFSW (International Association of Schools of Social Work/International Federation of Social Workers) (2004) *Global Standards for the Education and Training of the Social Work Profession*, http://www.ifsw.org/en/p38000868.html, accessed 23 June 2011.

IFSW/IASSW (International Federation of Social Workers/International Association of Schools of Social Work) (2000) *Definition of Social Work*, http://www.ifsw.org/f38000138.html, accessed 2 May 2009.

Ilich, I. (1983) *Gender*. London: Marion Boyars.

Ingoldsby, B.B. (2006a) 'Family origin and universality', in B.B. Ingoldsby and S.D. Smith (eds), *Families in Global and Multicultural Perspective* (2nd edn). London: Sage Publications. pp. 67–78.

Ingoldsby, B.B. (2006b) 'Mate selection and marriage', in B.B. Ingoldsby and S.D. Smith (eds), *Families in Global and Multicultural Perspective* (2nd edn). London: Sage Publications. pp. 133–46.

Ingoldsby, B.B. (2006c) 'Marital structure', in B.B. Ingoldsby and S.D. Smith (eds), *Families in Global and Multicultural Perspective* (2nd edn). London: Sage Publications. pp. 99–128.

Ingoldsby, B.B. (2006d) 'The history of the Euro-Western family', in B.B. Ingoldsby and S.D. Smith (eds), *Families in Global and Multicultural Perspective* (2nd edn). London: Sage Publications. pp. 41–60.

Kabeer, N. (2003) *Gender Mainstreaming in Poverty Eradication and the Millennium Development Goals: a Handbook for Policy-Makers and Other Stakeholders*. Ottawa: Commonwealth Secretariat.

Kelley, K. and Byrne, D. (1992) *Exploring Human Sexuality*. New Jersey: Prentice Hall, Inc.

Leeder, E.J. (2004) *The Family in Global Perspective: a Gendered Journey*. London: Sage Publications.

Leslie, G.R. and Korman, S.K. (1984) *The Family in Social Context*. New York: Oxford University Press.

Mason, J. (1991) 'Foster care and permanency: an analysis of the context for practice', *Australian Journal of Social Issues*, 26(4): 242–56.

McKenry, P.C. and Price, S.J. (2006) 'International divorce', in B.B. Ingoldsby and S.D. Smith (eds), *Families in Global and Multicultural Perspective* (2nd edn). London: Sage Publications. pp. 168–89.

Newman, M. (2005) *Socialism: a Very Short Introduction*. New York: Oxford University Press.

Nicholson, L.J. (1990) 'Introduction', in L.J. Nicholson (ed.), *Feminism/Postmodernism*. New York: Routledge.

Orozco, M. (2006) *Transnational Families: Lives on the Edge, but in Pursuit of Change*, http://www12.georgetown.edu/sfs/isim/Publications/RCRCCPubs/Orozco/Transnational%20Families%20Report%20with%20methodology.pdf, accessed 8 April 2011.

Pandhe, S. (1989) *Women's Subordination (Its Origins)*. New Dehli: Kanak Publications.

Pereira, W. (1997) *Inhuman Rights: the Western System and Global Human Rights Abuse*. Mapusa, Goa: The Other India Press.

Phillipson, C. (2006) 'Aging and globalization: issues for critical gerontology and political economy', in J. Baars, D. Dannefer, C. Phillipson and A. Walker (eds), *Aging, Globalization and Inequality: the New Critical Gerontology*. Amityville, NY: Baywood Publishing Co. pp. 43–58.

Rogers, E.M. and Sebald, H. (1962), 'A distinction between familism, family integration and kinship orientation', *Marriage and Family Living*, 24: 25–30.

Smith, H. (1958) *The Religions of Man*. New York: Harper & Row.

Smith, S.D. (2006) 'Global families', in B.B. Ingoldsby and S.D. Smith (eds), *Families in Global and Multicultural Perspective* (2nd edn). London: Sage Publications. pp. 3–24.

Strong, B., deVault, C. and Cohen, T.F. (2008) *The Marriage and Family Experience: Intimate Relationships in a Changing Society*. Australia: Wadsworth.

Toth, K. and Kemmelmeier, M. (2009) 'Divorce attitudes around the world: distinguishing the impact of culture on evaluations and attitude structure', *Cross-Cultural Research*, 43(3): 280–97.

Triandis, H.C. (1988) 'Collectivism and development', in D. Sinha and H.S.R. Kao (eds), *Social Values and Development: Asian Perspectives*. New Delhi: Sage Publications. pp. 285–303.

UNICEF (United Nations Children's Fund). (2004) *Child Protection: a Handbook for Parliamentarians*.

United Nations. (2007) *World Fertility Report 2007*, http://www.un.org/esa/population/publications/worldfertilityreport2007/wfr2007-text.pdf, accessed 17 May 2011.

United Nations. (2009a) *World Population Ageing 2009*, http://www.un.org/esa/population/publications/WPA2009/WPA2009-report.pdf, accessed 23 June 2011.

United Nations. (2009b) *Follow-up to the Tenth Anniversary of the International Year of the Family: Report of the Secretary-General*.

White, J.M. and Klein, D.M. (2008) *Family Theories* (3rd edn). London: Sage Publications.

Zechenter, E.M. (1997) 'In the name of culture: cultural relativism and the abuse of the individual', *Journal of Anthropological Research*, 53(3): 319–47, http://www.class.uh.edu/faculty/tsommers/moral%20diversity/cultural%20relativism%20abuse%20of%20individual.pdf, accessed 22 June 2011.

Zeitlin, M.F., Megawangi, R., Kramer, E.M., Colletta, N.D., Babatunde, E.D. and Garman, D. (1995) *Strengthening the Family – Implications for International Development*. Tokyo: United Nations University Press, http://archive.unu.edu/unupress/unupbooks/uu13se/uu13se00.htm#Contents, accessed 15 June 2011.

Zimmerman, S.L. (2001) *Family Policy: Constructed Solutions to Family Problems*. London: Sage Publications.

21

Childhood and Youth in International Context: Life-course Perspectives

Letnie Rock, Jeff Karabanow and Kathleen Manion

INTRODUCTION

Notions of childhood and youth are social constructs that vary across cultures and time. Regardless of how they are defined, children and youth constitute significant populations for social work in most communities. Encapsulating the vast array of perspectives on the subject is difficult and in this brief chapter we only provide an introduction.

Children's early physical dependency is unquestionable, but as they begin to make sense of the world around them their realities are shaped by their immediate environment, their families, their local communities and, increasingly, by forces which operate on a global level, such as climate change, migration or access to resources. Family, invariably intertwined with the cultural conceptualisation of childhood, directly impacts how beliefs, values, mores and customs are passed onto the next generation.

How children and youth are conceptualised informs how societies interact with them. Legal definitions of 'childhood', which are informed by contemporary cultural norms, have great impact on the level of power or agency a child is assumed to have. Montgomery (2001:15) suggests that welfare professionals tend to emphasise childhood as a time of powerlessness, vulnerability and ignorance, while others argue for a more rights-based approach as this better supports the notion of children's agency (Scott et al., 1998).

The United Nations Convention on the Rights of the Child (CRC) (UN, 1989) defines a child as 'every human being below the age of eighteen unless, under the law applicable to the child, majority is attained earlier' (Article 1). The CRC has been one of the most widely accepted UN Conventions and has wielded tremendous global influence – not least in offering a convenient definition, which, however, belies the complexity inherent in the lived experiences of children and young people.

Currently there are approximately 2.2 billion children and young people below the age of eighteen years in the world and of those approximately one billion children live in poverty and 24,000 die each day due to poverty (Shah, 2010). While governments may officially acknowledge the rights of children, they may lack the means or will to create the living environment which supports these rights, such as quality education and medical services. Even within a Western context, many families and children live a tenuous existence made more vulnerable by social exclusion, and lack of education or opportunities to access power.

In this chapter, we begin our discussion by providing an overview of definitions, theories and experiences of childhood including legal boundaries and ambiguities. The chapter then considers international influences on childhood, particularly the events leading up to the CRC and beyond, before exploring different perspectives on child protection with a particular focus on children living on the streets, children in disasters, and children who are orphaned as a result of HIV and AIDS. The concluding sections offer some insight into the role of social work with children and youth in a global context.

DEFINITIONS, THEORIES AND EXPERIENCES OF CHILDHOOD

Childhood is a transient state of development preceding adulthood. Although passing from one state to the other is often marked by rites of passage the boundaries between the two are often unclear. Children are not a homogeneous group. There are differences in ages and stages, gender, religious affiliations, cultures and ethnicities. Different stages of development within childhood include infants, toddlers, preschoolers, school aged children, adolescents (aged 10–19), teenagers (aged 13–19), and finally youth (defined by the UN as between the ages of 15 and 24) (Ansell, 2005).

Sawyer (2006) argues that family law considers children as part of families, often lacking a separate legal identity. Childhood is defined differently in different places and the legal 'age of majority' also varies across countries (Lundy, 1997). The promotion of a consistent age for children's involvement and participation in some activities is difficult because the age at which children are presumed to have reached adulthood varies between cultures. In some traditional societies including those where the life-expectancy is low, this may be as early as 12 years of age while in Western societies this may be 18 years of age or even later.

However, even among those countries where the age of majority is harmonised there may be anomalies in the legislation with respect to the ages at which children can perform certain tasks, potentially compromising how they are treated. For example, there are variations between states in America about the ages required to be able to vote, purchase alcoholic beverages or access contraception – and similarly, about the points when parents' duty to support or public schools' obligations to educate end (Giovannoni, 1985). Differences are even more apparent in international comparisons: for instance, in Chile one is criminally responsible at 14, can marry at 16 and can start work at 15; in Grenada the ages are 7, 21 and 14, respectively, and in Denmark they are 15, 18 and 13, respectively (Right to Education, 2010). Sometimes, the minimum ages set in different pieces of legislation are contradictory. In some Caribbean countries, for example, children can start full-time employment before they are legally permitted to stop attending school, creating a difficult paradox (CARICOM and UNICEF, 2000). Lundy (1997) argues that government policy on age of majority and responsibility, such as voting rights or criminal responsibility, can be arbitrary and lack logic.

Demarcating the journey into adulthood is often celebrated by rituals which also do not match with the legal ages of majority, for instance in the religious coming of age ceremonies, such as bar mitzvah and bat mitzvah in Judaism, upanayana in Dvija Hinduism, or the Sacrament of Confirmation in Christianity. Similarly, children themselves have their own definitions of what constitutes childhood: Kendall (2010) asked children in Malawi and Mozambique how they defined childhood and adulthood and their response was a gendered one, with girls seen as reaching adulthood at puberty and boys when they left school and entered the workforce. In Nigerian Hausa society men and women are relegated to specific roles which restrict them from certain spaces, but their children are afforded more liberty and given essentially a special 'go-between' status (Corsaro, 1997). This suggests that despite clear-cut national and international legal definitions of 'childhood' the reality of how children are defined is quite varied within and across cultures.

Western societies have a particular fixation on theories of childhood (Aries, 1962) and these constructs have influenced conceptualisations in other regions including parts of Africa, Asia and Latin America through colonisation, missionary activity, migration and influence over international conventions and the actions of international non-government organisations (NGOs) (Ansell, 2005).

Qvortrup (2009) suggests that until recently children were largely marginalised, but the growth in interest in children illustrates a healthy debate which now surrounds them and their realities. Theories of childhood are fairly recent, having emerged in the past few centuries. Kendall (2010) highlights the influence of 20th and 21st century Western concepts, which assume that children are distinct from adults and require special protection. There are different views on whether such concepts symbolised a more caring society (Aries, 1962) or whether they evidenced a more pervasive society seeking to regulate children and poor families (Hendrik, 1997).

Although theorisation of childhood may be a relatively recent activity, evidence indicates a focus on children and their activities has existed in various guises throughout history. For instance, the Ancient Greeks had distinct ideas about pedagogy (Post, 1994), which are seen to have influenced concepts of childhood in medieval Islam (Conrad, 1994). The latter involved dichotomous understandings: the 'innocent child' needing protection and the 'incorrigible child' needing discipline and moulding.

Theorists often propose these dualistic perspectives of children: as either active agents or untamed and sentimentalised threats (Corsaro, 1997); as either naturally evil and in need of shaping or innocent, untainted and in need of nurture and protection (Jenks, 1996); as unformed people, to be shaped into civilised adults (the Lockean view, cited in Post, 1994); or as innocent at birth, to be slowly corrupted by society's influence (Rousseau, cited in Post, 1994).

As more focus was placed on children, theories began to emerge in the area of psychosocial development, including Freud's theory of unconsciously developed psycho-sexual stages, Piaget's staged taxonomy of children's natural development, and Erikson's psychosocial understanding of children's development.

While the above theories of childhood are largely Eurocentric, it is noteworthy that there has been some cross-fertilisation of conceptualisation of childhood across other countries. Platt (2005) argues that in Japan children's reformers were heavily influenced by policy makers and thinkers in the West and discourse on theories of childhood began to spread with the proliferation of schools.

James et al. (1998) suggest that a growth of interest in childhood in the field of sociology led to different notions of childhood, including the socially constructed child, the tribal child, the minority group child, the social structural child, and the situated child. The 'tribal child' is a conceptualisation of children as autonomous beings, distinct from adults, but imbibing their own social agency with their own set of rules and rituals. The 'minority child' sees children as actors living in an adult-dominated world where they simply play the part of a minority, experiencing discrimination and alienation from the adult world. The 'socially structural child' proposes children are moulded by the social structures which they inhabit. Similarly, Brofenbrenner (1979) believes children are wholly influenced by their relationship to their environment. He proposed a way of understanding them in a series of nested systems: micro, meso, exo and macro systems.[1]

The 'situated child' is a conceptualisation of children as seen through spaces they inhabit, such as the schooled child, the urban child and children in domestic space (James et al., 1998). Holloway and Valentine (2000), attempting to integrate different components of the sociology of childhood (including the local and the global), suggest that ideas about childhood are connected with the spaces children occupy within society.

Alternate theories regarding childhood include 'nature versus nurture' debates, attachment theory and resilience theory. The nature versus nurture debate has been long-standing. Mead (1963) demonstrated that child rearing has an immense impact on how children develop, with prescribed, rather than innate, gender and age specific roles. However, Morris (2010) argues that children are shaped by both biology and socialisation, as recent evidence suggests some development milestones are reached without external influences.

Bowlby (1969) was one of the first proponents of attachment theory, which has become a quintessential principle in Western social work practice with children. The theory proposes that infants and toddlers form attachments with their caregivers forging later psychosocial development. Barriers to those attachments can adversely affect children. In a different vein, research on resilience provides an opportunity to explore the ways in which people overcome adversity following stressful situations (Ungar, 2009; Garbarino, 1999).

Ansell (2005) suggests that commonly discussed theories bear only slight resemblance to the lived experiences of children and young people in the West, and are markedly different from those in developing nations. Boyden

(1997) suggests that although the majority of children live in the developing world, children who fall outside of the Western ideals of childhood (of play and study) are considered deviant. The everyday experiences of children and young people are shaped by their internal resources and by the social, political, economic, and cultural dimensions that surround them. Children and youth are affected by the same discrimination and inequity that plagues adult populations, but perhaps their marginalised status exacerbates the effect.

The socio-economic environment in which children are reared indelibly marks their current and future well-being. How a child or young person's emerging physical, social, emotional, spiritual and psychological needs are responded to profoundly affects their life outcomes. While children in resource-rich communities and families may have access to better elements of care and in turn develop better resistance to stress (Prilleltensky et al., 2001), children and youth in under-resourced environments may not fare as well, particularly where primary caregivers have little time to devote to tending to their emerging needs. As an example, children in lone parent families, often headed by women, are more likely to be marginalised and lack basic needs (Lundy, 1997: 36). More generally, gender inequality and discrimination further compromise the well-being and advancement of women and children, particularly girls. Acute examples of this can be seen in instances of sexual exploitation or even cases of female infanticide.

Children take different roles within their families and communities. Traditional family structures reign in Melanesia where children provide for their wider family (Theis, 2007). Similarly, within the Maori tradition in New Zealand children are not seen as individuals, but rather as integral parts of the family and tribe.

The family, whatever its form, provides the foundation for a child's life and conversely can disrupt their life. Based on extensive multi-national research, Rohner and Kaleque (2002) found that a lack of parental acceptance profoundly affects children, youth and adults, often with negative emotional, behavioural and physical impacts. Similarly, children are affected by the changing nature of the family structure. Lam (2011) notes that in Hong Kong the spread of capitalism has undermined traditional family structures and increased the number of step families. While traditional China 'celebrates the wholeness of family' (p. 607), step-children are seen as a threat to this image and often face negative stereotypes.

Children and youth experience particular times of growth and change which can increase their vulnerability. Discourse in the West increasingly emphasises the importance of the first five years of life, including the importance of good pre- and post-natal care, which can affect both the child's and mother's chance of survival. The nations with the highest and lowest rates of infant and maternity mortality, Somalia and Canada, respectively, are vastly different. In 2010, the infant mortality rate in Somalia for children under five was estimated at 107.42 per 1000 live births (CIA, 2010a) and the maternal mortality rate was estimated at 1044 per 100,000 live births (UNICEF, 2010), whereas in Canada the same estimated infant mortality rate was 4.99 per 1000 live births (CIA, 2010b) and the maternal mortality rate was less than 5 per 100,000 live births (UNICEF, 2010). These figures are inevitably tied to numerous variables, but Canada's relative wealth and universal health care and Somalia's disrupted health care and ongoing conflict undoubtedly play a role.

Understanding these definitions, theoretical underpinnings and experiences of childhood, as well as the psychosocial development and the potential vulnerabilities imbibed in stages of childhood has particular relevance for social work professionals at individual, communal or societal levels.

INTERNATIONAL PERSPECTIVES ON THE RIGHTS, WELFARE AND PROTECTION OF CHILDREN

In 1924, the League of Nations endorsed the first Declaration on the Rights of the Child. UNICEF was founded in 1946 by unanimous

vote at the first UN General Assembly meeting to support relief to children after World War II. The Universal Declaration of Human Rights was introduced in 1948, which imparts basic human rights to all, including children, but does not specify protection for children (UN, 1948; Lundy, 1997). In 1959 the notion of children having rights and entitlements to special care and protection was formally acknowledged when the UN General Assembly adopted the Declaration on the Rights of the Child (UN, 1959).

By 1962 a widespread international movement to protect children from abuse and neglect emerged with the 'discovery of child abuse' and the publication of a paper entitled 'the Battered Child Syndrome' (Kempe et al., 1962). This seminal publication identified the physical harm some caregivers were inflicting on children. Public attention to the issue led children's welfare to be placed on the political agenda and child abuse legislation to be drafted in countries such as Canada, Australia, New Zealand, Ireland, the USA and the UK (Oates, 1986).

The UN celebrated and raised the profile of the plight of children and youth through symbolic initiatives: for instance, 1979 was declared the year of the child and 1985 (and 2010) were heralded as the years of youth. It was in 1989, however, after a decade of consultation, that the CRC was created and it has since been ratified by all but two of the world's nations. Although not without its critics, the CRC is one of the most influential international conventions and lays out basic human rights afforded to all children with the guiding principles 'of non-discrimination (Article 2), best interests of the child (Article 3), maximum survival and development (Article 6) and participation of children (Article 12).

Ratification by countries established their commitment and obligation to periodically report to the Child Rights Committee (an international monitoring mechanism) on their implementation of the CRC. This has led countries to consider their standards of care for children and obliges them 'to review, revise and reform [their] laws relating to children' (Lundy, 1997: 28). The CRC provides a rights-based approach to child protection that takes into consideration children's entitlement to care, the family's role in caring for children, children's participation in decisions which affect them, as well as the roles of civil society, government and the international community.

Since the introduction of the CRC several UN initiatives have tried to progress the well-being of children. Shortly after the introduction of the CRC, a World Summit for Children was held in 1990 to formulate a plan of action for implementing the CRC. It was the largest gathering of world leaders to that date. The World Programme of Action of Youth was adopted in 1995 by the UN General Assembly and UN World Youth Reports on those actions were released in 2003, 2005, 2007 and 2010. In 2000 the UN launched the Millennium Development Goals which were conceptualised as a way to galvanise key government, private sector and civil society agencies and individuals to actualise eight ambitious targets by the year 2015, half of which focused on children (including universal education, gender equality, child health, maternal health and combating HIV/ AIDS). Unfortunately, many nations will struggle to even approach these formidable targets. In 2001, the Global Movement for Children was launched to inspire and mobilise people to act for the betterment of children, and in 2010 the UN formed a new agency (UN Women) targeting issues concerning women and girls.

Despite the wide commitment to the CRC, much debate exists over its interpretation, in particular over how children are understood and how their rights are translated. According to Archard (2003), some argue children should have equal rights to adults, others suggest children have welfare but not liberty rights, still others suggest children hold rights in trust. Alternate interpretations purport that children are not qualified to be holders of rights in the same way as adults; that ascribing rights to children misunderstands the

notion of childhood; or that rights are unnecessary because children are protected via alternate means. Within the quagmire of different interpretations, Sawyer (2006) argues that the CRC confuses matters by embedding the concept of *partial* rights for children. Circumnavigating the debate altogether, Roose and De Bie (2011) suggest the CRC is best used as a discussion document which commits nations to principles supporting children and families.

In the context of children's welfare, debate exists over whether they require protection at all (Kendall, 2010). One perspective suggests that children's age makes them inherently vulnerable and dependent upon adults for their survival, placing them at increased risk of maltreatment. Indeed, UNICEF (2006) suggests that millions of children around the world are abused and neglected every year. Whether or not this assumption is accepted, an extensive recorded history exists of the ways in which children, particularly those without strong protectors or advocates, have suffered cruel treatment, including accounts of infanticide, abandonment, inappropriate housing and treatment (for instance children living on the streets, in prisons or in almshouses), exploitation through indentured and slave labour, trafficking, organised commercial sexual exploitation, internet abuse, or opportunistic abuse arising from conditions that prevail in the aftermath of disasters (UNICEF, 2006; Radbill, 1988; Jones and Trotman Jemmott, 2009).

Radbill (1988) notes that there have been efforts to protect children from abuse and neglect and to provide them with alternative care throughout history. Within the Anglophone literature, historical accounts of the evolution of child protection are particularly rich in the UK. The Elizabethan Poor Laws of 1602 provided poor families with some relief; however, poor, 'indigent' and 'wayward' children continued to be sorely mistreated and devalued. They were placed in institutions or to work in factories or on farms under harsh conditions. As the view of children as delinquent and inherently evil changed in the 19th century to one that saw them to be in need of shaping, interventions concerning children also shifted. Children living in poverty, on the streets, or having difficulties with families were placed in rural reformatories in order to remedy ill effects caused by parents or others (Platt, 1969). Initiated by the 'child savers' (a middle class, religious and philanthropic women's movement), reformatories transformed the child welfare system to a supposedly more gentle approach engendering the middle class values of family, work and religion (Platt, 1969) steeped in the belief that youths could be 'reformed' or 'transformed' into conscientious citizens.[2]

Currently, many state and civil society organisations make provisions for children in need of care and protection through a range of services ranging from preventive and supportive interventions through to alternative care arrangements such as adoption, foster care, kinship care, residential/institutional care, or through the provision of rehabilitative services and programmes. These child welfare services and programmes tend to vary in scope and adequacy from country to country. Some are institutional and residual in character and serve only the families most in need while others are universal and preventive. In comparing child welfare models in the Global North, Hetherington (2002) found that the UK, Ireland and Australia (Victoria) were characterised by a child protection perspective (emphasising individual rights and responsibilities and focusing on crisis), while Nordic countries and continental Europe (Belgium, France, Germany, Greece, Italy, Luxembourg and the Netherlands) were dominated by a welfare regime with a 'family service' orientation (valuing preventive work and family functioning).

Children's welfare is less explicit in policies in the global South and tends to be borrowed from international treaties heavily influenced by the North (Boyden, 1997).

CHILDREN AND YOUNG PEOPLE AT RISK IN PARTICULAR CONTEXTS

Through ratification of the CRC, governments commit to ensuring the survival, protection, development and participation rights of all children by implementing necessary policies and programmes. The CRC respects 'the importance of the traditions and cultural values of each people for the protection and harmonious development of the child ... as well as the importance of international co-operation for improving the living conditions of children in every country, in particular the developing countries' (Lundy, 1997: 108).

However, neo-liberal and neo-conservative policies shaping global economic and political realities have had tremendous impact on communities and families for several decades. Various international monetary policies have endorsed rationalisation and privatisation of services in many countries, exacerbating cuts to key health, education and social welfare services. Those most affected are families in impoverished and disenfranchised communities, with little or no access to resources to enable them to provide healthy and safe environments for their children. Such material deprivation may coexist with other problems like heightened levels of violence and crime, unemployment, child maltreatment and exploitation. The protection and/or escape of children from these situations depend on their level of resilience, the formal and informal social supports available to their families, access by the families to community resources to meet their needs, and the political will of governments.

A child's vulnerability can be exacerbated by a number of tragic one-off or endemic circumstances, for example when they are orphaned or abandoned, displaced, or left behind when carers migrate. Such circumstances may lead to children losing a significant person and protector in their life. In conflict situations children may be at risk of particular forms of abuse when they are forced to act as child soldiers or suicide bombers or are enslaved for sexual or labour exploitation. Children may also be vulnerable through abuse and maltreatment in their families and communities (including through cultural rituals that put them in physical danger such as female genital mutilation) or when their family is broken up (e.g. parental separation). Children and young people can also put themselves at risk through their own activities, for instance children who run away from home, abuse illegal substances or find themselves in conflict with the law.

Children orphaned or made vulnerable as a result of HIV and AIDS

Stories of orphaned children are as old as mankind. However the spread of the HIV/AIDS epidemic has shown us a new manifestation of this familiar story. HIV/AIDS became a global public health threat in the 1980s and it 'continues to be a major global health priority' (UNAIDS, 2009: 7). Table 21.1 demonstrates the extent to which children, especially in sub-Saharan Africa, have been affected by HIV/AIDS, either through infection or by being orphaned. The numbers are expected to rise particularly in this region, where it is estimated that 9 out of 10 people worldwide who are infected with HIV live (AVERT, 2010a).

There are also high rates of infection in the Caribbean region, where the US Agency for International Development (December, 2008, cited in UNAIDS, 2009) indicates that young women have especially elevated rates of the infection. In 2006 the estimated number of children who required care as orphans as a result of the disease in this region was 250,000 (with 200,000 of these in Haiti) (Sullivan, 2006). This number seems small when compared to other countries, for example in 2008 there were 1 million orphaned children in Uganda and 1.4 million in South Africa as a result of the epidemic (AVERT, 2010a).

In 2001, the UN General Assembly recognised the magnitude of the disease and its impact on human life and convened a Declaration of Commitment known as the United Nations General Assembly Special Session (UNGASS) on HIV/AIDS. The Declaration was adopted by member states of the UN and seeks an 'urgent, coordinated and sustained response to the HIV/AIDS epidemic' (UN, 2001). The Declaration provides guidelines for governments to ensure the care and protection of children orphaned and made vulnerable by HIV and AIDS (Sections 65–67), including 'increased access to essential services' (UNAIDS/UNICEF, 2004: 20). It notes that children orphaned and affected by HIV/AIDS may need special assistance including psychosocial support and protection from abuse. The Declaration calls on governments to guarantee that policies neither stigmatise nor discriminate against children orphaned and made vulnerable by HIV/AIDS and to ensure their human rights are upheld. The international community is urged to support programmes for children made vulnerable by HIV/AIDS in affected regions, particularly those in countries at high risk in sub-Saharan Africa (UNAIDS/UNICEF, 2004).

Issues for children who are orphaned tend to be similar regardless of where they live

Table 21.1   HIV/AIDS and its impact on children in selected regions (2008)

Region	Overall population infected with HIV/AIDS	Adults and children over 16	Children under 15	AIDS-related deaths	Children orphaned as a result of HIV/AIDS
World	33.4 million	31.3 million	2.1 million	2 million	15 million
Sub-Saharan Africa	22.4 million		1.8 million	1.4 million	14.1 million
Caribbean	240,000				11,000

Sources: UNAIDS (2009); AVERT (2010a, 2010b); Shah (2010).

and are often compounded when they or their caregivers suffer from HIV/AIDS (McLean et al., 2009). However, Kendall (2010) cautions against stereotyping children's vulnerability as a result of HIV/AIDS and argues that such stereotypes rely on Western constructions of ideal childhoods and ignore children's resiliency and agency. With this caveat, many children are orphaned, separated from siblings, expected to carry additional responsibilities and ultimately raised 'without parental love and care' (AVERT, 2010b). According to UNICEF (2002: 4)

(children) are often plunged into economic hardship because their sick parents are unable to work, and with savings being spent on health care, they are forced to take on the tremendous adult responsibility of supporting the family. The pressures of earning and caring for ailing parents and younger siblings can lead to children's withdrawal from school, even before the demise of their parents, intensifying to total abandonment of school when one or both parents die.

These experiences may have damaging and long-lasting effects on the well-being and development of affected children (McLean et al., 2009). The extreme psychosocial distress children may experience is exacerbated by the stigma and shame associated with the disease (UNICEF, 2002). Some children face discrimination from and/or abandonment by friends, relatives and other members of their communities, with extremely negative consequences for their self-esteem and psychological well-being.

A study conducted in the Republic of Trinidad and Tobago found that stigma and discrimination was at the core of many of the problems which orphaned children faced, including access to education, adequate housing, isolation, rejection and the lack of support from extended family and friends (McLean et al., 2009). The authors also found that orphaned children often turned to risky survival strategies (such as life on the streets) which made them even more vulnerable by exposing them to crime and sexual and other forms of abuse, heightening the risk of their own infection with HIV. At the

same time, their social marginalisation meant that the very people and institutions children approached for protection were often causing them further harm.

The situation is likely to be similar in countries like Haiti where fear about HIV/AIDS persists, where people avoid contact with anyone infected with HIV and where community resources available to affected children and their families are limited (UNAIDS, 2009). Until a cure is found for this disease many children will continue to be affected and their lives placed in jeopardy.

STREET CHILDREN

Young people who lived and worked on the streets were the most disparaged in early industrialised Europe and they were seen as the bane of the industrialised world. It was commonly believed they had *chosen* their street lifestyle, a perspective that has since been largely rejected as ill informed.

In many developing countries (for example, Guatemala), there are large populations of street children who are either orphaned (because their parents were killed in civil wars, by natural disasters or by disease) or displaced (by civil wars, natural disasters or extreme poverty) (UNICEF, 1990; Lave, 1995; Human Rights Watch, 1997). Moreover, within both developed and developing nations, families (predominately female headed) experience homelessness, often living on the street (in slums and shanty towns or on sidewalks, in parks and under bridges) (Lave, 1995; Smollar, 1999; UNICEF, 1999).

Much of the recent research on homeless children has associated them with 'running away' from their particular family setting which includes child maltreatment, family disruption, poverty and family dysfunction (see for example, Karabanow, 2004a; 2008; 2010). Related to this phenomenon are children who work on the street in order to eke out a living for themselves or their families. This is a near universal urban phenomenon, but takes on a local flavour in each city in the world, for instance children who wash windscreens at traffic lights, street vendors, shoeshine boys and flower sellers (Karabanow et al., 2010; Human Rights Watch, 1997; UNICEF, 1999). As Lusk (1992: 296) pointed out in his study of street children in Rio de Janeiro, 'they are on the street and earn money because there is not enough at home or because they have no alternative.' Lusk et al. (1989) suggested that street children in Latin America should be primarily viewed as 'workers'. Lusk (1989), Carizosa and Poertner (1992) and Rizzini and Lusk (1995) outline four overarching ideological assumptions that guide service provision with street youth. First, the 'correctional/institutional' approach understands street children as 'deviants' and 'threats to public safety' and thus intervention follows the ideology of removal from society and correction of personal pathologies. The 'rehabilitation' approach is more benevolent, yet it still assumes personal pathology or deficiencies. Street children here are perceived as inadequate, needy, abandoned or harmed. The intervention involves protection and rehabilitation – attempting to 'fix' the individual and integrate him/her back into mainstream society. The third approach is 'street education', which assumes street children are 'normal' adolescents who have been forced by a deficient society to live under difficult conditions. In other words, street children are in their predicament because of structural social deficiencies (such as lack of affordable housing and meaningful employment). This approach argues that the education and empowerment of street children can foster engaged collective action whereby solutions to problems can be forged. The last approach is 'prevention' and involves strategies of education and advocacy which explore responses to the root causes of homelessness. This approach attempts to prevent children from moving towards street life and promotes community-based programmes (such as after-school programmes, mentoring and peer support, and midnight basketball activities).

Agencies and programmes throughout the globe that have shown success in engaging with at-risk children have in general adopted 'street education' and 'prevention' strategies (see Karabanow, 2004a for case examples). The major characteristics of such initiatives include: providing for basic needs (e.g. shelter, food and clothing); fostering the strengths of participants through community building; linking with external communities and building more sustainable support structures; and advocacy on behalf of participants. When interrelated, these elements function to create a safe and caring environment where participants can build an empowered and resilient community. In other words, when taken together, these four elements forge a 'culture of hope' for an otherwise marginalised population (Karabanow, 2004a).

Young people are attracted to services/programmes deemed responsive to their needs; respectful, knowledgeable and considerate of their situations; non-judgemental and accepting of differences; participatory and democratic; supportive through the long-term; non-bureaucratic and action-oriented (Karabanow, 2004b).

Children and disasters

Around the world, disasters, both natural and man-made, have been occurring on different scales and magnitudes. Natural disasters such as tsunamis, floods, earthquakes, volcanoes, wild fires, hurricanes and landslides are tragic occurrences but they are 'an inevitable part of human life' (Azarian and Skriptchenko-Gregorian, 1998: 1). They affect individuals, families, organisations and communities (Pyles, 2007). In recent times the media have brought us news of the deaths and devastation for thousands of people in the aftermath of major natural disasters such as the Indian Ocean earthquake and tsunami (2004), Cyclone Nargis in Burma (2008), Hurricane Katrina in Louisiana, USA (2005), landslides in Taiwan and China (for instance 2010), avalanches in Pakistan and Afghanistan

(2010), and massive earthquakes in Armenia (1988), Japan (2011), Iran (2003), Haiti (2010) and Chile (2010) to name but a few.

Human interference (e.g. in influencing climate change) has played a role in the increasing rates of natural disasters around the world and children are always among those affected (Azarian and Skriptchenko-Gregorian, 1998; UWI/UNEP/ UNICEF, 2009). The impact on children and youth as a result of these catastrophic events is severe because many die, many others are injured, their homes and livelihoods are destroyed, their families are displaced and there is the 'abrupt collapse of community life' (Azarian and Skriptchenko-Gregorian, 1998: 1).

Children as well as adults who have been directly affected by the event may show symptoms of trauma and distress (Ehrenreich, 2001; Azarian and Skriptchenko-Gregorian, 1998; Lazarus et al., 2003). Apart from injury, displacement, homelessness and overcrowding, children may suffer as a result of hunger, poor nutrition, unsafe drinking water, poor hygiene (precipitating infectious diseases and other ill-health), lack of privacy, disrupted education, as well as maltreatment, abandonment, or the deaths of parents, relatives and friends. Issues may be exacerbated for special groups of children such as the very young, children with disabilities and other special needs, or migrant and refugee children. According to Ehrenreich (2001), school age children may display a range of symptoms following a disaster, including depression, withdrawal, generalised fear, defiance, 'acting out', resentfulness, suspiciousness, irritability, 'agitated' behaviour and somatic complaints. Children may also suffer from difficulties with concentration, intrusive thoughts, sleeping difficulties, regressive tendencies, as well as a range of problems relating to their sense of identity, their interactions with others and their outlook on the future. Symptoms may include post-traumatic stress disorder or other trauma-related psychological difficulties. In many cases, immediately after a disaster strikes, governments and emergency and relief organisations become overwhelmed by the magnitude of the destruction impacting the time it takes for those affected to receive adequate help. Reconstruction is generally slow and (on average), affected children may not experience normalcy in their lives for several months. However, the ways in which children and adolescents are able to survive these events are intertwined with their own resilience and the formal and informal support given by their families and communities. Therapy can help children and families to cope with their trauma (Azarian and Skriptchenko-Gregorian, 1998; UWI/UNEP/UNICEF, 2009). Papadopoulos (2007) advocates focusing therapeutic interventions not just on the trauma, but on resiliency and adversity affected development.

Currently the only international human rights principles or guidelines explicitly referring to the protection of children in natural disasters are found in the Convention on the Rights of Persons with Disabilities (CRPD; UN, 2006), and UNGASS (UWI/UNEP/UNICEF, 2009). The UNGASS Declaration calls on governments to recognise, in their national strategies for HIV/AIDS awareness, prevention and treatment, the increased vulnerability of populations affected by armed conflict, natural disasters and humanitarian emergencies. The CRPD requires governments to protect and ensure the safety of persons with disabilities in situations of risk (including armed conflict, humanitarian emergencies and natural disasters) (Article 75).

We cannot afford for the care and protection of children and their families in disaster situations to not be prioritised by governments and local and international disaster management and relief organisations.

CONCLUDING THOUGHTS: IMPLICATIONS FOR SOCIAL WORK

Socials workers have an important role in working with, and for, children and youth at the micro, meso and macro level, and increasingly with civil society at the international level (Lyons et al., 2006). Effective services for children target and view them within the context of their families and communities (Connolly, 2007). Social workers can also play an important role in advocating and agitating for preventive policies and programmes that foster children's agency and reach those children most in need.

The difficulties faced by some children and young people at risk leave social workers no shortage of motivation to effect change for them.

Numerous 'conceptual maps' exist on engaging children and youth at risk, with common tenets including locality development, social development, active participation, anti-oppressive approaches and consciousness-raising. Locality development promotes meeting people's basic needs in an immediate, caring, respectful, sensitive and compassionate manner through the building of safe community spaces. Social development engages a holistic exploration of the individual and confronts social, political and economic forces which shape their experiences. It implies an understanding of the complexities which make up an individual and avoids narrowly focusing upon the presenting problem issue. Active participation involves children and youth in the design, development and implementation of the service. It does not involve token involvement; rather, it allows for true experiences of being accepted and contributes positively to self-esteem as outlined in the CRC in Articles 12, 13, 14 and 15 (UN, 1989). Anti-oppressive approaches do not involve 'blaming the individual' but understand the political, economic, and social forces that greatly influence the individual's situation. Through individual and collective activities, anti-oppressive social work fosters safe community settings where individuals can build and rebuild a sense of identity, worth, and understanding of their immediate environments. And finally, social action implies a commitment to fundamental structural change in the form of demands for increased resources

and/or equal treatment through advocacy. Social action allows those without a voice to be heard through critical reflection and empowerment strategies (Karabanow, 2004b).

Social workers also have a role in engaging in research initiatives that would identify trends and emerging problems. As our increasingly global community is connected through social media and internet knowledge sharing there are increasingly numerous opportunities for social workers to contribute to and learn about children and young people's issues. As an example two such forums, the Better Care Network (www.bettercarenetwork.org) and the Child Rights Information Network (www.crin.org) provide platforms for providing and reading research, and policy and practice advice.

NOTES

1 This could be simply described as relations at the interpersonal level (such as family), relations between microsystems, systems that indirectly affect a person and relations at the socio-cultural level.

2 Around this time, agencies focusing on children's welfare began to emerge: an example was the London Society for the Prevention of Cruelty to Children, established in 1884 and renamed the National Society for the Prevention of Cruelty to Children in 1889, the same year that the Prevention of Cruelty to Children Act was passed in the UK (NSPCC, 2010).

REFERENCES

Ansell, N. (2005) *Children, Youth and Development.* Abingdon: Routledge.

Archard, D.W. (2003) *Children, Family and the State.* Aldershot: Ashgate.

Aries, P. (1962) *Centuries of Childhood: A Social History of Family Life.* New York: Vintage Books.

AVERT (2010a) *Averting HIV and AIDS.* 'Sub-Sahara Africa HIV/AIDS Statistics*, available at http://www.avert.org/africa-hiv-aids-statistics.htm accessed 14 August 2010.

AVERT (2010b) *Averting HIV and AIDS.* 'AIDS Orphans', available at http://www.avert.org/aids-orphans.htm accessed 14 August 2010.

Azarian, A. and Skriptchenko-Gregorian, V. (1998) *Children in Natural Disasters: An Experience of the 1988 Earthquake in Armenia*, available at http://www.aaets.org/article38.htm accessed August 2010.

Bowlby, J. (1969) *Attachment and Loss: Volume 1. Attachment.* New York: Basic Books.

Boyden, J. (1997) 'Childhood and the policy makers: a comparative perspective on the globalization of childhood', in A. James and A. Prout (eds), *Constructing and Reconstructing Childhood* (2nd edn). London: Routledge. pp.190–230.

Bronfenbrenner, U. (1979) *The Ecology of Human Development: Experiments by Nature and Design.* Cambridge: Harvard University Press.

CARICOM (Caribbean Community) and UNICEF (2000) *The Rights of Children in the Caribbean: Questions and Answers.* Barbados: UNICEF Caribbean Area Office.

Carrizosa, S. and Poertner, J. (1992) 'Latin American street children: Problems, programmes and critique'. *International Social Work*, 35 (4): 405–13.

CIA World Fact Book (2010a) available at https://www.cia.gov/library/publications/the-world-factbook/geos/so.html accessed August 2010.

CIA World Fact Book (2010b) available at https://www.cia.gov/library/publications/the-world-factbook/geos/ca.html accessed August 2010.

Connolly, M. (2007) 'Practice frameworks: Conceptual maps to guide intervention in child welfare', *British Journal of Social Work*, 37 (5): 825–37.

Conrad, L.I. (1994) 'Children of Islam: concepts of childhood in medieval Muslim society'. *Medical History*, 38 (1): 105–6.

Corsaro, W.A. (1997) *The Sociology of Childhood.* London: Pine Forge Press.

Ehrenreich, J.H. (2001) *Coping with Disasters: A Guidebook to Psychosocial Intervention* (revised ed.). Old Westbury, NY: Center for Psychology and Society, State University of New York.

Garbarino, J. (1999) *Lost Boys: Why Our Sons Turn Violent and How We Can Save Them.* New York: Ballantine Books.

Giovannoni, J.M. (1985) 'Child abuse and neglect: an overview', in J. Laird and A. Hartman (eds), *A Handbook of Child Welfare: Context, Knowledge and Practice.* New York: The Free Press. pp.193–212.

Hendrik, H. (1997) *Children, Childhood and English Society 1800–1990.* Cambridge: Cambridge University Press.

Hetherington, R. (2002) *Partnerships for Children and Families Project: Learning from Difference: Comparing Child Welfare Systems.* Waterloo: Wildfred Laurier University. Available at www.wlu.ca/pcf-project accessed 27 August 2004.

Holloway, S. and Valentine, G. (2000) 'Spatiality and the new social studies of childhood', *Sociology*, 34 (4): 763–83.

Human Rights Watch (1997) *Guatemala's Forgotten Children: Police Violence and Abuses in Detention.* New York: Human Rights Watch.

James, A., Jenks, C. and Prout, A. (1998) *Theorizing Childhood.* Cambridge: Polity Press.

Jenks, C. (1996) *Childhood.* London: Routledge.

Jones, A. and Trotman Jemmott, E. (2009) *Child Sexual Abuse in the Eastern Caribbean: The Report of a Study Carried Out Across the Eastern Caribbean During the Period October 2008 to June 2009.* Huddersfield: Action for Children, UK, University of Huddersfield and UNICEF Eastern Caribbean.

Karabanow, J. (2004a) *Being Young and Homeless: Understanding How Youth Enter and Exit Street Life.* New York: Peter Lang Publishing Inc.

Karabanow, J. (2004b) 'Making organizations work: Exploring characteristics of anti-oppressive organizational structures in street youth shelters', *Journal of Social Work*, 4 (1): 47–60.

Karabanow, J. (2008) 'Getting off the street: Exploring young people's street exits', *American Behavioral Scientist*, 51 (6): 772–88.

Karabanow, J. (2010) 'Street kids as delinquents, menaces and criminals: another example of the criminalization of poverty', in D. Crocker and V.M. Johnson (eds), *Poverty, Regulation, and Social Exclusion: Readings on the Criminalization of Poverty.* Halifax: Fernwood Publications. pp.140–7.

Karabanow, J., Hughes, J. and Kidd, S. (2010) 'Travailler pour survivre: exploration du travail des jeunes de la rue [Working to survive: Exploring street youth labor]', *Criminologie*, 43 (1): 7–29.

Kempe, C.H., Silverman, F.N., Steele, B.R., Droegamuller, W. and Silver, H.K. (1962) 'The battered child syndrome', *Journal of the American Medical Association*, 181 (July): 17–24.

Kendall, N. (2010) 'Gendered moral dimensions of childhood vulnerability', *Childhood in Africa*, 2 (1): 26–37.

Lam, G. (2011) 'Difficulties of stepchildren from reconstituted families in a westernized society challenged by traditional Chinese culture', *International Social Work*, 49 (5): 605–13.

Lave, T. (1995) 'Breaking the cycle of despair: Street children in Guatemala City'. *Columbia Human Rights Law Review*, 27 (1): 57–121.

Lazarus, P.J., Jimerson, S.R. and Brock, S.E. (2003) *Helping Children after a Natural Disaster*, available at http://www.nasponline.org/resources/crisis_safety/naturaldisaster_ho.aspx accessed August 2010.

Lundy, C. (1997) *An Introduction to the Convention on the Rights of the Child*. Ontario Canada: Full Circle Press.

Lusk, M. (1989) 'Street children programs in Latin America', *Journal of Sociology and Social Welfare*, 16 (1): 55–77.

Lusk, M. (1992) 'Street children of Rio de Janeiro', *International Social Work*, 35 (3): 293–305.

Lusk, M., Peralta, F. and Vest, G. (1989) 'Street children of Juarez: a field study'. *International Social Work*, 32 (4): 289–302.

Lyons, K., Manion, K. and Carlsen, M. (2006) *International Perspectives on Social Work: Global Conditions and Local Practice*. Basingstoke: Palgrave Macmillan.

McLean, R., Sogren, M. and Theodore, K. (2009). 'The impact of HIV-AIDS on children at risk – the case of Trinidad and Tobago', in A.D. Jones, J.A. Padmore and P.E. Maharaj (eds), *HIV-AIDS and Social Work Practice in the Caribbean: Theory, Issues and Innovation*. Miami, FL: Ian Randle.

Mead, M. (1963) *Sex and Temperament in Three Primitive Societies*. New York: William.

Montgomery, H. (2001) *Modern Babylon? Prostitution Children in Thailand*. Oxford: Berghahn Books.

Morris, D. (2010) *Child: How Children Think, Learn and Grow in the Early Years*. London: Octopus Publishing.

NSPCC (National Society for the Prevention of Cruelty to Children) (2010) *History of the NSPCC*. http://www.nspcc.org.uk/what-we-do/about-the-nspcc/history-of-NSPCC/history-of-the-nspcc_wda72240.html.

Oates, K. (1986) *Child Abuse and Neglect: What happens Eventually?* New York: Brunner/Mazel.

Papadopoulos, R.K. (2007) 'Refugees, trauma and adversity-activated development', *European Journal of Psychotherapy & Counselling*, 9 (3): 301–12.

Platt, A.M. (1969) *The Child Savers*. Chicago: The University of Chicago Press.

Platt, B. (2005) 'Japanese childhood, modern childhood: the nation-state, the school, and 19th-century globalization', *Journal of Social History*, 38 (4): 965–85.

Post, N. (1994) *The Disappearance of Childhood*. New York: Vintage Books.

Prilleltensky, I., Nelson, G. and Person, L. (2001) 'The role of power and control in children's lives: an ecological analysis of pathways toward wellness, resilience and problems', *Journal of Community and Applied Social Psychology*, 11 (2001): 143–58.

Pyles, L. (2007) 'Community organising for post-disaster social development: locating social work', *International Social Work*, 50 (3): 321–33.

Qvortrup, J. (2009) *Structural, Historical, and Comparative Perspectives*. Bingley, UK: Emerald Group Publishing Limited.

Radbill, S.X. (1988) 'Children in a world of violence: a history of child abuse', in R.E. Helfer and R.S. Kempe, *The Battered Child* (4th ed.). Chicago IL: University of Chicago Press. pp. 3–22.

Right to Education (2010) *At What Age? Comparative Table*, available at www.right-to-education.org/node/279, accessed February 2011.

Rizzini, I. and Lusk, M. (1995) 'Children in the streets: Latin America's lost generation', *Children and Youth Services Review*, 17 (3): 391–400.

Rohner, R.P. and Khaleque, A. (2002). 'Parental acceptance-rejection and life-span development: a universal perspective', in W.J. Lonner, D.L. Dinnel, S.A. Hayes and D.N. Sattler (eds), *Online Readings in Psychology and Culture* (Unit 11, Chapter 4). Washington USA: Center for Cross-Cultural Research, Western Washington University, Bellingham, available at http://www.wwu.edu/culture.

Roose, R. and De Bie, M. (2011) 'Children's rights: a challenge for social work', *International Social Work*, 51 (1): 37–46.

Sawyer, C. (2006) 'The child is not a person: Family law and other legal cultures', *International Social Work*, 28 (10): 1–14.

Scott, S., Jackson, S. and Backett-Milburn, K. (1998) 'Swings and roundabouts: Risk anxiety and the everyday worlds of children', *Sociology*, 32 (4): 689–705.

Shah, A. (2010). *Poverty and Facts and Stats,* available at http://www.globalissues.org/article/26/poverty-facts-and-stats, accessed August 2010.

Smollar, J. (1999) 'Homeless youth in the United States: description and developmental issues', in M. Raffaelli and R. Larson (eds), *Homeless and Working Youth Around the World: Exploring Developmental Issues*. San Francisco: Jossey-Bass Publishers. pp. 47–58.

Sullivan, M.P. (2006) *CRS Report for Congress RL32001: AIDS in the Caribbean and Central America*, available at http://fpc.state.gov/documents/organization/32921.pdf, accessed April 2011.

Theis, J. (2007) 'Performance, responsibility and political decision-making: child and youth participation in Southeast Asia, East Asia and the Pacific', *Children, Youth and Environments*, 17 (1): 1–13.

UN (United Nations) (1948) *The Universal Declaration on Human Rights*. New York: United Nations.

UN (United Nations) (1959) *United Nations Declaration on the Rights of the Child*. New York: United Nations.

UN (United Nations) (1989) *The Convention on the Rights of the Child*. New York. United Nations.

UN (United Nations) (2001) *UN General Assembly Special Session: Declaration of Commitment on HIV/AIDS*. New York: United Nations.

UN (United Nations) (2006) *The Convention on the Rights of Persons with Disabilities,* available at http://www.un.org/disabilities/convention/conventionfull.shtml accessed August 2010.

UNAIDS (2009) *AIDS Epidemic Update. UNAIDS/WHO*. Geneva, Switzerland: UNAIDS.

UNAIDS/UNICEF (2004) *The Framework for the Protection, Care and Support of Orphans and Vulnerable Children Living in a World with HIV/AIDS*. New York: United Nations.

Ungar, M. (2009) 'Resilience practice in action: five principles for intervention', *Social Work Now,* 43 (August): 32–8.

UNICEF (United Nations Children's Fund) (1990) *Children and Development in the 1990s*. New York: United Nations Children's Fund.

UNICEF (United Nations Children's Fund) (1999) *The State of the World's Children*. Oxford: Oxford University Press.

UNICEF (United Nations Children's Fund) (2002) 'The real casualties of HIV/AIDS are ... children', *Children in Focus,* 15 (1): 1.

UNICEF (United Nations Children's Fund) (2006) *The State of the World's Children: Childhood Under Threat*. New York: United Nations Children's Fund.

UNICEF (United Nations Children's Fund) (2010) available at http://www.unicef.org/infobycountry/somalia.html, accessed August 2010.

UWI/UNEP/UNICEF (University of the West Indies/United Nations Environment Programme/United Nations Children's Fund) (2009) *Gap Analysis: Children and the Environment in the Eastern Caribbean*. Final report prepared by the University of the West Indies, Cave Hill Campus for the UNEP and UNICEF Eastern Caribbean Area Office, UN House, Hastings, Christ Church, Barbados.

22

Adulthood: Some Comparative and International Perspectives

Ruby C. M. Chau

INTRODUCTION

This chapter, with an emphasis on the comparative and international perspectives of adulthood, has three aims. Firstly, it explores meanings of contemporary adulthood as a specific stage of life. Secondly, it examines the effectiveness of work and family as two major institutions in enabling adults to have their needs and social roles fulfilled, and considers the current welfare responses to the diverse needs of adults with different socio-economic characteristics. Last but not least, it suggests future directions in policy, research and practice in order to address both homogeneity and diversity in adulthood.

Corresponding to these three aims, this chapter is divided into three parts. The first part explores contemporary understandings of adulthood. The second part carries out two analytical tasks. The first task is the discussion of some of the ideological and social changes in recent decades which have brought about challenges to the conventional assumptions of work and family. The second task is the examination of how these changes have affected these two institutions in responding to the diverse needs of adults, especially those from disadvantaged socio-economic positions. The final part puts emphasis on the 'active agent approach' and searches for future directions in terms of policy, research and social work practice.

CONTEMPORARY PERSPECTIVES ON ADULTHOOD

As a life stage, adulthood is understood to be the period between youth and old age and is therefore of variable duration. When there is any change in the definition of the other two stages, the 'meaning' of adulthood changes accordingly. For instance, delay among young people in entering employment due to the increased length of formal education (particularly in the global North) means a shorter adulthood. However, if governments postpone the retirement age to encourage longer years of paid work (and fewer years for claiming retirement benefits), the period of adulthood extends correspondingly.

Erikson's classical theory suggested that adulthood contains three phases: young adulthood (20s to 30s), middle adulthood (40s to mid-60s) and late adulthood (65 years old or above) – although the last is more often now 'redefined' as 'old age' (see Chapter 23). In each stage, a person has to overcome certain life crises to achieve growth and to move on to the next phase. In young adulthood, a person has to overcome isolation and to experience close friendship and intimate relationships. In middle adulthood, one has a need to combat stagnation and to invest in a socially responsible future, such as building family, community and career. In late adulthood, one needs to review life accomplishments, to feel satisfaction and acceptance of past experience and present circumstances (Bentley, 2007). Despite the fact that Erikson's (eight) stages of psychosocial development have been highly influential in the understanding of human development, one major criticism of Erikson's view in general and on adulthood in particular lies in its assumption of the universality of human experiences and the applicability of one theory to the experiences of all (Bentley, 2007).

Despite the fact that adulthood takes up a long period in the life course, it has received less attention from policy and research than other life stages. By inserting 'adulthood' as the keyword in main academic search engines and library catalogues, a long list of results may appear. However, these are not all directly relevant. A certain proportion of the publications are concerned with 'emerging adulthood' or 'transition to adulthood'. These publications are actually about adolescents or young people growing up into adults (e.g. Konstam, 2007; Macmillan, 2007;

Arnett, 2006). Another section of the publications relate adulthood to ageing, emphasising the decline of physical functioning in (late) middle life and/or transition into retirement (e.g. Mason, 2011; Charles, 2009). The lack of direct research interest may be a reflection of a general view that adulthood is not a particularly important or interesting stage in its own right. It is perhaps regarded as comparatively stable, with less excitements and challenges than the other life stages. Another explanation could be that adulthood encompasses a wide range of life experiences in accordance with the heterogeneous characteristics of individual adults and the contexts in which they live. It is difficult to capture its multiple meanings. Understandings of adulthood vary within and between different countries, social groups, cohorts and individuals.

In recent decades, the expanding volumes of cross-national studies on how governments across the world organise their welfare services have shown that countries do not necessarily provide the same economic, social and political conditions for adults to manage their lives. Esping-Andersen (1990, 1997) presented 'three worlds of welfare' based on the examination of the labour market decommodification of 18 OECD (Organisation for Economic Co-operation and Development) members (mostly Anglo-Saxon and western European countries). His threefold classification of regimes identified: the liberal welfare state, the conservative welfare state and the social democratic welfare state. Adults in the liberal welfare regime are expected to make more use of the private market to meet their needs and handle social risks. Adults in the conservative welfare regime are expected to rely more on occupational welfare and the family to satisfy their needs and to deal with social risks. Adults in the social democratic regime are expected to rely more on the public welfare institutions to handle social risks and to fulfil needs. Gough (2004) draws our attention to the fact that the Anglo-Saxon and western European countries (such as most of the 18 OECD members studied by Esping-Andersen) share three key elements in the economy and polity – a legitimated state, a pervasive labour market as the basis for most people's livelihoods, and sophisticated financial markets providing insurance and a vehicle for savings. However, not all countries in the rest of the world have these three elements. In relation to this point, Gough (2004) presents two welfare regimes based on the studies of poor countries in South Asia and Africa – the informal security regime and insecurity regime. Adults in the informal security regime attempt to meet their needs and deal with social risks through participating in communities, in which social relationships are usually informal, hierarchical and asymmetrical (Wood, 2004). Adults in the insecure regime do not have any formal or informal mechanism to meet their needs and to deal with social risks, and as a result live a highly insecure life.

Comparative studies show not only the differences in the ways in which adults in different countries manage their lives but also raise our awareness of the inequalities between adults living in different parts of the world. According to the United Nations (2010), half the world's multi-dimensionally poor live in South Asia (844 million people), and more than a quarter live in Africa (458 million); life expectancy in the Gambia by 2010 was 57, that is 24 years fewer than for someone born in Norway. There were about 1 billion malnourished people (most of them in Asia and sub-Saharan Africa) in 2010. However, in contrast, many people in developed countries (such as the USA) eat too much and obesity is a growing problem. The unequal distribution of resources between people across the world affects how they shape their lives – for example, many adults in poor countries spend most of the time fighting against hunger; while some adults in rich countries seek medical assistance or coaching to eat less.

Attention should also be paid to international migrants, whose number increased from 155 million people in 1990 to 213 million in 2010 (United Nations, 2010). About 75 percent of all international migrants are located in 30 countries in the world. Once inside the first gate of admission, migrants may be deprived of some social, economic and political rights (Lister, 1997). As a result it is unlikely that they will enjoy a standard of living comparable with that of the mainstream population. It is important to note that migration is also a gendered subject (Castles and Miller, 2008). Female migrants exceed male migrants in many developed countries, e.g. Australia, Canada, France, Italy, Japan, the Netherlands and the United Kingdom. An important reason for migration is marriage and family reunion. It is likely that many female adult migrants spend their lives looking after their children in a foreign place, maintaining transnational contact with their place of origins; and work in a culturally different setting, vulnerable to both racial and sexual discrimination (Chau and Yu, 2001; Chau, 2008).

It is important to note that even within the same country, different interpretations of adulthood exist. In discussing the transition from youth to adulthood, Corijn (2001) suggests three interactive perspectives to understand what the transition entails, namely the start of a 'dual career' related to family and work; the focus on the structural constraints on the life course; and the transition from dependence to independence. By starting a family and a work career, a young person would be able to achieve economic, emotional, residential and other forms of independence. However, the establishment of one's own family and career happens in a particular social, economic, political and cultural context and is subject to various contextual constraints. Therefore there is no guarantee of a successful transition to adulthood for every individual.

Corijn's argument draws our attention to the importance of contextual factors (such as how jobs are allocated in society and the cultural expectations about the role of different members in the family) in people's experience of adulthood. Life course theorists suggest the significance of cohort effects which illustrate the impact of historical events and processes on individual lives (Alwin and McCammon, 2004). By studying two different age cohorts in Australia, Wyn and her colleagues (2008) conclude that there are similarities as well as differences in their adult lives between the post-1970s cohort and the post-1980s cohort. For instance, inequalities continue to be significant in both cohorts' experiences. Young people with low socio-economic backgrounds in both cohorts are disadvantaged in entering higher education and have poorer health. However, the meanings of career are quite different for the two cohorts. As employment has become more flexible and less likely to provide security in the 21st century, the younger cohort tends to see a career as a personal journey rather than as a position or pathway within an occupation or organisation (Wyn et al., 2008).

Some scholars (e.g. Janke et al., 2011; Levinson, 1996; Aiken, 1998) argue that individuals differ from each other in their understanding and experience of adulthood. Janke et al. (2011) point out that different people in their adulthood come across different life events which may be regarded as positive (career achievements, becoming a grandparent) and/or negative (divorce, job loss, loss of a loved one). Certainly those adults who have career success and a stable family life have a different experience of adulthood from those divorcees who suffer from long-term unemployment. Levinson (1996) suggests the concept of 'life structure', stressing that one's socio-cultural world (e.g. family, work, religion) interrelate with personal aspects (e.g. role experiences such as friend, spouse, parent) to lead to unique patterns or designs in adults' lives in any given time. Aiken (1998) starts his discussion on adult development with a list of scenarios, including a 35-year-old male who is severely mentally retarded; a mentally gifted 14-year-old who has been awarded a college degree in mathematics; and a 13-year-old female who is married and has a one-year-old child.

These scenarios indicate that, to different individuals, the meaning of adulthood would be different.

A study in the US disseminated by Furstenberg and his colleagues in 2005 shows that Americans have taken longer to complete the traditionally defined life tasks for transition to adulthood, including leaving home, finishing school, becoming financially independent, getting married and having a child. Only 46 percent of women and 31 percent of men aged 30 in 2000 had done so, compared to 77 percent of women and 65 percent of men of the same age in 1960. They suggest that the delay is mainly due to changes in the labour market in the past decades. Young people have to spend more time on education and job preparation now than in the past before they can get a full-time job which pays enough to support a family. The study also reports that not all young adults could complete the transition easily or complete it at all. For instance, young people from less well-off families sometimes move back and forth between work and school or combine both to gain their qualifications. With limited financial, time and mental resources, they may choose to postpone marriage or parenting and concentrate on career development.

How to construct adulthood involves not only handling events but also constructing and reconstructing identity. It is not uncommon for adults to have 'minority' identities such as lesbian, gay or other 'queer' sexualities for example. These 'minority' identities have historically been subject to the destructive disciplinary intentions of others (Cooper, 2004). In order to create the conditions for respecting vulnerable forms of difference, it is necessary for adults to fight for more than tolerance from the 'majority' in the community. For example, lesbian feminists have developed various analyses of what they term 'heterosexual privilege', in which they suggest that heterosexuality, far from being 'natural', is a political institution designed to restrict the sexual behaviour and choices of women and deny the lesbian possibility

(Hicks, 2005). Besides challenging the 'privileged identity', Cooper (2004) suggests that it is necessary to celebrate what are the most marginalised identities such as the transsexuals, butch dykes and leathermen. It is important to note that adults may have more than one 'minority' identity. How they associate themselves with their identity is related not only to their personal preference but also to the consideration of the political strengths they can gain from fighting for their interests and against the vested interests. Lloyd (1992) suggests that disabled women might do better to work with non-disabled women and disabled men to get their concerns accepted as 'central, to both disability and feminist agendas than to pursue a separatist strategy'. It is also important to note that identity exists in a fluid rather than essential form (Chau and Yu, 2010). It is possible that adults play an active role in changing their identity in order to secure an inclusive politics of voice and representation (Lister, 1997). However, it is equally possible that their identities are passively changed by the public policies.

The above discussion shows that adulthood is a multi-dimensional and dynamic life stage. The concept of intersectionality (e.g. Franken et al., 2009) is useful in analysing how different aspects of identity (notably age, gender and race, but also including sexuality and [dis]ability) combine and interact to make the individual experience of adulthood feel – and be – more or less privileged or oppressed. The reality of adulthood is therefore far more complex than suggested by Erikson's three phases. Adulthood can be a hazardous and difficult journey for many, and not a destination of safety and security to be reached easily (Côté, 2001).

RECENT CHANGES AND CHALLENGES

This section discusses some of the pro-market social changes in recent decades which have brought about challenges to the conventional assumptions of work and family, two major channels through which adults' needs and social roles are fulfilled. These changes have taken place mainly in Anglo-Saxon, European and some East Asian countries. As mentioned above, how people in Anglo-Saxon and (Western) European countries organise their welfare and life can be very different from people in other parts of the world. Despite these differences it is still worth discussing the ideological and social changes taking place in these locations due to the global scale of knowledge and policy transfer. Through the operation of international organisations, such as the World Trade Organization, the World Bank, the OECD and the International Monetary Fund, many ideas practised in Western countries are promoted to the rest of the world (Deacon, 2008; Yeates, 2008).

Not every adult can successfully attain independence through work and family. Instead, individuals rely on a welfare mix of different sectors in meeting their needs and to perform their social roles – these include the state, the market, the family and the voluntary sector (Powell, 2007; Gilbert, 2009). The debates on the ideal combination of these sectors to help individuals meet their needs have been vigorous and seem to be never-ending. Examples of these debates are those concerned with the relative desirability of the residual welfare model, the industrial achievement model and the institutional redistributive model (Titmuss, 1974); the relative importance of different claim systems (e.g. work, capital, family and government) (Rein, 1983); and the merits and demerits of the liberal, conservative and social democratic welfare regimes (Esping-Andersen, 1990, 1999; Powell and Barrientos, 2011). Since the late 1970s, the debate on the ideal form of this welfare mix has been significantly influenced by neo-liberalism. Supporters of these ideologies are keen not only to stress the private market as the most effective mechanism for creation and allocation of wealth but also attempt to demonstrate that the market-dominated welfare mix is the most efficient response to economic, political, cultural, social and technological changes (Hill, 2006). A number of these changes are highlighted below.

A major change in recent years is the replacement of Fordism by post-Fordism. Fordism is characterised by the harnessing of economic activity to the large-scale mass production of standardised goods for mass markets under the direction of hierarchical systems of centralised management and control (Purdy and Banks, 1999). Post-Fordism is marked by the features of 'localism' and 'adaptability'. These two concepts imply that the global economic web replaces hierarchical systems of centralised control with dispersed trans-global networks, which allow sub-national local sites to bypass national state structures, traverse national boundaries and link directly with any other site in the world. As a result, governments are required to help people adjust to the demands of the international market and increase their commodity values, for example, through promoting incentives to work.

A second change is the collapse of communism, and the keenness of the post-communist states to search for effective market reform formula (King and Szelwnyi, 2005). In his book, *The End of History and the Last Man* (1993), Fukuyama stresses that there is no alternative to liberal capitalism. Based on this 'common sense' view of many governments, measures such as privatisation of public services, deregulation, tax reform and fiscal discipline are seen to be the way to the development of a healthy and vibrant economy.

These national measures are reinforced by international activities. The increasing mobility of capital makes it difficult for national governments to tax capital to promote a redistribution of resources. International organisations such as the World Bank propose policies to reinforce the ideas of individual's self-reliance (Walker and Wong, 2005). For example, the World Bank advocates pension reforms in favour of a funded scheme at the expense of the ones based on the pay-as-you-go principle. Some countries such as Singapore promote Asian values that stress the economic hegemony against a more collective-based economy.

These changes have brought about challenges to both work and family, the two channels through which adults seek to have their needs and social roles fulfilled. For instance, the labour markets in many economies have been undergoing a process of 'flexibilisation' (Tangian, 2007). So that they can have better control over costs and expenditures, private companies and public bodies are seeking to establish a flexible workforce by offering short-term contracts and expecting employees to be employed on flexible working conditions, including flexible wages. Some commentators argue that flexibilisation of employment has caused increasing unemployment and underemployment, bad employment, and problematic relationships between work and the rest of socialisation (Nectoux and van der Maesen, 2003). According to a report disseminated by the International Labour Organisation (ILO) (Jansen and Uexkull, 2010), the global unemployment rate rose to 6.6 percent in 2009, an increase of 0.9 percentage points over 2007. Despite comprising less than 16 percent of the global workforce, the developed economies and the European Union region accounted for more than 40 percent of the increase in global unemployment from 2007 to 2009. The increasing difficulties in finding employment among the general population imply that there are even slimmer chances for socially disadvantaged groups (such as disabled people, single parents and women) to enter the labour markets. This also explains why the youth unemployment rate has always been higher than the rate for the general population. The same ILO report shows that the global youth unemployment rate rose by 1.6 percentage points to reach 13.4 percent in 2009 relative to 2007 (Jansen and Uexkull, 2010).

As highlighted by Esping-Andersen (1999), the family is also facing risks partly because of the insecurity faced by its members in the labour market. Alongside this, the family as a social institution has also been subject to increasing marital instability leading to divorce or separation, and, in many cases, single parenthood. Statistics show that there has been a constant decrease in the percentage of married households across OECD countries. For instance, in the US, only 50 percent of the total number of households contained married couples in 2008 as compared to 60.8 percent in 1980. This coincides with the increase in the percentage of single-parent households. For example, in the UK, lone parent families increased from 14.8 percent in 2001 to 16.2 percent in 2010 (Beaumont, 2011). For those couples who got married, there is no guarantee of a long-lasting relationship. The percentage of newly married couples ending up in divorce in 2002 was as high as 54.9 percent in Sweden; 52.9 percent in Belarus and 51.2% percent in Finland respectively (*Divorce Magazine*, 2011).

While work and family are facing these challenges, the capacity of social welfare to provide support for individuals has also been undermined by the global changes mentioned above. Wilding (1997) argues that globalisation has stimulated an ideology of competitiveness leading to changed priorities in social policy, from meeting needs to motivating and training people to seek paid employment. In the pursuit of global competitiveness, a 'public burden model of welfare' has been widely adopted by governments. There has been a general call for the reduction of social expenditure and the development of more productivist social policy (Wilding and Holliday, 2003).

Capitalism is marked by structural needs for capital accumulation and political legitimacy (Walker and Wong, 2004; Gough, 1979). To fulfil these needs, capitalist governments in both the East and the West have attempted to make use of the above changes to justify their reforms of the welfare mix in favour of the private market and individualism. Their reforms can be seen as a do-it-yourself (DIY) approach (Chau and Yu, 2009). Such an approach is marked by two major

characteristics – adults must learn to confront risks and simultaneously anticipate and expect their own lives to be less sure, less taken for granted (Giddens, 1994); and people and government should reconstruct their division of responsibility in the provision of welfare. In the new division, adults are expected to take a more active role in providing for their own welfare needs; and the government will only provide a basic minimum (Heron and Dwyer, 1999; Yu, 2008).

To promote these ideas of the DIY approach, governments have launched different types of reforms. Examples include residualisation measures; market-led measures; welfare-to-work measures; and 'flexicurity' measures. The residualisation measures are intended to maintain social welfare provisions as close to the residual welfare model as possible (Forrest and Murie, 1988; Chau and Yu, 2003). An important way to residualise social welfare is to make users feel that they are inferior to those who purchase services in the market. This can be done by requiring users to be means-tested for benefits and/or by lowering the benefits provided by social welfare agencies. The market-led measures are founded on the assumption that the private market and the government can mutually benefit by co-operating with each other. In order to motivate people to take part in the private market, the government can apply the market-led measure by actively playing the role of subsidisers and regulators (Abrahamson et al., 2005; Johnson, 1990; Powell and Barrientos, 2011). The welfare-to-work measures are intended to encourage welfare users to work instead of relying on social welfare. To achieve this goal, the government may encourage service users, by 'sticks and carrots', to receive training and to develop their work habits. Finally, the flexicurity measures are founded on the assumption that people should adjust to the increasingly flexible and insecure markets. In order to help them make this adjustment, the government provides some support through the provision of social welfare (Tangian, 2007).

All these changes suggest that governments have chosen to be more responsive to the needs of the market rather than to the needs of people. State welfare provision tends to focus on the production and reproduction of labour. In developed countries, such as the UK, welfare-to-work measures have dominated welfare developments in the last few decades (Powell and Barrientos, 2004). These measures are applied to different socio-economic groups including young people, lone parents and people aged over 50 (Yu, 2008). In China, welfare-to-work measures have been applied to adults with various disabilities (Chau, 2009). This has contributed to forming the general belief that paid work is the major, if not the only, means to eliminate poverty at a personal and at a national level. Disabled adults, regardless of their abilities and characteristics, are expected to seek self-reliance through taking part in the labour market, no matter how unfavourable the working conditions are. Those who 'choose' to rely on welfare (due to various reasons and constraints), have to bear the inferior quality of services and stigmatised status attached to them.

In carrying out the DIY approach, capitalist governments identify themselves not only as the defenders of capitalism but also as moral leaders. At the same time as promoting the work ethic and traditional family values, they also label some groups as the 'moral underclass' (Levitas, 1998). Examples of these groups include those who rely on welfare (e.g. single parents and long-term users of state benefits) and those seen as a threat to traditional family values (e.g. gays and lesbians) (Chau and Yu, 2002). The governments not only criticise these people as groups undeserving of social welfare but they also see them as a threat to social cohesion (Chau and Yu, 2009). As discussed above, adults have diverse characteristics and have different needs. However, the market has become more hegemonic and government policies further marginalise adults identified as 'minorities'. In addition, the market has significantly failed large proportions of the global population who, 'under normal circumstances', would expect to work and provide for their families, witness the effects of the Asian financial crisis in the late 1990s and the more recent (and still ongoing) financial crises in the US and Europe.

FUTURE DIRECTIONS

Social workers have a mission to facilitate adults in meeting their needs. Before discussing some important aspects of practice it is worth discussing briefly the concept of need. According to Gough (2004), need refers to a particular category of goals which are assumed to be universalisable. The universality of need is based on a belief that if need is not satisfied then serious harm of some objective kind will result. This harm can be seen as fundamental disablement in the pursuit of one's vision of good. It can also be seen as an impediment to successful social participation. These two ways of defining harm imply that human beings need both health and autonomy to participate in life. If human beings are impaired by mental illness or by poor cognitive skills and by blocked opportunities, they cannot make informed choices in terms of their own lives.

Given these ideas about 'need', it is not surprising that social workers have a deep concern about the difficulties faced by 'vulnerable adults'. This is a contested notion which can be understood in various ways according to national contexts. However, according to the Department of Health in the UK (2000), a vulnerable adult is defined as a person 'who is or may be in need of community care services by reason of mental or other disability, age or illness, and who is or may be unable to take care of him or herself, or unable to protect him or herself against significant harm or exploitation'. To meet the needs of the vulnerable adults, it is necessary to give them basic protection such as financial support and personal care. Leaving aside the context-specific and rather limited nature of this definition, evidence indicates that vulnerable adults need more than just provision of these services. For instance, analysts point out that it is not easy to reach disadvantaged adults who need mental health care because of mistrust of institutions, cultural insensitivity and stigma (Dobransky-Fasiska, et al., 2010). Studies also indicate that people with mental illness do not trust professionals such as the police even though they invariably have contact with them (Watson et al., 2008). In the US, there is evidence that black adults used psychiatric outpatient services less frequently than whites (Horvitz-Lennon et al., 2009). These and other findings suggest that vulnerable adults need not only material resources to maintain a decent standard of living, but also support for establishing an effective and trusting relationship with those who offer help and with the rest of society. To secure this relationship, it is necessary to create the conditions for the vulnerable adults to make informed choices for participating in decision making and in the consumption and production of services intended to meet their needs. This implies that we should not only take care of the health of vulnerable adults but also their autonomy.

To take another example, in searching for the ideal ways for conceptualising and meeting needs of disabled groups, there has been considerable debate on the relative merits of the individual model and social model. The individual model of disability locates the 'problem' of disability in the individual. The social model views disability as a situation of collective institutional discrimination and social oppression (Oliver and Barnes, 1998). Based on the social model of disability, social workers work with people with disabilities to focus on the barriers within society which serve to disable people with impairments. Boxall (2002: 213) points out, 'From a social model perspective, disability is not caused by people's impairments: it is the failures of society to accommodate people with impairments that cause disability'. It is

suggested that the ideas of the social model of disability should be borrowed to develop strategies for facilitating other groups of vulnerable adults to organise their lives. This implies that actions should be taken to remove the barriers to the work intended to strengthen the health and autonomy of vulnerable adults rather than focusing on forcing them to make individual changes.

It is important to note that while not all adults are seen as 'vulnerable adults', many people can be vulnerable to serious risks in some period of their adult lives. Hence, it is worth paying attention not only to those adults commonly identified as 'vulnerable adults' but also to the potential vulnerability of all adults. For instance, Dani and Harris (2005) cite a World Health Organization (WHO) estimate that one-third of the global adult population smokes. Since tobacco use is on the rise, particularly in developing countries, deaths resulting from tobacco use continue to rise disproportionately in countries with the least well-resourced health services. Because of the increasing flexibility of the labour market, more and more adults experience unemployment before retirement. To take another example, the pension reforms in favour of funded schemes in a large number of countries are causing anxiety to increasing numbers of middle-aged workers about whether they will receive sufficient pensions to support them in retirement (Yu, 2008). With the emphasis on the concept of health and autonomy, it is necessary not only to provide adults in need with health care or material support but also to empower them to play an active role in constructing their own lives.

Since the concept 'active' is highly related to autonomy, it is not surprising that this term has been attracting increasing attention since the early 1990s. As stressed by Titterton (1992), there is a need for an understanding of the individual as a creative; reflexive agent, who helps to create, but is also constrained by the social forces and conditions in which she or he exists. In response to this need, Titterton has developed a new paradigm for welfare, composed of three elements:

1 It should attempt to understand people's 'differential vulnerability' to threats to their welfare and well-being in terms of the complexity of social, material and personal forces.
2 It should examine the differential coping strategies that people use when faced with such threats and explore how these too, are shaped by differential access to material, social and personal resources.
3 The study of welfare outcomes should include those people who 'survive' and work through the threats to their welfare.

The three elements of this paradigm provide a challenge to assumptions about the universality of 'expert knowledge'. According to Leonard (1997), this worldview omits the experiences and forms of knowledge generated by women, non-Europeans, and the subordinated classes. In order to expose the defects of this worldview, it is necessary to enable all groups to speak for themselves, in their own voice, and have that voice accepted as legitimate (Harvey, 2005).

Some analysts (e.g. Williams et al., 1999; Dominelli, 2004; Ferguson, 2008) are calling for the expansion of the welfare research agenda to examine structural inequality at national and international levels and to see to what extent individuals can be shown the respect they need to be active agents in promoting their own well-being. Over a decade ago, Williams et al. (1999) made several important suggestions in the context of feminist approaches to research and policy formation. These included stressing the importance of people's own experiences, definitions and meanings of problems; developing new forms of coping strategies based on political perceptions of personal problems/risks; and avoiding seeing people simply as victims of inequalities by stressing a positive reappraisal of identity (such as survivor rather than victim).

The essence in these recent texts and debates is the emphasis on people being active, and the provision of opportunities and resources for playing an active role in developing themselves and structuring and restructuring their surroundings. Perhaps for this reason, the word 'active' is often mentioned in the development of concrete strategies for improving the lives of individuals – such as active citizens, active learners, active users. It is thus worth considering developing strategies that could promote active adulthood. To do so, the notion of active ageing, suggested by Walker (2002), can serve as a useful reference and some of his principles for active ageing are relevant, as follows:

1 Activity should consist of all meaningful pursuits which contribute to the well-being of the adult concerned, or of his or her family, or of the local community or of society at large and should not be concerned only with paid employment or production.
2 Active adulthood (instead of ageing) must encompass all adults (instead of older people).
3 Intergenerational solidarity should be maintained with the stress on fairness.
4 The concept should embody both rights and obligations.
5 The concept should stress participation and empowerment.
6 National and cultural diversity should be respected.

There are also some important suggestions in other aspects of the social work literature for helping individual adults to become active participants in making their own life decisions. Some of these are listed as follows:

1 Giving drug users the right to choose whether to access treatment rather than them being forced to receive treatment (Measham and Paylor, 2005).
2 Demystifying the research process so that service users can participate fully in research activities and projects (Dominelli, 2005; Barnes et al., 1999).
3 In order to reduce the oppression suffered by ethnic minority groups, it is necessary not only for their needs to be understood but also for the structural inequalities to be dealt with (Chau and Yu, 2010).
4 Unity in diversity should be strengthened among those involved in resisting different aspects of oppression and exploitation (Ferguson, 2008).

5   Ethnocentricism should be challenged in the policy transfer process and the development of international social work (Walker and Wong, 2004).
6   Attention should be paid to both universal and diverse dimensions of need (Chau and Yu, 2010).
7   Values should be given the central position in social work practices (Ferguson, 2008).

CONCLUSION

This chapter has highlighted issues about contemporary adulthood from a comparative and international perspective. It is noted that adulthood, often the longest stage in one's life course, has not received the amount of attention it deserves. One reason for this could be the general assumption that adulthood is a stable time in the life course with work and family as the main concerns. However, it may also be that the huge range of adult experiences and its contingent nature have made 'adulthood' too broad to be studied as a unified concept.

The above discussion suggests that these two observations are more apparent than real. With the global ideological and economic changes, the relationship between the state and the market has shifted to favour the latter to a great extent. Market values have become dominant in both the private and the public sector in the global North with implications also for people in the countries of the global South. Paid workers are in more vulnerable positions because of the process of flexibilisation of employment. Work is no longer a reliable means to attain independence and maintain living standards. Alongside the emergence of diverse family forms, the capacity of the family to fulfil the needs of individuals has been further weakened by the changes in the labour market.

There has been increasing research evidence showing the differential experiences of adulthood among women, people with disabilities, migrants and people with different socio-economic characteristics. However, welfare policies as a major response to these diverse experiences, especially those of disadvantaged groups, have not been flexible enough to respond to the heterogeneous reality. Against the backdrop of the globalised economy, social welfare has been increasingly geared to respond to the needs of maintaining a competitive market. Contemporary welfare policies have put the emphasis on enabling adults, through 'carrot and stick' measures, to contribute to the labour market, regardless of their needs and capacities.

As a cross-national and cross-cultural profession, social work holds strong beliefs about the right to self-determination of people (individually and collectively) and their capacity to seek change and personal growth. To empower people with different backgrounds and characteristics to pursue a better life, the social work profession has an obligation to promote 'active adulthood', in which, opportunities and support should be available for adults to have their needs met and their concerns heard. With the wider participation of adults at societal, national as well as global levels, the social work profession should also advocate for structural changes in the capitalist market and in welfare policies to make them more responsive to the diverse needs of different adult groups.

REFERENCES

Abrahamson, P., Thomas, P.B. and Greve, B. (2005) *Welfare and Families in Europe*. Burlington, VT: Ashgate.

Aiken, L.R. (1998) *Human Development in Adulthood*. Boulder, CO: netLibrary.

Alwin, D. and McCammon, R. (2004) 'Generations, cohorts and social change', in J. Mortimer and M. Shanahan (eds), *Handbook of the Life Course*. New York: Springer.

Arnett, J.J. (2006) *Emerging Adulthood: The Winding Road from the Late Teens through the Twenties*. Oxford; New York: Oxford University Press.

Barnes, C., Mercer, G. and Shakespeare, T. (1999) *Exploring Disability: A Sociological Introduction*. Cambridge: Polity.

Beaumont, J. (ed.) (2011) *Households and Families, Social Trends 41*. New Port: The Office of National Statistics.

Bentley, E. (2007) *Adulthood*. London: Routledge.

Boxall, K. (2002) 'Individual and social models of disability and the experiences of people with learning difficulties', in D. Race (ed.), *Learning Disability: a Social Approach*. London: Routledge.

Castles, S. and Miller, M. (2008) *The Age of Migration: International Population Movements in the Modern World* (4th edn). New York: Guilford Press.

Charles, S.T. (ed.) (2009) *Current Directions in Adulthood and Aging*. Boston: Pearson.

Chau, C.M. (2008) *Health Experiences of Chinese People in the UK, a Race Equality Foundation Briefing Paper*. London: Health Equality Foundation.

Chau, C.M. (2009) 'Socialism and social dimension of work – employment policies on disabled groups in China', *The Hong Kong Journal of Social Work*, 43: 19–29.

Chau, C.M. and Yu, W.K. (2001) 'Social exclusion of Chinese people in Britain', *Critical Social Policy*, 21 (1): 103–25.

Chau, C.M. and Yu, W.K. (2002) 'Coping with social exclusion: Experiences of Chinese women in three societies', *Asian Women*, 14: 103–27.

Chau, C.M. and Yu, W.K. (2003) 'Marketisation and residualisation – recent reforms in the medical financing system in Hong Kong', *Social Policy & Society*, 2 (3): 199–207.

Chau, C.M. and Yu, W.K. (2009). 'Social quality and the social harmony campaign in Hong Kong', *Development and Society*, 38 (2): 277–95.

Chau, C.M. and Yu, W.K. (2010) 'The sensitivity of United Kingdom health-care services to the diverse needs of Chinese-origin older people', *Ageing and Society*, 30: 383–401.

Chau, C.M., Yu, W.K. and Cheung, P.W. (2002) *Report for National Conference on Chinese Older People*. York: Joseph Rowntree Foundation.

Cooper, D. (2004) *Challenging Diversity: Rethinking Equality and the Value of Difference*. Cambridge: Cambridge University Press.

Corijn, M. (2001) 'Transition to adulthood: sociodemographic factors' in M. Corijin and E. Klijzing (eds), *Transition to Adulthood in Europe*. Dordrecht, Boston, London: Kluwer.

Côté, J.E. (2001) *Arrested Adulthood: The Changing Nature of Maturity and Identity*. Boulder, CO: netLibrary.

Dani, J. and Harris, R. (2005) 'Nicotine addiction and comorbidity with alcohol abuse and mental illness', *Nature Neuroscience*, 8 (11): 1465–70.

Deacon, B. (2008) 'Global and regional social governance' in N. Yeates (ed.), *Understanding Global Social Policy*. Bristol: Policy Press.

Department of Health (2000) '*No Secrets: Guidance on Developing and Implementing Multi-agency Policies and Procedures to Protect Vulnerable Adults from Abuse*. London: Department of Health. http://www.dh.gov.uk/prod_consum_dh/groups/dh_digitalassets/@dh/@en/documents/digitalasset/dh_4012248.pdf

Divorce Magazine (2011) *World Divorce Statistics*, http://www.divorcemag.com/statistics/statsWorld.shtml.

Dobransky-Fasiska, D., Nowalk, M., Pincus, H., Castillo, E., Lee, B., Walnoha, A., Reynolds, C. and Brown, C. (2010) 'Improving depression care for disadvantaged adults by partnering with non-mental health agencies', *Psychiatric Services*, 61 (2): 110–12.

Dominelli, L. (2004) 'Culturally competent social work: a way toward international anti-racist social work?', in L. Gutierrez, M. Zuniga and D. Lum (eds), *Education for Multicultural Social Work Practice: Critical Viewpoints and Future Directions*. Alexandria: Council on Social Work Education.

Dominelli, L. (2005) 'Social work research: contested knowledge for practice', in R. Adams, L. Dominelli and M. Payne (eds), *Social Work Futures: Crossing Boundaries, Transforming Practice*. Basingstoke; New York: Palgrave Macmillan.

Esping-Andersen, G. (1990) *The Three Worlds of Welfare Capitalism*. London: Polity.

Esping-Andersen, G. (1997) 'Hybrid or unique? The Japanese welfare state between Europe and America', *Journal of European Social Policy*, 7 (3): 179–89.

Esping-Andersen, G. (1999) *Social Foundation of Postindustrial Economies*. New York: Oxford University Press.

Ferguson, I. (2008) *Reclaiming Social Work*. London: Sage.

Forrest, R. and Murie, A. (1988) *Selling the Welfare State: The Privatisation of Public Housing*. London: Routledge.

Franken, M., Woodward, A., Cabo, A. and Bagilhole, B.M. (eds) (2009) *Teaching Intersectionality: Putting Gender at the Centre*. Athena.

Fukuyama, F. (1993) *The End of History and the Last Man*. New York: Free Press; Toronto: Maxwell Macmillan Canada; New York: Maxwell Macmillan International.

Furstenberg, Jr, F.F., Settersten, Jr, R.A. and Rumbaut, R.G. (2005) (eds) *On the Frontier of Adulthood: Theory, Research, and Public Policy*. Chicago: University of Chicago Press.

Giddens, A. (1994) *Beyond Left and Right: The Future of Radical Politics*. Cambridge: Polity Press.

Gilbert, N. (2009) 'Welfare pluralism and social policy', in J. Midgley and M. Livermore (eds) (2nd edn), *The Handbook of Social Policy*. California; New Delhi: London; Singapore: Sage.

Gough, I. (1979) *The Political Economy of the Welfare State*. London: Macmillan.

Gough, I. (2004) 'Welfare regimes in development contexts: a global and regional analysis', in I. Gough and G. Wood (eds), (2004) *Insecurity and Welfare Regimes in Asia, Africa, and Latin America: Social Policy in Development Contexts*. Cambridge; New York: Cambridge University Press.

Harvey, D. (2005) *A Brief History of Neoliberalism*. Oxford: Oxford University Press.

Heron, E. and Dwyer, P. (1999) 'Doing the right thing: Labour's attempt to forge a new welfare deal between the individual and the State', *Social Policy and Administration*, 33 (1): 91–104.

Hicks, S. (2005) 'Sexuality: social work theories and practice', in R. Adams, L. Dominelli and M. Payne (eds), *Social Work Futures: Crossing Boundaries, Transforming Practice*. Hampshire: Palgrave.

Hill, M. (2006) *Social Policy in the Modern World: A Comparative Text*. Oxford: Blackwell.

Horvitz-Lennon, M., Frank, R., Thompson, W., Baik, S., Alegria, M., Rosenheck, R. and Normand, S. (2009) 'Investigation of racial and ethnicity disparities in service utilization among homeless adults with severe mental illness', *Psychiatric Services*, 60 (8): 1032–8.

Janke, M., Carpenter, G., Payne, L. and Stockard, J. (2011) 'The role of life experiences on perceptions of leisure during adulthood: A longitudinal analysis', *Leisure Sciences: An Interdisciplinary Journal*, 33 (1): 52–69.

Jansen, M. and Uexkull, E.V. (2010) *Trade and Employment in the Global Crisis*. Geneva: International Labour Office, New Delhi: Academic Foundation.

Johnson, N. (1990) *Reconstructing the Welfare State: a Decade of Change 1980–1990*. New York: Harvester Wheatsheaf.

King, L. and Szelwnyi, I. (2005) 'Post-communist economic systems', in N. Smelser and S. Swedberg (eds), *The Handbook of Economic Sociology* (2nd edn). Princeton: Princeton University Press; NY: Russell Sage Foundation.

Konstam, V. (2007) *Emerging and Young Adulthood: Multiple Perspectives, Diverse Narratives*. New York: Springer.

Leonard P. (1997) *Postmodern Welfare: Reconstructing an Emancipatory Project*. London: Sage.

Levinson, D.J. (1996) *Seasons of a Woman's Life*. New York: Alfred A. Knopf.

Levitas, R. (1998) *The Inclusive Society?* London: Macmillan.

Lister, R. (1997) *Citizenship: Feminist Perspectives*. London: Macmillan.

Lloyd (1992) 'Panel on transitions to adulthood in developing countries; committee on population, division of behavioral and social sciences and education', in C.B. Lloyd et al. (eds) *The Changing Transitions to Adulthood in Developing Countries: Selected Studies*. Washington, DC: The National Academies Press.

Macmillan, R. (ed.) (2007) *Constructing Adulthood: Agency and Subjectivity in Adolescence and Adulthood*. Amsterdam : Elsevier JAI.

Mason, M.G. (2011) *Adulthood and Aging*. Boston, MA: Allyn & Bacon.

Measham, F. and Paylor, I. (2005) 'Legal and illicit drug use' in R. Adams, L. Dominelli and M. Payne (eds), *Social Work Futures: Crossing Boundaries, Transforming Practice*, Basingstoke; New York: Palgrave Macmillan.

Nectoux, F. and van der Maesen, L. (2003) 'From unemployment to flexicurity – opportunities and issues of social quality in the world of work in Europe', *European Journal of Social Quality*, 4 (1/2): 1–27.

Oliver, M. and Barnes, C. (1998) *Social Policy and Disabled People: From Exclusion to Inclusion*. London: Longman.

Powell, M. (2007) 'The mixed economy of welfare and the social division of welfare', in Powell, M. (ed.), *Understanding the Mixed Economy of Welfare*. Policy Press: Bristol.

Powell, M. and Barrientos, A. (2004) 'Welfare regimes and the welfare mix', *European Journal of Political Research*, 43 (1): 83–105.

Powell, M. and Barrientos, A. (2011) 'An audit of the welfare modelling business', *Social Policy and Administration*, 45 (1): 69–84.

Purdy, M. and Banks, D. (1999) 'Tracing continuity and diversity in health and exclusion', in M. Purdy and D. Banks (eds), *Health and Exclusion: Policy and Practice in Health Provisions*, London; New York: Routledge.

Rein, M. (1983) *From Policy to Practice*. New York: M.E. Sharpe.

Tangian, A. (2007) 'European flexicurity: concepts, methodology and policies', *Transfer*, April: 551–73.

Titmuss, R. (1974) *Social Policy: An Introduction*. London: Allen and Unwin.

Titterton, M. (1992) 'Managing threats to welfare: the search for a new paradigm', *Journal of Social Policy*, 21 (1): 1–23.

United Nations (2010) *Human Development Report*. United Nations.

Walker, A. (2002) 'A strategy for active ageing', *International Social Security Review*, 55 (1): 121–39.

Walker, A. and Wong, C.K. (2004) 'The ethnocentric construction of the welfare state', in P. Kennett (ed.) *A Handbook of Comparative Social Policy*. Cheltenham, UK; Northampton, MA: Edward Elgar. pp. 116–30.

Walker, A. and Wong, C.K. (2005) 'Introduction: East Asian welfare regimes', in A. Walker and C.K. Wong (eds), *East Asian Welfare Regimes in Transition*. Hong Kong: The Policy Press. pp. 3–20.

Watson, A., Angell, B., Morabito, M. and Robinson, N. (2008) 'Defying negative expectations: Dimensions of fair and respectful treatment by police officers as perceived by people with mental illness', *Administration and Policy in Mental Health* 35: 449–57.

Wilding, P. (1997) 'Globalisation, regionalism and social policy', *Social Policy & Administration*, 31 (4): 410–28.

Wilding, P. and Holliday, I. (2003) *Welfare Capitalism in East Asia: Social Policy in the Tiger Economies*. New York: Palgrave Macmillan.

Williams, F., Popay, J. and Oakley, A. (1999) 'Changing paradigms of welfare', in F. Williams, J. Popay and A. Oakley (eds), *Welfare Research: a Critical Review*. London: UCL Press. pp. 2–16.

Wood, G. (2004) 'Informal security regimes: the strength of relationships', in I. Gough and G. Wood (eds), *Insecurity and Welfare Regimes in Asia, Africa, and Latin America: Social Policy in Development Contexts*. Cambridge; New York: Cambridge University Press.

Wyn, J., Smith, G., Stokes, H., Tyler, D. and Woodam, D. (2008) *Generations and Social Change: Negotiating Adulthood in the 21st Century: Report on the Life-Patterns Research Program 2005–2007*. Australia: Australian Youth Research Centre, The University of Melbourne.

Yeates, N. (2008) 'The idea of social policy', in N. Yeates (ed.), *Understanding Global Social Policy*. Bristol: Policy Press.

Yu, W.K. (2008) 'The normative ideas underpinning the welfare to work measures for young people in Hong Kong and the UK', *International Journal of Sociology and Social Policy*, 28 (9/10): 380–93.

23

Older Persons and Social Work: a Global Perspective

Terry Hokenstad and
Amy Restorick Roberts

INTRODUCTION

This chapter addresses the social work response to global ageing. Rapid population ageing is taking place in both developed and developing countries. Greater numbers of older adults worldwide are creating demand for more supportive services for older persons and family caregivers that are accessible regardless of income, ethnicity, or gender. Internationally, important trends, including changes in family structure, migration, ageism, elder abuse, and human rights issues, contribute to an increased vulnerability among older persons. The social work response has been guided by the three priority directions of the United Nations Madrid International Plan of Action on Ageing (United Nations, 2002a). These include older adults and development, advancing health and well-being into old age, and ensuring enabling and supportive environments. Through direct practice and community organising roles, social workers advocate for the rights of older people, address age

discrimination, support family caregivers, reduce elder abuse, and improve the health and well-being of older persons. Future directions for social work in the field of ageing are also discussed. This chapter first reviews the demographic context of population ageing, followed by a consideration of older adults within a changing society, current issues and action among older persons, and the social work response.

A GREYING WORLD: THE DEMOGRAPHIC CONTEXT

Population ageing

Unprecedented demographic changes have created a worldwide phenomenon of population ageing. The expansion of the older adult population along with declining fertility rates is shifting the distribution of the world's population dramatically. For the first time, the number of older adults will soon be larger than the number of children between birth to fourteen years old (United Nations, 2006). As shown in Table 23.1, the current global population estimate of persons 60 years of age and above (737 million in 2009) will reach over 2 billion by 2050 (United Nations, 2009). While important demographic differences between regions and countries within the same region exist, older adults will comprise a larger portion of the population between 2009 and 2050 in all regions of the world (see Table 23.1). By 2050, there will be one older adult for every five persons worldwide (United Nations, 2009).

Population ageing is taking place in both developed and developing countries. As Table 23.1 shows, developed countries have a higher proportion of older people as a percentage of the total population compared to developing countries. However, more than 60 percent of the world's older adult population

lived in developing countries in 2008, and an estimated 79 percent of all older adults worldwide will live in developing nations by 2050 (United Nations, 2008a). While developed countries will continue to experience a substantial increase in the percentage of older adults, population ageing will occur at a much faster rate in developing countries (United Nations, 2009). Given the rapid pace of population ageing in developing countries, less time is available for the development and funding of health and social services infrastructures to support the needs of older persons.

Also, the senior part of the population is growing older. Many countries expect the 'oldest old' category (80 years and above) to increase faster over time than the overall older adult population. The increases in the 'oldest old' segment will be the most profound in developing countries, where the

Table 23.1   Demographic characteristics of global and regional population ageing

Geographic region	Number of adults 60 years and above (thousands)		Percentage of total population		Share of persons 80 years or over		Life expectancy at age 60 (2005–2010)	
	2009	2050	2009	2050	2009	2050	Men	Women
World statistics								
Total population 60 years and above	737,275	2,008,244	11	22	14	20	18	21
Developed countries (more developed regions)	263,905	416,055	21	33	20	29	20	24
Developing countries (less developed regions)	473,370	1,592,188	8	20	11	17	17	20
Regional statistics								
Africa	53,770	212,763	5	11	8	10	15	17
Asia	399,881	1,236,103	10	24	11	18	18	20
Europe	158,503	236,426	22	34	19	28	18	23
Latin America and the Caribbean	57,039	186,036	10	26	15	22	20	22
Northern America	62,744	124,671	18	28	21	29	21	25
Oceania	5338	12,246	15	24	19	27	21	25

Source: United Nations (2009).

Note: Developed countries include all regions of Europe, North America, Australia/New Zealand, and Japan. Developing countries include all regions of Africa, Asia (excluding Japan), Latin America and the Caribbean, and the regions of Melanesia, Micronesia, and Polynesia.

population aged 80 and above is projected to increase by a factor of 6.7 between 2005 and 2050 (United Nations, 2009).

Population ageing presents socioeconomic and geopolitical challenges. Older persons' participation in the labour market varies widely across nations. Older men and women in developing countries are more likely to actively work for compensation than those in developed countries (see Table 23.2). These differences are primarily attributable to the limited coverage of pension programmes and income support available to older adults in the developing world. As older adults make up a larger portion of the overall population, policies about a statutory retirement age influence participation in the labour market. In developed countries, men are typically eligible for pension benefits around the age of 65 and women are commonly eligible for pension benefits at a slightly younger age. Some developing countries have younger statutory retirement ages (between 55 and 60 years) for men and women. These younger ages are influenced both by lower life expectancies and the relative infancy of

social security systems (United Nations, 2009).

For countries that provide social security, income pensions, or public health benefits to older adults, the old-age support ratio measures the expected dependency of older adults on potential workers.[1] As shown in Table 23.2, the old-age support ratio will decrease between 2009 and 2050 both globally and in every region of the world. Europe, Northern America and Oceania have lower old-age support ratios, while the ratios are higher in Africa, Asia, and Latin America and the Caribbean. In Europe, there were only five persons of working age per older adult in 2000 – and it is predicted that this ratio will be less than 2:1 in 2050 (United Nations, 2002b). For all countries, changes in mortality, fertility, and international migration will have some influence on population ageing. Some countries have recognised the value of increasing the migration of younger workers as a potential solution to decreasing dependency ratios. But relative to the current demographic trends, this is probably negligible (United Nations, 2008b).

Table 23.2   Percentage of adults 60 years and older in the labour force and old-age support ratio trends

Geographic region	Percentage of adults, 60 years or over, in labour force	Old-age support ratio	
World statistics	Men / Women	2009	2050
Total population estimates	40 / 20	9	4
Developed countries (more developed regions)	24 / 14	4	2
Developing countries (less developed regions)	47 / 24	11	4
Regional statistics			
Africa	61 / 34	16	9
Asia	44 / 23	10	4
Europe	18 / 10	4	2
Latin America and the Caribbean	47 / 21	10	3
Northern America	32 / 22	5	3
Oceania	30 / 18	6	3

Source: United Nations (2009).

Note: Developed countries include all regions of Europe, North America, Australia/New Zealand, and Japan. Developing countries include all regions of Africa, Asia (excluding Japan), Latin America and the Caribbean, and the regions of Melanesia, Micronesia, and Polynesia.

Longevity

Another important aspect of population ageing is the global increase in longevity. In most regions, people are enjoying a longer lifespan. Due to medical and public health advancements, life expectancy worldwide has increased more than 20 years since 1950. On average, men who live to age 60 can expect to live another 18 years, and women of 60 can expect to live another 21 years (United Nations, 2009). Overall, in developed countries, the average life expectancy in 2005 was approximately 78 years, and this figure is expected to increase to 85 years by 2050 (United Nations, 2008a). Developing countries, on the other hand, have an average life expectancy of 63 years, which is anticipated to increase to 74 years in 2050 (United Nations, 2008a).

While most people can realistically expect to live longer, there are some exceptions to this trend. In the countries of sub-Saharan Africa, more than 22 million people are affected by the HIV epidemic. This has resulted in a decreased life expectancy in some countries (UNAIDS, 2008). Programmes to decrease the spread of HIV/AIDS have been initiated to prevent the spread of communicable diseases and increase life expectancy. The countries of the former Soviet Union also have a high mortality rate among younger adults. Deaths caused by external circumstances are three times higher for persons who live in Russia compared to Western countries (United Nations, 2008a). In response to this population crisis, programmes to improve the mortality of Russians have been implemented to promote healthy and active lifestyles. In other developed countries, most deaths from non-communicable diseases occur in old age.

Despite the overall positive trends in longevity, there are wide variations in life expectancies across countries. Even within the same region of the world, considerable differences exist in average life expectancy. In South-Eastern Asia, for example, men and women in most countries born between 2005 and 2010 have average life expectancies of 70 or above according to the UN's *World Population Prospects* (2008a). But several countries in the region, e.g. Cambodia, Lao People's Democratic Republic, Myanmar, and Timor-Leste, had an average life expectancy for men and women of approximately 10 years less than their neighbours. These countries are challenged to improve their national average of life expectancy through improving nutrition and reducing injuries and diseases.

Gains in life expectancy also differ by gender. In most regions, females have a higher life expectancy than males and are more likely to survive into old age. Thus, most older adults are women. Worldwide, at age 60 and older, there were 63 million more women than men in 2000, and this trend continues into the oldest-old category (United Nations, 2002a). In 2009, there were 83 men for every 100 women among people aged 60 and above, while the number decreased to only 59 men for every 100 women among people over 79 (United Nations, 2009). There was a greater difference between the sexes in terms of life expectancies in developed countries, where women live significantly longer, but in countries with lower mortality rates, women often spend a longer period in ill health (United Nations, 2008b).

Diversity within the older population

The older adult population is heterogeneous, and great diversity exists between and within groups of older persons. Around the world, cultural as well as demographic factors such as gender, race, and socioeconomic status contribute to diversity and determine education levels, job options, and the overall ability to amass wealth over the lifespan. For some, ageing is a positive experience of embracing new activities and a time of reflection, while for others it is defined by discrimination, marginalisation, and violence (Help Age International, 2009a). The experiences of older persons also differ according to the country of origin, urban or rural residence, marital status, health condition, and relationships with family members. In addition to cross-national comparisons, it is also important to examine diversity within specific national, cultural, and ethnic groups. Greater susceptibility to oppression in earlier life stages among vulnerable groups, such as women and racial minorities, leads to greater vulnerability in old age. According to Help Age International, 'the cumulative gender bias experienced by women throughout the life in education, the labour market and saving capacity, spells poverty and exclusion for women in old age' (Help Age International, 2005b: 3). Diversity is often related to social exclusion, and minority groups are at higher risk of marginalisation, facing many barriers to full participation in society.[2] Social exclusion can result in inequalities in wealth that present barriers to meeting basic needs for nutrition, sanitation, and healthcare.

In both developed and developing countries, the experience of ageing is strongly related to the degree to which an older person has financial or material resources. A minority of privileged older persons have accumulated substantial wealth, while many more live in poverty. In Asia, more than 55 million older people live on less than US$1 per day (Help Age International, 2008c). Poverty among older persons results in 'multi-dimensional deprivation – hunger, under-nutrition, dirty drinking water, illiteracy, having no access to health services, social isolation, and exploitation' (Chronic Poverty Research Centre, 2005: 12). Cumulative disadvantages of poverty, disability, or poor educational attainment over the life course negatively impact the position of older persons in society; for example, in South Africa older people living in poverty were 2–3 times more likely to be illiterate compared to the non-poor (Chronic Poverty Research Centre, 2005). The impact of poverty on the well-being of older persons and the continuation of poverty in old age is therefore of considerable concern to social workers.

OLDER PERSONS IN A CHANGING SOCIETY: INTERNATIONAL CHALLENGES

Changing family structure and living environments

Dramatic changes in the global ageing population are an aspect of changes in family structure (see also Chapter 20). Due to the longer lifespan, many middle-aged family members are likely to have an older parent or relative living into old age. The Parent Support Ratio gives an estimate of the demands placed upon family members aged 50–64 from caregiving requirements of elders (over 85 years of age). Globally, the Parent Support Ratio is increasing, indicating that fewer family caregivers will be available for the growing older adult population. In 1950, there were less than two persons over 85 years of age per 100 carers between 50 and 64 years old; by 2000 the ratio doubled, and by 2050 it is expected to reach 11 persons over 85 per 100 carers (United Nations, 2002b). This is concerning, because families provide vital support to older people who may be subject to chronic illness, frailty, and physical or cognitive disabilities over an extended period. Family caregivers are often the primary providers of support services to older adults in developing countries where formal support systems are not available; but, families also provide the majority of elder-care in developed countries and help many older adults to avoid institutional placement.

Increased industrialisation and modernisation globally contribute to challenges in the provision of care across generations, but decreasing fertility rates leave fewer adult children available to assist with caregiving. Additionally, adult daughters are usually the caregivers for frail elders, and more women participate in the formal labour market in developed countries. Many women must balance paid work with caring for older adults, sometimes as well as caring for children or other relations. Modern expectations and employment opportunities can require geographic relocation of younger adults, leaving older adults in rural areas (with distance complicating care giving) or isolated in unfamiliar urban areas. Developed countries offer some support to family carers, including through labour market support policies (e.g. flexible work schedules and family leave policies); economic supports (e.g. salaries and tax credits for caregiving); and social services that provide instrumental and emotional support to reduce the stress of family caregiving (Hokenstad, 2006). However, these supports are largely absent in developing countries.

The multi-generational residence with older and younger family members living together has traditionally been an important practical as well as cultural arrangement that supported caregiving in developing countries, but recent trends include a move to nuclear households and more older adults living alone or with only a spouse (United Nations, 2005). An increase in solitary living among older adults contributes to social isolation and barriers to family caregiving. Overall, challenges to family care have increased while formal care systems continue to be limited (Cowgill, 1972; United Nations, 2005).

Alternatively, many older people contribute to their families by providing caregiving to younger generations. In developing countries with high rates of HIV/AIDS, increasing numbers of grandparents are becoming the primary caregivers for their grandchildren (when parents are deceased or sick). However, worldwide, grandparents may take over major child rearing responsibilities when a parent is absent (e.g. due to violence, incarceration or substance abuse) or to assist working parents.

In the developed world, the 'Ageing in Place' movement has emerged as a strategy to enable older people to live independently in old age. Only a very small percentage of older people live in institutional environments, and the majority of older people prefer to age in their lifelong homes. The 'Ageing in Place' movement has produced a number of policies and programmes to assist older

people with personal care and home maintenance services, including enhancements in home design and assistive technology to improve the functionality of the home for people with disabilities. Various types of retirement communities, including Naturally Occurring Retirement Communities and Continuing Care Retirement Communities are also part of this movement and accommodate different housing patterns and living arrangements while providing social, recreational, and healthcare services for older adults (Hokenstad, 2006).

Migration

An increasing number of older persons are migrating, most frequently to countries in Europe and North America. The United Nations (2002a) estimated that 15 percent of all international immigrants are aged 60 years and above. In circumstances of 'voluntary migration' (see also Chapter 6), older adults arrive in receiving countries in pursuit of improved social and economic well-being or to maintain close proximity to younger members of their family. Vulnerable older persons are often forced to move in response to financial insecurity, war or conflict, ethnic or religious discrimination, natural disasters, or poor environmental conditions.

While international conventions promote the rights of all refugees, the Age, Gender, and Diversity Mainstreaming Programme of the United Nations High Commissioner for Refugees (UNHCR) assists older persons to participate in planning for emergency response activities and safeguards access to basic services for elders (UNHCR, 2009).

Relocation within countries also affects older persons. In developing countries, migration of younger adults to urban areas in search of work has already been alluded to, with consequences for the older generation, whether they remain in rural areas or relocate. Forced relocation may also be necessary due to infrastructure projects such as dams flooding rural areas or natural disasters preventing return to a traditional settlement. Such situations may also impact on older people in developed countries but some may also have the resources to relocate voluntarily (for a variety of reasons), either within or between countries. Knowledge of trends in elective and forced migration among older persons is important for social workers in the field of international ageing.

OLDER PERSONS IN THE 21ST CENTURY: ISSUES AND ACTION

Negative images, ageism and discrimination

Although many traditional cultures have accorded respect to the older generation, ageism and discrimination against older people exist worldwide, not least in post-industrial societies driven by economic goals. Negative attitudes to older people contribute to societal practices that compromise their freedoms and basic human rights. As indicated, many older persons live in poverty; many are isolated and some have been denied access to healthcare, social support services, and jobs because of their age. Vital public health information and documentation to qualify for aid may be withheld from older persons or made difficult to access. For instance, older adults without access to the internet may be excluded from important information sharing and communication. Those who are able to obtain services may be treated disrespectfully.

Older persons in socially and economically disadvantaged groups may be particularly subject to discrimination; for instance, older immigrants or refugees may be excluded from social programmes and separated from other support networks. Recommendations to remedy social exclusion consist of advocating for universal rather than means-tested social welfare systems to ensure full and equal inclusion of all persons; affirming the role of the state in changing exclusionary practices; supporting social movements and community empowerment; improving the coordination of policies among diverse sectors; and involving agencies, donors, and the private sector to extend the protection of human rights (Social Exclusion Knowledge Network, 2008).

Additionally, a more balanced view of ageing is needed which recognises the valuable experience of older persons and their ongoing roles in family and civic life. Older adults are often portrayed as dependent, weak, and a burden, yet many make a meaningful contribution to society, culture, and economic prosperity. The positive aspects of ageing, including manifestations of resourcefulness and expertise, tend to be overshadowed by negative views that support ageism and discrimination. One goal of the United Nations Madrid International Plan of Action on Ageing (United Nations, 2002a) is to improve 'public opinion' in respect of older persons. Initiatives that counter negative beliefs about ageing include the World Health Organization's 'Active Ageing Programme' to raise awareness of the positive aspects of ageing. This includes the 'Positive Images Gallery' of older persons involved with work, volunteer roles, and leisure activities supported by the Australian government; and a 'Myth Busters' campaign sponsored by the Benjamin Rose Institute in the United States. Such initiatives recognise the achievements of men and women over 70 years of age who actively contribute to society. Similarly, WHO Europe (2006) is emphasising the positive concept of 'enablement' in order to increase the participation of older people in all aspects of society and raise awareness of opportunities for civic engagement, regardless of age.

Human rights issues

The Universal Declaration of Human Rights (United Nations, 1948) states in Article 1 that 'all human beings are born free and equal in dignity and rights'. (See also Chapter 4 and

Appendix 5.) Every individual, regardless of age, is entitled to freedom from discrimination and abuse. Globally, older persons suffer violations of human rights, including rights to personal safety, health, work, property ownership, access to information, and social security. Help Age International (2009a) has reported that older men and women face discrimination related to their age in addition to other personal characteristics (e.g. gender, ethnic origin, disability, poverty, sexuality, and literacy levels). These violations are disproportionately experienced by women and other socially and economically disadvantaged groups.

Millions of older persons worldwide experience chronic and extreme poverty due to employment discrimination and inadequate social security protections. Approximately 80 percent do not have pensions and depend on their ability to work or support from their families to provide for their basic needs in old age (United Nations, 2007). Many older workers in low- and middle-income countries struggle with very low wages or unpaid work, unstable work, poor working conditions, difficulty with accessing capital and credit, and exclusions from skill development programmes (Help Age International, 2010a).

Discriminatory inheritance laws also contribute to poverty in old age. In many parts of the world, laws prohibit older women from owning property or inheriting property after their husband dies. Women who attempt to retain their property in Kenya and Ghana fear the accusation of witchcraft which can lead to violent abuse and brutal killings. Human rights interventions in Africa have created programmes to increase literacy, provide access to entitlements, and educate widows about legal property rights and inheritance (Help Age International, 2008c; United Nations, 2002c).

Disadvantaged groups, such as older immigrants, face additional systematic barriers in accessing services available to other citizens. In response to the differential access and coverage of social protections for older immigrants, the Madrid International Plan of Action on Ageing (United Nations, 2002a) has called for receiving countries to encourage supportive social networks, provide assistance with achieving economic and health security, and develop policies that reflect the respectful inclusion of older migrants in the social, cultural, political, and economic aspects of society.

In addition to losses associated with old age, those who move to another country must also deal with the losses of culture, familiar communications, a more limited social/family network, and difficulties in accessing formal services. A study of Israeli immigrants from the former Soviet Union reported that these immigrants had fewer resources and a high need for services, yet they were also less likely to use social services after hospitalisation due to barriers related to information sharing (Auslander et al., 2005). Among older Chinese immigrants in Canada, a recent study found that a number of individual characteristics (e.g. being female and/or single, length of time in the country, and living in poverty) predicted the likelihood that an older person would experience a barrier in utilising healthcare services (Lai and Chau, 2007). Thus, the social work role includes identifying barriers, reaching out to vulnerable groups, and adapting interventions and services to allow for flexible and culturally appropriate services for diverse groups.

Social worker roles in the area of human rights include drawing attention to the multiple forms of discrimination and rights violations in old age, empowering older people to understand and protect their rights, influencing the development of anti-discriminatory laws, and improving national responses to population ageing.

Elder neglect and abuse

Elder abuse is a serious problem worldwide. The World Health Organisation (WHO) has defined elder abuse as 'any type of action, series of actions, or lack of actions, which produce physical or psychological harm, and which is set within a relationship of trust or dependence' (WHO, 2008: 81). An estimated 4 to 6 percent of older persons internationally have experienced physical, psychological, financial abuse, or neglect in their own home (WHO, 2002).

Changing family structures and living arrangements are altering patterns of care and influencing the incidence of abuse, neglect, and violence against older persons. WHO has identified a number of risk factors, including a weakening of bonds between generations in a family; the social isolation of the older person; and the societal depiction of older people as weak and dependent. Research suggests that certain characteristics of the victim or the perpetrator are associated with elder abuse, such as alcohol or substance use, mental health disorders, physical impairment, economic dependency, chronic stress, social isolation, or living in an overcrowded household (WHO, 2002). Physical and emotional abuse may also take place in alternative care settings such as hospitals or nursing homes. In residential settings, stressful work conditions, staff burnout, and staff who are poorly trained in managing challenging behaviours are all risk factors for elder abuse (Hawes, 2003).

In many countries, elder abuse has been widely regarded as a private, family matter rather than an illegal or violent act. The cultural understanding of elder abuse varies considerably according to the country and region, although the perpetrators of elder abuse are usually family members or spouses. A study in South Korea found that physical abuse is often initiated by a spouse and was estimated to affect one in five older couples (Kim and Sung, 2001). In India, adult children are nine times more likely to inflict elder abuse compared to spouses (Chokkanathan and Lee, 2005). Similarly, daughters-in-law in Japan, who are most likely to provide elder care, are the most likely to abuse older adults (Soeda and Araki, 1999; Tsukada et al., 2001). The dynamics of dependency in the

relationship between the victim and perpetrator may alter the form of abuse. For example, neglect involves the victim's dependence upon the perpetrator for caregiving assistance, while financial exploitation more often involves the perpetrator's dependence upon the victim (Hokenstad, 2006).

THE SOCIAL WORK RESPONSE: THREE PRIORITY DIRECTIONS FOR ACTION

At the United Nations Second World Assembly on Ageing, the Madrid International Plan of Action on Ageing (MIPAA) was adopted to provide the international community with a set of recommendations to promote the rights of older people, address the challenge of age discrimination, and improve the health and well-being of older persons. Three priority directions for action were identified. These include older adults and development, advancing health and well-being into old age, and ensuring enabling and supportive environments (United Nations, 2002a). Subsequently, the International Federation of Social Workers (IFSW) issued an International Policy on Ageing and Older Persons to explicate the priority areas of the MIPAA for social workers globally and articulate the role of the profession in addressing the current and emerging needs of older adults. According to the IFSW Policy statement, 'social workers are in a unique position to create, implement, and advocate for policies, programmes, services, and research benefiting older adults' (IFSW, 2009: 3) and are actively involved in advancing the three priority directions of the MIPAA.

OLDER ADULTS AND DEVELOPMENT

The IFSW (2009) statement affirmed the role of social work in supporting the full integration of older adults in society, including recognition of their social, economic, and intellectual contributions. Older adults are particularly at risk of poverty on leaving the labour market, and social workers can engage in policy advocacy to improve the economic well-being of older persons through national policies that promote equitable wages and decent working conditions for people of all ages. Strategies for policy advocacy to protect older workers in the formal and informal economy vary according to national conditions, but can include: implementing any age discrimination legislation; lobbying for flexible economic policies to incorporate older workers' skills and experience; facilitating education and training programmes for men and women; supporting the accessibility of micro-finance programmes for older persons; and supporting removal of age-based mandatory retirement legislation (Help Age International, 2010a: 5). In Peru, Bangladesh, and Uganda, human rights workers address issues of age discrimination in employment and gender inequality in compensation (Help Age International, 2009b). As part of a social development project in Bangladesh, social workers help reduce the physical, social and psychological barriers faced by older women wishing to borrow small amounts of start-up capital through the Grameen Bank (or other micro-credit schemes). The securing of micro credit to engage in less physically demanding work roles in income-generating micro-enterprise businesses contributes to the financial stability of the wider family unit (Help Age International, 2008a).

To alleviate poverty in old age, social workers also advocate for universal social pensions that provide an adequate standard of living. A recent report to the UN endorsed non-contributory social pensions in order to achieve social security in old age through reducing extreme poverty for older persons as well as their families (Help Age International, 2010b). Pensions empower older women and men by improving nutrition, household food security, health outcomes, and reducing chronic poverty for children and grandchildren (Help Age International, 2008c).

With a universal social pension, older people have an increased ability to participate in the economy through saving, investing, and creating jobs without risk of exclusion or stigma. Furthermore, universal social pensions support human rights obligations and provide a better alternative to targeted pension schemes that often exclude the poorest older people (Help Age International, 2010b). Recent positive progress in social pension plans for older people has occurred in Russia, Thailand, the Phillipines, Lesotho, and Kenya through expanding the amount of cash transfer or coverage (Help Age International, 2009a). In addition to being involved with the development of policies for improving income security, social workers also identify barriers that limit the distribution of benefits and provide information to older persons about entitlements. For example, social workers in Bolivia help older people to obtain birth certificates that are required in order to register for social pensions (Help Age International, 2008e).

Advancing health and well-being into old age

The IFSW affirms the WHO's definition of health, as 'a state of complete physical, mental and social well-being and not merely the absence of disease or infirmity' (WHO, 1948: 100). Since primary healthcare services have proved to be the best strategy to promote healthy ageing, social workers collaborate with medical professionals to support primary healthcare programmes providing treatment for a range of basic health conditions. Social workers often facilitate greater access to primary healthcare by coordinating public transportation and removing barriers in the physical environment that may prevent older persons from receiving care. For example, social workers at Help Age India connect rural communities with mobile medical units: these provide primary medical care to people who cannot see a doctor due to reduced mobility and poverty (Krishnaswamy et al., 2008). In Denmark, social workers make home visits to all citizens over 74 to promote health and prevent disease (Vass et al., 2007).

Within primary care settings, social workers help medical professionals to provide services that are both age-friendly and responsive to the needs of diverse groups of older adults. An example of this includes human rights workers in Indonesia who educate primary healthcare workers about the specific needs of older people, work to change ageist views, and promote capacity-building for staffing community-based health centres in order to respond to the chronic conditions common among older people (Help Age International, 2006a). Social workers also advocate for affordable and universal healthcare for older persons: the affordability of medical care remains a challenge in many parts of the world. In Tanzania, social workers involved with an older citizen's monitoring project empowered elders to discuss healthcare concerns with local leaders, resulting in the local government granting lifetime free medical treatment for vulnerable older people with severe health problems, disabilities, or older persons living alone (Help Age International, 2005b).

In addition to supporting physical health, social work expertise is instrumental in providing vital mental health services to older adults. As members of interdisciplinary community mental health teams, social workers in England provide mental health screenings and assessments, education and training to manage symptoms, and case management services (Tucker et al., 2007). Alzheimer's disease and other forms of dementia are a growing issue in the field of ageing. In 2010, an estimated 35.6 million persons worldwide were living with dementia with an estimated global cost of US$604 billion (Alzheimer's Disease International, 2010). It is estimated that the number of people with dementia will triple between 2010 and 2050, and the sharpest increase in numbers will take place in low- and middle-income countries (Alzheimer's Disease International, 2009). Social workers will be increasingly involved

in addressing the social and medical needs of people with cognitive disabilities as well as supporting their family members.

Understanding the diversity among different ethnic and cultural groups is a critical skill that social workers bring to the development of effective, accessible, and meaningful programmes to improve the well-being of older persons. In rural areas of developing countries, older adults may have difficulty accessing health and social services due to language barriers, limited availability of transportation, and discriminatory practices. For example, although older people in Ghana should have free healthcare, it is difficult to travel long distances to reach a medical clinic, and poor attitudes from healthcare workers towards older persons have been reported (Help Age International, 2007a). Negative attitudes towards older persons can result in longer waiting periods for hospital care or withholding available medical treatments and prescription drugs. Many older people in Latin America speak diverse native languages and some are illiterate, hindering information sharing, the ability to qualify for social protections, and the utilisation of healthcare and social services (Help Age International, 2007b). Social workers advocate for the inclusion of language translators in healthcare and social services; support greater accessibility of primary healthcare and supportive services for older persons in rural areas through mobile clinics; and educate healthcare providers to shape culturally sensitive services. Thus, social workers help to identify unmet needs among all members of the community and promote the inclusion of otherwise excluded groups.

Social workers in many countries are involved in education and advocacy efforts to promote active ageing and healthy living. Important lifestyle factors such as not smoking, eating a balanced diet, exercising regularly, limiting alcohol use, and being included in society are associated with better health in old age (WHO, 1998). Social workers in direct service roles and community-wide education campaigns draw upon the profession's value of self-determination to provide older persons with public service information to delay the onset of illness, disease, or disability. Social workers can help older people, individually or in groups, to develop self-management skills to make lifestyle changes that support their health.

Social workers also encourage and arrange civic engagement to promote active ageing. For example, older adults who volunteer with the neighborhood-based Enrique Gross Fraternal Association of Grandparents in Columbia operate a food bank, visit sick members of the community to deliver meals, and run a recycling business. They themselves derive many benefits from their volunteer roles including better nutrition, improved health, and enhanced feelings of self-worth (Help Age International, 2006b). In the US, a recent study found that African American women over 55 years old in the Experience Corps programme (a volunteer tutoring programme for children) reported long-term positive physical and mental health outcomes, including decreased depression, improved social networks, and a better quality of life (Tan et al., 2009).

Ensuring and enabling supportive environments

The UN priority area of ensuring and enabling supportive environments includes action to support family caregivers of older persons and to reduce elder abuse and neglect.

Support of family caregivers

Social workers can be important resources to family caregivers, who provide the majority of elder care around the world. In direct practice, social workers, particularly in wealthier countries, visit older adults and family caregivers to identify unmet needs and to coordinate care plans. For example, in Sweden they connect older persons and their family caregivers to a continuum of health and social services, such as home-delivered meals, transportation, and housing. On an individual basis, social workers provide education and counselling to caregivers aimed at preventing role conflicts, reducing feelings of burden, and strengthening stress management skills.

Other examples of clinical and case management roles exist in many other countries. Social workers involved with a cognitive-behavioural psychotherapeutic programme in Spain decreased caregivers' depression, anxiety, and burden (Lopez and Crespo, 2008). In Singapore, social workers facilitate family mediation to balance the needs of the primary family caregiver and the older person, lead educational workshops to help family carers manage stress, and advocate for additional community-based services (Mehta, 2006). In care management and medical settings, social workers assist older people with acute or chronic illnesses and involve family carers in training and support to provide higher levels of specialised care over longer periods. In Japan, specialised dementia training and counselling services are provided to family caregivers of older persons with early dementia (Nomura et al., 2009).

Social workers around the world also organise and empower older persons and their families to discuss their needs for healthcare, social services, and economic supports with policymakers and other community members in order to influence social policy. Integral to the process of facilitating community development activities, they have used their expertise to develop a range of services and supports for older persons and family members. Social workers with social development organisations support the leadership of older women who care for younger family members with HIV/AIDS through mutual support groups in Vietnam to increase access to treatment, improve their ability to earn an income, and influence policy changes at the national level (Help Age International, 2008b).

Elimination of elder abuse and neglect

Internationally, social workers play an important role in the effective response to elder abuse by improving understanding of the problem and how to address it; increasing awareness of the problem and established interventions; facilitating problem detection; preventing the problem and treating its consequences; and promoting change to affect better problem resolution (Podnieks et al., 2010). Social workers in case management roles require cultural sensitivity to assess elder abuse and neglect problems within diverse contexts and relationships. For example, in South Africa, social workers are involved in an anonymous national hotline (the Halt Elder Abuse Line, HEAL) to provide counselling, referrals, and follow-up home visits (Marais et al., 2006). After a problem has been identified, social workers provide a variety of services, including shelters, caregiver respite, counselling, emergency funds, legal assistance, case management, witness assistance programmes, mental health assessments, support services, and guardianship services (Nerenberg, 2006). In the US, adult protective system social workers perform psychosocial assessments of the victim and his or her support network, question the victim, report suspected cases of abuse, provide immediate and follow-up counselling, and make referrals to hotlines and other community resources (Society for Social Work Leadership in Health Care, 2010).

Social workers also lend their expertise to educate older persons about their rights, and work with law enforcement and medical professionals to recognise and protect elders from abuse. For example, staff with Help Age Ghana increased awareness of abuse through advocacy materials, human rights education, and arranging legal assistance for older persons (Help Age International, 2007a). Some developed countries, such as Argentina, Canada, Sweden, the United Kingdom, and the United States, have established legal and social service systems to report perpetrators of elder abuse and to provide treatment to victims. The majority of nations in Latin America and the Caribbean have legislation in place to protect older persons from abuse and neglect, but systems of action and enforcement are in need of strengthening (WHO, 2002). However, some countries do not have laws against elder abuse, and many do not have programmes to address the problem (Podnieks et al., 2010).

Several international non-governmental organisations with social work staff focus on raising awareness of the issue of elder abuse. The International Network for the Prevention of Elder Abuse (INPEA) established the first World Elder Abuse Awareness Day on 15 June 2006. In partnership with WHO, the INPEA has started an international study of defining elder abuse to inform prevention and response programmes. WHO is also providing international leadership in identifying the risk factors and recommending responses to elder abuse. Over the last decade, the amount of research on the causes, nature, extent, and consequences of all forms of violence against older women and men has increased.

CONCLUDING COMMENTS: FUTURE DIRECTIONS FOR SOCIAL WORK IN AN AGEING WORLD

Population ageing and individual longevity provide increasing challenges and opportunities for social work in the coming decades. At the same time, as the IFSW Policy Statement (2009) points out, social workers have the opportunity to collaborate with older adults in developing 'ageing friendly' programmes, and providing culturally competent services to this population. Increased emphasis on 'ageing' in social work practice, education, and research are required to meet these challenges and opportunities.

Social work practice will have an ongoing focus on the UN priority directions of older adults and development; advancing health and well-being into old age; and ensuring enabling and supportive environments, with particular emphasis on caregiver support and anti-elder abuse programmes. In the developing world, social work will give continuous attention to the social isolation and exclusion of older people due to modernisation and the movement of younger family members from the countryside to the city. This requires a social development focus including micro-enterprise opportunities for older people. In the developed world emphasis will be given to providing services and support to caregivers of older people as well as seniors themselves. Case assessment and care management knowledge and skills will be particularly important in direct service social work with the growing senior population (Hokenstad, 2006).

The increased demand for services to ageing populations will require an increase in social workers with specialised education in social gerontology. In some countries the profession is already giving attention to the recruitment of more students and practitioners for this specialty area of practice, but the number of specialists available lags considerably behind the need (Whitaker et al., 2006). In addition, social workers practising in health, mental health, and family services will require increased knowledge about older people and skills in working with them. Thus, social work education faces a continuing challenge of providing both basic and advanced training for social workers in the field of ageing.

Effective service delivery to the growing older population, globally, will require increased knowledge of the environmental context in which older people live and an improved understanding of the different stages in the ageing process. Social work research in the field of elder care should include a focus on the social environment with studies on the interactions between formal and informal support systems. Further attention also needs to be paid to programme evaluation with particular emphasis on service coordination and accessibility. Research studies with the goal of improving needs assessment for older people in health, mental health, and social settings are also needed in order to maximise independent living and provide appropriate services for home- and community-based care. Finally, additional research is needed to evaluate practice interventions in social gerontology. Along with more focused social work practice and more specialised social work education, such an improved knowledge base will help the profession to better serve older people in the 21st century.

NOTES

1 The old age support ratio compares the number of workers age 15–64 to the number of adults 65 and older in order to determine demographic and economic trends that can predict the solvency of social security systems as well as the collective ability of younger workers to provide financial support to older family members. A greater old-age support ratio (indicating a larger number of potential workers to older adults) is economically desirable.

2 Social exclusion is defined as 'a dynamic, multi-dimensional process driven by unequal power relationships interacting across four main dimensions – economic, political, social and cultural – and at different levels including individual, household, group, community, country, and global levels' (Social Exclusion Knowledge Network, 2008: 2).

REFERENCES

Alzheimer's Disease International (2009) *World Alzheimer's Report 2009*. Retrieved from http://www.alz.co.uk/research/files/WorldAlzheimerReport.pdf.

Alzheimer's Disease International (2010) *World Alzheimer's Report 2010*. Retrieved from http://www.alz.co.uk/research/files/WorldAlzheimerReport2010.pdf.

Auslander, G.K., Soskolne, V. and Ben-Shahar, I. (2005) 'Utilization of health social work services by older immigrants and veterans in Israel', *Health & Social Work*, 30 (3): 241–51.

Chokkanathan, S. and Lee, A.E.Y. (2005) 'Elder mistreatment in urban India: A community based study', *Journal of Elder Abuse & Neglect*, 17 (2): 45–61.

Chronic Poverty Research Centre (2005) *The Chronic Poverty Report: 2004–2005*. Retrieved from http://www.chronicpoverty.org/uploads/publication_files/CPR1_ReportFull.pdf.

Cowgill, D.O. (1972) 'A theory of aging in cross-cultural perspective', in D.O. Cowgill and L.D. Holmes (eds), *Aging and Modernization*. New York: Appleton-Century-Cofts.

Hawes, C. (2003) 'Elder abuse in residential long-term care settings', in R.J. Bonnie and R.B. Wallace (eds), *Elder Mistreatment: Abuse, Neglect, and Exploitation in an Aging America*. Washington, DC: The National Academies Press.

Help Age International (2005a) *Millennium Development Goals Must Target Poorest, say Older People*. Retrieved from http://www.globalaging.org/elderrights/world/2005/mdgs.htm.

Help Age International (2005b) *Older Persons Monitoring in Tanzania*. Retrieved from www.helpage.org/download/4ece3d5fbfb6e.

Help Age International (2006a) *Age-friendly Community Health Services in Aceh, Indonesia*. Retrieved from http://reliefweb.int/node/222225.

Help Age International (2006b) *Active Ageing in Columbia*. Retrieved from http://helpage.org.

Help Age International (2007a) *Addressing the Abuse of Older People in Ghana*. Retrieved from http://helpage.org.

Help Age International (2007b) *Age Demands Action in Latin America: Progress on Implementation of the Madrid International Plan of Action on Ageing (MIPAA)*. Retrieved from http://www.helpage.org/what-we-do/rights/the-madrid-plan-mipaa/.

Help Age International (2008a) *Older People and Micro-credit: Bangladesh Experience*. Retrieved from http://www.docstoc.com/docs/36484307/Older-people-and-micro-credit.

Help Age International (2008b) 'Empathy clubs for older people affected by HIV and AIDS', *Ageways*, 71, 13–14.

Help Age International (2008c) *Poverty, Work and Pensions*. Retrieved from http://www.helpage.org/what-we-do/work/

Help Age International (2008d) *Older People in Africa: A Forgotten Generation*. Retrieved from http://eng.zivot90.cz/uploads/document/205.pdf

Help Age International (2008e) *Social Pensions in Bolivia*. Retrieved from http://www.globalaging.org/pension/world/2008/pensionsbolivia.htm.

Help Age International (2009a) *The Ageing and Development Report: A Summary*. Retrieved from www.helpage.org/download/4c461a5bf010d/.

Help Age International (2009b) *Older Women's Rights*. Retrieved from http://www.helpage.org/what-we-do/rights/.

Help Age International (2010a) *Forgotten Workforce: Older People and their Right to Decent Work*. Retrieved from http://www.helpage.org/what-we-do/work/forgotten-workforce-older-people-and-their-right-to-decent-work/.

Help Age International (2010b) 'Pensions "critical to rights"'. *Ageing & Development*, 28: 1–2.

IFSW (International Federation of Social Workers) (2009) *International Policy on Ageing and Older Persons*. Retrieved from http://www.ifsw.org/p38000214.html

Kim, J.Y. and Sung, K.T. (2001) 'Marital violence among Korean elderly couples: a cultural residue', *Journal of Elder Abuse & Neglect*, 13 (4): 73.

Krishnaswamy, B., Than Sein, U., Munodawafa, D., Varghese, C., Venkataraman, K. and Anand, L. (2008) 'Ageing in India', *Ageing International*, 32 (4): 258–68.

Lai, D.W. and Chau, S.B.Y. (2007) 'Predictors of health service barriers for older Chinese immigrants in Canada, *Health & Social Work*, 32 (1): 57–65.

Lopez, J. and Crespo, M. (2008) 'Analysis of the efficacy of a psychotherapeutic program to improve the emotional status of caregivers of elderly dependent relatives', *Aging & Mental Health*, 12 (4): 451–61.

Marias, S., Conradie, G. and Kritzinger, A. (2006) 'Risk factors for elder abuse and neglect: Brief descriptions of different scenarios in South Africa', *International Journal for Older People Nursing*, 1 (3): 186–9.

Mehta, K.K. (2006) 'A critical review of Singapore's policies aimed at supporting families caring for older members', *Journal of Aging & Social Policy*, 18 (3/4): 43–57.

Nerenberg, L. (2006) 'Communities respond to elder abuse', *Journal of Gerontological Social Work*, 46 (3/4): 5–33.

Nomura, M., Makimoto, K., Kato, M., Shiba, T., Matsuura, C., Shigenobu, K., Ishikawa, T., Matsumoto, N. and Ikeda, M. (2009) 'Empowering older people with early dementia and family caregivers: a participatory action research study', *International Journal of Nursing Studies*, 46 (4): 431–41.

Podnieks, E., Anetzberger, G.J., Wilson, S.J., Teaster, P.B. and Wangmo, T. (2010) 'World view scan of elder abuse', *Journal of Elder Abuse and Neglect*, 22 (1/2): 164–79.

Social Exclusion Knowledge Network (2008) *Understanding and Tackling Social Exclusion*. Retrieved from the World Health Organization Commission on Social Determinants of Health website: http://www.who.int/social_determinants/knowledge_networks/final_reports/sekn_final%20report_042008.pdf.

Society for Social Work Leadership in Health Care (2010) *Elder Abuse/Neglect Standard of Care*. Retrieved from http://www.sswlhc.org/html/standards-elderly.php.

Soeda, A. and Araki, C. (1999) 'Elder abuse by daughters-in-law in Japan', *Journal of Elder Abuse & Neglect*, 11 (1): 47.

Tan, E.J., Rebok, G.W., Qilu, Y., Frangakis, C.E., Carlson, M.C., Tao, W., Ricks, M., Tanner E., McGill, S. and Fried, L. (2009) 'The long-term relationship between high-intensity volunteering and physical activity in older African American women', *Journals of Gerontology Series B: Psychological Sciences & Social Sciences*, 64B (2): 304–11.

Tsukada, N., Saito, Y. and Tatara, T. (2001) 'Japanese older people's perceptions of "elder abuse"', *Journal of Elder Abuse & Neglect*, 13 (1): 71.

Tucker, S., Baldwin, R., Hughes, J., Benbow, S., Barker, A., Burns, A. and Challis, D. (2007) 'Old age mental health services in England: Implementing the National Service Framework for Older People', *International Journal of Geriatric Psychiatry*, 22 (3): 211–17.

UNAIDS (2008) *Sub-Saharan Africa*. Retrieved from http://www.unaids.org/en/CountryResponses/Regions/SubSaharanAfrica.asp.

UNHCR (United Nations High Commissioner for Refugees) (2009) *Global Report 2009*. Retrieved from http://www.unhcr.org/pages/49c3646c4b8.html.

United Nations (1948) *Universal Declaration of Human Rights*. Adopted and proclaimed by General Assembly resolution 217 A (III) of 10 December 11948. Retrieved from http://www.un.org/events/humanrights/2008/hrphotos/declaration%20_eng.pdf.

United Nations (2002a) *Report of the Second World Assembly on Ageing, Madrid, 8–12 April 2002*. Retrieved from http://www.c-fam.org/docLib/20080625_Madrid_Ageing_Conference.pdf

United Nations (2002b) *World Population Ageing: 1950–2050*. Department of Economic and Social Affairs, Population Division. Retrieved from http://www.un.org/esa/population/publications/worldageing19502050/.

United Nations (2002c) *Abuse of Older Persons: Recognising and Responding to Abuse in a Global Context*. New York: United Nations Press.

United Nations (2005) *Living Arrangements of Older Persons around the World*. Department of Economic and Social Affairs, Population Division. Retrieved from http://www.un.org/esa/population/publications/livingarrangement/report.htm.

United Nations (2006) *Population Ageing* (UN Publication No. ST/ESA/SER.A/251). Department of Economic and Social Affairs, Population Division. Retrieved from http://www.un.org/esa/population/publications/ageing/ageing2006.htm.

United Nations (2007) *World Economic and Social Survey 2007: Development in an Ageing World – 60th Anniversary Edition, 1948–2007*. New York: United Nations.

United Nations (2008a) *Ageing and Development*, in R. Vos, J.A. Oscampo and A.L. Cortez (eds). New York: United Nations.

United Nations (2008b) *The World Population Prospects: The 2008 Revision Population Database*. Department of Economic and Social Affairs, Population Division. Retrieved from http://esa.un.org/unpd/wpp/unpp/panel_population.htm.

United Nations (2009) *Population Ageing and Development 2009* (UN Publication No. 09-59532). Department of Economic and Social Affairs, Population Division. Retrieved from http://www.un.org/esa/population/publications/WPA2009/WPA2009_WorkingPaper.pdf

Vass, M., Avlund, K. and Hendriksen, C. (2007) 'Randomized intervention trial on preventative home visits to older people: Baseline and follow-up characteristics of participants and non-participants', *Scandinavian Journal of Public Health*, 35: 410–17.

Whitaker, T., Weismiller, T. and Clark, E. (2006) *Assuring the Sufficiency of a Frontline Workforce: A National Study of Licensed Social Workers. Executive Summary*. Washington DC: NASW Press.

WHO (World Health Organization) (1948) *Preamble to the Constitution of the World Health Organization*. International Health Conference, New York, 19–22 June 1946.

WHO (World Health Organization) (1998) *Health Promotion Glossary*. Retrieved from http://www.who.int/hpr/NPH/docs/hp_glossary_en.pdf.

WHO (World Health Organization) (2002) *World Report on Violence and Health: Abuse of the Elderly*. Retrieved from http://whqlibdoc.who.int/publications/2002/9241545615_chap5_eng.pdf.

WHO (World Health Organization) (2008) *A Global Response to Elder Abuse and Neglect: Building Primary Health Care Capacity to Deal with the Problem Worldwide: Main Report*. Retrieved from http://www.who.int/ageing/publications/ELDER_DocAugust08.pdf.

WHO Europe (World Health Organization Europe) (2006) *Active Ageing*. Retrieved from www.euro.who.int/ageing.

Regional Perspectives

Manohar Pawar

INTRODUCTION TO SECTION 5: REGIONAL PERSPECTIVES

The last section of this handbook presents regional perspectives from around the world. Although there is a substantial consensus that social work is a global profession, it is mostly rooted in the local. Local unique features of social work education and practice make it challenging and complex to understand the profession at a global level as a universal and all-encompassing entity – which it is not. In an interdependent world, a global perspective may be necessary, and it does provide a synoptic picture. However, it is further necessary to focus on particular aspects of that picture and enlarge them for better understanding. In this final section we shift the focus from a global social work picture to seven regions and a few countries within each of these. The regions discussed are Africa; South and East Asia; Australasia and the Pacific islands; Europe; the Middle East; Latin America; and North America and the Caribbean.

The regional analysis of social work shows that social work has taken root in various countries and is evolving according to their unique socio-economic and political contexts and stages of development. In Chapter 24 Mwansa and Kreitzer discuss social work in Africa in the light of the impact of colonialism and modernisation on African people, culture, polity, economy, conflicts and wars; entrenched poverty levels; and related problems (e.g. low levels of health and education). Not only have Western social work education models greatly influenced social work education patterns, but these have also intersected with racially discriminatory connotations. Although the origins of the profession in Africa date from the 1920s, it has since had a chequered history and uneven spread across 54 countries (including the case examples of Ghana, Mali, Ethiopia and South Africa). Major challenges facing social work in Africa now include racism and oppression; poverty and poor health; the impact of neo-liberal policies; developing professional associations; moving from Western-centric curricula to Afrocentric ones; and implementing a social development approach.

Southern and Eastern Asia is equally diverse and contrasting. In Chapter 25 Pawar with Tsui include a focus on the extent to which social work has developed national associations and whether (or not) these are linked to regional and international bodies, social work education models, practice patterns and research. While they give examples from a range of countries of developments and issues in social work and education, particular attention is paid to India and China. This partly reflects the political and economic power of these two countries in the region but also the challenges for social work, whether it is a long established or relatively recent form of professional activity. Although social work is new and not well resourced in some of the smaller countries in Southeast Asia, there are strong signs of development of indigenous research and challenges to the hegemony of the West from this region as a whole. However, the region generally also needs to localise social work education and practice, apply a developmental perspective and promote relevant quality standards and ethics.

The depiction of the Australasia region by Beddoe and Fraser (Chapter 26) shows the uneven and different developments in social work in Australia and New Zealand relative to the island nations of the Southwest Pacific. In the first two countries Anglo-American traditions of social work largely took root, with more recent development of critical approaches, while in the Pacific islands there has been relatively more attention to community development. In both Australia and New Zealand there are relatively well established professional associations (as well as more recently developed separate associations for social workers from the original/ Indigenous populations) and mechanisms exist for regulation of the profession. There is some reference to social worker mobility both within and outside the region and there are strong links with the international professional bodies. In contrast, social workers in the South Pacific islands may be isolated, despite facing similar challenges (e.g. struggling economies, poverty, civil war and natural disasters): such problems call for developments in social work education and practice, which to date have been limited.

In Chapter 27 Zaviršek and Lawrence introduce the European region and discuss both the origins of social work and current challenges and developments in a region which contains a high level of diversity (including of language) across nearly 50 nations. Although professional social work originated in Europe over one hundred years ago, its history and current status varies between European countries. It faces significant challenges as, on the one hand, minority populations face discrimination on the basis of race, gender, class and geographic movements, while on the other, welfare services are declining. The European Union is currently an important mechanism for pushing 27 nation states towards harmonisation, for example, in higher education awards. Despite this – and a rich (ongoing) experience of 'links and exchanges' within the region – there is no common recognition of social work qualifications. However, there are shared social concerns and the region has seen important developments (e.g. in the spread of anti-oppressive values and practices and in social work research) at the same time as the threat to the fundamental principles of social work appears to be increasing.

The discussion of social work in the Middle East provides an entirely different, mixed and challenging context. In Chapter 28 Al-Makhamreh and Libal suggest that despite high income levels (many countries have a developed status), economic status has not kept the region peaceful and free from major social problems emanating mainly from ongoing conflicts, war and post-conflict situations, with associated displacement, ethnic minorities and religion-based groupings, gendered practices, and changing demographic profiles. The authors consider the current status of social work in the Middle East, here taken as covering 16 countries, with case examples from Egypt, Israel, Jordan and Turkey. Although the Middle East has considerable global significance in geo-political and economic terms, this is not reflected in the development of social work, notwithstanding its presence in some countries for nearly a hundred years. Besides conveying some of the complexities, diversity and inequalities of the region, the authors also illustrate the efforts being made to develop forms of social work that are in tune with the needs and cultural traditions of individual countries.

Like many other regions, Latin America is very diverse and heterogeneous. Saracostti, Reininger and Parada in Chapter 29 argue that, despite having better income levels and natural resources than some regions, the region is experiencing growing poverty and inequality; vulnerability among children, women and older people; and privatisation alongside weaker welfare systems. Although social work was introduced in Latin America (under colonial influence) in the 1920s, it has periodically been significantly hampered due to prevailing socio-political-economic conditions and its development can be categorised into four phases: consolidation of the profession; the reconceptualisation movement; the role of dictatorships; and the return of democracy. Core issues for social work in most countries are the poverty and marginalisation of the majority of the population; and a concern that international, neo-liberal interventions have tended to destabilise and undermine national attempts to develop viable income support and welfare systems. Social work as a discipline itself is marginalised and debates continue in some countries about the extent to which social work should be theoretical or practical and be a more politicised activity, including resisting influences from the global North.

Finally, Watkins and Holder Dolly in Chapter 30 provide a North American and Caribbean regional perspective. The Caribbean islands context is quite different from those of the USA and Canada but the authors succinctly discuss the basic geographic and socio-economic profiles of the region, historical perspectives, and contemporary trends and challenges for social work education and practice. All the countries share different aspects of a colonial history but have subsequently developed differently. Social work in the USA is extensively developed and well regulated: it has the biggest professional body and the largest number of social work schools in the world. Social work in the USA, rather than focusing on poverty and unemployment issues, has significantly embraced private practice, notwithstanding the employment of many social workers in the public sector and NGOs. Social work systems and practices in Canada show some variations from American models, not least related to the country's different political leanings and welfare traditions. The socioeconomic situation of the Caribbean islands is markedly different (and their histories are varied) resulting in other differences in the development of social work.

The USA's contribution to the social work profession and knowledge within the region and beyond needs particular attention and (although the authors do not make this point) it is important to acknowledge the USA's role in social work globally. The USA has been a major creator and transmitter of social work knowledge internationally (it has played a significant role in the establishment of social work schools, training of social work educators and supply of textbooks), but in this act of 'helping' it has sometimes also prevented the emergence of indigenous social work, contributing to some of the tensions inherent in the very notion of international social work. However, some US academics have also contributed to our greater appreciation of power imbalances and the potential dangers of indiscriminate knowledge transfer.

These selective regional pictures by different authors provide 'snapshots' of social work around the world. The coverage is not comprehensive; particularities will change over time and others might have different perceptions. However, the chapters provide important insights into the different regions and complement material presented in the preceding sections. They provide a fascinating picture of the challenges faced by social workers around the world and also the richness and diversity of social work when considered from an international perspective. Despite the many differences there are also common themes, including poverty, diversity and inequalities. The blurring of the delineation of the North and South regions suggests that we need to change the status quo of the 'creator/ exporter' and 'borrower and importer' (often from North to South) to a new order of mutual sharers and learners in one interdependent world.

24

Social Work in Africa

Lengwe-Katembula J. Mwansa
and Linda Kreitzer

INTRODUCTION

The social work profession has a dream, a belief and a hope for the millions of people in the world. As a professional activity and creative enterprise in human service, social work remains committed to the promotion of social justice and human rights, focusing specifically on marginalised and disadvantaged people. It has a futuristic vision and mission to make a difference in people's lives by mediating between them and their environment (Ambrosino et al., 2005; Maluccio et al., 2002; Mullaly, 1997). However, in a rapidly changing and globalising environment, it has become increasingly important to give meaning to the profession's guiding standards and principles in relation to the specific needs of people in different countries and regions of the world. This chapter intends to share an overview of social work in the African continent in terms of the socio-political-economic situation, characteristics of social work education and core practice issues that influence social work practice. It is hoped that it will stimulate debate for the purpose of defining the terrain of the social work profession in Africa.

PRE-COLONIAL AFRICA

Africa, in general, had a long-standing tradition of social support systems even before the advent of modern social welfare and social work practice. In Botswana's pre-colonial times, for example, there were structures in place that dealt with the welfare of families and the communities at large. According to Hedenquist (1991) the chiefs, the villages (communities) and the extended families provided for and handled material, cultural, social and spiritual needs of its members. Communities were organised in such a way that social issues could be dealt with when the need arose – for instance, the upbringing of children and the inculcation of societal values and customs were the responsibility of the members of the extended family. The value of helping those who were in need was regarded as a responsibility of the communities, such that during the pre-colonial times it was customary for those who were well off to assist the poor (Hedenquist, 1991; Apt and Blavo, 1997). All this changed when European powers dominated Africa through colonialism.

COLONIALISM AND AFRICA

A great deal has been written about colonialism and how it has disrupted the fabric of the African continent (Fanon, 1961; Memmi, 1965), creating conditions that foster enmity between ethnic groups, leading to wars (Caselli, 2006) and the quagmire of underdevelopment. Unlike the tribal wars of the past, the colonisers used what Freire (2000) calls 'tactics of oppression' to subjugate Africans. Through manipulation, divide-and-rule and cultural invasion African people became a silenced people. For example, a favourite ploy was to incite jealousy and envy by showing favour to some and not to others and by arbitrarily installing chiefs who were manipulated to oppress and suppress other ethnic groupings. This sowed seeds of bitterness and anger directly into the foundation of many future nations and set the stage for intra- and inter-national conflict. In addition to separating indigenous ethnic groups, inter-tribal interactions were discouraged, creating prejudices and fostering tribalistic attitudes based on incorrect perceptions of others. Another poignant example of this strategy was the apartheid regime in South Africa that fortunately came to an end in 1994 (Guest, 2004; Onyeani, 1990). Finally, the most deadly influence was cultural invasion whereby the invader succeeds in convincing the society invaded of their intrinsic inferiority.

When independence came to African countries there was great hope for national unity and a common identity for the continent. This fairytale aspiration was short-lived in many parts of the continent in the face of realities. A very unfortunate consequence of this history that became a dominant truth was that the prejudices created and exploited did not disappear overnight, but continued to be a bone of contention both within and among the newly formed nations. A good example of this is the genocide in Rwanda (Des Forges, 1999; Wallimann et al., 2000).

Not only was the psyche of African people affected by colonisation, but a new form of colonialism emerged following independence in many countries – that of economic colonisation (Guest, 2004). The impact of the (neo-liberal) structural adjustment programme (SAP) fuelled the move of the already declining economies into negative growth. With harsh economic hardship biting, old prejudices resurfaced and ethnic battle lines were drawn. Ideas such as national unity, or a common identity were dismissed and there was a mad scramble to gain as many resources, through whatever means possible. Corruption set in and the rule of law broke down, engendering instability spreading across the continent; and at the root of the political instability was conflict, corruption, tribalism and xenophobia.

Long periods of political instability caused a complete lack of development in some countries, while in others economies became stagnant, leading to regression of developmental milestones, and subsequent widespread poverty. This poverty drove the cycle of conflict, further aggravating the poverty and having devastating effects on health, causing infrastructure to further deteriorate, and increasing human migration away from troubled regions. One of the legacies of human migration is the so-called 'brain drain' of highly skilled professionals migrating to the West in search of greener pastures, leaving behind them a large void in many sectors, most notably health and education.

DESCRIPTION OF THE REGION

In 1995 the population of Africa was 719 million, with projected estimated annual rates of growth of 2.37 percent for 1995–2000; 2.21 percent for 2000–2005; and 1.79

percent for 2020–2025. These rates were significantly higher than those for total global growth, which was estimated at 1.37 percent for 1995–2000; 1.20 percent for 2000–2005; and 0.84 percent for 2020–2025 (Heaps et al., 1999; Cohen and Malin, 2009). Notably, the population below 14 years of age was 44 percent in 1995 while the population above 65 years of age was 3.2 percent and, according to Bulatao and Lee (1983), is forecast to grow to 4.2 percent by 2025. This indicates that the economically active population of the continent has to shoulder a weightier burden than in other regions.

Today, the region is faced with unique challenges, such as highly disparate socio-economic development, widespread and complex conflicts and wars, large-scale poverty, orphanhood, domestic violence, endemic corruption, and a ravaging HIV and AIDS epidemic. However, in examining these challenges, caution must be exercised to realise the diversity of the African continent, extending beyond some of the more frequently reported countries such as Kenya, Somalia, Uganda or South Africa. A simple fact that is easily forgotten, even among scholars of international reputation, is that the continent of Africa contains 54 countries with multitudes of cultures, religious and traditional beliefs, socio-political and historical developments, but in most cases with common colonial historical heritages. Nwoye (2004) notes that Africa consists of a variety of nations distinguished by their 'lingua franca' of a colonial heritage, and which include English-, French-, Spanish-, Portuguese-, Arabic-speaking, and multi-lingual countries as a result of the partition of Africa in 1885 at the Congress of Berlin.

The misconception or misrepresentation of Africa's diversity has led to proposed solutions based on Western models of a dubious nature that have no merits or relevance to the socio-economic problems of the continent (Padayachee, 2010). The situation has continued to deteriorate steadily. The SAP approach was that of 'one size fits all' with disastrous consequences as evidenced by widespread economic hardships, massive unemployment created by privatisation of the parastatals, currency devaluation, and a drop in the general standard of living across the continent. Added to these hardships are demographic as well as health, education and poverty issues that affect Africa.

Health

Africa is beset with numerous debilitating health problems including HIV and AIDS, malaria, tuberculosis, hepatitis and malnutrition, which are all fuelled by poverty. The AIDS pandemic is perhaps the gravest of the many crises Africa faces in this millennium. Despite all the efforts directed towards prevention, HIV and AIDS remains a serious threat to development on the continent. According to the UNAIDS (2009), of the 38.6 million people living with HIV and AIDS worldwide, 70 percent of adults and 80 percent of children are in Africa. During 2008 and 2009 about 1.4 million and 1.3 million people respectively died from AIDS in sub-Saharan Africa. More than 14 million children have so far lost one or both parents to AIDS. However, although the epidemic seems to be levelling off in many countries of sub-Saharan Africa, the epicentre of the epidemic has shifted from central and eastern regions to the countries of Southern Africa. In Somalia and Senegal the HIV prevalence is under 1 percent of the adult population, whereas in Namibia, South Africa, Zambia and Zimbabwe around 15–20 percent of adults are infected with HIV. In three southern African countries, the national adult HIV prevalence rate now exceeds 20 percent. These countries are Botswana (23.9 percent), Lesotho (23.2 percent) and Swaziland (26.1 percent) (UNAIDS, 2008). Malawi, Namibia, South Africa, Swaziland, Zambia and Zimbabwe have prevalence levels well above 26 percent among those in the prime of their lives aged between 15–49 years (UNAIDS, 2008). The epidemic has taken its toll on these countries through unprecedented levels of morbidity and mortality, robbing them of productive human resources which they can ill afford to lose. The healthcare systems of these countries are barely coping with the burden of care created by the epidemic. This has been compounded by the declining economic status of most African countries which has made providing for healthcare in general (out of the meagre resources left over from other national priorities) virtually impossible.

The social and economic consequences are yet to be fully appreciated but are already widely felt at the personal, family and societal levels. What is most clear is that the epidemic has seriously reversed development gains made over decades in African countries. Life expectancy in Africa has decreased to become the lowest of all regions, currently at about 47 years instead of 62 years without AIDS (Sparks, 2002; Anderson and Maher, 2001; Bollinger and Stover, 1999). Many families have lost their bread-winners and cannot afford food or fees for medical care.

Education

Education is a socialising mechanism for a productive life for the young people throughout the world, and so it is in Africa. In most African countries, education has been seen as a vehicle for social mobility and a change in values. However, participation rates in many African countries are low. Schools often lack many basic amenities to facilitate learning and suffer from chronic overcrowding and poor resource availability. But most notable is the problem of out-of-school children in sub-Saharan Africa which sharply contrasts with other regions of the world. For example, only 0.5 percent of children are out of school in countries such as Japan, Malaysia, Spain, Uruguay and Uzbekistan. In comparison, half or more children in sub-Saharan Africa are not in school in countries such as Somalia (77 percent), Chad (64 percent), Niger (62 percent), Liberia (61 percent) and Ethiopia (55 percent) (Huebler, 2009).

According to UNICEF (2008) 93 million children worldwide were estimated to be out of school with the majority being found in sub-Saharan Africa. Of course it is notable that there has been some significant progress with a 13 percent increase in the net enrolment rate from 57 percent in 1999 to 70 percent in 2005. However, there remains a great deal to be done to increase the net enrolment rate to ensure universal education for children. Currently, three out of 10 children of primary school age do not go to school (Huebler, 2007). Based on this report, it is quite evident that the Millennium Development Goal of Universal Education may not be tenable for millions of children in many countries of sub-Saharan Africa by the year 2015. The lack of education for several millions of children creates a bleak future for poverty reduction and general social development in Africa. In other words, poverty, with all its attendant evils, will continue to suck in more and more people. While poverty is decreasing in other parts of the world, sub-Saharan Africa will experience an increase in the numbers of people living in poverty.

Conflict situations

The Democratic Republic of Congo has recently suspended mining activities in the eastern part of the country due to civil violence. The ever-existing tension between Ethiopia and Eritrea continues to impose a severe drain on opportunities for development in the two countries. Sudan and Somalia are virtual war zones leading to internal displacement, wanton loss of human life, and human suffering of catastrophic proportions. As always, women and children have borne the brunt of the suffering. Northern Uganda is still reeling from civil conflict waged by the Lord's Resistance Army for years on end, and here again, many women and girls are victims of rape and kidnapping to become sex slaves while many boys are turned into child soldiers. Madagascar, Ivory Coast and Guinea have yet to find some semblance of peace, as does Zimbabwe where flagrant human rights violations are openly perpetrated by the regime. Apart from in a few countries, most elections in Africa are a sham. Corruption goes on unabated to become the order of business. It is difficult to remain positive with regard to human development opportunities on the continent, and thus for social workers employing a strengths-based approach remains a challenge.

Poverty

In Africa, poverty is the underlying factor contributing to health issues, corruption and slow development. A child dies every three seconds from AIDS in Africa, and one in six children on the continent dies before the age of five. Most of these deaths could be prevented (UNICEF, 2008). Of the world's 50 poorest countries, 33 are found in Africa with more than 800 million people going to bed hungry every day (UNDP, 2009). Whereas 1.4 billion people in the developing countries lived on US$1.25 a day in 2005 (a decrease from 1.9 billion in 1981), the majority of people in sub-Saharan Africa live on less than US$1.25 a day. Poverty continues to suck in more today than was the case at independence of most countries in sub-Saharan Africa. This is against the background of declining levels of abject poverty in the rest of the world (World Bank, 2008). The largest proportion of the African poor (around 70 percent) lives in rural areas and in large households often headed by women (World Bank, 2007).[1]

However, there are observers such as Oppenheimer (2007) who portray a different scenario for Africa. While admitting that not all countries that make up the continent are on course to success, the foundation has been established for many countries in sub-Saharan Africa to succeed. His analysis is largely based on the evidence of economic growth, governance and reduction in conflict. He observes that the average continental economic growth

of 5.8 percent in 2006 (with similar figures in the two previous years) is a significant improvement compared to an average of 2 percent in the 1980s and 1990s. Many economies in Africa were not affected by the latest 2008 global economic crisis because they are basically not export oriented. There has also been a two-thirds decline in the number of conflicts on the continent from the 1990s. Equally important is the fact that many countries in Africa have ventured to adopt democracy against the dictatorial rule of a one-party state which was prevalent in the 1970s, 1980s and part of the 1990s. This coincided with the ushering in of a new economic outlook of free market enterprise as opposed to the socialist centralised economic model of previous years (World Economic Forum, 2011; Oppenheimer, 2007) as well as debt cancellation for many countries in Africa. The adoption of democracy, liberal economic reforms, decline in conflict, and the end of apartheid in South Africa in 1994 have attracted international attention and encouraged western donors to consider African countries more positively in terms of foreign aid. Weaning Africa off of foreign aid is now a goal for the future with some African economists like Moyo (2009) and other groups positively interested in Africa's future (Cultural Diplomacy, 2011). Perhaps one needs to be cautious in interpreting these as constituting a glimmer of hope for Africa today. While there are possibilities for economic success, it is too early to pronounce on the future. The average 5.8 percent growth for economies in Africa tends to mask disparities of growth among economies in Africa. For example, the Botswana economy grew by 10 percent for the past four decades (Maipose and Matsheka, 2008) while Zambia's economy managed to grow by only 3.8 percent in the same period. The food riots in Cameroon, Burkina Faso and Somalia in 2008 (Bank Information Centre, 2008) and in Mozambique in 2010, demonstrate the continuing economic hardships faced by countries where the national budget is donor driven.

SOCIAL WORK PRACTICE AND EDUCATION IN AFRICA

Not only has Africa had its share of challenges as mentioned above, but the social work profession has also had its challenges, trying to be effective in a continent as diverse as Africa. In fact, social work was imported into Africa by missionaries, European colonial administrators, and those involved in commercial enterprises of various forms (Mwansa, 2010, 2011). In the scheme of things, the missionaries were the forerunners of colonialism. They provided information from their travels or explorations to their countries of origin about the wealth of these new lands. Alongside their preaching, missionaries began to introduce some social welfare services such as schools and clinics and then later social work (Apt and Blavo, 1997; Grobler, 2007; Rea, 1970). Colonialism provided the socio-political context and general environment in which social work was initiated. The introduction of social work in Africa was characterised by case work, group work and community mobilisation, especially through rural development for specific community projects, which in the French colonies of West Africa, such as Niger, Cameroon, Upper Volta and Senegal, was popularly referred to as 'Animation Rurale' (Gellar et al., 1980). The concept of animation rurale embraced the idea of self-help which at the time was an approach in community development.

Social work practice in Anglophone countries was mainly remedial and social welfare departments were set up to hand out provisions to the less fortunate. For example, in Namibia, like in many other countries in Africa, missionaries began to provide social services in 1950; later on the government followed suit and then non-governmental organisations (NGOs) covered areas not provided for by the government. Social work grew as services became available and social workers came to be in demand to work for these organisations. In Namibia the first social worker was appointed by the Dutch

Reformed Church to provide social work services to 'church members in Tsumeb in the rural northern region of the country' (Grobler, 2007: 47). Similarly, in countries such as Ghana, the British began to provide social welfare in 1939 following an earthquake, and the Department of Social Welfare Services was established in 1946 to provide social work services to the victims and to Second World War veterans. There was a need to integrate the veterans into society after their absence from home (United Nations, 1950). The colonial system in Botswana established the Department of Social Welfare service in 1946 also following the return of the Second World War veterans (Hedenquist, 1991). Social services included cash benefits, information and counselling to the veterans, adult and audio-visual education and guidance for girls and boys. However, community development projects were initiated through the concept of 'Ipelegen' meaning self-help. Groups of young men and the communities were mobilised to undertake building of schools, bridges, roads and dams (Hedenquist, 1991). The introduction of copper mining in Zambia in the 1890s saw the introduction of social welfare services and social work in the early 1930s (Bancroft, 1961; Baldwin, 1966).

In the early beginning of social work in Africa, many workers were trained on the job by mainly European- or British-trained social workers. This trend continued until schools of social work were established in various parts of Africa. South Africa took the lead in starting a school of social work in 1924 followed by Egypt in 1936, Algeria in 1942 and Ghana in 1945 (ASWEA, 1974; Gray and Mazibuko, 2002; Healy, 2008). For most countries of Africa, a Western social work curriculum was transported to Africa with the assumption that it was transferable to an African setting (Kendall, 1995; Midgley, 1981). In fact it was encouraged to become more Western, thus perpetuating the notion that Western knowledge is civilized and perfect, and African knowledge is primitive and imperfect.

For most parts of Africa, with the notable exception of South Africa, documentation concerning the evolution of social work education in Africa mainly started with the establishment of the Association of Social Work Education in Africa (ASWEA). (Other documentation includes the *Journal of Social Development in Africa* which began in Zimbabwe in 1986.) Formed in 1971, the Association organised seminars, for the most part annually from 1971 to 1989, and documents were produced of the proceedings from these seminars (ASWEA, 1986). Concerned with a Western-dominated approach to social work training and practice, African academics and practitioners came together to discuss issues concerning social work education and practice including national social development planning, women's issues, rural issues, training in family welfare and social development versus social welfare trends of the 1970s and 1980s. Two volumes of case studies were also compiled for teaching purposes as well as two surveys of curricula around Africa. (ASWEA no longer exists and for a long time these documents were not available in Africa. However, through a joint project with the Association of Schools of Social Work in Africa [ASSWA], the International Association of Schools of Social Work [IASSW] and the University of Calgary these documents are now available online and in print in Africa.) These documents show important factors in the evolution of social work education and practice; three of which are: (1) for the most part, African social work curricula have followed Anglo-American and European theories and practice; (2) social workers have had to adapt their practice from a Western perspective; and (3) participants at the seminars were uncomfortable about this and advocated an Afro-centric social work curriculum but never managed to produce an African-centred curriculum. One reason for this reliance on Western social work education is a European influence on education.

The assumption that Western social work curricula were transferable to the African setting has been challenged by the conferences of the ASWEA and other African and non-African social work authors since the 1980s. The debate continues (Osei-Hwedie and Jacques, 2007) and in the meantime, many African social work students continue to be taught a Western approach to social work practice and an adaptation of theory and methods has to be completed in order to practice effectively in the community. Following are case examples of how social work started in four countries: Ghana, Mali, South Africa and Ethiopia. They feature important elements of these programmes and the kind of practice issues social workers are involved in.

Ghana

Social work in Ghana, like most other African countries, coincided with the introduction of a social welfare system through the colonial administration (Wicker, 1958). In 1946 the Department of Social Welfare and Housing was created and in 1952 the Department of Social Welfare and Community Development. The first recruits in Ghana for the social work profession were volunteers and experienced people 'who had acquired some knowledge of human beings ... they recruited experienced and mature people to do the work especially teachers and people who had worked in the villages' (Kreitzer, 2004: 25–6). Until the 1940s, in Ghana, both expatriate and indigenous social workers were trained overseas. The British welfare structures used primarily a remedial model in which clients' problems were identified and immediate needs sought to solve the problem. Preventive measures and structural changes were not addressed. Attention was given to physical and mental rehabilitation, with special attention to homeless children, disabled people, women and migrants. Asamoah and Beverly (1988) point out the short-sightedness of the colonial welfare policy as: '(a) failure to take a holistic view of the human condition, (b) an overriding importance of political considerations, (c) minimisation of the positive effects of traditional structures, and (d) emphasis on economic expediency or advantage for the colonial power instead of benefiting the colonies' (p. 178).

In 1948, an indigenous initiative took place in Ghana that used the skills of social/community workers. This was the community development movement (Sautoy, 1958) and grew 'during the 1950s as one of the most important factors in the social and economic development of the country' (Abloh and Ameyan, 1997). Community development provided 'adult literacy, home economics, self-help village projects, extension campaigns (teaching locals how to improve their lifestyle) and training' (Abloh and Ameyan, 1997: 282–3). Much of the success of community development was due to financial backing from the colonial government and the rise of nationalism. The rise of nationalism not only helped community development; it also helped the profession of social work become public.

In 1998 and in 2004, curricula re-evaluations were completed in Ghana with the hope that these suggestions would encourage a curriculum that is more African-centred and that meets the needs of Ghanaian society.

Mali

From 1970 to 1972, Mali initiated an economic and social development plan that would lay the foundations for long-term development. It was decided that social work should be integrated into these long-term development plans. Appropriately trained manpower was needed for this task and, as Mali had started out with a Francophone curriculum, this was determined to be inappropriate for training social workers for this development plan. The plan was to advance rural dwellers economically and socially and 'the people of Mali had to return to their own origins and evaluate their potential with a view to developing it wisely. They had to have the courage to question everything and

everybody to know their true aspirations' (ASWEA, 1973a: 61). A house-to-house survey was completed, and based on the findings of the survey, the two Schools of Social Work were closed down and a new curriculum developed that was compatible with Mali's priorities for development. Training included the fields of social science, law, economics, social legislation, live-stock rearing, agriculture, labour relations, accounting and home economics. The curriculum advocated for mental, physical and spiritual health. In 1982, the Centre National de Developpement Communautaire offered a four-year diploma in community development. The curriculum continued the original comprehensive training, including the above fields, as well as four years of training in community development, social research and rural geography (ASWEA, 1982: 151). The drive towards rural development should be a focus in social work training.

South Africa

According to Gray and Mazibuko (2002) and Sewpaul and Lombard (2004) South Africa had the first formal social work education in Africa. The evolution of social work in South Africa was also influenced by colonialism as well as subsequently by the apartheid system (Patel, 2005). 'The foundation of racial discrimination, denigration of indigenous ways, paternalism in social services and the distorted nature of social welfare policies favouring whites as the welfare elite, were laid during colonial times and permeated social welfare thinking for more than two centuries' (p. 67). During the 1920s and 1930s social work 'was born out of concern for white poverty' (Sewpaul and Lombard, 2004: 539). As the apartheid system developed in the late 1940s and early 1950s, blacks were discriminated against and their welfare needs unmet through this system. Social work was granted full professional status in 1978 but continued to discriminate between races. Since the formal end to apartheid in 1994, social work has taken up the challenge of including all races in its service delivery and education. There has been a strong change in social welfare policy and social work practice that is based on the social development model introduced by Midgley (1995) and spelled out in the White Paper for Social Welfare (1997) in South Africa. The system is evolving into one where all South Africans are included in services and resources.

Ethiopia

During the 1950s a School of Social Work was opened during the rule of Haile Sellasie. However it was closed when the military government came into power in 1974. It re-emerged in 2004 with a master's level degree (MSW) at the University of Addis Ababa after lengthy needs assessments and analysis of whether or not social work was needed in Ethiopia. The findings revealed that there was a need for training that concentrated on macro practice; in particular managing community-based services and developing new programmes focused on the reduction of poverty, counselling people with HIV and AIDS, family support to orphaned and abandoned children and community development. There is an emphasis on development of policy and programmes in organisational, community and governmental areas as well as the development of leadership and administrative skills. The PhD programme was created in 2006 and the bachelor's programme (BSW) in 2007. Continual re-evaluation of the curriculum with students, alumni, NGOs and government officials who employ social workers has produced changes to the curriculum. For instance, the family court president of Addis Ababa requested social workers to be assigned to the court to assist judges in investigating the needs of families that come through the family court. The BSW programme includes comprehensive social science training as well as courses specific to Ethiopia such as community mobilisation, ethnography of Ethiopia, ethnicity and

diversity, migration and refugees, and law. The MSW programme has three focuses: (1) children, youth and family; (2) healthcare; and (3) community and social development. The PhD programme is flexible with so as to be mindful of culturally specific content.

SUMMARY

For many parts of Africa, rural development continues to be an important part of the overall development of the country, and social workers work with groups and communities to empower people to work towards sustainable communities. Besides the regular casework scenario, social workers work in industry, probation services, family services, rehabilitation, child welfare, schools, programmes to address prostitution and health services. They also organise literacy/adult education, sports and recreation. To encourage wealth creation as a response to poverty reduction, social workers promote cooperatives, especially the small-scale industries and trade and skills development (Mupedziswa, 1996). They also work with grassroots organisations such as village development committees to mobilise the citizenry for development. Social work has also traditionally been part of sociology in African universities and there is a trend for it to form its own departments, separate from sociology. There is a growing understanding that social work training has to be more African-specific and needs to be re-evaluated on a regular basis. There is need for social work curricula to maintain the context, guard against brain-drain to the west and maintain a database of course materials.

Core issues

The core issues facing social workers in Africa on a daily basis include racism and the traumatic effects of oppression, health issues, an appropriate Afro-centric social work curriculum, strengthening professional associations, advocating a social development approach, and dealing with the effects of neo-liberal policies and poverty.

Racism and trauma from oppression

One of the most devastating forms of oppression known to the world is colonisation, whether it is by European countries or by one ethnic group over another. The social work profession is committed to the 'empowerment and liberation of people ... and to human rights and social justice' (IFSW, 2004) and all social work training and practice should concentrate on reducing racism, ethnic tensions and injustice for all citizens of each country. The effects of racism, colonisation and oppression should form part of training in social work programmes and this would include self-examination of students' own history and socialisation as well as how to fight injustices that discriminate against different ethnic groups (Bishop, 2002).

Health issues

Interdisciplinary approaches to working with individuals, groups and communities concerning health matters are imperative for effective social work interventions. Working with health staff in hospitals and communities, as well as working alongside traditional healers to educate communities concerning health issues, can not only reduce health issues but can affect the social welfare of families and communities.

Neo-liberalism and poverty

It is now very clear that the neo-liberal economic policies have largely failed Africa and many attempts at alleviating poverty have not worked. In fact the UN Millennium Goals of reducing poverty for many African countries will not be met by 2015. 'Africa's severe economic problems in the 1970s, made worse by the global recession of the 1980s and the implementation of structural adjustment programmes in some countries in the mid-1980s, posed new challenges for social work education' (Asamoah, 1995: 235). Today, Africa continues to have the largest share of the world's absolute poor. HIV and AIDS, education, civil war and corruption all add to the challenges faced by African countries. The challenge for social workers is to confront structural issues such as poverty reduction, promote transparency and the rule of law, fight corruption, and work for sustainable development to bring about lasting change for all.

Curriculum in Africa

One of the present challenges concerning training and practice is how to bring about reforms in social work training institutions to reflect a more Afro-centric curriculum and less of a European one (Kreitzer et al., 2009). This critical reflection needs to include structural and cultural societal issues in relation to human rights and the needs of society. 'Critical reflection based on critical theory requires that specific issues be raised in the reflection, such as the exercise of power, oppression and discrimination. The ultimate aim is to change what is malfunctioning' (Askeland and Bradley, 2010: 674). This is difficult in a continent where many in power view Western knowledge as better than traditional knowledge. It is also a challenge to identify exactly an 'African perspective', because of the influence of other cultures in many African societies. Additionally, many African social work students see Western-influenced social work training as an opportunity to leave Africa and practise in the Western world, especially given the existing high demand for professional social workers in the West. This perpetuates a brain-drain of social workers from Africa and leaves the profession in African countries depleted of social workers and academics that could enhance and contribute to the profession and associations. Research and writing play a key role in encouraging African academics and practitioners to discuss and incorporate African perspectives in teaching and practice and to continue the lively debate about what is 'African culture'. There is a continual lack of textbooks written by Africans with case studies that are about Africa.

The Association of Schools of Social Work could develop databases of information, to access online, including: (1) a collection of African case studies at the individual, group and community levels; (2) course outlines of each country's social work training; and (3) a collection of articles about social work in Africa to help in this process.

Strengthen the professional associations

The strength of a profession is often reflected in the strength of its professional association. National professional associations should be the voice of the people of the country and a critic of social policies as well as setting moral standards for the government. A combination of an increased acceptance by governments of the importance of social work's voice in social policy formulation, planning, recognition of this importance through financial reward, and developing strong association structures that monitor professional practice in each country would help increase social work's profile as an important profession. Codes of ethics of the associations should be African-centred and reflect social issues of the particular country and not those of the western world. Continentally, the Association of Schools of Social Work in Africa (ASSWA) needs to be strengthened as a voice for social work in Africa. It can also bring together social work education in African countries and unify social work on the continent. The

growing cooperation with the other international organisations like the International Federation of Social Workers (IFSW), International Association of Schools of Social Work and the International Council on Social Welfare (ICSW) is a welcome development.

Social development approach

Interestingly, the original ASWEA documents stressed the importance of social development, which has now been embraced by many school curricula in Africa. Three of the documents are entitled *Relationship between Social Work Education and National Social Development Planning* (ASWEA, 1973b), *The Role of Social Development Education in Africa's Struggle for Political and Economic Independence* (ASWEA, 1977) and *Social Development Training in Africa: Experiences of the 1970's and Emerging Trends of the 1980's* (ASWEA, 1981). As more African countries develop a social development approach, leaving behind the colonial/remedial type of social work, this needs to be reflected in social work training and practice.

CONCLUSION

The African continent, before colonisation, was a 'loose collection of ethnic communities or micro-nations' (Maathai, 2009: 186) that had been shaped over thousands of years. It had a long, involved, complex and cultured history with an immense diversity of ethnic groups, complete with appropriate social, economic and political infrastructure. With colonialism, these systems were threatened, weakened and often destroyed. During the colonial period, social welfare systems based on models in the colonising countries were introduced and Africans were sent to Europe to be trained in social welfare. Once they returned, new institutions replaced the traditional systems and were remedial in their approach to helping people. With the end of the two World Wars many African countries obtained their independence from the colonial powers, only to find themselves struggling to survive in the new economic order. European universities played a major role in the development of education in Africa, and this influence continues today with Western knowledge continuing its hegemony over African universities, including in social work training.

Poverty, disease and corruption continue to prevail in many African countries which cannot develop under such conditions including the present neo-liberal economic system. The challenges for social work, as a frontline profession, are multiple and complex. It needs to critically reflect on the present curricula and promote Afro-centric curricula, using Africans as important resources for teaching and practice and to create their own unique curricula, and a profession that suits the African continent.

NOTE

1   Among the worst casualties are women and children who suffer the severest forms of malnutrition and related diseases. Notably, the current estimates do not reflect the potentially huge impact of rising food and fuel prices on the world market since 2005. The poor suffer from a broad range of debilitating disadvantages that underlie the problem of hunger. They have less access to opportunity, infrastructure and other publically provided goods and services. They also tend to receive poor education or none at all. Perhaps more important is the fact that poverty is more pervasive with a wider array of adverse ramifications than once thought and that families may be trapped in poverty over generations. With its multidimensionality and interlocking dynamics connected to factors such as gender and geographical location, poverty continues to escalate, creating despair, powerlessness, dependency, shame, humiliation and loss of self-esteem. Such a state of being can translate into deprivation related to insufficiency in food, housing, health, education, employment and all that is required to maintain an acceptable standard or quality of life (Mwansa, 2010).

REFERENCES

Abloh, F. and Ameyan, S. (1997) 'Ghana', in H. Campfens (ed.), *Community Development Around the World: Practice, Theory, Research and Training*. Toronto: University of Toronto Press.

Ambrosino, R., Heffernan, J., Shuttleworth, R. and Ambrosino, R. (2005) *Social Work & Social Welfare: an Introduction* (5th edn). Belmont: Brooks/Cole – Thomas Learning.

Anderson, S. and Maher, D. (2001) *An Analysis of the Interaction between TB and HIV and AIDS Programmes in Sub-Saharan Africa*. WHO/CDS/TB/2001. 294. Geneva: WHO.

Apt, A.A. and Blavo, E.Q. (1997) 'Ghana', in N.S. Mayadas, T.D. Watts and D. Elliott (eds), *International Handbook on Social Work Theory*. Westport: Greenwood Press.

Asamoah, Y.W. (1995) 'Africa', in T.D. Watts, D. Elliott, and N.S Mayadas (eds), *International Handbook on Social Work Education*. Connecticut: Greenwood Press.

Asamoah, Y.W. and Beverly, C.C. (1988) 'Collaboration between Western and African schools of social work: Problems and possibilities', *International Social Work*, 31: 177–93.

Askeland, G.A. and Bradley, G. (2010) Linking critical reflection and qualitative research on an African social work master's programme. *International Social Work*, 50 (5): 671–85.

ASWEA (Association of Social Work Education in Africa) (1973a) *Compilation of Case Studies in Social Development in East Africa*. ASWEA: Addis Ababa.

ASWEA (Association of Social Work Education in Africa) (1973b) *Relationship between Social Work Education and National Social Development Planning, Document 6*. Addis Ababa: ASWEA.

ASWEA (Association of Social Work Education in Africa) (1974*) Curriculum of Schools of Social Work and Community Development Training Centres in Africa, Document*. Addis Ababa: ASWEA.

ASWEA (Association of Social Work Education in Africa) (1977) *The Role of Social Development Education in Africa's Struggle for Political and Economic Independence, Document 12*. Addis Ababa: ASWEA.

ASWEA (Association of Social Work Education in Africa) (1981) *Social Development Training in Africa: Experiences of the 1970's and Emerging Trends of the 1980's, Document 17*. Addis Ababa: ASWEA.

ASWEA (Association of Social Work Education in Africa) (1982) *Survey of Curricula of Social Development Training Institutions in Africa, Document 18* (2nd edn). Addis Ababa: ASWEA.

ASWEA (Association of Social Work Education in Africa) (1986) *Association for Social Work Education in Africa.* Addis Ababa: ASWEA.

Baldwin, R.E (1966) *Economic Development and Export Growth: A Study of Northern Rhodesia, 1920–60.* Berkeley and Los Angeles: University of California Press.

Bancroft, J.A. (1961) *Mining in Northern Rhodesia.* London: British South Africa Company.

Bank Information Centre (2008) *Food Riots in Africa.* http://www.bicusa.org/en/article.3702.aspx.

Bishop, A. (2002) *Becoming an Ally.* London: Zed Books.

Bollinger, L. and Stover, J. (1999) *The Economic Impact of AIDS.* Glastonbury, CT: the Futures Group International.

Bulatao, R.A. and Lee, R.D. (1983) *Determinants of Fertility in Developing Countries.* New York: Academic Press. V. 1 and 2.

Caselli, G. (2006) *Demography: Analysis and Synthesis.* Amsterdam; Boston: Elsevier.

Cohen, J.E. and Malin, M. (2009) *International Perspectives on Goals of Universal Basic and Secondary Education.* New York; London: Routledge.

Cultural Diplomacy (2011) 'The rise of Africa: Strategies to confront the challenges of the 21st century: does Africa have what it takes?' *International Symposium on Cultural Diplomacy in Africa.* Berlin, 14–17 July 2011. http://www.culturaldiplomacy.org/experienceafrica/index.php?en_the-rise-of-Africa.

Des Forges, A. (1999) *Leave None to Tell the Story: Genocide in Rwanda.* New York: Human Rights Watch and Paris: International Federation on Human Rights.

Fanon, F. (1961) *The Wretched of the Earth.* New York: Grove Press.

Freire, P. (2000) *Pedagogy of the Oppressed.* New York: Continuum.

Gellar, S., Charlick, R.B. and Jones, Y. (1980) *Rural Development, Senegal.* Rural Development Committee, Center for International Studies, Cornell University (Ithaca, NY 170 Uris Hall, Ithaca. Government of South Africa (1997) White paper for social developmental welfare. http://www.info.gov.za/view/DownloadFileAction?id=127937.

Gray, M. and Mazibuko, F. (2002) 'Social Work in South Africa at the dawn of the New Millennium', *International Journal of Social Welfare*, 11: 191–200.

Grobler, M. (2007) 'The indigenisation of social work in Namibia' in C. Rehklau and R. Lutz (eds), *Internationale Sozialarbeit Sozialarbeit des Sudens Band 2 – Schwerpunkt Afrika.* Oldenburg: Paulo Freire Verlag.

Guest, R. (2004) *The Shackled Continent: Africa's Past, Present and Future.* London: Pan Macmillan.

Healy, L. (2008) *International Social Work: Professional Action in an Interdependent World* (2nd edn). New York; Oxford: Oxford University Press.

Heaps, C., Humphreys, S., Kemp-Benedict, E., Raskin, P. and Sokona, Y. (1999) *Sustainable Development in West Africa: Beginning the Process.* Boston: Stockholm Environment Institute Publishers.

Hedenquist, J. (1991) *Introduction to Social and Community Development Work in Botswana.* Botswana: Ministry of Local Government and Lands.

Huebler, F. (2007) *International Education Statistics.* http://huebler.blogspot.com.

Huebler, F. (2009) *International Education Statistics. UN Millennium Goals.* http://huebler.blogspot.com.

IFSW (International Federation of Social Work) (2004) *Definition of Social Work.* http://www.ifsw.org/f38000138.html.

Kendall, K. (1995) 'Foreword', in T.D. Watts, D. Elliott, and N.S. Mayadas (eds), *International Handbook on Social Work Education.* Connecticut: Greenwood Press.

Kreitzer, L. (2004) *Indigenization of Social Work Education and Practice: A Participatory Action Research Project in Ghana.* Unpublished PhD thesis, University of Calgary, Alberta, Canada.

Kreitzer, L., Abukari, Z., Mensah, J., Kwaku, A. and Antonio, P. (2009) 'Social work in Ghana: a participatory action research project looking at culturally appropriate training and practice', *Social Work Education*, 28 (2): 145–64.

Maathai, W. (2009) *The Challenge for Africa.* New York: Pantheon Books.

Maipose, G.S. and Matsheka, T.C. (2008) 'The indigenous developmental state and growth in Botswana', in B.J. Ndulu, S.A. O'Connell, J. Azam, R.H. Bates, A.K. Fosu, J.W. Gunning and D. Njinkeu. *The Political Economy of Economic Growth in Africa 1960–2000.* Cambridge: Cambridge University Press.

Maluccio, A., Pine, B.A. and Tracy, E.M. (2002) *Social Work Practice with Families and Children.* New York: Columbia University.

Memmi, A. (1965) *The Colonizer and the Colonized.* Boston: Beacon Press.

Midgley, J. (1981) *Professional Imperialism: Social Work in the Third World.* London: Heinemann.

Midgley, J. (1995) *Social Development: The Development Perspective in Social Welfare.* London: Sage Publications.

Moyo, D. (2009) *Dead Aid: Why Aid is not Working and How There is a Better Way for Africa*. London: Penguin Books.

Mullaly, B. (1997) *Structural Social Work: Ideology, Theory, and Practice* (2nd edn). Ontario: Oxford University Press.

Mupedziswa, R. (1996) 'Community development in Zimbabwe', in M. Hutton, and L.-K. Mwansa (eds), *Social Work Practice in Africa: Social Development in a Community Context*. Gaborone: Print Consult.

Mwansa, L.-K. (2010) 'Challenges facing social work education in Africa', *International Social Work*, 53 (1): 129–36.

Mwansa, L.-K. (2011) 'Social work education in Africa: whence and whither?', *Social Work Education*, 30 (1): 4–16.

Nwoye, A. (2004) The shattered microcosm: Imperatives for improved family therapy in Africa in the 21st century', *Contemporary Family Therapy*, 26 (2): 143–64.

Onyeani, C. (1990) *The Capitalist Nigger: The Road to Success, a Spider Web Doctrine*. New York: Timbukutu Publishers.

Oppenheimer, N. (2007) 'Why Africa will succeed', *New Africa*, July: 464.

Osei-Hwedie, K. and Jacques, G. (2007) *Indigenising Social Work in Africa*. Accra: Ghana University Press.

Padayachee, V. (2010) *The Political Economy of Africa*. New York: Routledge.

Patel, L. (2005) *Social Welfare and Social Development*. Cape Town: Oxford University Press.

Rea, W.F. (1970) 'Agony on the Zambezi. The first Christian mission to Southern Africa and its failure', *Zambezia, A Journal of Social Studies in Southern and Central Africa*, 1 (2): 46–53.

Sautoy, P. (1958) *Community Development in Ghana*. London: Oxford University Press.

Sewpaul, V. and Lombard, A. (2004) 'Social work education, training and standards in Africa', *Social Work Education*, 23 (5): 537–54.

Sparks, D.L. (2002) *Economic Trends in Africa: South of Sahara* (32nd edn). Routledge: Europa Publications Limited.

The World Economic Forum Global Competitiveness Report (2010–2011) London: Oxford University Press.

UNAIDS (2008) *Report on the Global AIDS Epidemic*. Geneva: United Nations.

UNAIDS (2009) *Report on the Global AIDS Epidemic*. Geneva: United Nations.

UNDP (United Nations Development Programme) (2009) *Human Development Report*. New York: United Nations.

UNICEF (United Nations Children's Fund) (2008) *The State of the World's Children 2008*. New York: United Nations Plaza.

United Nations (1950). *Training for Social Work: An International Survey*. Lake Success: United Nations Department of Social Affairs.

Wallimann, I., Dobkowisk, M. and Rubstein, R. (2000) *Genocide and the Modern Age: Etiology and Case Studies of Mass Death*. Syracuse: Syracuse University Press.

Wicker, E.R. (1958) 'Colonial development and welfare, 1929–1957: The evolution of a policy', *Social and Development Studies*, 7 (4): 170–92.

World Bank (2007) *World Bank Report*.

World Bank (2008) *World Bank Report*.

25

Social Work in Southern and Eastern Asia

Manohar Pawar with the assistance of Ming-sum Tsui

INTRODUCTION

After introducing the unique features and socio-economic-political background of Southern and Eastern Asia, this chapter discusses the current status of social work in the region in terms of its development as a profession, social work educational models, practice patterns and research. It also looks at what can be done to initiate social work education and practice in areas where it is most needed. We argue that, despite references to social work as a global profession (e.g. Healy, 2001; Hugman, 2010), it has not yet become local in Southern and Eastern Asia and that it needs to be. The current issues and needs, as well as socio-economic-political developments, suggest that concerted efforts are needed both at local and global levels to qualitatively and quantitatively expand social work, particularly in the least developed areas of the region.

SOUTHERN AND EASTERN ASIA

Southern and Eastern Asia here refers to 26 countries (see Table 25.1); eight countries in

South Asia, seven in North East Asia and 11 countries in South East Asia. Of the eight South Asian countries, five are least developed (Afghanistan, Bangladesh, Bhutan, Maldives and Nepal), and of the 11 South East Asian countries, four are least developed (Cambodia, Lao PDR, Myanmar and Timor-Leste). According to the ESCAP (Economic and Social Commission for Asia and the Pacific), only Japan is classified as a developed country in the region, though the development level of the four Asian tigers (Hong Kong, Korea, Singapore and Taiwan) is higher than in the other countries in the region.

South and East Asia together make one of the largest, most fascinating regions in the world in terms of geographic location, natural resources, population size, diverse cultures, ethnicity, religion, historical legacies, external dependence and influences, power, and political and institutional arrangements (Todaro and Smith, 2003). It is also home to two major growing economies, China and India. Particular attention is therefore paid to these countries, given their population size and significance within the region and globally, but also as representative of countries with the longest and shortest social work histories in the region.

Southern and Eastern Asia is also one of the most challenging regions in the world, as significant proportions of the population experience low income and living standards with poor health and inadequate education. Many countries are characterised by high rates of population growth, substantial dependence on agriculture and primary-product exports, low productivity, imperfect markets, and vulnerability (Todaro and Smith, 2003). The region's least developed countries have persistently high levels of poverty, large rural-based populations, economies reliant on agriculture, poor infrastructures, high levels of under-nourishment and significant resource gaps (FAO, 2003; UNDP, 2005).

The region is diverse in many respects, including its resources and wealth. For example, thousands of languages and dialects are spoken that may or may not have a written script. All major religions are in evidence and they cut across countries and sub-regions. Most[1] of the people in Cambodia, Japan, Laos, Myanmar, Sri Lanka, Thailand and Vietnam follow Buddhism. In China, Hong Kong, Taiwan and Singapore, Chinese indigenous religions (Taoism, Buddhism, and Chinese folk religion) are popular. The majority of people in the Philippines follow Christianity. Hinduism is most common in India and Nepal, while Islam is the most widespread religion in Bangladesh, Indonesia, Malaysia and Pakistan (O'Brien and Palmer, 1993). Importantly, indigenous people across the region also have their own belief systems. Beyond religious diversity, within religions there are thousands of sects and castes (e.g. in India). Some traditional caring, sharing and helping functions appear to have originated in various religions and diverse cultural practices which have significant implications for human rights and gender equality. Culture, diversity, gender and human rights are important, complex and sensitive dimensions of the region that need to be well understood when developing professional social work practice (Yip, 2005).

Similarly, the region's political systems are also varied, and significantly influenced by the historical legacies of colonisation. Except for China, Japan and Thailand, all countries and islands in the region were colonised by other countries, notably the United Kingdom, France, Portugal, the Netherlands, Germany, Japan, China and Imperial Russia. Depending upon the political system, the governance structures and freedoms enjoyed by people in the region differ greatly. China, DPR Korea, Lao PDR and Vietnam are communist states. However, China has significantly decentralised and introduced elements of democracy at grassroots levels (Pawar, 2009; Yan and Tsui, 2007), both in urban and rural areas; Hong Kong and Macao enjoy limited democracy. In Myanmar, a military Junta dictates the terms. Mongolia follows a mixed parliamentary and presidential system. In South Asia, most of the countries are federal republics or parliamentary democracies. Through the process of decentralisation, India has provided significant power and resources to the local-level governing systems. Bhutan has recently transitioned from absolute monarchy to constitutional monarchy. Afghanistan has an Islamic republic system. Many East Asian countries have a background of dictator rulers, but have changed to different variations of constitutional monarchy (Cambodia, Brunei, Malaysia and Thailand) or to parliamentary republic systems (Indonesia, the Philippines and Singapore). The very nature of these political systems – including the quality of governance, level and style of democracy or its absence, conflicts, terrorism and wars – has significant impact on the way professional social work is developed, taught and practised in the various countries.

There is enormous economic diversity too. Depending upon the economic development levels, countries have been categorised into least developed, developing and developed countries. Almost every country in the region was affected by the global financial crisis in 2008 and 2009 and their economic growth declined to different degrees. However, with governments' fiscal interventions and stimulus packages many countries in the region have recovered. The UNESCAP (2010a) analysis suggests that the North East Asia region is forecast to grow by 4 percent (though it would be significantly less if China's growth is taken out of the equation); South East Asia by 5.1 percent; and South Asia by 6.1 percent in 2010. China is forecast to grow by 9.5 percent and India by 8.3 per- cent– two major emerging economies in the region and in the world. As a broad social policy measure, UNESCAP (2010a: 99) notes that:

> Looking beyond 2010, accelerating economic growth is crucial to bring down poverty levels. The challenge will be how to make growth more inclu- sive by spreading its benefits to larger segments of the population. More resources should be devoted to the provision of basic services such as educa- tion, health, sanitation and housing particularly for those belonging to lower income groups. Targeted programmes for the benefit of the poor in the broader framework of social protection should also be a priority.

This policy measure is relevant and challeng- ing to the social work profession in terms of how it facilitates the provision of human services and social protection, particularly for the marginalised and disadvantaged groups in every country. Many countries (Mongolia, Cambodia, Lao PDR, the Philippines, Bangladesh, India, Nepal and Sri Lanka) are making slow progress with regard to poverty eradication. Between 1990 and 2005, Asia and the Pacific reduced the number of people living on less than US\$1.25 a day from 1.5 billion to 979 million, but still nearly 70 percent of the world's poor live in the region. Although there is some good news with regard to progress towards achiev- ing the millennium development goals (MDGs, see Appendix 6), many countries in the region have lagged behind in the MDG indicators: reducing infant mortality and child malnutrition; increasing primary school enrolment and completion; attaining gender equality; and improving water and sanitation while also reducing CO_2 emissions (see UNESCAP, 2010b). Can social work contrib- ute to inclusive and sustainable growth,

particularly at the local level, or to enabling poor people to make use of opportunities created by such growth?

CONTEMPORARY DEVELOPMENTS IN SOCIAL WORK IN THE REGION

Development of social work as a profession

Development of social work and social work as a profession are two different aspects and quite complex, particularly in the Asian con- text. Almost every country in the region has its own social work practices, as understood in context, according to national culture and traditions, and most people seem to relate to this culturally and traditionally based social work. Given local, cultural contexts, it is often difficult, at least initially, to establish and develop professional social work. Our discussion here is limited to professional social work – defined as an occupation for which members have received specialist training that provides eligibility for member- ship of professional associations (if they exist). Some of the common indicators to identify the development of the social work profession are (1) the existence of professional associations, (2) their membership, (3) their roles and functions in developing and main- taining the profession, and (4) the general legitimacy and recognition among members and the public of social work in government and non-government organisations, and in society at large. The last indicator is difficult to measure directly, though it may be ascer- tained, for instance, by looking at how effec- tive the association is in influencing decisions that matter for the association, its members and society at large.

At the regional–global level the presence of some associations gives an impression that the social work profession does exist at this level. For instance, the International Associ- ation of Schools of Social Work (IASSW), Asia Pacific Association of Social Work

Table 25.1 Institution/association members of professional bodies in Southern and Eastern Asia

South and East Asian countries	IASSW member schools in 2010	IFSW member associations	APASWE member schools
Afghanistan	–	–	–
Bangladesh	–	1	–
Bhutan	–	–	–
Brunei Darussalam	–	–	–
Cambodia	–	–	1*
China	48	1	2
Hong Kong, China	4	1	2*
India	5	1	1
Indonesia	–	–	2
Japan	82	4	82
Korea (North)	–	–	–
Korea (South)	2	1	60
Lao PDR	–	–	–
Malaysia	1	1	2
Maldives	–	–	–
Mongolia	–	1	–
Myanmar	–	–	–
Nepal	–	–	1
Pakistan	–	–	–
Philippines	2	1	1
Singapore	1	1	2
Sri Lanka	1	1	–
Taiwan, (China)?	1	–	1
Thailand	2	1	1
Timor-Leste	–	–	–
Vietnam	–	–	2

Note: Accuracy of figures cannot be guaranteed. Individual members are not included.
IASSW: International Association of Schools of Social Work; IFSW: International Federation of Social Workers; APASWE: Asia Pacific Association for Social Work Education.
*Unclear whether member is individual or institutional.
? Independent country status is unresolved.
Source: IASSW (2010), IFSW (2008), APASWE (2009).

Education (APASWE), International Federation of Social Workers (IFSW), Asia-Pacific Region, and related associations such as the International Consortium for Social Development, Asia Pacific Branch, all have members. They organise periodic conferences and publish newsletters and/or journals and often facilitate regional or international collaboration on relevant activities (IASSW, 2010; APASWE, 2009; IFSW, 2008). However, a country-level examination presents a mixed picture of the development of the social work profession: in some countries the profession is relatively well established, but in others it is very weak. In some countries social work is just emerging, while in others it does not even exist.

Table 25.1 shows that of the 26 countries, only 11 countries' schools are members of the IASSW, only 12 countries' social work associations have membership of the IFSW, and social work schools from only 14 countries have institutional membership of the APASWE (2009). Nine countries (Afghanistan, Bhutan, Brunei Darussalam, North Korea, Lao PDR, Maldives, Myanmar, Pakistan and Timor-Leste) have no membership association with any of the international professional social work bodies.

Although there are a number of social work schools in Pakistan, its membership link is not visible in these international bodies. Social, economic and political problems in most of these nine countries are well known, but professional social work has little or no profile.

This mixed picture also shows how local, national, regional and international social work professional associations are connected and disconnected from each other (see Figure 25.1). It may be inferred that in some countries, e.g. Hong Kong, Japan and Singapore, where the profession is relatively well established, local schools, national associations, regional associations and international associations are well connected (unbroken innermost triangle). In other countries, e.g. Afghanistan, Bhutan, Lao PDR and East Timor, where professional social work is yet to emerge, there is no connectivity between local, national, regional and international associations, as it appears that very little exists at the local and national level and it is not clear what regional and international associations are doing to change that situation (next broken triangle). In a third group,

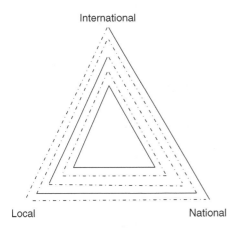

Figure 25.1 Connectedness and disconnectedness among professional associations in South East Asia at local, national and international levels

Source: Pawar (2010, unpublished).

e.g. India, Nepal and Sri Lanka, local associations are connected at the regional and international level, but not at the national level as there appears to be no national level functional social work association (middle triangle). Elsewhere, local and national associations may have links, but have remained isolated from the regional and international associations (fourth outer triangle). Finally, national associations may be well connected in some countries at the regional and international level, but not at the local level (outermost triangle).

China's professional social work seems to be speedily developing and relatively well connected at local, national, regional and international levels (Yuen-Tsang and Wang, 2002), but India appears to be lagging behind in its professional development. Social work development in China is largely driven by the government (Liu, 2003; Yan and Tsui, 2007), whereas in India social work mainly originated with the support of philanthropy and charity and with some support from the government (Ranade, 1987; Mandal, 1995; Nanavatty, 1997).

When we look at the core issues related to professional development, the analysis of the existence of social work schools, associations and their membership and links may appear peripheral, though important. As professional social work is generally taking roots in traditional societies, developing identity and recognition as a profession is challenging. Almost every country has a story to tell about this issue. Local populations have problems in understanding what professional social work from the West is and how it is different from other peoples' activities described as social work. Except in a few countries (e.g. Japan, Korea, Taiwan, Hong Kong and Singapore), social work educators and practitioners have not been able to organise a strong, functional and effective professional body at the national level, though a lot of good work is done by some in the region. However, there are variations in terms of quality and quantity; and the extent to which professional associations contribute to knowledge creation, skill development and maintaining professional standards is also doubtful. Whether professionalisation should lead to specialisation and then to professional registration are contentious issues, and their relevance to the region is debatable. On the other hand, could professionalisation lead to indigenisation; local knowledge and skills development; and the utilisation of a social development perspective to address the massive development issues (e.g. poverty and unemployment) in the region? It is not clear what international social work associations can and should do to address such professional development issues. Lack of and/or weak professional associations at regional, international and national levels and their disconnection at local levels have significant implications for the quality and quantity of social work education provided in different countries, and for initiating new social work education programmes where they do not exist in the region.

Developments in social work education

Accurate and reliable data as to the number and state of social work schools in each country are lacking, as is information about course structures and curriculum content. The following material is based on discussion with colleagues, and observations and experience in some of the countries in the region. The anecdotal evidence suggests that the spread of social work education in the Southern and Eastern Asian region is uneven and unbalanced when compared to needs; and is urban centred and still evolving in many countries. Information presented in Table 25.2 suggests that in 12 countries social work schools and education are relatively well established and expanding, particularly in India. In China, Mongolia and Vietnam, social work schools are being established and are rapidly expanding, particularly in China (Yan and Tsui, 2007; Yuen-Tsang and Wang, 2002). In Nepal, Cambodia, Lao PDR and Sri Lanka, one or two schools exist with varying capacity, but in these countries social work schools and education need to be better developed and appropriately expanded. In seven countries of the region, we were not able to access information about the existence of social work schools and we suggest that it does not exist (see for example, WHO-AIMS, 2007), though there may be plans and attempts to initiate social work education in some of these countries.

The context of the origin of professional social work education in each country is

Table 25.2   Social work schools and education in Southern and Eastern Asia

Established and expanding	Establishing and expanding	Developing and to be expanded	No information / to be developed
Bangladesh	China	Cambodia	Afghanistan
Hong Kong	Mongolia	Lao PDR	Bhutan
India	Vietnam	Nepal	Brunei
Indonesia		Sri Lanka	North Korea
Japan			Maldives
Korea (South)			Myanmar
Malaysia			Timor-Leste
Pakistan			
Philippines			
Singapore			
Taiwan (China)?			
Thailand			

? Independent country status is unresolved.

unique. Generally, a range of interactive factors have led to the development of social work schools, including: colonial history; contacts with the Western countries; industrialisation, urbanisation and development levels; non-government initiatives and efforts, particularly from missionaries and philanthropic and charititable organisations; government initiatives and welfare programmes; initiatives of higher education institutions; education and exposure in Western countries; and interest of Western scholars buttressed by Western aid. In some countries, e.g. India and South Korea, social work education was initiated by missionaries, philanthropic trusts and charitable organisations. As countries developed and, industrialised, government welfare programmes were established to address new needs and problems, and social work personnel were trained often with the support of Western countries. Most of the 12 countries listed in the first column of Table 25.2 have gained from such Western support and social work education has been available in many of these countries for more than 50 years. In China, Mongolia and Vietnam, governments have been the main initiators and drivers of social work programmes since the 1990s (although they are offered in universities). In Nepal (see Nikku, 2009), Cambodia, Lao PDR and Sri Lanka, missionaries, Western scholars, aid agencies, local universities or non-governmental organisations (NGOs) together or independently have initiated social work programmes on a small scale.

There is no uniformity in the level and structure of social work programmes. In India, for many years, two-year postgraduate social work programmes were offered either in a generic form or as specialisms related to employment opportunities, e.g. medical and psychiatric social work, family and child welfare, criminology and corrections, community organisation and labour welfare. Recently, many institutions have introduced three-year undergraduate programmes. Similarly, in Hong Kong three-year undergraduate and two-year full time postgraduate

programmes are offered, while in Malaysia, Singapore, and Japan, four-year undergraduate social work courses are the norm. Many well-established social work schools in the region also offer PhD programmes and one university in Hong Kong has recently developed a professional doctorate (DSW at Hong Kong Polytechnic University).

Although the depth and breadth of curriculum content differ significantly between school and countries, generally the social work curriculum is based on foundation subjects (e.g. sociology, psychology, politics, economics and local history); social work methods subjects (work with individuals/case work, groups/group work and communities/community organisation); policy and welfare administration and social research. Research-based dissertations may be undertaken by students in some schools (e.g. in India). In all the well-established schools field education has a central place in the curriculum. In many countries the social work curriculum appears to be highly prescriptive. For example, in India the curriculum is determined at the university level, with prescribed textbooks and an element of bureaucracy, so that any modification is difficult to achieve, though some schools do periodically revise their curricula.

Although awareness of the need for indigenisation of the curriculum is generally increasing in the region, by and large Western social work models remain dominant (Midgley, 1981; Cox, 1995, 1997; Hugman, 2010; Yan and Tsui, 2007) and most schools do not have a development orientation in their programmes. However, in many countries social work training is provided in local languages (e.g. in Japan, South Korea, India and China). The (rapid) increase in the number of social work schools in the region is raising doubts about quality and standards as, without adequate resources (including lecturers trained in social work and qualified practice teachers or field supervisors), it is difficult to maintain minimum standards. Many new social work programmes are offered under the auspices of other disciplines (e.g. sociology, psychology or business disciplines, e.g. in Japan and Lao PDR) and taught by academics without social work qualifications (e.g. in China and India). Fieldwork education has become a significant issue. While countries such as Hong Kong and Japan have developed social work education accreditation standards, no such standards have been developed in most countries. Even in India, where professional social work education has been provided for more than 75 years, accreditation standards do not exist. Finally, although some new schools are emerging in rural areas and small towns (e.g. in India), most social work schools are urban-centred. Indigenisation of social work education therefore remains the greatest challenge in the region, though some *local* efforts are noteworthy: such efforts are often a combination of global and local initiatives, as in Vietnam (Hugman, 2010).

Developments in social work practice

The foundation for social work practice is laid in field education programmes (AASW, 2008: 37; ALTC, 2010: 7), and, as mentioned, schools normally include field education to a significant extent (Cox et al., 1997). Students have opportunities to observe a range of government and non-government agencies and to develop their practice skills in at least two different settings focusing on work with individuals and groups, or on work with communities and organisations. This kind of field education is possible where social work schools are located in large urban centres where hospitals, NGOs and government welfare programmes can be accessed. Some schools have also initiated their own fieldwork projects, which are used for student placements.[2]

Where new social work schools have been established in small towns and rural areas and professionally trained social work educators are not available, the provision of quality field education for social work students is limited due to the inadequate number and range of field work agencies and non-availability of trained field work educators. This trend in field education could result in qualified social workers who lack practice knowledge and skills; and measures to address the issue (e.g. establishment of minimum standards, resources for field education, training of fieldwork educators and expectations regarding student supervision) could be encouraged through international collaboration.

Qualified social workers practise in a wide range of settings (e.g. hospitals, schools, governmental and non-governmental organisations) (Cox et al., 1997) and fields of practice include mental health, adoption, disability, labour welfare, disaster relief and rehabilitation. Client groups include families, children, youth, elders, migrants and refugees, and communities. A relatively small proportion of workers are found in development projects directly addressing poverty and unemployment issues, e.g. through micro credit and self-help groups. In Japan, Singapore and South Korea (where welfare and social security systems are relatively well developed) a large proportion of social workers are employed in government organisations or in government-funded welfare programmes. In the other countries, social workers mainly practise in NGOs; and only a small number of social workers work in the field of social policy and planning throughout the region.

Many countries in the region are disaster prone (e.g. the tsunami in South and East Asia in 2006, the earthquake in Sichuan, China in 2008 and the earthquake, tsunami and nuclear radiation leakage in Japan in 2011). So some schools have developed a focus on training for disaster-related work (Tan et al., 2006; Rowlands and Tan, 2008). While some social workers work in 'social worker' designated jobs, the positions and titles held by others might not reflect their professional qualification (e.g. community organiser/development officer, probation and parole officer, project manager or coordinator). Many countries in the region have neither developed their own code of ethics for social work practice nor acknowledge the international code of social work ethics. It is also concerning that a small number of social workers are leaving the field to work in other occupations and may or may not return to social work. Similarly, some jobs that could well be performed by social workers are performed by others, sometimes because there is not a sufficient supply of qualified social workers.

Despite these concerns, innovative social work practice is notable in some countries, for instance, with street children in India (e.g. Butterflies, 2010; see also Dabir and Athale, 2011) and scavengers' cooperatives in the Philippines (Medina, 2000). Some social workers from the region have assumed social activist roles and demonstrated extraordinary achievement in mobilising marginalised people to work for social change. For example, Ms Medha Patkar, an environmental activist has done remarkable work with indigenous people in Western India and has been fighting for their land and human rights (see the Right to Livelihood Award, 1991). Similarly, Evelyn Balais-Serrano, a social worker from the Philippines, has made a significant contribution to asserting social work's role in human rights work at national, regional and international levels (see Balais-Serrano, 2000, 2007).

Developments in social work research

Social work research is an important part of the social work profession, as knowledge creation and skills development depends on it. Most of the social work schools provide research methodology training as part of the social work curriculum. Although social work educators and practitioners perform several research roles (see Tripodi and Potocky-Tripodi, 2007), research undertaken in the social work field may be broadly delineated into five categories: course work dissertations; research higher degrees; funded research projects; research publication and dissemination; and workshops/seminars/conferences (Pawar, 2010).

As mentioned, a number of students complete a minor dissertation on a relevant topic as part of their undergraduate or postgraduate courses; and social work research is undertaken at PhD level often by social work educators in their own country or overseas. Increasingly, social work educators undertake funded research projects on a range of social issues and competitive grants may be awarded by research organisations (e.g. the Indian Council of Social Science Research) by relevant ministries or international/national NGOs.[3] With regard to research publication and dissemination, a number of peer-reviewed social work journals are published in the region, including *Asia Pacific Journal of Social Work and Development*, *China Journal of Social Work*, *Hong Kong Journal of Social Work*, *The Indian Journal of Social Work*, *Perspectives in Social Work*, *Contemporary Social Work* (earlier named *Lucknow University Journal of Social Work*) and *Rajagiri Journal of Social Development*. Some authors have published in international journals (see Chapter 1) and social work professionals from the region have also published a number of authored and edited books both in English and local languages. As in other regions, well-established social work schools located in research-oriented universities generally have better research output than others.

Finally, research activity includes the organisation of workshops, seminars and conferences to discuss research outcomes and related issues. Although statistical data are not available, such academic gatherings are organised with varied frequencies at all levels. However, many social work educators and practitioners find it difficult to participate in such events due to lack of resources, and more frequent organisation of such events at local level would be beneficial.

Given the size of the region, including 26 countries and the growing number of social work schools, it is questionable whether this research is adequate in terms of quality and quantity. Social work research output still lags behind research in other social sciences, and research does not reflect the range of innovative and interesting practice being undertaken in challenging settings. The lack of systematic research and publication mechanisms in some countries leads to an absence of effective systems for disseminating practice knowledge with evidence. There is still considerable reliance on word of mouth and informal networks for sharing information, and social work educators generally need to do a lot more research, writing and publishing either in their own language or in English.

CORE ISSUES AND PROSPECTS FOR SOCIAL WORK IN THE REGION

In nearly a century of professional social work in the region, much has been accomplished in terms of professional development, education, practice and research. However, considering the magnitude of the issues faced, it appears that more can and should be done. Poverty, unemployment, urbanisation and migration; conflicts, refugees and inter- and intra-national displacement of people; violation of human rights and gender discrimination; weak governance systems; limited health, education and housing provision; and the special needs of children, women, elderly and disabled people all need to be addressed at local, national and international levels. In a way social work appears to have remained as a 'caged non-violent tiger': it needs to be thoughtfully released for the benefit of the whole region and beyond.

Social work prospects in the region are promising. To realise those prospects, social work itself needs to change its perspectives to meet the needs of people and the region. Whether the profession is ready or not, social work schools are growing fast in the region. For example, in China, by 2010 there were 240 BSW programmes and, in the same year,

26 top universities in China recruited the first cohort of MSW students, with the expectation that the number of MSW programmes will increase to 50 in the near future. The Chinese government plans to increase the number of professional social workers from 400,000 in 2010 to 3,000,000 in 2020. In India social work schools are also increasing, though accurate or estimated figures are not available. Unstructured and informally collected data suggested that one of the states (Maharashtra) in India has nearly 150 social work programmes. In another state, 32 BSW programmes have been initiated, affiliated to just one university. One MSW programme had to expand to two new campuses as the main campus could cope with an increasing number of students (Pawar, 2010). In Lao PDR, a the landlocked and one of least developed countries in the world, in 2006 the National University started a BA in sociology and social development (BSSD) programme in which social work is also taught. The BSSD has become a popular programme among young people and about 500 students were studying on this programme in 2008–2009.[4] In seven countries (see Table 25.2) of the region, there is no formal social work programme, although most of these countries are listed among the UN's 'least developed'.

The claim that social work is now a global profession (Healy, 2001; Hugman, 2010) may be true as, in many capital cities and large urban centres, largely Western-modelled social work exists. But such social work has mostly remained isolated from the majority of rural and remote parts of the region. Thus, the answer to the question, 'is social work a local profession?' is 'no' for most of the Southern and Eastern Asian region. The question, therefore, is how can we make social work also a local profession in the region?

The major requirement is for a shift in the perspective of professional social work. It needs to shift from mostly a clinical and remedial focus on individuals to local-level social-development- oriented social work (Pawar and Cox, 2010). Local-level social development involves comprehensive growth of grassroots level communities and villages, along nine dimensions – cultural, political, economic, ecological, education, health, housing, equity groups, citizens and their institutions – by the local-level communities themselves (e.g. see chapters 2 and 3 in Pawar and Cox, 2010; also Midgley and Conley, 2010). These dimensions have been largely neglected by the mainstream development efforts.

Opportunities and necessary resources, including infrastructure for social work education and practice, need to be provided in rural and remote areas in all countries of the region, particularly in the least developed countries and the least developed areas within countries, targeting the most disadvantaged and marginalised population groups. One of the most neglected groups in the region are indigenous populations and local minority groups, which have been often marginalised and sometimes even persecuted.

A pertinent issue with great potential for the region is indigenisation of its social work education and practice. While many social work educators and practitioners are conscious of this issue, and have made this suggestion several times (Gray, 2005; Gray et al., 2008; Pawar, 1999; Tsang and Yan, 2001; Tsui and Yan, 2010) very little has been achieved. Where indigenisation has occurred, it has grown as a natural course of action, often serendipitously. There seem to be adverse forces that consciously or inadvertently perpetuate Western social work models that do not dovetail with the region and local conditions. Conscious and concerted efforts need to be made to indigenise social work education and practice and some strategies have been suggested (Pawar, 1999) as follows:

1   Acknowledgement of the fact that current teaching is based on US/Western social work models.
2   Questioning the relevance of the models and the specialisations often resulting.
3   Identifying what is irrelevant and why – and retaining only what is relevant.
4   Identifying the national and local special circumstances and factors which need to be addressed.
5   Identifying and documenting country-specific coping methods, interventions and solutions, and incorporating these into classroom teaching and field education.
6   Organisation of curriculum development workshops at the school and inter-schools levels involving educators, practitioners and student representatives.

Through these processes an entire social work curriculum can be revised to indigenise and fit better with local contexts.

One of the critical issues within the region relates to quality assurance and maintenance of standards in a time of rapidly expanding social work education and practice. Many conscientious social work professionals are concerned that the consequences of this expansion – without sufficient and appropriately trained social work educators; without adequate books, information technology facilities and libraries; with only a limited number of field education placements and variable supervision opportunities – will be the qualification of social workers insufficiently and inappropriately trained to meet the challenges. This could result in unintentional harm to people and communities rather than achieving the goals and standards the profession sets. Global social work standards (Appendix 3) were expected to address this issue to some extent. However, they may not help to maintain quality social work education practice as there is some resistance to these standards, which have been the subject of considerable controversy in the region (Gray and Fook, 2004; Noble, 2004; Sewpaul and Jones, 2004; Yip, 2004). There is a clear need to establish functional professional associations which can develop social work standards and ethics appropriate to the development of social-development-oriented social work programmes. These would build on local knowledge and resources to address contemporary and emerging issues including gender inequalities, human rights infringements, and climate change adaptation and mitigation strategies.

Following a process of indigenisation, social work programmes drawing on and creating local knowledge and resources may not require aid from the West for this or any other purpose. As the economies of China, India and the four Asian tigers grow and others develop, the similarities could become more important than the differences between North and South or East and West, which could become blurred or irrelevant. Resources could be mobilised within the region to indigenise the social work curricula, create local knowledge and develop social work programmes where they are most needed. Given current development trends, many countries should be able to mutually help each other with their own development. This would not negate positive aspects of the globalisation process, but its text and context would be different. It is important to learn from economic development experience of the West, where, in the midst of economic growth and wealth, poverty and related social ills persist and social work has consciously or inadvertently maintained that status quo in a reactive manner or failed to change it. On the other hand, in the East, in the midst of poverty and related problems, economic growth and wealth persist, albeit unequally distributed. Here the aim of social work should be not to replicate and recreate Western models, but to develop indigenous ways to address the issues so as to achieve comprehensive local-level social development where economic and social changes work together to combat poverty and related social problems.

Mobilising and employing local resources, and the necessary training and capacity building could lead to development of social work schools and growth of research, writing and publishing which emphasises indigenisation of social work education and practice. As this occurs, more avenues for publication and dissemination are needed, including books and journals both in local and English languages at less cost, so that they are readily accessible to social workers in the region.

To achieve the above, and to make social work truly a local profession, local, regional,

national and international cooperation and collaboration within Southern and Eastern Asia and beyond is needed and should be cultivated. This can be done by employing the available information technology and establishing and developing networks and connections within social work to better connect at local, national and international levels (see Figure 25.1).

CONCLUSION

This chapter has aimed to provide a broad overview of the current status of professional social work in East and South Asia. To this end, we have analysed developments in social work as a profession and in social work education, practice and research. Drawing on this analysis, we have presented core issues, particularly the need for localisation of social work education and practice; a developmental perspective in social work; and the promotion of relevant quality standards and ethics with necessary resource support. Given the economic growth forecast for the region and associated social changes, the potential for social work growth in the region is significant, particularly in the least developed areas of all countries. The analysis unequivocally lends support to our core argument that professional social work needs to be locality-specific, and to achieve this concerted cooperative and co-ordinated efforts are needed at local, national and global levels. We believe that the ideas expressed in this chapter may facilitate the realisation of this hope for the region.

NOTES

1   Most or majority refers to about 66 percent of the population belonging to a particular religion.
2   For example, the well-known Tata Institute of Social Sciences in India has initiated a number of fieldwork projects (a child guidance clinic; social

work at police stations; rehabilitation work at Prayas; and several community development oriented projects) with varying degree of success.

3 A number of evaluation and action research projects are also undertaken by social work schools. In fact, for one rural-based social work school in India, such projects were an important means for running the school programme as staff members were expected to teach during morning hours and work for the projects in the afternoon, this being an important source of their income.

4 Based on an email communication from Saychai Syladeth, an academic at the National University of Laos.

REFERENCES

AASW (Australian Association of Social Workers) (2008) *Australian Social Work Education and Accreditation Standards.* Canberra: AASW.

ALTC (Australian Learning and Teaching Council) (2010) A *Guide to Supervision in Social Work Field Education.* Sydney: ALTC.

APASWE (Asian and Pacific Association for Social Work Education) (2009) *APASWE Membership 2010.* Retrieved on 5 June 2010 from http://www.apaswe. com.

Balais-Serrano, E. (2000) 'International displacement in Southeast Asia', *Refugee Survey Quarterly*, 19 (2): 58–63.

Balais-Serrano, E. (2007) *Rome Statute of the International Criminal Court Ratification and Implementation in Asia: Some Prospects and Concerns.* Retrieved on 4 December 2010 from http://www.icclr.law.ubc.ca/Site%20Map/ICC/ AsiaProspectsandConcerns.pdf.

Butterflies (2010) *Buttlerflies.* View an NGO's work at http://www.butterflieschildrights.org/home.php.

Cox, D. (1995) 'Asia and the Pacific', in T.D. Watts, D. Elliot and N.S. Mayadas (eds), *International Handbook on Social Work Education.* Westport: Greenwood Press. pp. 321–38.

Cox, D. (1997) 'Asia and the Pacific', in N.S. Mayadas, T.D. Watts and D. Elliot (eds), *International Handbook on Social Work Theory and Practice.* Westport: Greenwood Press. pp. 369–82.

Cox, D., Pawar, M. and Picton, C. (1997) *Social Development Content in Social Work Education.* Melbourne: RSDC, La Trobe University.

Dabir, N. and Athale, N. (2011) *From Street to Hope.* New Delhi: Sage.

Drucker, D. (2009) 'Whither international social work? A reflection', *International Social Work*, 46 (1): 53–81.

FAO (Food and Agriculture Organization) (2003) *Activities of FAO in Support of Least Developed Countries, Land-Locked Developing Countries and Small Island Developing States.* Retrieved on 2 March 2009 from http://www.fao.org/docrep/meeting/006/y9308e.htm.

Gray, M. (2005) 'Dilemmas of international social work: Paradoxical processes of indigenisation, universalism and imperialism', *International Journal of Social Welfare*, 14 (3): 231–8.

Gray, M. and Fook, J. (2004) 'The quest for a universal social work: Some issues and implications', *Social Work Education*, 23 (5): 625–44.

Gray, M., Coates, J. and Yellow Bird, M. (eds) (2008) *Indigenous Social Work around the World. Towards Culturally Relevant Education and Practice.* Burlington: Ashgate.

Healy, L.M. (2001) *International Social Work: Professional Action in an Interdependent World.* New York: Oxford University Press.

Hugman, R. (2010) *Understanding International Social Work: A Critical Analysis.* Basingstoke: Palgrave Macmillan.

IASSW (International Association of Schools of Social Work) (2010) *List of Member Schools 2010.* Retrieved on 5 June 2010 from http://www.iassw-aiets.org/ index.php?option=com_content&task=blogcategory&id=69&Itemid=103.

IFSW (International Federation of Social Workers) (2008) *IFSW Member Organisations.* Retrieved on 5 June 2010 from http://www.ifsw.org/f38000017. html.

Liu, J.T. (2003) 'A review of documents: A critical analysis of ten important issues in the development of social work education in China', *Hong Kong Journal of Social Work*, 37 (1): 41–59.

Mandal, K.S. (1995) 'India', in T.D. Watts, D. Elliot and N.S. Mayadas (eds), *International Handbook on Social Work Education.* Westport: Greenwood Press. pp. 355–65.

Medina, M. (2000) *Scavenger Cooperatives in Asia and Latin America.* Retrieved on 1 January 2009 from http://www.wiego.org/occupational_groups/ waste_collectors/Medina%20Scavenger%20 Cooperatives%20in%20Asia%20and%20LAC.pdf.

Midgley, J. (1981) *Professional Imperialism: Social Work in the Third World.* London: Heinemann.

Midgley, J. and Conley, A. (2010) *Social Work and Social Development: Theories and Skills for Developmental Social Work.* New York: Oxford University Press.

Nanavatty, M.C. (1997) 'India', in N.S. Mayadas, T.D. Watts and D. Elliot (eds), *International Handbook on Social Work Theory and Practice*. Westport: Greenwood Press. pp. 245–62.

Nikku, B.R. (2009) 'Social work education in South Asia: a Nepalese perspective', in C. Noble, M. Henrickson and Y. Han (eds), *Social Work Education: Voices from the Asia Pacific*. Melbourne: Vulgar Press.

Noble, C. (2004) 'Social work education, training and standards in the Asia-Pacific region', *Social Work Education*, 23 (5): 527–36.

O'Brien, J. and Palmer, M. (1993) *State of Religion Atlas*. London: Simon & Schuster.

Pawar M. (1999) 'Professional social work in India: Some issues and strategies', *Indian Journal of Social Work*, 60 (4): pp. 566–86.

Pawar, M. (2009) 'Community development in China: Problems and prospects', in P. Basu and Y. Bandara (eds), *WTO Accession and Social Economic Development in China*. Oxford: Chandos Publishing.

Pawar, M. (2010) *Social Work in Southern and Eastern Asia: Contemporary Developments and Issues*. Paper presented at the 2010 Joint World Conference, Social Work and Social Development: the Agenda, 10–14 June 2010, Hong Kong, China.

Pawar, M. and Cox, D. (eds) (2010) *Social Development: Critical Themes and Perspectives*. New York: Routledge.

Ranade, S.N. (1987) 'Social work', in *Encyclopaedia of Social Work in India* (Volume 3). New Delhi: Ministry of Welfare, Government of India. pp. 134–42.

Right to Livelihood Award (1991) http://www.rightlivelihood.org/narmada.pdf.

Rowlands, A. and Tan, N.T. (2008) 'Social development following the Indian Ocean tsunami: an international social work response through the Fast project', *Social Development Issues*, 30 (1): 47–58.

Sewpaul, V. and Jones, D. (2004) 'Global standards for social work education and training', *Social Work Education*, 23 (5): 493–513.

Tan, N.T., Rowlands, A. and Yuen, F.K.O. (2006) *Asian Tsunami and Social Work Practice: Recovery and Rebuilding*. New York: Haworth.

Todaro, M.P. and Smith, S.C. (2003) *Economic Development* (8th edn). Harlow, England: Pearson.

Tripodi, T. and Potocky-Tripodi, M. (2007) *International Social Work Research: Issues and Prospects*. New York: Oxford University Press.

Tsang, A.K.T. and Yan, M.C. (2001) 'Chinese corpus, western applications: the Chinese strategy of engagement with western social work discourse', *International Social Work*, 44 (4): 433–54.

Tsui, M. and Yan, M.C. (2010) 'Editorial: developing social work in developing countries: experiences in the Asia Pacific region', *International Social Work*, 53 (3): 307–9.

UNDP (United Nations Development Programme) (2005) *Voices of the Least Developed Countries of Asia and the Pacific: Achieving the Millennium Development Goals Through a Global Partnership*. Retrieved on 20 March 2009 from http://www.unescap.org/unis/Library/pub_pdf/LDCMDG-Voices.pdf

UNESCAP (United Nations Economic and Social Commission for Asia and the Pacific) (2010a) *Economic Social Survey of Asia and the Pacific 2010: Sustaining Recovery and Dynamism for Inclusive Development*. Bangkok: UNESCAP.

UNESCAP (United Nations Economic and Social Commission for Asia and the Pacific) (2010b) *Achieving the Millennium Development Goals in an Era of Global Uncertainty: Asia-Pacific Regional Report 2009/10*. Bangkok: UNESCAP.

WHO-AIMS (World Health Organisation Assessment Instrument for Mental Health Systems) (2007) *Report on Mental Health System in Bhutan*. Thimphu: WHO and Ministry of Health, Bhutan.

Yan, M.C. and Tsui, M.S. (2007) 'The quest for western social work knowledge: literature in the USA and practice in China', *International Social Work*, 50 (5): 641–53.

Yip, K.-S. (2004) 'A Chinese cultural critique of the global qualifying standards for social work education', *Social Work Education*, 23 (5): 597–612.

Yip, K.-S. (2005) 'A dynamic response to globalization in cross cultural social work', *International Social Work*, 48 (5): 593–607.

Yuen-Tsang, A.W.K. and Wang, S.B. (2002) 'Tensions confronting development of social work education in China', *International Social Work*, 45 (3): 375–88.

26

Social Work in Australasia

Liz Beddoe and Heather Fraser

INTRODUCTION

Australasia is a large, complex region in the South Pacific which has a rich mix of developed and developing nations, comprising diverse cultures, geographies and histories. The term Australasia is used to describe Australia and the islands of the south-west Pacific Ocean, including New Zealand and New Guinea (Everett-Heath, 2010). Combining the Latin word 'australis' (or 'southern') with the word 'Asia', 'Australasia' became a popular term in the late nineteenth century (Everett-Heath, 2010) and was mostly used by those in the northern hemisphere to refer to Australia and New Zealand (Doyle, 2001). Since then 'Australasia' has sometimes been used to refer to Australia, New Zealand and Asian countries, such as Indonesia and Malaysia, while others include the Pacific island groups, which include many sovereign nations, and related territories in Antarctica. For our purposes we are including Australia, New Zealand, Papua New Guinea and the islands of the south-west Pacific region.[1]

While some problems such as those relating to violence, abuse, poverty and rising sea levels are shared across and within the region

there is great diversity with regard to culture, social conventions, the distribution of wealth, political participation, the rights and aspirations of Indigenous peoples and the diverse nature of social welfare systems. Similarly, social work developments have been uneven across the region, reflected in the availability of research and literature. These factors, as well as the experiential knowledge of the authors, lead to an emphasis on the largest countries in the region, Australia and New Zealand.

Our aim in this chapter is to present an overview of key socioeconomic features of the countries in the region as a background against which we explore social work in its many forms. In particular we wish to recognise the aspirations of Indigenous peoples[2] in a region shaped by colonisation over more than two centuries, and the role of social work in addressing oppression. Western models of social work do not fit Indigenous cultures and are frequently associated with 'what Durie (1997) calls colonial narratives – stories of displacement, discontinuity and cultural oppression' (cited in Ruwhiu, 2009: 113). Finally, we consider current issues in social welfare which present considerable challenges to social work, as well as the need to develop more appropriate forms of post-colonial social work, relevant to local conditions in each country.

COUNTRY CONTEXTS

As suggested above, sharp differences exist between the post-industrial countries of Australia and New Zealand and the smaller south Pacific islands in which adherence to traditional lifestyles, subsistence agriculture or fishing and primary industries predominate. In 2009, the Organisation for Economic Co-operation and Development (OECD) ranked New Zealand and Australia second and ninth, respectively, in terms of economic performance, while Tonga and Fiji were ranked 52nd and 54th, with Papua New Guinea ranked as 102nd out of 183 countries (Doing Business, 2010). In many countries in the region, processed food is increasingly replacing traditional foods. This in turn has meant that diabetes has become an important health concern in addition to other chronic diseases (e.g. malaria), particularly in the islands least resourced to address health problems. We now provide a brief profile of the main countries in the region.

Australia

Australia is a large island continent with a population of 22 million people residing predominantly in urban centres, dotted around the coast. In 2009, the median age of the Australian population was 36.8 years, up from 36.3 years in 2004. When completing national census surveys the majority of Australians identify themselves as Christian but a much smaller proportion attend church. Notably, almost one quarter of people living in Australia were born elsewhere and many more are first or second generation Australians, the children and grandchildren of recently arrived migrants and refugees (Australian Government, 2010).

Originally, an estimated 250 Indigenous cultural groups inhabited the area (Australian Bureau of Statistics (ABS, 2010), over a period of approximately 40,000 years. In 1788, however, Australia became an outpost for British empire-building efforts and a solution to their overflowing prisons. This was followed by 'free settlers' or Europeans looking for a new life and way to acquire land that they could use for farming. In 1901 the Commonwealth of Australia was established as a Constitutional Monarchy. However, it was not until 1967 that Indigenous Australians were formally recognised as Australian citizens, after non-Indigenous Australians voted for it in a national referendum. Today, Indigenous people make up 2.4 percent of the total Australian population (about 460,000 people) and the legacy of colonisation has continued with chronic poverty, unemployment, high morbidity, mortality and incarceration rates constituting some of the indicators of ongoing oppression against Indigenous Australians (Briskman, 2008).

Australia is now regarded as a developed, post-industrial capitalist society with a liberal, representative form of democracy operating across three tiers of government: local councils; state governments; and the federal government. The voting system is preferential and for Australian citizens and permanent residents, voting is compulsory, with fines occasionally levelled at those failing to vote.

Agriculture, mining, manufacturing, tertiary education and tourism are Australia's main industries. Cattle and sheep farming and grain growing continue to dominate, along with forestry (ABS, 2010).

Australians consume vast quantities of fossil fuels. Arguments about whether to sign up to international carbon emissions reduction targets and trading schemes have been fierce. To date, Australia has done neither in spite of significant levels of concern in the wider Australian society about fossil fuel use, proposed nuclear power plants, carbon trading schemes and the environment more generally. However, a carbon tax commenced July 2012.

Drought and salinity problems, particularly in regional areas, have also dogged Australia. These problems have not been helped by farming and domestic practices that consume the relatively scarce fresh water supply with an ever-increasing appetite. The effects of rising temperatures from climate change are also being felt, and the devastation from the recent floods has been profound. Aggressive settlement, particularly in low-density expansions, has seriously threatened outer-city multi-species habitat. Yet, housing shortages and rising housing costs, particularly in the major cities, have bolstered arguments to expand suburban 'development', so as to ease pressure on 'average families' (Property Wire, 2010).

In 2007–2008 the Australian average household income was AU $811 per week (ABS, 2010) and by 2010 the unemployment rate was 5 percent (OECD, 2010). Relative to other nations, Australia has fared well in the recent 'global financial crisis' (OECD, 2010). In part this has been attributed to Australia's natural resources boom, the easing of drought and the Rudd Labour federal government's AU$42 billion 'Stimulus Package' in 2009–2010. The Stimulus Package used a form of neo-Keynesian economics to stimulate demand for goods, services and labour by making direct cash payments to millions of individuals and strong reinvestment into infrastructure projects (for example, schools) (Grattan, 2009). Yet, what these figures hide is the growing evidence of social stratification, poverty and social inequality (Gorey, 2007; Pease, 2010).

New Zealand

New Zealand is a small country in the southwestern Pacific Ocean with two main islands (the North Island/Te Ika-a-Maui and the South Island/Te Wai Pouamu), and numerous smaller islands. New Zealand is regarded as the last land mass in the world to be discovered, and inhabited by Māori most probably in the 13th century. Large-scale European colonial settlement began in the 1840s and since then New Zealand has changed from a British colony to a modern, developed democracy with considerable cultural diversity (Wilson, 2009).

The Treaty of Waitangi is of great significance in New Zealand social policy (Belgrave et al., 2005). Signed in 1840, the Treaty is an agreement between the joint tribes of New Zealand and the British Crown, the latter, in the modern social democracy, becoming the New Zealand government. There were two different versions, in Māori and in English. The Treaty provided protection and governance but does not, according to the Māori version, cede sovereignty in exchange for British citizenship (Fleras and Spoonley, 1999). The key principles are partnership, protection and participation. In the present day the Treaty of Waitangi is legally effective in the New Zealand Courts to the extent that it is recognised in many Acts of Parliament and 'is central to New Zealand political life' (Fleras and Spoonley, 1999: 13). Many of the references in statutes are not to the actual text of the Treaty but rather to the 'principles' in order to apply the Treaty to present-day circumstances and issues. The major principle, partnership, embeds biculturalism in government policy – especially in relation to environment, health, education, welfare and justice. The principle of redress arose from the partnership principle and reflects the New Zealand government's duty to actively address Treaty breaches, for example land confiscation. This entails recognition and recompense for wrongdoing and has resulted in many settlements where land and financial benefits have been applied to ensure redress. In social work this is reflected in the Bicultural Code of Practice (ANZASW, 2008) which requires members to advocate for equal Māori participation in policy, decision making and equal access to resources. Social workers need an appreciation of Māori culture and protocol and aspire to support Māori social workers to work with Māori services users.

From the 1840s until the 1990s citizenship was largely linked to the British Empire with this reflected in narrow immigration policies (Bartley and Spoonley, 2005: 137). Since the early 1990s a liberalised immigration policy has led to increased migration from Asia with a view to developing trade and attracting investment. New Zealand's population is estimated at over 4 million with roughly three-quarters of the population identifying their ethnicity as either European or Other, 565,000 people identifying as Māori, 354,000 as Asian, 265,000 as of Pacific islands heritage and 34,000 as either Middle Eastern, Latin American or African (Statistics New Zealand, 2007). The growth of migration from Asia, Africa and the Middle East has raised tensions between the 'new' multiculturalism and the bicultural stance developed over the last three decades. Multicultural policies and programmes offer legitimation of migrants' status and contributions in New Zealand society while biculturalism is fundamental acknowledgement of 'indigeneity and original occupancy' (Fleras and Spoonley, 1999: 248).

New Zealand is regarded as a post-industrial developed nation with a democratic government in Westminster style, and a mixed member proportional representation system of electing a government since 1993. New Zealand's main sources of income are from manufacturing, services, construction, agriculture, education and tourism (New Zealand Government, Careers, 2010). Natural beauty abounds alongside the serious challenges associated with climate change.

Papua New Guinea

Papua New Guinea (PNG) is the largest developing country in the South Pacific region. It comprises 600 separate islands and one of the most diverse repositories of geographic, biological, linguistic and cultural wealth on earth, with more than 5 percent of the world's biodiversity in less than 1 percent of the world's total land area. Papua New Guinea's population in 2009 is estimated at 6.6 million, growing by an annual average rate of 2.7 percent; about 40 percent of the total population is under 15 years old (National Statistical Office of Papua New Guinea, 2000). About 86 percent of the people inhabit rural communities based on traditional village structures and dependent on subsistence farming supplemented by cash cropping; a minority inhabit coastal villages, dependent on fishing; and others have migrated to the capital (Port Moresby). PNG has a relatively small dual (formal and informal) economy with the formal economy dominated by large-scale resource projects, particularly in mining and petroleum, providing a large proportion of government revenue. The informal economy supports 85 percent of the people (mainly through semi-subsistence agriculture). With an abundance of natural resources including minerals, forestry, fishery and agriculture, PNG also has an increasing interest in ecological and cultural tourism.

Fiji

Fiji is made up of 322 islands and atolls, inhabited by 837,000 people, of whom there are 475,000 Indigenous Fijians, 313,000 Indian Fijians and 47,000 Others. Agriculture and mining are key sources of the country's income. Tourism is important though it has recently been impacted by a volatile political situation. In 2006 Fiji experienced a military takeover of its elected civilian government (partly related to ethnic rivalries) and consequently faces an uncertain future and many challenges. However, it is a central location for the University of the South Pacific and has air links and trade with other Pacific islands, such as Vanuatu, so could resume a previous path to economic development if ethnic tensions could be resolved and democratic rule re-established.

Western Samoa

The estimated population of Western Samoa is 187,000 (Samoan Bureau of Statistics, 2011) with most Samoans living on the two main islands of Savai'i and Upolu, mainly in small, coastal villages. Around 60 percent of

Samoan households depend on a mixture of subsistence and commercial agriculture. The main sources of income for the country are remittances and tourism. Participatory poverty assessments undertaken by the government confirm that a significant number of households experience hardship arising from 'poverty of opportunity' that is manifested in three ways: the lack of access to basic services; inadequate resources to meet basic household needs and customary obligations to family, village community and church; and limited opportunities to participate fully in the socioeconomic life of the community. Those most vulnerable to hardship include landless people, unemployed adults (especially unskilled youth), single income households, isolated rural households, people with disabilities and elderly persons without family support. In September 2009 a tsunami struck Samoa: 143 people were killed, 500 injured and 5247 people were directly affected with losses to housing, agriculture and small business.

Tonga

Tonga is a kingdom with a population of around 120,000 people spread across 36 of its 169 islands, with most living on the main island of Tongatapu. Agriculture, fisheries and tourism are the basis of the Tongan economy. The larger islands are fertile and support crops for local consumption and export. However, Tonga's small, open economy is vulnerable to fluctuations in world commodity prices and susceptible to natural disasters such as cyclones. The public sector plays a large role in the economy together with remittances, the latter signalling the importance of emigration by people seeking work in other countries.

Raratonga and the Cook Islands

Approximately 20,000 people live on the 15 islands which constitute the Cook Islands

with another 37,000 Cook Islands people living in neighbouring New Zealand. Polynesians comprise at least 80 percent of the total population and many converted to Christianity in the colonial era. As with so many other countries in the region, subsistence farming is central. Tourism is the major industry, and fruit processing provides some employment. Yet, in Western terms, the economy of the Cook Islands is fragile, even if the people themselves are robust. New Zealand is the major export partner and also provides international aid. English is now the dominant language and the legal system is based on that in operation in New Zealand.

CHARACTERISTICS OF SOCIAL WORK IN THE REGION

While there are many common features, there is great diversity in how social work is practised throughout the region (Noble et al., 2009). Greater international labour mobility, trends towards greater regulation of social workers and changing pre-service educational requirements have raised awareness of issues stemming from the internationalisation of social work (Beddoe and Duke, 2009). The IASSW (International Association of Schools of Social Work) Global Qualifying Standards document recognises the increasing mobility of social workers and raises hopes for greater comparability of broad curricula between qualifications in order to facilitate portability of the qualifications (IASSW, 2005). Yet the development and regulation of the profession of social work has not been without debate.

Regulation and professional bodies

Increased regulation of social work in many countries, together with greater labour mobility, is a potential source of tension in the region. For instance, New Zealand requires a minimum of a three-year qualification for registration, although New Zealand and Australian universities offer both four-year Bachelor of Social Work degrees and two-year qualifying masters degrees for those who hold a relevant undergraduate degree. An agreement between the two governments includes mutual recognition principles relating to the registration of occupations, thus the disparity in qualification requirements might pose difficulties for the regulating bodies, should Australian social work move towards statutory regulation (Beddoe and Duke, 2009). One of the consequences of increasing regulation is that, having regulated qualifications and standards for social work, professional bodies need to reconcile their standards with the need to recruit those with overseas qualifications to meet any shortfall in 'home-grown' graduates. While there are clearly regulatory issues here, there are also challenges for social work practice contexts, training and cultural awareness (Welbourne et al., 2007).

In Australia the professional social work body is the Australian Association of Social Workers (AASW), which approves social work qualifications. In New Zealand, the Aotearoa New Zealand Association of Social Workers (ANZASW) does not approve qualifications (which are assessed for recognition by the Social Workers Registration Board). Both professional social work associations are affiliated to the International Federation of Social Workers (IFSW). The role of associations in the development of social work is complex and national histories are often poorly recorded (Mendes, 2005). Many professional associations have struggled to manage tensions between working for social justice and promotion of the interests of the profession by achieving enhanced professional legitimacy (O'Brien, 2005). Both Gillingham (2007) and O'Brien (2005) suggest that professional registration need not lead to diminished public advocacy; but can be used to voice concerns, particularly about the impact of public policy on groups already disadvantaged by structural inequality, poverty and marginalisation.

Developments related to professional registration, the scope of practice and other forms of credentialing indicate that social work across the region is in a process of change (Nash, 2009). In New Zealand (but not Australia) limited registration has been achieved, albeit still voluntary beyond the state sector (Beddoe and Duke, 2009).

In 2001 there were an estimated 10,000 people employed in Australia who possessed an AASW recognised social work qualification. Today the AASW has 6000 members and takes an active role in the accreditation of social work programmes. Membership is voluntary and members must hold a qualification approved by the AASW. In 2011, 2841 of an estimated 6000 social workers were registered in New Zealand and the ANZASW has approximately 4000 members. However, precise data on the size of the social work workforce is difficult to obtain without 'protection of title', as people who would not be eligible for registration can describe themselves as social workers. A similar situation pertains in Australia making it difficult to get an accurate picture of the size of the workforce from government statistics in both countries. Both professional associations have set expectations for practitioners to meet continuing education requirements; and involvement in these processes has increased visibility, leading to an increase in membership.

In both Australia and New Zealand, Indigenous social work organisations have formed. For instance, in Australia the National Coalition of Aboriginal and Torres Strait Islander Social Workers Association offers full membership to Indigenous Australian social workers and associate membership to non-Indigenous Australian social workers (NCATSISWA, 2011). Unlike New Zealand, there is no treaty between Indigenous and non-Indigenous Australians. In the most recent Australian Social Workers' Code of Ethics (AASW, 2010) Indigenous interests and the importance of practising culturally sensitive social work are clearly stated. It is another example of Australian social workers collectively trying to come to terms with the contradictory and, at times, deeply coercive roles enacted with and over Indigenous people (Briskman, 2007).

More recently a new organisation, the Tangata Whenua Social Workers Association has formed in New Zealand, with self-determination for Māori practitioners a major goal, recognising that over the last 20 years '*By Māori for Māori* services have grown and produced practice models, Māori frameworks, Māori fields of practice and *iwi* (tribes) and Māori social services. Together these models and services are all assertions of *rangatiratanga* (self-determination and governance)' (Tangata Whenua Social Workers Association, 2010).

The region is developing greater involvement in international social work bodies (Gray and Rennie, 2007: 45–7). For example, from the early 1990s New Zealand social work has developed from being very isolated through extending its international relationships. International contact occurs at the professional body level (IFSW); amongst educators via IASSW, particularly through the Asia Pacific regional networks; and for employers and practitioners via international communities of policy and practice development.

While development of professional associations and accreditation has not been high on the agenda of social workers in the Pacific islands, both Fiji and the Papua New Guinea have professional associations. These in turn have links to regional and international bodies and significant efforts are made to enable representatives to attend global conferences, as well as participating in regional events closer to home.

Education and research

In any country the profession of social work is also linked to the educational opportunities available. Social work education across Australasia varies dramatically and while Anglo-American oriented social work programmes have long been established in Australia and New Zealand, community organising and development work has been more common in the Pacific, with Western forms of social work making their way into curricula only more recently. Social work education programmes contribute to the profession developing a more articulate, knowledge-informed, reflexive and critical professional stance.

Most social work educators hope that graduates will be critically reflective practitioners, imbued with a spirit of social inquiry, and with an orientation towards career-long learning and innovation. Nevertheless, variation exists among social workers in terms of how they define just practice and how willing they are to involve themselves in social activism. The battle over theoretical perspectives is ongoing, with structural, critical, and anti-oppressive and post-colonial social work approaches providing counterpoints to psychodynamic, medical and eco-systemic perspectives. Critical perspectives are strong, as demonstrated in recent publications (see, for example, Briskman, 2007; Gray et al., 2008; Mendes, 2008; Allan et al., 2009; Pease, 2010).

Accreditation processes relate not only to the length of programme or level at which awards are granted, but also to the structure and content of programmes. Specific courses on child protection, cross-cultural communication, work with Indigenous peoples and in the mental health field have moved from elective status to become core parts of curricula in Australia and in New Zealand, where competencies to work with Māori and cultural and ethnic groups must be demonstrated. In Australia, schools of social work wrestle with the multiple and diverse interests within and beyond Indigenous communities. The political landscape is complicated by recent measures introduced as 'Emergency Intervention' in selected Indigenous communities, where more coercive welfare practices have been trialled (e.g. the quarantine of welfare payments, by the Northern Territory National Emergency Response Act, 2007).

In New Zealand, the recognition of the Treaty of Waitangi principles in legislation and practice promoted a journey towards the development of both Māori and bicultural policies and practices. In health, social, education and justice services, the particular needs of Māori service users are addressed through teams and cultural advice services, all sharing the aim of ensuring that Māori values and practices are respected and Māori participation included as a matter of course. In social work this commitment has been codified in the Bicultural Code of Practice within its Code of Ethics (ANZASW, 2008). Specifically, 'Māori concepts of child welfare and family wellbeing became the norm and were no longer seen as alternative' (Bradley, 1996: 3). A significant impact is seen in the development of family decision making processes enshrined in legislation (Connolly, 1994) and the use of family group conferencing which has spread as a global practice (Connolly, 2006; Healy and Darlington, 2009).

Pasifika social workers[3] have an interest group in the ANZASW and publish an occasional issue of the local journal. Pasifika social workers and researchers have articulated approaches to practice to work with Pasifika communities and to raise awareness in social work education (Passells, 2006; Meo-Sewabu et al., 2008; Mafile'o, 2009). The new migrant social workers are also collectively organised, with groups meeting who share Chinese, African and other cultural heritages, rather supporting the contention of Fleras and Spoonley (1999: 248) that in New Zealand there is a 'mutual coexistence' of multiculturalism and biculturalism 'since neither competes with the other for the same space'.

In social work, culturally responsive practice is underpinned by notions of self-determination, partnerships and indigenous rights (Briskman, 2008; Ruwhiu, 2009). Western social work interventions do not always adequately recognise the breadth of

culture, economy, community and family, and consequently, the need to indigenise the social work curriculum is a current theme. Tiong (2006: 282) writes that 'indigenisation in the Asia-Pacific region is the process of assessing the local values and cultural context as well as the strengths and resources for appropriate social work intervention'. There is however a tension in social work education between 'the push for practice and education to become more indigenous ... and the pull to prepare graduates for the growing international labour market for social workers' (Beddoe, 2007: 48).

There is growing contact and increasing cross-fertilisation of ideas through the region's several journals, (e.g. *Australian Social Work, Aotearoa New Zealand Social Work Review*) and there are efforts to make these more relevant trans-nationally. For instance, in 2010, AASWE added a New Zealand co-editor and four New Zealand based members to the editorial board of its journal, *Advances in Social Work and Welfare Education*. There is also increasing collaboration in writing and research 'across the Tasman' with several recent books aiming to serve the needs of social work students and practitioners in both Australia and New Zealand (Beddoe and Maidment, 2009; Connolly and Harms, 2009; Noble et al., 2009).

Social work in many Pacific islands has been strengthened through development of social work education at the University of the South Pacific (USP) in Fiji and by distance in collaboration with Massey University in New Zealand (Yeates, 2006). This raises hopes for professionalisation and the development of local indigenous models of practice and research (Kuruleca, 2005; Nainoca, 2005). Some courses in the programmes are available through distance learning in the USP's 12 member countries (Cook Islands, Fiji Islands, Kiribati, Marshall Islands, Nauru, Niue, Samoa, Solomon Islands, Tokelau, Tonga, Tuvalu and Vanuatu). The Fiji Association of Social Workers has produced a journal, the *Fiji Social Workers Journal*.

Finally, the University of Papua New Guinea offers an undergraduate degree in humanities with a social work specialisation emphasising community work.

ISSUES IN SOCIAL WELFARE AND CHALLENGES FACING SOCIAL WORK

Across the region economic conservatism has increased, with many countries, including Australia and New Zealand, instituting New Public Management regimes in public health, welfare and education (Rees and Rodley, 1995). This has made both the practice and receipt of social work services and programmes ever more difficult. Health inequalities are significant issue in the region as they are elsewhere (Bywaters et al., 2009). The social determinants of health relate to the circumstances, in which people are born, grow up, live, work and age, and the systems put in place to deal with illness (Commission on Social Determinants of Health, 2008). The poorest of the poor, around the world, have the worst health. Within even developed countries, the evidence shows that in general the lower an individual's socioeconomic position the worse their health. For example, in New Zealand Māori between 45 and 64 years of age are three times more likely to die than others in the same age group (Dew and Matheson, 2008: 9). In Australia the life expectancy for Indigenous Australians is around 17 years less than for non-Indigenous Australians (ABS, 2006). Refugees and migrants are more likely to experience negative health outcomes because of additional risk factors including: experience of a major trauma (especially relevant for refugees); being isolated from their families and communities; being underemployed or unemployed; and experiencing a reduction in socioeconomic status. Both countries' governments claim commitment to reducing health inequalities, though the government rhetoric of 'closing the gaps' in New Zealand was dropped because of political pressure (Matheson and Dew, 2008: 10).

Australia

In Australia the demand for social workers is high, reflecting problems associated with growing social inequality. In spite of claims that Australia is a classless, egalitarian society, social classes exist along with other social divisions based on ethnicity, gender, sexuality, age, (dis)ability and religion (Pease, 2010). Members of the Australian upper class continue to enjoy immense wealth and many forms of unearned privilege (Pease, 2010). In the much larger middle-class there is diversity and mobility. Among the working class there is even more racial and ethnic diversity. People who are long-term unemployed and those who live in chronic poverty experience significant forms of material deprivation, stigma, alienation, exploitation and exclusion (Saunders et al., 2008). Those most susceptible include: young people leaving state care (Mendes, 2009); single adults with severe mental illness or with substance misuse problems; women and their children fleeing domestic violence (Fraser, 2008); newly arrived asylum seekers from the Middle East; and Indigenous Australians (Fraser and Briskman, 2005; Briskman et al., 2008). As Western et al. (2005: 12) note, '[N]o amount of pulling on one's individual bootstraps can change the statistical likelihood that groups with particular characteristics will be prevented from enjoying the benefits more readily available to other social groups'.

Significantly, most Aboriginal and Torres Strait Islanders grow up in families living in poverty. For most Indigenous Australians access to decent housing, education, healthcare and employment continues to be well below that of non-Indigenous Australians. While some Indigenous communities are doing well and are publicly 'showcased', many others suffer poor health in intolerable living conditions and with few resources.

A formal apology was made to members of the 'Stolen Generations' of Indigenous people forcibly and systematically removed from their families as children with the intent of fully integrating them into white society (Briskman, 2008). However, no economic reparations have followed and the overall rate of Indigenous poverty continues to be high. Dilemmas continue over whether to grant mining rights for the royalties they need so badly, or to protect sacred cultural and environmental sites, often at the expense of their own wellbeing. In most accredited social work programmes in Australia, these injustices are well known either through Indigenous electives or Indigenous case studies, yet very few Australian social workers, and even fewer academics, are Indigenous.

Many rights and entitlements long associated with Australia's welfare state have been dismantled, with many citizenship rights now conditional upon people's preparedness to carry out paid labour, even if the pay is meagre, tenure shaky and working conditions poor (Mendes, 2008). In contrast to the sunny images often associated with Australia, those receiving unemployment benefits, single-parent pensions or disability support know that the penalties for non-compliance can be severe. For example, unemployed people are expected to fulfil strict 'active citizenship obligations', or risk having their income support cut off. Welfare-to-work programmes and other expressions of 'mutual obligation' have become so embedded that two societies (or 'worlds') have been created, in one of which the fruits of global capitalism are enjoyed while in the other, some of the most basic human rights are trivialised if not denied. As Gorey (2007: 516) observes: 'Australia is fast becoming a country where the perpetual positive images force the grim facts to stay in the background'.

Over the last two decades the convergence of the two major Australian political parties has prompted some voters to question how much 'choice' they can exercise through the ballot box. Some have looked beyond the major parties and have voted for the Greens.

Some have become involved in internet activism (e.g. Get Up!), or a range of campaigns, e.g. relating to gay rights, women's rights and the refugee movement (Briskman et al., 2008). However, traditional forms of civic participation – evidenced by rates of volunteering, preparedness and availability to provide unpaid care, and informal acts of neighbourliness – have waned, especially among younger Australians, precipitating what some describe as a 'crisis in care' and 'the care deficit'. The ageing population of Australia makes the growing shortfall in quality care provision difficult to ignore, especially given the challenges facing care providers.

As Keevers et al. (2008) explain, even the smallest community organisation dependent on state support in Australia is expected to be driven *most* by cost imperatives (not human need). Community organisations of all sizes are expected to win tenders through government sponsored tendering processes and are encouraged to join up with others in 'consortiums' so that their bids are more 'competitive'. Common problems that ensue involve the mismatch of organisational values and visions, and the under-pricing of bids that often leave the winning group under-resourced to administer the programmes.

New Zealand

The previous Labour Government in New Zealand (1999–2008) opted for a self-described 'social development' framework, acknowledging that many people receiving social security benefits 'were there not because of being work-shy or facing adverse labour market conditions, but due to a range of other social conditions – domestic violence, psychiatric conditions, substance abuse, absence of labour market skills, or physical disability' (Fletcher, 2009: 31). The 'Working for Families' scheme was designed to take advantage of a strong labour market by encouraging beneficiaries with children to move off benefits and into paid work. In general terms this government shifted the focus from income assistance to lifting 'individual capacity and aggregate capability to contribute to wider economic growth' (Humpage and Craig, 2009: 47). Thus an economic agenda dominates, and social (as opposed to economic) development is minimal.

In 2008 a National government was elected, supported by the right-wing ACT party and by the Māori Party. Social policy is therefore in a state of flux, related to both this new political configuration and the economic recession (Stephens, 2009: 24).

As elsewhere, official projections indicate an ageing population (the baby-boom generation): between 2011 and 2021 the elderly population is projected to grow by about 200,000 and in the following 10 years by 230,000 (Statistics New Zealand, 2007). Stephens (2009: 24) notes the potential for ethnic tension, especially if the current differentials in employment rates, benefit receipts, poverty rates and income distribution are maintained. More recently the immense cost of the 2010 and 2011 Christchurch earthquakes will impact on social spending and will be used to fuel the National-led government's desire to control welfare expenditure. Child poverty remains a stubborn problem unlikely to be improved in the current scenario (St John, 2009). O'Brien (2009: 77–8) writes that in New Zealand child poverty is not experienced equally; 'although in total there are more Pakeha (European origin) children experiencing poverty ... Māori and Pasifika children are over-represented'.

The previous decades have seen a partnerships model expand the role of the non-government sector in the provision of social services and some health promotion and prevention services at primary healthcare level. This has resulted in a strong non-government sector, especially in the area of family support and non-statutory child welfare, increasing the employment opportunities of professional social workers. At the time of writing this chapter the New Zealand government is developing a new approach to child and family welfare, a policy plank of the Māori party known as 'Whanau Ora', the main objective being to strengthen extended family capabilities and develop an integrated approach to family wellbeing via a broadening of relationships between government and community agencies beyond contractual arrangements. The impact of this scheme on other sectors of the voluntary welfare sector and social work employment is difficult to predict at this stage.

The wider Pacific

Social workers in developing countries in the region write of the impact of globalisation both on traditional economies and on cultural values at the same time as new social problems have increased (Yeates, 2006). For example, in Papua New Guinea gambling, the sex industry, HIV and AIDS, alcohol and drug abuse require attention alongside poverty and family violence (Wrondimi, 2005; Kuruleca, 2005). Additionally, high levels of unemployment in the small formal economies that exist have sometimes resulted in temporary or permanent migration of younger adults in search of work. While this strategy can lead to the valuable addition of remittances to family finances and national economies it also deprives communities of (potential) leadership and familial care. It can also be noted that poor governance, political instability or natural disasters in specific islands increase inequalities in society and strain existing limited health and welfare services. The need to develop forms of social work and development that are appropriate to the cultures and needs of separate islands, in a context of very constrained resources, poses a significant challenge across the South Pacific islands.

CONCLUSIONS

This chapter has provided an introduction to, and overview of, the challenges faced in the

Australasian region, where social work has developed in diverse forms. While social work in Australia and New Zealand have been publicly recognised and internationally developed, South Pacific social workers are often isolated and confronted with growing social problems in the context of struggling economies, exacerbated in some case by civil war and natural disasters. In both New Zealand and Australia inequality has grown over the last decade and more punitive attitudes towards social problems now tend to prevail. Across the region, poverty, housing instability, family violence and child abuse continue to be major social challenges. There is also the need to maintain or develop policies and practices that respect the traditions and self-determination of minority groups, not least Indigenous populations. Increasing opportunities for training and employment of minority social workers (along with development of relevant curricula) are important goals throughout the region. Finally, social workers in the region face the challenge of meeting the often contradictory expectations of funding bodies while addressing injustice with diminishing resources.

NOTES

1   In recognition of this and the fact that we, the authors, are white women from New Zealand and Australia (respectively), we speak most confidently about the trends and practices in our home countries but more tentatively about other countries in the South Pacific, especially those in the Pacific island group.
2   It is customary to capitalise Indigenous when applied to Indigenous Australians.
3   Pasifika is the formally accepted term utilised to describe the communities of people from Pacific islands' heritages who have settled in New Zealand for 100 years.
4   In New Zealand it is particularly important to maintain the momentum of bicultural practice, strongly supported in the Code of Ethics (ANZASW, 2008) and in registration legislation (SWRA, 2003) and while much has been achieved, there is a risk of complacency. Social workers are also challenged to respond positively to growing cultural diversity while

recognising the tensions inherent in the struggles for self-determination of Indigenous peoples and the multiculturalism that emerges through the contributions, needs and aspirations of growing migrant and refugee communities. So far, there is far from adequate provision for ethnic and migrant minorities, in part a political response to public unease about migration and the social change it brings relative to the expectation that the government will primarily address biculturalism (Bartley and Spoonley, 2005: 141–2).

REFERENCES

AASW (Australian Association of Social Workers) (2010) *Code of Ethics*. Canberra: AASW.

ABS (Australian Bureau of Statistics) (2006) *The Health and Welfare of Australia's Aboriginal and Torres Strait Islander Peoples*. Canberra, Australia: Accessed 13 September 2008 from http://www.abs.gov.au/.

ABS (Australian Bureau of Statistics) (2010) *1301.0 Year Book 2009–2010* http://www.abs.gov.au/ausstats/abs@.nsf/mediareleasesbytitle.

Allan, J., Briskman, L. and Pease, B. (2009) *Critical Social Work, Theories and Practices for a Socially Just World* (2nd edn). Crows Nest, N.S.W: Allen and Unwin.

ANZASW (Aotearoa New Zealand Association of Social Workers) (2008) *Code of Ethics*. Christchurch: ANZASW.

Australian Government (2007) *Northern Territory National Emergency Response Act*, Australian Parliament, Canberra, 10 December 2010. Accessed 17 January 2012 from http://www.comlaw.gov.au/Details/C2011C00065/Download.

Australian Government (2010) *About Australia*. Accessed 11 November 2010 from http://australia.gov.au/about-australia/our-country/our-people#PopulationToday.

Bartley, A. and Spoonley, P. (2005) 'Constructing a workable multiculturalism in a bicultural society', in M. Belgrave, M. Kawharu and D. Williams (eds), *Waitangi Revisited: Perspectives on the Treaty of Waitangi*. Melbourne: Oxford University Press. pp. 136–.

Beddoe, L. (2007) 'Change, complexity and challenge in social work education in Aotearoa New Zealand', *Australian Social Work*, 60(1): 46–55.

Beddoe, L. and Duke, J. (2009) 'Registration in New Zealand social work: the challenge of change', *International Social Work*, 52(6): 785–797.

Beddoe, L. and Maidment, J. (2009) *Mapping Knowledge for Social Work Practice: Critical Intersections*. Melbourne: Cengage.

Belgrave, M., Kawharu, M. and Williams, D. (eds.). (2005)*Waitangi Revisited: Perspectives on the Treaty of Waitangi*. Melbourne: Oxford University Press. pp. 136–50.

Bradley, J. (1996) 'Iwi and cultural social services policy: the state's best kept secret', *Social Work Review Te Komako*, 8(4): 3–5.

Briskman, L. (2007) *Social Work with Indigenous Communities*. Sydney: Federation Press.

Briskman, L. (2008) 'Decolonizing social work in Australia: Prospect or illusion', in M. Gray, J. Coates and M. Yellow Bird (eds), *Indigenous Social Work around the World, Towards Culturally Relevant Education and Practice*. Aldershot: Ashgate. pp. 83–96.

Briskman, L., Latham, S. and Goddard, C. (2008) *Human Rights Overboard: Seeking Asylum in Australia*. North Melbourne: Scribe Publications.

Bywaters, P., McLeod, E. and Napier, L. (eds) (2009) *Social Work and Global Health Inequalities*. Bristol: Policy Press.

Commission on Social Determinants of Health (2008) *Closing the Gap in a Generation: Health Equity Through Action on the Social Determinants of Health*. Geneva, Switzerland: World Health Organisation. Accessed 6 September 2010 from http://whqlibdoc.who.int/publications/2008/9789 241563703_eng.pdf.

Connolly, M. (1994) 'An act of empowerment: the Children, Young Persons, and Their Families Act (1989)', *British Journal of Social Work*, 24 (1): 87–100.

Connolly, M. (2006) 'Fifteen years of family group conferencing: coordinators talk about their experiences in Aotearoa New Zealand', *British Journal of Social Work*, 36 (4): 523–40.

Connolly, M. and Harms, L. (eds) (2009) *Social Work: Contexts and Practice* (2nd edn). Melbourne: Oxford University Press.

Dew, K. and Matheson, A. (eds) (2008) *Understanding Health Inequalities in Aotearoa New Zealand*. Dunedin: University of Otago Press.

Doing Business (2010) *Economy Rankings*. Accessed 11 November 2010 from http://www.doingbusiness. org/economyrankings/.

Doyle, H. (2001) 'Australasia', in G. Davison, J. Hirst and S. Macintyre (eds), *The Oxford Companion to Australian History*. Oxford: Oxford Reference Online.

Everett-Heath, J. (2010) 'Australasia', *Concise Dictionary of World Place-Names*. Oxford University Press. Oxford Reference Online.

Fleras, A. and Spoonley, P. (1999) *Recalling Aotearoa: Indigenous Politics and Ethnic Relations in New Zealand*. Auckland: Oxford University Press.

Fletcher, M. (2009) 'Social policies in the recession', *Policy Quarterly* 5 (1): 29–35.

Fraser, H. (2008) *In the Name of Love, Women's Narratives of Love and Abuse*. Toronto: Women's Press.

Fraser, H. and Briskman, L. (2005) 'Through the eye of a needle: The challenge of getting justice in Australia if you're indigenous or seeking asylum', in I. Ferguson and M. Lavalette (eds), *Globalisation, Global Justice and Social Work*. London: Routledge. pp. 109–23.

Gillingham, P. (2007) 'The Australian Association of Social Workers and the social policy debates: a strategy for the future?', *Australian Social Work*, 60 (2): 166–80.

Gorey, A. (2007) 'Inequity in the Australian education system', *Policy Futures in Education*, 1 (4): 516–18.

Grattan, M. (2009) 'Splashing the cash', *The Age*, February: p. 3.

Gray, M. and Rennie, G. (2007) 'International social work: bodies with organs', *Social Work Review*, 19 (2): 42–58.

Gray, M., Coates, J. and Yellow Bird, M. (eds) (2008) *Indigenous Social Work around the World: Towards Culturally Relevant Education and Practice*. Aldershot: Ashgate.

Healy, K. and Darlington, Y. (2009) 'Service user participation in diverse child protection contexts: principles for practice', *Child & Family Social Work*, 14 (4): 420–30.

Humpage, L. and Craig, D. (2009) 'From welfare to welfare-to-work', in N. Lunt, M. O'Brien and R. Stephens (eds), *New Zealand New Welfare*. Melbourne: Cengage. pp. 41–8.

IASSW (International Association of Schools of Social Work) (2005) *Global Standards for Social Work Education*. Joint Statement by IASSW and IFSW. Accessed 4 September 2010 from http://www.ifsw. org/cm_data/GlobalSocialWorkStandards2005.pdf.

Keevers, L., Treleaven, L. and Sykes, C. (2008) 'Partnership and participation: contradictions and tensions in the social policy space', *Australian Journal of Social Issues*, 43 (3): 459–77.

Kuruleca, S. (2005) 'Returning home: Making sense of social work in Fiji', *Fiji Social Workers Journal*, 1 (1): 1–5.

Mafile'o, T. (2009) 'Pasifika social work', in M. Connolly and L. Harms (eds), *Social Work: Contexts and Practice* (2nd edn). Melbourne: Oxford University Press. pp. 121–34.

Matheson, A. and Dew, K. (2008) 'Health, justice and politics', in K. Dew and A. Matheson (eds), *Understanding Health Inequalities in Aotearoa New Zealand*. Dunedin: University of Otago Press. pp. 9–16.

Mendes, P. (2005). 'The history of social work in Australia: A critical literature review', *Australian Social Work*, 58 (2): 121–31.

Mendes, P. (2008) *Australia's Welfare Wars Revisited*. Sydney: UNSW Press.

Mendes, P. (2009) 'Young people transitioning from out-of-home care: a critical analysis of Australian and international policy and practice', *Australian Social Work*, 62 (3): 389–403.

Meo-Sewabu, L., Walsh-Tapiata, W., Mafile'o, T., Havea, S. and Tuileto'a, R. (2008) 'Developing a Pacific strategy for social work at Massey University, New Zealand', *Fiji Social Workers Journal*, 3: 13–29.

Nainoca, M.G. (2005) 'Nai dabedabe: a model of practice of social work in Fiji', *Fiji Social Workers Journal*, 1: 8–12.

Nash, M. (2009) 'Histories of the social work profession', in M. Connolly and L. Harms (eds), *Social Work: Contexts and Practice* (2nd edn). Melbourne: Oxford University Press. pp. 363–77.

National Statistical Office of Papua New Guinea (2000) *2000 National Census*. Accessed 1 May 2011 from http://www.spc.int/prism/country/pg/stats/2000_Census/census.htm.

NCATSISWA (National Coalition of Aboriginal and Torres Strait Islander Social Workers Association) (2011). Accessed 27 April 2011 from http://www.atsisw.org/vision.htm.

New Zealand Government, Careers. Accessed 11 November 2010 from http://www2.careers.govt.nz/major_industries_new_zealand.html.

Noble, C., Henrickson, M. and Han, I.Y. (eds) (2009) *Social Work Education in the Asia Pacific Region: Issues and Debates*. Melbourne: Vulgar Press.

O'Brien, M. (2005) 'A just profession or just a profession', *Social Work Review*, 17 (1): 13–22.

O'Brien, M. (2009) 'Poverty and disadvantage', in M. Connolly and L. Harms (eds), *Social Work: Contexts and Practice* (2nd edn). Melbourne: Oxford University Press. pp. 68–80.

OECD (Organisation for Economic Co-operation and Development) (2010) *Employment Outlook 2010 – How Does Australia Compare?* Accessed 1 May 2011 from www.oecd.org/dataoecd/14/38/45603025.pdf.

Passells, V. (2006) 'Pasifika 'location and privilege: Conceptual frameworks from first year Pasifika social work students', *Social Work Review (Tu Mau II)*, 18 (1): 14–21.

Pease, B. (2010) *Undoing Privilege, Unearned Advantage in a Divided World*. London: Zed Books.

Property Wire (2010) 'Australia's housing prices heading higher due to shortage of development', *Nu Wire Investor* 22 March, accessed December 2010 from, http://www.nuwireinvestor.com/articles/australias-housing-prices-heading-higher-due-to-shortage-of-development-54891.aspx.

Rees, S. and Rodley, G. (1995) *The Human Costs of Managerialism*. Sydney: Pluto Press.

Ruwhiu, L. (2009) 'Indigenous issues in Aotearoa New Zealand', in M. Connolly and L. Harms (eds), *Social Work: Contexts and Practice*. Melbourne: Oxford University Press. pp. 107–20.

Samoan Bureau of Statistics (2011). Accessed 1 May 2011 from http://www.sbs.gov.ws/.

Saunders, P., Naidoo, Y. and Griffiths, M. (2008) 'Towards new indicators of disadvantage: Deprivation and social exclusion in Australia', *Australian Journal of Social Issues*, 43 (2): 175–94.

Statistics New Zealand (2007) *Population Ageing in New Zealand*. Accessed 8 December 2010 from http://www.stats.govt.nz/browse_for_stats/people_and_communities/older_people/pop-ageing-in-nz.aspx.

Stephens, R. (2009) 'Social policy, cold climates and economic recessions', *Policy Quarterly*, 5 (1): 24–8.

St John, S. (2009) 'Working for families: work, families and poverty', in N. Lunt, M. O'Brien and R. Stephens (eds), *New Zealand New Welfare*. Melbourne: Cengage. pp. 78–91.

SWRA (Social Workers Registration Act) (2003) Wellington: NZ Government.

Tangata Whenua Social Workers Association (2010) Accessed 17 August 2010 from http://twswa.org.nz/.

Tiong, T.N. (2006) 'Regional perspectives from Asia-Pacific', *International Social Work*, 49 (2): 277–84.

Welbourne, P., Harrison, G. and Ford, D. (2007) 'Social work in the UK and the global labour market: Recruitment, practice and ethical considerations', *International Social Work*, 50 (1): 27–40.

Western, J.S., Dwan, K. and Kebonang, Z. (2005) 'The importance of visibility for social inequality research', *Australian Journal of Social Issues*, 40 (1): 125–41.

Wilson, J. (2009) 'History – Māori arrival and settlement', *Te Ara - the Encyclopedia of New Zealand*. updated 3 March 2009. Accessed from http://www.TeAra.govt.nz/en/history/1.

Wrondimi, G.H. (2005) 'Social work in Papua New Guinea today', *Fiji Social Workers Journal*, 1 (1): 45–6.

Yeates, B. (2006) 'Social and community work education and practice at the University of the South Pacific', *Fiji Social Workers Journal*, 2 (1): 36–7.

27

Social Work in Europe

Darja Zaviršek and Susan Lawrence

INTRODUCTION

At different points in history the geopolitical boundaries of Europe bordering Africa, Asia and the Arctic and Atlantic Oceans have shifted, variously including and excluding different nation states. The two most prominent of Europe's institutions define Europe differently, the European Union (EU) having 27 member states (Europa, 2011) (with a population of 495 million inhabitants), whilst the Council of Europe (representing over 800 million people) counts 47 member countries covering all countries in the continent (with the exception of Belarus) (Council of Europe, 2010).

Lyons and Huegler (2010) describe Europe's geographical spread as stretching from the Nordic and Baltic countries in the Northwest, encompassing Russia in the Northeast, and in the Southwest including the Iberian Peninsula, and extending Southeast to Turkey (to the West of the Bosporus). The countries within this continent vary enormously in size of both land mass and demography. Compare for example, Malta with 408,333 people and occupying 316 square kilometres with Russia with a population of over 138,739,892 and covering over 17 million square kilometres.[1]

The United Nations (UN) divides Europe geographically into four regions based on the main compass points. Northern Europe includes the Nordic and Baltic countries along with the United Kingdom and Ireland; Southern Europe comprises mainly the countries bordering the Mediterranean Sea; Western Europe includes Belgium, France, Germany, the Netherlands, Switzerland and some of the smaller countries of 'continental Europe', and Eastern Europe includes former Soviet Union countries. The UN categorises the countries of Europe as amongst the world's economically 'developed' areas (United Nations Statistics Division, 2011). Further sub-divisions of these four regions are variously utilised when attempting to explain or describe commonalities and differences within and between countries in Europe. The rationale given or implied for such groupings can be tenuous and the countries included in these regions often differ.

The cultural diversity of Europe is exemplified by its range of languages. Within the EU, there are currently 23 official working languages and over 60 indigenous or minority language communities (Europa, 2010). Historically, Europe has been and remains connected with its colonial legacy. Migration has contributed significantly to its rich tapestry of cultural and ethnic diversity, encouraged since the late 20th century by policies of 'multiculturalism' in countries such as the Netherlands, Sweden and the UK. Elsewhere, policies of 'assimilation' sought to indigenise newcomers into the dominant culture of the receiving country, as was the case in France (Lyons and Huegler, 2010).

HISTORICAL PERSPECTIVES

As with the region itself, social work in Europe, since its professional origins around the beginning of the 20th century, has been prone to political and ideological interpretations. The largest European country, Russia (which extends into Asia), has sometimes been seen as part of Europe and at other times been pushed beyond its borders. Some parts of Europe, which were geographically embraced, were culturally seen as strangers (Turkey for instance). The Cold War division of Europe (between NATO and the Warsaw Pact countries), had built a political and social border as well as a physical barrier (the Berlin Wall), a division reflected in the history of European social work.

Since the early 1990s a growing internationalisation and the establishment of networks among social work schools and scholars have contributed towards a better understanding of social work across Europe. Examples are the ECSPRESS Network (Chytil and Seibel, 1999) the European Platform for World-Wide Social Work (EUSW)[2] and the Network for Historical Studies on Gender and Social Work in Europe.[3] Many social work researchers previously thought that social work was only known in the 'West' and that professional social work was established with the aid of those from the 'West' following the collapse

of communism. This type of thinking, known as the 'cold-war methodology' had constructed Eastern Europe as a homogenous entity and overshadowed the specific social work traditions of various European countries in different periods of the 20th century (Hering and Waaldijk, 2005).

The attempts to establish professional social work could be seen across Europe, beginning with courses in Germany, the Netherlands and the UK in the last years of the 19th century. A school of social work was established in Amsterdam in 1899 (Healy, 2001) while Alice Salomon (1872–1948) founded the first women's school for social work in Berlin (in 1908). In 1912, another Jewish Austrian 'welfare theorist', Ilse Arlt (1876–1960), opened a school of social work in Vienna (Maiss, 2009). Similar schools were also established in Budapest (in 1926, by Margit Slachta); in Bucharest (in 1929, by Princess Ileana); and in Warsaw (in 1925, by Helena Radlinska).

These vibrant social work activities were halted in many countries by events from the 1930s onwards, including a growing economic recession and the rise to power of the Nazi regime. Yugoslavia was the only post-war European country where communist leaders established several schools of social work (Zaviršek, 2005, 2008). Perceived as an activity for petit-bourgeois women, social work was deemed unsuitable within state socialism. The dominant belief was that socialism would eradicate the need for such intervention and ensure the well-being of every human being. Therefore, social work in Eastern Europe had apparently been erased when communism ended in the 1990s. After the historic fall of the Berlin Wall (in 1989) and the demise of different forms of state socialism (by 1991) an intensive process of European integration took place, which led to the expansion of the Council of Europe and the EU. The EU enlargements in 2004 and 2007 included 10 former socialist countries.[4] These events also influenced social work developments. Two important associations assisted integration: the International Association of Schools of Social Work (IASSW; established in 1927) and the European Association of Schools of Social Work (EASSW; established in 1995).

The early professionalisation of European social work (up to 1938) occurred at a time when capitalist societies realised that economic and social stability required support structures for people who were vulnerable or disadvantaged. The consequences of the Second World War strengthened the secular concept of welfare and the development of European welfare states. In the aftermath of the Holocaust, the Universal Declaration of Human Rights (1948) and the Convention for the Protection of Human Rights and Fundamental Freedoms (1953) seemed to signal a commitment towards humanity, equality, and the well-being of everyone (Appendix 4). Later on, the European Social Charter (adopted in 1961 revised in 1996)[5] aimed to guarantee the social and human rights of people in Europe, including the right to social security (Article 12); the right to social and medical assistance and appropriate public and private services (Article 13). Article 14 explicitly mentions the right to benefit from social welfare services and the promotion of services 'which, by using *methods of social work*, would contribute to the welfare and development of both individuals and groups in the community, and to their adjustment to the social environment' (emphasis added). In the post-war climate, therefore, the value base and ethical discourse within European social work and social policy shifted from 19th century thinking (help to the deserving needy) to a focus on human and citizen rights; and equality among European populations, regardless of age, gender, ethnicity, sexual orientation and disability.

Paradoxically, the division of Europe into two competing political and economic systems of capitalism and communism that lasted for nearly 50 years, had importantly influenced the development of European welfare states and professional social work.

Scheppele (2010) has suggested that the period of 'compassionate liberalism' of Western societies actually started with the Russian Revolution (in 1917) and ended with the collapse of the Soviet Empire. When European liberalism lacked the competition of another political system, it started to promote a more aggressive competitiveness, increased the neo-liberal ideology of work, and started to re-organise state institutions (ministries, welfare and educational institutions including universities) to serve the private rather than the public sphere. The neo-liberal ideology and processes have substantially transformed social work and social policy throughout Europe.

THE SHRINKING DOMAIN OF SOCIAL POLICY AND SOCIAL WORK

Some commentators have utilised comparative social policy models when attempting to typologise social work in different countries, on the basis that social policy and welfare systems are significant for the way social work is formed and organised (Meeuwisse and Sward, 2007). Lorenz (1994) argued that the ideological basis informing different welfare regimes permeates the practice of social work and from this perspective he identified four broad categories of social work in Europe, largely building on work on welfare regimes (Esping-Andersen, 1990; Leibfried, 1992).

In Lorenz's (1994) typology, the *Scandinavian model of social work* (e.g. in Sweden) saw state agencies as the principal employers of social workers within networks of multidisciplinary services, existing to promote democracy and solidarity. Social workers were expected to evaluate and develop services and enjoyed a relatively high status. This model is based largely on social democratic political approaches. The *residual model* (dominant in the UK), largely described countries where the state and market jointly operate in the provision of social work services and privatisation of welfare has been evident since the later part of the 20th century. Services are mainly means-tested, largely targeted at the poorest members of society and there is an orientation towards individualised approaches that often emphasise a 'polarisation of care and control', relying more on coercion than social cohesion (Lorenz, 1994: 24). The *corporatist model* exists mainly in countries following the principles of Bismarck's welfare state organisation and based on Catholic principles of subsidiarity. The responsibility for welfare resided in the institution closest to the point of need, i.e. the individual, family, community, non-governmental organisation (NGO) before the state. The state funded NGOs to deliver services and because of the lack of centralisation, the social professions diversified. State social workers were often left to carry out tasks associated with 'control' and such positions were not attractive (examples are Germany and the Netherlands). The final model offered in this typology is the *rudimentary model*. In some countries, Lorenz suggests that because the state offers very limited social protection and has patchy provision of social services it is difficult to generalise about social work. In some countries a number of social workers are employed by the state, but more typically by NGOs. (This grouping includes 'Southern' or 'Mediterranean' countries such as Spain but also Ireland.)

Meeuwisse and Sward (2007) identify a series of objections to such typologies in their review of cross-national comparisons of social work, e.g. that they are built upon dubious assumptions – for example male wage-labour models. They also question the direct link between welfare models and social work. Further, Wilensky (2002) argues that 'convergence theory' has made such models irrelevant as the processes of economic globalisation and changing demography have blurred distinctions in the 'welfare mix' in different countries, resulting in welfare systems having greater similarity. Others propose profession- or practice-oriented comparisons as useful perspectives for

comparison (Hokenstad et al., 1996; Jergeby and Soydan, 2002). However, Meeuwisse and Sward point to the danger that 'sweeping and one-sided generalisations' and 'similarities and differences in social work are either underestimated or overemphasised' (2007: 494) when using comparative modelling techniques, and that such studies inevitably become quickly outdated. The study by Lorenz illustrates this point as it pre-dated the accession of the ten Central and Eastern European (CEE) countries into the EU which consequently were excluded from the typology.

Over the last 20 years Europe has undergone (and is still experiencing) multi-dimensional welfare state transformations in financing, provision and regulation accompanied by the export of jobs from Europe. Current social issues include mass unemployment of young and older people; the exploitation of workers, e.g. through flexible employment and low wages; and privatisation of the public sector across the region. Exacerbated by the economic crisis in Europe that began in the United States in 2008, poverty and social inequalities are growing and elements of 'social Darwinism' are returning as the rich grow richer and the deprivation of the poor is individualised and sometimes punished. In 2010 mass protests of workers and trade unions in several European countries demonstrated reactions to these processes. The more conservative analysts describe these changes as 'refocusing of state interventions and redefinitions of the mixed economy of welfare' (Seeleib-Kaiser, 2008: 211) but do not yet see this as signalling the 'end of the welfare states', while more radical thinkers see these processes as the withdrawing of public responsibility, the shifting of public savings into private hands and a retrenchment in the domain of welfare policy with harmful long-term consequences. In the view of many social work scholars the European commitment towards welfare and human rights is shrinking (Jordan, 2004; Fortunato et al., 2008).

Critical researchers in social work and social policy have variously described recent trends as: from welfare to workfare (Ginsburg and Lawrence, 2006); from welfare safety net towards a scarcity of resources (Dobkowski and Walliman, 1998); from managing resources to managing people (Littlechild, 2009); from welfare entitlements to the criminalisation of the poor (Wacquant, 2009 [2004]); from a structural understanding of inequality to the individualisation of responsibility for poverty, illness and old age (Dominelli and Hoogvelt, 1996; Moussu, 2008); from welfare activities of the state to policies and practices directed at governing the social (Clarke, 2004); from welcoming immigrant labour to the system of border controls, detention centres and deportation policy known as 'Fortress Europe' (Humphries, 2004; Zorn, 2009), and from secular-based social work towards the re-religionisation of welfare services (Rommelspacher, 2010).

Measurements of income distribution within the EU indicate that levels of inequality are connected to the risk of poverty and point to a gap between CEE countries, Mediterranean countries and other Western European countries. Income inequality is highest in CEE and high in some Mediterranean countries, but lower in the majority of Western countries (e.g. especially in Sweden and Denmark). Poland, Hungary, Greece, Spain, Italy, Ireland and the UK all face above-average levels of inequality while other EU member states have a middle level of inequality (Ward et al., 2009). The increasing level of poverty is partly related to a growing number of migrant and domestic workers in flexible and precarious jobs across

Europe (Pena-Casas and Latta, 2004). During 2008 and 2009 the number of people working in flexible or short working day employment increased dramatically, as shown in Table 27.1.

Current welfare transformations show differences in the design and arrangements of social welfare provision across Europe but, as emphasised by Seeleib-Kaiser (2008), also evidence a strong convergence of social policies, institutions and welfare regimes. The welfare changes evidently show a common trend of states' withdrawal from their responsibilities in most areas of social welfare, social housing, pensions, health and even education.

Many other issues are also of concern for social work in Europe today, for instance racism towards migrants, ethnic and religious minority groups; the slow process of interethnic reconciliation after ethnic wars in former Yugoslavia and the former Soviet Union; and the rise of new political conflicts (e.g. in Georgia) (Ramon, 2008). Uncertainty and disappointment are replacing a period of great hope and trust in stable European welfare states, which impacted upon social work values in the second part of the 20th century. These changes are having a profound effect on social work practice and education. The shrinking of people's social rights has been one of the reasons for an increased interest in ethics. Social workers are currently actively engaged in debates about social work ethics and different codes of ethics that exist across Europe (Banks, 2006; Staub-Bernasconi, 2007). They acknowledge that social work ethics have to be connected with other areas

Table 27.1   People in flexible forms of employment in Europe

	2008	2009
Belgium	120,000 persons	185,000 persons
Ireland	20,800	89,250
Austria	8800	62,000
Germany	50,000	1,400,000

Source: Leskošek, 2010.

such as feminist ethics, disability ethics and the area of human rights and democracy. For example, one of the ongoing ethical dilemmas for social work is that people with disabilities are partially excluded from ordinary life by the disability label in order to be re-included through welfare system provision. They are part of society, but their participation is exclusionary and their identity formation is based upon negative images, stereotypes, stigma and parallel institutional provision (e.g. special schools and segregated employment places or occupational activities) (Zaviršek, 2002, 2007). It can be noted that social workers are sometimes complicit with these types of exclusionary provision but sometimes advocate against them. Another ethical dilemma across Europe concerns whether religion should transcend the private sphere and influence human rights issues and social work interventions within the public sphere.

Social work in Europe is inevitably connected with social movements, political activities and regional,[6] international and professional networks. In its early stages, members of the women's and feminist movements and those who advocated for workers' rights were among the most important agents of change. Today, critical social work thinkers and practitioners are contributing to European networks and global initiatives against the negative effects of global capitalism, climate change and environmental and human made disasters (Climate Change and Disaster Intervention task force groups of the IASSW); against managerialism, marketisation and stigmatisation of service users (Social Work Action Network – SWAN[7]); against the negative effects of inequalities on people's health (Social Work and Health Inequalities Network[8]); and for the increase of social work knowledge on interventions in times of political conflict (International Social Work and Political Conflict Resolution Network[9]). These innovations and critical approaches are likely to have important consequences for the future of social work education and practice in Europe.

PROFESSIONALISATION OF SOCIAL WORK THROUGH EDUCATION

Although the ethos of caring for and protecting the more vulnerable members of a community or society can be traced back many centuries (Adams et al., 2000), organised social work education and training courses emerged in Europe in the late 19th and early 20th centuries (Kantowicz, 2005). This was based variously upon ideological concepts from the four broad traditions of Judeo-Christianity, philanthropy, feminism and socialism (Lorenz, 1994). Early attempts at internationalisation were documented by pioneers during the 1920s and early 1930s, and continued after the Second World War when social, community and group work methods were utilised in social and political reconstruction (Lorenz, 2006).

The convergence of social work training and education in many European countries from the late 1940s onwards could have resulted in casework-based approaches becoming the only dominant pattern. However, challenges to such uniform ideas (from the late 1960s on) came from several sources: from attempts to indigenise social work to pre-war forms in some countries; and from more radical perspectives associated with mental health and disability user-led movements as well as feminist and anti-racist social work that emphasised structural and collective explanations and interventions. In several European countries the allied discipline of social pedagogy with its own epistemological paradigm was influential for social work's development (Hämäläinen, 2003).

EU education policy included student and staff mobility programmes from the late 1980s and these have facilitated the sharing of knowledge about and broadening of the social professions throughout Europe. Scholars, practitioners and students, facilitated by EU-funded mobility grants, began to discover and experience different and unfamiliar approaches and interventions (Seibel and Lorenz, 1996; Lyons and

Lawrence, 2006). Exchanges revealed a rich diversity of education and training forms. The location of education programmes within academia and the differential status afforded to social work academics in different countries point to cultural, political and historical differences and similarities within Europe. A key issue in this context is whether education for the social professions is considered as an academic discipline, impacting on the roles and status of professionals (Frost and Camapanini, 2005).

The so-called 'Bologna Process' in Europe in the early 21st century sought to establish a European Higher Education Area and furthered the recognition of qualifications both within Europe and internationally through a common pattern of undergraduate (bachelor), postgraduate (master) and doctoral (PhD) study. The result is that most social work education qualifying programmes subject to the Bologna initiative now conform to a recognisable pattern of awards at bachelor and/or masters level (Ginsburg and Lawrence, 2006: 35). They are delivered in the tertiary education sector, mainly but not exclusively in universities or 'universities of applied science' (formerly institutions providing vocational or applied professional education) (Labonté-Roset, 2005). Most programmes include practice placements as well as an academic focus although there remain differences in programme length (between 3 and 5 years) and named award (e.g. Bachelor, Diploma, License) (Kantowicz, 2005: 303).

The Bologna reform, however, opened the gates for the corporatist orientation of education and commercialisation of public universities. The reforms helped to mask the high rate of youth unemployment across Europe. There was also an ideological shift concerning the purpose of science, seen increasingly as serving the needs of industry and capital through an emphasis on 'skills acquisition' over the potentially transformative intellectual power of critical thinking. Conversely, the same reform has (at least formally) provided an opportunity for the rapid academisation of social work education. Research has become more highly valued within social work departments and, increasingly, the internationalisation of social work schools is becoming an everyday reality. Postgraduate European courses have emerged within social work. An example is the long established MA Comparative European Social Studies (MACESS), a collaborative course delivered since 1994 at Zuyd University in Maastricht and validated by London Metropolitan University. MACESS is taught by a pan-European team drawn from a network of partner Universities throughout Europe (Lawrence, 2006). In 2009 the very first joint European doctoral programme INDOSOW (International doctoral studies in social work) was established by six social work schools in Europe.[10] This programme promotes critical thinking, comparative perspectives and innovative methodologies such as service-user and academic joint research (Zaviršek and Videmšek, 2009).

But such developments are far from typical. In many Western European countries (paradoxically often those with the longest and strongest traditions in social work) the social work discipline has been traditionally placed in universities of applied science, which are still not eligible to validate doctoral programmes. The opposite is true for most East European and Scandinavian countries, as well as Ireland and the UK, where social work is taught at university level with relevant PhD opportunities. In some countries, such as Ukraine, the new doctoral social worker programmes have to compete with potentially more profitable programmes, such as 'management in public health' or 'social administration', which better fit into the corporatist logic of the higher education business, favouring more practical and managerially oriented approaches (Zaviršek, 2009a). This diverse and hesitant pattern of development reflects ambivalence towards social work as an academic discipline with its own theoretical foundations.

Today, a variety of different occupational roles and titles exist within the landscape of activities known as 'social work' within Europe, and, in an endeavour to be more inclusive, the term social professions has been used by some European commentators since 1996 (Seibel and Lorenz, 1996; Lyons and Lawrence, 2006: 7). Shardlow and Payne (1998) argue that in some countries social work and social pedagogy are seen as having closely linked theoretical paradigms (Germany, Poland, etc.), while in other countries they have been developed as two separate social science disciplines (Croatia, Macedonia, etc.). However, broader disciplines within Europe in fields such as youth and community work, social care, residential work, 'special educators' and 'animators' could also be categorised as being allied to the social pedagogic tradition (Shardlow and Payne, 1998).

Some authors are critical of the fragmentation of social work and believe that 'social work' should be kept as the wider name of a social science discipline which includes different professional activities (Staub-Bernasconi, 2006). The fragmentation into many different occupations (e.g. rehabilitation, social management, case and care management) might have a future negative effect upon social work's scientific knowledge base and fuels an on going debate about whether social work is a social science discipline or 'just a profession'.

MULTI-SECTOR APPROACH IN SOCIAL WORK RESEARCH AND PRACTICE

The multi-sector approach, intersectionality, and multidimensional research are similar concepts which are gaining fundamental importance in social work research and are reflected in social work practice across Europe. These concepts consider more than one dimension of a person's condition and focus at the intersection of different analytic categories (age, gender, ethnicity, disability, etc.) in order to gain a better understanding of the person's needs, strengths and life-course prospects. A person's life, desires and future opportunities are shaped by their life context (e.g. gender, educational skills, age, family and ethnic background, employment, disability); household characteristics (e.g. composition and size of the household, number of earners, housing situation, social networks, caring responsibilities); structural factors (social welfare provision, social and economic policies, social values and morals, diversity and discrimination against minority groups); and global conditions (economic crises, neo-liberalism, international migration, asylum politics).

While it is obvious that people traditionally defined as vulnerable (e.g. children, single mothers, elders, people with disabilities) remain disadvantaged, the intersectionality approach helps us understand how disadvantage varies according to class, welfare and value systems. For example, unemployed women face a high risk of poverty overall and this risk increases among older women, especially in Eastern Europe, but not, remarkably, in the Netherlands (Expert Group on Gender, Social Inclusion and Employment, 2006). The difference is caused by two dominant value systems with regard to gendered definitions of old age.

Another example shows the interrelatedness of economic vulnerability and welfare provision. While lone-parent households are generally vulnerable to poverty, this is less so in Scandinavian countries than in the UK and Ireland, demonstrating that the combination of more comprehensive welfare benefits and employment systems prevent impoverishment among female-headed households (Expert Group on Gender, Social Inclusion and Employment, 2006). When the risk of unemployment, poorly paid jobs, the absence of a strong welfare system and public prejudices come together, they create discrimination and disadvantage for individuals, families and groups which might not exist in other countries to the same extent. Therefore, a more radical and historically aware social work practice embracing advocacy and empowerment is needed to support the person in a specific context.

This approach also has implications for the use of the strengths perspective in social work. Research undertaken by Schultz (2007) has shown that professionals often view members of ethnic minorities as being needy, dependant and less capable of solving every-day difficulties; 'the stranger is always thought to be very much in need of help, even though this person has many abilities' (2007: 62). The intersectionality approach considers home culture; age; ethnic group networks; the status of a particular ethnicity in the larger society; racism; gender; and personal resources and resilience. This provides a complex and diverse picture about the every-day life and needs of people and collectives.

Working with families seems to be the most commonly shared focus of social work across Europe, both in relation to teaching curricula and everyday practice. In countries with a stronger tradition of diversity approaches in social work, the notion of a 'family' encompasses diverse forms and cir-cumstances while in countries with more traditional curricula social workers are still oriented towards 'desirable norm families' and less responsive to the support needs of differently constituted families. Although lone-parent households are increasing in absolute numbers and as a proportion of all households, images of the family have yet to change accordingly. Intra-familial violence and child abuse remain significant topics, as do poverty among young families and the particular economic vulnerability of single-parent households in countries such as the UK, Luxembourg, Lithuania and Malta (where poverty levels are higher compared with other households; Expert Group on Gender, Social Inclusion and Employment, 2006). A recent study which compared pov-erty in Nordic countries with that in Belgium and the Netherlands has shown that female labour market behaviour influences the pov-erty rates in these countries (Fritzell and Ritakallio, 2010). If Belgium and the Netherlands developed similar practices

towards dual-earners and single working persons to those common in Nordic countries, poverty would decline dramati-cally. Nevertheless, the multi-sector approach would additionally need to consider the dif-ferences in gender regimes, child welfare, employment and housing policies in order to contextualise differences in female labour market behaviours among these countries.

Families and individuals from ethnic minorities who need social services face additional disadvantages because most wel-fare services fail to provide culturally sensi-tive brokering for people from different ethnic backgrounds (Dominelli, 1988 [1997], 2002; Rommelspacher, 1995).

When working with people with disabili-ties and their families, social workers in many countries have adopted the social model of disability initiated by disability activists, service-users and academics (Oliver, 1983; Morris, 1993; Pečarič, 2002). The major contribution made by social work includes methods for assisting, encouraging, and implementing governmental policies to provide extra resources; and also for redirect-ing existing policies towards inclusionary transport, schooling, housing, supported employment and community-based services. Advocacy, citizenship rights, meaningful participation (especially in the field of work) and inclusion (especially in education) have become key concepts in social work. One of the most visible changes has been the rejec-tion of the spatial segregation of people with disabilities and mental health problems as well as the recognition that acts of violence (including gendered violence) and abuse were being committed against people with disabilities at home and in institutions (Zaviršek 2002, 2009b).

Social parenthood, too, has become a reality for a growing number of adults and children. The increase in divorce, medically assisted reproductive technology, co-habitation, blended families, same-sex-parent families and international adoptions have been changing the traditional understanding of 'family' based on blood ties between adults and children (Zaviršek 2009c). Instead of 'the demise of the family', social workers across Europe emphasise more inclusive understandings of 'family' and families' rights to self-definition.

Social work research has acknowledged the interrelatedness of unemployment and the pathologisation of people with different skin colours and minority ethnic backgrounds. For example, approximately 10–12 million Roma people live in Europe and their unemployment level has risen from 60 to 90 percent in some countries (Kosovo, Romania). This is partly as a consequence of poor education received by Roma children who are frequently labelled as 'intellectually disabled' and sent to special schools (Zaviršek, 2007). This form of medical-pathological intervention stems from an approach which sees the culture of ethnic minorities as fixed and inherently different and destructive. To counteract discrimination, the European Roma Summit in 2008 agreed a Platform for Roma Inclusion (2008). In 2010 priority was given to equal access to education for Roma children. This has profound implications for social professionals who work with Roma families across Europe. Several 'good practice' projects (against discrimination toward Roma children and families) have been developed (e.g. in Finland, Sweden, Austria and the UK) (Guy et al., 2010).

The long history of discrimination against Roma people cannot be detached from their expulsions from France during 2010. Like other citizens of EU countries, Roma people have the right to stay unconditionally in another EU member state for up to three months, after which they have to prove employment or sufficient living resources (*European Directive 2004/38/EC*, Articles 6; 7).[11] People who are considered an 'unreasonable burden on the social assistance system of the host Member State' (Article 14) may lose their residence rights and in extreme cases face expulsion. This is more likely to affect those who are poor, unemployed and in need of social assistance. It is obvious that several conflicting ethics

simultaneously exist in Europe. While documents such as the Charter of Fundamental Rights of the European Union[12] ensure 'social security benefits and social advantages' and 'a decent existence for all those who lack sufficient resources' 'for everyone residing and moving legally within the European Union' (Article 34), these rights are shrinking, especially for the poorest in society.

From a social work perspective the entire notion of someone being seen as a 'burden' to the social assistance system shows how labels of social problems and potential criminality are ascribed to the poor in ahistorical and individualised ways. Despite historically-based racism towards the Roma on the grounds of skin colour, poverty and particular occupations, social workers in many countries are not sufficiently proactive in engaging in anti-racist practice, promoting empowerment and raising societal awareness against prejudice.

When such conditions prevail alongside the rising power of hate politics and right-wing governments in many European countries, the Roma are easily reconstructed as 'wandering travellers' representing scapegoats for the majority population. Therefore, social workers need to be vocal against political practices which discriminate against minority ethnic groups and which make them more vulnerable to racist attacks and further impoverishment. The European Union Charter of Fundamental Rights and the European Social Charter, together with the Global Standards of professional ethics (IFSW and IASSW, 2004), should ensure the foundations for protecting the human rights of minority groups.

Another analytical dimension is age. Within the EU, 85 million people (or 17 percent of the EU's total population) are aged over 65 years, with 22 million (or 4 percent) being over 80 years old (the majority of whom are women). Europe is considered to be the world's 'oldest' region with a rapidly ageing population: those aged over 65 are projected to constitute 30 percent of the EU population by 2060 (Eurostat, 2008).

Throughout Europe rural areas tend to have older populations than urban areas, partly due to younger people migrating in search of better employment opportunities, particularly in Greece, Moldova, Estonia and Southern Italy (Manthorpe and Livsey, 2009). A rare exception is the Republic of Kosovo (with a population of approximately 2 million people), where more than one-third of the population is under 19 years of age; with an average age of 22–23 years; and only 5.5 percent are older than 64 years (Labour Market Statistics 2007; 2008). Ageing populations in Europe are also becoming increasingly diverse, as migrants often 'age in place' rather than returning to their country of origin, either by choice or through necessity (Lawrence and Simpson, 2009).

Ageing populations typically lead to increased requirements for support, provided variously in different European states by families, communities, non-governmental organisations or health and social services – though more often a combination of some or all of these. In more affluent European countries, there has been a general shifting of social service provision from institutional to community-based care for elders requiring additional support. Poorer countries can barely afford social services and home care for elderly people. Some authors speak about the 'Central and Eastern European model' of home care, which denotes an almost complete lack of publicly supported and affordable home care, for instance as in Poland, where home care is almost exclusively provided by relatives (mostly women) (Prochazkova and Schmid, 2009: 144).

Migration has impacted on European elders in a variety of ways. Some more affluent elders themselves choose to migrate across borders, typically from Northern to warmer Southern European countries. Whilst EU citizens are entitled to emergency healthcare when resident in another EU state, they are not entitled to social or domestic care and help (Warnes, 2006). This has sometimes required specialist, often bilingual provision delivered largely by NGOs in areas where large numbers of older migrants settle and require support in times of need. An example of this is in Spain, particularly in coastal resorts, where large numbers of British, German and Dutch elders have settled after retirement.

Migration also impacts on elders in Europe through the trend to employ people from other countries as domestic or live-in care staff, either because nationals do not want to do this type of demanding and challenging work, or because staff from other countries can be employed more cheaply, flexibly or precariously, particularly if they are undocumented workers. Migration flows in this context are typically from East to West Europe, for example, from Poland to the UK, from Ukraine to Poland, from Albania to Italy. Migrant social care workers are commonly employed in residential care settings and nursing homes but also in private domestic settings, the last particularly in Greece and Italy (Warnes, 2006; Lawrence and Torres, 2012). A study in Austria identified between 27,000 and 30,000 mostly Slovakian, Romanian and Czech caregivers working for approximately 15,000 families in need of 24-hour long-term care. Often their initial illegal status was regulated through new legislation enacted in 2007 and 2008 (Prochazkova and Schmid, 2009).

However, it can be noted that many European elders are also providing important intergenerational solidarity and social capital by caring for siblings, friends, children and grandchildren; offering financial and material resources and both paid and voluntary labour in a variety of commercial and charitable settings, in groups and in communities (Lawrence and Simpson, 2009). The importance of grandmothers as childminders is not confined only to day care. In countries such as Romania and Lithuania, for example, grandmothers are often sole carers of grandchildren whose parents have temporarily migrated west for employment. Social workers are required to register grandmothers as carers in such circumstances, although many of these arrangements remain 'informal' and below the radar of the authorities (Lawrence and Torres, 2012). When young people migrate West an inevitable shortage of care workers in poorer parts of Europe can result. The question of who is going to care for sick, disabled and elderly people remains as yet unanswered.[13]

CONCLUSION

The fluidity of the boundaries of Europe over time and the different cultural and historical developments have given rise to a rich variety of occupational groupings present in the landscape of social care, social services and the social professions: these are sometimes called social work and sometimes not. Increasingly, social workers are expected to raise their critical voices and develop more radical forms of practice to counter the shrinking domain of welfare rights. Dignity, equality, justice and freedom as fundamental social work principles need to be protected not only for those living in Europe, but for everyone in a globalised world.

NOTES

1 Figures from CIA World Factbook https://www.cia.gov/library/publications/the-world-factbook/geos/rs.html (14 December 2011).

2 Established in 2001; cf. Camapanini (2007).

3 Established in 2001; cf. Hering and Waaldijk (2005).

4 Poland, the Czech Republic, Slovakia, Hungary, Slovenia, Lithuania, Estonia and Latvia joined the EU in 2004, and Romania and Bulgaria in 2007.

5 European Social Charter, 1961. http://conventions.coe.int/Treaty/EN/Treaties/html/035.htm (10 October 2010).

6 A recent regional social work network is the Eastern European sub-regional Association of the Schools of Social Work, established in 2008 as part of the IASSW and the European Association of Schools of Social Work (EASSW). www.eesrassw.net (12 September 2010).

7 http://www.socialworkfuture.org/ (12 September 2010).

8 http://www2.warwick.ac.uk/fac/cross_fac/healthatwarwick/research/devgroups/socialwork/swhin/ (15 November 2010).

9 http://www.isw4peace.org/ (15 November 2010).

10 University of Ljubljana (Slovenia), Anglia Ruskin University (UK), University of Siegen and Alice Salomon in Berlin (Germany), St Poelten (Austria) and the University of Jyväskylä (Finland).

11 Directive 2004/38/EC of the European Parliament and of the Council, of 29 April 2004 on the Right of citizens of the Union and their family members to move and reside freely within the territory of the Member States. http://europa.eu/LexUriServ/LexUriServ.do?uri=CONSLEG:2004L0038:20040430:EN:PDF.

12 Official Journal of the European Communities C 364/1, 18 December 2000, http://www.europarl.europa.eu/charter/pdf/text_en.pdf.

13 The notorious demand for nursing staff in Bulgaria and Romania today is even more alarming if compared with the 8000 requests for documents allowing Romanian doctors to work abroad in the last three years, as has been reported by the Romanian health ministry (Mason, 2010).

REFERENCES

Adams, A., Erath, P. and Shardlow, S. (2000) *Fundamentals of Social Work in Selected European Countries.* Lyme Regis: Russell House Publishing.

Banks, S. (2006) *Ethics and Values in Social Work.* Basingstoke: Palgrave Macmillan.

Camapanini, A. (2007) 'Introduction. Educating social workers in the context of Europe', in E. Frost, M.J. Freitas (eds), *Social Work Education in Europe.* Rome: Carocci. pp. 9–20.

Chytil, O. and Seibel, F. (1999) *European Dimensions in Training and Practice of Social Professions.* Blansko: Albert.

Clarke, J. (2004) *Changing Welfare, Changing States.* London: Sage.

Council of Europe (2010) *The Council of Europe: An Overview,* http://www.coe.int/AboutCoe/media/interface/publications/tour_horizon_en.pdf, accessed 31 August 2011.

Dobkowski, M.N. and Wallimann, I. (1998) *The Coming Age of Scarcity.* Syracuse, NY: Syracuse University Press.

Dominelli, L. (1988 [1997]) *Anti-Racist Social Work.* London: Macmillan.

Dominelli, L. (2002) *Anti-Oppressive Theory and Practice.* London: Palgrave.

Dominelli, L. and Hoogvelt, A. (1996) 'Globalisation and the technocratisation of social work', *Critical Social Policy*, 6 (2): 45–62.

Esping-Andersen, G. (1990) *The Three Worlds of Welfare Capitalism*. Cambridge: PolityPress.

Europa (2010) *Languages of Europe*. http://ec.europa.eu/education/languages/languages-of-europe/doc141_en.htm, accessed 11 November 2010.

Europa (2011) *Basic Information on the European Union*. http://europa.eu/about-eu/basic-information/index_en.htm, accessed 31 August 2011.

Eurostat (2008) *Population and Social Conditions* 72/2008.

Expert Group on Gender, Social Inclusion and Employment (2006) *Gender Inequalities in the Risks of Poverty and Social Exclusion for Disadvantaged Groups in Thirty European Countries*. European Commission, Directorate-General for Employment, Social Affairs and Equal Opportunities, Unit G.1., accessed 10 October 2010.

Fortunato, V., Friesenhahn, G.J. and Kantowicz, E. (2008) *Social Work in Restructured European Welfare Systems*. Rome: Carocci.

Fritzell, J. and Ritakallio, V.-M. (2010) 'Societal shifts and changed patterns of poverty', *International Journal of Social Welfare*, 19: 25–41.

Frost, E. and Camapanini, A. (2005) 'Inclusivity, process and product in writing for European social work education. Le implicazioni nella composizione di testi per il Servizio Sociale a livello europeo', *European Journal of Social Work*, 8 (3): 317–22.

Ginsburg, N. and Lawrence, S. (2006) 'A changing Europe', in K. Lyons, and S. Lawrence (eds), *Social Work in Europe: Educating for Change*. Birmingham: BASW/Venture Press.

Guy, W., Liebich, A. and Marushiakova, E. (2010) *Improving the Tools for Social Inclusion and Non-discrimination of Roma in the EU*. Luxembourg: Publications Office of the European Union.

Hämäläinen, J. (2003) 'The concept of social pedagogy in the field of social work', *Journal of Social Work*, 3 (1): 69–80.

Healy, L. (2001*) International Social Work: Professional Action in an Interdependent World*. Oxford: Oxford University Press.

Hering, S. and Waaldijk, B. (eds) (2003) *History of Social Work in Europe (1900–1960)*. Opladen: Leske & Budrich.

Hering, S. and Waaldijk, B. (2005) 'Information about the activities of the "Network for Historical Studies on Gender and Social Work in Europe" (www.sweep.uni-siegen.de). The foundation of the network in 2001 and further activities', *European Journal of Social Work*, 8 (2): 201–4.

Hokenstad, M.C., Khinduka, S.K. and Midgley, J. (1996) *Profiles in International Social Work*. Washington, DC: NASW Press.

Humphries, B. (2004) 'An unacceptable role for social work: Implementing immigration policy', *British Journal for Social Work*, 34: 93–107.

IFSW and IASSW (International Federation of Social Workers and International Association of Schools of Social Work) (2004) *Ethics in Social Work, Statement of Principles*. http://www.ifsw.org/f38000032.html.

Jergeby, U. and Soydan, H. (2002) 'Assessment processes in social work practice when children are at risk: A comparative, cross-national vignette study', *Journal of Social Work Research and Evaluation*, 3: 127–44.

Jordan, B. (2004), *Sex, Money and Power. The Transformation of Collective Life*. Cambridge: Polity.

Kantowicz, E. (2005) 'Dilemmas in comparative research of education for social work in Europe', *European Journal of Social Work*, 8 (3): 297–309.

Labonté-Roset, C. (2005) 'The European higher education area and research-orientated social work education', *European Journal of Social Work*, 8 (3): 285–96.

Lawrence, S. (2006) 'Postgraduate provision in Europe', in K. Lyons and S. Lawrence (eds), *Social Work in Europe: Educating for Change*. Birmingham: BASW/Venture Press.

Lawrence, S. and Simpson, G. (2009) 'International aspects of social work with elders', in S. Lawrence, K. Lyons, G Simpson and N. Huegler (eds). *Introducing International Social Work*. Exeter: Learning Matters.

Lawrence, S. and Torres, S. (2012) 'Older people and migration: challenges for social work' (Special Issue) in *European Journal of Social Work*, 15 (1).

Leibfried, S. (1992)'Towards a European welfare state?' in Z. Ferge and J.E. Kolberg (eds), *Social Policy in a Changing Europe*. Boulder, CO: Campus/Westview. pp. 245–80.

Leskošek, V. (2010) 'Načeti temelji socialne države: revščina', *Sobotna pril*, 14 August: 12.

Littlechild, B. (2009) 'Social work in the UK: The professional debate in relation to values and managerialism', in D.M. Maglajlič (ed.), *Social Work Theory and Practice*. Dubrovnik; Zagreb: InterUniversity Center. pp. 239–50.

Lorenz, W. (1994) *Social Work in a Changing Europe*. London: Routledge.

Lorenz, W. (2006) 'Education for the social professions', in K. Lyons and S. Lawrence (eds), *Social*

Work in Europe: Educating for Change. Birmingham: BASW/Venture Press.

Lyons, K. and Huegler, N. (2010) 'Immigration and the European Union', in U. Segal, N. Mayadas and D. Elliott (eds), *Immigration Worldwide*. New York: Oxford University Press. Chapter 29.

Lyons, K. and Lawrence, S. (eds) (2006) *Social Work in Europe: Educating for Change*. Birmingham: BASW/Venture Press.

Maiss, M. (2009) 'Sozialarbeit im Dienst der Ermöglichung substanzeller/materieller Bedingungen von Freiheit und Wohlleben', in P. Pantucek and M. Maiss (eds), *Die Aktualität des Denkens von Ilse Arlt*. Wiesbaden: VS.

Manthorpe, J. and Livsey, L. (2009) 'European challenges in delivering social services in rural regions: A scoping review', *European Journal of Social Work*, 12 (1): 5–24.

Mason, D. (2010) *Reading Room: Health in Bulgaria/Romania, and the Plight of Minorities*. 23 August.

Meeuwisse, A. and Sward, H. (2007) 'Cross-national comparisons of social work – a question of initial assumptions and levels of analysis', *European Journal of Social Work*, 10 (4): 481–96.

Morris, J. (1993) *Community Care or Independent Living?* York: Joseph Rowntree Foundation.

Moussu, G. (2008) 'Social-political and cultural changes in social work practices in France from 1973 to the present', in V. Fortunato, G.J. Friesenhahn and E. Kantowicz (eds), *Social Work in Restructured European Welfare Systems*. Rome: Carocci. pp. 129–38.

Oliver, M. (1983) *Social Work with Disabled People*. London: Macmillan.

Pečarič, E. (2002) 'Personal assistance for disabled people', in *National Congress of Social Work Slovenia, Book of Abstracts: Global-Local-Social*. Ljubljana: University of Ljubljana, School of Social Work.

Pena-Casas, R. and Latta, M. (2004) *Working Poor in the European Union*. Dublin: The European Foundation for the Improvement of the Living and Working Conditions. http://www.eurofound.europa.eu/pubdocs/2004/67/en/1/ef0467en.pdf.

Platform for Roma Inclusion (2008) *European Commission, Employment, Social Affairs and Inclusion*. http://ec.europa.eu/social/main.jsp?catId=761&langId=en, accessed 7 February 2011.

Prochazkova, L. and Schmid, T. (2009) 'Homecare aid: a challenge for social policy research', in S. Ramon and D. Zaviršek (eds), *Critical Edge Issues in Social Work and Social Policy*. Ljubljana: FSD.

Ramon, S. (ed.) (2008) *Social Work in the Context of Political Conflict*. Birmingham: Venture Press.

Rommelspacher, B. (1995) *Dominanzkultur. Texte zu Fremdheit und Macht*. Berlin: Orlanda.

Rommelspacher, B. (2010) 'Ethics in social work between secularism and re-Christianisation', in D. Zaviršek, B. Rommelspacher and S. Staub-Bernasconi (eds), *Ethical Dilemmas in Social Work. International Perspectives*. Ljubljana: FSD. pp. 65–77.

Scheppele, K.L. (2010) 'Liberalism against neoliberalism: resistance to structural adjustment and the fragmentation of the state in Russia and Hungary', in C.J. Greenhouse (ed.), *Ethnographies of Neoliberalism*. Philadelphia: Universty of Pennsylvania Press.

Schultz, D. (2007) 'Resource- and resilience-oriented work with immigrant and black patients', in D. Zaviršek, J. Zorn, L. Rihter and S. Demšar (eds), *Ethnicity in Eastern Europe. A Challenge for Social Work Education*. Ljubljana FSD.

Seeleib-Kaiser, M. (2008) 'Welfare state transformations in comparative perspective: shifting boundaries of "public" and "private" social policy?', in M. Seeleib-Kaiser (ed.), *Welfare State Transformations. Comparative Perspective*. Hampshire and New York: Palgrave Macmillan.

Seibel, F. and Lorenz, W. (1996) *Social Professions for a Social Europe*. Frankfurt: IKO-Verlag fur Interkulturelle Kommunikation.

Shardlow, S. and Payne, M. (1998) *Contemporary Issues in Social Work: Western Europe*. Aldershot: Ashgate.

Staub-Bernasconi, S. (2006) 'Social work as a profession: cross-national similarities and differences', in I. Weiss and P. Welbourne (eds), *Social Work as a Profession: a Comparative Cross-national Perspective*. Birmingham: Venture Press.

Staub-Bernasconi, S. (2007) *Soziale Arbeit als Handlungswissenschaft*. Bern: Haupt Buchhandlung.

United Nations Statistics Division (2011) *Composition of Macro Geographical (Continental) Regions, Geographical Sub-Regions, and Selected Economic and other Groupings*. http://unstats.un.org/unsd/methods/m49/m49regin.htm#europe, accessed 31 August 2011.

Wacquant, L. (2009 [2004]) *Punishing the Poor. The Neo-liberal Government of Social Insecurity*. Durham and London: Duke University Press.

Ward, T., Lelkes, O., Sutherland, H. and Toth, I.G. (2009) *European Inequalities*. Budapest: Tarki.

Warnes, T. (2006) 'Older foreign migrants in Europe: multiple pathways and welfare positions', in

S. Daatland and S. Biggs (eds), *Ageing and Diversity: Multiple Pathways and Cultural Migrations.* Bristol: Policy Press.

Wilensky, H.L. (2002) *Rich Democracies: Political Economy, Public Policy, and Performance.* Berkeley, Los Angeles and London: University of California Press.

Zaviršek, D. (2002) 'Pictures and silences: memories of sexual abuse of disabled people', *International Journal of Social Welfare*, 11 (4): 270–85.

Zaviršek, D. (2005) '"You will teach them some, socialism will do the rest!": history of social work education in Slovenia during the period 1940–1960', in K. Schilde and D. Schulte (eds), *Need and Care: Glimpses into the Beginnings of Eastern Europe's Professional Welfare.* Opladen, Blommfield Hills: Barbara Budrich Publishers. pp. 237–72.

Zaviršek, D. (2007) 'Communities of gatekeepers and communities of advocates: being disabled in Eastern Europe', in L. Dominelli (ed.), *Revitalising Communities in a Globalising world.* Aldershot: Ashgate. pp. 207–17.

Zaviršek, D. (2008) 'Engendering social work education under state socialism in Yugoslavia', *British Journal of Social Work*, 38 (4): 734–50.

Zaviršek, D. (2009a) 'Can development of the doctoral studies in social work resist the neo-liberalism within academia? Some comparisons', in R. Ramon and D. Zaviršek (eds), *Critical Edge Issues in Social Work and Social Policy. Comparative Research Perspective.* Ljubljana: Faculty of Social Work. pp. 219–37.

Zaviršek, D. (2009b) 'Social work with adults with disabilities: an international perspective. Critical commentary' *British Journal of Social Work*, 39 (7): 1393–405.

Zaviršek, D. (2009c) 'Between blood and care: social parenthood as the enlargement of the concept of parenthood in the current societies', *Socialno delo*, 48 (1/3): 3–16.

Zaviršek, D. and Videmšek, P. (2009) 'Service users involvement in research and teaching: is there a place for it in Eastern European social work'. *Ljetopis socialnog rada*, 162: 207–22.

Zorn, J. (2009) 'The right to stay: challenging the policy of detention and deportation', *European Journal of Social Work,* 12 (2): 247–60.

28

The Middle East: Expanding Social Work to Address 21st Century Concerns

Sahar Al-Makhamreh and Kathryn Libal[1]

INTRODUCTION

This chapter introduces important trends in social work professionalisation, social work education, and social work practice and research in the Middle East. The authors underscore that while some countries in the region have developed a social work profession that resembles many other countries globally, social work is still in its nascent stages of development and efforts to indigenise or localise practice in many contexts remains a vital arena of work. Discussion of social, economic, and political processes, such as urbanisation, economic globalisation, migration, armed conflict in some countries, and demographic trends that signal a boom in the number of youth in most countries, provide a backdrop for understanding the place of social work in the Middle East. The authors assert that enhancing both traditional local forms of social support and state-sponsored programmes for low-income and vulnerable populations should be a priority in coming years. As with the assessment of

Pawar with Tsui on Southern and Eastern Asia (Chapter 25), local, regional, and global initiatives to support the expansion of social work education and professional opportunities are necessary. This is true not only of the least developed areas, but also for targeted populations in even the most developed and economically robust states (including oil-rich Gulf States and countries such as Turkey, Israel, and Iran). In this chapter first we provide contextual background on the Middle East; second we address trends in the development of social work in the region, focusing on Egypt, Jordan, Turkey, and Israel, respectively; and finally we focus on key challenges that social work faces in the region.

CONTEXTUAL BACKGROUND ON THE MIDDLE EAST

The Middle Eastern countries we address in this chapter are diverse in terms of culture, ethnicity, religious affiliation, and political and economic structures. For our purposes the Middle East here includes 16 countries extending from Egypt to Iran[2] and Turkey. It is not possible to provide detailed descriptions of the unique social and political aspects of each country; thus we endeavor to highlight key trends common to the region and identify unique circumstances in several countries where social work as a profession has developed more fully than in other countries.

Nation-states in the Middle East and North Africa (MENA) bear the historical legacy of colonialism and imperialism, including notably the Ottoman, British, and French Empires. The crucible of World War I and the dissolution of the Ottoman Empire and eventual demise of Western colonialism in the region remade the geo-political and social landscape. The Armenian Genocide perpetrated by Ottoman leaders in 1915 (Watenpaugh, 2010) and mass exchange of Greek and Turkish populations initiated by the League of Nations in 1923 engendered the first large-scale displacements of peoples on the basis of ethnicity and religion (Hirschon, 2003). One of the most challenging issues of forced migration has been the long-standing Israeli and Palestinian conflict over territory and the right of Palestinian refugees to return to Israel, and this displacement has had profound impacts on neighbouring Arab states throughout the region (Peteet, 2009). Conflict has been chronic in other parts of the Middle East as well, including domestically in southeastern Turkey (between the Turkish military and Kurdish separatists) and in Iraq (between Kurds, Shia, and Sunni groups), and the suppression of opposition groups in Iran. Moreover, interregional conflict has episodically occurred with wide-ranging effects for many countries in the Middle East, including the decade-long Iran–Iraq War of the 1980s, the Persian Gulf War, and the US-led Iraq War that began in 2003 (Harding, 2007). At the time of writing during what has been widely called the 'Arab Spring' of 2011, political instability and conflict are rife in several countries and regime change or shifts in governance seem likely in some.

The majority of people in the Middle East practise Islam, though within this religious tradition there is great diversity in terms of levels of religiosity and specific beliefs. Turkey remains a staunchly secular state (officially), while a large proportion of the population practises Sunni, Sufi, and Alevi forms of Islam. It also has small Christian and Jewish populations. While Sunni Muslims are numerically the largest group of Muslims in the entire region (including Arabs and Turks), significant Shia minorities exist in Lebanon, Syria, Saudi Arabia, and other Gulf States. Moreover, Shia Islam is the dominant form of practice in Iran and Iraq. Judaism, while historically spread throughout the region, now is concentrated in Israel, but with small populations continuing to reside in Egypt, Turkey, Iran, Iraq, Lebanon, and other states. Armenian, Arab, and Turkish Christians also form important minority ethno-religious groups in the region. A significant number of Christian Palestinians continue to reside in the West Bank and Jerusalem, though their presence is often eclipsed by politics related to Palestinian Muslims who oppose Israeli occupation through membership in Hamas. This only briefly sketches the parameters of religious and ethnic diversity that must be attended to when considering culturally sensitive social work practice in the Middle East.

Countries in the Middle East vary widely in terms of the strength of their economies – Turkey, Israel, Iran, and the oil-rich Gulf States boast the most stable economies and relatively low poverty and unemployment rates. Yet, even within these states, considerable economic inequality and marginalisation of groups persists. For example, Kurds in Turkey disproportionately make up the poor (Saatci and Akpinar, 2007) and have more limited access to quality education than ethnic Turks (Yıldız, 2005). Likewise, in Israel, while Arab Israelis make up more than 20 percent of the population, they are more likely to face joblessness, earn lower wages, and fail to enter the university system (Lewin et al., 2006). For Palestinians in Gaza and the

West Bank, poverty, unemployment, and underemployment remain a fact of life for many individuals and families (Roy, 2004). Likewise, many Arab Iraqis, a significant proportion of whom are either internally displaced or are refugees in Jordan, Syria, or Lebanon, face serious challenges in meeting basic needs such as housing, food, water, healthcare, and primary education (Al-Qdah and Lacroix, 2010; Harding, 2007; Libal and Harding, 2011). Social and economic dislocation is pronounced even in the oil-rich Gulf States, as global economic recession continues to reverberate and labor markets fail to match the abilities of young educated Arabs seeking work (Dhillon et al., 2009).

Scholars and analysts examining social development throughout the Middle East point to significant challenges posed by the large youth population in the region. An initiative at the Brookings Foundation calls for 'youth-inclusive development', in light of the fact that 32 percent of the population in the Middle East is comprised of individuals between 15 and 29 years of age (Constant and Kreisch, 2010). The study notes that although population growth is slowing in many countries in the region, young people still make up a high proportion of the overall population facing high unemployment and underemployment. The United Nations Development Programme (UNDP) and League of Arab States estimate that approximately 51 million jobs must be created by 2020 to 'meet the demand of the total unemployed and those entering the work force. A significant proportion of these jobs are needed for currently unemployed youth and new youth labour force entrants during the next decade' (as cited in Constant and Kreisch, 2010).

Informalisation of labour, inadequate pathways to training programmes and higher education, and rising costs of living all contribute to other significant social changes, including delay of marriage and the inability to establish separate households among urban middle class youth (Dhillon et al., 2009). Lack of adequate educational systems,

programmes for job creation, and other welfare supports throughout the region has generated heightened interest in developing social work education. The relatively small numbers of trained social workers in most countries will require educational programmes to 'scale up' training efforts, as well as to collaborate more effectively with other community leaders, those working within charitable and religious institutions and non-governmental organisations (NGOs), as well as professionals trained in psychology, sociology, and the medical fields.

DEVELOPING SOCIAL WORK IN THE REGION

Social work in MENA is a profession with a genealogy rooted in religious and ethnic-based philanthropy of the late 19th century and state-sponsored developmentalist approaches that gained ascendancy in the post-colonial period following World War II (Ragab, 1995). Government-initiated programmes to secure social welfare throughout most of the region have a recent history and the practical 'reach' of such efforts has been relatively limited.[3] The family, extended kin, and neighborhood support comprised immediate 'safety nets' to meet individual and family needs. Moreover, religious institutions, whether Islamic, Christian, or Judaic, have long been recognised sites of social assistance (Bonner et al., 2003; Singer, 2008). Indeed religious voluntary and institutional forms of welfare remain dominant forms of social assistance for individuals throughout the region (e.g. Harmsen, 2008; Clark, 2004; White, 2002).

While social work has developed throughout the region in diverse ways, a number of processes and themes can be identified that play a vital role in shaping the profession. Social work education sponsored by institutions of higher learning was initiated in the 1950s and 1960s in a number of countries, including Egypt, Turkey, Lebanon, Israel,

Iran, and Iraq. The development of 'the profession' – adapted from Western traditions of social work – has been less robust than in other allied fields, such as medicine. As is highlighted above, local kinship, neighbourhood and religious institutional supports have been crucial in addressing individual and family needs. Yet, despite the centrality of local forms of charity and social support, state ministries charged with social welfare seek to develop social policies and social work practice responsive to the realities of an increasingly urban, service-based socioeconomic structure. They also recognise the continuing need for developing rural responses that are not solely structured as 'social development initiatives', and the increasing urgency of working with marginalised groups, including ethnic and religious minorities, undocumented migrant workers, female-headed households, elderly, and disabled people.

With the exception of Israel, national professional social work organisations remain nascent or aspirational bodies. The Israel Association of Social Workers is active in advocating for the interests of social workers, focusing in recent years on challenges professionals face with large caseloads (Auslander, no date; Mansbach and Kaufman, 2003). In Turkey, an Ankara-based Association of Social Workers has recently formed to address similar concerns (Yazıcı, 2008). Both the Israeli and Turkish bodies are members of the International Federation of Social Workers (IFSW). Morocco and Lebanon also have their own national unions for social workers and are IFSW members. In Egypt, the Egyptian Society for Social Workers (formed first in 1940), operates alongside other organisations, yet has not been recognised by the government as an independent voice for the profession. In 2008 Jordanian professionals established the Jordanian Association of Social Workers. Yet Ragab's observation (1995) that professional organisations in the region are either nonexistent or very weak is still true: unionisation is politically difficult in most countries in the region and where

social work degrees exist, graduates are often grouped in organisations with allied professions.

Regionally, associations of schools of social work are only in the nascent stages of formation although informal collaboration and sharing of information among schools of social work within Arab states has accelerated in recent years and, as the number of social work educational programmes grows in Israel, such an association is likely to be formalised. Participation in the International Association of Schools of Social Work (IASSW) is also limited. In 2010, IASSW membership included seven universities in Israel, one in Lebanon, one in the United Arab Emirates, and one in Turkey (IASSW, 2011). Current membership is not a sufficient indication of involvement, however, as other social work programmes from Turkey, Jordan, Iran, and Egypt have been members. Moreover, a number of social work educators from the Middle East are individual members in IASSW and participate actively in international social work conferences and advocacy and policy-making efforts.

Social workers also are active in numerous charitable governmental and non-governmental organisations, such as community-based NGOs, national chapters of the International Red Cross and Red Crescent Association (Benthall and Bellian-Jourdan, 2003), and national chapters of United Nations intergovernmental organisations, such as UNICEF (United Nations Children's Fund), UNDP, and UNHCR (United Nations High Commissioner for Refugees). Scant research has been conducted detailing how social work in the Middle East contributes to such developmental, charitable, and community-based organisations. Tracing the influence of social workers in regional and global policy-making is a vital arena of potential research and practice.

An important consideration for social work is how to promote cooperation between often secular, state-centred social work educational institutions and the considerable number of religious institutions involved in providing

THE MIDDLE EAST

social care through informal networks (Benthall and Bellian-Jourdan, 2003; Harmsen, 2008; White, 2002). Ragab (1995) noted a movement to reorient social work to an Islamic framework in many countries: such an endeavour is being led by social workers trained in the United Arab Emirates (UAE) (Ashencaen Crabtree, 2008; Holtzhausen, 2010) and Egypt (Soliman and Abd Elmegied, 2010). This process is embedded within the broader trend of re-Islamicising the public sphere in many societies in general. Yet, as Yazıcı (personal communication, 2010) notes, social work educational institutions are often highly secular in their orientation and have yet to fully grapple with developing curricula to address local needs.

In addition, strengthening social work education requires fuller attention to the diverse cultural and religious groups within countries in the region, and the specific needs of migrants and refugee populations which have grown considerably in the past two decades. This is true for the countries with the most developed social work programmes, such as Israel, Turkey, and Egypt (Roer-Strier and Haj-Yahia, 1998; Spiro, 2001), and those now expanding their social work education programmes, such as the United Arab Emirates and other Gulf States (Ashencaen Crabtree, 2008) and Jordan (Al-Makhamreh and Sullivan, 2010).

We have chosen to focus on several cases that provide opportunities to consider how social work in each of these countries reflects distinctive historical trajectories of development as well as opportunities and challenges to expansion in the coming decades. We have selected two Arab countries: Egypt due to its role as an early leader in social work education and Jordan because of recent expansion of social work education and the country's pivotal role in the region. We include Turkey due to its status as a rapidly developing country seeking to use European social welfare models in a largely Islamic society.[4] Finally, we address Israeli social work, which has arguably the most deeply institutionalised social work education and practice, and yet

faces substantial challenges in addressing the effects of structural inequality faced by diverse Arab and Jewish populations in the coming years.

Egypt: an early leader in social work education and practice

Egypt in many ways led social work education in the region in the first part of the 20th century. The profession emanated from charitable and voluntary work by individuals in local communities of various religious backgrounds and as part of the legacy of British colonialism and Christian missionary endeavours.[5] By the early 1930s the government began to pass social welfare laws to address poverty and the needs of marginalised groups, such as orphans, disabled people, and widowed women (Salem, 2010). In the 1930s, the first social work unions or organisations were formed, and these early institutionalisation efforts led to the establishment of the Ministry of Social Affairs in 1939. In 1941 the Egyptian Association for Social Workers was formed to advocate for the profession, followed by the creation of the Higher Institution for Social Work Education, which was open only to women (Salem, 2010).

During this era, professional practice was deeply influenced by Western models and by those Egyptians who studied abroad and returned to teach or practice social work (Al-Krenawi and Graham, 2003). Educational curricula prepared social workers to follow a case-work approach to solving individual problems that resulted from poverty and illiteracy (Soliman and Abd Elmegied, 2010). The legacy of the adoption of what Al-Krenawi and Graham characterise as a 'largely Northern conception' of social work must be understood as a 'product of colonialism' (2003: 75) – the effects of which are felt today in teaching and the training of social workers.

The introduction of Arab socialism, following the establishment of the Egyptian republic in 1953, marked an era of expansion and a shift in emphasis from case work to a collectivist model stressing community organisation and social and economic development (Soliman and Abd Elmegied, 2010). By the early 1960s women and men could earn a bachelors degree in social work at Helwan University in Cairo.

Despite the fact that professional social work has existed in Egypt for almost a century, the relative status of the profession remains precarious, particularly in light of the scale of poverty and the inadequacy of state-level supports for marginalised groups. Indeed, alongside state-supported social services there operate robust and more informal types of social care supported by Islamic and Christian institutions (Atia, 2008; Clark, 2004). Soliman and Abd Elmegied (2010) highlight the need to assess social work's contribution to society and to establish a national association that is capable of monitoring and contributing to a culturally relevant, engaged social work profession. Moreover, efforts must be made to improve the popular image of Egyptian social workers, particularly in light of Soliman and Abd Elmegied's findings that social work's status has diminished in recent years.

Since the late 1960s, social work education and professional practice has expanded considerably, just as the Egyptian population has grown to more than 70 million people. Helwan University, which has both masters and doctoral-level programmes, is a leader in social work education, and other programmes have been developed since the 1970s at Kufer, Alshiek, Eswan, and Damanhor. The first doctorate programme degree in social work was formed in 1972 at Helwan University. Despite these gains, social work is still accorded a 'lower status' compared to other human service professions in the health fields and psychology. Student selection processes based on the outcomes of generalised tests taken while in high school have meant that often students who have little interest in social work are 'tracked' into the profession (Mahara Professional Consultancies in Development, 2008; Soliman and Abd Elmegied, 2010). Moreover, fuller state support for developing social work programmes and professional associations is needed to allow the field to expand to meet growing social needs in coming years. Unprecedented numbers of protesters who captured global attention in early 2011, called not only for the removal of the long-time president Hosni Mubarak but also (and perhaps more importantly) for sustained efforts to reform the economy, tackle corruption, and address entrenched poverty and inequality experienced by the majority of the population.

Jordan: scaling up responsive social work for the 21st century

Like Egypt, social work in Jordan emerged from a hybridisation of philanthropic activities by ethnic and religious groups with Western social work models (Al-Makhamreh, 2005; Ibrahim, 2010). Earliest charitable efforts for the poor were organised by Christian and Caucasian immigrants groups in the early 20th century. Between the 1930s and 1950s voluntarism through charitable and relief organisations coexisted alongside sophisticated tribal system supports in rural communities (Cocks et al., 2009). In the 1950s and 1960s as part of a state-sponsored project for development, social assistance was increasingly administered by the government and a mix of national and international non-governmental organisations and religious groups. The institutionalisation of social welfare was initiated in 1951 with the founding of the Department of Social Affairs under the Ministry of Health and the passage of legislation on social welfare (National Conference for Social Work in Jordan, 1998).

In the 1970s–1990s the Jordanian government accelerated efforts to support social development, prioritising social welfare for the domestic agenda. This reflected growing needs of the population caused by rapid industrialisation and urbanisation; the continuing influx of Palestinian (and later Iraqi) refugees; economic migrants from Egypt and other countries; and population growth

(Sullivan et al., 2010). Political tension between some officials in Parliament and governmental institutions and the Muslim Brotherhood, which had gained in influence in the country, made the question of state accountability for social welfare provision a key concern (Harmsen, 2008). These factors presented substantial challenges, stretching the capacity of previous systems and prompting the state to scale up social work education and initiatives through the state and emerging non-governmental sector (National Conference for Social Work in Jordan, 1998).

In response, the National Assistance Fund (in 1986) and Employment and Development Fund (in 1992) were created and welfare-related legislation was passed, such as laws regulating *zakat* (religious charitable donations) and addressing the needs of persons with disabilities. National NGOs, including the Queen Alia Fund, the Nour Al-Hussein Foundation and the Higher Board Net for Social Assistance, accelerated efforts to deliver social services not adequately addressed by the state (National Conference for Social Work in Jordan, 1998).

In this context, governmental and non-governmental institutions increasingly began seeking trained social workers to work in community-based programmes. Social work education in Jordan is relatively new (Al-Makhamreh, 2005; Sullivan et al., 2010). The oldest two-year diploma programme was established in 1965. By the late 1990s, civil servants, politicians, and local leaders understood that while local support to address social problems and individual needs was still the accepted ideal, personal and familial ties could not alone tackle these issues. In 1998, a two-year programme at the Institute of Social Development was upgraded to a four-year bachelor degree programme located in Princess Rahma University College, which was in turn affiliated with Al-Balqa Applied University (Maharah Professional Consultancies in Development, 2008; Cocks et al., 2009). By 2006, four colleges of social work had been established that operated as satellite programmes affiliated with the Al-Balqa Applied University. Other bachelors programmes at the Hashemite University and Yarmouk University have been added.

Social work educators at Al-Balqa Applied University, Jordan University, and the Hashemite University are now working to build capacity in the arenas of education, training and practice. They also aim to develop social work's professional status, set up a national standard for training and job descriptions, and establish a national code of practice and ethics (Sullivan et al., 2010). In another sign of institutionalisation efforts, in 2009 the Ministry of Higher Education has begun to establish guidelines for accreditation due to be implemented in 2011. In addition, several universities have sponsored the doctoral training of a number of educators at institutions in several European countries.

Turkey: bridging state-based and charitable social service practices

Social work emerged as a profession in Turkey in the 1960s, though its roots can be seen in efforts of early pioneers like Sabiha Zekeriya Sertel, who trained in community organisation at the Columbia School of Social Work in New York in the early 1920s (Libal, 2001). Prior to the formation of the General Directorate of Social Services and Child Protection in the 1980s, welfare supports were offered to individuals through a variety of institutions, both public and charitable (Libal, 2001; Yazıcı, 2008). In 1983, the government established the Social Services and Child Protection Agency charged with providing basic services to children taken into institutional care and a variety of programmes for elderly or disabled people, and women and their children seeking shelter from domestic violence (Yazıcı, 2008). State-sponsored welfare programmes remain relatively modest and do not universally address the needs of the population; arguably only a fraction of those qualified receive support, and even this is only at very modest levels.

Moreover, as the Turkish state embarks on its own 'welfare reform' programme, even these minimal supports are in jeopardy (Yazıcı, 2007).

While programmes offered through the Social Services and Child Protection Agency play an important role in meeting some of the basic needs of Turkey's population, the majority of 'front-line' workers have not been trained in professional social work programmes. Bulut (2003) notes that between 1982 and 2002 the School of Social Work at Hacettepe University, which was the only university-based social work programme until 2002, produced 3000 social workers. When considered in light of Turkey's more than 70 million citizens, this number is small indeed. Turkish social workers largely have not benefitted from formal university-based training, instead 'learning on the job', as they do in many entry-level social service positions in highly industrialised countries like the USA.

Another obstacle to the development of the profession is the low regard accorded to social workers. As in other countries in the region, state-run social welfare institutions and those working in them are stigmatised. Moreover, widespread ideals that stress the necessity of seeking social support from family, neighbours, or charitable institutions (*vakıf*) rather than the state continue to dominate (White, 2002). Because of the relatively small number of formally trained social workers, some Turkish officials and community-based activists are pressing for the development of other departments and schools of social work at a number of higher education institutions in Turkey.

Until the late 1990s, social work education at the School of Social Work in Hacettepe University was divided into case work, group work, and community organisation. Following analysis of trends in social work education in Europe and the USA, Hacettepe University and the newer Başkent University Department of Social Work implemented generalist practice bachelors programmes (Bulut, 2003). Expansion of social work education at the university level is now a priority: no longer can one or two educational institutions train enough professionals to work in a range of settings and community organisations. Moreover, as the government devolves social welfare work to the non-governmental and charitable sectors, social workers are likely to be in higher demand, for example in private shelters and group homes. Başkent University's Department of Social Work was created in 2002 and, like Hacetteppe, Başkent's undergraduate programme promotes educational models influenced by curricula in Europe and the USA. As Turkey continues to press for accession to the European Union, they are eager to conform to European standards in social work education and practice. Hacettepe University's School of Social Work has been a sporadic member of IASSW since 1965 and also has membership of the European Association of Schools of Social Work (EASSW). Başkent University's programme has also participated in the EASSW and IASSW. Turkey, which participates in the Bologna Process to create a European Higher Education Area, has committed to taking part in regular exchanges between academics from Turkish universities and Turkish social workers with other European educators and practitioners (Agten, 2006).

While scaling up social work education is a priority, 'localising' the curricula to reflect particular cultural, religious, or socioeconomic realities is still nascent. Few social work educators stress such topics in annual meetings of social work educators. A need exists to develop social work modules that foster social inclusion of low-income Turkish and Kurdish families. Concerns about relevant social work practice with Kurds are pronounced, as many have migrated to cities in Turkey's west in the past decades and face specific needs as newcomers in the region; it is also crucial to develop localised, relevant practice addressing social development and social welfare work for rural Turks and Kurds in the Southeast and Black Sea regions.

Israel: social work education for a diverse society

Social work education in Israel, as in Egypt, can be traced to the 1930s. Henrietta Szold was a central figure in this early history and is credited with early efforts to create a professionally trained staff for social welfare departments serving the Jewish population in Jerusalem (Guttmann and Cohen, 1995; Spiro, 2001). Ten years after Israel achieved statehood, the first university-based programme in social work was founded at the Hebrew University in Jerusalem. A number of social work educators were invited from the USA to help craft its curriculum, which emphasised 'the role of social work as society's instrument for promoting social justice, particularly distributive justice' (Guttmann and Cohen, 1995: 307). Three more schools were formed at universities in Tel-Aviv, Bar-Ilan, and Haifa in the 1960s and in 1982 Ben Gurion University (Beer-Sheva) was also established. Guttmann and Cohen (1995) note that, with professionalisation, a shift has occurred away from earlier social justice mandates towards clinical practice. Yet, a social justice foundation persists in many programmes, where human rights issues, such as addressing hunger and food insecurity, strengthening the safety net for poor and low-income individuals, addressing discrimination toward new-immigrant Jewish groups, and tackling the structural marginalisation of both Bedouin and Palestinian Arab-Israelis, have been a focus.

One challenge – not unlike that faced in all the other countries in the region – is the fact that the exam system for students entering university tracks students to the field of social work, even if it is not a primary career interest (Guttmann and Cohen, 1995). However, a more recent study finds that social work as a career path has grown in popularity in the 2000s, ranking as the fifth most preferred educational track among applicants to universities in Israel in 2005 (Segal-Engelchin and Kaufman, 2008). Even as Israel implemented its own welfare reform processes, including privatisation of some social services, four new colleges of social work were established in the 2000s. While students in the Segal-Engelchin and Kaufman study (2008) cited the desire to work in private practice, the study also found that almost half of all students surveyed are interested in community-based work, policy practice and social change.

Another challenge is the lack of trained Israeli-Arab social workers within Israel, despite relatively robust funding by the state to develop social work education and the profession (Roer-Strier and Haj-Yahia, 1998). Building a culturally and politically sensitive curriculum in Israel's schools of social work remains a challenge, particularly in light of the larger ongoing conflict between Israel and the Palestinian (Occupied) Territories. Roer-Strier and Haj-Yahia (1998) noted more than a decade ago that no schools of social work required a course on human oppression or systemic racism. Positive developments have since occurred on an institution-by-institution basis, where schools of social work have integrated educational instruction and field practice units addressing human rights concerns of Palestinians within Israel. Course content includes, for example, attention to Palestinian women's experiences of militarisation and violence in Israel, Palestine, and Jordan (Shalhoub-Kevorkian, 2011), the rights of unrecognised Bedouin villages, and the realisation of Bedouin children's rights.[6]

KEY CHALLENGES IN STRENGTHENING SOCIAL WORK IN THE MIDDLE EAST

Contextual challenges

Social workers practising throughout the region face significant emerging social problems that require not only more robust training and governmental supports for practice, but also the advocacy and insights of front-line workers who are engaged at the community-level. Economic migration, both into the region and by locals seeking jobs in Europe or other countries in the Middle East, poses substantial new social problems for individuals and families. Often males migrate for work and send home remittances, leaving women and other extended family members to care for children, work, and address the challenges of 'female-headed' household status. Forced migration, especially in the wake of US-led invasion and occupation of Iraq, presents deep challenges to local systems for support (Libal and Harding, 2011; Al-Makhamreh and Lewando-Hundt, 2011); yet long-standing populations of Palestinian refugees residing primarily in Jordan, Syria, Lebanon, Egypt, or in camps in Gaza and the West Bank remain one of the most intractable social problems in the region. Moreover, as Roer-Strier and Haj-Yahia (1998) assert, the need for trained Arab social workers in Israel is also a paramount concern, as Arabs continue to grapple with discrimination and a status as second-class citizens who are disproportionately poor, face malnutrition, joblessness or underemployment, and discrimination in educational fields as a result of their nationality.

Other social problems also remain pronounced, many linked to widespread poverty and the lack of adequate education at the primary, secondary, and university levels, as well as inadequate healthcare systems. Other key concerns include addressing exploitative child labour practices, homelessness among children, domestic violence, shaping programmes for supporting individuals with disabilities and their families, addressing increasing chemical dependency and alcoholism (especially among male youth), and the spread of HIV/AIDS. Each of these domains illustrates not only the need for qualified social workers to develop new modes of social work practice, but also the necessity for social work to partner with other professions in developing more comprehensive approaches to addressing social inequalities (Soliman and Abd Elmegied, 2010).

Professional status and employment opportunities

As discussed above, social work in the Middle East, despite a fairly long history in several countries, is still at an early developmental stage. Lack of recognition accorded to the profession compared with other human service professions has resulted in limited capacity for developing social work education, and institutions such as unions and associations to help foster the profession.

Part of the problem can be linked to the feminisation of the profession. While it is considered an appropriate career path for women seeking work in the public sphere, it is accorded relatively lower status than other male-dominated professions (Ashencaen Crabtree, 2008; Yazıcı, 2008). As Al-Makhamreh (2005) notes, women are thought to be particularly well-suited to doing work within the domestic sphere in care-giving roles. A typical feature of social work practice in Jordan and some other Arab countries is the use of 'fictive kinship'. Creating a sense of imagined kin connection through outreach by women allows social workers to overcome many religious sensitivities and cultural constraints. Yet, this feminisation can also create challenges, especially in official institutions where social work may take place, such as in hospitals. Al Makhamreh's (2005) study of hospital social workers in Jordan showed that women faced discrimination in their interprofessional relations with doctors due to the dominance of male power and medical models of assistance in this setting (Al-Makhamreh, 2005). Thus, while a feminised profession may facilitate access to households, the overall status of women within society affects their ability to effectively advocate for clients and communities in the public sphere.

Social workers throughout the region do not play a significant role in policy practice or formal political advocacy. Alsaid Amer's (2007) study in Egypt finds that the national Association of Social Workers did not empower social workers to participate in policy making or the political process more generally. Enmeshment in a large bureaucratic system hindered Egyptian social workers from policy advocacy on behalf of their clients; and Alsaid Amer noted that most social workers themselves lacked the motivation or sense of efficacy to participate in such decision making.

One of the most significant challenges to professionalisation and expanding opportunities for social workers in the labour market is the availability of social work educators at the university level. For example, in Jordan, among the 30 social work academics identified in a recent study, less than half held a degree (at any level) in social work, while the majority held degrees in sociology and had no practice experience. Other key needs include the development of a more robust regionally-based body of knowledge on both contextual factors that shape human needs and promising approaches to social work practice and the integration of technology into delivery systems for social care (Mahara Professional Consultancies in Development, 2008, Cocks et al., 2008; Al-Makhamreh and Sullivan, 2010).

Compounding the stigma often associated with social work is the lack of a sufficient number of positions for graduates once they complete their degrees. For example, in Jordan, an average 165 students have graduated each year over a seven-year period but, on average, only 18 graduates per annum secured jobs (Mahara Professional Consultancies in Development, 2008; Soliman and Abd Elmegied, 2010). What Ashencaen Crabtree (2008) notes for the UAE specifically holds true for most countries in the region: 'Although there is an increasing awareness of the value of an established profession, post-qualifying posts are few in number despite a clear social need for more' (2008: 537).

Developing pathways to employment and addressing the relatively low status accorded the profession must be addressed at the policy level and may require more effective forms of mobilisation among social work educators and practitioners.

Promoting localisation of knowledge and diversity-based approaches to social work education

A number of scholars point to the relatively limited role that research plays in informing social work practice in the region (Salem, 2005; Sullivan et al., 2010). Several collaborative initiatives between Middle Eastern and European or US schools of social work have been developed as one approach to accelerate the development of the profession. In Jordan, Al-Balqa Applied University collaborated with Reading and Brunel Universities (UK) on exploring needs for social work education in Jordan (Cocks et al., 2008; Mahara Professional Consultancies in Development, 2008; Sullivan et al., 2010). The U-based Columbia University has partnered with the Jordan River Foundation and other non-profit organisations to develop short-term training projects. A fundamental concern has been to leverage such collaborations in the creation of programmes that reflect the local needs of Jordanians and the current capacity of educational institutions and the state. This entails paying particular attention to culturally relevant practice and avoiding wholesale adoption of curricula from the global north. The social work faculty at the UAE University similarly reflects North–South efforts to collaborate in social work education. The faculty is split almost evenly between European or North American and Arab professors. As UAE social work programmes expand, they aim especially to localise an international social work curriculum (familiar to IASSW member schools) to meet the needs of UAE social work practitioners (Holtzhausen, 2010). This entails a strong focus on family well-being, child development, individual and family counselling, and community services (Ashencaen Crabtree, 2008).

More broadly, social work programmes throughout the Middle East endeavour to develop contextually relevant practice (Al-Krenawi and Graham, 2000; Furman et al., 2004; Al-Makhamreh and Lewando-Hundt, 2008). This is vital in light of social workers' practice shifting to meet the new needs that have emerged with rapid urbanisation, the influx of large numbers of migrant workers from outside of the region, ongoing struggles to meet the needs of refugees (primarily Palestinians and Iraqis), and the stresses of a demographically young population where youth often struggle to enter the labour force and delay marriage and family formation. A key gap in both research and social work education is in attending to the considerable cultural diversity and social inequalities.

Moreover, social work educators throughout the region must navigate specific challenges in balancing religious-based and secular aspects of social care. As Ragab (1995) noted in the mid-1990s, an Islamic reorientation of social work education has been underway in the Gulf State societies. Other officially secular states, such as Turkey, have also begun to engage 'culturally relevant' approaches to social work practice that include recognition of the role of religious belief and institutions in social care (White, 2002). This process of incorporating modes of social work practice that draw upon religious aspects of social identity represents a formal recognition of what social workers had long done in their direct and community-based practice.[7] Little research has been conducted in any of the countries of the region to examine what it is that trained social workers (and allied para-professionals and non-professionals) do in their daily practice (but see Yazıcı, 2007). Yet, it is clear that social workers must grapple with localised cultural sensitivities in their everyday practice. Recognising that service provision will often take place within a family-based context and that families will be centrally involved in decision making is key to the reception of social welfare providers in communities (Ashencaen Crabtree, 2008).

CONCLUSION

Social work educators throughout the region are increasingly mobilising to craft curricula and models that better fit the socio-economic, political, and cultural realities of the Middle East in all its diversity. They also note the need to engage international social work in the social work curriculum, focusing on cross-cultural understanding and concerns with global social problems. Attending both to localisation and globalisation is necessary to grapple with the considerable challenges that social workers and their clients will face in coming years. One of the most significant challenges to professionalisation and expanding opportunities for social workers in the labour market is the availability of social work educators at the university level. At the associational or organisational level, efforts to establish collaborative frameworks that create bridges between schools of social work and with other organisations centrally involved in social care are in the earliest stages. Moreover, building understanding among clients and communities and with governmental agencies supporting social welfare must be a primary focus for social workers in the next decade.

NOTES

1 The authors wish to thank Aviva Ron, MSW graduate student at the School of Social Work, University of Connecticut, for her research assistance.

2 The inclusion of key non-Arabic speaking countries (Iran, Turkey, and Israel) represents a departure from earlier survey chapters (Ragab, 1995).

3 The most notable exception to this is Israel (Guttmann and Cohen, 1995), as well as Turkey (Yazıcı, 2007) and to a lesser extent Iran and Egypt (Ragab, 1995) in urban areas.

4 We wanted to address social work in Iran in this chapter, but due to limitations in sources and on access to Iranian social workers we have not addressed this important case here. Yet, we want to stress how critical it is to foster research on social work and allied professions in Iran and to rebuild bi-lateral and international relationships with Iranian institutions working in social work and allied fields in coming years. Iran has a sizeable and well-educated population, yet the country also faces a number of challenging social problems, including poverty,

unemployment and underemployment, and population growth. While scholarly and professional exchange has been taking place with Iran for a number of years, this has not been as common for social workers and their national and international institutions.

5 This included charitable efforts on behalf of Muslim, Coptic Christian, Jewish, and other religious groups. Christian missionaries from Europe and the United States also played roles in establishing orphanages, homes for widows, and other disenfranchised groups (Baron, 2005, 2008).

6 These examples are drawn from efforts at The Paul Baerwald School of Social Work at Hebrew University and the Department of Social Work at Ben-Gurion University of the Negev, respectively. The authors thank Dr Roni Kaufman at Ben-Gurion University's Department of Social Work for his insights into recent developments in Israeli social work.

7 An intriguing study on social work training for ultra-orthodox Jewish women underscores the trend of attempting to reach communities through cultural mediators that bridge religious belief and practice and social work values and practice (Garr and Marans, 2001).

REFERENCES

Agten, J. (2006) *EASSW Bulletin*. Geel, Belgium: European Association for Schools of Social Work. Accessed from http://www.eassw.org/bulletins/Ankarabulletin.pdf.

Al-Krenawi, A. and Graham, A. (2000) 'Culturally sensitive social work practice with Arab clients in mental health settings', *Health and Social Work*, 25 (1): 9–22.

Al-Krenawi, A. and Graham, A. (2003) 'Principles of social work practice in the Muslim Arab world', *Arab Studies Quarterly*, 25 (4): 75–91.

Al-Makhamreh, S. (2005) *Social Work as an Emerging Profession in the Middle East: An Ethnographic Case Study of Jordanian Hospital Social Work*. Ph.D. dissertation, University of Warwick, UK.

Al-Makhamreh, S. and Lewadno-Hundt, G. (2008) 'Researching at home as an insider/outsider: Gender and culture in an ethnographic study of social work practice in an Arab society', *Qualitative Social Work*, 7 (1): 9–23.

Al-Makhamreh, S. and Lewando-Hundt, G. (2011) 'An examination of models of social work intervention for use with displaced Iraqi households in Jordan',

European Journal of Social Work. Early view available at: DOI:10.1080/13691457.2010.545770.

Al-Makhamreh, S. and Sullivan, M.P. (2010) 'Professionalising social work in Jordan: challenges and implications', *Joint World Social Work Conference*. Hong Kong, 13 June 2010.

Al-Qdah, T. and Lacroix, M. (2010) 'Iraqi refugees in Jordan: lessons for practice with refugees globally', *International Social Work*. First published 6 December doi:10.1177/0020872810383449.

Alsaid Amer, M. (2007) *Recent Studies in the Social Work Field*. Cairo: Al-Maktab Algamei Alhadeth (in Arabic).

Ashencaen Crabtree, S. (2008) 'Dilemmas in international social work education in the United Arab Emirates: Islam, localisation and social need', *Social Work Education*, 27 (5): 536–48.

Atia, M.A. (2008) *Building a House in Heaven: Islamic Charity in Neoliberal Egypt*. Ph dissertation, University of Washington, Seattle.

Auslander, B. (n.d.) *Israeli Social Workers Fight for Professional Conditions*. International Federation of Social Workers website. Accessed on 1 February 2011 at http://www.ifsw.org/p38001390.html.

Baron, B. (2005) 'Women's voluntary social welfare organizations in Egypt', in I.M. Okkenhaug and I. Flaskerud (eds), *Gender, Religion and Change in the Middle East: Two Hundred Years of History*. Oxford: Berg Publishers. pp. 85–102.

Baron, B. (2008) 'Orphans and abandoned children in modern Egypt', in N. Neguib and I.M. Okkenhaug (eds), *Between Missionaries and Dervishes: Interpreting Welfare in the Middle East*. Leiden: Brill. pp.12–34.

Benthall, J. and Bellion-Jourdan, J. (2003) *The Charitable Crescent: the Politics of Aid in the Muslim World*. London: I.B. Tauris.

Bonner, M., Ener, M., and Singer, A. (2003) *Poverty and Charity in Middle Eastern Contexts*. Albany, NY: State University of New York Press.

Bulut, I. (2003) 'A generalist approach to social work education in Turkey', *Social Work and Society*, 1 (1): 128–37.

Clark, J.A. (2004) *Islam, Charity, and Activism: Middle-class Networks and Social Welfare in Egypt, Jordan, and Yemen*. Bloomington, IN: Indiana University Press.

Cocks A., Forrester D., Sullivan M.P. and Victor, C. (2008) *Developing Social Work in Jordan: Report on a Project to Support Social Work Education in Jordan*. Amman: The British Council.

Cocks A., Al-Makhamreh S., Abuieta S., Al-Aledein J., Forrester, D. and Sullivan, M.P. (2009) 'Facilitating the development of social work in the Hashemite Kingdom of Jordan: a Jordanian/UK collaboration', *International Social Work*, 52 (6): 799–810.

Constant, S. and Kreisch, M. (2010) *Taking Stock of the Youth Challenge in the Middle East: New Data and New Questions*. Washington, DC: Brookings Institution. Accessed on 31 January 2011 at http://www.brookings.edu/articles/2010/06_middle_east_youth.aspx.

Dhillon, N., Salehi-Isfahani, D., Dyer, P., Yousef, T., Fahmy, A. and Kraetsch, M. (2009) *Missed by the Boom, Hurt by the Bust: Making Markets Work for Young People in the Middle East*. Middle East Youth Initiative. Dubai: Dubai School of Government and Wolfensohn Center for Development at Brookings.

Furman, L., Benson, P., Grimwood, C. and Canda, E. (2004) 'Religion and spirituality in social work education and direct practice at the millennium: a survey of UK social workers', *British Journal of Social Work*, 34 (6): 767–92.

Garr, M. and Marans, G. (2001) 'Ultra-orthodox women in Israel: a pilot project in social work education', *Social Work Education*, 20 (4): 459–68.

Guttmann, D. and Cohen, B.Z. (1995) 'Israel', in D. Elliott, N. Mayadas and T. Watts (eds), *International Handbook on Social Work Education*. Westport, CT: Greenwood Publishers. pp. 306–319.

Harding, S. (2007) 'Man-made disaster and development: the case of Iraq', *International Social Work*, 50 (3): 295–306.

Harmsen, E. (2008) *Islam, Civil Society, and Social Work: Muslim Voluntary Associations in Jordan between Patronage and Empowerment*. Amsterdam: Amsterdam University Press.

Hirschon, R. (ed.) (2003) *Crossing the Aegean: Compulsory Population Exchange between Greece and Turkey*. London: Berghahn Books.

Holtzhausen, L. (2010) 'When values collide: Finding common ground for social work education in the United Arab Emirates', *International Social Work*, 54 (2): 191–208.

IASSW (International Association of Schools of Social Work) (2011) http://www.iassw-aiets.org/index.php?option=com_content&task=blogcategory&id=69&Itemid=103, accessed 11 February 2011.

Ibrahim, R.W.Z. (2010) *Making the Transition from Residential Care to Adulthood: the Experience of Jordanian Care Leavers*. Ph dissertation, University of East Anglia, Norwich, UK.

Lewin, A.C., Stier, H. and Caspi-Dror, D. (2006) 'The place of opportunity: Community and individual determinants of poverty among Jews and Arabs in Israel', *Research in Social Stratification and Mobility*, 24 (2): 177–91.

Libal, K. (2001) *National Futures: The Child Question in Early Republican Turkey*. Ph dissertation, University of Washington, Seattle.

Libal, K. and Harding, S. (2011) 'Humanitarian alliances: local and international NGO partnerships and the Iraqi refugee crisis', *International Journal of Immigrant and Refugee Studies*, 9 (2): 162–78.

Mahara Professional Consultancies in Development (2008) *Identifying the Current Situation of Social Work within the Jordanian Context*. Unpublished paper delivered at the conference Exploring Reality Expanding the Vision. Amman, Jordan, 7–8 August.

Mansbach, A. and Kaufman, R (2003) 'Ethical decision-making of social workers' associations: a case study of the Israeli Association of Social Workers' responses to whistle-blowing', *International Social Work*, 46 (3): 303–12.

National Conference for Social Work in Jordan (1998) *The Historical Reality of Social Work in Jordan*. Amman, Jordan: Ministry of Social Development.

Peteet, J. (2009) *Landscape of Hope and Despair: Palestinian Refugee Camps*. Reissue version. Philadelphia, PA: University of Pennsylvania Press.

Ragab, I.A. (1995) 'Middle East and Egypt', in D. Elliott, N. Mayadas and T. Watts (eds), *International Handbook on Social Work Education*. Westport, CT: Greenwood Publishers. pp. 281–304.

Roer-Strier, D. and Haj-Yahia, M.M. (1998) 'Arab students of social work in Israel: Adjustment difficulties and coping strategies', *Social Work Education*, 17 (4): 449–67.

Roy, S. (2004) 'The Palestinian-Israeli conflict and Palestinian socioeconomic decline: A place denied', *International Journal of Politics*, 17 (3): 365–403.

Saatci, E. and Akpinar, E. (2007) 'Assessing poverty and related factors in Turkey', *Croatian Medical Journal*, 48: 628–35.

Salem, S. (2005) *The Role of Social Research in Developing the Group Method of Social Work in Egypt: An Evaluation a Study on Juveniles Delinquency Care*. Ph dissertation, Helwan University.

Salem, S. (2010) 'The historical development of social work in Republic of Egypt from 1930–2010'. Unpublished paper, Yarmouk University. Jordan.

Segal-Engelchin, D. and Kaufman, R. (2008) 'Micro- or macro-orientation? Israeli students' career interests in an antisocial era', *Journal of Social Work Education*, 44 (3): 139–57.

Singer, A. (2008) *Charity in Islamic Societies*. London: Cambridge University Press.

Shaloub-Kevorkian, N. (2011) *Militarization and Violence Against Women in the Middle East: A Palestinian Case Study*. London: Cambridge University Press.

Soliman, H.H. and Abd Elmegied, H.S. (2010) 'The challenges of modernization of social work education in developing countries: the case of Egypt', *International Social Work*, 53 (1): 101–14.

Spiro, S.E. (2001) 'Social work education in Israel: Trends and issues', *Social Work Education*, 20 (1): 89–99.

Sullivan, M.P., Forrester, D. and Al-Makhamreh, S. (2010) 'Transnational collaboration: Evaluation of a social work training workshop in Jordan', *International Social Work*, 53 (2): 217–32.

Watenpaugh, K.D. (2010) '"A pious wish devoid of all practicability": Interwar humanitarianism, the League of Nations and the rescue of trafficked women and children in the Eastern Mediterranean, 1920–1927', *American Historical Review*, 115 (4): 1315–39.

White, J.B. (2002) *Islamist Mobilization in Turkey: a Study in Vernacular Politics*. Seattle, WA: University of Washington Press.

Yazıcı, B. (2007) '*Social Work and the Politics of the Family at the Crossroads of Welfare Reform in Turkey*'. Ph dissertation, New York University.

Yazıcı, B. (2008) 'Social work and social exclusion in Turkey: An overview', *New Perspectives on Turkey* 38: 107–34.

Yıldız, K. (2005) *The Kurds in Turkey: EU Accession and Human Rights*. London: Pluto Press.

29

Social Work in Latin America

Mahia Saracostti, Taly Reininger
and Henry Parada

INTRODUCTION

Latin America can be defined as a heterogeneous region with a diversity of populations
and social problems. The continent has been
marked by common histories of colonialism,
imperialistic interventions, dictatorship, and
violations of human rights and striking levels
of inequality within and between countries.
In this chapter, we attempt to explore social
work as a discipline, education and practice
in the region. We understand the concept of
Latin America as a suitable expression that
covers social, national and regional complex
and diverse realities (Esquivel, 2000).

DESCRIPTION OF THE REGION

Main demographic features

Central America is the tapering isthmus of
southern North America, extending from the
Isthmus of Tehuantepec in southern Mexico
south-eastward to the Isthmus of Panama,
while South America is considered a continent forming the southern portion of the
American landmass. Central America has an
area of 524,000 square kilometres, or almost
0.1 percent of the earth's surface, and in
2009, its population was estimated at
41,739,000. South America has an area of
17,840,000 square kilometres, or almost 3.5
percent of the earth's surface and, in 2005,
its population was estimated at more than
371,090,000. The sustainability of the
regional ecosystems is currently threatened
by inefficient management and indiscriminate exploitation of natural resources, contamination and poor air quality, ineffective
management of waste and climate change.

The countries of Latin America have
undergone profound demographic changes,
such as the decrease in population growth
(1.3 percent in the period from 2005 to 2010)
and population ageing. The region's leading
countries in terms of ageing include Cuba
and Uruguay. This change results from a
rapid fall in fertility, preceded by a sustained
reduction in mortality, which began towards
the end of the first half of the 20th century
and has now resulted in a life expectancy at
birth of 73.4 years (CEPAL, 2007).

Indigenous peoples make up the majority
of the population in Bolivia and Peru;
two-fifths in Ecuador, and the Mayan population has a strong presence in Guatemala.

The demographics of Venezuela and Colombia include approximately 25 percent white European descendants. People of white European descent constitute the majority in Argentina and Uruguay. African descendants are significantly present in Guyana, Brazil, Colombia Venezuela, Suriname, French Guiana, and Ecuador. Mestizos (mixed white and Amerindian) are the largest ethnic groups in Paraguay, Venezuela, Colombia, Ecuador and Central American countries. East Indians form the largest ethnic minority groups in Guyana and Suriname. Brazil and Peru have the largest Japanese and Chinese communities in South America (Lizcano, 2005).

Spanish and Portuguese are the dominant languages in South and Central America, along with indigenous languages in some countries. The Roman Catholic Church maintained its dominant role in Central and South American society, but its hegemony has been slowly eroded by the growth and development of Pentecostal religious organisations (Fraser, 2005).

Political systems and governance issues

The continent became a battlefield of the Cold War during the second half of the 20th century. The democratically elected governments of Argentina, Brazil, Chile, Uruguay, Paraguay, El Salvador, Guatemala and Honduras were overthrown or displaced by military dictatorships in the 1960s and 1970s. During the last two decades, the majority of Latin American and Caribbean countries have completed their transition to liberal electoral democracy. Several Latin American democracies are neoliberal economic models for the region (e.g. Chile, Costa Rica, Uruguay), while others, severely deficient across a wide range of measures, are also called 'democracias de fachada' (fake democracies).

The widespread adoption of 'electoral' democracy as a political regime has so far not been accompanied by greater capacities of political organisations and civil society to effectively channel and resolve social demands, particularly from excluded groups (Villarreal, 2007; UNDP, 2004). Although most populations in the region believe that democracy is the best political system, frustration with democracy has been exacerbated by the inability to resolve social concerns and create employment particularly when democracy was associated with neoliberal ideology (Latino Barómetro, 2006). Participative democracy has been considered one of the top challenges faced by the region and this is exemplified in phrases such as: 'Little real enforcement of rules and accountability for politicians', 'Weak democratic culture', 'Crisis of representation', 'Political intimidation and violence', 'Traditional parties losing traditional constituencies', and 'No real separation of powers' (Jones, 2007: 5).

Today, the countries of Latin America face numerous challenges to the quality of their democracies (Berkman and Cavallo, 2006). The first challenge relates to the weak level of institutionalisation of the political parties and party systems in the region (see above and Jones, 2007). The second challenge relates to the under-representation of women and other social groups such as ethnic and racial minorities, youth, and the poor in the region's national legislatures (Van Cott, 2007).

Better democratic governance depends on its ability to deliver improvements in the quality of life of citizens, as well as on poverty reduction and sustainable and equitable growth. These latter dimensions will be developed in the following section.

Predominant economic and social factors

The region is facing a paradoxical situation at the beginning of the 21st century. On the one hand, it enjoys an extraordinary wealth of human and natural resources and has been benefiting, for the past few years, from a positive economic upturn (UNDP, 2007). On the other hand, the region continues to have high income inequalities compared to other regions. While a majority of countries are middle income and rated as having mostly high or medium levels of human development, a large proportion of the population in Latin America lives in poverty or extreme poverty, a minority have huge wealth and the proportion of people in the 'middle class/ middle income' group is relatively small.

The global economic crisis of 2008 also impacted on the region and put the brakes on five consecutive years of economic growth. Regional growth, which averaged 5.3 percent between 2003 and 2008, plummeted into negative territory at the onset of the crisis, with Caribbean economies and Mexico faring worse than their South American counterparts. On average, the growth rate fell 6 percentage points in 2007–2009 but countries such as Argentina, Costa Rica and Mexico experienced a contraction of 10 percentage points of real gross domestic product (World Bank, 2010).

Consistently, the decline in the poverty rate from 2007 to 2008 – 1.1 percentage points – is notably smaller than the two-point average annual decrease from 2002 to 2007. Moreover, the indigence rate rose 0.3 percentage points from 2007 to 2008 after having decreased an average of 1.4 points per year since 2002 (CEPAL/OIT, 2009). In Brazil, Peru and Uruguay the poverty rate fell in urban areas by at least 3 percentage points; in Colombia it came down by 4 percentage points; in Costa Rica and Paraguay it declined by more than 2 points; and in Venezuela and Panama it dropped by about 1 point. In the Dominican Republic and Ecuador, the rate did not vary significantly. In Mexico the situation worsened, as the poverty rate rose 3.1 percentage points between 2006 and 2008 (CEPAL, 2010).

There was an overall increase in poverty, with only Brazil, Paraguay and Peru managing to reduce their figures, by around 1 percentage point. This is in contrast with the increases recorded by Venezuela, the Dominican Republic, Ecuador, Mexico and Panama, of between 1.4 and 2.5 percentage points, and by Costa Rica and Uruguay, which

had very slight increases. In Colombia, indigence rose by 2.7 percentage points between 2005 and 2008, which corresponds to 0.9 of a percentage point per year (CEPAL, 2010).

According to the United Nations Development Program (UNDP, 2005) approach, a human poverty index (HPI)[1] attempts to bring together the different features of deprivation in the quality of life. At the top of the ranking were Uruguay, Chile and Costa Rica due to the fact that they had reduced human poverty to the point at which it affected less than 10 percent of their populations. The worst Latin American countries during 2004 in the HPI index were Guatemala, Honduras, Nicaragua and Haiti.

In general, during 2008, 33 percent of the region's inhabitants were poor, including 12.9 percent who were indigent, equivalent to 180 million poor and 71 million indigent persons (CEPAL, 2010). One aspect of concern relating to poverty in Latin America is the persistence of vulnerability gaps tied to demographic characteristics, particularly age, gender and ethnicity. Poverty among children under the age of 15 is, on average, 1.7 times higher than poverty among adults (CEPAL, 2010; CEPAL/UNICEF, 2009). The poverty rate of women is 1.15 times higher than that of men, and the widest gender gaps are found in Argentina, Venezuela, Chile, Costa Rica, the Dominican Republic, Panama and Uruguay. The poverty rate is 1.2–3.4 times higher for indigenous people and those of African descent than for the rest of the population, and that gap has grown in all countries studied, except for Brazil (CEPAL, 2010).

The Gini index, which measures inequality, decreased by an average of 5 percent during the period analysed. A number of countries posted significant declines – at least 8 percent in Argentina, Venezuela, Nicaragua, Peru, Panama, Paraguay and Bolivia, while Colombia, the Dominican Republic and Guatemala increased their income concentration during this period (World Bank, 2010).

Despite progress, income concentration levels in Latin America are among the highest in the world. The inequality in the region is reinforced by the large presence of the informal sector and is reflected in wage income (CEPAL/OIT, 2009), education, health and in access to land and credit (UNDP, 2007). In the case of education, for instance, the low quality of public education, together with the cost of going to school, results in high failure and dropout rates in secondary education. Peru, for example, has undergone a massive expansion of its educational system with little benefit for social mobility (Benavides, 2004; Escobar et al., 1998). Wage inequality has increased in the majority of countries in the region, decreasing only in Brazil and Colombia, and remaining unchanged in Argentina, Chile and Guatemala (Azevedo and Bouillon, 2009).

Neoliberalism, social welfare provisions and marginalisation

During the eighties and the nineties, Latin America went through a process of neoliberalisation – structural adjustment that brought retrenchment of the underdeveloped social welfare systems. Central America went through a series of civil wars that brought forced migrations from Honduras, Nicaragua, Guatemala and El Salvador to northern countries such as the USA, Canada, Mexico and Europe (Garcia, 2006; Torres-Rivas, 2009). Liberalisation of the underdeveloped informal welfare system made the people in Central America face their economic and social situation without any support from weak governments and rely more on the remittances from family members living outside the region (Martinez Franzone, 2008).

Governments in South America, particularly those with more developed welfare systems (Argentina, Chile and Brazil) have increasingly recognised the need to provide protection for marginalised populations in the face of the economic fluctuations of the market economies. During the past three decades, Latin America became a laboratory for economic and social policy experiments

aimed at reducing poverty. Some countries have taken an economic approach, aiming to increase income and consumption capacity among the poor, while others have focused on social abilities, understood as the ability to take part in community and social activities and to feel a sense of belonging in large groups (Sen, 1997). Some Latin American countries have developed poverty programmes with additional investment components for human capital through education and health (Attanasio et al., 2005, 2006).

A recent example is the 'Oportunidades' programme in Mexico, which combines cash transfers with support for keeping children in school and investing in health and nutrition. Another example would be the 'Chile Solidario System' (MIDEPLAN, 2003; Saracostti, 2008). Finally, in recent years poverty has been linked also to vulnerability (Mosser, 1999). A number of public system alternatives dealing with poverty have been introduced in Latin America. According to Hicks and Wodon (2001), the main alternatives to dealing with poverty in Latin America have been emergency employment programmes including, especially, public works; systems of direct cash grants which may be conditioned on favourable behaviour; nutrition and food interventions, particularly those targeted at vulnerable groups such as children and pregnant women; and other instruments, such as pensions and unemployment insurance.

Central American countries have developed a different welfare system from South American countries. Martinez Franzone (2008) argues that these countries have developed high levels of informal economy with very low incomes, and the few welfare programmes are closely dependent on international cooperation, making them highly unreliable. The participation of communities in the development of their own wellbeing have become extremely important. Domestic work and a high reliance on the informal work of women have become the norm. A high level of migration has also become a source of national economic resources as well as family support. One-fifth of the El Salvador and one-tenth of the Honduran populations live outside those countries (Martinez Franzone, 2008). Welfare policies are a residual format of support in which states do not respond to the social pressures but to the definitions of social needs as defined by international cooperation.

HISTORY OF SOCIAL WORK IN THE REGION

Social work has a long and turbulent history in Latin America that can be divided into four principal phases shaped by the socio-political climate of the region. The four phases can be classified as (1) consolidation of the profession; (2) the Reconceptualisation movement; (3) the role of dictatorships; and (4) the return of democracy.

The first school of social work to open its doors in Latin America was the Dr Alejandro del Rio School of Social Work in Chile in 1925 (Di Carlo, 1992). The school was strongly influenced by and linked to medicine. Argentina holds a similar history with its first school offering degrees in social work in 1930, also strongly influenced by the medical profession and regarded as an auxiliary profession whose role was to aid by 'educating' people mainly in health matters (Queiro-Tajalli, 1997a). Social work education during these formative years had strong European influences, with social work school directors and leaders educated in European countries such as Belgium and France (Cornely and Bruno, 1997). As the profession formed its roots in Latin American society, it also found a home within the legal sphere in Argentina, establishing itself in law and social science faculties and becoming known as a paralegal, paramedical profession throughout the region (Melano, 2007).

In comparison, in Brazil, the Catholic Church played a central role in the first years of the profession. Brazil's first school of social work was founded in 1936 in the Pontificia Universidad Catolica de Sao Paulo

and provided the profession in its early years with a conservative, moralist and individualistic perspective (Siqueria da Silva and Rodrigues, no date; Wanderley and Yazbek, 2007). Colombia also presents a similar history of Catholic Church influence in social work education which led to a conservative form of social work practice within the country (Torres, 2007).

As social work took hold and consolidated during the 1940s and 1950s, foreign US influence played a key role in its development. This period is also known as the 'traditional' social work era with emphasis on case, group and community levels of practice under a strong structural functionalist perspective (Araneda Alfero, 2007; Faleiros, 2007; Queiro-Tajalli, 1997a). Social work education in Latin America was strongly influenced by Mary Richmond's classical text 'Social Diagnosis', thus creating the image that social work practice in the United States had a primary positivistic focus on individual deficiencies rather than on macro-level change (Torres, 2007). Parra (2005) defines this phase of social work in Latin America as conservative due to its lack of discussion on ethical and political issues and the neutrality of social workers. It was the critique to this traditional perspective, the political changes and activism of the mid-1960s that sparked a heterogeneous movement within the social sciences known as Reconceptualisation which also influenced social work. This movement also influenced student organisations, unions and rural agricultural worker associations, creating a widespread and extremely diverse movement seeking structural and political changes in the region (Hernandez and Ruz, 2007a).

The Reconceptualisation movement initially began in Latin America's southern cone[2] and rapidly spread throughout the region, sparking intense debates on the role of social work, its ethical and political dimensions, and the need to create a Latin American social work capable of responding to the specific problems and needs of the region. This movement took a stance which assumed that revolutionary change was necessary in the profession as well as in the region (Parra 2005). The movement critiqued capitalist society and the possibility of change coming from government agencies that aimed for change on an individual rather than societal level (Quiero-Tajalli, 1997b). Alayon and Molina (2006) identify four primary formative methods of this period: (1) the Belo Horizonte method; (2) Paolo Freire's alphabetisation; (3) Orlando Fals Barda's Participatory-Action Research method; and (4) popular education.[3] The Reconceptualisation movement sought to empower communities, seeking change from below, and was strongly influenced by the Marxist perspective.

It was during this time that social work schools within the region came together and in 1965 created the Latin American Association of Social Service Schools, ALAESS. The first Latin American Congress of Social Service took place during November, 1965 in Lima, Peru and included representatives from 25 social work schools from Argentina, Bolivia, Brazil, Colombia, Costa Rica, Chile, Ecuador, Guatemala, Honduras, Panama, Paraguay, Peru and Venezuela. Social work schools felt motivated and compelled to initiate profound changes in social work education, veering away from what was considered a charity profession to one with a more critical focus. In 1975 ALAESS, together with economic support from the Konrad Adenaur foundation, formed CELATS (Latin American Social Work Education Centre), the first such Latin American Centre, located in Lima, Peru. CELATS' mission was to advance research in social work, offer continuous education and specialisation courses, as well as to promote and publish social work research in Latin America (Araneda Alfero, 2009; Parada, 2007).

The 1970s Reconceptualisation movement faded due to the proliferation of dictatorships in the region: Argentina 1966–1973 and 1976–1983; Bolivia 1969–1979; Brazil 1964–1985; Chile 1973–1990; Ecuador 1972–1979; Guatemala 1970–1986; Honduras 1972–1982; Nicaragua 1967–1979; Panama

1968–1989; Peru 1968–1980; Uruguay 1981–1985. Social work schools were closed during these years and social workers throughout the region suffered persecution and witnessed the reduction of their influence (Melano, 2007; Hernandez and Ruz, 2007b). In Chile, social work was stripped of its university status, which had a profound effect on the profession up to this day.

The end of dictatorships in the region led social work to actively participate in the reconstruction of democracy through the promotion of democratic processes and participation in the formulation of social policies through organisation and education group and community levels (Ramirez, 2004). Social workers played a key role in defending human rights and denouncing violations during military regimes, working with victims, their families, and communities at large. In Argentina, the return to democracy led to the reopening of social work schools that had been closed by the military regimes and in Chile, after many years of struggle, social work regained its university status (Melano, 2007; Hernandez and Ruz, 2007b).

CONTEMPORARY SOCIAL WORK

Social work education – brief comparative analysis

Today social work education in Latin America remains heterogeneous, presenting an interesting evolution from the founding of the first school of social work in Chile in 1925. Social work education throughout the region is offered in public and private universities as well as professional institutions, as in Argentina and Chile. The majority of countries in Latin America offer 4–5-year degrees (Acotto, 2008).

Most schools of social work in the region belong to social sciences and law faculties with a few exceptions such as the Social Work Faculty at the Universidad Nacional de Entre Rios in Argentina and the Social Work

School of the Universidad Nacional de Asuncion in Paraguay, belonging to the Philosophy Faculty. Most schools in the region offer a multidisciplinary focus in their course structures, with courses such as introduction to psychology, sociology, anthropology, social policy and economics. Another common feature is the focus on field practice with some schools beginning internship placements in the fourth semester (e.g. the Universidad Andres Bello in Chile) or fifth semester (as at the National Autonomous University of Santo Domingo in the Dominican Republic). Research courses as well as courses on ethics are other common characteristics.

Social work schools in the region have begun to differentiate amongst themselves with some embracing a more 'traditional' social work with a clear distinction between case, group and community level of interventions. Other schools embrace a more critical focus and attempt to integrate intervention practices and social work theoretical approaches. According to Lorena Molina, president of the Latin-American Association for Teaching and Investigation in Social Work (ALAEITS), it is common to find these different focuses within countries but also coexisting within schools (personal communication[4]). Brazil is known in the region for approach academic formation (Faleiros, 2007) and it is interesting non-Brazilian to note that two social work schools which have embraced the same perspective offer electives in Portuguese, perhaps due to the large social work bibliography in Portuguese or to prepare their students for postgraduate education in Brazil (Universidad de Costa Rica and Universidad Nacional de Entre Rios, Argentina).

Apart from Portuguese, few schools offer language courses and even fewer offer courses on the indigenous languages and cultures. One that does is Universidad Nacional de Asuncion in Paraguay which offers two courses on Guarani language and culture; another is Universidad Nacional Mayor de San Marcos in Peru which offers two courses on Quechua. Perhaps this is a challenge social work faces in the future – embracing and including cultural diversity in its course structures.

A more clinical focus in social work education is rare to find in the region although it is now becoming more common to find one or two courses on family, family therapy, social work and mental health in undergraduate education. In Peru, for example, the school of social work at Universidad Nacional Federico Villarreal has clearly embraced a more clinical stance offering four courses on systemic family therapy (http://www.unfv.edu.pe/facultades/fccss/escuelas/trabajo-social#).

Postgraduate education in social work is widespread in the region, with many countries having masters-level programmes (Argentina, Brazil, Chile, Costa Rica, Honduras, Guatemala, Mexico, Paraguay, and Uruguay to name a few). Regarding doctoral degrees, Brazil is in the forefront in Latin America, having created the first programme in the region in 1981 (Queiro-Tajalli, 1997a). This has had a profound effect on social work in the region for two primary reasons. Firstly, having a doctoral programme the since the 1980s has allowed Brazilian social work to develop as a respected and consolidated discipline within the social sciences, producing and specialising in social work research. Secondly, for many years Brazil was the only country in Latin America offering doctoral programmes in the region; social work professionals from other Latin American countries received their doctorates from Brazilian universities, thereby spreading Brazilian social work and influence within the region (Wanderley and Yazbek, 2007).

Social work doctorate programmes are still scarce and relatively new in 2010 with three programmes in Argentina (Universidad Nacional de la Plata, Universidad Nacional de Rosario and Universidad Nacional de Entre Rios), and programmes in Uruguay (Universidad de la Republica de Uruguay), Mexico (Universidad Autónoma de Nuevo

León in collaboration with the University of Texas Arlington), Honduras (Universidad Nacional Autónoma de Honduras which offers a doctorate in social science), and Puerto Rico. The lack of options to receive doctorates in social work to Latin America and the existing language barriers has led many social work professionals to seek doctorates in other disciplines, primarily in sociology, education, philosophy and psychology. This has played another influential role in social work education in the region since the majority of those in academic education (with the exception of Brazil) are specialised in other disciplines (Matus and Ponce de Leon, no date).

Theoretical debates and repercussions in research

Social work as a discipline enjoys little recognition in Latin America, with the exception of few countries. One important historical academic debate that has marked the development of social work as a discipline in the region has been the debate on whether social work qualifies as an academic discipline or not. On the one side Ander-Egg (1996) argues that social work lacks a proper theoretical body and borrows its theoretical foundations from other social sciences and therefore cannot be labelled a science or scientific practice. He bases his argument on the idea that social work is practical in its core and not capable of producing knowledge.

On the other side of the debate, defenders of social work as an academic discipline argue that social work is capable of producing knowledge as well as systemising and critically analysing practice (Kisnerman, 1998: 154–5, cited in Moran, 2006). According to Netto (2008), in order for social work to overcome its 'ugly duckling' status (a product of it being labelled social technology) in the social sciences, it is necessary to solidify academic theoretical and research, thus producing professionals

qualified in planning, executing, and evaluating social policies as well as producing knowledge at the doctoral level.

This disciplinary debate has had profound effects on the development of social work in the region not only within the profession but also in its dialogue with other disciplines. Lopez et al. (2007) recognise that in Mexico, social work enjoys little social recognition, which has affected its capacity to produce research. This lack of social recognition throughout the region, with the exception of a few countries (Brazil, Venezuela, Colombia, Argentina and Uruguay) has had profound repercussions on the possibilities for social workers to apply for government grants and funding in research. A concrete example is found in Chile with social work being considered a sub-discipline of sociology in the government's National Commission on Science and Technology, CONICYT (personal communication with Teresa Matus[5]).

Dominant features of social work

It is important to note that social work in Latin America differs widely regarding its development and spheres of action, influenced by the socio-political and historical context of each country (personal communication Lorena Molina). It is, however, possible to recognise several common features within the region.

One such feature is the role of social work in implementing social policies (Faleiros, 2007; Guerra, 2005; interview with Carlos Montaño in *Revista Electrónica Sintesis*, 2008; Quiero-Tajalli, 1997b). This embryonic relationship between social work and social policy (interview with Carlos Montaño in *Revista Electrónica Sintesis*, 2008) has led many in the academic world to embrace a critical perspective wary of the neoliberal economic social policies being implemented in Latin America, particularly the changes from universal social policies to targeted social policies, decentralisation and privatisation of social services (Rivera, 1998, cited in Chinchilla, 2008). Today, the discussion in academic circles is whether or not social work has an ethical and political responsibility in working towards challenging neoliberal policies responsible for the rampant inequalities and exclusion found within the region, arguing they violate human rights (Lizana, 2007; Alayon and Molina, 2006).

Issues of poverty, inequality, marginalisation and social exclusion are high priorities for social work in Latin America since the inequality gap continues to grow within and between countries in the region (Netto, 2008). Melano (2007) identifies a 'new poverty' in the region, due to a decrease of the middle classes. Social workers in the region are primarily found implementing targeted poverty programmes, but a social work presence is seen in the design and evaluation of social programmes (Melano, 2007; Saracostti, 2008, 2010).

Social workers in Latin America can be found working in public, private and not-for-profit sectors. Traditionally, the public sector has been the main employer of social workers in the region (Melano, 2007; Wanderley and Yazbek, 2007). In Bolivia, for example, the state continues to be the major employer of social workers in health and infant care programmes but with decentralisation to municipalities, social workers face a challenge as today only 10 percent of municipalities in Bolivia employ social workers (Castro Ortega, 2007).

While employment in the public sector continues to diminish, social workers are employed in increasing numbers by NGOs. This has had some positive effects on the profession in the region, leading to development of new social interventions, BUT it has also provoked instability since most professionals are hired on a project basis (Caballero, 2007).

In the region, there are examples of social work in the private sector, specifically in employee assistance programmes, as well as in human resources departments in countries such as Brazil, Chile and Peru. Social workers administer benefits and work directly with employees (Lopez et al., 2007; Queiro Tajalli, 1997a). In Argentina and Chile, social workers are active in mediation (Hernandez and Ruz, 2007b; Melano, 2007; Queiro Tajalli, 1997a). They are also active in risk management specifically related to natural disasters since Latin America is frequently affected by earthquakes, hurricanes, landslides and floods (personal communication with Lorena Molina).

New programmes have been developed which have allowed social work to be recognised socially and accepted as a professional discipline with a particular approach and method of knowledge creation, as is the case for social work programme at the Autonomous University of Santo Domingo, created in 2007.

CHALLENGES

The challenges found in contemporary social work in Latin America are numerous. Social workers in the region today are faced with poor labour conditions in a low-status profession; separation between theory and practice; neoliberal policies; and complex social problems that require alternative interventions.

One such challenge is found in the precarious labour conditions of professionals in the region. It is common to find professionals working on short-term contracts, receiving low wages and lacking benefits (Melano, 2007). Labour flexibilisation is another challenge facing social workers in the region. This is partly due to the saturation of the labour market caused by the proliferation of social work schools in the region, graduating more social workers than the labour market can absorb and compounded by precarious employment conditions, low wages and non-professionals entering into traditional social work positions (Benito and Chinchilla, 2005; Vidal, 2009). According to Benito and Chinchilla (2005), the flexibilisation of labour in social work will have profound consequences in the profession, leading to its deprofessionalisation, lack of credibility in society, and the debilitation of professional bodies.

Ander-Egg (1996) argues that social work faces challenges in Latin America due to the influx of other professions, such as community psychology, social pedagogy, and socio-cultural animation, to name a few, into what have traditionally been social work roles. A challenge for contemporary social work is to differentiate itself from other similar professions and solidify its role, finding its specificity in its intentions and actions, revaluing and socially legitimising a profession that has been undervalued in the region (Diaz Argueta, 2006). Strengthening professional bodies in order to advocate for the profession and improve its social status is another challenge faced by social work in the region.

Theoretical and academic social work in Latin America also faces challenges. There is still a strong Eurocentric epistemological influence within several curricula across the continent. Despite the recognition of the indigenous populations, their worldviews are still invisible in many countries. The process of indigenisation and knowledge development needs to continue growing. Strong emphasis on one social category (class) has silenced other elements important to understanding the intersectionality of oppression. Disabilities, sexual orientation, and race, among other social categories, are still underrepresented in curricula. Universities in general have made attempts to introduce liberal notions of multiculturalism but without introducing indigenous worldviews to their curricula (Ba Tiul, 2007).

Research as an academic practice has been limited in many programmes within Latin America; some academics teach many hours and have full-time jobs outside the university that do not allow them to engage productively in knowledge creation and community participation. There are fewer full-time professors who have the privilege of time and job security to engage in research, and there is a huge majority who mostly teach, creating a disjunction between research, dissemination,

teaching and community engagement. Many school curricula limit themselves to the reproduction of knowledge.

This phenomenon is particularly visible in countries where neoliberal influence in higher education brought cuts to funding for public universities, which reach a more extensive student population. The development of private universities, with or without subsidies from governments, narrows the number of students and the class diversity of those students accessing higher education. This situation has created two-tier higher education programmes within these countries. Most private universities spend most of their efforts in teaching and their production of research is low. Labour conditions are precarious for most professors who are forced to have full-time jobs outside the university in order to support themselves (Torres and Schugurensky, 2002; Arocena and Sutz, 2005). There are also examples of highly developed private universities which have a high level of knowledge production but are considered to be a form of university entrepreneurship (Bernasconi, 2005).

Social work in Latin America also faces a challenge in unifying academic spheres to social work practice (personal communication with Cecilia Aguayo[6]). The large separation between the theoretical/analytical and the technical/practical side of social work in Latin America has been a major debate that has not yet been resolved and requires providing more instances for dialogue and interaction between those who 'theorise' and those who 'intervene' (Siqueira da Silva and Rodrigues, no date). This also raises the need for more research in and from social work and how research can be used in practice (Matus, 2002).

CONCLUSIONS

In conclusion, social work in Latin America has had a rich and diverse history since the opening of the first school of social work in

1925. The constant transformation of the profession in the region must reflect the changing
realities the continent faces. There are many
challenges to face as a (an article 'a' is needed
between as a discipline) discipline, but at the
same time there are opportunities to engage
and build alliances with social movements that
are inclusive of those populations that have
been marginalised and continue to be marginalised. Social work in Latin America needs to
continue working with minority populations,
specifically afro-descendent, LGBT (lesbian,
gay, bisexual and transgender), women and
people with disabilities, and with other social
movements that require our support. Social
work also needs to continue working to solidify its status, role, and impact in the region.

NOTES

1   The HPI index concentrates on deprivation
in three elements of human life: longevity (the
vulnerability to death at a relatively early age), knowledge (percentage of adults who are illiterate),
and decent living standard (percentage of people
with access to health services, safe water, and
percentage of malnourished children under the age
of 5).

2   The geographic region known as the Southern
Cone of Latin America generally refers to Argentina,
Chile, Paraguay and Uruguay. With regard to the
Reconceptualisation movement, Araneda Alfero
(2009) includes Brazil in what he defines as the
Southern Cone of Latin America.

3   The four formative methods mentioned by
Alayon and Molina (2006) are community development approaches that originated in Brazil and spread
throughout the region during the Reconceptualisation
movement.

4   The authors would like to thank Lorena Molina,
president of the Latin-American Association for
Teaching and Investigation in Social Work (ALAEITS)
and professor at the Universidad de Costa Rica for
her collaboration on this chapter.

5   The authors would like to thank Teresa Matus,
professor of the School of Social Work at the
Pontificia Universidad Católica de Chile for her collaboration on this chapter.

6   The authors would like to thank Cecilia
Aguayo, Director of the School of Social Work at
Universidad Andrés Bello for her collaboration on this
chapter.

REFERENCES

Acotto, L. (2008) *Reporte Acción Julio 2006 a Julio 2008
Región Latinoamérica y Caribe.* Federación
Internacional de Trabajo Social. Available online at:
http://www.ifsw.org/cm_data/9.6_Latin_America_
and_Caribbean_Report.doc (accessed 20 June 2010).

Alayon, N. and Molina, M.L. (2006) 'La desigualdad
social: desarrollo y desafíos del Trabajo Social desde
la Reconceptualización en América Latina',
Perspectivas 17: 43–65.

Ander-Egg, E. (1996) *Introducción al Trabajo Social.*
Latinoamericano: a 40 anos de la Reconceptualización.

Araneda Alfero, L.D. (2007) 'La Reconceptualización
del Trabajo Social Latinoamericano. Su Analisis y
Prospectiva', in N. Alayon (ed.), *Trabajo Social
Latinoamericano: a 40 anos de la Reconceptualización.*
Buenos Aires: Espacio. pp. 149–62.

Araneda Alfero, L.D. (2009) *Las Escuelas de Trabajo
Social del Continente. Su Organización Apostillas
para su Historia. 1965–2009.* XIX Seminario
Latinoamericano de las Escuelas de Trabajo Social
Asamblea General Alaeits. Universidad Católica de
Santiago de Guayaquil.

Arocena, R. and Sutz, J. (2005) 'Latin America universities: from an original revolution to an uncertain
transition', *Higher Education*, 50: 573–92.

Attanasio, O., Gómez, L., Heredia, P. and
Vera-Hernandez, M. (2005) *The Short-term Impact
of a Conditional Cash Subsidy on Child Health and
Nutrition in Colombia.* Report Summary. London:
Institute of Fiscal Studies.

Attanasio, O., Fitzsimons, E., Gomez, A., Lopez, D.,
Meghir, C. and Mesnard, A. (2006) *Child Education
and Work Choices in the Presence of a Conditional
Cash Transfer Programme in Rural Colombia.* IFS
Working Paper, W06/01. London: Institute of Fiscal
Studies

Azevedo, V. and Bouillon, C. (2009) *Social Mobility in
Latin America: a Review of Existing Evidence.* Inter-
American Development Bank.

Ba Tuil, K. (2007) 'Los Pueblos Indígenas: Derechos a
la Educación y la Cultura', in M. Berraondo (ed.),
Pueblos Indígenas y Derechos Humanos.
Publicaciones de la Universidad de Deusto, Serie
Derechos Humanos, vol. 14.

Benavides (2004) 'Educación y Estructura Social en el
Perú: Un Estudio acerca del Acceso a la Educación
Superior y la Movilidad intergeneracional en una
Muestra de Trabajadores Urbanos', in *¿Es Posible
Mejorar la Educación peruana?: Evidencias y
Posibilidades.* Lima, Peru: Grupo de Análisis para el
Desarrollo (GRADE).

Benito, L. and Chinchilla, M. (2005) 'Flexibilización laboral y desprofesionalización del Trabajo Social', in A. Ruiz (ed.), *Búsquedas del trabajo social latinoamericano: urgencias propuestas y posibilidades*. Buenos Aires: Espacio Editorial. pp. 69–80.

Berkman, H. and Cavallo, E. (2006) *The Challenges in Latin America: Identifying what Latin Americans Believe to be the Main Problems Facing their Countries*. Washington, D.C.: Interamerican Development Bank. Unpublished Manuscript.

Bernasconi, A. (2005) 'University entrepreneurship in a developing country: the case of the P. University Católica de Chile, 1985–2000', *Higher Education*, 50: 247–74.

Caballero, E. (2007) 'Reconceptualizacion y Trabajo Social en Honduras', in N. Alayon (ed.), *Trabajo Social Latinoamericano: a 40 años de la Reconceptualizacion*. Buenos Aires: Espacio Editorial. pp. 211–22.

Castro Ortega, N. (2007) 'A 40 años de la Reconceptualizacion del Trabajo Social en Latinoamérica. Una aproximación sobre el caso boliviano', in N. Alayon (ed.) *Trabajo Social Latinoamericano: a 40 años de la Reconceptualizacion*. Buenos Aires: Espacio Editorial. pp. 41–55.

CEPAL (Economic Commission for Latin America and the Caribbean) (2007) *Demographic Trends in Latin América*, Observatorio Demográfico N°3.

CEPAL (Economic Commission for Latin America and the Caribbean) (2010) *Social Panorama in Latin Latinoamericano: a 40 años de la Reconceptualizacion*.

CEPAL/OIT (Economic Commission for Latin America and the Caribbean/International Labour Organisation) (2009) 'Crisis en los mercados laborales y respuestas contracíclicas', *Boletín CEPAL/OIT coyuntura laboral en América Latina y el Caribe*, N° 2, Santiago de Chile, Septiembre.

CEPAL/UNICEF (Economic Commission for Latin America and the Caribbean/United Nations Children's Fund) (2009) *Pobreza infantil, desigualdad y ciudadanía*. Informe final. Iniciativa. CEPAL/UNICEF en Latinoamericano: a 40 años de la Reconceptualizacion.

Chinchilla, M. (2008) *Globalización y Trabajo Social ¿Nuevos Compromisos o Viejos Retos*. Revista Electrónica Síntesis. Available online at: http://www.revistasintesis.cl/sintesis1chinchilla.pdf (accessed 23 July 2010).

Cornely, S. and Bruno, D. (1997) 'Brazil', in N. Mayadas, T.D. Watts and D. Elliot (eds) *International Handbook on Social Work Theory and Practice*. Westport, CT: Greenwood Publishing. pp. 93–110.

Diaz Argueta, J.C. (2006) 'Naturaleza y Especificidad del Trabajo Social: un desafío pendiente de resolver. Reflexiones para el debate', *Revista Katálisis*, 9 (2): 217–26. Available online at http://www.scielo.br/scielo.php?pid=S1414-49802006000200009&script=sci_arttext (accessed 19 July 2010).

Di Carlo, E. (1992) 'El Trabajo Social Latinoamericano. Hacia un Modelo de Acción Social Transformadora', in C. de Robertis, *Metodología de la Intervención en Trabajo Social*. Barcelona: Editorial El Ateneo. pp. 28–35.

Escobar, J., Saavedra, J. and Torero, M. (1998) *Los Activos de los Pobres en el Perú*. Documento de Trabajo 26. Lima, Peru: Grupo de Análisis para el Desarrollo (GRADE).

Esquivel, G. (2000) *Neoliberalismo y su Impacto en el Trabajo Social*. Available online at: http://www.ts.ucr.ac.cr/perspectiva.htm (accessed 15 December 2010).

Faleiros, V. (2007) 'Reconceptualizacion del Trabajo Social en Brasil: una cuestión en movimiento?', in N. Alayon, *Trabajo Social Latinoamericano: a 40 años de la Reconceptualizacion*. Buenos Aires: Espacio Editorial. pp. 57–70.

Fraser, B.J. (2005) 'In Latin America, Catholics down, church's credibility up, poll says', *Catholic News Service*. 23 June.

Garcia, M. (2006) *Seeking Refuge, Central American Migration to Mexico, the United States and Canada*. London: University of California Press.

Guerra, Y. (2005) 'Instrumentalizad del proceso de trabajo y Servicio Social', in A. Ruiz (ed.), *Búsquedas del trabajo social latinoamericano: urgencias propuestas y posibilidades*. Buenos Aires: Espacio Editorial. pp. 19–37.

Hernandez, J. and Ruz, O. (2007a) 'La Reconceptualizacionen Chile', in N. Alayon, *Trabajo Social Latinoamericano: a 40 años de la Reconceptualizacion*. Buenos Aires: Espacio Editorial. pp. 85–113.

Hernandez, J. and Ruz, O. (2007b) 'El Trabajo Social en Chile', in J.P. Desauriers and Y. Hurtubise (eds), *Trabajo Social Internacional: Elementos de Comparación*. Buenos Aires: Lumen-Hvmanitis. pp. 115–38.

Hicks, N. and Wodon, Q. (2001) 'Social protection for the poor in Latin America', *CEPAL Review*, 73: 93–113.

Jones, M. (2007) *Democracy in Latin America, Challenges and Solutions: Political Party and Party System Institutionalization and Women's Legislative Representation*. Houston, Texas, United States of America.

Latin Barómetro (2006) *Informe Latin Barómetro*. pp.1–95.

Lizana Ibaceta, R. (2007) 'Desigualdad Social y Trabajo Social', *Revista Perspectivas*, 18: 145–158.

Lizcano, F. (2005) *Composición Étnica de las Tres Áreas Culturales del Continente Americano al Comienzo del Siglo XXI*. Universidad Autónoma del Estado de México, Centro de Investigación en Ciencias Sociales y Humanidades, 38: 185–232.

Lopez, R., Ribeiro, M. and Cabello, M. (2007) 'El Trabajo Social en México', in J.P. Desauriers and Y. Hurtubise (eds), *Trabajo Social Internacional: Elementos de Comparación*. Buenos Aires: Lumen-Hvmanitis. pp. 59–82.

Martinez Franzone, J. (2008) *Arañando Bienestar? Trabajo Remunerado, Protección Social y Familias en América Central*. Buenos Aires Argentina CLACSO Libros.

Matus, T. (2002) *Escenarios y desafíos del Trabajo Social en América Latina*. Boletín Electrónico Sura #69. Escuela de Trabajo Social: de Costa Rica. Available online at www.ts.ucr.ac.cr (accessed 16 July 2010).

Matus, T. and Ponce de Leon, M. (no date) *Trabajo Social al Sur del Mundo*. Unpublished Manuscipt, Escuela de Trabajo Social, Pontificia Universidad Católica de Chile.

Melano, M.C. (2007) 'Trabajo Social en la Argentina', in J.P. Desauriers and Y. Hurtubise (eds), *Trabajo Social Internacional: Elementos de Comparación*. Buenos Aires: Lumen-Hvmanitis. pp. 31–57.

MIDEPLAN (2003) *Sistema Chile Solidario: Integral Social Protection to the Poorest 225.000 Households of the Country*. Gobierno de Chile, Chile.

Moran, J.M. (2006) *Epistemología, Ciencia y Paradigma en Trabajo Social*. Sevilla: Aconcagua Libros.

Mosser, C. (1999) 'The asset vulnerability framework: reassessing urban poverty reduction strategies', *World Development*, 6 (1): 1–19.

Netto, J.P. (2008) 'El orden social contemporáneo como desafío central', *Revista Trabajo Social*, 74: 31–46.

Parada, H. (2007) 'Regional perspectives from Latin America: social work in Latin America history, challenges and renewal', *International Social Work*, 50 (4): 560–9.

Parra, G. (2005) 'Hacia la construcción del proyecto ético político profesional critico', in A. Ruiz (ed.), *Búsquedas del trabajo social latinoamericano: urgencias propuestas y posibilidades*. Buenos Aires: Espacio Editorial. pp. 135–59.

Queiro-Tajalli, I. (1997a) 'Latin America', in N. Mayadas, T.D. Watts and D. Elliot (eds), *International Handbook on Social Work Theory and Practice*. Westport, CT: Greenwood Publishing. pp. 51–9.

Queiro-Tajalli, I. (1997b) 'Argentina', in N. Mayadas, T.D. Watts and D. Elliot (eds), *International Handbook*

on *Social Work Theory and Practice*. Westport, CT: Greenwood Publishing. pp. 76–92.

Ramirez, F. (2004) *Adios 'Señorita Asistente' Construyendo la Historia del Trabajo Social en Chile*. *Revista Electrónica Síntesis*. Available online at http://redalyc.uaemex.mx/pdf/708/70801410.pdf (accessed 20 July 2010).

Revista Electrónica Síntesis (2008) *Discusiones urgentes del Trabajo Social Critico Conversación con Carlos Montaño*. Available online at http://www.revistasintesis.cl/sintesis1montano.pdf (accessed 23 July 2010).

Saracostti, M. (2008) 'The Chile Solidario system: the role of social work', *International Social Work*, 51 (4): 566–72.

Saracostti, M. (2010) 'Constructing Chile's social protection system: from early childhood to the elderly', *International Social Work*, 53 (4): 568–74.

Sen, A. (1997) *Social Exclusion: a Critical Assessment of the Concept and its Relevance*, Asian Development Bank.

Siqueira da Silva, J. and Rodrigues, M. (no date) *Servicio Social, Trabajo y Formación Profesional: Desafíos Contemporáneos*. Available online at http://www.internacionaldelconocimiento.org/documentos/ponenciascompletasm4/JoseFernandoSiqueiraYMAngela.pdf (accessed 12 July 2010).

Torres, C. and Schugurensky, D. (2002) 'The political economy of higher education in the era of neoliberal globalization: Latin America in comparative perspective', *Higher Education*, 43: 429–55.

Torres, L. (2007) 'Reflexiones en torno al Movimiento de Reconceptualizacion', in N. Alayon, *Trabajo Social Latinoamericano: a 40 años de la Reconceptualizacion*. Buenos Aires: Espacio Editorial. pp.103–13.

Torres-Rivas, E. (2009) *CentroAmerica Entre Revoluciones y Democracia*. Buenos Aires Argentina, Libros Prometeo CLACSO coediciones.

UNDP (United Nations Development Program) (2004) *Cultural Liberty in Today's Diverse World*. Human Report, United Nations Development Program, New York USA.

UNDP (United Nations Development Program) (2005) *Human Development Report*, United Nations Development Program, New York.

UNDP (United Nations Development Program) (2007) *Draft Regional Programme Document for Latin America and the Caribbean, 2008–2011*, New York.

Van Cott, D. (2007) *From Movements to Parties: the Evolution of Ethnic Politics*. New York: Cambridge University Press.

Vidal, P. (2009) *Condiciones Labourales de la Profesion: ¿Precariedad Laboural o Condition Sine Qua Non?* Boletín Electronica Sura 153. Available online at www.ts.ucr.ac.cr (accessed 13 July 2010).

Villarreal, G. (2007) 'Guatemala's current and future globalization: social work's continuing education role', *International Social Work*, 50 (1): 41–51.

Wanderley, M. and Yazbek, M. (2007) 'El Servicio Social en Brasil: Origen, Prácticas y Desafíos', in J.P. Desauriers and Y. Hurtubise (eds), *Trabajo Social Internacional: Elementos de Comparación*. Buenos Aires: Lumen-Hvmanitis. pp.139–59.

World Bank (2010) *Latin American and the Caribbean Regional Brief*. Available online at http://web.worldbank.org/WBSITE/EXTERNAL/COUNTRIES/LACEXT/0,,contentMDK:20340156~pagePK 146736~piPK:64909335~theSitePK:258554,00.html (accessed 16 December 2010).

30

Social Work in North America and the Caribbean

Julia Watkins and Jennifer Holder Dolly

INTRODUCTION

The vastness of the North American continent and the Caribbean in close proximity are matched only by the vastness and diversity of their populations and surpassed only by the scale of their challenges and abundance and yet disparity of their resources. This diverse group of peoples, with their needs, aspirations, and interactions, works to secure a more productive and sustainable quality of life aligned with the social work tenets of social justice, equality, and empowerment. For this chapter, as defined by the editors, North America encompasses the nations of Canada and the United States. The Caribbean, in this case, refers to a region situated near the Caribbean Sea, which consists of the Greater and Lesser Antilles, Suriname, Guyana, Belize, and Trinidad and Tobago, and reference is made primarily to the English-speaking Caribbean. This chapter discusses these distinct geographic areas, and the authors – one from the United States and the other from the Caribbean – have attempted to highlight briefly the social and cultural uniqueness of each, while also drawing together the common threads of social work practice and education.

GEOGRAPHIC, DEMOGRAPHIC AND OTHER CHARACTERISTICS

Within North America and the Caribbean region, robust, enterprising, and relatively young and affluent societies also contain examples of extreme poverty and unequal access to resources. The effects of the treatment of indigenous peoples and the legacy of slavery in North America and the Caribbean endure in the present day. While there are some commonalities and interdependencies related to population mobility within and between the United States, Canada, and the Caribbean, we here describe separately the main geographic and demographic characteristics of the two largest countries and of the Caribbean sub-region, respectively.

The United States

The United States has a land mass of 9,372,610 sq km – the fourth largest country in the world. It is composed of states, including the non-contiguous states of Hawaii and Alaska; the District of Columbia; the Commonwealth of the Northern Mariana Islands; and the territories of American Samoa, Guam, Puerto Rico, US Minor Outlying Islands; and the US Virgin Islands. The geography is varied, with a spectrum of arid deserts, fertile plains, towering mountains, and wet lowlands, bounded on the east and west by the North Atlantic and Pacific Oceans. It has an abundance of resources: fossil fuels, natural gas and oil, timber, minerals, and water, as well as human and educational capacity (*The Economist*, 2009). Its 310 million people are as diverse as its geography. The white population of European heritage comprises 79.6 percent of the population while indigenous peoples now account for only 1 percent. Other groups represented in the population are people of African-American heritage (12.9 percent) Hispanic heritage (15.8 percent), and Asian and Pacific Islander heritage (4.8 percent) (United States Census Bureau, 2010).

What is more telling about the US population, however, is that, according to 2006–2008 US Census data, 13.2 percent of the population live in poverty, unevenly distributed between the different racial groups. The percentage of non-Hispanic whites below the poverty level was 9.2; African-Americans below the poverty level accounted for 24.7 percent, and Hispanics 21.2 percent (United States Census Bureau, 2008). The indicator frequently used in evaluating health status is that of infant mortality. The US infant mortality rate was 6.86 infant deaths per 1000 live births in 2005. The United States ranked 29th in the world in 2004 (the latest year that data are available for all countries), comparable with Poland and Slovakia (MacDorman, 2008). These statistics are contrasted with the fact that the United States has the world's largest economy (by gross domestic product [GDP]). The United States' largest trading partner is its neighbour to the north, Canada (*The Economist*, 2009).

Canada

Canada is an enormous land mass of 9,970,610 sq km: only Russia is larger.

Much of this area, however, is almost uninhabitable terrain in the Northern Territories and only 5 percent of the total landmass is arable. Like its neighbour to the south, Canada also enjoys an abundance of natural resources in the form of oil and natural gas, timber, minerals, and water as well as human and educational capacity. Its geography is strikingly varied, from the farms and fisheries of the Maritime Provinces of the east coast (bounded by the North Atlantic Ocean) to the vast fertile agricultural plains of the midsection and the towering mountains and fisheries of the west (bounded by the Pacific Ocean). A significant proportion of Canada's population lives in its major cities spread across the southern belt of the country, and yet it is sparsely populated by the standards of much of the developed world. In spite of being the second largest country in land mass, it ranks 36th in size of population with 32.6 million inhabitants. Canada is an officially bilingual nation (French and English). The median age of its population is 38.6 years with 17.6 percent under the age of 15 and 17.8 percent over the age of 60 years (*The Economist*, 2009).

Canada has the eighth largest economy in the world by GDP (*The Economist*, 2009). Its relative affluence is contrasted with a rate of poverty equivalent to that in the United States: 9.4 percent with low income after taxes (Statistics Canada, 2010a). Compared to the 19th century, when the majority of the population were white European descendants (predominantly British or French), the population in the 21st century reflects much greater ethnic diversity (particularly in Canadian cities), but descendants of the indigenous population (First Nations people) comprise only 2 percent of the population overall (Statistics Canada, 2010b; *Encyclopedia of the Nations*, no date). The infant mortality rate for Canada is better than that of the United States but is still high: Canada ranks 15th compared to 17 peer countries, with a rate of 4.99 deaths per 1000 live births (Conference Board of Canada, 2010).

The Caribbean

The Caribbean's diverse population reflects a history of European colonialism, the slave trade, and the practice of indentureship. African, British, East Indian, French, Portuguese, Spanish, and Syrian are just a few of the nationalities represented, with Christian, Muslim, and Hindu religions all being represented in the region. Islands such as Guyana, Trinidad and Tobago, and Suriname are more ethnically heterogeneous than others in the region. Differences in language also affect interrelationships in the region. The economies of each country have developed along different trajectories. For example, Trinidad and Tobago's economy is mainly based on petroleum and natural gas, whereas countries such as Barbados and Jamaica rely heavily on tourism. The sugar industry, which once played a major role in countries such as Cuba and small islands such as St Kitts and Nevis, has changed dramatically over the last decade, as has the position of the banana industry in nations such as St Lucia and Dominica.

Most of the countries are independent; islands such as Martinique and Guadeloupe are French territories. Premdas (2003: 163) notes that the 'political systems vary widely from parliamentary democracies to presidential dictatorships to virtual anarchism'. Countries such as Grenada and Jamaica are democracies based on capitalism, whereas Cuba can be defined as communist.

THE EMERGENCE OF SOCIAL WORK IN NORTH AMERICA AND THE CARIBBEAN

In seeking to serve the needs of its multifaceted populations, the profession of social work in North America and the Caribbean has had to develop and change to meet new demands within and across borders.

In the United States and Canada social work is recognised as a profession, with specific legal and societal expectations for its educational institutions and individual practitioners. It emerged as a profession 'at the turn of the twentieth century as a response to the serious health and social problems that accompanied industrial expansion and the rise of immigration' (Watkins et al., in press). Its beginnings are found in the European traditions of the Elizabethan Poor Laws, the German system of social insurance, and the British traditions of education and community action to better the conditions of people affected adversely by the exploitive nature of the industrial revolution (Stuart, 2008).

European and other immigrants to the North American continent were the first to seek the American dream of a better life – to own property, to speak freely, and to worship according to their own dictates. However, they were faced with the daunting tasks of acculturation and assimilation, requiring hard work, a strong faith, and education. On the other hand, they expected access to the more general benefits accruing to society. Social workers frequently facilitated this access, as they pursued the mission of the profession: to guarantee social justice for the socially, economically, and politically disadvantaged, seeking new and greater economic, social, and religious opportunity (Watkins et al., in press; Stuart, 2008).

Drawing from European antecedents, social work emerged in this unique context as a way of fulfilling that dream through social and political action, securing the rights of disenfranchised and economically disadvantaged populations, arguing for racial and gender equality, and seeking social justice and full participation in society demanded as a constitutional right (Watkins et al., in press).

Navigating between the often contradictory demands of individual aspiration and collective action for the common good, the North American system of service provision has included equally diverse and sometimes competing elements: private philanthropy and a public safety net, charitable gifts and community activism; creation of work opportunities contrasted with cash relief; and educational opportunities relative to sheer hard work. Such elements could risk dividing populations in need of services into two groups: the worthy and the unworthy. One point of view would suggest that adherence to an ideological stream will trump the need for a flexible and progressive system of meeting human need. A more sophisticated analysis would find a complex society in which some individuals cannot achieve their aspirations because of structural constraints (e.g. racism, economic recession, global economic and educational competition) and the seismic shift from an economy based on agriculture and manufacturing to one focused on knowledge production.

Social work in North America, particularly in the United States, emerged from the social activism of the late 19th century that was performed out of a sense of charity and philanthropy. The Charity Organization Societies (COS) and later the Russell Sage Foundation promoted participation in community life particularly through education, employment, and services for children. From the friendly visitors of the COS to the Settlement House Movement – both heavily modelled on the European experience – social work was identified as an occupation, and only emerged with professional status requiring a professional education in the 1920s and 1930s (Stuart, 2008).

As the emerging profession moved from requiring certificates to requiring degrees from actual colleges or universities, tensions were endemic to the process. Two schools of thought predominated. The American Association of Schools of Social Work (AASSW), a group primarily representing those sponsored by 'private social agencies and located in or near urban areas' (Kendall, 2002: 4), limited its membership in 1937 to graduate schools. AASSW's opposite, which represented social work programmes in state-supported universities, was the National Association of Schools of Social Administration (NASSA). NASSA's mandate was the promotion of baccalaureate social work education in response to the

workforce needs generated by the Social Security Act of 1935. Not until 1952 did AASSW and NASSA merge to form the Council on Social Work Education (CSWE) (Kendall, 2002).

In 1955 seven practice organisations joined together to form the National Association of Social Workers (NASW); following the merger the organisation had 22,000 members (NASW, 2010a; Stuart, 2008). Initially, the organisation was open only to social workers with a graduate degree, but in 1969 membership was extended to include social workers with an undergraduate degree (Stuart, 2008). NASW developed a code of ethics for social workers and has outlined practice guidelines in many areas (NASW, 2010b). Social work practice in the United States is now further regulated by state boards of licensure, which are represented by the Association of Social Work Boards. All NASW members are expected to adhere to the national Code of Ethics and there are procedures for enforcing ethical practice, both through NASW and through the licensing boards.

The Canadian developmental experience parallels that of the United States, and although there are separate educational and practice associations, a close relationship endures under a 2007 memorandum of agreement for reciprocity of degrees in social work between the two countries. The Canadian Association of Social Workers (CASW) was established in 1926, and the Canadian Association of Schools of Social Work (CASWE) dates from 1967. Until 1970 Canadian schools of social work relied on CSWE accreditation for quality assurance. Also, many Canadian social work faculty members relied on US conferences and journals for professional development for many years (Jennissen and Lundy, no date). Some of the differences between US and Canadian social work can be attributed to factors such as French cultural traditions and also to social work's relationship to the First Nations people in Canada. In the United States the relationship of the federal government with the indigenous populations

(Native Americans) has been characterised by 'policies that perpetuate dependency and undermine self-determination' (Weaver, 2008: 298).

Tracing the history of Caribbean social work can be difficult due to a dearth of well-documented material and a lack of consensus regarding the definition of social work in the region. Like Great Britain and the United States, social work in the Caribbean had its roots in social welfare practices of the mid- to late-19th century. Following the emancipation of enslaved African people in 1838, mass poverty occurred, with relief services mostly provided by the state. In countries such as Jamaica, the functions of relief personnel 'included identifying, screening and paying out benefits to the indigent poor, recommending them for medical care or for institutional care in alms house, as well as providing services for children of destitute adults' (Maxwell, 2002: 14). Friendly Societies in Jamaica were formed among ex-slaves and ethnic groups to improve self-reliance and religious groups (e.g. the Anglican Church) also played a role, providing funds, education, and health care for ex-slaves and their children (Maxwell, 2002). Associations such as the United Negro Improvement Association (UNIA), founded by Jamaica native Marcus Garvey in 1914, 'spoke of the need for self-affirmation, economic self-reliance and political independence' (Baker, 1997: 6). Baker also notes that 'there is a tremendous silence about the contribution of this movement to social welfare policy and practice in the "official historiography" of social work' (1997: 6). In the early 20th century social services provided by government and private groups tended to focus on community development and services to children, older adults, and individuals with disabilities (Maxwell, 2002). Examples include the school meal service of the Coterie of Social Workers in Trinidad and Tobago, the Baby League Clinic in Barbados, and Jamaica Welfare Ltd in Jamaica (Guy, 1997; Maxwell, 2002).

Unrest in the 1930s, notably in countries such as Trinidad and Tobago, spurred the formation of the Moyne Commission in 1938. It studied social and economic conditions in the British territories of the Caribbean and published a report in 1945, although some of the report's provisions were enacted earlier (Institute of Commonwealth Studies Library, 2004). This report recommended that 'persons designated "social welfare officers" were to be employed in each of the then colonies to develop effective social welfare services' (Maxwell et al., 2001: 58). In 1940 the Central Council of Voluntary Social Services was established in Jamaica to coordinate the work of private social service organisations and received government subsidies to undertake this role (Girvan, 1949). Some training courses for social welfare personnel were held in the 1940s and early 1950s in Jamaica, and some individuals were sent to universities in the UK (such as London, Liverpool, and Swansea) for further preparation (Williams et al., 2001).

Guy (1997: 4) notes that 'in the mid 1950's, another generation of graduates emerged from England with post-graduate Diplomas in Hospital Social Work'. In the Caribbean, a 2-year professional certificate was launched in 1961 at the University of the West Indies, Mona Campus (UWI–Mona), modelled on that of British universities. Changes occurred in the certificate programme during the 1970s, 'bringing it more in line with the professional requirements of North America and Britain' (Williams et al., 2001: 58). The University of Guyana initiated a 2-year diploma programme in 1970 similar to the UWI–Mona certificate and moved to a baccalaureate-level degree programme in 1992. In 1980 the College of the Bahamas began to offer a 2-year associate degree in social work (Williams et al., 2001) and added a baccalaureate-level programme in 2001. In 1988 UWI–Cave Hill Campus in Barbados began a 2-year certificate programme, followed by that of UWI–St Augustine Campus in Trinidad in 1990. Later both campuses' offered a baccalaureate-level programme.

The BSW programme was initiated at UWI–Mona in 1989 followed by an MSW programme in 1993; UWI–St Augustine began to offer an MSW programme in 2002 (Healy, 2004; Williams et al., 2001). Both UWI campuses at Mona and St Augustine now offer a Ph programme. Other institutions in Jamaica offer associate-level programmes. In 1996 the University College of Belize, now known as the University of Belize, began an associate-level programme and later added a baccalaureate-level degree programme. In Trinidad and Tobago, the University of the Southern Caribbean offers a BSW programme, and the College of Science Tertiary and Applied Arts of Trinidad and Tobago (COSTAAT) offers an associate-level programme. In Barbados an associate level programme is offered at Barbados Community College. Social Work education in the Caribbean has therefore become more comparable with that in its northern neighbours, and is becoming more accessible to the dispersed population of this sub-region but is still considered insufficient given the challenges of the Caribbean.

CONTEMPORARY SOCIAL WORK EDUCATION AND PRACTICE

According to the United States Bureau of Labor Statistics (2009) there are currently more than 640,000 social workers practising in the United States, primarily in the areas of children and families, school social work, health, mental health, and substance abuse. Additionally, there are 673 CSWE-accredited social work programmes, which together have more than 86,000 students enrolled and more than 6000 full-time faculty members. An additional 41 social work programmes are in candidacy (CSWE, 2010b). 145,000 social workers and students are NASW members (NASW, 2010b).

Social work education is offered at the baccalaureate, masters, and doctoral levels in the United States. The baccalaureate degree is the entry level of practice and generalist practitioners are qualified to work with individuals, families, groups, organisations,

and communities. The masters-level degree prepares graduates for advanced practice in a specific area of concentration. The Educational Policy and Accreditation Standards developed by CSWE outline the competencies required of all social workers – what a graduate must know and be able to do to practise social work effectively. Both degrees include a combination of time in the classroom and experience in the field (CSWE, 2008). At the doctoral level the majority of social work programmes are focused on preparing individuals for research, teaching, and administration with a PhD in social work. However, in the last few years some doctor of social work (DSW) degree programmes have emerged that prepare social work practitioners for clinical practice or social service agency administration. Practice is regulated by the states through licensure boards. Qualifications and regulations differ by state, but all require a postsecondary degree in social work (Watkins et al., in press).

In Canada there were 30,970 registered social workers in 2006, more than double the number in 1997. The largest concentration is in Ontario, followed by Quebec. More than 80 percent of social workers in each province are female (Canadian Institute for Health Information, no date). CASW, the major professional organisation, now has 15,000 members, representing almost half of all registered social workers in the country (CASW, 2010a). Social workers are registered in each province. Professional associations manage the registration process in six of the provinces, whereas external organisations manage registration in the other four (CASW, 2010b). The Association of Social Work Boards allows for membership of regulatory bodies in the United States and Canada.

The Canadian Association of Social Work Education (CASWE) accredits 67 social work programmes at the baccalaureate and master's levels (CASWE, 2010). At the baccalaureate level the students are prepared for generalist practice leading to entry-level social work positions. Field education is also an integral component of education. At the masters level, students are prepared for 'advanced, specialized, or supervisory social work roles' (CASWE, 2008: 15). There are also four social work PhD programmes in Canada (CASWE, 2010).

Social work practice in North America is grounded in a commitment to improve well-being for individuals, families, groups, and communities. It is based on person-in-environment and strengths-based perspectives. Contemporary social work also recognises and responds to the global context of practice (CASW, 2008; CSWE, 2008). Weismiller and Whitaker (2008: 165) identified key tasks carried out by social workers as '(a) enhancing problem-solving, coping, and development of capacities of people; (b) link people with systems that provide resources, services, and opportunities; (c) promote effective and humane operations of systems; and (d) develop and improve social policy'. Practice in North America is also increasingly moving toward an evidence-based practice model, which uses research to inform practice (CASW, 2008; CSWE, 2008).

The Caribbean

At all the UWI campuses, the current social work baccalaureate-level programme offers courses in 'social work methods for practice with individuals, groups and communities' as well as courses in 'social policy, social legislation and social agency administration; and the organisation and monitoring of 800–900 hours of practice in a wide variety of field agencies' (Maxwell et al., 2003: 16). Additionally, classes in sociology and psychology as well as courses in related areas, such as economics, are mandatory for social work students (Maxwell et al., 2003). The programme's emphasis on strengths, resilience, and the ecosystemic perspectives rather than a Freudian-based orientation reflects the evolution of social work over the last few decades (Van Breda, 2001). Within the last decade, there has been a strong call for broadening the social work curriculum

even further - Nettleford (2005) calls for social workers to become more aware of global policies and decisions and their ramifications for Caribbean peoples. The social activist Verna St Rose Greaves argues that 'We need to pay greater attention to human rights issues and social justice issues' (interview with St Rose Greaves, by JHD in 2010). It is proposed that 'issues such as globalisation must feature as critical components of social work education' (Sewpaul, 2008).

The practicum, where students can apply the theoretical perspectives learned in the classroom, presents some challenges. There are insufficient trained personnel who can provide teaching and supervision on a voluntary basis. In Trinidad and Tobago some graduates have been reluctant to act as practice teachers. The UWI–St Augustine programme, in response recently developed a 1-year certificate programme for practice teachers.

In research, social work is affected by a perception that it is not a science, which 'places it low on the list of institutions' priorities for necessities such as research facilities, scientific support teams, funding and collaborative opportunities' (Videka et al., 2008: 296). Also, on an international scale, there are difficulties in defining the boundaries of research, given social work's similarities to fields such as psychology and sociology (Nygren, 2006; Sunesson, 2003; Sandstrom, 2007). In addition, the size of the population of the Caribbean region and the uniqueness of its circumstances, including its resources and approaches, often provide challenges in building research agendas, conducting such research, or its dissemination. Notwithstanding, social work scholars are taking up the challenge to create a body of knowledge that is relevant to the needs and environment of the region as well as to the Caribbean Diaspora.

To date, infrastructure issues and different needs within Caribbean nations have precluded an accreditation process that can be applied to social work education across the region; however, programmes are influenced by standards-setting developments in North America and Great Britain (Healy, 2004). Incremental progress has been made in Trinidad and Tobago with the establishment of a regulatory framework that governs social work as a profession allied to medicine.

Contemporary social work practice has expanded to incorporate fields such as school social work, medical social work, social work in corrections, employee assistance programmes, family life and parent education, and HIV/AIDS counselling (Guy, 1997; Maxwell, 2002). Some have argued that the predominant orientation of social work education has been toward clinical social work, or micro-practice (Baker, 1997), and that social workers need to become more involved in macro-level practice. To address the latter, some social work education programmes offer courses that foster analysis of social policies and equality-related issues, as well as developing skills in the management of social work agencies. However, Maxwell (2002) cautions that although there has been an increase in macro-level practice, much of this is done by individuals without professional social work qualifications. Those with such qualifications are restricted to the provision of 'primary management services, as heads of departments, or units that provide ameliorative or distributive type services' as well as casework and counselling (Guy, 1997: 13).

Educators point to the emergence of social workers in trade unions, in policy-making entities, on national boards, and in politics as positive examples of involvement at the macro level. For example, one of the authors (JHD) took a lead in the recovery efforts in Grenada after Hurricane Ivan in 2004. In Trinidad and Tobago, social workers were part of an advocacy group for school social work, and attempts have been made to move toward an organisation that could convey professional status for social work. At the same time the weakness of national associations in the overall region belies the capability of social workers to advocate for themselves (Williams et al., 2001). Some

local associations of social workers exist in countries such as Barbados, Guyana, Jamaica, and Trinidad and Tobago. The region's educators were the initiators of the Association of Caribbean Social Work Educators (ACSWE), a regional body of those involved in social work education and practice that sponsors the peer-reviewed journal *Caribbean Journal of Social Work* and biennial conferences; and interacts with the North American Congress of Social Workers (NACSW) and the International Association of Schools of Social Work (IASSW). However, in the absence of a recognised organisation for the regulation of the profession in the region, the ability of these groups to advocate for the professional status of social work is limited.

CHALLENGES TO SOCIAL WORK IN THE REGION

There are economic, political, and societal challenges to contemporary social work practice: specifically, changes in population, changes in the nature of work, and globalisation. Social work education and practice must respond to these changes in the practice context. Foremost among the current challenges is the global economic downturn. The economic environment has led to an increase in demand for social work services, often from those who have never accessed services before. This increased demand is coupled, in many cases, with reduced resources available to social service agencies and education and in government assistance progammes (NASW, 2009; Watkins et al., in press).

Another example of a change in context is the ageing of the US population. According to CSWE, 'By 2020, one in six Americans is projected to be aged 65 and older, with the most dramatic growth among those over age 85, elders of color, and women' (CSWE, 2010a). Similarly, in Canada one in five Canadians will be aged 65 or older by 2026 (Health Canada, 2002). Demand for geriatric social workers has already grown as the population ages and older adults live longer; but more and better prepared social workers will be needed to work effectively with this group.

Another rapidly growing area of social work practice is military social work. As a result of wars in Afghanistan and Iraq there is now an influx of more than 1 million veterans and more than 2 million military members who have served in combat deployments. Beyond the military service members and veterans, their family members and communities are also profoundly affected by deployment (CSWE, 2010c). Although the number of Canadian military service members who have been deployed recently is much lower than that of the United States (25,000 to Afghanistan since 2002), this number still represents a substantial increase in the need for services (Naumetz, 2010). Social workers interacting with the military services or veterans' departments and those working in external social service agencies who are likely to encounter military personnel, veterans, or their families in the course of practice also need preparation to work competently with this population (CSWE, 2010c). Many social work education programmes have already begun developing courses, concentrations, or certificate programmes to address the need for additional content in this area of practice.

There are also changes in the scope of social work practice, based on changes in the health and mental health of communities. For instance, there have been advances in genetic and genomic research in recent years. Some social workers have been speaking of the need for social work training in genetics for many years, and the issue is likely to remain at the forefront as the implications of genetic conditions and availability of genetic testing further develop. NASW's (2003) standards on genetic practice state

> it is imperative that social workers become more aware of the ethical, legal and psychosocial implications of a genetic diagnosis, genetic testing and genetic research in order to empower individuals and families to speak out for their rights as public citizens. (2003: 2)

As social work seeks to respond to these external demands, another situation confronts the profession, related to its boundaries and spheres of activity: other professions undertaking similar work are challenging the roles of social workers. The social work title is only given protection on a state-by-state basis in the United States, so there may be places where individuals can practice under the name *social worker* without the necessary training, or employers may relabel posts so that they are open to differently qualified staff. Encroachment from other professions and work by those without appropriate training are serious threats to the continued health of the profession and the populations served. To address these challenges, the profession in the form of education, research, and practice must work in partnership for comprehensive change.

For countries such as Guyana and Trinidad and Tobago, race relations and the inequitable distribution of resources remain leading concerns (Premdas, 2003). Crime, homophobia, and poverty continue to affect countries such as Jamaica (Carr, 2003), and World Trade Organization rules and decisions place countries such as Dominica and St Lucia at a disadvantage (Bernal, 2003). Countries such as Grenada, Guyana, and Haiti have grappled with the psychosocial and economic effects of severe natural disasters (Rogers, 2006). In addition, mass Caribbean emigration (Goulbourne, 2009) and the HIV–AIDS epidemic have greatly affected nations such as the Bahamas, Haiti, and Trinidad and Tobago (McLean et al., 2009) and thus the role of social workers in the region.

The perception of social workers both inside and outside of the profession is also a concern of social work professionals in the Caribbean region. Franklyn Dolly, chief executive officer of Trinidad and Tobago's Dolly and Associates, which provides counselling, training, and other services, points out that

> Social workers usually exist as support systems to other professionals and not as a core part of institutions (e.g. probation officers support the court,

medical social workers support doctors). Social workers believe that they are inferior. This is their 'story' and so they behave this way and 'bring it on' the profession. (Interview with Dolly by JHD, 2010)

Solomon adds:

Persons who have made significant contributions and are professional social workers rarely receive awards. In St Vincent and the Grenadines, there are very few trained social workers but many deem themselves to be social workers. There is still a view that social work is mainly about welfare work ... To some extent, there has been a change. Social workers are taking positions in authority; they are authors, researchers, etc. There has been some progress [... even though] those who hold esteemed positions in the job market and in education do not respect or understand social work and its role. (Interview with Roselle Solomon, MSW graduate student, UWI–St Augustine, 2010)

Evident here are the profession's search for definition of the boundaries of its practice, the esteem of professionals, and the ambivalence about the profession in society, which provide important aspects of the agenda for social work in the sub-region.

CONCLUSION

Advances in social work education have resulted in individuals working in both micro- and macro-practice environments; in governments broadening their outreach efforts; and in regional and international linkages continuing to be created and strengthened. However, challenges remain in both interior and exterior perceptions of the profession; the range of responses to socioeconomic realities that are urgent and sometimes dichotomous; and the need to draw on the knowledge and experience of professionals in the region to provide culturally appropriate services. If the profession is to mature, social workers must acknowledge their worth; understand and use their full repertoire of skills, including those employed in advocacy activities; and build strong professional

organisations so that they can best serve the many peoples in the region.

REFERENCES

Baker, P. (1997) 'Discerning the future in the past: Notes on the bases of transformative social work in the Caribbean', Paper presented at *Effecting Change and Social Transformation for the 21st Century: Challenges For Social Work Education – The Third Conference of Caribbean and International Social Work Educators*. Trinidad Hilton, Port-of-Spain, Trinidad, 6–10 July.

Bernal, R. (2003) 'The Caribbean in the international system: Outlook for the first 20 years of the 21st century', in K. Hall and D. Benn (eds), *Contending with Destiny: The Caribbean in the 21st Century*. Kingston, Jamaica: Ian Randle. pp. 295–25.

Canadian Institute for Health Information (no date) *Canada's Healthcare Providers, 1997 to 2006, a Reference Guide*. Retrieved from http://www.cihi.ca/cihi-ext-portal/internet/en/applicationleft/spending+and+health+workforce/workforce/other+providers/cihi009900.

Carr, R. (2003) 'On "judgements": poverty, sexuality-based violence and social justice in 21st century Jamaica', *Caribbean Journal of Social Work*, 2: 71–87.

CASW (Canadian Association of Social Workers) (2008) *Social Work Scope of Practice*. Retrieved from http://www.casw-acts.ca.

CASW (Canadian Association of Social Workers) (2010a) *About CASW*. Retrieved from http://www.casw-acts.ca.

CASW (Canadian Association of Social Workers) (2010b) *Regulation of Social Work in Canada*. Retrieved from http://www.casw-acts.ca.

CASWE (Canadian Association for Social Work Education) (2008) *CASWE Standards for Accreditation*. Retrieved from http://www.caswe-acfts.ca/vm/newvisual/attachments/866/Media/StandardsofAccreditationMay200825012010sl.pdf.

CASWE (Canadian Association for Social Work Education) (2010) *Universities*. Retrieved from http://www.caswe-acfts.ca/en/Universities_37.html.

Conference Board of Canada (2010) *Infant Mortality*. Retrieved from http://www.conferenceboard.ca/HCP/Details/Health/infant-mortality-rate.aspx.

CSWE (Council on Social Work Education) (2008) *Educational Policy and Accreditation Standards*.

Retrieved from http://www.cswe.org/Accreditation/2 008EPASDescription.aspx.

CSWE (Council on Social Work Education) (2010a) *About the Gero-Ed Center.* Retrieved from http:// www.cswe.org/CentersInitiatives/GeroEdCenter/ AboutGeroEd.aspx.

CSWE (Council on Social Work Education) (2010b) *Accreditation.* Retrieved from http://www.cswe.org/ Accreditation.aspx.

CSWE (Council on Social Work Education) (2010c) *Advanced Social Work Practice in Military Social Work.* Alexandria, VA Council on Social Work Education.

Encyclopedia of the Nations (2010) *Canada – Ethnic Groups.* Retrieved from http://www.nationsencyclo- pedia.com/Americas/Canada-ETHNIC-GROUPS.html.

Girvan, D.T.M. (1949) 'Social welfare developments in Jamaica and the Jamaica Social Welfare Commission', in *Educational Approaches to Rural Welfare.* Washington, DC: Food and Agricultural Organization of the United Nations. pp. 11–37.

Goulbourne, H. (2009) 'Forced and free Caribbean migration', in E. Thomas-Hope (ed.), *Freedom and Constraint in Caribbean Migration and Diaspora.* Kingston, Jamaica: Ian Randle. pp. xi–xxiv.

Guy, R. (1997) 'Revisiting professionalism in Trinidad and Tobago: a social worker's perspective', Paper presented at *Effecting Change And Social Transformation for the 21st Century: Challenges For Social Work Education – The Third Conference Of Caribbean And International Social Work Educators.* Trinidad Hilton, Port-of-Spain, Trinidad, 6–10 July.

Health Canada (2002) *Canada's Aging Population.* Ottawa: Division of Aging and Seniors.

Healy, L. (2004) 'Standards for social work education in the North American and Caribbean region: current realities, future issues', *Social Work Education*, 23: 581–95.

Institute of Commonwealth Studies Library (2004) *Caribbean Online – Routes to Roots: Moyne Commission.* Retrieved from http://commonwealth. sas.ac.uk/libraries/caribbean/moyne.htm.

Jennissen, T. and Lundy, C. (no date) *Keeping Sight of Social Justice: 80 Years of Building CASW.* Retrieved from http://www.casw-acts.ca/.

Kendall, K.A. (2002) *Council on Social Work Education: its Antecedents and First Twenty Years.* Alexandria, VA: Council on Social Work Education.

MacDorman, M.F. (2008) 'Recent trends in infant mor- tality in the United States', *NCHS Data Brief*, 9: 1–9.

Maxwell, J. (2002) 'The evolution of social welfare services and social work in the English-speaking Caribbean (with major reference to Jamaica)', *Caribbean Journal of Social Work*, 1: 11–27.

Maxwell, J., Williams, L., Ring, K. and Cambridge, I. (2003) 'Caribbean social work education in the University of the West Indies', *Caribbean Journal of Social Work*, 2: 11–35.

McLean, R., Sogren, M. and Theodore, K. (2009) 'The impact of HIV–AIDS on children at risk. The case of Trinidad and Tobago', in A.D. Jones, J.A. Padmore, and P.E. Maharaj (eds), *HIV-AIDS & Social Work Practice in the Caribbean.* Kingston, Jamaica: Ian Randle. pp. 71–99.

NASW (National Association of Social Workers) (2003) *NASW Standards for Integrating Genetics into Social Work Practice.* Retrieved from http://www.naswdc. org/practice/standards/geneticsstdfinal4112003. pdf.

NASW (National Association of Social Workers) (2009) *Social Workers Speak on the Economy.* Retrieved from http://www.naswdc.org/pressroom/2009/ sweconomiccrisis.pdf.

NASW (National Association of Social Workers) (2010a) *The History of NASW.* Retrieved from http://www. naswdc.org/nasw/history.asp.

NASW (National Association of Social Workers) (2010b) *About NASW.* Retrieved from http://www.naswdc. org/nasw/default.asp.

Naumetz, T. (2010) 'Afghanistan veterans on disability now 6000', *The Hill Times Online*. 8 February. Retrieved from http://www.thehilltimes.ca/page/ view/afghanistan-02-08-2010.

Nettleford, R. (2005) 'Social work with Caribbean people: perspectives from home and abroad - Caribbean social work education in the University of the West Indies', *Caribbean Journal of Social Work*, 4: 9–12.

Premdas, R. (2003) 'Diversity and liberation in the Caribbean: the decentralist policy challenge in the new millennium', in K. Hall and D. Benn (eds), *Contending with Destiny: The Caribbean in the 21st Century.* Kingston, Jamaica: Ian Randle. pp. 161–78.

Rogers, T. (2006) 'De day we see wind in Grenada: community dialogue and healing through playback theatre', *Caribbean Journal of Social Work*, 5. Retrieved from http://portal.unesco.org/culture/en/ files/30186/11415087821Tracie_Rogers.pdf/ Tracie%2BRogers.pdf.

Sewpaul, V. (2008) 'Social work education', *Caribbean Journal of Social Work*, 6–7: 16–35.

Statistics Canada (2010a) *Persons in Low Income After Tax (in percent 2004–2008).* Retrieved from http:// www40.statcan.gc.ca/l01/cst01/famil19a-eng.htm.

Statistics Canada (2010b) *Ethnic Origins, 2006 Counts, for Canada, Provinces and Territories*

*–20% Sample Dat*a. Retrieved from http://www12.statcan.ca.

Stuart, P.H. (2008) 'History', in T. Mizradi and L. Davis (eds), *Encyclopedia of Social Work* (20th edn). Washington, DC: NASW Press and Oxford University Press. pp. 156–64.

The Economist (2009) *Pocket World in Figures: 2009 Edition*. London: Profile Books Ltd.

United States Bureau of Labor Statistics (2009) *Social Workers in Occupational Outlook Handbook* (2010–2011 edn). Retrieved from http://www.bls.gov: http://www.bls.gov/oco/ocos060.htm.

United States Census Bureau (2008) *S1701. Poverty Status in the Past 12 Months*. Retrieved from http://factfinder.census.gov.

United States Census Bureau (2010) *Annual Estimates of the Resident Population by Sex, Race, and Hispanic Origin for the United States: April 1, 2000 to July 1, 2009 (NC-EST2009-03)*. Washington, DC.

Van Breda, A.D. (2001) *Resilience Theory: a Literature Review*. Pretoria, South Africa: South African Military Health Service. Retrieved from http://www.van-breda.org/adrian/resilience.htm.

Videka, L., Blackburn, J.A. and Moran, J. (2008) 'Building research infrastructure in schools of social work: a university perspective', *Social Work Research*, 32: 294–301.

Watkins, J., Jennissen, T. and Lundy, C. (in press) 'Social work in North America: an introduction', in L. Healy and R. Link (eds) *Handbook on International Social Work*. New York: Oxford University Press.

Weaver, H.N. (2008) 'Native Americans', in T. Mizradi and L. Davis (eds), *Encyclopedia of Social Work* (20th edn). Washington, DC: NASW Press and Oxford University Press. pp. 295–9.

Weismiller, T. and Whitaker, T. (2008) 'Social work profession: workforce', in T. Mizrahi and L. Davis (eds), *Encyclopedia of Social Work* (20th edn). Washington, DC: NASW Press and Oxford University Press. pp. 164–8.

Williams, L., Maxwell, J., Ring, K. and Cambridge, I. (2001) 'Social work education in the West Indies', *Social Work Education*, 20: 57–73.

Appendix 1: International Definition of Social Work (IFSW/IASSW)

This document can be viewed at:

(IFSW) http://www.ifsw.org/f38000138.html
(IASSW) http://www.iassw-aiets.org/index.
  php?option=com_content&view=category
  &layout=blog&id=26&Itemid=51&lang=
  english

The *International Definition of Social Work* is arguably the single most important document for the profession since it sets out the role and function of social work and applies across the globe. The first definition was approved and adopted by the General Meeting of the International Federation of Social Workers (IFSW) at its General Meeting in Brighton in 1982, as follows: 'Social work is a profession whose purpose it is to bring about social changes in society in general and in its individual forms of development'. While this served the profession for many subsequent years it was seen to be rather limited and a more comprehensive definition was required that also committed the profession to a value-base which social workers around the world could aspire to.

Between 1996 and 1999, IFSW set up a Task Force, part of a joint working party constituted with members of the International Association of Schools of Social Work (IASSW) to draft a contemporary definition of social work that aimed to have global applicability. A variety of national and international source materials was consulted and extensive reviews undertaken by a number of practitioners, academics, experts and representatives of national and international organisations. At its biennial general meeting held in Montreal in July 2000, IFSW agreed a new international definition of social work, while IASSW also adopted this definition at its General Assembly.

The core concept of this new Definition is that of 'person-in-environment', where it was accepted that '...the central organizing and unifying concept of social work universally was intervention at the interface of human beings and their environments, both physical and social, thereby reaffirming the thinking of previous social work theorists' (Hare, 2004: 409). This is a generic view, where *environment* can be interpreted in a holistic sense at micro, meso and macro levels, reflecting the broad range of activities, interactions and change strategies that social workers engage in, from individual counselling and therapy to working with families, groups and communities, advocating change at a social policy level and engaging in social action. In addition, the definition emphasizes the principles of empowerment, respect for human rights and social justice which are seen as key to social work practice.

The *International Definition of Social Work* was formally adopted by both IASSW and IFSW on 27 June 2001 and reads as follows:

DEFINITION

The social work profession promotes social change, problem solving in human relationships and the empowerment and liberation of people to enhance well-being. Utilising theories of human behaviour and social systems, social work intervenes at the points where people interact with their environments. Principles of human rights and social justice are fundamental to social work.

COMMENTARY

Social work in its various forms addresses the multiple, complex transactions between people and their environments. Its mission is to enable all people to develop their full potential, enrich their lives, and prevent dysfunction. Professional social work is focused on problem solving and change. As such, social workers are change agents in society and in the lives of the individuals, families and communities they serve. Social work is an interrelated system of values, theory and practice.

VALUES

Social work grew out of humanitarian and democratic ideals, and its values are based on respect for the equality, worth, and dignity of all people. Since its beginnings over a century ago, social work practice has focused on meeting human needs and developing human potential. Human rights and social justice serve as the motivation and justification for social work action. In solidarity with those who are disadvantaged, the profession strives to alleviate poverty and to liberate vulnerable and oppressed people in order to promote social inclusion. Social work values are embodied in the profession's national and international codes of ethics.

THEORY

Social work bases its methodology on a systematic body of evidence-based knowledge derived from research and practice evaluation, including local and indigenous knowledge specific to its context. It recognises the complexity of interactions between human beings and their environment, and the capacity of people both to be affected by and to alter the multiple influences upon them including bio-psychosocial factors. The social work profession draws on theories of human development and behaviour and social systems to analyse complex situations and to facilitate individual, organisational, social and cultural changes.

PRACTICE

Social work addresses the barriers, inequities and injustices that exist in society. It responds to crises and emergencies as well as to everyday personal and social problems. Social work utilises a variety of skills, techniques, and activities consistent with its holistic focus on persons and their environments. Social work interventions range from primarily person-focused psychosocial processes to involvement in social policy, planning and development. These include counselling, clinical social work, group work, social pedagogical work, and family treatment and therapy as well as efforts to help people obtain services and resources in the community. Interventions also include agency administration, community organisation and engaging in social and political action to impact social policy and economic development. The holistic focus of social work is universal, but the priorities of social work practice will vary from country to country and from time to time depending on cultural, historical, and socio-economic conditions.

This definition and associated commentary has received wide acceptance by most social work organisations, educational bodies and associations and is used extensively today. It is understood that social work is a dynamic and evolving profession, and the definition needs to be continually reviewed to keep up with the changes in the profession as well as reflect the diversity of social work practice. Consequently IFSW and IASSW have agreed a procedure to review the definition every ten years. Although a review was considered at the Hong Kong Joint World Conference on Social Work and Social Development in 2010, no changes were made to the definition at that time, and the results of an international survey (EASSW, 2010) will be presented to the Joint Conference of the IASSW, IFSW and the International Council on Social Welfare (ICSW) in Stockholm in June 2012, which may lead to further changes. Translations of the definition are available from http://www.eassw.org/definition.asp in Arabic, Chinese, Danish, Dutch, Finnish, French, German, Greek, Japanese, Portuguese, Russian, Spanish, Swedish and Turkish.

Nigel Hall
Co-editor

REFERENCES

EASSW. (2010) 'Review of the International Definition of Social Work'. Available at: http://www.eassw. org/Review%20Definition%20presentation%20 Hong%20Kong2010-6-9.pdf, accessed 18 July 2011.

Hare, I. (2004) 'Defining social work for the 21st century. The International Federation of Social Workers' revised definition of social work', *International Social Work*, 47(3): 407–24.

Appendix 2: Ethics of Social Work: Statement of Principles

This document can be viewed at:

(IFSW) http://www.ifsw.org/f38000032.html
(IASSW) http://www.iassw-aiets.org/index.php?option=com_content&view=category&layout=blog&id=27&Itemid=50&lang=english

The *Ethics in Social Work: Statement of Principles* developed by the International Federation of Social Workers (IFSW) and the International Association of Schools of Social Work (IASSW) demonstrates an initiative to develop global ethical standards for the social work profession. Prior to publication, the document was reviewed extensively by social workers in the 80 professional organisations of IFSW, as well as by social work educators from around the world, and then approved at the 2004 World Conference in Adelaide, Australia, and adopted formally in October 2004.

The *Statement of Principles* is based on the 1976 International Code of Ethics of IFSW which represented the first code of ethics adopted to apply to social workers globally, supplemented in 1986 by a Declaration of Ethical Principles. These were merged in July 1994 into the *International Ethical Principles and Standards for Social Workers*.

This led in 2004 to an agreed joint document with IASSW: *Ethics in Social Work:*

Statement of Principles. This document was designed to be shorter than the 1994 version and to remain at the level of general principles. The Statement needs to be acceptable in all countries and consequently cannot be too specific, but needs to spell out broad principles that social workers may generally aspire to. As with the other joint policies this was not seen as a final and complete document, but one in the process of constant revision. Both IFSW and IASSW have formed a joint Ethics Committee to try to operationalise the Statement and consider any possible changes.

The *Statement of Principles* is incorporated into national statements and codes of ethics around the world and is an essential element in social work education and training. The development of international statements of value and principle is part of the process of building a unifying framework for the social work profession based on, or influenced by, international human rights declarations.

The *Statement of Principles* has four main sections. First, a Preface which emphasises that ethical awareness is a fundamental part of professional practice. This suggests that by staying at the level of general principles, the aim is to '...encourage social workers across the world to reflect on the challenges and dilemmas that face them and make ethically informed decisions about how to act in each particular case'. Complicating factors are that: often these decisions may be complex and nuanced; social workers may find themselves in the middle of conflicting interests, they also function both as 'helpers' and 'controllers', there may be a conflict between protecting the interests of people and 'demands for efficiency'; and resources are limited.

Second, the Statement includes the *International Definition of Social Work* which emphasises that the social work profession promotes social change in a context where human rights and social justice are fundamental. The third section notes that the common standards where human rights and justice are specified can be found in international statements and covenants such as the Universal Declaration of Human Rights (1948) and the United Nations Convention on the Rights of the Child (1989), which form common standards of achievement, and recognise rights that are accepted by the global community.

Finally the Statement specifies the ethical principles themselves and divides these into three main areas: (1) human rights and human dignity; (2) social justice; and (3) professional conduct. These are reproduced below:

HUMAN RIGHTS AND HUMAN DIGNITY

Social work is based on respect for the inherent worth and dignity of all people, and the rights that follow from this. Social workers should uphold and defend each person's physical, psychological, emotional and spiritual integrity and well-being. This means:

1 Respecting the right to self-determination – social workers should respect and promote people's right to make their own choices and decisions, irrespective of their values and life choices, provided this does not threaten the rights and legitimate interests of others.
2 Promoting the right to participation – social workers should promote the full involvement and participation of people using their services

in ways that enable them to be empowered in all aspects of decisions and actions affecting their lives.
3 Treating each person as a whole – social workers should be concerned with the whole person, within the family, community, societal and natural environments, and should seek to recognise all aspects of a person's life.
4 Identifying and developing strengths – social workers should focus on the strengths of all individuals, groups and communities and thus promote their empowerment.

SOCIAL JUSTICE

Social workers have a responsibility to promote social justice, in relation to society generally, and in relation to the people with whom they work. This means:

1 Challenging negative discrimination[1] – social workers have a responsibility to challenge negative discrimination on the basis of characteristics such as ability, age, culture, gender or sex, marital status, socio-economic status, political opinions, skin colour, racial or other physical characteristics, sexual orientation, or spiritual beliefs.
2 Recognising diversity – social workers should recognise and respect the ethnic and cultural diversity of the societies in which they practise, taking account of individual, family, group and community differences.
3 Distributing resources equitably – social workers should ensure that resources at their disposal are distributed fairly, according to need.
4 Challenging unjust policies and practices – social workers have a duty to bring to the attention of their employers, policy makers, politicians and the general public situations where resources are inadequate or where distribution of resources, policies and practices are oppressive, unfair or harmful.
5 Working in solidarity – social workers have an obligation to challenge social conditions that contribute to social exclusion, stigmatisation or subjugation, and to work towards an inclusive society.

PROFESSIONAL CONDUCT

It is the responsibility of the national organisations in membership of IFSW and IASSW to develop and regularly update their own codes of ethics or ethical guidelines, to be consistent with the IFSW/IASSW statement. It is also the responsibility of national organisations to inform social workers and schools of social work about these codes or guidelines. Social workers should act in accordance with the ethical code or guidelines current in their country. These will generally include more detailed guidance in ethical practice specific to the national context. The following general guidelines on professional conduct apply:

Social workers:

1 are expected to develop and maintain the required skills and competence to do their job;
2 should not allow their skills to be used for inhumane purposes, such as torture or terrorism;
3 should act with integrity. This includes not abusing the relationship of trust with the people using their services, recognising the boundaries between personal and professional life, and not abusing their position for personal benefit or gain;
4 should act in relation to the people using their services with compassion, empathy and care;
5 should not subordinate the needs or interests of people who use their services to their own needs or interests;
6 have a duty to take necessary steps to care for themselves professionally and personally in the workplace and in society, in order to ensure that they are able to provide appropriate services;
7 should maintain confidentiality regarding information about people who use their services. Exceptions to this may only be justified on the basis of a greater ethical requirement (such as the preservation of life);
8 need to acknowledge that they are accountable for their actions to the users of their services, the people they work with, their colleagues, their employers, the professional association and to the law, and that these accountabilities may conflict;
9 should be willing to collaborate with the schools of social work in order to support social work students to get practical training of good quality and up-to-date practical knowledge;
10 should foster and engage in ethical debate with their colleagues and employers and take responsibility for making ethically informed decisions;
11 should be prepared to state the reasons for their decisions based on ethical considerations, and be accountable for their choices and actions;
12 should work to create conditions in employing agencies and in their countries where the principles of this statement and those of their own national code (if applicable) are discussed, evaluated and upheld.

The *Ethics Statement* is subject to revision in a similar way to the *International Definition of Social Work* through the joint Ethics Committee, while discussion at Conferences also focuses on areas for possible change. In the context of this discussion, social work can be viewed on two levels. As noted in Banks et al. (2008), while at one level it is a professional practice rooted in particular nation states, cultures, and legal and policy frameworks, at another level it represents an international social movement, concerned to work for social justice worldwide: 'The international statement on ethics embodies both these senses of social work and contributes to dialogue about values, practices and ideals across boundaries' (2008: 14). This suggests the importance of a continual process of constructive dialogue between the two organisations and an ongoing debate about the purpose, role and mission of the social work profession.

Nigel Hall
Co-editor

NOTE

1 In some countries the term 'discrimination' would be used instead of 'negative discrimination'. The word negative is used here because in some countries the term 'positive discrimination' is also used. Positive discrimination is also known as 'affirmative action'. Positive discrimination or affirmative action means positive steps taken to redress the effects of historical discrimination against the groups named.

REFERENCE

Banks, S., Hugman, R., Healy, L., Bozalek, V. and Orme, J. (2008) *Global Ethics for Social Work: Problems and Possibilities*. Papers from the Ethics and Social Welfare Symposium, July 2008, Durban. Available at: http://dro.dur.ac.uk/6530/1/6530.pdf. Accessed 21 August 2011.

Appendix 3: Global Standards for the Education and Training of the Social Work Profession

This document can be viewed at:

(IASSW) http://www.iassw-aiets.org/index.
php?option=com_content&task=blog
category&id=28&Itemid=49
(IFSW) http://www.ifsw.org/p38000255.html

The *Global Standards for the Education and Training of the Social Work Profession* were developed by the Global Minimum Qualifying Standards Committee, established in 2000 and comprising members from the International Association of Schools of Social Work and the International Federation of Social Workers: the resulting document was approved at the separate General Meetings of the two bodies in Adelaide in 2004. The document was developed on the basis of wide consultations (including about the need for such standards) but has not been accepted without criticism in some quarters (see later): they have, however, been described by the joint chairs of the international bodies as 'aspirational' and dynamic and not intended to be prescriptive (Sewpaul and Jones, 2004).

In prefacing the document, the international organisations gave several reasons for adopting international standards. These include the need to take account of the impact of globalisation on social work training and practice, recognising the changing world in which social workers function and the responsibilities of social work education to adequately prepare practitioners for this globalised environment. A corollary to this principle is the facilitation of partnerships, including international student and staff exchange programmes. The standards seek to encourage exchange while respecting cultural diversity.

Other reasons noted for adoption of the standards focus on protection of clients and recognition of social work practitioners. The standards are not intended to be a substitute for licensing or other legal certification of professional expertise, but aspire to assure a baseline of knowledge and skills for programme graduates around the world. This will help both clients and officials to draw a distinction between social workers and non-social workers in all countries, as well as facilitating the movement of trained social workers from one country to another by assuring equivalency of educational background.

SUMMARY CONTENTS

The document commences with an introduction which refers readers to appendices detailing the processes involved in its production and caution that should be exercised in its use. It accepts and reiterates the international definition of social work and provides a short summary of the core purposes of social work (broadly described as being 'targeted at interventions for social support and for developmental, protective, preventive and/or therapeutic purposes' [ISW, no date: 15]).

The document then lists a range of standards to be aimed for in the following nine areas:

- School's core purpose or mission statement
- Programme objectives and outcomes
- Programme curricula including field programmes
- Core curricula
- Professional staff
- Social work students
- Structure, administration, governance and resources
- Culture and ethnic diversity and gender inclusiveness
- Values and ethical codes of conduct of the profession

The section on core curricula is prefaced by the statement that curricula should be identified and selected according to 'local, national and/or regional/international needs and priorities' (ISW, no date: 19) and is then subdivided into four sections suggesting core curricula relating to:

- the domain of the social work profession (4.2.1);
- domain of the social work professional (4.2.2);
- methods of social work practice (4.2.3);
- (epistemological) paradigm(s) of the social work profession (4.2.4).

COMMENTARY AND CRITIQUES

The elaboration of and agreement on global standards in education for social professionals (including social pedagogues) can be seen as a major step in the internationalisation of social work education. The standards are designed to encourage the development of high quality education for social workers in countries around the world. In adopting the Global Standards, IASSW and IFSW were aspiring to move social work graduates closer to a global equivalency where the professional qualifications obtained by social workers in one country are accepted as comparable with those achieved elsewhere. Globalisation has resulted in increased migration in the general population, including, more specifically, increased international mobility of social workers. In addition, the growing number of social workers employed by international organisations often need to confirm professional credentials including educational qualifications. In some (primarily Western) countries, there is increasing governmental regulation of social workers, which requires documentation of credentials received from an accredited educational institution. While the global standards are an aspirational document and there is no monitoring, control, or accreditation function connected to them, they do provide a baseline of comparison that may assist social workers working out of the country in which they received their training (Sewpaul and Jones, 2004).

Additionally, anecdotal evidence suggests that in countries where social work is relatively new (or recently re-established) and lacking in formal structures for accreditation, or even in precedents with regard to expectations, social work educators can find it helpful to have external (international) criteria and standards against which to develop their programmes and to promote their own needs and values in higher education institutions unfamiliar with the requirements of professional education programmes (Lyons and Lawrence, 2006). It can be argued then that the standards provide a broad universal framework for the education of social professionals that can be adapted to local contexts and conditions (Hokenstad, 2008).

However, the advent of even an aspirational set of global standards has not been without controversy. A major point of debate has been their relevance to local cultures and conditions. This issue concerns both the value base and curriculum content addressed in the document. Some educators argue that sections are based on assumptions of universality based in Western societies and grounded in Western experiences. The argument suggests a form of intellectual imperialism that attempts to determine the nature of social work education around the globe. It further states that the standards fail to give attention to indigenous cultures and their contributions to human wellbeing. For example, Yip (2004), taking the international definition, the ethics statement and the global standards document together, suggests that these still embrace an ideology of Western social work imperialism reflecting values which do not sit comfortably with Chinese experience and expectations (e.g. where responsibilities and stability are at least as much valued as rights and change, respectively). Gray (2005) also argues that much greater emphasis must be placed on culture and cultural context and that in any debates and assumptions about globalisation, internationalisation and universalism, we should not perpetuate imperialistic tendencies, but rather aim to promote indigenous practices, educating social workers accordingly.

Thus the standards are not accepted as globally appropriate by all, nor even as necessary by some. However, the criticisms were to some extent anticipated and the dangers of devising such a document have been articulated (e.g. Sewpaul, 2005). It is ultimately the responsibility of social work educators (and their national organisations, if any) to promote or ignore the standards. If the former, they need to be adopted in ways which are appropriate to national conditions and respectful of both local values and the aspirations of the international authors of this document.

Karen Lyons and Terry Hokenstad
Joint editors

REFERENCES

Gray, M. (2005) 'Dilemmas of international social work: paradoxical processes in indigenisation, universalism and imperialism', *International Journal of Social Welfare*, 14(3): 231–8.

Hokenstad, M.C. (2008) 'International social work education', in T. Mizrahi and L.E. Davis (eds), *Encyclopedia of Social Work*, (20th edn). New York, NY: Oxford University Press. Vol. 2, pp. 488–93.

ISW (International Social Work). Supplement issued with *International Social Work*, containing the Definition, Ethics and Global Standards documents. London: SAGE.

Lyons, K. and Lawrence, S. (2006) *Social Work in Europe: Educating for Change.* Birmingham: IASSW/BASW, Venture Press.

Sewpaul, V. (2005) 'Global standards: promise and pitfalls for re-inscribing social work into civil society', *International Journal of Social Welfare*, 14(3): 218–30.

Sewpaul, V. and Jones, D. (2004) 'Global standards for social work education and training', *Social Work Education*, 23 (5): 493–513.

Yip, K.S. (2004) 'A Chinese cultural critique of the global qualifying standards for social work education', *Social Work Education*, 23 (5): 597–612.

Appendix 4: The United Nations

The United Nations website, www.un.org/en/ provides a comprehensive outline of the organisation.

Some key objectives of the United Nations (UN) system, namely peace-keeping, human rights, humanitarian assistance, and social and economic development, closely reflect, albeit on a different level and scale, fundamental goals of social work. Moreover, the UN can often support workers and agencies engaged in international social work. Hence it is important that social workers understand the UN and cooperate with it wherever possible.

Founded in 1945 by 51 nations as a response to the experience of World War II, the UN is engaged in assisting its current 193 member states to work together on a wide range of fronts to maintain peaceful relationships, improve people's lives, respect rights and harmonise action. While essentially a member states organisation, operating under a Charter, the UN relates also to over 13,000 civil society organisations, some of which have consultative status and various other roles through the Department of Economic and Social Affairs of the Economic and Social Council. The UN is thus the only international organisation that enables states and a wide variety of other organisations to work together to the extent that they are willing to do so. It has, however, little ability to oblige any state or organisation to do anything.

The UN has six principal organs established under its Charter. *The General Assembly*, composed of the member states on the basis of 'one state one vote', receives many reports, discusses a wide range of issues and makes recommendations. While it represents nigh universal coverage, it can only reflect essentially the positions of the current political leadership of its members, rather than peoples, specific populations or civil society. This can be a significant drawback in its effectiveness, leading at times to the suggestion that one or more parallel assemblies are required, representing perhaps people and civil society.

The Security Council, with its five permanent members (France, Republic of China, Russian Federation, United Kingdom and the United States) and ten elected members with two-year terms, is charged with peace and security issues. The arrangement of five permanent members, each with a veto power in regard to substantive resolutions, has greatly reduced the Council's effectiveness and cries out for reform. Alternative arrangements have been advanced in recent years and may not be too far off. The Council has been accused of not acting in relation to various states infringing people's rights and jeopardising peace, but the prevailing voting system is largely responsible for this failure. Where it is able to intervene, the Council encourages and facilitates negotiations between warring parties and may deploy a peace-keeping force, with personnel made available by member states. In 2011, fifteen peace-keeping operations were deployed.

The Economic and Social Council, with a revolving membership of 54 states, promotes economic and social development, and oversees many of the agencies with which social workers are likely to be involved. This Council also has active regional commissions and standing committees: social workers can be very active at these levels.

The remaining three central organs are *the Trusteeship Council, the International Court of Justice* (with the related International Criminal Court emerging in 2002), and *the Secretariat*. In June 2010, the Secretariat had some 44,000 staff members located at various centres around the world. It requires a large budget and a complex administration, and the UN has been criticised as being too expensive, bureaucratic and hierarchical.

Apart from affiliation with the Economic and Social Council and involvement in UN conferences through, for example, a parallel civil society organisations conference, most social work involvement with the UN is with the range of specialised agencies, funds and programmes, offices and other entities, reporting variously to the General Assembly, Security Council or Economic and Social Council. The list of these agencies and other entities is a very long one (see the UN websites). Some of them come under the UN budget, to which all member states contribute, and some of them must raise their own funds. Some are essentially operational while others have coordinating, promoting, overseeing, and other roles. Some are also independent of the central organs of the UN, apart from reporting to and at times cooperating with them. These include the World Bank (WB) Group, the International Monetary Fund (IMF) and the various courts and tribunals. Among the UN agencies best known to social workers are the World Health Organization (WHO), the United Nations Children's Fund (UNICEF), the United Nations High Commissioner for Refugees (UNHCR), the United Nations Development Program (UNDP), and very recently, UN-Women, but social work in the field engages with a very wide range of UN entities.

In international social work, as commonly defined, social workers are often working in partnership with, collaborating with, or being assisted by various elements of the UN system. In addition, some draw on, and sometimes contribute to, publications emanating from the UN, or draw inspiration from the work of its agencies and their personnel. However, it should be noted that the UN is often limited by the influence of state members' current leadership over what it can report, say, or do about many situations. Hence discussions with UN personnel will often provide important insights at variance with published reports or even actions in the field. Not only may reports be biased by states' demands and statistics, but the field work is limited in scope and direction by the funds, personnel and other resources made available to UN agencies in the field seeking to respond to specific situations. In these ways, particular activities of the various arms of the UN can be significantly circumscribed by specific member states, and it is important to appreciate this when evaluating the agency's work in any context.

Over the years, the UN has enacted a large number of conventions, frequently aimed at protecting either universal rights or those of specific populations. Not all member states choose to sign these conventions, and even more fail to reflect them in state legislation or seek to enforce them. However, their very existence enables social workers at any level to campaign around these conventions. These conventions cover not only basic human rights but also the rights of virtually all populations with which social workers commonly work, as well as others.

The UN is not engaged in world governance, even though some states have feared that it could be and have campaigned against this. Whether it should become so by being reformed is debated. For example, could it be more representative of peoples and non-government agencies, and given the power to enforce the many conventions, agreements and recommendations that already emanate from the organs of the UN? A similarly controversial area is its role in relation to the formulation and enforcement of international law. It has clearly played a role over the period of its existence in the emerging field of international law, and the established international courts, together with the tribunals set up in the aftermath of conflict, do represent some of the first tentative steps towards the enforcement of an international legal system. However, the effective functioning of such a system still has a long road ahead, and it remains controversial as to whether the UN should be given this role.

A further area of debate is that of global social policy. Much of what the UN has achieved to date can be seen as contributing to that end, but the extent to which it should play a pro-active role in this regard remains an open question. One key issue is that of the sovereignty of states versus the capacity of an international body to hold states to account in various ways: this is likely to remain controversial. A second issue is the relative roles of the UN as an international body and the emerging regional bodies, such as the European and African Unions. These clearly have the potential to carry out a range of roles, at least within the confines of their regions but sometimes with consequences well beyond.

The UN is a large and complex structure that currently operates in the face of a range of restrictions. Despite its limitations, it has achieved much over the decades of its existence and possesses the potential to do even more. To be effective, however, it needs to work in close cooperation with all nation states and a range of other organisations, and that aim can best be achieved through the active involvement and support not only of governments but also of the professions and civil society. To this end, international social work can, and should, certainly contribute.

David Cox

FURTHER READING

www.unsystem.org/ provides alphabetic and thematic indexes of the names and websites of United Nations organisations, and the separate websites are the best current introduction to any United Nations body.

A further comprehensive outline of the United Nations system can be found in Weiss, T.G. and Daws, S. (eds) (2007) *The Oxford Handbook on the United Nations*. Oxford: Oxford University Press.

Robertson, G. (2000) *Crimes Against Humanity: The Struggle for Global Justice*. London: Penguin Books, provides an excellent discussion of the history of, and difficulties confronting, the United Nations in the field of global justice.

For an overview and discussion of the World Bank, International Monetary Fund and World Trade Organization, see Todaro, M.P. and Smith, S.C. (2003) *Economic Development*. 8th edn. Harlow, England: Pearson. pp. 584–7 and 626–30.

For good discussions of the United Nations System, its strengths and limitations, see Gordon, W. (1994) *The United Nations at the Crossroads of Reform*. New York: M.E. Sharpe; and Mingst, K.A. and Karns, M.P. (2007) *The United Nations in the Twenty-First Century*. 3rd edn. Boulder, CO: Westview Press.

Appendix 5: Human Rights: The Human Rights Triptych

Given that social work is considered a human rights profession[1], it is necessary to have an adequate understanding of human rights principles. Having arisen from the ashes of World War II, they are essentially international legal mandates to fulfill human need, a world response to human rights abuses and declarations that they should never happen again. To fully understand the entire body of human rights principles, Rene Cassin, often referred to as the Father of Human Rights, urged the peoples and nations of the world to understand and appreciate the 'Human Rights Triptych'. The Universal Declaration of Human Rights (UDHR), the authoritative definition of human rights standards, a document increasingly referred to as customary international law, is at the centre. On the right are the guiding principles, declarations and conventions that elaborate upon the Universal Declaration and can have more judicial force: on the left are implementation measures, such as reporting to human rights committees, the Universal Periodic Review, and world conferences (see Wronka, 2008: 52, for a tabular representation of this triptych). Taken altogether, human rights principles can serve as the bedrock of social justice, asserting values that can ultimately move the world community towards a 'human rights culture,' that is,

a 'lived awareness' of human rights principles in our minds and hearts and dragged into our everyday life (www.humanrightsculture.org).

THE CENTRAL PANEL: THE UNIVERSAL DECLARATION OF HUMAN RIGHTS (UDHR)

Endorsed with no dissent by the General Assembly on 10 December 1948, by January 2012 virtually every member nation of the UN has signed this document. The most translated document in the world, it can be found on the internet at http://www.ohchr.org/EN/UDHR/Pages/SearchByLang.aspx.

For a summary of the UDHR's historical, philosophical, and religious antecedents, as well as, country debates prior to its endorsement, see Wronka (1998, 2008). Very briefly, the UDHR, a philosophic/historic compromise, consists of five interdependent crucial notions: human dignity (Article 1, a major teaching in nearly every religion); non-discrimination (Article 2, also a major teaching); negative freedoms (Articles 3–21, also called civil and political rights, largely reflective of the US Bill of Rights, urging governments *not to* interfere with fundamental freedoms, like speech and the press); positive freedoms (Articles 22–27, also called economic, social, and cultural rights, indicative of the Soviet Constitution of 1923, which pose governmental obligations *to provide for* the fulfillment of human needs like physical and mental health); and solidarity rights (Articles 28–30, *urging duties* towards one another and the need for a socially just national and international order requiring *governmental cooperation* to fulfill human rights for everyperson, everywhere).

For the sake of brevity, below is an educated layperson's[2] summary of the UDHR's substantive provisions, with some commentary as appropriate.

The Universal Declaration of Human Rights

Preamble
Given that disregard and contempt for human rights have resulted in barbarous acts that have shocked the conscience of humanity and that recognition of the inherent dignity of human beings and equal rights of the human family is the foundation of freedom, justice, and peace in the world, the General Assembly proclaims UDHR as a common standard of achievement for all peoples and nations.

Article 1
All human beings are born free and equal with dignity and rights and should act towards one another in a spirit of brotherhood [and sisterhood].[3]

Article 2
Everyone is entitled to human rights *without discrimination as to race, color, sex, language, religion, political opinion, national origin, property, birth, or other status* (italics added).[4]

Article 3
Everyone has the right to life, liberty, and security.

Article 4
No one shall be held in slavery or servitude.

Article 5
No one shall be subjected to torture or cruel, inhuman, or degrading treatment or punishment.

Article 6
Everyone has a right to recognition everywhere as a person before the law.

Article 7
Everyone is equal before the law and has the right to equal protection before the law.

Article 8
Everyone has the right to an effective remedy should a right be violated.

Article 9
No one shall be subjected to arbitrary arrest, detention, or exile.

Article 10
Everyone is entitled to full equality in a fair and public hearing by an independent, impartial, and competent tribunal.

Article 11
Everyone has the right to be presumed innocent until proven guilty in a public trial with all guarantees necessary for a proper defense.

Article 12
Everyone has the right to privacy in the family, home, or correspondence and to protection against attacks upon honour and reputation.

Article 13
Everyone has the right to freedom of movement within one's country and the right to leave one's country and the right to return to it.

Article 14
Everyone has the right to seek and enjoy asylum from persecution in other countries.

Article 15
Everyone has the right to a nationality.

Article 16
Men and women of full age have a right to marry, with free and full consent, and to found a family, the fundamental unit of society, which is entitled to protection by the state.

Article 17
Everyone has the right to own property, which shall not be arbitrarily taken away.

Article 18
Everyone has the right to freedoms of thought, conscience, and religion.

Article 19
Everyone has the right to seek, receive, and impart information and ideas and to freedoms of opinion and expression.

Article 20
Everyone has the right to peaceful assembly and association.

Article 21
Everyone has the right to take part in government directly or through freely chosen representatives and the right to equal access to public services. The will of the people shall be the basis of government.

Article 22
Everyone has the right to social security through national and international cooperation and is entitled to the realisation of economic, social, and cultural rights, which are indispensable to human dignity and development.

Article 23
Everyone has rights to: meaningful and gainful employment which shall ensure to the worker's family an existence worthy of human dignity and supplemented by social protections as necessary; equal pay for equal work; and to form and join unions.

Article 24
Everyone has the right to rest, leisure, and periodic holidays with pay.

Article 25
Everyone has the right to an adequate standard of living for the health and well being of the family, including but not limited to: food, clothing, housing, medical care, necessary social services, security in the event of unemployment, sickness, disability, widowhood, or old age. Motherhood and childhood are entitled to special care and assistance. Children born in or out of wedlock shall enjoy the same social protection.

Article 26
Everyone has the right to education, which shall be directed to the full development of the human personality and the promotion of understanding, tolerance, and friendship among all nations, racial, or religious groups.

Article 27
Everyone has the right to the free participation in the cultural life of the community; to enjoy the arts; and to share in the benefits of scientific advancement.

Article 28
Everyone is entitled to a social and international order in which human rights can be realised.

Article 29
Everyone has duties to the community in which the free and full development of the human personality is possible. Rights have limits solely for the purpose of securing recognition and respect for the dignity of others.

Article 30
No person, group, or government has the right to engage in the destruction of any of these human rights.[5]

THE RIGHT PANEL: CONVENTIONS, DECLARATIONS, AND GUIDING PRINCIPLES

Mentioned below are first, articles from two major conventions, at times, called covenants and treaties: The International Convention on Civil and Political Rights (ICCPR) and the International Convention on Economic, Social, and Cultural Rights (CESCR). Following are mention of other core and timely human rights documents, including not only conventions, but also declarations and guiding principles, the former having the most judicial force. (They can be found in their entirely at: http://www2.ohchr.org/english/law/ and scrolling down to the appropriate document.) In brief, guiding principles often become declarations, if not conventions. A case in point is the Guiding Principles to Eradicate Extreme Poverty. In March 2012 at the Human Rights Council meetings, IASSW urged governments to consider drafting a legally binding International Convention to Abolish Extreme Poverty (CAEP) (see www.humanrightsculture.org, also this author's website and portal for resources for human rights/social justice advocates). It is important to keep in mind that many state constitutions have an article that asserts in essence that international treaties ought to become law, such as Article 6, the Supremacy Clause of the US Constitution, stating they should become "law of the land… and the judges bound thereby."

The International Convention on Civil and Political Rights (ICCPR)[6]

Endorsed 16 December 1966; entered into force on 23 March 1976. September 2011: 72 signatories, 167 parties. At: http://treaties.un.org/Pages/ViewDetails.aspx?src=TREATY&mtdsg_no=IV-4&chapter=4&lang=en[7]

Article 1 – All peoples have the right to self-determination meaning that they can freely pursue their economic, social, and cultural development, based upon the principle of mutual benefit. They cannot be deprived of their own means of subsistence.

Article 2 – Everyone has the right to non-discrimination and a remedy by competent state authorities should their rights be violated.

Article 3 – All men and women have equal rights.

Article 6 – Everyone has the right to life and survival.

Article 7 – No one shall be subjected to torture, cruel, inhuman or degrading punishment, nor to medical or scientific experimentation without full consent.

Article 8 – No one shall be held in slavery; slavery and the slave trade in all their forms shall be prohibited.

Article 9 – Everyone has the right to liberty and security of person, including freedom from arbitrary arrest and detention and the right to a fair and prompt trial. Upon arrest, persons must be informed of the reasons for their arrest and the charges brought against them.

Article 10 – Persons deprived of liberty shall be treated with humanity and respect for the inherent dignity of the human person. Juveniles shall be separated from adults and be treated appropriately for their age. The essential aim of treatment of prisoners is for their reformation and social rehabilitation.

Article 11 – No one shall be imprisoned due to debt.

Article 12 – Everyone has the right to liberty of movement, including the right to leave and return to one's country and the right to choose one's residence.

Article 13 – Aliens have the right to submit reasons against possible expulsion, which ought to be reviewed by specially designated competent authorities.

Article 14 – Everyone has the right to equality before the law. This should include the right to a fair and public trial by competent impartial authorities; the presumption of innocence until proven guilty; trial without undue delay; an understanding of charges in language the accused understands; and an adequate legal defence.

Article 17 – No one shall be subjected to arbitrary unlawful interference with his privacy, family, home, or correspondence, nor to unlawful attacks upon his/her honour or reputation.

Article 18 – Everyone has the right to freedom of thought, conscience and religion, including the right to practice his/her religion individually or in community.

Article 19 – Everyone has the right to freedom of expression, to seek, receive, and impart information and ideas of all kinds, either orally, in writing, in the form of art, or through any other media of choice.

Article 20 – Advocacy of national, racial, or religious hatred, propaganda for war that constitutes incitement to discrimination, hostility, or violence shall be prohibited.

Article 21 – Everyone has the right to peaceful assembly.

Article 22 – Everyone has the right to freedom of association with others, including the right to join or form trade unions for the protection of his/her interests.

Article 23 – The family, as the natural and fundamental unit of society, is entitled to protection by society. Everyone has the right to marry and found a family with free and full consent of intending spouses.

Article 24 – Every child has rights to non-discrimination and protection by society. They shall be registered immediately after birth, have a name, and the right to acquire a nationality.

Article 25 – Everyone has the right to take part in public affairs either directly or through freely chosen representatives and the right of equal access to public service.

Article 26 – Everyone has the right to equality before the law and to equal protection.

Article 27 – Ethnic, religious, or linguistic minorities shall not be denied the right in community with other members of their group to enjoy their own culture, profess and practice their own religion, or use their own language.[8]

First Optional Protocol[9] – Individuals, who feel that they were victims of violations, as defined by the ICCPR, have the right to send communications to appropriate human rights committees (Endorsed 16 December 1966; entered into force 23 March 1976. At August 2011: 35 signatories; 114 parties).

Second Optional Protocol – Governments shall take all necessary measures to abolish the death penalty (Endorsed 15 December 1989; entered into force 11 July 1991. At August 2011, 35 signatories; 35 parties).

The International Convention on Economic, Social, and Cultural Rights (CESCR)

Endorsed 16 December 1966; entered into force 3 January 1976. At August 2011, 69 signatories; 160 parties. At: http://treaties.un.org/Pages/ViewDetails.aspx?src=TREATY&mtdsg_no=IV-3&chapter=4&lang=en

Article 1 – All peoples have the right to self-determination meaning that they can freely pursue their economic, social, and cultural development, based upon the principle of mutual benefit. They cannot be deprived of their own means of subsistence.

Article 2 – States shall take steps to progressively realise economic, social, and cultural rights and with non-discrimination.

Article 3 – Men and women shall have equal rights as enunciated in this Covenant.

Article 4 – In enjoying economic, social, and cultural rights, states may pose limitations, but only in so far as they are compatible with promoting the general welfare in a democratic society.

Article 5 – No state, group, or person has the right to destroy any of the rights in this Convention.

Article 6 – Everyone has the right to work, including the opportunity to gain one's living by work freely chosen and accepted. States shall take steps like technical, vocational, and training programs and policies to achieve steady, economic, social, and cultural development and full and productive employment.

Article 7 – Everyone has the right to just and favourable conditions at work, which at minimum includes safe and healthy working conditions; fair wages to ensure a decent living for workers and their families; equal pay for men and women for equal work; and rest, leisure, and reasonable limitation of working hours and periodic holidays with pay.

Article 8 – Everyone has the right to form and join trade unions, to strike in conformity with laws necessary for a democratic society, and to establish national and international confederations of unions.

Article 9 – Everyone has the right to society security, including social insurance.

Article 10 – The widest possible protection and assistance should be accorded to the family, the natural and fundamental unit of society, particularly while responsible for the care and education of dependent children. Special protections should be accorded to working mothers during a reasonable period before and after childbirth, including paid leave or leave with adequate social security benefits. Children should not be discriminated against because of parentage. They should be protected from economic and social exploitation, which would prohibit employment in work harmful to their morals or health and likely to hamper their normal development.

Article 11 – Everyone has the right to an adequate standard of living for himself and his family, including adequate food, clothing, and housing. Everyone has the right to be free from hunger. States individually and through international cooperation shall promote programs to improve methods of production, conservation, and distribution of food; disseminate knowledge of the principles of nutrition; reform agrarian systems to ensure the efficient development and utilisation of natural resources; and ensure the equitable distribution of world food supplies in relation to need.

Article 12 – Everyone has the right to enjoy the highest attainable standard of mental and physical health. Steps taken to achieve this right shall include provision of the reduction of stillbirth and infant mortality rate; the improvement of all aspects of environmental and industrial hygiene; the prevention, treatment, and control of epidemic, endemic, occupational and other diseases; and conditions to ensure to all medical service in the event of sickness.

Article 13 – Everyone has the right to education, which shall be directed to the full development of the human personality and the sense of its dignity and shall strengthen respect for human rights. Furthermore, education shall enable all persons to participate effectively in a free society, promote understanding, tolerance, and friendship among all nations and all racial, ethnic, or religious groups and the maintenance of peace. Primary education shall be compulsory and available free to all.

Article 14 – If states, when becoming a party to this Convention do not have compulsory primary education free of charge, they shall undertake measures within two years to work out a detailed plan of action for its progressive implementation.

Article 15 – Everyone has the right to participate in cultural life, to enjoy the benefits of scientific progress, to benefit from the protection of the moral and material interests resulting from any scientific, literary or artistic production of which he/she is the author. States shall respect the freedom indispensable for scientific research and creative activity and encourage the development of international contacts and cooperation in the cultural and scientific fields.[10]

Select core and other timely human rights documents[11]

International Convention on the Elimination of All Forms of Racial Discrimination (CERD) – Endorsed 7 March 1966; entered into force 4 January 1969. At August 2011, 85 signatories; 174 parties. At: http://www2.ohchr.org/english/law/cerd.htm

Convention on the Elimination of Discrimination Against Women (CEDAW) – Endorsed 18 December 1979; entered into force 3 September 1981. At August 2011, 98 signatories; 187 parties. At: http://www2.ohchr.org/english/law/cedaw.htm

Convention on the Rights of the Child (CRC) – Endorsed 20 November 1989;

entered into force 2 September 1990. At August 2011, 143 signatories; 140 parties. At: http://www2.ohchr.org/english/law/crc.htm

Convention Against Torture (CAT) – Endorsed 10 December 1948; entered into force 26 June 1987. At August 2011, 77 signatories; 149 parties. At: http://www2.ohchr.org/english/law/cat.htm

Genocide Convention – Endorsed 9 December 1948; entered into force 12 January 1951. At August 2011, 41 signatories; 141 parties. At: http://www2.ohchr.org/english/law/genocide.htm

Declaration on the Rights of Indigenous Peoples – Endorsed on 13 September 2007 with 143 for; 4 against (USA, New Zealand, Australia, and Canada, who have now voted in favour); 11 abstaining; 34 absent. http://en.wikipedia.org/wiki/Declaration_on_the_Rights_of_Indigenous_Peoples

Guiding Principles for the Protection of Persons with Mental Illness and the Improvement of Mental Health Care – Endorsed 19 December 1991. Other information not available. At: http://www2.ohchr.org/english/law/principles.htm

Guiding Principles to Eradicate Extreme Poverty – Still in the process of endorsement. At: http://www.ohchr.org/EN/Issues/Poverty/Pages/DGPIntroduction.aspx

THE LEFT PANEL: IMPLEMENTATION[12]

A Major Portal to Human Rights Initiatives: The UN Office of the High Commissioner on Human Rights (http://www.ohchr.org/EN/Pages/WelcomePage.aspx).

Countries' Reports to Human Rights Committees (http://www.unhchr.ch/tbs/doc.nsf/newhvdocsbytreaty?OpenView&Start=1&Count=750&Collapse=1#1)

Portal to the Universal Periodic Review (UPR) (http://www.ohchr.org/en/hrbodies/upr/pages/uprmain.aspx)

Proceedings of the Human Rights Council in general (http://www2.ohchr.org/english/bodies/hrcouncil/)

World Human Rights Conferences (http://www.conferencealerts.com/humanrights.htm).

A Human Rights Portal for the African Union (AU) (http://www.au.int/en/content/african-charter-human-and-peoples-rights)

A Human Rights Portal for the Organization of American States (OAS) (http://www.cidh.oas.org/Basicos/English/Basic2.American%20Declaration.htm)

A Human Rights Portal for the European Union (EU) (http://www.eucharter.org/).

A Human Rights Portal for the Association of Southeast Asian Nations: (http://www.aseanhrmech.org/international.html). Author's Website serving as a portal for human rights/social justice advocates, particularly those in the discipline of social work: (http://www.humanrightsculture.org)

Joseph Wronka

NOTES

1   See, for example, Ife (2008), Reichert (2011) and Wronka (1998, 2008).

2   Please note that Eleanor Roosevelt, chair of the drafting committee for the Universal Declaration, wanted a document for the educated layperson, not for the doctorate in jurisprudence. Whereas summaries of articles may not be total or precise, they ought to agree with their substance and sense and provide an adequate platform discussing the values inherent in the UDHR.

3   Eleanor Roosevelt wanted a document using non-sexist language, a rather novel initiative given the tenor of the times. However, the committee by and large felt otherwise.

4   It is important to emphasise that this article's emphasis is that being human, rather than such characteristics like race, sex, or religion, is the sole criterion to have the rights to be enumerated. Roughly, this article, also reflective of the spirit of the times, was a prelude to considering other areas of discrimination, such as sexual orientation, age, disability, medical condition, or marital status. As Eleanor Roosevelt said, the UDHR was 'a good document... not a perfect one'.

5   Originally intended to be elaborated upon by later UN documents, the Women's International League for Peace and Freedom (WILPF) of which Jane Addams was first co-president radically departed from

this intent by calling upon the world community to amend the UDHR to include an Article 31, the right to clean and potable drinking water, indicative of perhaps the most pressing concern in the 21st century.

6 Continuing with the intent of Eleanor Roosevelt, this section states what appears to substantively represent a major theme (or themes) of select articles, including either direct or paraphrased clauses from the articles. Although an unofficial summary, the purpose here is to expand debates concerning the values that these documents represent, generally going beyond the UDHR and working on the assumption that only chosen values endure. Here, for purposes of expediency only the first two major human rights conventions, the ICCPR and CESCR (to be discussed), given their widespread familiarity in the international arena, will be elaborated upon. Their familiarity is further buttressed by the fact that taken collectively with the UDHR, they have traditionally been referred to as The International Bill of Rights. Later, mention of other select core and other timely human rights documents will be mentioned only cursorily for purposes of expediency. For a tabular summary of all those documents, see Wronka (2008).

7 Websites for conventions will include countries' concerns, that is, reservations and understandings as pertaining to each document and whether they have signed and/or ratified that document. Being a signatory means that a country has decided to consider ratification in its legislative bodies. Once ratified, however, it poses a legal obligation, especially if the state constitution has a clause as in the USA's Constitution's Article 6 (sec. a) called 'The Supremacy Clause', which states that a treaty must be considered 'Supreme Law of the Land', and 'the judges bound thereby' (see, for example, Steiner et al. (2007) and Weissbrodt et al. (2001). But ratification may include a 'non-self-executing' clause, giving the human rights document a mere symbolic, rather than judicial significance, as the USA did when it ratified the ICCPR (Buergenthal et al. (2002).

8 The rest of the Covenant, articles 28–53, deal essentially with procedural and other matters pertaining to states' ratification and submission of periodic reports before the monitoring committee of the ICCPR. These reports, substantive to the left side of the Human Rights Triptych can be found on the internet at: http://www.unhchr.ch/tbs/doc.nsf/newhv docsbytreaty?OpenView&Start=1&Count=750&Expa nd=4.13#4.13

9 Roughly, such a protocol serves as an amendment to the foregoing document.

10 As in the ICCPR, the rest of the Covenant deals essentially with procedural and other matters pertaining to states' ratification and submission of periodic reports before the monitoring committee of CESCR.

11 These documents are here given their importance in the human rights arena. At first glance, it may seem that they set us up against one another because, for example, working on behalf of the rights of women, we might forget the rights of children. However, if we acknowledge the interdependence of human rights and the fact that social justice is, indeed, a struggle, all of our efforts can and should integrate all human rights principles in creative ways which call in part for a just social and international order, until every person, everywhere has their rights realised.

12 Concerning implementation, generally considered the weakest part of the triptych, ultimately the will of the people is necessary to enforce human rights principles. Consequently, this Second World Decade for Human Rights Education (2005–2015) can continue to play a pivotal role in bringing a global consensus towards creating a human rights culture. Listed here are select resources, not only for UN implementation measures, but also for other regional organisations that have evolved.

REFERENCES

Buergenthal, T. Shelton, D. and Stewart, D. (2002) *Buergenthal's International Human Rights in a Nutshell.* Eagan, Minnesota: West Publishing Company.

Ife, J. (2008) *Human Rights and Social Work: Towards Rights Based Practice.* Cambridge: Cambridge University Press.

Reichert, E. (2011) *Social Work and Human Rights: A Foundation for Policy and Practice.* New York: Columbia University Press.

Steiner, H., Alston, P. and Goodman, R. (2007). *International Human Rights in Context: Law, Politics, Morals.* 3rd edn. New York: Oxford University Press.

Weissbrodt, D., Fitzpatrick, J., Newman, F., Hoffman, M. and Rumsey, M. (2001). *International Human Rights: Law, Policy, and Process.* Cincinnati, OH: Anderson.

Wronka, J. (1998). *Human Rights and Social Policy in the 21st Century: a History of the Idea of Human Rights and Comparison of the United Nations Universal Declaration of Human Rights with United States Federal and State Constitutions* (rev. edn). Lanham, MD: University Press of America.

Wronka, J. (2008). *Human Rights and Social Justice: Social Action and Service for The Helping and Health Professions.* Thousand Oaks, CA: SAGE.

Appendix 6: Millennium Development Goals

This document can be viewed at:

http://www.unmillenniumproject.org/goals/gti.htm

www.un.org/millennium/declaration/ares552e.htm

The Millennium Development Goals (also known as the MDGs) are a set of social objectives that the member states of the United Nations (UN) have agreed to meet by the year 2015. They are contained in a UN resolution, known as the Millennium Declaration which was unanimously adopted by the organisation's 189 member states at a Special Session of the General Assembly (known as the Millennium Summit) in September 2000 (United Nations, 2000). The Declaration contains eight broad goals which are broken down into 18 specific, measurable targets that range over topics such as poverty reduction, improvements in school attendance, the enhancement of gender equity, reductions in child and maternal mortality, the promotion of sustainable development and improvements in international cooperation.

HISTORY

The UN and its member states have been committed to improving the well-being of the world's people since the organisation's Charter was signed in 1945. Numerous resolutions and other international instruments have been adopted and various international gatherings have been convened to mobilise support for this effort. One especially important international meeting was the *World Summit on Social Development* held in Copenhagen in 1995. This was convened at a time of global economic adversity, financial crises and the promotion of neoliberal policies by the International Monetary Fund (IMF), the World Bank and the governments of some Western countries such as Britain and the United States. All used their political influence and aid programmes to promote market liberalisation and reduce government involvement in social and economic affairs. By the 1990s, these policies had resulted in severe spending cuts, retrenchments in government services and an increase in the incidence of poverty and deprivation in many countries. The summit was convened to challenge these developments and to secure a renewed commitment from the member states to use public resources to improve the well-being of their citizens. A particularly noteworthy feature of the summit was that 117 heads of state including presidents, prime ministers and monarchs from different parts of the world attended and endorsed the summit's call for international action. The summit concluded with the unanimous adoption of the Copenhagen Declaration which contained 10 broad commitments to address pressing global problems such as poverty, hunger, unemployment, gender discrimination, child mortality and HIV/AIDS among others (United Nations, 1996). These subsequently formed the basis for the MDGs.

Following the World Summit, staff at the UN Secretariat began to plan for the implementation of the commitments through closely collaborating with governments, donor countries and other international agencies. It was agreed that a follow-up meeting would be held in 2000 to assess progress. Initially this meeting was known as Copenhagen +5 but when it was realised that it would be held at the beginning of a new millennium, the title of the meeting was changed to the Millennium Summit. This time, 147 heads of state attended and many of them addressed the General Assembly and declared their support for the Dec laration.

IMPLEMENTATION

With the exception of Goal 8 which deals with global partnerships, national governments are given primary responsibility for implementing the goals. Most have established implementation plans, allocated funds and created reporting and monitoring systems. Responsibility for particular goals was usually assigned to government ministries such as health, education and housing while overall direction was provided by the government's central planning agency or the office of the president or prime minister. Nongovernmental organisations and the business community were also encouraged to participate. The UNs' Millennium Project (based in New York) provides policy direction, promotes coordination and monitors progress.

Although many governments have increased budgetary allocations to programmes designed to meet the goals, international aid has also been required, especially to assist low-income countries. In addition to funding from the UN and its different agencies, resources have been provided by the IMF, the World Bank and the regional development banks. Official development assistance, from high-income donor countries as well as international nongovernmental organisations and foundations, has also been mobilised. A special effort has been made to integrate the poverty alleviation policies of the World Bank with the longer-term MDGs. Today, the Bank is a major advocate and funder of government efforts to achieve the goals.

In addition to meeting the MDGs through nationally directed programmes and policies, the adoption of what are described as Quick Win projects has been encouraged. These can be more readily implemented than longer-term national programmes often at a relatively affordable cost. Among others, they include the provision of mosquito nets to poor families, the abolition of school fees and user charges for health services, legislative reforms guaranteeing property and inheritance rights to women and local community-based forestry projects. International donors and large foundations have made a significant contribution to funding these projects.

PROGRESS SO FAR

Although it is intended that most of the goals and targets will be reached by 2015, some goals may be met sooner, while it is recognised that others will require longer. For example, it is anticipated that a target date of 2020 will be required to meet the goal of improving the lives of people residing in informal settlements. On the other hand, it was hoped that gender disparities in primary and secondary education could be eliminated by 2005 and that universal access to HIV/AIDS treatment could be provided by 2010. In some cases, such as halving the proportion of the population living in poverty by 2015, a baseline of 1990 is used so that the time to achieve this target is actually 25 years.

In addition to establishing an international system of data collection and monitoring, the UN convened two high-level meetings of the General Assembly in 2005 and 2010 to evaluate progress. The meeting of 2005 was overshadowed by the invasions of Afghanistan and Iraq and vigorous criticism by Mr John Bolton, the US ambassador at to the UN, of the work of the organisation in general and the goals in particular. His views reflected the disdain in neoconservative circles in the United States government for the UN and its activities. Mr Bolton raised a number of objections to the goals arguing that more progress would be made if governments adopted free-market economic policies and liberal democratic political systems. Much was made of the fact that progress since 2000 had been decidedly mixed (United Nations, 2005).

The 2010 meeting was less contentious and the progress report presented by the Secretary General, Ban Ki-Moon, was generally well-received (United Nations, 2010). The report stated that significant progress had been made in achieving many but not all of the goals. The incidence of absolute poverty had fallen steadily and is on target to decline to 920 million people or about half the number who were in poverty in 1990. The most dramatic reduction in the incidence of poverty had taken place in East Asia but declines were also recorded in other regions including South Asia, Sub-Saharan Africa and Latin America. School attendance has increased significantly and the enrolment of girls had improved, particularly in sub-Saharan Africa. There were also what the report described as 'remarkable' improvements in combating HIV/AIDS. The incidence of other infectious diseases such as malaria and measles had also fallen largely because of effective immunisation campaigns. These programmes played a major role in reducing the incidence of child mortality which fell from about 12.5 million in 1992 to

8.8 million in 2008. The report was optimistic that most countries were on target to reach these goals.

On the other hand, less progress had been made in reducing the incidence of hunger, maternal mortality and providing access to safe water and improved sanitation. Although the incidence of hunger has fluctuated over the years, food insecurity remains endemic in South Asia and sub-Saharan Africa. Despite progress in combating infectious diseases, tuberculosis infections in South Asia and sub-Saharan Africa were still a serious problem even though infection rates had levelled off. With the exception of Central Asia, little progress had been made in reducing the rate of maternal mortality, and complications arising from pregnancy remain the primary cause of death among young women in developing countries. Similarly, minimal progress had been made in providing access to adequate sanitation and it was unlikely that the target of reducing the proportion of people without sanitary access by 2015 would be met. This was also the case with access to clean water but some gains had been recorded in East Asia and Latin America. With regard to the goal of developing a more effective global partnership between the Western and developing nations, official development assistance flows from high-income donor to low-income countries fell short of agreed targets. The report called for a renewed commitment to increasing international aid. The report also pointed out that much more needed to be done to address the limitations of the global financial system which had experienced a major crisis in 2008 with serious repercussions for many countries. On the other hand, there were positive indications that the financial situation in highly indebted low-income countries had improved. Also, it appears that multinational, pharmaceutical firms were more amenable to reducing the costs of essential drugs and increasing their availability in poor countries.

The report noted that some countries had made little progress because of the effects of the global financial crisis; a lack of political commitment and dedication to development; and insufficient funding. Violence, dictatorship and food insecurity continue to be a problem in a number of countries. Major disparities between social conditions in urban and remote rural areas remain a serious problem. Nevertheless, the report claimed that many governments supported by international agencies had made significant progress, justifying the view that states can adopt policies and programmes that promote the wellbeing of their citizens. This is true even of a number of low-income countries which were able to mobilise the political will and resources to improve social conditions. Although the report made little reference to the role of direct income transfers in reducing poverty, the expansion of conditional cash transfers and other means tested programmes in regions such as Latin America and Southern Africa had made a significant contribution to poverty reduction. Economic growth has also played a major role, particularly in the East Asian and Southeast Asian countries, India and parts of Latin America. Poverty reduction, the report pointed out, would depend on both antipoverty programmes and long-term sustainable growth.

CRITIQUE

The MDGs have been the subject of lively debate ever since they were first adopted in 2000 and a number of criticisms of their limitations as well as the underlying philosophy have been made. Some of these criticisms are concerned with technical issues such as the way particular targets are operationalised and how data is collected while others address more substantive issues.

There has been some discussion about the limitations of using official data to assess progress. It is recognised that data collection procedures in many countries are inadequate and it is on this basis that some have questioned whether data have been presented in a particularly favourable light by governments for political advantage. There are doubts about the claims of some governments, particularly in very poor African countries, that they have dramatically reduced the incidence of poverty. A related question is whether improvements in numerical indicators actually reflect substantial qualitative changes in the social services. For example, it cannot be claimed on the basis of increases in school enrolments that the quality of education has improved and that children are better educated than before. This is equally true of the quality of services in many clinics and hospitals. In some cases, the data also fail to address delivery problems such as whether food distribution programmes actually reach poor people. In this regard, it is recognised that high levels of 'leakage' have often impeded performance even though the extent of the problems of mismanagement and even corruption is not officially documented.

As may be expected, different groups have claimed that the goals do not adequately address their needs. Women's groups have pointed out that gender equality is largely confined to reducing gender disparities in education and maternal health and that the goals have failed to address problems of discrimination, violence and the blatant oppression of women. Human rights advocates want more emphasis on civil and political rights and the promotion of liberal democratic forms of governance. Others have claimed that the goals do not place sufficient emphasis on promoting peace and addressing the perennial problem of civil wars, ethnic conflicts and the oppression of minority groups. It has also been pointed out that the goals are minimal standards and that more ambitious efforts could have been made particularly with regard to reducing inequalities in income, wealth and power at both the national and global levels. On the other hand, some critics have argued that the goals are another example of a failed, wasteful and ineffectual statist approach that will not bring about sustained improvements in people's well-being. They believe that a market-based approach is more likely to be successful.

Questions about the way the goals have been conceptualised have also been raised. It has been argued that the goals are an *ad hoc* collection of targets that do not coherently address the challenges facing the global community today. In this regard, it has been claimed that the Commitments contained in the Copenhagen Declaration offer a more effective programme of action and that they should have been more effectively used to set targets in the Millennium Declaration. Another criticism is that the great majority of the goals are directed at the developing countries even though they are supposed to have universal relevance. While it is true that high-income countries have already met many of the goals, more effort should have been made to link the experience of these countries with efforts to achieve the MDGs in the global South.

Although these criticisms raise important questions, there is general agreement that the adoption of the MDGs by the member states of the United Nations in 2000 was in itself a remarkable achievement. Efforts to respond to social problems at the global level have been evolving since the formation of the League of Nations in 1919, but it was only with the World Summit in 1995 and the Millennium Summit in 2000 that the governments of the world's nations made an unprecedented collective commitment to improve social well-being throughout the world. Despite the fact that primary responsibility for the implementation of the MDGs lies with national governments, implementation has been a global affair. Although much more needs to be done, the goals have formed the basis for significant progress in the first decade of the 21st century. Hopefully, these historic efforts to eradicate poverty, address the challenges of ill-health, ignorance and social deprivation and improve the well-being of the world's people will continue well beyond 2015.

James Midgley

REFERENCES

United Nations (1996) *Report of the World Summit for Social Development: Copenhagen, 6–12 March 1995.* United Nations: New York.

United Nations (2000) *The United Nation Millennium Declaration.* (Resolution 55/2) United Nations: New York.

United Nations (2005) *Investing in Development: a Practical Plan to Achieve the Millennium Development Goals.* United Nations: New York.

United Nations (2010) *Keeping the Promise: a Forward-looking Review to Promote an Agreed Action Agenda to Achieve the Millennium Development Goals by 2015.* United Nations: New York.

Index